The U.S. ARMY in Frontier Montana

RONALD V. ROCKWELL

POMPEYS PILLAR

Bureau of
Land Management

NATIONAL MONUMENT

In memory of my lovely wife
and partner of forty years
Gabriele M. Rockwell
1945 – 2007

ISBN 10: 1-59152-065-7
ISBN 13: 978-1-59152-065-8

Published by Ronald V. Rockwell

© 2009 by Ronald V. Rockwell

Cover Design: Margot Boland

Cover Art: Gabriele M. Rockwell & Donita Powell

Front Cover: Photo of Nez Perce Chief Looking Glass courtesy
of the National Archives

Back Cover: U.S. Army emblems courtesy of The Institute of
Heraldry, U.S. Army

Cataloging-in-Publication Data is on file at the Library of Congress.

Created, produced, and designed by Sweetgrass Books,
PO Box 5630, Helena, MT 59604, 800-821-3874.

sweetgrassbooks
a division of Farcountry Press
Printed in the United States.

13   12   11   10   09   1   2   3   4   5   6

Table of Contents

Preface

IN APRIL 1945 MY PARENTS PURCHASED A FARM APPROXI-
mately one and a half miles southeast of the old Fort Shaw post. I was
six years old at the time. I attended Fort Shaw Public Elementary School,
located in a renovated adobe building that had originally been one of the
old post buildings. All of my elementary school years were spent there. In
1945 most of the buildings on the south side of the post were still standing,
some portions in use as teachers' quarters, although no longer in the best
condition. The school building stood on the west side of the old post and,
to its south on the southwest corner of the original post, a few portions of
adobe wall ruins remained, none more than a few feet tall. I only recently
determined that this was likely all that was left of the old post hospital.

I recall a building still standing on the north side—it was also used
as a teacher's quarters—and one building on the east side. One summer,
German prisoners of war were briefly housed at the fort. They worked in
the sugar beet fields in the valley. Some excitement arose in the area when
it was reported that one of them had escaped. The word was that he was
located sleeping under a nearby tree. So much for the dangerous German!

During my elementary school years the demise of the old post continued. I recall the building on the north side burning down during the school
year. Also, one summer the building on the east side burned to the ground.
Large columns of dark smoke rose skyward; my father told me that it was
the storage facility for Cascade County Weed Control. In those days no one

was concerned about toxic waste. Little concern was voiced, and there was no EPA cleanup. Times were different.

For a short period of time we occupied ourselves during recess playing among the old adobe ruins. I recall my schoolmates and I pushing down some of the old stubby adobe walls still standing. As I stated before, they were not very high; maybe two or three feet. There was little concern about preservation in those days. The teachers put a stop to this activity more out of concern for our safety than any concern for preservation of an old ruin.

Sometimes, walking about the fields on our farm, I would find bulky lead rifle slugs, usually lying at or very near the surface. Although they are no longer in my possession, they were likely slugs from the old caliber .45-70 rifles utilized by the army personnel at the post during target practice. Our farm, which was simply barren prairie at the time, was probably directly downrange from the shooters.

After graduating from the eighth grade at Fort Shaw School—no small accomplishment for me in those days—I attended high school a few miles up the Sun River Valley in Simms, MT. Nearly every Saturday or Sunday, at least one day a week, when I was free for a few hours from chores—milking cows on our farm was a 24/7 duty occupying my time from 5:15 A.M. to 7:30 A.M. and 5 P.M. to 7 P.M. daily—I would ride my saddle horse along the Sun River Valley bottom with my friend Roger Carrier. Although I was unaware of it at the time, Roger was five-eighths Cree-Chippewa Indian and French-Canadian. Living apart from his parents, he had been taken in by a neighbor family from the time he was about twelve until his completion of high school. Although I was an able horse rider, Roger was the real cowboy. His dream was to be a champion bronco rider. When we were about fourteen or fifteen years old, we took our two saddle horses and a pack horse, Nellie, and packed into the upper Dearborn River about thirty miles up from the trailhead for one week.

At one point during the first day we got on the wrong trail, which became treacherous. In a moment of panic, old Nellie reared up and tumbled down a slide area for about one hundred feet. The pack saddle was broken into small pieces, the groceries destroyed, and the stock was broken off my caliber .30-30 Winchester Model 94 carbine, which had been secured on top of the pack. We worked our way down to Nellie, who was lying in a depression breathing heavily and bleeding from a wound in her side. We were unable to get her on her feet. Convinced that she was mortally wounded, I decided to do the right thing by giving her the coup-de-grace with my carbine. Although the gun could still be fired without the stock, I hesitated, fearing that the barrel might be bent, possibly resulting in my own premature demise!

I was pondering whether to shoot, when Nellie suddenly decided to get up. Other than a ruptured blood vessel in her side, she had no broken bones. Somehow we managed to get her back up to the trail (she lived on another fifteen years). We backtracked to the trailhead, drove into Augusta, MT, and purchased another week's worth of groceries for about $16.! The trip was successfully completed.

In our later high school years Roger and I drifted apart but remained friends. I contacted him after being out of touch for over forty years. I do not know if he ever became a champion at it, but he certainly spent a great deal of his life riding broncos in rodeos throughout the West, and he had a lot of broken bones to prove it! Roger passed away in 2002.

My closest friends in later high school years were Robert Lynes, Jr., and James Fleming. We did a lot of jack rabbit, prairie dog, pheasant and big game hunting together in our allotted free time. Much of it was done on or near Square Butte. From the 1930's until approximately 1952 the greater portion of the butte including the entire top had belonged to my grandparents, Walter and Dana Woodrow. During the 1930's my granddad had gone out on a financial limb by borrowing $5,000 to purchase this 5,000-acre property for the grand price of $1.00 per acre! Lewis and Clark had referred to it as "Fort Mountain." We also hunted throughout the Birdtail country near St. Peter's Mission and the areas around Lincoln, MT, where my uncle, Donald Evans, owned a sawmill.

Although always very interested in history, particularly Montana history, I learned very little factual information regarding the past in these areas. We knew that the army had been stationed at the post for a time and then it had become an Indian school for some years. Both these periods were in the distant past. While in the eighth grade we took a course in Montana history. I still recall the little textbook; I wish I had a copy of it today for comparison purposes. We learned a lot about Lewis and Clark, but very little about the old fur traders, the American Indians of the area or any specifics about the military personnel stationed at the post. We were, of course, aware of the importance of the American Indians, who had been the sole occupants of the area in the distant past, but learned few specifics. In addition to my friend Roger, part Indian, there were, on occasion, one or two full-blooded American Indians in our class, but only for brief periods of time.

My first experience with the U.S. Army was a stint of six months active duty with the U.S. Army Reserve commencing after my graduation from Simms High School in 1956. By this time my academic performance was somewhat improved. I then began attending the University of Montana in Missoula and, after working a summer at the Lincoln Ranger Station, was hired and trained as a smokejumper for the U.S. Forest Service in Missoula, parachuting to and suppressing forest fires in remote areas. After two years at the University of Montana and two fire seasons as a smokejumper out of the base at Missoula, I traveled to Germany with my saved wages and eventually attended universities there for four years, studying German. This period was interrupted by working an additional two fire seasons as a smokejumper for the Bureau of Land Management in Fairbanks, AK. I eventually ended up with master's degree in German literature granted by Middlebury College, Middlebury, VT.

During the period 1967 to 1968, subsequent to marrying my wife Gabriele, my lover, partner and best friend for forty years until her early death in 2007, I was hired by the U.S. Agency for International Development and served as a civilian advisor in South Vietnam. Most of this service was spent occupying the position of Deputy District Senior Advisor on the CORDS advisory team in Nhon Trach District, Bien Hoa Province. I was the only civilian on the team.

My immediate superior was a U.S. Army major, and my co-workers were a captain, a lieutenant and enlisted men. We were a small unit averaging about ten men in size, stationed in a small district capital in the Vietnamese countryside. Needless to say, the job was extremely hazardous. My civilian predecessor had been captured and shot on the spot by the Viet Cong three weeks prior to my arrival. About six weeks later my army superior was killed by a roadside booby trap. The Viet Cong occasionally attacked our small compound at night with harassing automatic weapons fire, but never a direct assault. They also set off road mines and attempted ambushes on two occasions in an attempt to kill members of our team. In addition to the deaths, our small unit also had one man wounded by shrapnel and one man shot in the leg by an AK-47 round in a roadside ambush.

Many of the officers and enlisted men I worked with were career army personnel. They knew that after completing one twelve-month tour, they would be called upon for future tours for as long as the war lasted. It was their duty in their chosen career. For such men, and now in our modern army, women as well, I have great respect. They are often vilified by armchair pundits viewing the field of battle from the comfort of their homes, and quietly judged as fools for taking on such a career. The country, however, has always needed and will continue to need such people. The members of our frontier army were no different.

After returning from Vietnam, I spent five years teaching in public school and college and then was hired and trained as a Special Agent for the Drug Enforcement Administration (DEA). After many years conducting drug investigations in such diverse areas as Albuquerque, District of Columbia, Baltimore, Germany, Lebanon, Cyprus, Sweden and Thailand, I supervised an enforcement group that worked primarily in the slums of Washington, D.C. This was, as were my previous assignments with the DEA, a very challenging public service, not entirely unlike the military in a combat zone. We worked under very dangerous circumstances, investigating and arresting armed and dangerous subjects. As an enforcement unit supervisor I had to tackle dangerous tasks with my team, always with one thing in mind: accomplish a dangerous mission in the safest way possible with the least possible prospect of harm to my team members and innocent civilians. As with the military in a combat zone, the mission was such, however, that the danger of instant and violent death was always great. This experience further enhanced my respect for dedicated servants of our country who are willing to take on dangerous tasks at great personal risk to carry out public policy, voted on by majority rule, but not always agreed to by a large number of our citizens.

This book has one purpose only. It is to tell the story of the U.S. Army's mission and its conduct of that mission in frontier Montana. Naturally, it began with the Lewis and Clark Expedition, which is well-known to most amateur historians. It was, however, the first U.S. Army mission into what would later become Montana Territory. I have therefore included a brief sketch of the expedition as it progressed through the future Montana Territory.

I have also included a chapter on the fur trade era, with which many Montanans are far less familiar in any detail. It was during this period that future army scouts such as Jim Bridger and Mitch Boyer would cut their teeth. It was also during this period that the American Indians inhabiting our future territory and the white trappers came to know one another. I have relied a great deal on Hiram Chittenden's excellent work, *The American Fur Trade of the Far West,* first published in 1902.

My sources for the remainder of this book are primarily U.S. government documents in the form of old army reports, letters and telegrams now located in the National Archives in Washington, D.C. I have also utilized sober, responsible, first-hand accounts written by people who were on the scene, such as books later written by some of those officers and men, and in one case a news reporter who actually participated in the various campaigns. I made an exception to this rule in my description of the attack by the U.S. Army on the Piegans on the Marias River in 1870. In writing on this matter, specifically the attack itself, I make reference to Mr. Robert Ege's book, *Tell Baker To Strike Them Hard! Incident on the Marias, 23 Jan. 1870.* This informative book was first published in 1970.

I do not seek to pass moral judgment on the military or the various American Indian tribes, which the military at times fought, at times supplied with subsistence, at times guarded or imprisoned, and at times protected. The army carried out established government policy, as was their mission. I have attempted to document all statements made, and to avoid quoting too many latter-generation authors, who, in my opinion, frequently cloud factual information with modern-day moral judgments, fabulous 20-20 hindsight, and, sometimes, questionable sources. To many modern-day citizens the frontier army is simply seen as a bunch of craven killers of innocent American Indian men, women and children. Many readers will be so inclined. I would hope, however, that they will familiarize themselves with the facts as presented in this book. They may arrive at the same conclusion, but it will be a much better informed judgment.

Serious students of Montana history will learn much from reading this book. It is my hope that it will serve many in the future as a great source of historical information regarding the activities of the U.S. Army in frontier Montana as well as those of some of the various American Indian tribes occupying the area. I do not, however, profess to be an expert on the various tribal cultures. I leave that to others. Any references to Indians in this book, and there are obviously many, stem primarily from white sources and documentation. Exceptions are the recollections of the Cheyenne warrior Wooden Leg and a few interviews of Sioux and Northern Cheyenne Indians subsequent to the Battle of the Little Bighorn. Duncan McDonald's interviews of the Nez Perce exiles in Canada also provide valuable information from the Nez Perce perspective. McDonald was half white, half Nez Perce, and spoke their language. The only Indians discussed in this book are the American Indians who populated frontier Montana and areas adjacent to the old territory. I do make brief mention of Cree Indians who made their home primarily in Canada.

Although the army remained on station in Montana throughout the 1880's, I have chosen to end this history with the termination of most serious clashes between the army and hostile Indian bands. This coincided to some extent with the surrender of Sitting Bull and his remaining band in July 1881 at Fort Buford, Dakota Territory, located just across the Montana–North Dakota boundary. During the 1880's and early 1890's the primary role of the army units stationed in Montana was one of securing reservation supplies and preserving an at times fragile peace. With few exceptions very little open hostility occurred within Montana during this period. Exceptions include a short-lived uprising by some Crow warriors under Sword Bearer and a very tense situation among the Flatheads, which was resolved by civil authorities. I have not covered the outbreak at Wounded Knee in 1890, which occurred in the Dakotas and did not spread into Montana, by then a state.

Ronald V. Rockwell
Virginia City, MT
Fall 2009

CHAPTER ONE

Lewis & Clark in Montana, 1805–1806

THE FIRST U.S. MILITARY EXPEDITION TO WHAT IS NOW Montana evolved from a real estate transaction conducted in the year 1803 between representatives of U.S. President Thomas Jefferson and Napoleon Bonaparte, emperor of France. Jefferson, who, through family heritage and natural interest, had an eye to expanding our young nation westward, was attempting to negotiate the purchase of New Orleans. It had just been reacquired by France from the Spanish crown. Americans were rapidly settling the Ohio Valley, and Jefferson wished to secure access to the sea via the mouth of the Mississippi at New Orleans, "…through which the produce of three-eighths of our territory must pass to market."[1] While the French emperor, Napoleon, had experienced unparalleled success on the European continent with his land army, the British navy still reigned supreme on the high seas. It posed a considerable threat to any future plans for French colonial expansion in distant North America. Napoleon therefore offered to sell the entire Louisiana Territory to a surprised Jefferson. The president moved quickly, taking advantage of this golden opportunity to peacefully double the size of our country. Napoleon had made the correct decision. Two years later, in 1805, British Admiral Nelson soundly defeated the French fleet off the Spanish coast at Trafalgar.

President Jefferson made plans to survey the newly acquired territory, which ranged from the Mississippi westward to the Continental Divide. He

---

[1] Charles and Mary Beard, *History of the United States:* 228.

selected a young Virginian and captain in the U.S. Army, Meriwether Lewis, to organize an expedition into this new territory and also seek a navigable route to the Pacific Ocean. It is of interest to note that the expedition was tasked not only to explore the newly acquired Louisiana Territory but also to press on to the Pacific through some 500 or 600 miles of British territory. Like many political leaders of our new nation, Jefferson believed in our "manifest destiny" to eventually control and establish settlements on the entire continent from coast to coast. Little was known in those days of the country west of the Mississippi. The Missouri River was believed to offer the best route to a "northwest passage." Celestial observations made by Spanish sea captain Bruno Hecta in 1775 and a visit to the mouth of the Columbia by American sea captain Robert Gray in 1792 had determined that the continent was approximately 3,000 miles wide.[2] However, the topography of this vast region was an unknown. The western mountains were assumed to be similar in size to the Appalachian Mountains.

Captain Lewis selected as his second-in-command, William Clark, younger brother of the famed George Rogers Clark. Although he always bore the honorary title of captain, William Clark held the rank of an army 1st lieutenant during this expedition. The party departed St. Louis, Louisiana Territory, in May 1804 and by October 24th had made its way to the Mandan villages near present-day Bismarck, ND. Here they spent the winter and, on April 7, 1805, resumed their voyage upriver. Upon their departure from the Mandan villages their party consisted of Captains Lewis and Clark, three sergeants, twenty-three privates, interpreters George Drewyer (Drouillard) and Toussaint Charbonneau, Captain Clark's African-American slave York, Charbonneau's Shoshone Indian wife, Sacagawea, and their baby.[3]

On April 25th they arrived at the mouth of the Yellowstone River near the future sites of that famous trading post, Fort Union, and the later military post, Fort Buford. The expedition had now entered the area of the future Montana Territory.[4] On the 8th of May they passed the mouth of the Milk River. While looking up the valley of the Milk River, Captain Clark, "... could not be certain but thought he saw the smoke and some Indian lodges at a considerable distance up Milk river." However, fearing that any Indians at this location might cause them potential trouble, they made no effort

---

[2] HistoryLink.org, Essay 5051.

[3] Reuben Gold Thwaites, *Original Journals of the Lewis and Clark Expedition*, Vol. I, Pt. II: 284.

[4] Ibid.: 334–335.

to seek them out.[5] On June 3rd they encountered the mouth of the Marias River approximately eleven miles below the future location of Fort Benton, a site that would play a significant role in the future of Montana Territory. After overcoming the initial confusion regarding the proper river to follow, they pressed on up the Missouri, arriving at the Great Falls on June 13th. Just prior to his arrival at the falls, Lewis remarked upon climbing to a high point for observation, "I overlooked a most beatifull and level plain of great extent or at least 50 or sixty miles; in this there were infinitely more buffaloe than I had ever before witnessed at a view." Shortly thereafter Captain Lewis came in sight of the Great Falls of the Missouri.[6]

The party spent one month in the general area of present-day Great Falls, MT. Most of this time was spent portaging equipment and supplies around the falls and making preparations to continue their voyage upriver. They noted a river flowing into the Missouri from the west at this location and named it the Medicine River. This was, of course, the latter-day Sun River.[7] Although the party had seen numerous signs of Indians since their departure from the Mandan villages, including the smoke sighted by Captain Clark on the Milk River, they were mostly old signs. This illustrates the vastness of this new territory, very thinly populated by a sprinkling of Indian tribes. That Lewis and Clark could travel over 600 miles up a major waterway without coming into contact with Indians is hard to imagine, but is a historical fact. This, however, does not preclude that the expedition may have been observed by Indians at various points along the Missouri.

This would also become cause for great concern. Now much closer to the Rocky Mountains, Lewis and Clark were anxious to make contact with the natives. They knew that at some point the waterway would diminish as they entered the mountains. They would then need horses to continue their journey. These they hoped to procure from the Indians. Sacagawea and her husband had been brought along for this purpose.

Sacagawea was a Shoshone (Snake) Indian. The Shoshones were known to inhabit a mountainous area in the upper waters of the Missouri. Not a powerful tribe, they ventured out into the Great Plains only when forced by necessity of hunger. Once they had secured a supply of buffalo meat, they quickly returned to the safety of the mountains. They greatly feared

---

[5] Thwaites, Vol. II, Pt. I: 12.

[6] Ibid.: 113–147.

[7] Ibid.: 155–156.

the Sioux, Blackfeet and other more powerful tribes who generally inhabited and roamed about the lower areas on the plains. Five years earlier near present-day Three Forks, MT, Sacagawea had been captured by a war party of Hidatsa (Minnetaree) Indians from the Knife River.[8] She had been in a group of Shoshones when they were attacked by the Hidatsas, who killed four men, four women and several boys. Four boys and several women, among them Sacagawea, had the good fortune to be taken prisoner.[9]

Departing the Great Falls area on July 15th and marching upriver, Lewis observed Square Butte looming up to the southwest and designated it "Fort Mountain." On July 17th they passed one river flowing in from the east, which they named the Smith River after the Secretary of the Navy, Robert Smith. Later they encountered a river flowing in from the west, which they designated as the Dearborn River after Secretary of War, Henry Dearborn. By the 20th of July they had reached the Gates of the Mountains near present-day Holter Dam.[10] In this general area they sighted a column of smoke that they believed to be man-made. "Capt. C. saw a smoke today up the valley of Pryor's creek which was no doubt caused by the natives likewise."[11] This was their second sighting of suspected man-made smoke in the territory, the first being on the Milk River. In the course of the next few days they pressed on toward the Three Forks and arrived there on July 27th. They had still not made contact with any Indians. Here three rivers flowed in to form the Missouri: from the southeast the Gallatin, from the south the Madison, and from the southwest the Jefferson. These tributaries were respectively named after the Secretary of the Treasury, Albert Gallatin; the Secretary of State, James Madison; and the President, Thomas Jefferson.[12]

The party elected to follow the southwesterly course of the Jefferson River, and on August 11th, far up the Beaverhead, a tributary of the Jefferson, Lewis sighted an Indian on horseback observing him from a safe distance. Attempts to approach the Indian failed and he rode off. By now the waterways had become small streams, scarcely passable, even for small canoes. Finally, on the 13th near Lemhi Pass, approximately thirty miles west of present-day Clark Canyon Dam, Lewis encountered a small group of Shoshone

---

8 The Knife River empties into the Missouri about fifty miles above Bismarck, ND.

9 Thwaites, Vol. II, Pt. I: 282–283.

10 Ibid.: 230–251.

11 Ibid.: 253.

12 Ibid.: 281.

women digging roots and was able to befriend two of them. When a large Shoshone war party came riding to the rescue of these women, Lewis's luck held and, after some tense moments, he was able to establish amicable relations with the chief of this formidable band, who, it was later learned, was actually Sacagawea's brother. Successful contact with the Shoshones had been made. The first recorded meeting between American whites and red men (Native Americans) in Montana had been a peaceful one. Earlier meetings with French-Indian traders from the British Possessions (Canada) cannot be ruled out. The party was able to negotiate the purchase of horses from the Shoshones.[13]

Although the Shoshones were rich in horses, food was apparently scarce for these mountain dwellers, who dared not follow the great buffalo herds on the plains at their leisure. One quote from Captain Lewis describes a deer hunt in which the famished Indians literally pounced on a deer shot by the party and consumed it raw, one Indian eating on one end of an intestine while squeezing the contents out the other end with his free hand. This reference underscores their feast-and-famine existence.[14] Most readers will find this hard to contemplate, but then, scarcely anyone in our modern-day western world has faced such hunger.[15]

The Shoshones provided Lewis and Clark with a guide who allegedly knew the way through the mountains to the west. By now just over the border in latter-day Idaho, they proceeded to the vicinity of Lost Trail Pass, reentering latter-day Montana and then proceeded down the Bitterroot Valley. Before turning westward toward Lolo Pass they learned from natives of the much shorter route back to the Missouri, which Lewis would follow on his return trip.[16]

On September 11th the expedition, following their Shoshone guide, headed up the Lolo Trail into the Bitterroot Mountains en route to the Pacific, which they eventually reached in November 1805. They very nearly perished

---

[13] Ibid.: 281–340.

[14] Ibid.: 355.

[15] In the early 1960's I was employed by the U.S. Forest Service and later the Bureau of Land Management as a smokejumper, parachuting to and suppressing forest fires in remote areas of Alaska and the western United States. Some of my colleagues were later employed in Laos with Air America, dropping air cargo to the Hmong tribesmen, enemies of the Pathet Lao. One, Eugene Debruin, was shot down and with other crew members parachuted into harsh captivity. While close to starvation they killed a snake that had crawled into their cell in the darkness. Not only did they eat the snake, but also cut out two mice it had eaten and consumed them as well. Phisit Intharathat, Phisit, "Prisoner in Laos": 16.

[16] Thwaites, *Original Journals*, Vol. III, Pt. I: 58.

crossing the Bitterroots. On September 20, 1805, now in the future Idaho, they had the good fortune to come upon a Nez Perce village. All members of the expedition were near starvation. The Nez Perce provided them with food and shelter; later, on the return trip, they supplied them with guides back through the Bitterroots.[17] By rescuing the Lewis and Clark Expedition from starvation, the Nez Perce Indians made a significant contribution to recorded Montana history. Although this tribe resided in Idaho and Oregon, members traveled annually via the "Buffalo Road" to the Montana Great Plains to hunt their supplies of buffalo meat. Thus, they were very familiar with the geography of the area later to become Montana Territory. A portion of the Nez Perce nation, the non-treaty Nez Perce, would play another important role in Montana history some seventy-two years later.

On July 1, 1806, the Lewis and Clark Expedition arrived back at Traveler's Rest Creek, having explored portions of the Snake, Clearwater and Columbia rivers and wintered on the Pacific coast. A decision had been made to split up the party into smaller groups for part of the return journey, in order to gain maximum possible information on routes and waterways in what is now Montana. Lewis would, with nine men, explore the shorter route to the Missouri and conduct a more thorough exploration of the Marias River drainage. Clark would proceed with the remainder of the force back to retrieve canoes cached at the headwaters of the Jefferson River. After sending some of his men downriver to transport the canoes to Captain Lewis near Great Falls, Clark would lead his remaining group, consisting of thirteen men and Sacagawea with her child, across the divide between the Missouri and the Yellowstone by the most direct route. Clark would then proceed down the Yellowstone River, eventually meeting Lewis at the mouth of the Yellowstone.[18] Evidence of Captain Clark's leg of the return is revealed in landmarks along their route that bear the names of expedition members. Among these are the Shields River, the Pryor Mountains and Pompeys Pillar, which was named after Sacagawea's baby boy. Clark's leg of the journey passed without serious mishap, although they did have some horses stolen.

Once Captain Lewis reached the Great Falls, he would leave three men to retrieve cached equipment while they awaited the later arrival of the party coming from upriver. Lewis would then proceed with three men to explore

---

[17] Ibid.: 77–96.

[18] Thwaites, Vol. V, Pt. I: 175–179.

the Marias and later rendezvous with the other group at the mouth of the Marias.

Captain Lewis parted company with his Nez Perce guides on July 4, 1806, near present-day Missoula. The Nez Perce were fearful of a Hidatsa raiding party they believed to be in the area. Lewis and his party proceeded up the Blackfoot River, passing through the area around present-day Lincoln, MT. They turned up Alice Creek and, on July 7th, crossed over into the Atlantic drainage. Once again Fort Mountain (Square Butte) and Haystack Butte, another landmark familiar to present-day residents of the Sun River Valley, received mention in Lewis's journal. "N. 45. E. 2 M. passing the dividing ridge between the waters of the Columbia and Missouri rivers at ¼ of a mile. From this gap which is low and an easy ascent on the W. side the fort mountain bears North East, and appears to be distant about 20 Miles."[19] The next day Lewis wrote, "N. 25 W. 3½ M. to the top of hill from whence we saw the Shishequaw mountain [Haystack Butte] about 8 M. distant, immediately before us...the Shishequaw mountain is a high insulated conical mountain standing several miles in advance of the Eastern range of the rocky mountains."[20]

Lewis and his party then proceeded across the prairie to the South Fork of the Sun River, which they referred to as Shishequaw Creek, followed it down to the Sun River, passing the future site of Fort Shaw on July 10th, and encamped that night near present-day Vaughn, on the south side of the Sun River. Lewis reported, "we killed five deer 3 Elk and a bear today saw vast herds of buffaloe in the evening below us on the river. We he[a]rd them bellowing about us all night. Vast assemblages of wolves. Saw a large herd of Elk down the river."[21] On the next day, July 11th, they arrived at the Great Falls. "I sincerely belief that there were not less than 10 thousand within a circle of 2 miles around that place."[22]

Regarding buffalo, it is of interest to note that by the time Fort Shaw was established in 1867 they were no longer as numerous in the area. In 1870 Colonel John Gibbon, an avid hunter, reported sighting only a few antelope on a ride from Fort Shaw to the South Fork of the Sun River in the area of Haystack Butte (vicinity of present-day Augusta, MT). However,

---

[19] Ibid., Pt II: 194.

[20] Ibid.: 194–196.

[21] Ibid.: 198.

[22] Ibid.: 199.

Montana pioneer Robert Vaughn reported large herds to the north of the river in 1869. Fort Benton's *River Press* reported on November 21, 1882, that cowboys had sighted and chased buffalo on Flat Creek and that these were the first buffalo sighted in that area for at least ten years.[23] The author assumes that the Flat Creek mentioned is the same creek that crosses Montana Highway 200 near Bowman's Corners.

As late as 1876 and 1877, there were still large herds of buffalo reported in the areas between the Missouri and the Yellowstone rivers and in the Powder River country. Troops under Colonel Nelson Miles also sighted a large herd of buffalo near the Bear Paw Mountains during the Nez Perce campaign in 1877. Montana rancher Granville Stuart reported that in the spring of 1880 he sighted numerous buffalo herds on the Rosebud River and the Musselshell River. Stuart would report, however, that by "…the fall of 1883 there was not one buffalo remaining on the range."[24]

Naturally, it would be impossible for such a large herd of buffalo as that sighted by Lewis to remain in any given area for an extended period of time. The buffalo sighted by Captain Lewis and his party were obviously on the move through the area, constantly looking for greener pastures. They had to move on as a matter of necessity, for such a large number of animals would have eaten all available grass in any given area in very short order—a matter of days or weeks. This is not rocket science. Ask any Montana cattle rancher.

Leaving three men at Great Falls, Lewis departed on the 16th of July with six men to explore the headwaters of the Marias. During his stay in the area of the Great Falls, they were obviously under observation by Indians, who managed to steal several of the party's horses. On July 26th, Lewis encountered a band of eight Indians, who identified themselves as Piegans. This encounter was, according to Reuben Gold Thwaites, "…on the south side of the Two Medicine River, about four miles below the mouth of Badger Creek on eastern edge of the [present-day] Blackfoot reservation."[25] They informed him that there was a white man living with them at their camp and that they traded with the British at a location north of the American-Canadian boundary. After camping overnight with the Indians, they encountered trouble, when the Indians attempted to steal their horses. This resulted in a violent exchange in which one Indian was knifed to death and another gut

[23] (Fort Benton, M.T.) *River Press*, November 21, 1882.

[24] Granville Stuart, *Forty Years on the Frontier*, Vol. II: 109, 124, 188.

[25] Thwaites, Vol. V, Pt. II: 220. This location is perhaps twenty miles southeast of present-day Browning.

shot. The remainder of the Indians hastened out of the area, presumably back to their main village for help. Lewis and his men made equal haste to vacate the area and put as much distance as possible between them and the Indians. Moving as fast as their horses would carry them, the party arrived at the mouth of the Marias on July 28th, where they had the good fortune to quickly rendezvous with the other group coming downriver.[26] They reached the mouth of the Yellowstone on August 7th and, a short while later, departed present-day Montana. At a point farther down the Missouri in present-day North Dakota they were reunited with Captain Clark's party. The date was August 12, 1806.[27] This was the end of the first phase of U.S. military involvement in Montana and the beginning of an enmity between the Blackfeet and the "Americans" that would last for several decades.

---

[26] Ibid.: 220–228.

[27] Ibid.: 237, 243.

CHAPTER TWO

The Fur Trade Era in Montana, 1806–1862

T HE ACQUISITION OF THE LOUISIANA TERRITORY AND the success of the Lewis and Clark Expedition quickly resulted in a migration of wealth-seeking adventurers into the upper reaches of the Louisiana Territory. These were not prospectors seeking mineral wealth but rather fur traders and trappers. From this point forward until the discovery of gold half a century later, the fur trade would dominate in the future Montana Territory. The presence of fur traders in the territory in the interim years between 1806 and the discovery of gold in Montana in 1862, and their experiences gained, were also significant for future military involvement in Montana Territory and adjacent western territories. It was primarily during the fur trade era that the white man's knowledge of the western Indian tribes and their customs and habits was more extensively developed. Many future U.S. Army scouts and guides would learn their skills as frontiersmen during the fur trade era.

To a lesser extent, the Indians populating these areas came to know the white man, but it was not until many years later, with the onslaught of the gold seekers, settlers, the iron horse, and the ever more rapid demise of the buffalo, that the western Indian began to realize his way of life was being engulfed by white society. Clashes between the different cultures would then become more frequent and, as white civilization advanced, such clashes would also have more potent political consequences. The death of a lone trapper at the hands of an Indian in a West populated with scattered Indian tribes and but a handful of white men scarcely raised any eyebrows in Congress. However, as towns arose in the territory's midst, with appointed and elected officials, the protection of the federal government was soon demanded by the local citizenry.

"Local citizenry" did not include the American Indians, for our national government treated them as members of Indian nations with which the United States made treaties just as they would with foreign powers. Therefore, the Indians were not only looked down upon by the white culture from a purely racist standpoint, sometimes as ignorant savages, but they also lacked the right to vote and, thus, had no opportunity to make their voices heard by democratic means. The only legitimate recourse afforded them within the bounds of the U.S. government was to complain through Indian agents appointed by the Commissioner of Indian Affairs. Unfortunately, the Office of Indian Affairs was all too frequently noted for corruption and ineptitude during the period covered by this book.

Even before reaching St. Louis, Lewis and Clark had encountered enterprising fur trappers on their way up the Missouri. John Colter, a member of the Lewis and Clark party, would join them and return upriver to the future territory. Colter thus became one of the first of a generation of famous and to some extent fabled American mountain men, many of whom spent a great deal of their time on future Montana soil. Hiram Chittenden would write in 1902 that the goods sought out by the fur traders and trappers were "…the fine furs obtained from the beaver, otter, mink, fox and other animals and the coarser products such as buffalo robes, bear and deer skins, which were not used as furs so much as for lap robes, heavy coats, and the like."[1] There was also considerable commerce in buffalo tongues, buffalo and bear tallow and wolf skins. Although initiated for the most part by the demands of the white culture in North America and Europe, the commerce was carried on by not only white and half-breed trappers and hunters but also to an even greater extent by the Indians, who sold directly to traders at points of rendezvous or fixed trading posts. The Indians had quickly discovered that these items, which they could easily obtain in their domain, brought them the ability to procure desired white man's goods otherwise beyond their reach. "Thus, in the early intercourse of the white man with the Indian, each gave to the other something that he valued lightly, and received in return something that he valued highly, and each felt a keen contempt for the stupid taste of the other."[2]

---

[1] Chittenden, *The American Fur Trade of the Far West*: 4.

[2] Ibid.: 5.

Up until the time of the acquisition by the United States of the Louisiana Territory and later the Oregon Territory, the Hudson's Bay Trading Company, based in the British Possessions, or latter-day Canada, reigned supreme in the fur trade business throughout most of the West and Northwest. However, once this territory was acquired by the United States, American competitor companies quickly stepped up to the plate. Some of them were quite successful and others not; the best known were the Missouri Fur Company, the Rocky Mountain Fur Company and, last but not least, John Jacob Astor's American Fur Company. These companies and lesser competitors pursued their commerce principally by trade with the Indians, but to a lesser extent also hired white and half-breed trappers and hunters at fixed wages to procure their goods on the frontier. A third method of commerce was carried on by independent operators or free agents. "These men worked on their own account, being bound to no company and generally sold the product of their labor at some regular trading post or rendezvous, although they occasionally went to St. Louis with it themselves."[3]

At the time of Captain Meriwether Lewis's violent encounter with the Blackfeet (Piegans) on the upper Marias River, the Indians had reported that there was a white man living among them. However, we do not know his identity. One can only speculate that he was a French-Canadian or half-breed trader associated with the Hudson's Bay Company, which carried on an active trade with the Blackfeet. We do know that the first man responsible for the establishment of a fixed trading post in Montana was Manuel Lisa, founder of the Missouri Fur Company. He was born a Spaniard in New Orleans in 1772 and by late 1820 had already passed away, a short lifespan of some forty-eight years. In 1807 Lisa, along with other members of his Missouri Fur Company, traveled up the Missouri to the mouth of the Yellowstone and then up to its junction with the Bighorn River, and established a trading post in the heart of Crow Indian country. The post was located on the right bank of the Bighorn near present-day Bighorn, MT, and was "...variously known as Fort Lisa, Fort Manuel and Manuel's Fort. No relic of it has survived and the precise spot where it stood is unknown, but to it belongs the honor of being the first American trading post established on the upper rivers and the first building erected within the limits of the present state of Montana."[4]

---

[3] Ibid.

[4] Ibid.: 119.

Among the men with Lisa was John Colter, who, on his way down the Missouri in early 1807 after spending a winter upriver trapping after he left Lewis and Clark, encountered Lisa's party heading up the Missouri. He was engaged by Lisa and returned upriver without reaching St. Louis that year. Lisa's operation out of Fort Manuel lasted until 1810. Colter served with him during this time. Sent out to make contact with the Blackfeet for fur trading purposes, Colter, in the company of Crow Indians, journeyed up the Wind River, then through Jackson Hole in present-day Wyoming and on westward to Pierre's Hole in present-day Idaho. There a battle took place between the Crows and a Gros Ventre or possibly a Blackfeet band. Colter, fighting on the side of the Crows, was wounded in the leg. After this encounter the Crows returned to the Wind River country and Colter, wisely deciding to give up his attempt to contact the Blackfeet for the time being, took the most direct route, via Yellowstone Park, back to Fort Lisa. It was on this journey that he became the first known white man to view the wonders of the park. At the time, most dismissed his narratives as tall tails. This information was, nevertheless, taken seriously by Captain William Clark, who received it directly from Colter at a later date in St. Louis. Clark thought enough of Colter's narrative to include a map of his return route through the park area in his report on the Lewis and Clark Expedition. He entitled it, "Colter's Route of 1807."[5]

Manuel Lisa, believing that the ultimate success of his upper Missouri and Yellowstone endeavors depended upon trade with the Blackfeet, once again dispatched Colter into Blackfeet country. Colter journeyed, this time with others, directly to the Three Forks area. It was here, while trapping with a companion named John Potts, also a former member of the Lewis and Clark Expedition, that another hostile encounter with the Blackfeet occurred. The location of this encounter was somewhere on a branch of the Jefferson River at a point about six miles from the Jefferson. The branch was obviously large enough to handle canoe traffic, since they were reported to be in a canoe when they encountered the Indians. Potts was killed and Colter was captured but eventually given an opportunity to run for his life. Thus, the famous account of Colter's escape, which he one year later personally recounted to the author John Bradbury. Bradbury then printed it in his *Travels in North America*.[6]

[5] Ibid.: 706.
[6] Ibid.: 704–715.

In the late autumn of 1809, Lisa, after making a return trip to St. Louis, arrived back at Fort Manuel with a strong party of trappers and hunters. The party was probably in excess of fifty men. They spent the winter trapping in the area of the fort, and in the very early spring moved a large party to Three Forks. The party was led by Pierre Menard and Andrew Henry, partners in the Missouri Fur Company. "Upon the arrival of the party at Three Forks, the erection of a post was promptly begun on the neck of land between the Jefferson and the Madison rivers, about two miles above their confluence."[7] All went well initially and the beaver were plentiful, but on April 12th the Blackfeet struck, killing five men at a loss of two of their own and stealing guns, ammunition and horses. This made it too risky to send trappers out in small teams, which was the preferred method of operation. It was now necessary to maintain a sizeable force at the post at all times for sufficient protection of life and property, thus slowing the potential for profit.

On April 21st, Pierre Menard wrote the following letter to his brother-in-law, Pierre Chouteau. The letter has been translated from French:

> Three Forks of the Missouri,
> April 21, 1810
>
> Dear Sir and Brother-in-Law:
>
> I had hoped to be able to write you more favorably than I am now able to do. The outlook before us was much more flattering ten days ago than it is today. A party of our hunters was defeated by the Blackfeet on the 12th inst. There were two men killed, all their beaver stolen, many of their traps lost, and the ammunition of several of them, and also seven of our horses. We set out in pursuit of the Indians, but unfortunately could not overtake them. We recovered forty-four traps and three horses, which we brought back here, and we hope to find a few more traps.
>
> This unfortunate affair has discouraged our hunters, who are unwilling to hunt anymore here. There will start out tomorrow, however, a party of thirty…They go to the place where the others were defeated. I shall give them only three traps each, not deeming it prudent to risk more, especially since they are not to separate, and half are to remain in camp.
>
> The party which was defeated consisted of eleven persons, eight or nine of them were absent tending their traps when the savages pounced upon the camp. The two persons killed are James Cheeks,

---

[7] Ibid.: 141.

and one Ayres, an engagé of Messrs. Crooks and McLellan whom
Messrs. Silvester and Auguste (Chouteau) had equipped to hunt on
shares. Besides these two, there are missing young Hull who was of
the same camp, and Freehearty and his man who were camped two
miles farther up. We have found four traps belonging to these men
and the place where they were pursued by the savages, but we have
not found the place where they were killed.

In the camp where the first two men were killed we found a Blackfoot
who had also been killed, upon following their trail we saw that another had been dangerously wounded. Both of them, if the wounded man dies, came to their death at the hand of Cheeks, for he alone
defended himself.

This unhappy miscarriage causes us a considerable loss, but I do not
propose on that account to lose heart. The resources of this country in beaver fur are immense. It is true that we shall accomplish
nothing this spring, but I trust that we shall next Autumn. I hope
between now and then to see the Snake and Flathead Indians. My
plan is to induce them to stay here, if possible, and make war upon
the Blackfeet so that we may take some prisoners and send back one
with propositions of peace—which I think can be easily secured by
leaving traders among them below the Falls of the Missouri. Unless
we can have peace…or unless they can be destroyed, it is idle to
think of maintaining an establishment at this point.

Assure Madame Chouteau of my most sincere esteem as well as your
dear children, and believe me always your devoted Pierre Menard.

We are daily expecting to see the Blackfeet here and are desirous of
meeting them.[8]

Things did not improve and Menard, leaving Andrew Henry in command, decided in late July to return to St. Louis. Before his departure,
however, they experienced two more attacks by the Blackfeet, the second
resulting in the death of another former member of the Lewis and Clark
Expedition, George Drouillard. He was killed in early May 1810 attempting
to trap about two miles from the main camp with several Delaware Indians,
who were also employed by the company. During the attack Drouillard
and two Delawares were killed. Before the summer ended, another battle
occurred in which a party of twenty hunters fought off about 200 Blackfeet,
losing only one man while claiming to have killed about twenty Indians.

8 Ibid.: 882–883.

That fall Andrew Henry decided to abandon the post at Three Forks and made his way up the Madison and over what is now known as Raynolds Pass to Henry's Lake and Henry's Fork of the Snake River. On Henry's Fork "…he built a temporary post at a point near where the village of Egin, Idaho, now stands."[9] There they spent the winter. By the spring of 1811 the enterprise fell apart and Henry returned to St. Louis.

In the autumn of 1811 a small party of American Fur Company trappers—LaChapelle, Turcot and Landry—accompanied by some Snake Indians (Shoshone) entered the Missouri headwaters country from Henry's Fork and the Snake River in latter-day Idaho but were robbed by the Blackfeet. They returned to the Snake River country and were joined by fellow trappers Dubreuil, Carson, Delauney, St. Michael and DeFaye, then returned to the Missouri River country in the spring of 1812. Here they were attacked by Crow Indians, who robbed them and killed DeFaye.[10] They then retreated back to the Snake River country. In observing the ultimate fates of the members of this party, one derives a sense of the dangers faced daily by these mountain men. By 1815, scarcely three years later, LaChapelle, Turcot, Landry and Delauney had also joined DeFaye in the mountain man's heaven. Of these five, three were killed by Indians, one fell from a horse and one died of disease.[11]

The War of 1812 brought about a lull in fur trading activity on the Upper Missouri. Later, in 1819, Congress and the Monroe administration became interested in launching a military and scientific expedition up the Missouri to establish a post at the mouth of the Yellowstone. Amid great expectations for this enterprise, President Monroe wrote to Secretary of War Calhoun:

> The people of the whole western country take a deep interest in the success of the contemplated establishment at the mouth of the Yellowstone River. They look upon it as a measure better calculated to preserve the peace of the frontier, to secure us the fur trade and to break up the intercourse between the British traders and the Indians, than any other which has been taken by the government. I take myself very great interest in the success of the expedition, and am willing to take great responsibility to ensure it.[12]

---

9 Ibid.: 143–144. Egin, ID, has apparently disappeared from the map since Chittenden's turn-of-the-century reference to it.

10 Chittenden: 205–206.

11 Ibid.: 224–225.

12 Ibid.: 561.

Instead of utilizing the tried and proven method of moving men and equipment up the Missouri River by keelboats, it was decided to use steamboats. The reader will recall that the first steamboat had been built only five years earlier, in 1807, by Robert Fulton. Unfortunately, the design of steamboats had not yet been adapted to the needs of the shallow and hazardous waters of the Missouri, and the boats were only able to make it as far as Council Bluffs before winter, arriving there on September 26th with 500 soldiers on board. During the winter, 300 of them contracted scurvy and over 100 of them died. In addition to this a scandal arose regarding the government contracts for the procurement of the steamboats, which had proven unsatisfactory for service on the Missouri. By the summer of 1820, amid discouragement, scandal and national budget shortages, it was decided to limit the expedition in size and scope. As a result a smaller group under Major S.H. Long explored the upper reaches of the Platte River to the Colorado mountains (Denver area), returning to the Mississippi by a southerly route along the Arkansas River.[13]

Manuel Lisa died on August 12, 1820, and Joshua Pilcher took over the management of the Missouri Fur Company. Under his management two more intrepid pioneers, Jones and Immel, led another party of trappers totaling twenty-nine men to the Three Forks area in 1823. They trapped up Jefferson Fork or the Jefferson River, but found that the rich supply of beaver had been depleted by heavy trapping by the Blackfeet, who sold their furs to the Hudson's Bay Company traders just north of the U.S. boundary with Canada. They garnered over thirty packs on the Jefferson, which, along with packs caught in other areas, made up a total of fifty-two packs. A pack usually consisted of a bundle of beaver skins weighing approximately one hundred pounds.[14] They decided to return via the Yellowstone with their cache, but on coming down the Jefferson on May 17th they met with a party of thirty-eight Blackfeet. The meeting did not result in hostilities, and the two parties spent the night together and discussed setting up a post near the Great Falls of the Missouri, a plan that seemed to please the Blackfeet. They parted company the next day on friendly terms.

The party had traveled on some two weeks and were still making their way down the Yellowstone when on May 31, 1823, at a point less than a day's travel above the mouth of Pryor Creek, "…probably in the vicinity of the mouth of Canon [Canyon] Creek…,"[15] they were ambushed by a force

---

[13] Ibid.: 560–583.

[14] Ibid.: 39, 148.

[15] Ibid.: 157.

of about 400 Blackfeet while strung out moving uphill along a buffalo trail. As Pilcher wrote later that year:

> The Indians did not show themselves until the rear of the party had entered the pass, when they rushed furiously upon them from every rock and bush. Knowing Immel and Jones, their chief aim was first to kill them. An Indian, supposed to be one of their principals, rushed boldly upon Immel, covering himself with his shield. Immel by a well directed shot, brought him down. His gun was hardly empty when he was literally cut to pieces. About thirty Indians fired and rushed on him at the same instant and immediately after gave away.
>
> Jones seized the moment and although he had received two severe wounds, rallied and assembled his men, collected the scattered horses, and was pressing forward with some prospect of success to pass the defile and gain the river plain when the Indians rushed upon them with great fury. They attacked the whites with lances, battle axes, scalping knives and every weapon used by the Indians. Jones, pierced on every side, fell…Nothing but defeat under such circumstances could be looked for and how so many of them escaped is indeed wonderful.[16]

The party lost seven men killed and four wounded. They also lost horses, traps and over one half of their beaver packs—all valued at about $15,000— a serious financial blow to the company. The survivors managed to build a raft and float down to a Crow village on Pryor Creek.[17] Thus ended all fur trading and trapping activity by the Missouri Fur Company on the Upper Missouri, and, of course, the reputation of Blackfeet hostility toward whites was preserved.

Former members of the Missouri Fur Company, Joshua Pilcher and nine men, did conduct a fur trading exploration from the Green River country in Wyoming north to Flathead Lake in western Montana where they spent the winter of 1828–1829. They were, however, not the first American fur traders to visit Flathead Lake. Mountain man Jedediah S. Smith had passed through there in 1824 and once again in March 1829 en route to the Jackson Hole area.[18] During his stay at Flathead Lake, Pilcher is said to have attempted to get the Hudson's Bay Company to operate on American territory east of the

---

16 Ibid.: 149–150.

17 Ibid.

18 Ibid.: 287.

mountains under his sponsorship. They declined.[19] Moving north from that point in February 1829, the party had their horses stolen. Encountering some other trappers from St. Louis, the band eventually dissolved. Pilcher returned east by way of the Hudson's Bay Company posts Fort Colville (Washington), the Jasper House (British Columbia), Fort Assiniboine and Edmonton House (Alberta), Carlton House, Cumberland House, Moose Lake, Selkirk's Settlement and the Brandon House, from where he traveled to the Mandan villages on U.S. territory.[20] As Hiram Chittenden recounted:

> His long expedition [gave Pilcher] an acquaintance with the British posts such as that time was possessed by no other American. He was treated by the Hudson Bay traders with the hospitality so well understood by that company, but which, when dispensed to rival traders, was always accompanied with a firm refusal to assist in any way in their trading operations.[21]

It should be remembered that all that portion of Montana west of the Continental Divide was at the time British territory. American fur traders often speculated but never proved that some Hudson's Bay traders may have encouraged the Blackfeet hostility toward the American companies to preserve their commercial interests on the Upper Missouri. Hiram Chittenden wrote on this subject:

> Rightly or wrongly the Missouri traders attributed these acts of persistent hostility on the part of the Indians to the instigation of British traders. It was about the same time that Ashley was attacked by the Aricaras and several of his men killed, while Henry's party near the mouth of the Yellowstone suffered a similar though less disastrous experience. It seemed impossible that these Indians would of their own free will maintain an attitude of such uncompromising hostility. Indignation at repeated outrages may have made the American traders unduly suspicious of the British. Whether these suspicions were well founded or not, it was a fact that the firearms with which the Indians attacked the traders came from across the line, and the furs which they took from our people quickly found their way back there in payment.[22]

---

[19] Ibid.: 159. Chittenden quotes Merk, *Fur Trade and Empire*: 307.

[20] Ibid.: 152–153.

[21] Ibid.: 153.

[22] Ibid.: 150–151.

The Hudson's Bay traders occasionally had their own problems with the Blackfeet, as is obvious from Chittenden's descriptions of the Edmonton House:

> …this post is of particular interest, not only as being one of the most important of the Hudson's Bay Company posts, and the distributing point for the trade of a large section of country at the eastern base of the mountains, but it was the post at which the Blackfeet traded. Even the British found this tribe a troublesome one to deal with, and their post at this point was unusually strong. Pilcher says it was a "strong stockade, with six bastions, and ten twelve pieces of small ordnance.[23]

In 1823 the Rocky Mountain Fur Company was organized under the leadership of William H. Ashley and Major Andrew Henry. On March 20th they placed the following ad in the *Missouri Republican,* a St. Louis newspaper:

> To enterprising young men. The subscriber wishes to engage one hundred young men to ascend the Missouri river to its source, there to be employed for one, two, or three years. For particulars inquire of Major Henry, near the lead mines in the county of Washington, who will ascend with and command the party…[24]

They departed St. Louis about April 15th with initial plans to winter near the Great Falls of the Missouri. However, they lost a boat underway and had their herd of fifty horses stolen by the Assiniboines. Eventually reaching the mouth of the Yellowstone, they established a post (name unknown) and spent the winter. The next spring Henry set out upriver for Three Forks, but "…he was attacked by the Blackfeet in the neighborhood of Great Falls with the loss of four men killed, and was driven out of the country. He returned to the mouth of the Yellowstone sometime in June, 1823."[25]

In the meantime Ashley had organized another party of about one hundred men and was heading upriver when on May 30th the party was attacked by the Aricara (Ree) Indians, downriver from the Mandan villages. Ashley had hoped to trade with the Aricaras for horses badly needed by Henry. However, the attack badly decimated his command, forcing him to withdraw downriver. This party contained many men who would later

---

[23] Ibid.: 158.

[24] Ibid.: 261.

[25] Ibid.: 263.

become famous in the annals of mountain men. Among them were Jedediah Smith, James Bridger, William Sublette, David Jackson, Edward Rose, and Hugh Glass. Young Smith volunteered to deliver a message to Henry—a very hazardous undertaking—in the company of an unidentified French-Canadian through hostile Indian country. Upon receiving news of Ashley's defeat, Henry left twenty men at the post on the Yellowstone and returned downriver to join and assist Ashley. The Aricaras were eventually defeated in a military campaign. Then Henry, leading a force of about eighty men, moved overland directly to his post on the Yellowstone. En route, on August 20th, he was once again attacked by Indians, losing two men killed with two wounded. Arriving at his post he determined that Blackfeet and Assiniboine Indians had stolen twenty-two of his horses and within a short period of time he lost seven more.

Abandoning his post at the mouth of the Yellowstone, he headed up that river. He made contact with Crow Indians near the mouth of the Powder River and they sold him forty-seven horses. In the fall of 1823 Ashley dispatched a party toward the southwest, believed to be led by Etienne Provost, while he proceeded with his remaining force to establish a post at the mouth of the Bighorn River (name unknown). The Provost party is generally thought to be the first known white men to traverse the South Pass in Wyoming—the point at which the famous Oregon Trail later crossed the Continental Divide. Both trapping parties reunited in the summer of 1824, having had a successful trapping season. "This was the first of the famous annual rendezvous in the mountains."[26]

To turn to the protégés of Ashley and Henry in later years, i.e. the spring of 1829, Jedediah S. Smith, who had just returned from a trip to the Flathead Lake area, joined up with David Jackson, who is believed to have wintered in Jackson Hole, thus the name. Along with William L. Sublette, Joseph Meek and others (among them possibly James Bridger), they proceeded north into the Gallatin Valley. While crossing from the Gallatin over to the Yellowstone River, they were attacked by the Blackfeet and two of their men were killed. The party was scattered but reunited in the Bighorn Basin where they joined Milton Sublette, William's younger brother. Eventually members of this group moved to the Powder River country to winter. Buffalo were plentiful there.

In April 1830, Jackson returned to Jackson Hole, but James Bridger guided Smith and others (we may presume that this was a fairly large party, per-

---

[26] Ibid.: 278.

haps as many as eighty men) up the Yellowstone then across the country into Judith Basin. Later, in August 1830, James Bridger, William Sublette, Thomas Fitzpatrick and others formed the Rocky Mountain Fur Company while in the Wind River country at a rendezvous. Departing the Wind River country in August, they conducted an expedition with 200 men to the Bighorn Basin and then directly cross-country from the Yellowstone to the Great Falls area, upriver to Three Forks, and up the Jefferson to the Continental Divide, from where they eventually arrived at the Salt Lake. The trip was highly successful. The Indians caused no problems, doubtless due to the size of the party. Bridger and others frequently repeated these trapping expeditions into Montana country, usually wintering in the Powder River country. In the spring of 1831 the Crow Indians robbed them of all their horses but the trappers were able to recapture their animals along with those of the Crows![27]

By the autumn of 1831 the number of Americans involved in the Rocky Mountain fur trade had greatly increased. This was evidenced by the big turnout at the rendezvous in Pierre's Hole in the summer of 1832 (present-day Victor, ID, area west of Jackson, WY). Held near the base of Teton Pass, the rendezvous included trappers from both the Rocky Mountain Fur Company and the American Fur Company. Milton Sublette had a party of about sixty men present. All were Rocky Mountain Fur Company trappers and traders. Besides a large number of whites, including Henry Vanderburgh and other members of the American Fur Company, there were hundreds of Indians visiting the valley, mostly Nez Perce and Flatheads. The Blackfeet (Gros Ventres) also roamed throughout the entire area and, as in the case of the Flatheads, were far from their Montana home. The Blackfeet were considered the enemies of all.

Upon departing this rendezvous with his company of trappers, Milton Sublette encountered a large party of Blackfeet within a few miles of the rendezvous site. A battle ensued in which friendly Nez Perce and Flatheads were also involved. It became known as the Battle of Pierre's Hole. Five whites were killed and six wounded; among the wounded was William Sublette. The Indian allies lost seven killed and six wounded. The Blackfeet are said to have lost twenty-six warriors and twenty-four horses. They fortified themselves for the fight in the face of superior numbers and were able to withdraw from the scene at night.[28] Eyewitness accounts of the

---

[27] Ibid.: 292–296.

[28] Ibid.: 650–655.

aftermath of this battle reported that the Indians involved gave "no quarter" to captured enemies:

> In their advance upon the Blackfoot redoubt some of the trappers saw an Indian woman [reported by Meeks to be wounded] leaning against a tree. Surprised that she should thus indifferently expose herself to certain death, they looked for the cause and found that she was standing beside the corpse of her dead warrior. The trappers would have saved her, but no sooner did the Indian allies see her than they fell upon and slew her.[29]

Another member of the expedition, W.A. Ferris, provided another eyewitness account:

> Our Indians followed the route of the fugitives for several miles, and found their baggage which they had concealed in divers places, as well as the bodies of five more Indians, and two young women who were yet unhurt, though their heartless captors sent them to the shades in pursuit of their relations without the least remorse.[30]

Apparently, 1832 was not a good year for either the Blackfeet or the Gros Ventres roaming about Wyoming. Shortly after the battle of Pierre's Hole, a large force of Gros Ventres were engaged by the Crow Indians in the Wind River country and badly defeated, losing some forty killed. "The remainder were scattered like fugitives throughout the Crow country."[31]

As competition increased, James Bridger and his partners were frequently incensed by the tendency of American Fur Company trappers Henry Vanderburgh and Andrew Drips to constantly shadow them in an effort to discover their trapping grounds. In the autumn of 1832, Bridger and his Rocky Mountain Fur Company associates were particularly exasperated by the presence of these two competitors following them on the Jefferson and Madison rivers. At one point Henry Vanderburgh, a veteran of the previously described battle with the Aricaras, was in the Madison Valley but no longer on the trail of Bridger and his Rocky Mountain Fur Company

---

[29] Ibid.: 655.

[30] Ibid.: 656.

[31] Ibid.: 655. The author realizes that these actions did not occur in Montana; however, as in the case of the U.S. military effort to secure the Bozeman Trail, and portions of the Yellowstone Campaign of 1876, these extra-territorial occurrences involved Indians who made their home in Montana. Further, knowledge of these events enhances the understanding of the reach of the Blackfoot Nation, of which the Gros Ventres were then considered a part in those earlier years.

compatriots. Vanderburgh was also operating separate from his partner, Drips. He decided to move his party from the Madison drainage over the mountains toward the Jefferson. En route he camped on a small stream believed to be Alder Creek. Moving down the creek he came to its junction with the Ruby River (Stinking Water). This would be at a point just below present-day Alder, MT. Freshly killed buffalo were sighted at this point, a sure sign of Indians in the area.

Vanderburgh was anxious to ascertain more information regarding these Indians. He wished to put his trappers at ease; otherwise they would be unwilling to move out of camp in small teams to set traps, as was desirable. With six others from his party (including W.A. Ferris, R.C. Nelson and a Frenchman

Jim Bridger, trapper and U.S. Army scout.
PHOTO COURTESY OF MONTANA HISTORICAL SOCIETY RESEARCH CENTER PHOTOGRAPH ARCHIVES, HELENA, MONTANA.

named Alexis Pillion), they moved up the Ruby River reconnoitering for the Indians. After traveling for about six miles, they approached a stand of timber where they were ambushed by about one hundred Indians, probably Gros Ventres.

> Three of the party of hunters turned instantly and fled. Vanderburgh's horse was shot under him, but he calmly disengaged himself, aimed his gun at his assailants and called out to his men, "Boy's don't run." The situation was, however, hopeless. Both he and Pillon [sic] were slain. The Blackfeet cut off the arms of the slain leader and "…these were later exhibited as trophies of victory at Fort McKenzie on the Missouri [mouth of the Marias].[32]

Around the time of Vanderburgh's unfortunate demise, Bridger also had some hard luck. He and Fitzpatrick, while trapping near the headwaters

---

[32] Ibid.: 660–662.

of the Madison, also had a scrape with the Blackfeet. Bridger received two arrow wounds in the back. One of the arrows was not removed for almost three years. Dr. Marcus Whitman accomplished this task while visiting the rendezvous at Green River in the summer of 1835.[33] Dr. Whitman and his wife would be killed by Indians some years later near Walla Walla in latter-day Washington.

In the meantime and in spite of the loss of their valuable man Henry Vanderburgh, the American Fur Company had made significant inroads in Montana. On October 1, 1828, the company established a post at the mouth of the Yellowstone and christened it Fort Floyd. It is believed to have been built under the leadership of James Kipp,[34] who worked under his very able superior, Kenneth McKenzie. McKenzie was a British subject who had formerly been employed by the Hudson's Bay Company. In the year 1829 another post was constructed about 200 miles up the Missouri from Fort Floyd. It received the name Fort Union. By the end of 1830, Fort Floyd had been renamed Fort Union. The name is appropriate for it sat at the confluence, or union, of the Missouri and Yellowstone rivers.[35] The first objective of this post was to facilitate trade with the Assiniboine Indians who made their home in that general area. McKenzie's second objective was to endeavor to open a lucrative trade with the ever hostile Blackfeet, with whom the Assiniboine Indians maintained a hostile relationship.

In the autumn of 1830, after arriving back at Fort Union from a trip downriver, McKenzie met a former Hudson's Bay trapper by the name of Jacob Berger. Berger had gained experience trading with the Blackfeet while with the Hudson's Bay Company and spoke their language. McKenzie proposed to send him on a mission to open relations with the Blackfeet, and Berger accepted this dangerous assignment. He traveled west for four weeks with four or five men and eventually located a Blackfeet village on the Marias River. Although odds were strong that his party would be slaughtered on site, they entered the village and conducted successful negotiations. The Indians, no doubt Piegans, were receptive to the idea of a post at their village.[36] Berger persuaded about forty Blackfeet along with some chiefs to return to Fort Union with his party. McKenzie later reported to his superiors:

---

[33] Ibid.: 663.

[34] Kipp's son, Joseph Kipp, would play an important role in the attack on the Piegans on January 23, 1870.

[35] Ibid.: 329–330.

[36] Ibid.: 332.

> On my arrival at Fort Union last fall I fortunately found a Blackfoot
> interpreter, Berger, and by this means have been enabled to make
> those Indians acquainted with my views regarding them. I sent him
> with four or five men to their village, where they were kindly re-
> ceived and well treated. On their return to the fort they were ac-
> companied by some of the principal chiefs. They expressed great
> satisfaction and pleasure at having a post at their village…[37]

McKenzie then dispatched a trader with a few men to the Piegan village
on the Marias, where they spent the winter of 1830–1831. In the summer
of 1831 he sent James Kipp with a party of twenty-five men to establish a
new trading post on the Marias. They arrived there and began construct-
ing the post in October 1831. The location was a good one for McKenzie,
for the Piegans were generally considered to be the "beaver hunters" of the
Blackfoot Nation. They were hostile to anyone else attempting to trap in
their country.

> The site selected by Kipp for the post was immediately in the angle
> between the Marias and the Missouri… During the first ten days af-
> ter the post was built there were traded, according to McKenzie, two
> thousand four hundred beaver skins with the prospect of bringing
> the number up to four thousand before the winter was over.[38]

The post, christened Fort Piegan, came under siege by the Bloods, also of
the Blackfoot Nation. This attack was believed to have been at the instiga-
tion of the British Hudson's Bay traders. Kipp plied them with alcohol and
the siege eventually dissolved. Also in the summer of 1831 McKenzie moved
to establish peaceful relations between his trading partners, the Blackfeet
and the Assiniboines, which would further enhance his potential for profitable trade. He therefore encouraged the Piegans and Bloods to forge a peace
treaty with the Assiniboines, which was negotiated that summer. The U.S.
government had no involvement in this treaty.[39]

The following spring Kipp traveled downriver with the procured furs.
His men refused to stay on during the summer of 1832 even though the
Piegans wished them to. That summer, while the post was abandoned,
it was burned down. Attempting to maintain the post and the lucrative
trade, McKenzie sent David Mitchell upriver with a party and a boatload

---

[37] Ibid.: 343.

[38] Ibid.: 334.

[39] Ibid.: 344.

of trading supplies for the Indians. On the way up, the boat sank, drowning two of Mitchell's men. Some Blackfeet were along on the trip and Mitchell had great difficulty convincing them that the loss of these supplies was not due to white treachery. In this he succeeded. Eventually he arrived at the old fort, finding it burned down. A new site was selected some six miles up the Marias "…on the left or north bank of the river in what [as of 1902] is now known as Brule bottom."[40] Living on their keelboat, the traders erected the new post in great haste, for their very lives depended on the security it could provide them. During the construction they were visited by large numbers of Indians, many of them hostile. The new post, called Fort McKenzie, which stood 120 yards from the river and was 140 feet square, represented over the next eleven years a permanent foothold in Blackfeet territory. Fort McKenzie was finally abandoned in 1843.[41]

In 1832 another important milestone in Montana history was achieved with the arrival of the steamboat *Yellowstone* at Fort Union on or about June 17th. The use of steamboats in the fur trade had been strongly promoted by McKenzie and, with advanced technology, the idea was now being put into practice. On board the *Yellowstone,* along with Pierre Chouteau, was the famous Indian artist George Catlin.[42]

Having established trade with the Blackfeet, McKenzie now turned his attention to the Crow Indians. In the summer of 1832 he sent Samuel Tulloch to build Fort Cass at the mouth of the Bighorn River.

> The following extracts from Wyeth's Journal of August 17 and 18, 1833, give the essential facts relating to [Fort Cass]: About 3 miles below the mouth of the Bighorn we found Fort Cass; it is situated on the east (right) bank of the Yellowstone River, is about 130 feet square, made of sapling cottonwood pickets with two bastions at extreme corners…[43]

Captain Bonneville's party reported that as of August 18, 1833, Fort Cass was manned by Tulloch and twenty men.[44]

The American Fur Company eventually dominated the fur trade in the Upper Missouri and Yellowstone regions. The company's success was,

---

[40] Ibid.: 334–335.

[41] Ibid.: 936.

[42] Ibid.: 338–339.

[43] Ibid.: 938.

[44] Washington Irving, *The Adventures of Captain Bonneville*: 297.

doubtless, due to the able but at times harsh leadership of Kenneth McKenzie. Born in Scotland in 1801, he was a well-educated and strong-willed man. He had served British fur companies before joining the American Fur Company in 1827. Describing McKenzie, Hiram Chittenden wrote:

> Of distinguished birth, he always carried himself as one born to command. His discipline was severe, and he had little regard for human life when it stood in his way…when news came of an Indian attack on a party of hunters, he was heard to inquire if the horses had been saved. On hearing that they had all been lost and that only the men had escaped, he exclaimed: "D–n the men! If the horses had been saved, it would have amounted to something!" No one about Fort Union ever doubted his ability; no one but dreaded his authority.[45]

Fort Union was described by Chittenden as "… the best built and most commodiously-equipped post west of the Mississippi …"[46] During their visit to Fort Union on August 24, 1833, the Bonneville party reported that McKenzie was raising domestic cattle at this post.[47] These may have been the first beef cattle to ever reach Montana! On August 29, 1833, William Sublette and his partner, Robert Campbell, established a competing post across the Missouri opposite the mouth of the Yellowstone. It was referred to as Fort William. It lasted only one year before fading into oblivion. The military post Fort Buford was later built on this site.[48]

Late in August 1833 a large band of Assiniboines with some Cree allies (the Crees generally made their home in the British Possessions), about 600 strong, attacked a small camp of Piegans just outside the gates at Fort McKenzie, thus breaking their peace agreement with the Blackfeet.

> The Assiniboines first fell upon the Piegan camp, tore their tents to pieces, killed several of the Indians, and threw the remainder into panic. The employees of the fort made haste to let in the friendly Indians, but the women, by a foolish endeavor to save their property, encumbered themselves with saddles, etc., blocked the door to the fort, and several of them were massacred before they could get in.[49]

---

[45] Chittenden: 384.

[46] Ibid.

[47] Irving: 302.

[48] Chittenden: 935.

[49] Ibid.: 665.

Fighting raged, with the Piegans retreating into the fort from where they maintained fire on the Assiniboines and Crees, who eventually retreated to the surrounding hills.

The German Prince Maximilian von Wied and the artist Karl Bodmer were present at the post when attacked. Maximilian described events during the battle:

> While all this was passing the court yards of the fort presented a very strange scene. A number of wounded men, women and children were laid or placed against the walls; others in their deplorable condition, were pulled about by their relatives amid tears and lamentations. The White Buffalo…who had received a wound in the back of his head was carried about in this manner, amid singing, howling, and crying. They rattled the shischikue in his ears, that the evil spirit might not overcome him, and gave him brandy to drink. He himself, though stupefied, sang without intermission and would not give himself up to the evil spirit. Otsequa-Stomik, an old man of our acquaintance, was wounded in the knee by a ball which a woman cut out with a pen knife, during which operation he did not betray the least symptom of pain. Natah-Otanee, a handsome young man with whom we became acquainted…was suffering dreadfully from severe wounds. Several Indians, especially young women, were likewise wounded.[50]

Reinforcements arrived from the other Piegan villages, and with the aid of the whites from the fort, the enemy was driven from the area. No whites were killed. Losses to the Piegans were seven killed and twenty wounded. The Piegans were initially disappointed with the response of the whites to this attack. However, by the time the enemy had been driven from the area they had become duly impressed with white prowess in battle.[51]

Another violent incident occurred at Fort McKenzie in the summer of 1843. At that time the post was under the direction of a man named Francis A. Chardon, who had a black servant he thought highly of. This servant was killed by some Blackfeet, and Chardon hatched a plot to get even. He was assisted by Alexander Harvey, another fur trader noted for his lack of scruples. The plan was to train a cannon on the post gate the next time the guilty Indian band came in to trade, then as they entered the gate, to set off the cannon, killing as many as possible, panicking the others, then stealing

---

[50] Quoted in Chittenden: 665–666.

[51] Ibid.: 667–668.

Alexander Culberston—Montana pioneer.
PHOTO COURTESY OF MONTANA HISTORICAL
SOCIETY RESEARCH CENTER PHOTOGRAPH
ARCHIVES, HELENA, MONTANA.

Mrs. Alexander Culberston (Natawista).
PHOTO COURTESY OF MONTANA HISTORICAL
SOCIETY RESEARCH CENTER PHOTOGRAPH
ARCHIVES, HELENA, MONTANA.

their goods. The plan was not a complete success, but three Indians were killed and three wounded. One of the dead was a chief.[52] The Blackfeet were, of course, bitter—and the fort had to be abandoned. Another one was built down the Missouri at the mouth of the Judith and christened Fort Chardon. It was soon abandoned, too.

In 1845, Alexander Culbertson, who would become another notable figure in Montana history, established a new post called Fort Lewis about eighteen miles above the present-day Fort Benton bridge. After one year it was decided to move the post downstream to the present site of Fort Benton. It kept the name Fort Lewis, in honor of Meriwether Lewis, until 1850 when it was rebuilt in adobe. It was then christened "Fort Benton, in honor of Thomas H. Benton, who had so often rescued the company from disaster."[53] Fort Benton would remain an American Fur Company post until 1864 when it was sold to the Northwest Fur Company. In 1867–1868 the U.S. Army stationed a company of infantry troops there for the purpose of

---

[52] Ibid.: 685–686.

[53] Ibid.: 937.

guarding military and government stores being shipped up the Missouri to the head of navigation at Fort Benton. The U.S. Army would continue this practice until the 1880's.

Upon the retirement of Kenneth McKenzie, Alexander Culbertson, who had joined the company in 1829, became the American Fur Company's most important man in Montana Territory. He was born in 1809 in Pennsylvania. He is believed to have been present at the Battle of Fort McKenzie in 1833. For some time he headed up operations at Fort Union. He was married to a "...Blood Indian woman of extraordinary intelligence, named Natawista Iksana and with the aid of his wife gained the complete confidence of the Blackfoot Nation."[54] He would later serve as U.S. Indian agent to the Blackfoot Nation. He and his Indian wife were persons of note in Montana Territory.

Eighteen forty-three became a watershed year for the fur trade, in particular the trade in beaver skins. Beaver hats began to be replaced by silk hats, resulting in decreased demand for beaver skins, and, consequently, the importance of the fur trade began to decline in the West. Even James Bridger, who had joined up with the American Fur Company in 1834, opted that year to build Fort Bridger on Black's Fork of the Green River in Wyoming. The primary purpose of this fort was not fur trade, but rather trade with westbound emigrants. Bridger would remain in this business for many years to come, gradually assuming more and more assignments as a guide or scout with various U.S. Army expeditions and campaigns.

Because of his ability, he was highly praised by U.S. Army officers. James Bridger became one of the best known, if not the best known, mountain man from among his original peers, not only because he stayed on the frontier for his entire able life, but also because he succeeded in living a long life. Born in Richmond, Virginia, in 1804, he was only eighteen years old when he joined the Henry expedition in 1822. As late as 1866, at age fifty-two, he still served as a scout for the U.S. Army at Fort Phil Kearny in Wyoming. He did not die until July 17, 1881. Contrast that longevity with Jedediah S. Smith, who was killed by Indians on the Cimarron fifty years earlier in 1831, or with William L. Sublette, who died at age thirty-two.[55] Bridger could speak the Flathead language and doubtless had some ability in other Indian languages. It is documented, however, that he utilized

---

[54] James McClellan Hamilton, *History of Montana*: 87.

[55] Chittenden: 251–259.

Flathead to communicate with a band of Blackfeet in central Montana in the year 1860. His ability to communicate with the Crow Indians is also documented by the Raynolds Expedition.[56] Captain Raynolds, who utilized and praised the services of James Bridger in the years 1859 and 1860, wrote:

> From all that I hear I conclude that in the balmy days of the fur trade, before the silk hat was invented, and when the beaver was the great object of attraction, the bands of trappers in the west were little more than bands of white Indians, having their Indian wives, and all the paraphernalia of Indian life, moving from place to place, as the beaver became scarce, and subsisting like the Indians upon the products of the country. Bridger says that one time he did not taste bread for 17 years.[57]

I have in the course of this essay on the fur trade in Montana mentioned the names of many forts. These were not military posts, for the first military post was not established in Montana Territory until July 11, 1866, with the opening of Camp Cook at the mouth of the Judith River, followed shortly thereafter with the construction of Fort C.F. Smith. The forts mentioned so far were for the most part temporary bastions erected for the protection of the traders against hostile Indians. They were in effect fortified trading posts. These posts were frequently abandoned after a single winter, the exceptions being posts like Fort Union (lying just east of the present-day Montana–North Dakota border), Fort McKenzie and Fort Benton. For example, in 1839 the predominant American Fur Company listed four posts, all of which had a profound impact on trade in Montana: Fort Union, Fort McKenzie, Fort Alexander, and Fort Van Buren. Fort Van Buren originated in 1835 and lasted until 1843. It was located "...on the right bank of the Yellowstone near the mouth of the Tongue River." Fort Alexander was located "...on the left bank of the Yellowstone opposite the mouth of the Rosebud. It was abandoned in 1850."[58]

By 1859 the company still maintained Fort Union, Fort Benton and another post, Fort Sarpy. Fort Sarpy was built in 1850. Its location was on the right bank of the Yellowstone about twenty-five miles downriver from the mouth of the Bighorn River.[59] By the summer of 1860 it was abandoned,

---

[56] W.F. Raynolds, *Report on the Exploration of the Yellowstone River.* 164–167.

[57] Ibid.: 77.

[58] Chittenden: 938–939.

[59] Ibid.

which, as reported later by 1st Lieutenant John Mullins of the Raynolds Expedition, was much to the consternation of the Crow Indians.[60] We will hear later about another fur trading post, Fort Pease, established in late 1875, lying just opposite the mouth of the Bighorn River. The occupants of this short-lived post were rescued by troops from Fort Ellis in March 1876.

Although the economic significance of the fur trade in the American West began its decline in the year 1843, it remained the only industry of any significance in Montana until the discovery of gold in the territory in 1862. Beaver had declined in demand, but trade continued in such items as wolf skins and buffalo robes. Wolf hunters were still active in the territory in the year 1860.[61] As of 1867, French-Canadians along the Missouri in the Dakotas were receiving five to six dollars per buffalo skin.[62]

Cattle herds began to appear in the Deer Lodge and Beaverhead valleys in the late 1850's. They were purchased in a worn-out condition from the transcontinental wagon trains, then driven north to Montana for fattening and eventual resale to westbound pioneers on the Oregon and California trails.[63]

[60] Raynolds: 167.

[61] Ibid.: 112.

[62] Trobriand, *Military Life in Dakota*: 31–32.

[63] Granville Stuart, Vol. II: 97–98.

CHAPTER THREE

The Northern Pacific Railroad Exploration and Survey; The Mullan Road; Indian Tribes Encountered; Early White Settlement

T HE SETTLEMENT OF THE DISPUTE WITH GREAT BRITAIN over the Oregon Territory in 1846 and the subsequent military occupation of that region by the United Sates, as well as technological advances that had occurred since the days of Lewis and Clark, resulted in increased interest in the construction of transcontinental rail routes. By March 1853 Congress authorized funding for the surveying of four such routes. Intense competition between northern and southern sympathizers in Congress during this final decade before the onset of the Civil War rendered them incapable of agreeing on a single route. Therefore, the decision was made to conduct topographical surveys of four potential routes: a northern route, a central route from St. Louis to San Francisco, another route farther south from Memphis via Santa Fe, and a southern route from New Orleans to San Diego.

The administration of President Franklin Pierce and his Secretary of War, Jefferson Davis, selected Isaac I. Stevens (1818–1862) to lead a topographical survey of the northern route. It became known as the Northern Pacific Railroad Exploration and Survey. Stevens was a West Point graduate and former U.S. Army engineer who had seen service and was wounded in the Mexican War. In early 1853 he had received an appointment as governor of the newly formed Washington Territory. Here, we must recognize that our government was not always inefficient and impractical in its actions. Since the governor would be traveling to Washington Territory, why not make better use of his travel by conducting the survey? In so doing, he also gained greater insight into that portion of the future Montana Territory west of the Rockies still incorporated in his assignment.

The U.S. government was not satisfied in killing two birds with one stone; it also accomplished an additional mission. The Commissioner of Indian Affairs, George W. Manypenny, appointed Governor Stevens to serve as Superintendent Ex Officio of Indian Affairs for Washington Territory.

Far more significant for the future Montana Territory was Manypenny's decision to authorize Governor Stevens to report on, meet with, and negotiate treaties with those Indian tribes occupying the vast expanse of territory along the survey route from St. Paul westward to the Rocky Mountains. Stevens was also authorized to appoint and assign Indian agents to the various tribes and make recommendations complete with cost estimates for the establishment of Indian agencies throughout that region.[1] The governor carried out this task diligently, providing thorough reports on the Indian tribes encountered as his survey party passed westward through present-day Montana in 1853. He would return to the area in 1855 to complete treaties with the Flatheads, Pend d'Oreilles and Kootenais (the Treaty of Hellgate), and with the tribes of the Blackfoot Nation—the Blackfoot Treaty of Fort Benton.

These treaties represented the first concrete steps at establishing permanent U.S. government oversight of these Montana tribes. The treaties restricted the recognized domain of these Indian nations and sought to establish peace between the various Indian tribes and nations, and with the whites. By signing these treaties the Indians also granted the whites permission to build and utilize transportation routes through the Indian domain. Compensation was made for loss of Indian land, although very limited, particularly in light of its value in modern times. Promises were made to provide for the Indians and offset the dwindling supply of buffalo and other wild game, already foreseen with the arrival of white settlers. In spite of the treaties, peace did not always reign between the tribes nor were government promises of support always fulfilled.

Governor Stevens was ably assisted in his survey by a recent West Point graduate, 2nd Lieutenant John Mullan. Lieutenant Mullan, a U.S. Army topographical engineer, would for the next nine years play an important role in frontier Montana. The reports generated by these two men give us a consid-

---

[1] George W. Manypenny, "Instructions to Gov. I. I. Stevens": 215–216, in Report of Governor Isaac I. Stevens, Superintendent Ex Officio, Annual Report of the Commissioner of Indian Affairs 1853, National Archives.

erable written record of the future territory during the period 1853–1862. Governor Stevens would go on to serve in his post in Washington Territory and later in Congress. At the onset of the Civil War in 1861, he entered the 79th New York Volunteers as a colonel. He would advance to major general and fall in 1862 at the Battle of Chantilly.

The Northern Pacific Railroad Exploration and Survey party departed St. Paul in the spring of 1853. They traveled by wagon over the prairie, surveying the route to Fort Benton via the Bois de Sioux River in southeastern North Dakota; to Fort Union near the junction of the Missouri and the Yellowstone rivers on the North Dakota–Montana border; then along the north bank of the Missouri to the Milk River; up the Milk River valley to Box Elder Creek, passing near modern-day Havre; and then down the northwest bank of the Missouri to Fort Benton. Here the party left their wagons to proceed on with pack animals. As had been the case with Lewis and Clark on their return voyage, Governor Stevens split up his party, sending Lieutenant Mullan along the more southerly route via Three Forks while he and others proceeded directly from Fort Benton, passing over the return route taken by Meriwether Lewis in 1806, from the Bitterroot up the Clark's Fork and then up the Blackfoot River. On September 8, 1853, while at Fort Benton, Governor Stevens issued the following instructions to Lieutenant Mullan:

> Dear Sir: With a select party, consisting of the Pegan [Piegan] guide, the White Crane, Mr. Rose, Mr. Burr, and two voyageurs, you will visit the Flathead camp on the Muscle Shell [Musselshell] river, about 100 miles south of this place, and procuring the most reliable and intelligent Flathead guides, will make your way to the St. Mary's village, exploring the best pass to that point from the headwaters of the Missouri river. You will collect every possible information as to routes, streams, prominent landmarks, and characteristic features of country—noting particularly the general quality of the soils—the forest trees, grasses, quality of water, and particularly of the route for the passage of wagon trains. With the barometer you will make the best profile time will allow of the route you pass over, and such facts as your limited means will allow, as to the feasibility of the route for a railroad.[2]

To avoid confusing the reader, it should be explained at this point that the Flathead Indians made their permanent home in the Bitterroot Valley.

[2] Isaac I. Stevens, "Instructions from Gov. Stevens": 222–223, ibid.

The camp on the Musselshell River referred to in this quotation was a temporary hunting camp for the procurement of buffalo meat.

Governor Stevens proceeded with the remainder of the party to Sun River Crossing, then on to the Dearborn River, making preliminary examinations of both the Cadotte and Lewis and Clark passes as possible railroad routes. Both of these passes were utilized by various Indian tribes, fur traders and hunters, and were known to the Indians as the Road to the Buffalo. It may interest the reader to note that estimates for these routes foresaw a one-half-mile-long tunnel at the Bird Tail Divide and a 2.1-mile-long tunnel at Lewis and Clark Pass. Crossing at Cadotte's Pass, adjacent to present-day Rogers Pass (Montana Highway 200) would have required a 4.19-mile-long tunnel![3] We must take into account that these estimates were based on the capabilities of the railroad equipment of the time. The steam and diesel engines of later generations could deliver more power and surmount steeper grades. For instance, General William T. Sherman, in discussing the logistical requirements to supply his army on its march to Atlanta some ten years later, estimated one locomotive for every ten cars, at ten tons per car.[4] Locomotives of that era did not have the ability to move the hundred car trains we have become accustomed to seeing behind them in the late 20th century.

After crossing the Continental Divide at Cadotte or Lewis and Clark passes, the Stevens party proceeded down the Blackfoot River to the Hellgate Canyon and the Bitterroot Valley near present-day Missoula. Arriving there in October 1853, it met with Lieutenant Mullan's party. Governor Stevens ordered Lieutenant Mullan to remain with a small party at Cantonment Stevens in the Bitterroot Valley throughout the winter and explore the region for a suitable railroad route as well as a wagon road leading from Fort Benton to Fort Walla Walla.

During the winter of 1853–1854, Lieutenant Mullan and members of his party traveled over 1,000 miles within the Rocky Mountains examining potential routes in a vast region bounded by the Kootenai River in the north and Fort Hall on the Oregon Trail over 400 miles to the south (near present-day Pocatello, ID). He collected and followed up on information provided by Hudson's Bay Company fur traders with knowledge of the region. Such information gave him clues on potential routes, but his sources

---

[3] John Mullan, *Report on the Construction of a Military Road*: 157–164.

[4] William T. Sherman, *Memoirs*: 11.

of information were accustomed to travel through these areas with pack animals and had no need to consider the feasibility of a wagon road through these passes. In the case of a railroad route, they also had no knowledge of the grade requirements, etc. Considerable assistance was provided by a half-breed, Gabriel Prudhomme, who had traveled extensively through the area with the Jesuit fathers in prior years.[5] Prudhomme would die shortly thereafter at Fort Owen, on January 15, 1856.[6]

Mullan selected a wagon route from the Bitterroot Valley via the Hellgate Canyon up the Clark's Fork River to Gold Creek, American Gulch and the Deer Lodge area. From there the road led up the Little Blackfoot River and over Mullan Pass just north of present-day MacDonald Pass, then north making several crossings of Little Prickly Pear Creek. It passed near present-day Wolf Creek, MT, and then paralleled present-day U.S. Highway 287 to the Dearborn Crossing. From here the trail crossed the Birdtail Divide west of Birdtail Rock and passed between Shaw and Square Buttes, then ran either direct to the Sun River Crossing or direct to a point approximately three miles below the Sun River Crossing. This crossing was referred to a few years later by surveyors stationed at Fort Shaw as the Middle Bridge. Both the Sun River Crossing and the Middle Bridge routes led to a point near present-day Vaughn, MT, known as the Leavings of Sun River. Here the road left the Sun River valley and took more or less a direct line past Benton Lake and Twenty-Eight Mile Springs to Fort Benton.

Aware of the political and promotional value of a quick, practical use of the route, Lieutenant Mullan effected sufficient preparations of this road to bring the wagons, left earlier at Fort Benton by the Stevens party, over the road to Cantonment Stevens near present-day Missoula. He completed the trip by March 31, 1854. This resulted in a congressional appropriation of $30,000 for work on the route.[7] Mullan continued his exploration westward, searching for the most suitable route over the mountains to Spokane and then to Fort Walla Walla. In September 1854 he and his party were ordered from the field.[8]

In January 1855, Lieutenant Mullan departed Washington Territory en route to the nation's capital in hopes of influencing a decision to

---

5 Mullan: 4.

6 John Owen, *The Journals and Letters of Major John Owen*: 115.

7 Mullan: 4.

8 Ibid.: 7.

Captain John Mullan.
PHOTO COURTESY OF MONTANA HISTORICAL
SOCIETY RESEARCH CENTER PHOTOGRAPH
ARCHIVES, HELENA, MONTANA.

appropriate sufficient funds for the completion of his project. He was to be disappointed, however, for that same year he was ordered south to Florida to participate in the Seminole campaign. By 1858 the former territorial governor Isaac Stevens was serving in Congress and continued the campaign for the completion of the road.

On April 5, 1858, Lieutenant Mullan departed New York for The Dalles, Oregon Territory, arriving there on May 15, 1858, anticipating a prompt resumption of his project, but he was deterred by another Indian war, this one between the U.S. Army and the Spokane, Coeur d'Alene and Pelouse Indian tribes in eastern Washington Territory. In December 1858, Mullan again returned to Washington, D.C., to lobby for the road.[9] He was successful and returned in the spring of 1859 with an appropriation of $100,000 for the project. Work was promptly commenced, with one hundred men assigned to the project, working from west to east, and by December 1859 construction was completed up to the vicinity of present-day Lookout Pass on the Montana-Idaho border.[10] At the time it was named Sohon's Pass after Gustavius Sohon, a member of Mullan's party. It crossed the Continental Divide on the border about one mile south of present-day Interstate 90 over Lookout Pass. Mullan was aided in his selection of this location by Aeneas, an Iroquois Indian guide.[11]

The party made winter camp at Cantonment Jordan, located near present-day De Borgia, MT.[12] Since Mullan had already brought wagons over the

---

[9] Ibid.: 9.

[10] Ibid.: 18.

[11] Ibid.: 6. It is of interest that Aeneas is described by Granville Stuart as an Iroquois Indian adopted into the Flathead tribe (Stuart, *Forty Years on the Frontier*, Vol. I: 196). According to Stuart he passed through American Fork on February 13, 1862, in search of a Snake Indian known as Peed-ge-ge. He and another Flathead Indian located Peed-ge-ge near present-day Deer Lodge, killed him and took one of his wives. (Ibid.: 197).

[12] Ibid.: 15a.

route between Fort Benton and the Bitterroot Valley in 1854, he was confident that he could now complete the route by the following summer of 1860. He was also aware that the U.S. Army posts in Oregon and Washington territories would be receiving recruits during the summer of 1860. He sent a dispatch to Washington, D.C., urging that these recruits—some 300 in number—be sent up the Missouri by steamboat to Fort Benton to await his completion of the road. Mullan wrote later in his report:

General Isaac I. Stevens.
PHOTO COURTESY OF THE LIBRARY OF CONGRESS.

> ...nothing should be left undone to secure the full success of the movement recommended; this was to send three hundred recruits from St. Louis to Fort Benton in the spring by steamers P. Choteau & Co., with four months supplies, and that I would meet them at Fort Benton with my train, with which they could make the trip to Walla-Walla in sixty days.[13]

In the meantime Mullan was in need of additional supplies. He engaged the assistance of the Flathead tribe, who made their home in the Bitterroot Valley. Responding to his request they provided him with over one hundred horses and fifteen to twenty men for the purposes of obtaining provisions from Fort Benton.

> They were paid for the use of their animals and the services of their men and made the trip in the month of March safely across the Rocky Mountains [to Fort Benton] bringing me back 11,000 rations...Such nobleness of character as is found among some of the Flatheads is seldom seen among Indians; and I here record to their credit that I have never had a want but which, when made known to them, they supplied, and that they always treated myself and my parties with a frank generosity and a continuous friendship.[14]

---

13 Ibid.: 21.

14 Ibid.

Although some rerouting of the wagon road occurred, particularly in the Deer Lodge Valley, Mullan and his party followed the route to Fort Benton utilized in 1853–1854, making necessary grading and other improvements. They reached Sun River Crossing on July 28, 1860.[15] Shortly thereafter Fort Benton was reached. There Mullan found Major George Blake waiting with the 300 U.S. Army recruits. Mullan, along with his wagons, led Major Blake and his men back over the newly constructed road, and they accomplished their march to Fort Walla Walla in fifty-seven days. Lieutenant Mullan estimated that their utilization of his new wagon road saved the U.S. government approximately $30,000 in travel expenses.[16] The Mullan party would continue working on the road making improvements, building bridges, and making repairs until September 11, 1862. When he departed Fort Walla Walla for Washington, D.C., Mullan wrote:

> Thus ended my work in the field, costing seven years of close and arduous attention, exploring and opening up a road of six hundred and twenty-four miles from the Columbia to the Missouri river, at a cost of $230,000…suffice it to say, we succeeded to our own satisfaction in accomplishing the full object of our mission, and those who by their cheerful aid lent me their cooperation have here my most heartfelt thanks…Our road involved one hundred and twenty miles of difficult timber-cutting, twenty-five feet broad, and thirty measured miles of excavation, fifteen to twenty feet wide. The remainder was either through an open, timbered country, or over open, rolling prairie.[17]

At the time of the construction of the Mullan Road, the changes to be wrought by the Civil War (1861–1865) and the subsequent rapid construction of the first transcontinental railroad (1869) were not foreseen. The section of the road running from Fort Benton to Helena, and to a lesser extent from Helena westward to Missoula, saw extensive utilization upon the discovery of gold in the early 1860's, in particular for moving freight goods south from Fort Benton to Helena and then by other routes to Virginia City and other settlements in southwestern Montana. However, some portions fell into disuse. By 1877 that portion running from Missoula to present-day Coeur d'Alene, ID, had so deteriorated that it was no longer passable by

---

[15] Ibid.: 26.

[16] Ibid.

[17] Ibid.

wagon without considerable repairs. That same year, General of the Army William Tecumseh Sherman, in contemplating a journey westward from Missoula, wrote, "For years it was traveled, but now has gone into disuse. Its bridges are all gone, and fallen timber so obstructs it, that I expect to drop my wagons at Missoula and take horses and packs."[18]

Of interest to the Montana historian are the records of the Indian tribes, missionaries, and early settlers who were residing in Montana at the time of the Northern Pacific Railroad Survey and the construction of the Mullan Road. The first to mention are the Indian tribes. During his westward movement within the region that later became Montana Territory, Governor Stevens provided thorough and extensive reports to the Commissioner of Indian Affairs on the Indian tribes he and members of his party encountered. These tribes were the Assiniboines; the tribes of the Blackfoot Nation known as the Bloods, the Blackfeet proper, the Piegans and the Gros Ventres; the Flatheads; and the Pend d'Oreilles.

The Assiniboines generally occupied the northeast corner of Montana Territory with some of them dwelling north of the border in Canada (the British Possessions).[19] The Stevens party first encountered them near the juncture of the Yellowstone and the Missouri in July 1853. They described the camp as "...numbering about one hundred and fifty lodges, and containing some twelve hundred persons."[20] They were at that time led by Chief Grizzly Bear and two lesser chiefs, Blue Thunder and Little Thunder. The Assiniboines were described as very friendly and possessing many dogs, which they utilized as beasts of burden. They also possessed many horses, some of very good quality. Governor Stevens wrote, "The Assiniboine Indians are, by no means, neat in their appearance, and seemed to be very poor, if we can judge from the meagreness of their clothing, which evidently had been worn a great length of time."[21]

Already in 1853 these Indians were lamenting the gradual demise of the buffalo on which they depended for their sustenance, which is of interest, since as of that time in our history, American whites had scarcely penetrated their area. Governor Stevens promised them that the "Great Father in

---

[18] William T. Sherman and Philip Sheridan, *Reports of Inspection Made in the Summer of 1877*: 59.

[19] Annual Report of the Commissioner of Indian Affairs, 1870, "Annual Report of Lieutenant Colonel A. Sully," United States Army: 189, National Archives.

[20] Annual Reports of the Commissioner of Indian Affairs, 1853, "Report of Gov. Isaac Stevens": 392, National Archives. We should note that this estimate approximates eight persons per lodge.

[21] Ibid.: 393.

Washington" would provide them with necessary provisions after the inevitable disappearance of the buffalo. One of the chiefs is quoted by Stevens:

> My Father, not long ago the Indian tribes of the Missouri river were called to council at Fort Laramie [referring to the Treaty of Fort Laramie concluded 1850 at Fort Laramie, Nebraska Territory]. A treaty was there made, fixing the hunting grounds of each tribe, and restraining each of them from encroaching on those of any other tribe. We have sacredly observed the treaty, and have never gone out of the grounds set apart for us. But the Sioux, on the one side, have come into our hunting grounds, and the half-breeds, on the other, have hunted over our plains.[22]

The half-breeds referred to were also known as the Red River Hunters, people of a French-Canadian and Indian mixture, who resided along the Red River near the present-day North Dakota–Canada–Minnesota borders. A number of them resided across the boundary in Canada. They subsisted to a considerable degree on agriculture but also conducted very large and efficient hunting expeditions westward into the buffalo country of the Sioux and the Assiniboines to procure buffalo meat and skins. Some of these expeditions numbered as high as 1,300 men, women, and children.[23] It is of little doubt that the results of such hunts on the food supply of local natives did not go unnoticed. Understandably, the Assiniboines sought the assistance of the powerful white tribe in driving their enemies from their hunting grounds.

The most significant and dangerous tribes in Montana at the time of the Stevens expedition were the members of the Blackfoot Nation. As we recall from the chapter on the fur trade era, they had a well-deserved reputation as very hostile. They were greatly feared not only by whites but by the other Indian tribes as well. Their hunting grounds were considered to extend west to east from the Rocky Mountains to the Judith River to the east and south of the bend of the Missouri River and to the mouth of the Milk River on the north bank of the Missouri. From north to south their domain stretched from the Saskatchewan River in present-day Alberta to points south of present-day Helena, MT. Governor Stevens encountered one Blackfeet hunting party near Fort Union, close to the mouth of the Yellowstone. During the fur trade era they were also found in the Powder River country; in the Wind

---

[22] Ibid.: 396.
[23] Ibid.: 399.

River country, the Green River country, and Jackson Hole in Wyoming; and Pierre's Hole in Idaho. The Flatheads in the Bitterroot Valley also experienced on occasion depredations by the Blackfeet.[24]

The Blackfoot Nation consisted of three distinct tribes: the Bloods, the Piegans and the Blackfeet proper; at the time, the U.S. Army also considered the Gros Ventres to be a Blackfeet tribe. Governor Stevens reported the Bloods (numbering at least 350 lodges amounting to a population of 2,450 with 875 warriors) and the Blackfeet proper (numbering at least 250 lodges amounting to a population of 1,750 with 625 warriors) shared an area at the headwaters of the Marias and Milk rivers. This area extended northward to the 50th parallel in Canada. With the exception of that portion north of the Canadian boundary, this would approximate the present location of the Blackfeet Reservation in Montana. The Piegans, consisting of 350 lodges and a population of 2,450 with 875 warriors, occupied an area generally extending from the Milk River south to the Marias and Teton rivers and bounded on the south and east by the Missouri River. The Gros Ventres numbered 360 lodges and a population of 2,520 with 900 warriors.[25] They were located in the country extending westward from the junction of the Milk and Missouri rivers to the territory of the Piegans. The Piegans, Bloods and the Blackfeet proper spoke the same language, but the Gros Ventres spoke the "...Arrapahoe language, which is not [as of 1853] understood by any white man or Indian, not of their tribe...Most of the Gros Ventres, however, speak the Blackfoot sufficiently for purposes of trade."[26]

The Gros Ventres came to be considered part of the Blackfoot Nation circa 1823. They had broken off with their Arapahoe kin around 1813 and settled for a time with the Crow Indians. After a brief period of mistreatment by their new hosts, "...they wandered over this country [general area of their homeland at the time of Stevens's visit] several years, plundered forts at the north, were driven away by the Kootenais, and, finally, in a destitute and miserable condition, settled some thirty years since in the country they now occupy."[27] They eventually established generally friendly relations with the other tribes of the Blackfoot Nation. They became prosperous through this relationship and their relationships with traders. Governor Stevens found them to have a friendly disposition toward his party, but he

---

[24] Ibid.: 415.

[25] Ibid.: 402.

[26] Ibid.: 403.

[27] Ibid.: 402–403.

nevertheless described them as "…now more independent, saucy, and more unfriendly to the whites, than any other band of the Blackfeet."[28]

The first encounter between the Stevens party and members of the Gros Ventre tribe occurred in late August 1853 upon their arrival at the Milk River.

> Among them were Eagle Chief, and his son; White Eagle; Little Soldier; and among the squaws a very pretty woman, wife of the Eagle Chief's son, called White Antelope.[29] Stevens learned that a family dispute had arisen between them and the Blackfeet proper. The Gros Ventres were preparing for hostilities. The governor urged them to maintain peace with their Indian neighbors in compliance with the wishes of the "Great Father in Washington." The Indians agreed to do so, and treated the governor and his party with kind hospitality. He was invited into numerous Gros Ventres lodges where he was always offered "… a mess made of buffalo-marrow, berries, and the scrapings of buffalo-lodge skins. I felt bound to partake of the proffered repast in each case, and found it quite palatable."[30]

Governor Stevens dispatched Mr. Stanley, his artist, in the direction of "the Cypress Mountain" in search of the Piegans with a request that they come to Fort Benton to meet him in council. This is believed to be the area of the Cypress Hills located near present-day Eastend, Saskatchewan, approximately seventy air miles straight north of Havre, MT. Mr. Stanley's party located the Piegan camp on September 14, 1853, "…160 miles north 20° west of Fort Benton."[31] The camp consisted of about one hundred lodges and 1,000 persons under the leadership of Chief Low Horn. Mr. Stanley was well received and treated in numerous lodges with a dessert consisting of "… boiled buffalo blood and dried berries."[32]

The chief agreed to travel to Fort Benton for the council meeting. Thus was Mr. Stanley witness to the high degree of mobility possessed by the Indian tribes of the plains. The reader may recall a scene from the popular movie *Dances with Wolves* in which the hero, Lieutenant Dunbar, marvels at the ability of his Indian hosts to strike their entire village and move out in a matter of hours. Mr. Stanley reported:

> At an early hour the town crier announced the intention of the chief

[28] Ibid.: 403.

[29] Ibid.: 405.

[30] Ibid.: 406.

[31] Ibid.: 408.

[32] Ibid.

to move camp. The horses were immediately brought in an[d] secured around their respective lodges, and in less than one hour the
whole encampment was drawn out in two parallel lines on the plains,
forming one of the most picturesque scenes I have ever witnessed...
Preparation for their transportation was made in the following manner: The poles of the lodge, which are from twenty to thirty feet in
length, are divided, the small ends being lashed together and secured
to the shoulders of the horse, allowing the but[t]-ends to drag upon
the ground on either side. Just behind the horse are secured two
cross-pieces to keep the poles in their respective places, upon which
are placed the lodge and domestic furniture. This also serves for the
safe transportation of the children and infirm, unable to ride on
horseback, the lodge being folded so as to allow two or more to ride
securely...The horses dragging this burden, often of three hundred
pounds, are also ridden by the squaws, with a child astride behind
and one in her arms, embracing a favorite young pup. Their dogs, of
which they have a large number, are also used in transporting their
effects in the same manner as the horses, making with ease twenty
miles a day, dragging forty pounds...In this way this heterogeneous
caravan, comprised of a thousand souls; with twice that number of
horses, and at least three hundred dogs, fell into line and trotted
gaily until night; while the chiefs and braves rode in front, flank, or
rear, ever ready for the chase or defence against a foe.[33]

On September 21, 1853, the governor held his council in Fort Benton. Three
of the Blackfeet tribes—the Piegans, the Bloods and the Blackfeet proper—
were in attendance. The Gros Ventres had, after accompanying the governor to
Fort Benton, lost patience with the wait and returned to their hunting grounds.
Although the governor does not mention this in his report, the Gros Ventres
were doubtless still festering over their dispute with the Blackfeet proper. He
impressed upon the Indians the desire of the "Great Father in Washington" for
peace among the various Indian tribes as well as peace between the Indians
and the whites. The Piegan chief, Low Horn, spoke for the Indians and after
the council "...he assembled his braves and...addressed them with great fervor
and eloquence; commanded them to cease sending out war parties henceforth,
and threatened them with severe punishment if they disobeyed."[34]

In his report on the Blackfeet the governor notes the lack of one white
man's evil which by 1853 had not yet made its debilitating impact on these

[33] Ibid.: 408–409.
[34] Ibid.: 411.

Indians. "Most of these Indians have never tasted whiskey, and only know it by their traditions of the white man's fire-water."[35] The governor described their diet as principally derived from the buffalo, i.e. buffalo meat, and a turnip or root referred to as *typsina* and dried berries. The liver of the buffalo was eaten raw, preferably while still warm.[36] The domestic behavior of the Indians was "kind and cheerful," with the wives and children well treated. As was the case with most Plains Indian tribes, the domestic labor was performed by the women.

Although the Blackfeet possessed some guns referred to by Governor Stevens as "northwest trading guns," they were more adept with the bow and arrow.

> The arrows have steel heads [obviously obtained from traders] and are feathered. When an Indian attacks a buffalo, if he fails with his gun he instantly brings his bow and arrows from his back, and discharges his arrows with great rapidity, firing from twelve to fifteen in a minute. At fifty yards the Indians are as certain in their aim with the bow and arrows as with a rifle. But it is remarkable that they never sight the arrow, and never elevate it to the eye, but always fire from the breast.[37]

The tribes of the Blackfoot Nation were not only noted for their hostility to whites at that time in history but were also greatly feared by other Indian tribes in the area. Since the Road to the Buffalo led into Blackfeet country, the numerous tribes from west of the Rockies frequently clashed with them during their buffalo hunts. As was the case with most of the Plains Indian tribes, nearly all other tribes were viewed as either deadly enemies, potential enemies or occasional enemies. During the period of his travels in the Northwest in 1845–1846, preceding the Stevens party by some eight years, Father Pierre-Jean De Smet reported frequent clashes between the Blackfeet and the Crees, located at the time north of Blackfeet country in southern Alberta. "The Cree nation is considered very powerful and numbers more than six hundred wigwams. This tribe is one of the most formidable enemies of the Blackfeet…The preceding year [1844] they carried off more than six hundred horses."[38]

---

[35] Ibid.: 412. We know, however, that the Bloods had been plied with alcohol during their siege of Fort McKenzie in the 1830's. We may assume that as of Stevens's visit the use of alcohol was not entirely unknown but not widespread among the Blackfeet.

[36] Ibid.

[37] Ibid.: 413.

[38] Pierre-Jean De Smet, *Oregon Missions*: 167.

There were also frequent clashes between the Blackfeet and their neighbors to the southeast, the Crows. Prior to his travels in Blackfeet country, Father De Smet had spent time west of the Rocky Mountains among the numerous Indian tribes living in the Columbia drainage. He commented:

> The difference of physiognomy existing between the Indians inhabiting the plains east of the mountains and those near the upper waters of the Columbia, is as great as the stupendous rocks that separate them. The latter are remarkable for their mildness, serenity and affability, while cruelty, craft—the word BLOOD, in fine, may be read in every feature of the Black-Foot Indian.[39]

The other two prominent tribes the governor and members of his party came into contact with were the Flatheads residing in the Bitterroot Valley and the Pend d'Oreilles, the two larger tribes of what the Office of Indian Affairs would later call the Flathead Nation. The governor estimated the Flatheads to number about sixty lodges, some devoid of men, totaling about 350 persons. Their village also contained sixteen log houses. They were led by Chief Victor. "The tribe was once a very powerful one, but has been much diminished by the Blackfeet...At a council held at Fort Owen, the Flatheads pointed out to me six or seven orphan boys whose fathers had been, within two or three years, killed by the Blackfeet."[40]

Indeed, that well-known landmark, the Hellgate Canyon, near present-day Missoula, MT, received its name as the result of clashes between the Blackfeet and the Flatheads. Lieutenant Mullan, upon passing through this canyon, was told of a battle in which approximately forty Flatheads had ambushed eleven Blackfeet who were the vanguard of a larger war party en route to Flathead country. The eleven Blackfeet were wiped out entirely. The Hellgate was so named by the Flatheads, for it was a favorite ambush site utilized by both sides.[41]

The demise of so many Flathead warriors at the hands of the Blackfeet resulted not only from Blackfeet incursions into Flathead territory, but also from losses sustained while the Flatheads were on their buffalo hunts out on the plains, where they frequently clashed with the more numerous Blackfeet. The Flathead warrior was noted for his bravery and his inclination to go into battle regardless of the number of enemies arrayed against

---

[39] Ibid.: 175.

[40] Annual Report of the Commissioner of Indian Affairs 1853: 419, National Archives.

[41] Ibid.: 417.

him. This may also have accounted for their heavy losses of manpower.

By 1853 the Flatheads were engaged in agriculture and also possessed about 1,000 head of domestic cattle, which had been introduced by the Jesuit missionaries during the 1840's. The Flatheads also subsisted on

> ...elk, moose, black and white tailed deer, the Bighorn, and bears. Beaver and otter are abundant. Their custom is to make two hunts annually across the mountains—one in the spring, returning in the fall; another in the fall, returning about mid-winter.[42]

Other tribes living west of the Rocky Mountains often joined the Flatheads in these hunts, especially their neighbors, the Pend d'Oreilles, as well as the Nez Perce, Coeur d'Alenes, etc. The Reverend N. Point, a Jesuit missionary, once accompanied the Flatheads on one of these hunting expeditions. He wrote, "On one occasion they returned [to the hunting camp] laden with the spoils of 344 fat [buffalo] cows."[43]

In 1863 Lieutenant Mullan described the Flatheads as

> ...the best Indians in the mountains. They have treaty arrangements with the government, but have never gone upon their reservation upon the Jocko river; no steps have been taken to remove them thence, and they still reside in St. Mary's valley [Bitterroot Valley], which, by terms of the treaty was guaranteed to them. They think the government has not kept its faith in not confirming this valley to them...They own great numbers of horses and cattle, and cultivate the soil more than any Indians except the Pend d'Oreilles. They are friendly, and under their chiefs, Victor, Ambrose, and Moïse, will always remain so unless some great injustice is done to them.[44]

The Pend d'Oreilles, pronounced *pon-der ray*,[45] were the largest tribe of the so-called Flathead Nation. At the time of the arrival of the Stevens party, they numbered about sixty lodges with approximately 420 persons. They made their home in the Jocko River Valley around the St. Ignatius Mission, which had been established by the Jesuits in their midst about 1844. "When the missionaries came among the Indians, they found them to be a poor, miserable, half-starved race, with an insufficiency of food, and nearly

---

[42] Ibid.: 415–416.

[43] De Smet, *Oregon Missions*: 385.

[44] Mullan: 49.

[45] Those fluent in French may choose to differ with me on this pronunciation. It is, however, the pronunciation given to me by an American Indian official at the Flathead agency.

naked; living upon fish, camash and other roots, and as the last extremity, upon the pine-tree moss."[46]

The missionaries gradually adapted the Pend d'Oreilles to a degree of subsistence from agriculture. They found the Indians inclined to learn and willing to work. Loyola was their chief at that time. He was very popular. At the time of his death in 1851, he was succeeded by Chief Victor—not the same man as Chief Victor of the Flatheads. The missionaries maintained about 160 acres under cultivation. "This is kept up for the natives, as but a few acres would be amply sufficient for the missionaries."[47] In addition to the supplies of buffalo meat procured on their annual hunts with the Flatheads, Nez Perce, and other Indians, they also subsisted on fish, venison and bear. The camash, or camas, root was a popular staple of the Pend d'Oreilles. Father De Smet described it as

> ...a small white vapid onion when removed from the earth, but becomes black and sweet when prepared for food...Baked in the ground over a period of several hours]...camash thus acquires a consistency equal to that of jujube [date-like fruit or gum drop]...It is sometimes made into loaves of various dimensions. It is excellent, especially when boiled with meat. If kept dry, it can be preserved a long time.[48]

On their deer hunts, the Pend d'Oreilles frequently took advantage of heavy snows, which rendered the deer relatively immobile in some areas: "...the deer cannot escape and are readily pursued and killed with clubs. They hunt over the whole section so thoroughly as to exterminate these animals in that locality, leaving none to breed....Last winter they killed eight hundred deer, these were but just sufficient for their wants."[49]

The Pend d'Oreilles, like their Flathead brothers, demonstrated friendship and good faith toward members of the Stevens party. Once, while on a buffalo hunt on the Musselshell River, the leaders learned that some newly "acquired" horses had been stolen by young Pend d'Oreille braves from Lieutenant Mullan's camp on the Bitterroot, over 150 miles distant. It was decided that a delegation of Indians would return these horses to Mullan

---

[46] Annual Report of the Commissioner of Indian Affairs, 1853: 419.

[47] Ibid.: 421.

[48] Ibid.: 423.

[49] Ibid.: 422. Although it is not mentioned by Governor Stevens, one must speculate that the Indians were equipped with snowshoes, which would enable them to move more rapidly in deep snow than the unfortunate deer.

without delay. "Thus the…Indians proved themselves not only honest but brave in the highest degree, coming as they did, five days and nights into an enemy's country, simply to do an act of justice to strangers."[50] Lieutenant Mullan would later describe the Pend d'Oreilles as "…friendly although there are some bad fellows among them."[51]

A third, smaller tribe known as the Kootenai Indians also dwelled just to the north of the Pend d'Oreilles. They resided about the shores of Flathead Lake and subsisted mostly on fish and roots. They also accompanied the Flatheads and Pend d'Oreilles on the annual buffalo hunts. Members of this tribe also migrated farther north into Canada on occasion. They were a relatively poor tribe with fewer horses than the Pend d'Oreilles and the Flatheads.[52] The Treaty of Hellgate in 1855 incorporated them into the Flathead Reservation along with the Pend d'Oreilles and the Flatheads.

Lieutenant Mullan would later make limited mention of the Shoshone (Snake) and Bannock Indians who roamed about the southwestern portion of Montana in the Beaverhead and Deer Lodge valleys and in the Salmon River country of Idaho. He commented, "I do not know their number or condition. I only know that they are adept horse thieves, have no treaty arrangements with the government, and need to be looked after both for the security of the frontier settlements and their own good."[53]

Although the Nez Perce did not reside in Montana in great numbers, there were some who regularly wintered in the Bitterroot Valley. Mullan referred to them as "Mountain Nez Perce," living among the Flatheads upwards of 200 in number. He stated that they were "…an annoyance both to the [Flatheads] and the whites. They should be either incorporated with the Flatheads or made to live with their tribe. They are generally disaffected and cause much trouble and disturbance in the country."[54]

This particular band of Nez Perce was referred to by John Owen as "Buffalo Indians." In 1859 he wrote:

> I would like the attention of Agent Cain called to that portion of the Nez Perces tribe known as the Buffalo Indians. They…are in the habit of wintering in the Bitterroot valley some thirty miles above

---

[50] Ibid.: 424.

[51] Mullan: 50.

[52] Report of the Commissioner of Indian Affairs, 1868: 211, National Archives.

[53] Mullan: 50.

[54] Ibid.

the agency [somewhere near present-day Darby], and I do assure you they are a source of great annoyance; killing cattle and stealing horses from the neighboring tribes.[55]

In view of the role they play in Montana military history, note that Lieutenant Mullan's opinion of the Nez Perce Indians residing in their homelands in eastern Washington and Oregon territories contrasted greatly from his remarks about the "Mountain Nez Perce." The Nez Perce, treaty and non-treaty, had not participated with the Spokanes, Coeur D'Alenes and Pelouses in their war with the whites in eastern Washington Territory in 1858. Instead, Chief Lawyer of the treaty Nez Perce had provided the U.S. Army with approximately thirty of their warriors to assist in the war with the hostiles. Colonel George Wright, in command of the campaign, had placed Lieutenant Mullan in charge of this cadre of Nez Perce scouts. While still in the field during this campaign, Mullan addressed a letter regarding the Indian problem to Charles E. Mix, Commissioner of Indian Affairs, Washington, D.C. The letter was written at the "Camp at the Four Lakes, Spokane Plains, Washington Territory," on September 5, 1858. In this letter Mullan sought to distinguish three tribes from the hostile Indians, namely the Nez Perce, the Flatheads and the Pend d'Oreilles. He noted that the Nez Perce were

> ... far advanced already in civilization—much further than any tribe west of the Rocky mountains, except the Flatheads. They are inclined to agriculture; already raise wheat, corn, and vegetables, with the rudest of means. When asked by Colonel Wright what they wanted, their reply was well worthy of a noble race: "Peace, ploughs, and schools."...I ask that a special appropriation be made to give these people schools, farms, and seeds; that means be taken to so build them up in their mountain homes that we may be enabled to point with joyous pride to a first few tutored savages reclaimed from their wild, nomadic habits; and while asking, aye petitioning for these, I cannot forget my old mountain friends the Flatheads and Pend d'Oreilles.[56]

To turn to the status of white settlement in the future Montana Territory at the time: The only white settlements of any size mentioned by Mullan along his construction route were at Frenchtown—about fifteen farms, a

---

[55] Annual Report of the Commissioner of Indian Affairs 1859: 424, National Archives.

[56] Mullan: 281–282.

sawmill and a gristmill, a few more farms along creeks in the Hellgate area, including a house belonging to a Frenchman named Brown, Higgins & Worden's store and Van Dorn's blacksmith shop in Hellgate (likely on Rattlesnake Creek), Fort Owen in the Bitterroot Valley near present-day Stevensville operated by Mr. John Owen, and a farm operated by Mr. Dempsey between Flint Creek and American Gulch. John D. Brown, who worked on the Mullan Road, would later refer to Mr. Dempsey as "...Bob Dempsey, an old discharged soldier, who lived between Gold Creek and what is now Radersburg."[57] In the summer of 1862 members of Mullan's party encountered a gold mining settlement near Deer Lodge, "...where we found Messrs. Blake, McAdow, Higgins, Dr. Atkinson and Gold Tom at work sluicing, and at the time they were taking out about ten dollars per day to the hand, and with fair prospects of extensive digging."[58]

Gold Tom is reported by John D. Brown as being the first person to successfully prospect gold in Gold Creek.[59] Mr. P.M. Engle reported that as of November 1859, "... Mr. John Grant has settled near the junction of the Hell's Gate river and built two log houses."[60] Grant had first wintered in the Deer Lodge Valley in 1857–1858 and by 1859 had some 250 horses and 800 cattle. By the time of the gold discovery in Bannack in July 1862, he had been joined in the valley by the families of Louis Deschenau, Leon Quesnelle, Louis Demers, David Contais, Fred Burr, the Stuart brothers, the Cosgrove brothers, Mr. Jackson, Jake Meek and the Leclair brothers. They all settled on Cottonwood Creek about eleven miles from the Little Blackfoot River.[61]

No other settlements or houses were reported until the road reached the Sun River Crossing, where Colonel A.J. Vaughan operated the Blackfeet agency farm, with some thirty to forty acres under cultivation raising wheat and vegetables. The farm was also in possession of a small hand-operated gristmill.[62] Besides Colonel Vaughan and his Indian wife and child, there was another white family consisting of J.H. Vail, his wife and two children,

---

[57] Quoted in Robert Vaughn, *Then and Now:* 188.

[58] Mullan: 34, 42.

[59] Vaughn: 190. According to Montana historian James McClellan Hamilton, Gold Tom was Henry Thomas, and his nickname had been given to him by Granville Stuart. Hamilton, *History of Montana:* 214.

[60] Mullan: 140.

[61] Lyndel Meikle, *Very Close to Trouble:* 66–77.

[62] Mullan: 42

and his sister-in-law, Miss O'Brien.[63] A Joseph Swift also wintered there in 1862–1863.[64] Of course, there was at the beginning of the Mullan Road the trading post settlement at Fort Benton. This was an American Fur Company post operating under the direction of Alexander Culbertson.

---

[63] Miss O'Brien would marry Henry Plummer, who was later hanged by vigilantes at Bannack.

[64] Vaughn: 51.

CHAPTER FOUR

The Jesuit Missionaries;
Steamboat Navigation to Fort Benton;
The Raynolds Expedition 1859–1860

NOT TO BE OVERLOOKED WAS THE CONTRIBUTION made to the settlement of the territory by the Jesuits. We have already made note of the Jesuit mission at St. Ignatius in the Jocko River Valley. This served as the mission for the Pend d'Oreille Indians. At the time of the arrival of the Stevens party, it was staffed by Father Adrian Hoecken, Brothers Francis and McGean and others unidentified. It had been in operation for about eight years, having been established in the spring of 1845.[1] The mission possessed over 1,000 head of cattle, a hand-operated gristmill on which the Indians could grind three bushels of wheat per day into flour, and about 160 acres under cultivation.[2]

Farther to the south, in the Bitterroot Valley, the Jesuits had also founded the St. Mary's Mission in the year 1841. By 1846 the mission consisted of a little log church and twelve log houses, a flour mill capable of milling ten to twelve bushels of wheat per day, a sawmill, forty head of cattle, domestic waterfowl, and a farm where wheat, potatoes, parsnips, beets, beans, and peas were harvested. As of 1845 this mission was staffed by Father G. Mengarini, Father Serbinati and four Brothers. The mission was located near present-day Stevensville, MT.[3]

As an integral part of their effort to bring Christianity to the Indians,

---

[1] Pierre-Jean De Smet, *Oregon Missions*: 259.

[2] Annual Report of the Commissioner of Indian Affairs 1853: 420, National Archives.

[3] De Smet: 288–292.

the Jesuits wished to establish a mission among the tribes of the Blackfoot Nation. The Blackfeet were, however, very hostile to whites and the much feared enemy of the Flatheads and the Pend d'Oreilles, host tribes of the St. Mary's and St. Ignatius missions. On October 25, 1845, Father Pierre-Jean De Smet met with a delegation of Blackfeet in Canada in the vicinity of present-day Edmonton, Alberta. They invited him to their village but hostilities in the area persuaded the Father to "...await a more favorable moment for visiting the Blackfeet."[4] Finally, in April 1859, Father Hoecken and Brother Vincent Magri were able to visit the Blackfeet, and they attempted to establish a mission on the Teton River near Priests Butte just southeast of present-day Choteau, MT. They built three cabins, were later joined by Father Camillus Imoda, and wintered there.

On March 3, 1860, they abandoned this site for a more suitable one on the Sun River. Once again they started cabins, but by August 1860 they decided to abandon this site as well. The Sun River site is described as being near the site of the future Fort Shaw. Lieutenant Mullan wrote, however, that it was located ten miles up the Sun River from the Sun River Crossing,[5] which would locate it near present-day Simms, MT. After departing the Sun River site, Father Imoda and Brother Magri returned to St. Ignatius and Father Hoecken departed for St. Louis.

In 1861 Father Imoda and Brother Francis DeKock traveled to Fort Benton and held services there that winter. In 1862 they were joined by Father Joseph Menetrey and Brother Lucian D. Agostino and eventually settled on a new site six miles up the Missouri River from the mouth of the Sun River near present-day Ulm; seven cabins and corrals were constructed. The site was named St. Peter's Mission after the Apostle Peter. It was staffed by Fathers Imoda, Giorda and Menetrey and two Jesuit brothers, presumably Brother Agostino and Brother DeKock. However, many of the Blackfeet remained hostile. The mission herder, John Fitzgerald, was killed by the Blackfeet within sight of the mission. Fathers Joseph Giorda, Imoda and L.B. Palladino, assisted by Mr. Vail (likely J.H. Vail from the Sun River Agency farm) and a Blackfoot guide, sought another location and settled on the current site of St. Peter's Mission near Birdtail Rock. The old mission was closed and camp established at the new site in the spring of 1866.[6]

---

4 Ibid.: 185.

5 John Mullan, *Report on the Construction of a Military Road*: 53.

6 Luise K. Cummings, *A Pictorial History of the Sun River Valley*: 27–28.

Another important event in the years prior to the Civil War, these of great economic impact in future Montana Territory, was the arrival of the first steamboats in Fort Benton in 1858 and 1859.[7] Indeed, the American Fur Company had been bringing steamboats as far up the Missouri as possible in earlier years, but never reaching Fort Benton. Mr. Edward A. Lewis reported leaving St. Louis in May 1857 aboard the steamer *Star of the West*, bound for Fort Benton with American Fur Company supplies. They only made it as far as Culbertson, some fifty-five miles east of present-day Wolf Point, MT. They then had to build Mackinaw boats and tow them over a period of sixty-five days to Fort Benton.[8] As already noted, the steamboat *Yellowstone* had made it as far up as Fort Union in 1832. Gradual improvements in the design of these boats, specifically adaptations for use on the treacherously shallow waters of the Missouri River, made this possible. The Missouri River steamers were of very shallow draft—less than four feet—and had unique features that were best described by General Philippe Regis de Trobriand, a future commander of the Montana Military District, during his ascent of the Missouri from Omaha to Fort Stevenson near Bismarck, Dakota Territory, in 1867. His entry for August 10, 1867, describes the method by which these steamers overcame troublesome sandbars frequently blocking their path:

> We lost a lot of time this afternoon. At a wide place in the river… we took the channel with no navigable outlet. We had to go back more than a mile, but then we ran into a sandbar twenty to thirty yards wide. To get across this obstacle, we had to make a passage or channel by steam power with the help of two props with which the bow of the boat was lifted. These props were two strong spars suspended from a powerful crane above each cathead. The crew rests the ends of the spars on the river bed, which is only two or three feet deep here. Then a system of ropes and pulleys is attached to an enormous ring on the front of the boat; one end fastened to the end of the spar and the other to a steam-driven winch. Lifted by the bow, the boat slowly forces her way on the surface of the sand, which is kept in motion by the current. After an hour or more of repeated effort, we got back into the channel again, and went on our way.[9]

---

[7] Mullan: 21.

[8] Robert Vaughn, *Then and Now*: 117–118.

[9] Philippe Regis de Trobriand, *Military Life in Dakota*: 29–30.

Woodcutters along the river earned three to six dollars per cord of wood delivered to the steamboats, which burned $100 worth of wood daily. In addition to the cost of the wood, another $150 per day in operating expenses were incurred by these steamers, making daily operating expenses $250. This made freight costs to points upriver very expensive. Freight charges from St. Louis to Fort Benton ran from 10 to 15 cents per pound. Trobriand described the crew of his steamer *Deer Lodge* as follows:

> There are on board 30 deck hands…all Negroes: two pilots, 2 mechanics, 2 boatswains, 6 firemen, 1 clerk, 1 barkeeper , 3 or 4 cooks, 1 barber who also takes care of the baggage, 6 chambermaids and 1 laundress. Everyone in the last classification is white but the barber, the chambermaids, and the cooks.[10]

From the area of Fort Sully, approximately forty miles upriver from present-day Pierre, SD, the steamboats as late as 1867 were often sniped at by hostile Indians along the banks, who sometimes wounded or killed passengers and crew. In defense, the pilot houses were covered with armor plate, and cargo such as lumber was often stacked on the outer edges of the decks to provide the passengers and crew with some degree of protection. An ample supply of arms and ammunition was maintained and the boats were often armed with howitzers. Every male passenger was usually armed at all times.[11]

Aside from the extensive contribution to Montana military history made by Lieutenant Mullan and Governor Stevens, there was another U.S. Army topographical engineer's exploration commissioned in 1859 that, in addition to portions of the Dakotas, Nebraska, Wyoming and Idaho, played itself out in southeastern, southern and east-central Montana. This was an expedition under the leadership of U.S. Army Captain William F. Raynolds. He received his orders from the U.S. War Department on April 13, 1859. Captain Raynolds was ordered to proceed up the Missouri to Fort Pierre near present-day Pierre, SD, and then follow the Cheyenne River and its North Fork west-northwest to its source. From there he was to proceed on

---

10 Ibid.: 34. Although freight charges were expensive, the advent of the steamboat on the Missouri made freight movement far cheaper and faster than it had been in the past. In a later chapter we will mention the presence of the steamboat *Far West* at the mouth of the Little Bighorn in 1876. Lieutenant Edward McClernand wrote that it carried 160 tons of freight; Edward J. McClernand, *On Time for Disaster*: 52. Contrast that to a large freight wagon pulled by six or more mules, which carried about five tons of freight. To move 160 tons would require over thirty large freight wagons pulled by 180 or more mules—mules that had to be fed and cared for.

11 Ibid.: 33–34.

to the source of the Powder River in northeastern Wyoming. His task was to ascertain if wagon routes could be established.[12]

Captain Raynolds was provided with a budget of $60,000 and the services of up to eight assistants, among them "…J.D. Hutton, as topographer and assistant artist; J.H. Snowden, as topographer; H.C. Fillebrown, as astronomer and assistant meteorologist and artist; Dr. F.V. Hayden, as naturalist and surgeon; Dr. M.C. Hines, as surgeon and assistant naturalist; [and] George Wallace as timekeeper and computer."[13] In all, the party numbered over forty-five persons including an infantry detail of thirty soldiers that served as an escort. Captain Raynolds also had the good fortune to procure the services of James Bridger as guide. The expedition included several six-mule-team wagons.

Upon reaching the Powder River near its source, the river was followed down to the Yellowstone and then up the Yellowstone to the mouth of the Tongue River, which was then explored to its source. The Yellowstone was also further explored upriver to the mouth of the Bighorn River. At that point the party proceeded up the Bighorn River to its source.[14] The expedition then wintered near Fort Laramie and continued its explorations the following summer. It should be noted that the very territory explored by Captain Raynolds in the summer of 1859 would, in the case of the portion later known as the Bozeman Trail, be the scene of dramatic clashes between the Sioux and Northern Cheyenne and the U.S. Army in 1866 and 1867. In 1876 it would be the scene of the so-called Yellowstone and Bighorn Campaign against the Sioux and their Cheyenne allies, in which General George Crook, General Alfred Terry, and Colonels George Custer and John Gibbon would participate with disastrous results for Colonel Custer and a large portion of his command. This campaign will be treated in later chapters, but the observations of Captain Raynolds taken in 1859 are of interest here.

Raynolds described the Sioux Indians, or Dakotas, as

> …by far the most numerous and powerful [in relation to the Crow Indians]… a confederacy of ten bands, speaking the same language, but separately organized under their own chiefs. These subdivisions are so decided that it is not uncommon for some of the bands to be engaged in a war in which others do not take part, although they

---

[12] W.F. Raynolds, *Report on the Exploration of the Yellowstone River*: 4.

[13] Ibid.: 18.

[14] Ibid.: 4.

never war upon each other. They occupy the country on both sides of the Missouri from the mouth of the Yellowstone [downriver] to Fort Randall, and from Powder river, on the west, to Minnesota river, on the east.[15]

He noted a difference in the bearings of some bands toward the whites. "Those to the south or near the Platte seem disposed to be peaceable, while those in the north are fierce, ill-tempered, and war-like."[16]

Captain Raynolds described the Crow Indians as occupying

> ...the country west of the Powder river, as far as the valley of the Three Forks of the Missouri, on both sides of the Yellowstone. They have had little or no intercourse with the whites save traders. They are divided into three bands—the mountain, middle, and lower— together numbering about 3,000 souls. They have never had trouble with the whites [in general this was true but there had been clashes between Crows and whites] and are disposed to be peaceable. They occupy the best buffalo ground in the west, but are jealous of intrusion...[17]

We may assume that much of the information provided by Raynolds regarding the Indians was derived direct from Jim Bridger. It is of interest to note that by 1866 the Sioux and their Cheyenne allies had driven the Crows out of much of their traditional homeland and pushed them some 120 miles westward to the west bank of the Bighorn River.

Although the captain commented on the immense buffalo herds observed on the Yellowstone, he made some rather interesting observations and predictions regarding these animals:

> ...the wholesale destruction of the buffalo is a matter that should receive the attention of proper authorities. It is due first and mainly to the fact that the skin of the female is alone valuable for robes. The skin of the male, over three years old, is never used for that purpose, the hair on the hind quarters being no longer than that on a horse, while, on the fore quarters, it has a length of from four to six inches. The skin is also too thick and heavy to be used for anything but lodge coverings, while the flesh is coarse and unpalatable, and is never used for food when any other can be had. The result is that

---

15 Ibid.: 16.

16 Ibid.

17 Ibid.: 16–17.

the females are always singled out by the hunter, and consequently the males in a herd always exceed the females, in the proportion of not less than ten to one.

Another, but far less important, cause of their rapid extinction is the immense number of wolves in the country, which destroy the young. The only remedy that would have the slightest effect in the case would be a prohibition of the trade of buffalo robes and a premium upon wolf skins. I fear it is too late for even this remedy, and notwithstanding the immense herds that are yet to be found, I think it is more than probable that another generation will witness almost the entire extinction of this noble animal.[18]

The reader will recall the quote in the last chapter from Reverend N. Point, a Jesuit missionary, where reference was made to the killing of 344 buffalo cows by Flathead hunters. The fact that buffalo cows were the preferred diet is further supported by a notation made by the Lewis and Clark Expedition in 1804 while proceeding up the Missouri and approaching the Mandan villages on October 22, 1804. "The hunters killed a buffalow bull, they Say out of about 300 buffalow which they Saw, they did not, see one Cow."[19] Apparently, the cows from among the buffalo they observed on that day had already been culled out by Indian hunters, for there were, indeed, very few white men in that area in 1804. In any case, the prediction of the demise of the buffalo within a generation was very accurate, for by 1883 scarcely any buffalo remained in Montana Territory.[20]

In the summer of 1860 Captain Raynolds sent Lieutenant Henry E. Maynadier with a group directly cross-country to the Yellowstone to explore the upper areas of this valley and later meet with Captain Raynolds's group at Three Forks. The captain then proceeded with his portion of the exploration party up the Wind River to its source, passed over a divide and down the Gros Ventre River into Jackson Hole, and then crossed the Tetons to Pierre's Hole in latter-day Idaho. This is in the area around Victor, ID, just to the west of the Tetons. From Pierre's Hole the group

---

[18] Ibid.: 11. It is the opinion of the author that considerable credence should be given to Captain Raynolds's comment on the buffalo, in particular due to the presence of his much respected guide, James Bridger, who had known the area and its trends since the 1820s and possessed considerable knowledge of the buffalo. The captain would certainly have drawn on Bridger's comments and knowledge in the formulation of his own opinion on the matter.

[19] Reuben Gold Thwaites, *Original Journals of the Lewis and Clark Expedition*, Pt. II, Vol. II: 202–203.

[20] Granville Stuart, *Forty Years on the Frontier*, Vol. II: 188.

proceeded northward to Henry's Lake and through what is now known as Raynolds Pass into the Madison Valley. They followed this valley down to the Three Forks of the Missouri, where they met with Lieutenant Maynadier's party on July 3, 1860.

Lieutenant Maynadier reported passing up the Yellowstone then following a well traveled Indian lodge-pole trail some twenty-two miles in a northwesterly direction to the Shields River, to a point where it led westward over a pass between the Yellowstone and Gallatin valleys, which he referred to as Blackfoot Pass.[21] Captain Raynolds then sent Lieutenant Maynadier back to the Yellowstone and down that river past Fort Sarpy to a later reunite with the main party at Fort Union. On his way down the Yellowstone the lieutenant took measurements of the depth of the river, surveying its navigation potential.

Raynolds and his party then proceeded toward Fort Benton, traveling over the country to the east of the Missouri, and eventually followed the Smith River from its headwaters down to the Missouri, just south of present-day Great Falls, MT. Of interest is the captain's comment about the Smith River:

> The valley of the Smith's river of which such frequent mention has been made in my journal for the past few days, is one of the finest upon the continent. It is very narrow, being barely half a mile in width, but the bottom and the adjacent hill-sides are covered with a luxuriant growth of grass, while the immediate banks of the river are fringed with considerable timber.[22]

When passing the mouth of the Medicine River (Sun River), Raynolds reported:

> ...we reached a spot upon the bank opposite the mouth of the Sun or Medicine river. This stream is about one-half the width of the Missouri at the point of junction, and flows through a wide and beautiful valley. By the aid of our glasses we endeavored to see the Indian agency or mission station upon its banks, but although 10 or 15 miles of country were visible, nothing that could be identified as the buildings in question could be seen.[23]

---

[21] Raynolds: 140–141. Lieutenant McClernand described three passes through which the Indians conducted raids into the Gallatin Valley: 1) Bozeman Pass, present-day Interstate 94; 2) Flathead Pass twenty miles north; and 3) Blackfoot Pass, ten more miles north—perhaps present-day Sixteen Mile Creek Road; McClernand, *On Time for Disaster*: 23.

[22] Ibid.: 106.

[23] Ibid.

Captain William F. Raynolds.
PHOTO COURTESY OF THE U.S. DEPARTMENT
OF COMMERCE.

Arriving at the Great Falls of the Missouri, Raynolds compared the physical features of the area to those described by Captain Clark in his journal and pronounced Clark's description extremely accurate in detail. Of particular interest to Raynolds was Clark's report of an active eagle's nest on what Clark referred to as Cottonwood Island, which was located "532 poles" upriver from Giant Springs. Raynolds noted that the eagle's nest remained in the same location some fifty-five years later.[24]

The captain and his party arrived in Fort Benton, remaining there from July 15 to July 22, 1860. From there he dispatched a twenty-man land party under 1st Lieutenant John Mullins (not to be confused with Lieutenant John Mullan of Mullan Road fame) to proceed directly overland from Fort Benton to Fort Union, making a topographical survey of that portion of the future Montana Territory lying between the Missouri and the Yellowstone rivers. The captain, with a smaller detachment, then floated down the Missouri to Fort Union. The captain's leg of the journey was relatively quiet; however, one quote may be of interest to the reader. "At one point [above Big Dry Creek] passed we landed two men who had come with us from Fort Benton for this purpose, who propose to remain there through the winter hunting wolves. As the nearest post is Fort Union, which is fully 200 miles distant, they plainly have no especial dread of Indian hostilities."[25]

Lieutenant Mullins was accompanied in his journey through central eastern Montana by "…James Bridger, guide; Dr. F.V. Hayden, naturalist; A. Schonborn, artist and meteorologist; and W.D. Stuart, topographer."[26] At one point along the Judith River, on July 24th, the party encountered a band of Blackfeet Indians. The band was called the Little Robes.

---

[24] Ibid.: 108–109.

[25] Ibid.: 110–112.

[26] Ibid.: 161.

> They were delighted to meet me, and I accompanied them to their
> village, half a mile distant, where to my surprise, I saw waving from
> the top of the chief's tent the "Star Spangled Banner". I counted
> 54 lodges and estimated the number of Indians to be about 150 or
> 200…I was enabled to talk to them through my guide and interpret-
> er, James Bridger, who spoke the Flathead language and was readily
> understood, as there were several members of the band who were
> Flatheads and could interpret to the rest.

The lieutenant noted the coordinates for this location as 47 degrees
6 min, 39 secs 2.[27]

Nine days later, as the party reached a branch of the Sandy, they encountered another band of Indians; this time they were identified by Bridger as
friendly Crow Indians. But these Crows were in a bad mood. After greeting
the Indians and identifying them, Bridger brought them, twelve in number,
into the white camp. Lieutenant Mullins wrote:

> I observed that they were all dressed in war-costume; their bows
> strung and arrows and rifles in their hands, and seemed to have an un-
> friendly scowl on their faces. Having with me only 14 available men, I
> stationed half of them as guard over the animals under the charge of a
> sergeant, and the other half placed over the property in camp. In a few
> minutes three of the Indians fired their rifles into the air, and on my
> asking what it meant, they informed me that their "hearts were bad,"
> and they had come to avenge themselves upon the white men. The
> answer was hardly given before my camp was charged by about 250
> Crow warriors. Yelling at the tops of their voices and firing about 30
> shots into my camp, but, fortunately, doing no damage except shoot-
> ing a few holes through one tent, and riding over another. I cautioned
> my men not to fire on the Indians unless someone of my party was
> hit. The object of the Indians in charging in this manner was to stam-
> pede my animals, and by that means get possession of them, but as I
> had taken the precaution to have the animals hobbled and tied up, the
> Indians failed to accomplish their object.[28]

Incredibly, the lieutenant, with the aid of Bridger, was able to calm
the Indians down without bloodshed and speak to their chief, known as Great
Bear. The Crows were angry with the whites because their intended annuities

---

[27] Ibid.: 161–164. We may note here that although the Flatheads and the Blackfeet were generally
considered implacable enemies, intercourse was carried on between some members of the tribes.

[28] Ibid.: 167.

had been allegedly delivered to their Sioux enemies. Furthermore, Fort Sarpy was now closed, and since Fort Union—the next available trading post—was in territory now controlled by the Sioux, they had, in effect, been deprived of a place to trade. This is corroborated by the fact that on his arrival at Fort Sarpy on July 20, 1860, while traveling downstream on the Yellowstone with his party en route to Fort Union, Lieutenant Maynadier had found the fort abandoned. The lieutenant was able to dissuade the Indians from further violence and extricate his party from the area without further incident. The location was given as Latitude 47 degrees, 5 min, 18 sec .72.[29]

Lieutenant Mullins's party reached Fort Union on August 11, 1860, where it reunited with Captain Raynolds's party and the party led by Lieutenant Maynadier, which had come down the Yellowstone. All members of the Raynolds expedition then departed Montana and proceeded down the Missouri. It should be noted that they made special mention of the American Fur Company representative in charge of Fort Union, Mr. Robert Meldrum. They had high praise for his friendliness and knowledge of the Crow Indians:

> He is undoubtedly the best living authority in regard to the Crows, outside of the tribe, having spent over 30 years in their country, during that time visiting the regions of civilization but once, and on that occasion spending only 19 days in St. Louis. He has long lived among these Indians, assuming their dress and habits, and by his skill and success in leading their war parties has acquired distinction, rising to the second post of authority in the tribe. He of course speaks their language perfectly, and says that it has become more natural to him than his mother tongue.[30]

Interestingly enough, Captain Raynolds identified James Bridger and Robert Meldrum as the only two white men he knew of who had seen the wonders of Yellowstone Park. He made no mention of John Colter.[31] This is perhaps not surprising for Colter is believed to have died in 1813, almost fifty years previously, when James Bridger was scarcely nine years old. Bridger did not go into Indian country until 1822.[32]

---

[29] Ibid. This location was likely near present-day Sand Springs, on Montana Highway 200. It is of interest to note that although the Blackfeet were considered hostile to whites and the Crows friendly, Lieutenant Mullins's party experienced exactly the opposite in his two encounters with Indians—proof positive that there were exceptions to this general rule.

[30] Ibid.: 49.

[31] Ibid.

[32] Chittenden, *The American Fur Trade:* 255, 712.

CHAPTER FIVE

The Gold Mining Era; The Establishment of Territorial Government in Montana; and The Montana Road 1862–1867

THE SETTLEMENT OF MONTANA BEGAN IN EARNEST with the discovery of gold placer deposits and the rush of miners and settlers that followed. Meantime, in the East—or, better said, in the states—the Civil War raged. The location of the first discovery of gold in the future territory is believed to have been on Gold Creek in 1858 by Henry Thomas. He was referred to by Granville Stuart as Gold Tom. There are references to a prospector named Francois Finlay, known as Benetsee, finding small quantities of gold on Gold Creek in 1852.[1] The Stuart brothers and Gold Tom followed up on rumors of this discovery and by 1862 were mining a profitable placer deposit. Alexander Culbertson also informed Lieutenant James Bradley in the 1870's that a prospector, named Silverthorne had arrived at his trading post in Fort Benton in 1856 with approximately $1,500 worth of gold dust that he claimed to have mined in the mountains to the west.[2] This gold could have been from the placer deposits in Idaho or Washington. In any case, by 1862 prospectors began arriving in large numbers in the future territory.

On July 28, 1862, John White and a party en route to the Salmon River in Idaho from Colorado discovered gold on Grasshopper Creek, which led to the establishment of Bannack. It populated rapidly. On May 26, 1863, an

---

[1] James Bradley, *March of the Montana Column:* 25; James McClellan Hamilton, *History of Montana:* 108.

[2] Bradley: 25.

even larger discovery was made in Alder Gulch, some seventy miles to the east, by William Fairweather, Henry Edgar, Tom Coover, Barney Hughes, Mike Sweeney and Harry Rodgers.[3] This led to the rise of Virginia City, Nevada City, Summit and other towns along the gulch. By the autumn of 1863 Captain James L. Fisk reported that over 1,000 persons populated Bannack, and between 7,000 and 8,000 people resided in Alder Gulch. A rancher named Morgan settled in the Little Prickly Pear Valley, and Deer Lodge consisted of about thirty houses and 150 inhabitants. John Grant's herd of cattle had now grown to about 4,000 head, and he was getting rich supplying beef to hungry prospectors.[4]

Bannack soon began a gradual decline while the Alder Gulch communities continued to grow, reaching a combined population of about 14,000 inhabitants. In September 1864 a rich quartz deposit was discovered in Last Chance Gulch by James W. Whitlatch, which gave rise to Helena, soon to become the largest town in the territory. Quartz mining also spread rapidly to other areas throughout the southern part of the future territory, among them Diamond City in Confederate Gulch, Jefferson City, Lincoln Gulch, Beartown, Blackfoot City and numerous other locations. An examination of the federal census of 1870 reveals towns containing 500 or more residents that are totally unknown to present-day Montanans. Diamond City, for example, still contained 460 inhabitants in 1870.[5] Granville Stuart visited Diamond City in May 1880 and reported that the town was "… now a mere wreck of a once prosperous placer mining camp."[6] Today, the only remains of this once significant town are dredger tailings and a lonesome U.S. Forest Service sign. Blackfoot City is now represented by a few piles of tailings in a lonely creek.

Along with the miners came the farmers, ranchers and merchants. The Bitterroot, Deer Lodge, Beaverhead and Gallatin valleys as well as the area around Helena and the Little Prickly Pear began to fill up with farms and ranches, ever ready to supply the needs of hungry prospectors and miners. Government began to arrive in Montana along with settlement. The first area of the state to contain any settlement of significance was the Bitterroot Valley. In 1860 it was a part of Washington Territory, which then formed

---

[3] Hamilton: 230.

[4] Ibid.: 154.

[5] U.S. Census 1870.

[6] Granville Stuart, *Forty Years on the Frontier*, Vol. I: 138.

Missoula County, covering all areas of present-day Montana west of the Continental Divide. On March 3, 1863, some months after the rise of Bannack and a few months prior to discovery of gold in Alder Gulch, Idaho Territory was formed, which contained all of present-day Montana and Wyoming and portions of Washington Territory. Montana became the third judicial district of the three districts in Idaho Territory, and Sidney Edgerton was appointed chief justice, with a seat in Bannack. On January 16, 1864, Idaho Territory formed new counties east of the Continental Divide in Montana, retaining Missoula County with a county seat at Wordensville. The new counties were Deer Lodge,

Thomas F. Meagher—
acting governor Montana Territory.
PHOTO COURTESY OF MONTANA HISTORICAL
SOCIETY RESEARCH CENTER PHOTOGRAPH
ARCHIVES, HELENA, MONTANA.

Beaverhead, Madison, Jefferson and Chouteau. The designated county seats for the new counties were Deer Lodge, Bannack, Virginia City, Gallatin City and Fort Benton, in that order.[7]

Sidney Edgerton was able to impose on an Ohio friend and congressman to introduce a bill forming Montana Territory, which was passed and signed into law on May 26, 1864.[8] Edgerton became the first territorial governor and Bannack the first territorial capital. Thomas Francis Meagher was later appointed secretary of Montana Territory by President Andrew Johnson on August 4, 1865. Meagher, a former Irish rebel and newspaper editor, had served gallantly during the Civil War as commander of the Irish Brigade. This unit was heavily engaged at the battles of Fredericksburg and Antietam. In the absence of the territorial governor, the secretary served as acting governor. Meagher would serve in this post as acting governor during the often extended absences of Edgerton and his successor, Green Clay Smith (1866–1868). Thus, Meagher actually served close to two years as the

---

[7] Ibid.: 273–275.

[8] Ibid.: 276–277.

John Bozeman, Montana pioneer.
PHOTO COURTESY OF MONTANA HISTORICAL
SOCIETY RESEARCH CENTER PHOTOGRAPH
ARCHIVES, HELENA, MONTANA.

de facto governor of Montana Territory until his death by drowning in July 1867. His aggressive style strongly influenced the politicians in Washington, D.C., and resulted in the decision to station federal troops in the territory, thus establishing the Montana Military District.[9]

White settlers in the new territory greatly feared a general Indian uprising, in particular in the months after the Fetterman Massacre in Wyoming, which occurred in December 1866. There were also false reports of the massacre of the entire U.S. Army garrison at Fort Buford on the Missouri just across the Montana Territory–Dakota Territory border in Dakota Territory. On March 21, 1867, John Bozeman wrote to Acting Governor Meagher regarding raids by hostile Indians into the Gallatin Valley. Less than one month later word arrived that Mr. Bozeman had been killed by hostile Blackfeet in the Yellowstone Valley. He had been en route to Fort C.F. Smith with a Mr. Thomas Cover, who survived the attack. According to Granville Stuart, Nelson Storey was operating a cattle camp at Benson's Landing, the site of present-day Livingston, MT, at the time of Bozeman's death. The well-known scout and guide Mitch Boyer, who later fell with Custer, was also present at this camp. Mr. Storey and a ranch hand went to the site of Bozeman's body and buried him. Stuart wrote, "These Indians were found later to be some renegade Blackfeet who had been expelled from their tribe and had taken refuge with the Crows."[10]

Following Bozeman's murder, Governor Green Clay Smith was petitioned by citizens in Bozeman to form a militia.[11] The request was granted and a militia was formed in Bozeman in 1867. The force was stationed at a post designated Camp Meagher near the mouth of the Shields River.[12] Also

9 Ibid.: 285–286.

10 Stuart, Vol. II: 64.

11 Ibid.: 294.

12 Ibid.: 295.

during late 1866 and 1867, the U.S. Army moved to establish posts at Fort Shaw[13] and Fort Ellis and later disband the militia. U.S. Army officers were not enthusiastic about a state militia, generally believing that it was made up of a rowdy, unruly element capable of causing more trouble with the Indian population than it prevented. Obviously, they had the Sand Creek Massacre in Colorado Territory on their minds. This had been carried out three years earlier by the Colorado militia. By October 23, 1867, the Montana militia had been disbanded.

The sudden growth of the gold mining areas, in particular Bannack, Virginia City and Last Chance Gulch (Helena) created a strong demand for services and supplies. The mining population was not self-sufficient. Vast amounts of equipment and supplies had to be freighted or packed into these frontier areas from great distances. As has always been the case in our history, American enterprise jumped to the task.

Freight companies and other entrepreneurs moved large quantities of freight northward into the Montana gold fields from faraway points such as Salt Lake City and Fort Hall, which was located on the Oregon Trail between the present-day towns of Pocatello and Blackfoot, ID. Many of these supplies had even more distant origins such as Omaha, Nebraska Territory, and Independence, MO. From these faraway points of U.S. civilization, the Oregon Trail followed the Platte River westward and then, near present-day Ogallala, NE, turned northwest up the valley of the North Platte, following it all the way to the South Pass near present-day Lander, WY. After crossing the Continental Divide, the trail split for distant points such as Salt Lake City, California and Oregon, with the Oregon portion passing near Fort Hall near present-day Pocatello, ID. This was the departure point for supplies moving north into Montana Territory.

The other route to the Montana gold fields was also a circuitous one. It was a water route following the Missouri River from St. Louis to Fort Benton in Montana Territory. The river was navigable only during periods of relatively high water during the spring and summer months. In dry years and in the late summer seasons, the Missouri frequently became too shallow to support steamboat traffic beyond the mouth of the Yellowstone. A more frequently used port was Cow Island, approximately 123 miles downriver from Fort Benton. The freight not able to reach Fort Benton by steamboat was then freighted in wagons on to Fort Benton. From here all arriving

---

13 Ibid.: 67.

goods and passengers traveled over land by stagecoach and freight wagon via the Mullan Road to Helena, and then on to Virginia City and Bannack. The distance from Fort Benton to Helena was 145 miles, to which Virginia City–bound passengers had to add another 100 miles!

This long river and road route was by no means a secure one. As previously noted, hostile Indians frequently fired on steamboats passing on the river. Parties of woodcutters were frequently attacked, robbed and sometimes murdered. In his book *Military Life in Dakota*, Colonel Philippe Regis de Trobriand, later commander of the Montana Military District while stationed at Fort Stevenson, Dakota Territory, during the years 1868–1869, wrote, "…seven whites settled above Buford [Fort Buford at the mouth of the Yellowstone] to cut wood were massacred by the savages. A steamboat discovered the scalped and mutilated bodies, and they were given a decent burial."[14]

The railroads had not yet been built coast to coast but, by the end of the Civil War in 1865, they were coming on fast, far outpacing earlier forecasts. In 1854 the first railroad had reached the Mississippi River. At that time scarcely anyone believed that intercontinental railroads were anywhere in the near future. In 1846 the *New York Evening Post* had predicted, "It will be time enough for the Government of the United States to make railroads beyond St. Louis or the Mississippi River…such a railroad will be, but not within forty years."[15] The mineral wealth of the Rockies and beyond changed this timetable. Scarcely twenty years were to pass before the first intercontinental railroad was completed in 1869, thus resulting in Montana's land-bound freight originating at the railhead in Corinne, UT. Montana Territory would have to wait at least another decade before being reached by railroads.

A third, more direct, route to the Montana gold fields from civilization also existed. It was at least 500 miles shorter than either of the two aforementioned routes, but by no means without problems. The U.S. Army would make a failed attempt to secure this shorter route for travel to the Montana gold fields. Although most of the action would take place in present-day Wyoming, this effort had a great impact on events in Montana Territory for years to come. This significant event will therefore be described in detail in this chapter.

14 Philippe Regis de Trobriand, *Military Life in Dakota*: 33–34, 311.

15 J.P. Dunn, Jr., *Massacres of the Mountains*: 52.

The route referred to as the Montana Road or the Bozeman Trail had been pioneered by John Bozeman. The trail commenced at Fort Laramie near the present-day Nebraska-Wyoming border, then passed near present-day Buffalo, WY, at the site of Fort Philip Kearny. From this point, one traveled ninety-one miles to Fort C.F. Smith (present-day Fort Smith, MT). From there the trail proceeded another sixty-three miles to the Clark's Fork, then ninety miles to Yellowstone Ferry near present-day Springdale, MT. The distance from Yellowstone Ferry to Bozeman was fifty-one miles. After an additional seventy miles, most of it up the Madison Valley, Virginia City was reached. Total distance from Fort Philip Kearny to Virginia City was 365 miles.[16] This route led directly through Sioux and Northern Cheyenne hunting grounds, the so called Powder River country, formerly occupied by the Crow Indians. The Crow Indians had only recently been driven out of most of this prize hunting ground by the Sioux and their Northern Cheyenne allies.[17]

Immediately following the end of the Civil War, public and eventually congressional pressure grew to establish military posts along the Montana Road to secure safe passage for persons and goods en route to and from the gold fields in Montana. On March 10, 1866, the commander of the Department of the Missouri, General John Pope, ordered the establishment of military posts "near the base of Bighorn mountain," and "on or near the upper Yellowstone."[18]

Some fifteen years earlier, on September 17, 1851, the government had negotiated a treaty with the western plains Indians known as the Treaty of Fort Laramie. This treaty laid out the recognized boundaries of the various Indian nations. Interestingly enough, the treaty recognized the greater part of the territory through which the Montana Road passed as Crow territory. Article II of the treaty stated, "The aforesaid nations do hereby recognize the right of the United States Government to establish roads, military and other posts, within their respective territories."[19] The territory in question, however, was no longer occupied by the Crows. They had been pushed out by the various bands of the Sioux nation and some of their Arapahoe and Cheyenne allies. Nevertheless, the government deemed it prudent to open

---

[16] Margaret Irvin Carrington, *Absaraka*: 252.

[17] Ibid.: 14–15.

[18] Report to the President by the Indian Peace Commission, National Archives.

[19] Charles J. Klapper, *Indian Affairs: Laws and Treaties*, Vol. II (Treaties): 595–596.

negotiations with the Sioux for the right to operate a road and construct posts. It is probable that they believed an arrangement could be easily reached with the Sioux and Northern Cheyenne, who were now in the area in force, by possibly increasing annuities or promises thereof. Negotiations were commenced with the Indians at Fort Laramie in June of 1866.

Government authorities were so confident of their ability to obtain an agreement from the treaty signatories that the 2nd Battalion of the 18th Infantry Regiment under Colonel Henry B. Carrington was ordered to depart from Fort Kearny on the Platte River at present-day Kearney, NE, on May 19, 1866. The battalion, eventually consisting of approximately 700 men, was accompanied by 226 mule teams with supplies for the purpose of establishing three posts along the Montana Road. One was to be Fort Phil Kearny, the other Fort C.F. Smith, and a third was to be constructed on the upper Yellowstone River, presumably at the location of the Yellowstone Ferry. Although the 2nd Battalion was strictly an infantry unit, it was also stocked with some 200 horses for use by mounted infantry.[20]

On June 13, 1866, Colonel Carrington's troops arrived at Fort Laramie on the North Platte (near present-day Fort Laramie, WY). This fort had been established by the American Fur Company in 1846 and sold to the government in 1849, at which time it became one of the most important military posts in the West. It was a well-known waypoint on the Oregon Trail and had been the site of previous councils and treaties with the various Indian tribes populating the region. Just prior to the arrival of Colonel Carrington's troops, the Presidential Peace Commission had begun talks with representatives of the various Indian tribes for the purpose of negotiating a right of passage for the white man along the Montana Road.

Margaret Carrington wrote:

> The proposed general peace with the Sioux, the Arapahoes, and the Cheyennes, and their anticipated surrender of the right of way to Virginia City, by Powder Run and along the Bighorn mountains— our very route—were matters of personal interest, independent of the difficulties that would be in the way of successfully building new forts and fighting Indians with a command that was barely sufficient to do its expected work on the basis of a permanent and reliable peace.[21]

---

[20] Carrington: 38–39, 42, 45.

[21] Ibid.: 74.

The U.S. peace commissioners ran into a problem that had not existed in such stark terms during prior peace treaties negotiated with the Indians. Those Indians who had opted for the white man's peace terms and were willing to remain on the reservations and accept rations provided by the Office of Indian Affairs were not a problem. They were willing to sign a new amended treaty. But other Indian bands, who had remained relatively independent, pursuing their native lifestyle of living off the land rather than waiting on the white man's handouts, were confronted with a stark reality. They knew that the buffalo were rapidly disappearing from the plains as the white settlers moved in. The buffalo herds were the mainstay of the Indian's sustenance. With the buffalo gone, only the deer, antelope and elk and other small game remained, and it was impossible for the Indians, even with all their skill and cunning as hunters, to secure enough food from these alternate sources to survive in any great numbers. The Ogallalla and Minneconjou bands of the Sioux, the Northern Cheyenne, the Arapahoe tribes and the Mountain Crows viewed the Powder River country as their last best hunting ground. The Mountain Crows had been driven from the major portion of this area by the Sioux and their Northern Cheyenne allies in recent years and were now usually confined to the Upper Yellowstone drainage west of the Bighorn River.

During the explorations of Captain Benjamin Bonneville in the years 1832–1835, the Powder River country, that portion of the Yellowstone River drainage extending west to east from the Bighorn River across the drainages of the Little Bighorn, the Tongue and the Powder rivers, was considered Crow hunting ground. Bands of the various Blackfeet tribes and other Indian tribes hunted this area, but at great risk of Crow vengeance. The Sioux occupied at that time areas farther east in the Black Hills and along the Little Missouri River.[22] Although the Crows had generally maintained peaceful relations with whites throughout the years since the Lewis and Clark Expedition, by 1866 they were much inclined to view the white man as an ally in their struggle against the Sioux and their Cheyenne allies, perhaps even as their last hope for survival.

The Sioux chief, Red Cloud, correctly foresaw the rapid demise of the buffalo and other game in this region once the white man had established a permanent road and a line of posts through it. In the past it had always been possible for the Indians to move on to a new area and continue to pursue the

22 Washington Irving, *The Adventures of Captain Bonneville*: 383–384.

independent lifestyle of the prairie nomad, with the exception of the presence of a more powerful Indian tribe. Now, there was nowhere else to go, and no choice but to surrender to the white man's ways. The following excerpt from U.S. Senate Document No. 13, 1867, reveals a lack of foresight and timing on the part of the government in its efforts to secure an agreement from the Indians.

> While negotiations were going on with Red Cloud and their leading chiefs to induce them to yield to the government the right to peaceably establish these military posts, which right they persistently refused to yield, saying that it was asking too much of their people—asking all they had—for it would drive away all the game, Colonel H. B. Carrington, 18th United States Infantry, with about seven hundred officers and men, arrived at Laramie, en route to their country to establish and occupy military posts along the Montana Road, pursuant to General Orders No. 33, Headquarters Department of Missouri, March 10, 1866, Major General Pope commanding. The destination and purpose of Colonel Carrington and his command were communicated to their chiefs. They seemed to construe this as a determination on the part of the government to occupy their country by military posts, even without their consent or that of their people, and as soon as practicable withdrew from the council with their adherents, refusing to accept any presents from the commission, returned to their country, and with a strong force of warriors commenced a vigorous and relentless war against all whites who came into it, both citizens and soldiers.[23]

It is not my purpose to dwell on the righteousness of either cause, that of the white man's manifest destiny or the red man's quest for survival. Events in the course of the history of all mankind have proven that eventually the stronger force overcomes the weaker force and prevails. In more recent years we have had trouble distinguishing the stronger from the weaker—a case in point is the Vietnam War.

Events were overtaking all concerned. Had the U.S. government strictly forbidden the advancement of the white man beyond the Mississippi River, it is doubtful that a significant change in the turn of events would have been achieved. The settlement by whites of the vast, for the most part empty Great Plains would have been delayed by some years, but the end result would have been similar—if not by U.S. citizens, then eventually by citizens

---

[23] Quoted in Carrington: 260.

settling under the auspices of some other "civilized" nation such as Great Britain, Spain or France. As the Sioux had pushed back the Crows and the Blackfeet had terrorized the Shoshones and the Flatheads, so the white nation was eventually overwhelming the traditional way of life of the various Indian tribes. The discovery of gold in California and, at a later date, in the Rocky Mountain regions would have occurred sooner or later with its inevitable consequence—a large influx of outsiders, mostly white Americans but also settlers from other parts of the globe.

The military man is sworn by oath to serve his government and is frequently tasked with enforcing its policies. He does not have the option of debating every policy decision made by his government. Many career military officers like Colonel Carrington, John Gibbon and others, such as George Armstrong Custer, recognized that in many ways the Indian was receiving unjust treatment at the hands of the whites, particularly the appointed agents of the Office of Indian Affairs. Indeed, in the year 1876, Custer found himself summoned to testify before the Heister Clymer Committee in the impeachment trial of Secretary of the Army William W. Belknap, an appointee of President Ulysses S. Grant. In his testimony Custer explained how the men in his command were forced by existing rules and regulations to buy goods at exorbitant prices from one post trader, a Mr. Siep. One of Custer's captains began purchasing goods in St. Paul and distributing them at cost to his men. Mr. Siep complained to Washington and Custer received an order that the captain cease the practice. In his testimony Custer pointed to persons at the right hand of Secretary Belknap as responsible for this policy. Thus Custer incurred the wrath of President Grant. As a result the president initially forbade him to lead the 7th Cavalry on its fateful expedition against the Sioux and Northern Cheyenne in 1876.[24]

It is also true that for the most part the majority of military men, as was the case with the general populace, believed in the white man's manifest destiny to occupy, exploit and cultivate these vast lands. General John Gibbon's *Journal of the Plains Trip* revealed such visions.

> We left Fort Kearny on Tuesday the 26th [of July, 1860] and have ever since been travelling along the valley of the Platte or Nebraska River…The valley is a dead level in the middle of which flows the river, now rapid & muddy as if from the rains and nearly up to the top of its banks. In places the stream is very wide and intersperced

---

[24] Charles Kuhlman, *Legend into History*, Appendix: 311.

with numerous islands generally covered with timber or tall brush-
wood. I amused myself as we rode along fancying the time when,
from the crowded population in the east, this country will be thickly
settled up this valley cut up into beautifully cultivated farms with
fruit and ornamental trees in abundance & the sand hills on the left
crowned with fine country residences...[25]

On June 17, 1866, Colonel Carrington and his troops marched out of
Fort Laramie en route to Fort Reno and then onward to select their building site for the new Fort Phil Kearny, which was eventually to be located
approximately fourteen miles north of present-day Buffalo, WY. The primary task was to secure sites and erect the posts—Fort Phil Kearny, Fort
C.F. Smith and the post at the Yellowstone Ferry—before winter overtook
them. It was not anticipated by U.S. military authorities that strong bands
of hostile Indians would confront them while performing this task, but Red
Cloud and his Northern Cheyenne allies had other plans.

On July 15th the site for the construction of Fort Phil Kearny was selected on a plateau overlooking the fork of Big Piney and Little Piney creeks
on the Montana Road, a distance of 235 miles from Fort Laramie. The site
contained an ample supply of grass, water and timber within the immediate area. No time was wasted getting started with construction. Horse-
powered sawmills were set up, pending the arrival of steam-powered mills,
and troops (wood details) were sent out along the stream bottoms to cut
timber while others surveyed the site. Yet others using horse-drawn mowers
cut available grass in the area, harvesting hay with which to feed the post's
animals—horses and a herd of beef cattle—throughout the coming harsh
winter months.

As work on Fort Phil Kearny progressed, Colonel Carrington dispatched
Brevet Lieutenant Colonel N.C. Kinney with two companies to the Bighorn
River, ninety-one miles distant, to establish Fort C.F. Smith in early August
1866. By August, events began to foretell increasing problems with the
Indians, and the post planned for the upper Yellowstone was abandoned for
lack of sufficient manpower.[26]

Commencing prior to the arrival of the troops at the site, Red Cloud's
warriors had begun to shadow them, observing their movements and activities. On July 14th three soldiers deserted and attempted to proceed via the

---

[25] John Gibbon, *Adventures on the Western Frontier:* 16.

[26] Carrington: 125.

Montana Road to the gold fields in Montana. They were stopped by Indians "...and instructed to return at once with a message to the white chief, that he must take his soldiers out of the country."[27] A series of harassing actions were carried out by the Indians from the first days at this new site. On July 17th attempts were made to steal some of the post's cattle herd.[28] The herd detail pursued the Indians over Lodge Trail Ridge to a distance several miles from the post. It was promptly surrounded by several hundred Indians. A relief column of two companies was sent to the rescue. Two men were killed and three wounded. Additionally, they found a party of six civilians massacred on the road.[29] Timber-cutting details were constantly harassed, and supply trains arriving from Fort Reno and Fort Laramie were attacked.

Colonel Carrington's wife, Margaret Irving Carrington, provided a detailed chronology of events in the area during the period July 22nd through September 27th.

> JULY 22D. At Buffalo Springs, on the Dry Fork of Powder River, a citizen train was attacked, having one man killed and another wounded.
>
> JULY 22D. Indians appeared at Fort Reno driving off one public mule.
>
> JULY 22D. Mr. Nye lost four animals near Fort Phil Kearney, and Mr. Axe and Mr. Dixon each had two mules stolen by Indians.
>
> JULY 23D. A citizen train was attacked at the Dry Fork of the Cheyenne, and two men were killed.
>
> JULY 23D. Louis Cheney's train was attacked; one man was killed, and horses, cattle, and private property were sacrificed.
>
> JULY 28TH. Indians attempted to drive off public stock at Fort Reno, and failed; but took the cattle of citizen John B. Sloss. Pursuit; recovered them.
>
> JULY 29TH. A citizen train was attacked at Brown Springs, four miles east of the East Fork of the Cheyenne, and eight men were killed, two were wounded, and one of these died of his wounds...

---

[27] Ibid.: 103.

[28] The reader should note at this point that the troops were accompanied by herds of cattle from which a sufficient number could be slaughtered on an as-needed basis. In the 1860's freezers were obviously not available; therefore beef was kept alive on the hoof until needed.

[29] Carrington: 119–120.

(Exact date Unknown) Grover, the artist, correspondent of Frank Leslie, was scalped one Sunday morning, only a few minutes walk from the post...

AUGUST 9TH. In one of the frequent attacks upon the timber train, four mules were taken after the driver had cut them loose; but a party from the fort under Corporal Phillip recaptured the mules, killing one Indian and wounding a second.

AUGUST 12TH. Indians drove off horses and cattle belonging to citizens encamped on the river bank near Reno. The cattle were recaptured.

AUGUST 14TH. Joseph Postlewaite and Stockley Williams were killed within four miles of Fort Reno...

SEPTEMBER 8TH, at 6 o'clock A.M. Twenty mules were driven from a citizen herd, during a severe storm, within a mile of Fort Phil Kearney...The colonel with one party, and Lieutenant Adair with another, were out until after 9 o'clock at night in pursuit.

SEPTEMBER 10TH. Ten herders were attacked a mile south of the fort, losing thirty-three horses and seventy-eight mules. Pursuit was vigorous, but unsuccessful.

SEPTEMBER 13TH. At midnight a summons came from the hay contractors. Messrs. Crary and Carter, at Goose Creek, for help, as one man had been killed, hay had been heaped upon five mowing-machines and set on fire, and two hundred and nine cattle had been stolen by the Indians, who had driven a herd of buffalo into the valley, and thus taken buffalo and cattle together out of reach. Lieutenant Adair went out at once with reinforcements, but found Indians in too large force for continuance of the work...Private Donovan came in with an arrow in his hip...

SEPTEMBER 14TH. Private Gilchrist was killed.

SEPTEMBER 16TH. Peter Johnson, riding a few rods in advance of his party, which was returning from a hay field near Lake Smedt, was suddenly cut off by Indians. Search was made that night by Quartermaster Brown, but his remains were not recovered.

SEPTEMBER 17TH. A large force demonstrated from the east, and took forty-eight head of cattle; but all were recaptured in pursuit.

SEPTEMBER 20TH. Indians attacked a citizen outfit lying in the angle of the two Pineys; but were repulsed by aid from the fort, losing one red man killed and another wounded.

SEPTEMBER 23D. Indians attacked and drove off twenty-four head of cattle. They were pursued by Quartermaster Brown, in company with twenty-three soldiers and citizens, and after a sharp fight at close quarters, the cattle were recaptured, and a loss was inflicted upon the Indians of thirteen killed and many wounded.

SEPTEMBER 23D. Lieutenant Matson, with an escort, bringing wagons from the hay field, was surrounded and corralled for some time by a superior force. He found upon the road the body of contractor Grull, who had been to Fort C.F. Smith with public stores, and was killed on return with two of his drivers...

SEPTEMBER 27TH. Private Patrick Smith was scalped at the Pinery, but crawled a half mile to the block-house, and survived twenty-four hours. Two of the working party in the woods were also cut off from their comrades by nearly one hundred Indians, and were scalped before their eyes...Captain Bailey's mining party lost two of their best men.[30]

One has to marvel at the ability of the post to maintain the pace of the construction work in the face of the Indian threat. But work went on. Indians appearing on hillsides near the fort were frequently scattered to the four winds by cannon shot. They were never bold enough to directly assault the fort, choosing instead to pick off single individuals or very small parties as the opportunity arose. For the most part, the red man of the plains had always been very averse to any unnecessary risk such as a frontal assault en masse, unless they perceived a very strong likelihood of victory with minimal losses. They were individualists as fighters, each warrior hopeful of counting coup, i.e. collecting scalps to enhance his personal standing within the tribe. These warriors believed in taking advantage of every weakness the enemy offered, attacking from sudden ambush or utilizing ruses such as feigning friendship and then suddenly attacking their surprised victims.[31] They shied away from unnecessary loss of life among their tribal members whenever possible. General Philippe de Trobriand, later commander of the Montana Military District, wrote in his book *Military Life in Dakota* that in September 1867,

[30] Ibid.: 123–128.

[31] Philippe Regis de Trobriand, *Military Life in Dakota*: 62.

In order to give an account of how the Indians make war—the plains Indians in particular—one must understand their ideas about warrior bravery and their complete ignorance of what we call heroism. To them the highest good is in stealing and killing as much as they can with the least possible risk to themselves. Since they have no conception of the feeling that makes us scorn danger they, quite on the contrary, take it into serious consideration, and even a scalp or booty will not bring them to gamble their life on a fifty-fifty chance. They will not venture an engagement unless they hold all the winning cards.[32]

One must take a degree of exception to this rule. When considering individual acts of heroism, countless examples can be found in a study of the Plains Indian. When cornered or when it was necessary to defend their women and children, the Plains Indian would fight regardless of the odds, and fight they did. Another exception was one-on-one fights with antagonists, such as the younger Sitting Bull in one-on-one combat with a Crow leader, which will be discussed in a later chapter. However, Colonel Trobriand's point is well taken. Indians did not recklessly sacrifice their numbers in suicidal charges as often depicted in old Hollywood movies.

General John Gibbon, in describing Indian tactics, wrote in 1879:

We frequently hear accounts of the most desperate acts of bravery by individual Indians, but these are usually isolated cases of bravado, and generally performed at a safe distance. An Indian who would unnecessarily expose his life with no prospect of benefiting his comrades would be looked upon as a fool. The absurd spectacle, so often laughed over, of the two idiots who (was it at the battle of Crecy?) stepped in front of their comrades, and with bows and salutes begged that each might first open fire, has no place whatever in Indian warfare. The Indian's delight is to take every advantage possible of his enemy; surprise him if within his power, do him all the harm he can, without suffering any himself. He is all the more pleased with himself if he can slaughter a whole party, the larger the better, without receiving a shot in return.[33]

The tactics so frequently employed by the Indians lulled the command at Fort Phil Kearny into continuing their preconceived belief that a large U.S. Army unit could not be defeated by any number of Indians. This was

---

[32] Ibid.: 62.

[33] Gibbon: 230–231.

reinforced by the knowledge that the Indians' manpower resources were very limited—that at the most an Indian leader could not possibly muster a unified force of more than a few hundred warriors. The September 1866 Post Return (monthly report) for Fort C.F. Smith reveals that a detail of twenty soldiers en route from Fort Phil Kearny to Fort C.F. Smith was attacked by a force estimated at 200 Indians on September 26, 1866. Private Charles Hackett was badly wounded and later died of his wounds. This group of soldiers was harassed by the Indians for two days but managed to arrive intact at Fort C.F. Smith.[34] Captain William J. Fetterman, assigned to Fort Phil Kearny in November 1866 with Co. C, 2nd Cavalry, had boldly asserted, "…a company of regulars could whip a thousand and a regiment could whip the whole array of hostile tribes."[35]

On December 6th, there was a decided change in the Indians' tactics. That morning the wood train was attacked by a large body of Indians about two miles from the fort. This had occurred frequently. The wood train consisted of approximately ninety men, half of whom were occupied with timber cutting while the other half stood guard. Captain William Fetterman rode out with seventeen mounted infantry and thirty-five cavalry troops to the relief of the besieged wood detail. Simultaneously, Colonel Carrington rode out with twenty-five mounted infantry in an attempt to cut off the Indians retreating from Fetterman's unit. The Indians fell back from Fetterman's oncoming unit to a point about five miles from the fort, on Peno Creek, where they elected to make a strong stand nearly surrounding Fetterman's detail. At this point problems arose. Twenty-five of the thirty-five cavalrymen panicked and, ignoring Captain Fetterman's orders, began a retreat toward the fort. This encouraged the Indians to even greater effort to induce panic among Fetterman's remaining infantry and Colonel Carrington's infantry unit; however, they were not successful. The infantry stood its ground, obeying orders to stand and fight. Colonel Carrington's detail was able to join with Fetterman's remaining troops and successfully withdraw from the field. However, that day's action foretold worse things to come.

On December 21, 1866, the wood detail again came under strong attack by the Indians. Colonel Carrington dispatched Captain Fetterman with a mounted force of eighty soldiers, including fifty-two mounted

---

34 September 1866 Post Return, Fort C.F. Smith, Records of the Adjutant General's Office, ca. 1775– ca. 1928, Record Group 94, National Archives.

35 Carrington: 171.

infantry, twenty-seven cavalrymen and two civilians to relieve the wood detail. Captain Fetterman was instructed to punish the Indians and push them back over Lodge Trail Ridge, a hill visible from the fort. This was the usual route of the Indians' retreat, which led in a northerly direction up the Montana Road. Colonel Carrington cautioned Captain Fetterman not to follow the Indians beyond Lodge Trail Ridge. At 11:45 A.M. Fetterman's troops were sighted by the observers at the fort in pursuit of the Indians near the top of Lodge Trail Ridge. They were then observed to disappear from sight over the ridge. Shortly thereafter heavy firing was heard from behind the ridge. A relief column consisting of seventy-six men under Captain Tenedor Ten Eyck was sent to Fetterman's relief.

Captain Eyck's force reached the summit of Lodge Trail Ridge at approximately 12:45 P.M. just as the last two shots were heard from the direction of Fetterman's column. From his vantage point on the ridge, Captain Eyck could see a large number of Indians grouped below. The Indians then departed the area and Captain Eyck advancing down the ridge discovered the naked bodies of Captain Fetterman and sixty-six of his men all lying within a circle approximately thirty-five feet in diameter. Some distance farther down the trail the remaining bodies of the detail were located, and at the farthest point were the bodies of the civilians and four or five of the older more experienced soldiers. Fetterman's force had been wiped out to the last man.[36]

The U.S. Army later concluded

> ...that the Indians, in force from fifteen to eighteen hundred warriors, attacked [Fetterman's command] vigorously in this position, and were successfully resisted by him for half an hour or more; that the command then being short of ammunition, and seized with panic at this event and the great numerical superiority of the Indians, attempted to retreat toward the fort; that the mountaineers and old soldiers, who had learned that a movement from Indians, in an engagement, was equivalent to death, remained in their first position, and were killed there; that immediately upon commencement of the retreat the Indians charged upon and surrounded the party, who could not now be formed by their officers, and were immediately killed. Only six men of the whole command were killed by balls, and two of these Lieutenant-Colonel Fetterman and Captain Brown, no doubt inflicted this death upon them-selves...[37]

---

[36] Ibid.: 262–269.

[37] Ibid.: 268.

The loss of Fetterman and his men, not unlike the loss of Custer and his troops ten years later, was greeted with disbelief on the part of many in the U.S. Army as well as the public at large. As is frequently the case when disasters occur, scapegoats were sought. Some U.S. Army officers criticized Fetterman's conduct as a commander,[38] expressing the belief that had the troops been better commanded they would have escaped. One critical factor may have been the availability of ammunition. At one point Fort C.F. Smith was down to ten rounds per man, Fort Phil Kearny to thirty-five rounds per man and Fort Reno to thirty rounds per man. Requests for more ammunition had not been answered.[39] Also, of the 700 men Colonel Carrington had arrived with in July, nearly 500 were recruits. There had been little time to train them since the primary task was to get Forts C.F. Smith and Phil Kearny sufficiently completed for the onset of winter. Furthermore, these 700 men were dispersed to three forts: Fort C.F. Smith, Fort Phil Kearny and Fort Reno, located on the road southeast of Fort Phil Kearny toward Fort Laramie. The limited availability of both time and ammunition prevented these recruits from receiving sufficient target practice. Therefore, proficiency in firearms was definitely not their strong suit! Fire discipline may have been also lacking due to insufficient training. Their targets, the Plains Indians, noted for their unsurpassed ability at horsemanship, were likely able to draw off fire from the troops with little harm to themselves. Custer described this ability in his book *My Life on the Plains:*

> [The Indians would] with war whoops and taunts dash over the plain in a line parallel to that occupied by the soldiers, and within easy carbine range of the latter. The pony seemed possessed of the designs of his dusky rider, as he seemed to fly unguided by bridle, rein or spur. The warrior would fire and load and fire again as often as he was able to do, while dashing along through the shower of leaden bullets fired above, beneath, in front, and behind him by the excited troopers, until finally, when the aim of the latter improved and the leaden messengers whistled uncomfortably close, the warrior would seem to cast himself over on the opposite side of his pony, until his foot on the back and his face under the neck of the pony were all that could be seen, the rest of his person completely covered by the body of the pony. This maneuver would frequently deceive the recruits among the soldiers; having fired probably about

---

[38] Trobriand: 47.

[39] Carrington: 263–264.

the time the warrior was seen to disappear, the recruit would shout exultingly and call attention of his comrades to his lucky shot. The old soldiers, however, were not so easily deceived, and often afterwards would remind their less experienced companion of the terrible fatality of his shots.[40]

Once the Indians realized that the soldiers of Fetterman's command had nearly expended their ammunition and were attempting to retreat or escape, they no doubt closed in on horseback, clubbing those troops now on foot and knocking those still mounted from their horses or killing them with arrows. The Indians were unsurpassed in their fighting ability as horsemen. Further, not even the Indians, but far less the cavalrymen, could effectively hit targets while firing rifles from horseback. It was standard procedure for cavalrymen, when making a stand against a strong enemy force, to dismount with every fourth man holding the horses while the remainder knelt or went into the prone position from where they could deliver a more accurate fire, but this required discipline in the ranks, which had likely broken down. Since the soldiers were still armed with Civil War muzzle-loaders, it took them some time to reload after firing. With these weapons and undisciplined firing, it would be possible for the Indians to rapidly close on the soldiers. Once they were within fifty yards, the Indians were very accurate with bows and arrows, which they could fire at the rate of twelve to fifteen per minute,[41] a much faster rate than that made possible by muzzle-loading rifles. This may explain the above quote that only six of the victims were killed by balls! It is of note that the Indians in the attack on December 6th were led by Red Cloud. But on December 21st Red Cloud and his band had left the area and were believed to be conducting a siege of Fort Buford at the junction of the Missouri and the Yellowstone.

The attack on the 21st was reportedly carried out by Minneconjous under Chief High Backbone. They were assisted in their endeavor by Ogallalla, Brule, Cheyenne, Arapahoe and some Crow Indians, numbering about 2,000 warriors. Years later, in 1876, U.S. Army scout Frank Grouard stated to Lieutenant John G. Bourke, one of General Crook's staff officers, that the Sioux had reported their losses to him as 185 killed and wounded.[42] Through repeated small-scale attacks the Sioux and their allies had been

---

[40] George A. Custer, *My Life on the Plains:* 220–221.

[41] Annual Report of the Commissioner of Indian Affairs, 1853: 413, National Archives.

[42] John G. Bourke, *On the Border with Crook:* 291–292.

able to develop a strategy for success. Under the able leadership of chiefs such as Red Cloud and High Backbone, sufficient numbers of warriors were brought together to pull off the big coup. No doubt, every warrior in the field that fatal day knew the plan of action from A to Z.

The blame for the disaster was, for the most part, laid at Colonel Carrington's feet. The U.S. Senate called for a report from the commanding officer, Colonel Carrington, in April 1867, but not before he had been relieved of command and replaced by Brevet Brigadier General H.W. Wessels. President Grant called for an investigation. The investigating commission later exonerated Colonel Carrington of responsibility for the disaster.

In January and February 1867, the months immediately following the massacre, very severe weather was experienced, cutting off contact with Fort C.F. Smith. In February, Sergeant Grant Graham was sent out on foot with a small detail to walk the ninety miles to C.F. Smith and then report back with news. It was feared that the smaller post may have been overwhelmed by hostiles. Sergeant Graham was able to accomplish his mission and report back that all was well at C.F. Smith.[43] In April the Indians killed one member of a mail party on the Dry Fork of the Powder River between Fort Phil Kearny and Fort Reno. On May 16, 1867, Indians drove off twenty-four head of government stock and on the 25th stole twenty-five ponies from friendly Crows encamped at the post. In June, Indians made additional attempts to stampede stock and on the 11th three soldiers were attacked while out hunting and one died of his wounds. On the 22nd the Sioux drove off twenty-five horses belonging to a large camp of friendly Crows encamped at the post. The Crows managed to recapture the horses and kill three Sioux. In July there were additional attempts to steal animals from the post.[44]

On August 2, 1867, a major engagement took place that became known as the Wagon Box Fight. This battle occurred six miles west of the fort, near the headwaters of Big Piney Creek, between a very large force of Sioux, Cheyenne and Arapahoes under the command of Red Cloud and a company of soldiers guarding the wood-cutting detail under the command of Captain James W. Powell. This time the tables were turned, and the Indians were defeated in their attempt to repeat the Fetterman Massacre. We are

---

[43] February 1867 Fort Phil Kearny Post Return, Records of the Adjutant General's Office, ca. 1775–ca. 1928, Record Group 94, National Archives.

[44] April, May, June, July 1867 Fort Phil Kearny Post Returns.

Red Cloud—Sioux chief.
PHOTO COURTESY OF THE NATIONAL ARCHIVES.

fortunate to have an excellent description of this battle in the book *Fighting Indian Warriors,* by E.A. Brininstool. About 1915, Brininstool interviewed Sergeant Samuel S. Gibson, a veteran of forty-eight years of service with the U.S. Army. It is from this interview that I have drawn information and quotes for the following account of the battle.[45]

The sergeant was just beginning his service as a young private when he accompanied the troops upon their arrival at the future site of Fort Phil Kearny. He was a member of the force that recovered the bodies of the victims of the Fetterman Massacre. On July 31, 1867, Company C of the 27th Infantry under the command of Captain Powell took up guard duty for the firm of Gilmore and Porter, civilian contractors responsible for cutting and delivering logs to the fort. The contractors had formed a defensive corral made of fourteen wagon boxes that they had removed from the wagons. They would place their stock inside this corral at night to protect them from theft by hostile Indians. The wagons were placed so close together that no full-sized animal could slip out between them, yet they were wide enough for a man to pass through. In case of attack by hostile Indians, plans were for the company and civilian contractors to fall back into this wagon-box corral for defense. Just prior to this fight

---

[45] E.A. Brininstool, *Fighting Indian Warriors*: 47–78.

an event had occurred that drastically altered the balance of opposing forces that had existed during the Fetterman Massacre—the delivery of new weapons. They were Springfield Model 1866 "Second Allin" Conversion caliber .50-70 centerfire breech-loaders. These rifles were originally Civil War–era Model 1863 Type II Springfield .58 muskets, which had been converted to .50 caliber breech-loaders.[46] Sergeant Gibson reports on the arrival of the new breech-loading rifles:

> It was well toward June [1867] when Gilmore & Porter's bull trains came up the trail with supplies for our post. When they did come, they were loaded to the guards with provender. But the thing that brought joy to our hearts was a huge lot of new improved breech-loading rifles (Springfield, 50-caliber). These were the very first rifles of this type ever issued to troops in Indian country. One hundred thousand rounds of ammunition accompanied these weapons. We now felt that we would stand a better chance in our battles with the savages. The guns we had been using were old antiquated muzzle-loaders, relics of the Civil War. The Indians knew this, and they also knew that once these old guns were fired, it took some time to reload them. Had it not been for these breech-loaders we had received, the Wagon Box fight would have ended with our scalps dangling at the belts of Red Cloud's savage hordes.[47]

The sergeant, at that time Private Samuel Gibson, was on picket duty on the morning when Indians were spotted in the distance, riding to the attack. The following quote of the sergeant reveals the range of the new rifle, the sergeant's marksmanship, and the riding skill of the Indians. Upon hearing a warning shout,

> [Private] Deming and I jumped to our feet, and sure enough, away to the west of us we counted seven Indians mounted, coming across the divide from the north at a dead run and in single file, riding toward the Little Piney and chanting their war song. As the Indians were coming in an oblique direction toward us, and as not a man in the company had yet fired a shot at an Indian from the new breech-loading fifty-caliber Springfield rifles with which we had just been armed, I sat down and adjusted my sights to seven hundred yards, and laying my rifle on top of a stone breastwork, took steady aim at the Indian in advance and fired. My bullet struck a stone in front of

---

[46] "Thrifty Innovation," Utah Gun Collectors Association website.

[47] Brininstool: 51.

the Indian, ricocheted off and wounded his pony. The Indian was thrown off, but immediately sprang to his feet as his pony fell, and was taken up behind a mounted warrior who was following closely in his rear.

About this time Deming and I looked toward our main camp, and over to the Big Piney, to the foothills toward the north, and there we saw more Indians than we had ever seen before. Deming explained in an excited tone: "Look at the Indians!" and pointing toward the foothills across Big Piney Creek, he added: "My God! There are thousands of them!"[48]

As planned, the troopers retreated under fire, returning fire until they reached the wagon-box corral, where they had 7,000 rounds of ammunition stored.[49] Upon his arrival at the wagon-box corral, Private Gibson reported to his commander, Captain Powell, as hordes of Indians began to surround them.

I reported [to Captain Powell] why we had left the picket-post without orders, as it was impossible for us to hold it against such overwhelming odds. Looking me straight in the eye Captain Powell exclaimed: "You have done nobly my boy. You could not have done better!" Then addressing the three of us, he said "Men, find a place in the wagon boxes. You'll have to fight for your lives today!" ...To my dying day I shall never forget the fierce "do-or-die" look on Captain Powell's face that morning.[50]

Most of the soldiers involved in this engagement had been witness to the slaughter of comrades less than seven months previous in the Fetterman Massacre and had no illusions about their fate should they lose this fight. Gibson observed Sergeant Frank Robertson during the interval just prior to the first assault on the corral

...taking the shoestrings out of his shoes and tying them together, with a loop at one end, which he fitted over his right foot, and a smaller loop at the other end to fit over the trigger of his rifle. I did not ask him what he was doing, because the awful horror of our isolated position seemed to dawn upon my mind, but I knew too well

---

[48] Ibid.: 55.

[49] Ibid.: 51.

[50] Ibid.: 51, 59.

the meaning of those grim preparations—that the red devils would never get old Frank Robertson alive![51]

The other men followed his example.

The hostile Indians—Sioux, Cheyenne and Arapahoe—surrounded and repeatedly assaulted the corral from shortly after breakfast until about 3 P.M. The men, concealed in the wagon boxes consisting of regulation boards no more than one inch thick, were able to deliver a rapid and accurate fire from their new breech-loaders, inflicting large numbers of casualties among the Indians. The defenders lost three killed—Lieutenant John C. Jenness and Privates Thomas Doyle and Henry Haggarty. At about 3 P.M. a relief column arrived from the fort and the hostiles withdrew.

> Captain Powell, in his official report, estimated the Indian loss at over three hundred killed and wounded, but we—the men of Company C—estimated that there must have been seven or eight hundred killed and wounded.[52]

Nevertheless, hostilities with the Indians continued. Later, on August 16, 1867, a unit was attacked by a force of about 200 Indians at O'Connor's Springs, leaving three soldiers wounded. In September the Indians stampeded the stock on one occasion and on the 24th of the month they scalped a citizen herder within sight of the post. The following month they killed another citizen contractor near the post. In November there were more attempts at theft of stock, and in December 1867 they once again attacked troops escorting a wagon train near O'Connor's Springs, killing one soldier and wounding three soldiers and eleven citizens. In January 1868 five citizen contractors cutting lumber were attacked, with two wounded. February, March and April were quiet, although the weather was good. In July 1868 the Indians "...made several hostile demonstrations near post"[53]

This would be their last opportunity to wreak havoc on the inhabitants of Forts C.F. Smith, Phil Kearny and Reno. On April 29, 1868, the U.S. government had signed a peace treaty with the Brule, Ogallalla, Yanktonai and Minneconjou bands of the Sioux Nation, ceding them the right to the territory they had so fiercely defended, and denying settlers and transients the use of the region. The government further agreed to abandon all three

---

[51] Ibid.: 61–62.

[52] Ibid.: 78.

[53] August, September, November 1867, January, July 1868, Fort Phil Kearny Post Returns.

forts on the Montana Road, or Bozeman Trail, within ninety days of signing the treaty, and to closing the road to white civilian traffic. As mentioned
earlier, this very territory had been recognized in the Fort Laramie Treaty of
1851 as constituting a portion of the homeland of the Crow Nation. It had,
however, been since conquered by the Sioux and their Northern Cheyenne
allies. Interestingly enough, this new treaty made no mention of the Crow
Nation and was not signed by a single representative of the Crow Nation. In
a space of less than twenty years, "Might had made right"—in this case for
the Sioux Nation.

Before closing this chapter on the Montana Road, it should be noted that
ninety miles farther up the Montana Road, the garrison at Fort C.F. Smith
also had to contend with hostile Indians. This post, while even more remote
in location, had one significant advantage. It was located near the Bighorn
River on the boundary of that portion of the country still controlled for the
most part by the Mountain Crows, who were the bitter enemies of the Sioux
and their Cheyenne allies. As stated earlier, the Crows saw a useful ally in
the white man. The Crows were friendly to the garrison and were encamped
nearby during December 1867, the month of the Fetterman Massacre. They
moved on to the Wind River country on January 4, 1868. The Crows provided the garrison with intelligence on the intentions of the Sioux, including the stated intention of the Sioux to attack the post with a force of 3,000
warriors.[54] This attack did not occur.

Margaret Carrington informs us that

> … parties of Crows came to Fort C.F. Smith to hunt and trade in
> that vicinity, and not only showed uniform friendliness toward the
> whites and the new road, but offered two hundred fifty young war-
> riors to engage in operations against the Sioux. Major Bridger had
> great confidence in this proposition; but the officers had, it would
> seem, no authority to employ so many, as well as no means of arm-
> ing and equipping them when employed.[55]

It would be ten more years before the U.S. Army in Montana Territory
would be authorized to recruit American Indian scouts. These would prove
very valuable in confronting hostile Indian bands.

---

[54] December 1867, January 1868, Fort C.F. Smith Post Returns.

[55] Carrington: 132. The Major Bridger is none other than our famous mountain man, James
Bridger, who as a relatively old man in his early sixties, suffering from rheumatism, served as
chief guide at Fort Phil Kearny.

Although manned by only two companies with a total strength of approximately 160 men, the garrison at Fort C.F. Smith fared better than their brothers at Fort Phil Kearny. While they experienced their share of action, fighting off horse thefts and other harassment at the hands of the hostile Sioux, some losses also occurred among their mail and supply details on the Montana Road between their base and Fort Phil Kearny. I refer to my previous description of the action on September 26 and 27, 1866, in which Private Hackett was fatally wounded. Additionally, an examination of Post Returns for Fort C.F. Smith during the two years of its existence reveals the following actions:

> SEPTEMBER 1866—Hay and timber details frequently attacked. Corporal Alvah H. Staples and Private Thomas Fitzpatrick were killed.

> MAY 1867—A large party of Sioux, Cheyenne, Arapahoe and Gros Ventre lurked about the vicinity of the post. On 5/26 they ran off several horses belonging to the Crow as well as the Post Suttler's entire stock of mules.

> JUNE 1867— One skirmish with Indians on 6/25.

> AUGUST 1867—Hayfield Fight.

> NOVEMBER 1867—Troops escorting train from Fort Phil Kearney were attacked on 1¼ by a large party of Indians. Two troopers killed and three wounded.

> APRIL 1868—On 4/16, 4/28 and 4/29 Indians attempted to run off horses and were thwarted.

> MAY 1868—A party of 50 Indians charged by the fort on 5/5.[56]

The most significant action at Fort C.F. Smith was the famous Hayfield Fight. I quote the Post Return for the month of August 1867:

> On the 1st inst. a party of nineteen soldiers and six citizens under command of 2nd Lieutenant S. Steinberg [Sigmund Steinberg], 27th Inf. who were guarding a party cutting hay were attacked by a force of Indians variously estimated at from 500 to 800. The troops were partly protected by a brush and log corral and fought

---

56 August 1866 through July 1868, Fort C.F. Smith Post Returns.

heroically three or four hours until relieved by troops sent from this post. The Indians were seriously punished and sustained a loss estimated at eight killed and thirty wounded. With the exception of one they carried off all their killed and wounded. Our loss was Lieutenant Steinberg, one private and one citizen killed and one Sergeant, and two privates wounded.[57]

On July 31, 1868, Forts Phil Kearny, C.F. Smith and Reno were abandoned in accordance with the terms of the treaty with the Sioux. The transcontinental railroad was rapidly advancing across the West and was completed by 1869. The government was now more interested in securing an agreement with the hostiles to leave the railroad unmolested. Furthermore, with the railroad finished, the route north into Montana from the new Corinne railhead—the Corinne Road—was now a more accessible route than the old Bozeman Trail. In spite of the treaty, however, intrepid groups of miners continued to use the trail. On his way down the Yellowstone in 1876 to partake in the campaign against the Sioux, Colonel John Gibbon noted in a telegram sent from the field that while at the Crow Agency on the Sweetwater, a group of 200 miners had just departed there en route down the Bozeman Trail to Fort Laramie. This was at a time when the U.S. Army was confronting overwhelming numbers of hostile Sioux in the region.[58]

As General Crook's column advanced northward in 1876 approaching Fort Reno from Fort Fetterman, which was located seven miles north of present-day Douglas, WY, they encountered the trail of some Montana miners heading for the Black Hills. They discovered the following inscription on a piece of board:

Dry Fork of the Powder River, May 27, 1876. Captain St. John's party of Montana miners, sixty-five strong, leave here this morning for Whitewood. No Indian trouble yet. Don't know exactly

---

[57] August 1867 Fort C.F. Smith Post Return. On January 21, 2006, the History Channel ran a program discussing the successes of the Henry Rifle. The Hayfield Fight was discussed and it was stated that a civilian with a Henry Rifle—a lever-action repeating rifle—had accompanied the detail and was involved in the fight that was alleged to last seven to eight hours. It was stated that the civilian killed some 200 Indians with his repeater. This obviously does not square with the information provided in the Fort Post Return. The thrust of the television program was to illustrate that the Henry Rifle saved the day for the detail. This may well be partially true, but no mention is made of the contribution made by the new .50-70 caliber Springfield Model 1866, which had been issued to the soldiers of the 27th Infantry in the summer of 1867.

[58] April 10, 1876, District of Montana Letters and Telegrams Sent and Received, Record Group 393.5, National Archives.

how far it is to water. Filled nose bags and gum boots with the liquid and rode off singing, "There's Room Enough in Paradise!" The board was signed...Daniels, Silliman, Clark, Barrett, Morill, Woods, Merrill, Buchanan, Wyman, Busse, Snyder, A. Daley, E. Jackson, J. Daley and others.[59]

[59] John F. Finerty, *War Path and Bivouac:* 77–78.

CHAPTER SIX

Establishment of the Montana Military District and Construction of Fort Shaw and Fort Ellis; Life at Fort Shaw

PRIOR TO THE BEGINNING OF THE CIVIL WAR IN April 1861, the Montana countryside contained scarcely a permanent structure in the entire realm, save an occasional trading post. However, the discovery of gold quickly resulted in the rapid growth of small and large boomtowns surrounded in choice valley bottoms by small farms and large, open-range cattle ranches. With few exceptions, all of these settled areas were located around Helena and to its south (Virginia City), southeast (Gallatin City and Bozeman), southwest (Deer Lodge and Bannack) and west (the Bitterroot Valley). The large influx of settlers soon resulted in contact and friction with the Indians of the area.

The tribes occupying the territory immediately after the Civil War were primarily the members of the Flathead Nation residing mostly west of the Continental Divide; the Blackfeet tribes residing mostly north of the Sun River Valley, extending beyond the Canadian line and, to some extent, east and south of the bend of the Missouri River in northern Montana; the Mountain Crows occupying the area of the upper Yellowstone River after having been driven out of the Powder River country by the Sioux and their Cheyenne allies; the Sioux occupying the Powder River country and eastern Montana extending into the Dakotas; and the Assiniboines occupying the northeastern portion of the territory.

It should be emphasized, however, that describing an area occupied or controlled by one Indian tribe or another was not an exact science. These tribes all pursued nomadic lifestyles, living for the most part off the hunt.

They were highly mobile and moved their encampments frequently to areas with greener grass and more game or to safer areas to avoid contact with enemy raiders. Their camps or villages were limited in size by their way of life, i.e. the logistics of finding and providing sufficient food from the hunt prevented their villages from becoming too large. A band had to be large enough to provide a sufficient mobile defense against its enemies but not so large it could not sustain itself by the hunt on the prairie. Smaller, more mobile groups also had greater survivability from disease than a large static group. An example is the near extermination of the stationary Mandan villages by smallpox in 1837.

Regarding the mobility of these tribes, we need only to digress to the previous chapter on the fur trade era to observe that the Blackfeet were found in hunting parties or camps consisting also of women and children, roaming as far south as the Green River country in Wyoming and also into the Powder River country. The Mountain Crows, then centered in the Powder River country and Wind River country, roamed throughout the Missouri River country and into the Jefferson Valley and the Sun River Valley. Hidatsa warriors roaming far from their North Dakota area homeland captured the Shoshone Sacagawea near Three Forks around 1799. Lewis was also warned by the Nez Perce of the presence of Hidatsa warriors on the Road to the Buffalo through the Lincoln (Blackfoot Valley) area in the summer of 1806. Even the Nez Perce residing as far away as eastern Washington and western Idaho traveled to the buffalo country periodically to procure buffalo meat and hides in the Judith Basin and the Powder River country.

The relative numbers of Indians occupying Montana Territory were small. In 1872 the Office of Indian Affairs provided the following estimates: Blackfeet, Bloods, and Piegans: 7,500; Assiniboines: 4,790; Gros Ventres: 1,100; Santee, Yanktonai, Uncpapa, and Cut-Head Sioux: 2,625; River Crows: 1,240; Mountain Crows: 2,700; Flatheads: 460; Pend d'Oreilles: 1,000; Kootenais: 320; Shoshones, Bannocks and Sheep-Eaters: 677; and "roving Sioux": estimated at 8,000. The total estimated Indian population in Montana Territory was 30,412.[1] We need only recall that Lewis and Clark traversed the entire distance between the Mandan villages, near the present-day Bismarck, ND, area, and the Beaverhead Valley, near present-day Dillon, MT, during a period of over four months without sighting a single Indian. This did not occur simply because the Indians avoided them, for they also

---

[1] Annual Report of the Commissioner of Indian Affairs for the Year 1872, National Archives.

saw only old signs and few fresh signs of Indians during this portion of their journey. This vividly illustrates a vast and nearly empty territory.

During the years immediately preceding the establishment of Fort Shaw in 1867, there were accounts of white-Indian incidents in the immediate vicinity of some of the numerous gold mining areas scattered throughout the southern half of the territory. Also, there were doubtless a number of killings of lone prospectors in remote areas by either Indians or white outlaws that were never recorded. While members of the Flathead Nation to the west of the Continental Divide remained peaceful, most settlers in the territory were fearful of the Blackfeet tribes, who had in earlier years developed a reputation for their hostility to whites. It was this tribe occupying the northern half of the territory, for the most part to the west of the Missouri, that most of the territorial settlers came into contact with. Various parties of Blackfeet, particularly Piegans, frequently wandered south of the Sun River boundary and stole horses and butchered cattle as they perceived the need and the opportunity. It was, of course, natural for them to do so in the universe they had lived in up to that time. One lived off the land and roamed free.

The white settler, after moving onto and settling unoccupied areas, perceived the Indian as a beggar, thief and sometimes murderer that one would be better off not having around. It fell to the U.S. Army not only to provide protection to the white citizenry but also to protect the peaceful Indians from vengeful whites, whiskey traders and hostile Indian tribes.

The Treaty of 1855 entered into by the Blackfoot Nation and Governor Isaac Stevens stipulated that the Blackfeet remain north of the Sun River and also allowed whites the right of passage along the Mullan Road (later the Fort Benton–Helena Road) from Fort Benton insofar as it passed through their reservation and eventually crossed the Sun River. Fort Benton was, at the close of the Civil War, the only settlement of any size in the northern half of the territory or north of the Sun River. Its population did not exceed 500 even in the very active summer season when the steamboats were coming up the Missouri.

The summer of 1865 saw increased hostility between Indians, settlers and miners. This trend continued into 1866, and fear of Indians increased in the territory. Mrs. Sidney Edgerton, wife of the first territorial governor, expressed her feelings toward Indians in one of her letters home from Bannack in 1865:

> Since Mr. E. went away [on business travel to Helena], we have heard great stories about the Indians killing whites who were on their way

to Fort Benton. I don't know how much truth there is in the reports, but, if they are true, Mr. E. will raise a company of men while in Helena to go after the Indians. I hope he will not have to go, but I do want to have the Indians killed.

In fact, the governor did issue a proclamation on May 31, 1865, calling out a volunteer militia of 500 men, but few answered the call. By June 6th, Mr. Edgerton had given up his attempt to form a militia.[2]

The general feeling and fears of the white populace in Montana Territory regarding Indians, in particular the Blackfeet tribes, is further described by an editorial in the *Montana Post* in June 1865, which was responding to the governor's call for volunteers:

> If ever there can be a time when men should remember that prudence is the better part of valor, it is the present epoch in our territorial history. We have in the game about to be played an immense stake. The lives of our friends, the safety of our communications, the preservation of merchandise and machinery—in fact, all that this Territory has, and by far the greater part of what it needs, depend for their salvation, depend upon the foresight, energy and capability of the officers in charge of the expedition now fitting out to protect our people from the red ruffians, the aboriginal and murdering road agents, who curse with their presence and desolate with their ravages the frontier settlements lying west of the United States.
>
> The real service that our small force can hope to accomplish at present, is to maintain the line from Benton to Last Chance, and afford protection to the immigration coming up the river. Any attempt at general war on the redskins would result in consequences to fearful to contemplate. The Blackfeet, the Sioux, the Bannacks, the Piegans, Gros Ventres, Pen d'Orreilles, Nez Perces, Bloods, Crows, and others would all join in a crusade against the Whites, were our soldiers to commence and indiscriminate plunder and slaughter of all Indians they might encounter, while a wholesome chastisement of the wrong doers, who all belong to the Blackfeet, will gratify the remainder of the tribes, many of who would assist us and the remainder stand honestly neutral from hatred to the Blackfeet.[3]

Public pressure for the presence of U.S. troops in the territory increased. The following is quoted from the *Congressional Record* of January 26, 1866:

---

[2] Mary Wright Edgerton, *A Governor's Wife on the Mining Frontier*: 125.

[3] Quoted in John Owen, *Journals of John Owen*, Vol. II: 313.

Mr. Donnelly, by unanimous consent, submitted the following preamble and resolution; which were read, considered, and agreed to, viz:

Whereas the development of the gold producing regions of the country is of the utmost importance to the financial success of the nation; and whereas communication between the northern tier of States and the gold fields of Idaho and Montana is now possible only by a long detour to the southward as far as St. Louis:

Resolved, that the Committee on Military Affairs be directed to inquire into the expediency of directing the Secretary of War, by bill or otherwise, to establish a line of military posts from the western boundary of Minnesota to the Territories of Montana and Idaho, by the most direct and advantageous route, and to facilitate communication along said route by the construction of a military road with proper bridges over water-courses.

Events such as the Fetterman Massacre in northern Wyoming in December 1866 as well as a widely circulated rumor of a Sioux massacre of the entire garrison at Fort Buford near the junction of the Yellowstone and Missouri rivers during the winter of 1866–1867 by the Sioux increased pressure for military support. Fort Buford was manned during the winter by a single company under the command of Captain William G. Rankin, a brevet colonel. The location of the fort near the junction of the Yellowstone and the Missouri rendered it very isolated during the winter months when the river was frozen. Communication was spotty at best and the fort was frequently harassed by hostile Sioux. Immediately following the Fetterman Massacre nearly 250 miles to the southwest, which had occurred on December 21, 1866, there was great anxiety regarding the fate of the Buford garrison. Seizing on rumors as it is quick to do even in our modern times, the press began circulating stories of a massacre. On April 6, 1867, the *Army-Navy Journal* reported that the garrison had been wiped out. Also on April 6th and on April 11th, the *Montana Post* and the *Helena Herald* respectively printed stories of the massacre. The *Herald* wrote:

…the sad and shocking story is told, of [the post's] entire annihilation—the Indians, coming upon the post in renewed force, succeeded after a most desperate battle in which the savages lost some 300 killed…in capturing the post and in barbarously butchering every officer, soldier and civilian connected therewith! It is stated that

Col. Rankin shot his devoted wife to prevent her from falling captive
to the savage fiends![4]

One can only imagine the effect this report, coupled with that of the
Fetterman Massacre, had on isolated Montana settlers and miners. The reports regarding Fort Buford were almost entirely false; the garrison, albeit
under some pressure from hostile Sioux, survived the winter. These erroneous reports were finally corrected by the *Army Navy Journal* on May 18th,
but many continued to believe that the post had been wiped out. In his book
Then and Now, Montana pioneer Robert Vaughn reported the massacre at
Fort Buford, and his book was not published until 1900![5] On February 24,
1867, Colonel I.V.D. Reeve, commander of the 13th Infantry Regiment, expressed little doubt that the Indians in the territory would commence hostilities as soon as the weather allowed.[6]

Throughout the summer of 1866, the U.S. Army moved up the Missouri
to establish posts in Montana Territory. Their mission was to secure the
freight and stage line between Fort Benton, Helena and Virginia City
and prevent incursions of hostile Indians southward, in the case of the
Blackfeet tribes, and westward, in the case of the Sioux, Cheyenne and
Crow, into Montana settlements. On July 11, 1866, the 1st Battalion of
the 13th Infantry under Colonel I.V.D. Reeve arrived at the mouth of the
Judith River on the Missouri. Here they established Camp Cooke, a temporary post. During the autumn of 1866 one company of the 13th Infantry,
Company E, was ordered from Camp Cooke to the Sun River area to locate a suitable site for a six-company post. The purpose of this post was
to secure the 137-mile-long stage and freight route between Fort Benton
(population approximately 500) and Helena (population 6,000–8,000). By
1867 this road, which was handling "...immense amounts of freight...,"[7]
also served the settlements in the Gallatin Valley, various mining camps
and, last but not least, Virginia City. This transportation artery, a portion
of that surveyed and established by Lieutenant John Mullan during the period 1853–1862, became much utilized after the discovery of gold in 1862,
especially during the summer months when steamboats could bring their

---

[4] Quoted in Philippe Regis de Trobriand, *Military Life in Dakota*: 46–47.

[5] Quoted in Robert Vaughn, *Then and Now*: 273.

[6] February 24, 1876, Department of Dakota, Letters and Telegrams Sent and Received, Record Group 393.4, National Archives.

[7] F.L. Lown, "Medical History of Fort Shaw Post, 6/1867–1/1873," Fort Shaw Letters and Telegrams Sent and Received, Record Group 393.7, National Archives.

abundant cargo up to Cow Island and Fort Benton. During periods of low water and/or ice, river traffic ceased.

The failure to secure the Bozeman Trail had left only one other transportation route to Montana open. That was the road beginning at Fort Hall in Idaho Territory on the Oregon Trail and, later, the Union Pacific Railroad at Corinne, UT, leading north to Virginia City and on to Helena. Branch roads led to Gallatin City (the Bozeman area), Deer Lodge and Missoula. An additional purpose of the post was to shield Montana settlements from the Blackfeet tribes occupying the country north of the Sun River. With the exception of Fort Benton, all Montana settlements of any significant size were located south of the Sun River Valley.

The task of locating a suitable site for the new post fell to Company E. The company spent the winter of 1866–1867 at St. Peter's Mission on the Missouri south of the mouth of the Sun River.[8] This was the old St. Peter's Mission, located near present-day Ulm, MT. (The St. Peter's Mission with which residents of Fort Shaw are now familiar is not located on the Missouri River, but rather west of that location in the Sullivan Valley.) The new military post site was selected and, by June 1867, Major William Clinton with five companies of the 13th Infantry moved onto it to commence construction. The post was initially named Camp Reynolds. Clinton's force amounted to 5 officers and 310 enlisted men. Of these, 17 were sick, 9 were under arrest and 1 officer and 1 enlisted man were absent without leave. The Post Return for the month of June noted that the site was located six miles west of Sun River Crossing, fifty-five miles southwest of Fort Benton and eighty-two miles north of Helena. It was further noted that "…timber was scarce… sufficiency of hay…[and] grazing good year around."[9]

The July 1867 Post Return reports the next month's progress:

> Temporary sheds for storing commissary & qtr master property have been erected and are still in the progress of erection. A temp Blacksmith's Shop has been built and a steam saw mill put up. The enlisted men have been employed in making adobe and cutting lumber for building purposes.[10]

On July 4, 1867, the Department of Dakota directed that the post be

---

[8] Ibid.

[9] June 1867 Fort Shaw Post Return, Records of the Adjutant General's Office, ca 1775–ca. 1928, Record Group 94, National Archives.

[10] July 1867 Fort Shaw Post Return.

renamed Fort Shaw in honor of Colonel Robert Gould Shaw, who fell while leading his regiment of African-American soldiers at Fort Wagner, SC, during the Civil War.

Plans to establish a six-company post at Fort Shaw were later modified to a four-company post, with two companies detailed to the Gallatin Valley to construct a new post, to be named Fort Ellis. This was done in response to requests from the territorial government that the U.S. military provide protection for settlers in Bozeman and the Gallatin Valley, particularly against incursions by hostile Indians from the Yellowstone drainage. This would also do much to eliminate the necessity for an armed Montana militia. On August 21st, the headquarters for the District of Montana and the headquarters for the 13th Infantry Regiment arrived to take up duties at Fort Shaw.[11]

By the month of September there were thirty-three civilians employed at the post, as listed by position and wage or salary:

Head Clerk (1)	$150/month
Clerk (1)	$125/month
Adobe Maker (1)	$125/month
Head Carpenter (1)	$125/month
Carpenters (12)	$100/month each
Masons (10)	$125/month each
Masons (2)	$100/month each
Blacksmiths (2)	$100/month each
Engineer (1)	$100/month
Sawyer (1)	$100/month
Saddler (1)	Salary not fixed[12]

Upon examination of two letters received at the post in August 1867, the author has been able to identify seventeen civilians employed at the Fort Shaw post: E.A. Casteller, James L. Connor, Joseph Dobrey, Edward Hurley, Bernard Killand, James Moran, John Milton, John Mitchell, William A. McConologue, Joseph D. Reilly, Jacob Standley, John A. Joyce, John McCarty, Jeramiah Carroll, David Duffy, William Buckley and J.B. Stewart. At least two other names were located but illegible. Apparently, under obvious pressure to get the fort building completed before onset of winter, the

---

[11] August 1867 Fort Shaw Post Return.

[12] September 1867 Fort Shaw Post Return.

post commander had ordered that the civilians work not eight but rather ten hours per day. This order resulted in a letter to the post commander from concerned workers:

> Col. G.L. Andrews
> Commandant Fort Shaw
>
> Sir,
>
> The undersigned citizen employees of the US Government now working at this post respectfully requests instructions from you in relation to the two hours extra work to [be] performed by us according to your order of the 20th, inst. We prefer to work but eight hours per day but if the exigencies of the time demand it we are content to work the two hours you demand of us provided you gaurentee that we shall receive extra pay in proportion to the amount of time in which we were engaged in performing extra labor believing that as citizens of the U S we have the undoubted right to comprehend the condition upon which we may perform any extra labor and feeling unwilling to leave our case to the consideration of the Sec of War we the undersigned respectfully submit the case for your consideration.[13]

The author was unable to locate a response to this request.

Post Surgeon F.L. Lown arrived at the post on August 23, 1867. His thorough documentation of the situation at the post and the surrounding area in his "Medical History of Post," dated December 31, 1868, is the author's primary source for the following paragraphs. At the time of his arrival all personnel were still living in tents. He wrote:

> By hard labor the troops erected that fall 1867 a part of each set of company quarters, three sets of officers quarters, a small part of the Post Hospital and a temporary store house. The troops did not get into quarters until late in the fall, and after the weather became very cold. Even then the buildings occupied were far from completed. The officers were still later getting into quarters. Necessarily men and officers both were much crowded during the winter 1867–68 but no one suffered. The winter of 1867–68 fortunately was not of unusual severity. In the spring 1868 the building of the post was resumed and pushed vigorously forward during the entire summer and late into the fall. The walls of all the quarters and most of the other buildings were now up and roofed. The entire Post will be

---

[13] August 21, 31, 1868, Fort Shaw Letters and Telegrams Sent and Received.

well built of adobe bricks with wooden roofs. The dimentions of the adobe brick used are six inches by twelve inches and four inches thick. The walls of the buildings are eighteen inches outside; the inside walls are one foot thick.[14]

Additional comments by Lown about the area will be of great interest to readers familiar with the Fort Shaw area. He frequently mentioned the alkaline content of the soil in the area of the post, stating that buffalo wallows near the post, which contained water in the springtime, would appear as white as snow after drying out during the summer and fall. The author had always assumed that the alkali in the soil in the Fort Shaw area was the result of the man-made irrigation project built around 1908–1910. It is now obvious that the alkali in the area predated the irrigation project.

> ... [A] large living spring, or springs, comes up in the prairie bottom opposite the Post (within about one and one-half miles 1½ miles), which forms an extensive slough; this slough remains year round, and is a favorite resort of ducks...The water is not however usually wholesome, or suitable for use, owing to holding in solution saline matters...[15]

Lown stated that he was aware of only one well in the valley, but the water was not suitable for drinking; he added that wells containing suitable drinking water would have to be dug below river level. Consequently, the personnel at the post drank river water, pumped up from the Sun River by a steam engine through wooden pipes into two large tanks of 3,724 gallons each. The pipes broke frequently, and Lown expressed the need for iron or lead pipes. Drainage was initially over the ground, presumably in small ditches, back toward the river. He noted that due to the extreme dryness of the climate, drainage over the ground had not yet caused a problem. Readers will not be surprised that the prevalent malady during the first year was diarrhea.

Lown stated that the countryside was generally unsuited for agriculture but that grazing was fair to good. "Irrigation is indispensable."[16] He mentioned that water could be brought to the post by way of an irrigation ditch from the Sun River, but that such a ditch would necessarily be very long and entail considerable effort. He pointed out that for the summer of 1868 a

---

14 F.L. Lown, "Medical History," December 31, 1868, Fort Shaw Letters and Telegrams Sent.

15 Ibid.

16 Ibid.

ditch was constructed from a point about one mile below the post to carry water from the river and irrigate a five-acre post garden, which was located near the river bottom. The river rose and flooded a large portion of this garden that first year, resulting in an unsatisfactory crop.

There were three ranches located in the valley downriver from the post; one of these grew good vegetables and sold them to the post. Lown stated that the post procured its hay from a supplier in the Missouri Valley. According to Lown the uniformly brown prairie, green only after the springtime rains, was the likely cause of homesickness among the troops. No doubt most of them stemmed from greener pastures in the East! Although it would be of great interest to most readers to observe the valley in its more virgin form, the more permanent greenness of the summer and the countryside now speckled by farms surrounded by trees as a result of the irrigation project are doubtless more pleasing to the eye. Lown believed that the only arable land in Montana Territory was located in the Gallatin, Deer Lodge and Bitterroot valleys and stated these areas were being settled rapidly.

Reading Lown's comments regarding year-round grazing in the area as well as the comment in the Post Return for June 1867, reported above, we can see the seeds of the disaster that befell Montana ranchers in the winters of 1880–1881 and 1886–1887.[17] Lown stated that freighters wintered their oxen on the open prairie without problems. He specifically mentions a large herd of livestock successfully wintered at a point about twenty miles above the post during the winter of 1867–1868. Harsh winters have since quickly ridded Montana cattle growers of any notion that they can survive every winter without hay on hand!

Of interest is the fact that a well-known landmark in the Fort Shaw area, Square Butte, had different designations in army reports. Lown mentioned the buttes in the area and stated, "The more easterly of these [buttes] is widely known throughout the country as the 'Crown Butte'."[18] Colonel John Gibbon also later referred to present-day Square Butte as "Crown Butte."[19] It is of interest, however, that U.S. Army, Department of Dakota, General Order No. 69, dated St. Paul, MN September 14, 1869, referred to Square Butte as "Square Butte." This particular order designated the boundaries of the Fort Shaw Military Reservation and made reference to the north-west angle of Square Butte. It may well be that this was a new designation to

---

[17] Ibid.

[18] Ibid.

[19] Gibbon, *Adventures on the Western Frontier*: 39.

distinguish this landmark from the other Crown Buttes referred to above. This is, however, purely speculation on the author's part.

According to Lown, the Sun River bottom was lined with brush and a few trees that he described as willow trees. He made no mention of cottonwood trees, of which there is a comparative abundance along the present-day Sun River. As noted in the June 1867 Post Return above, timber was scarce. Lown stated that even getting sufficient wood for fuel was a problem.

> The necessary supply of fuel for the past winter almost swept the valley of trees. Wood, and building material is procured by contract from the vicinity of the Missouri River, south of here; the former is obtained about fifteen or twenty miles distant, and the pine timber for building is found in the mountains higher up the Missouri; some forty or fifty miles from the post.[20]

He extended hope that there were coal supplies in the area, particularly about thirty miles distant on the Dearborn, where coal had been reported. Lown further commented that, as of the close of the year 1868, no Indians lived in the valley and that they seldom visited the post.

Post Surgeon F.L. Lown occupied a very important position at Fort Shaw. Post surgeons in our frontier army were usually officers with the rank of major or captain. As before stated, a great deal of information about life at the posts of the Montana Military District can be gained by studying their "Medical Histories," which are found in the original post ledgers at the National Archives. The post surgeon had many important responsibilities. The most obvious was care for the sick and the wounded at the post. It may surprise the present-day reader to note that preventative care was also very high on the U.S. Army's list of priorities, even in 1867. Each post surgeon was required to submit a "Monthly Sanitary Report," which addressed the state of the quarters and buildings, the character and cooking of rations, the water supply and drainage, and the clothing and habits of the men. With regards to the posts of the Montana Military District, many of these reports were either not properly recorded or lost, but a sufficient number are on record in the National Archives to provide the reader with a very good picture of everyday life and living conditions at the posts.

Naturally, the post surgeon was responsible for the post hospital. At Fort Shaw, the post hospital was located as the southernmost building on the west side of the square. Its contents were indeed sparse when compared

---

[20] August 31, 1868, Fort Shaw Letters and Telegrams Sent and Received.

to anything we would refer to as a hospital in the last half of the twentieth century. It was staffed by the post surgeon and/or assistant surgeons, who did their best with the medical knowledge and medicines of their era to perform amputations, combat infections, fight illnesses and assist in child-births. The nurses were enlisted men chosen from the ranks to perform this duty. Doubtless for many, this duty assignment was not a favorite one. An assistant surgeon later assigned to Fort Shaw, L.K. Werner, complained in June 1872 that the post commander was assigning excess duties to nurses, contrary to army regulations. In a report dated December 31, 1875, John D. Hall, another assistant surgeon wrote, "Nursing. Performed as well as could be expected by men untrained and often changed, to suit the short-sighted views of company officers."[21]

It is obvious from reading these reports that the post surgeons of the day were acutely aware of the value of cleanliness and good hygiene in pre-venting illnesses. Many of the matters requiring their attention are taken for granted by the modern-day citizen. In reading these reports it becomes ever more clear what a significant and revolutionary improvement in our standard of living was brought about by the arrival of hot and cold running water and indoor plumbing. Such items were an unknown to occupants of Fort Shaw and other Montana Military District posts.

Each company barracks or dormitory at Fort Shaw consisted of an adobe and wood structure thirty feet long and twenty feet wide with a nine-foot ceiling, which contained bunks for up to eighteen men. This amounted to 600 square feet of floor space for eighteen men. Each barracks had what was referred to as a washroom and a sink, the latter not being a sink in the mod-ern-day sense of the word, but rather a hole dug in the ground to accom-modate waste water from the wash room. These sinks had an overflow that led into irrigation ditches, which in the years subsequent to the summer of 1870 flowed past the post quarters and eventually into the Sun River during the months of April through September. During the summer months, while the ditch was unencumbered by ice, waste water was carried handily away from the living quarters. During the winter months, the irrigation ditch was dry and the sinks were often frozen. In this circumstance the men would throw waste water into the ditch immediately adjacent to the barracks. This water would then dry up in the ditch or, if of sufficient quantity, flow down the ditch toward the river. In periods of extreme cold the water would freeze

---

[21] Fort Shaw Sanitary Reports, June 1872, December 1875, ibid.

in place shortly after being thrown into the ditch. As long as it remained frozen, there was little danger of its breeding vermin or disease.

Mrs. George Armstrong Custer, in her book *Following the Guidon*, accurately described the acceptable sanitation practices of the day at Fort Abraham Lincoln in Dakota Territory:

> There was no sink in the kitchen or outside. The cook opened the door and flung the contents of the dishpan or garbage bucket as far to one side as the vigorous force of her arms would send it. This always left an unsightly spot, to which we were compelled to shut our eyes as there was no remedy.[22]

Although the barracks were each amply heated by a large woodstove, one can well imagine that no great quantity of hot water for washing was available at reveille to allow for any great comfort in daily hygiene. At best the soldier could enjoy a cold wash pan filled with cold water. One can easily imagine them splashing just enough cold water in their faces to wake up for roll call, then tossing the waste water into the ditch and ducking back into the warm barracks! There were no bathrooms anywhere on the post, i.e. rooms equipped with any type of bath tub. Full-body baths for the men were nonexistent, especially in the winter months. Indeed, in his February 1875 Monthly Sanitary Report, Assistant Surgeon J.D. Wall wrote, "I recommend that a wash-room be constructed for each company, & that each man be required to bath the whole body at least once a week." The reader is reminded that this was eight years after the establishment of the post![23]

Toilets were in the form of outdoor privies, one structure for each company, one structure for the hospital, and one structure for each of the other living quarters such as officers' quarters and married enlisted men's quarters. The holes or vaults of these privies, as well as the sinks and removal of waste water, received the constant attention of the post surgeon. In the winter months there was little danger of strong odors or accumulation of vermin, etc., at the privies. In the summer months, however, the problem could become acute and a source of cholera and other diseases. The post surgeon was constantly recommending that odorous contents of the privy vaults be covered with a layer of charcoal or lime and then dirt, and a new vault dug at a new location, no doubt a few feet removed from the old location. For example, on May 31, 1878, Assistant Surgeon Paul R. Brown

---

22 Elizabeth B. Custer, *Following the Guidon:* 229.

23 February 1875 Fort Shaw Sanitary Report, Fort Shaw Letters and Telegrams Sent and Received.

recommended that lime be thrown into the privies on the post on a weekly basis, particularly during the hot summer months. On September 13, 1882, Assistant Surgeon H.S. Kilbourne noted that privy vaults at some of the officers' quarters were full to the surface. He recommended that privy vaults filled to within thirty inches of the surface be covered over and their privies moved to new locations. In his recommendation he also raised the possibility of installing slide-out boxes for periodic waste removal.[24]

Another matter that received the constant attention of the post surgeon was the frequent lack of proper ventilation in the barracks. On February 28, 1879, Post Surgeon Major Charles R. Greenleaf addressed a letter on this subject to the post adjutant:

> Sir: In submitting the Monthly Sanitary Report required General Orders No. 125, A.G.O. 1874, I have the honor to invite attention to the large number of men on Sick Report since January 1st, 1879.
>
> The percentage of Sick to the mean strength of the Command, during January was 31.87, during Febr. was 36.79; nearly 60 per cent of the cases treated have been for rheumatism and affections of the air passages, and there has been a daily average of 10+, prescribed for at the Dispensary, for the same cause, who were not on sick report.
>
> A total of 554 days service have been lost to the Government since Jan 1st, through diseases of this character.
>
> There has been a notable falling off in the Sick Report since Feb. 18th, at which time the Commanding Officer issued certain orders, having in view the general hygienic improvement of the men.
>
> There are, in my opinion, three good causes for the production of these effects:
>
> 1st Overcrowding of the Company Quarters,
>
> 2nd An absence of proper ventilation in the quarters,
>
> 3rd An extremely variable temperature, with a tendency of catarrhal affections becoming epidemic.
>
> This subject has been commented on, by my predecessors in their several Annual Sanitary Reports since 1872, and recommendations to diminish the size of the garrison, with a view of averting sickness,

---

[24] May 31, 1878, September 13, 1882, Fort Shaw Letters and Telegrams Sent and Received.

have been made by all of them, as also by Medical Director, Surgeon Jno F. Head, U.S. Army, at two of his official visits of inspection.

The remedy consists:

1st In diminishing the size of the command, and 2nd in properly ventilating *all* the quarters occupied as barracks.

This can readily be done by putting outlet ventilators and cold air inlet boxes, in the buildings, after the pattern now in the Hospital wards; these wards, with a cubic air space nearly five times greater than the barracks, (952 cubic feet in hospital—203 cub. Ft. in [illegible] become offensive if the inlet and outlet ventilating tubes are closed over night, but are quite free from impurity, and of a comfortable temperature, when they are kept open; I refer to them as a practical evidence of the good effects of ventilation, and ample air space.

No better comparison of well and poorly ventilated quarters can be made than of those at Ft. Benton, and Ft. Shaw; at the former each man in quarters has a cubic air space of 496 feet; at the latter a cubic air space of 203 ft. The company on duty there has been exposed to the same malarial influence in the South, and has done the same amount of field service in the North, as the companies of the 3rd Infantry on duty here; yet, not a single case of sickness has occurred among them since their arrival at that Post, which can be attributed to bad air, or overcrowding.

I would respectfully recommend that estimates be made and forwarded to the proper authorities, for sufficient galvanized iron to make outlet ventilators, and lumber to make cold air inlet boxes, for every building at this Post now occupied, or to be hereafter occupied as quarters by soldiers, and that, without erecting additional barracks, the garrison be limited to a *maximum* of (4) four companies.

The cooking, general police, and condition of the Command is, in other respects, good.

> Very resp.
> Your Ob. Servt.
> Chas. R. Greenleaf
> Major & Surg., U.S.A.[25]

The post surgeon also addressed overcrowding in the guardhouse on

[25] February 28, 1879, ibid.

June 23, 1872, noting that it was too small for the twenty-nine prisoners held at the time and thus presented a danger to the prisoners and others as well. By December 1875 the average occupancy of the guardhouse was entered as fourteen.[26] We may therefore assume that twenty-nine was either an unusually high number or that the problem was remedied.

The barracks initially contained two-story wooden bunks, which the post surgeon found lacking.

> ...old wooden two-story bunks, for four men each, is much to be deprecated. Besides the other objections to their use they afford harbor for vermin, which certainly in some instances at this post, have availed themselves of it, and which no amount of care can dislodge.[27]

A June 17, 1872, entry in the Medical History noted that this problem had been remedied by the issuance of single-story iron beds. An entry on the same date addressed the bedding "As usual for some years in our Army, the clothing and bedding (especially the blankets) are ill-adapted, a swindle on the soldier, and generally beneath contempt."[28]

By December 31, 1873, we see evidence of renovations at the post. Assistant Surgeon A.H. Maiselis wrote:

> A new Bakery has been erected on the north side of garrison, nearly on a line with the new Q. M. Store House, built of stone, 60 X 20 x 9 ft, 18 inch walls, shingle roof. Inside measurement 47 [he wrote 47 but must have intended 57] X 17 feet, this is divided by a wooden partition into two rooms, one the Bakery proper 44½ X 17 feet and the other 12½ X 17 feet—used as a sleeping room for the Bakers well furnished and capable for all demands.

> A new Stable has been erected at the corrall on the site of the old one. Stone foundation. Balloon frame. Clapboarded with shingle roof. Dimensions 30 x 232½ feet X 9 feet, divided into one stable proper with accommodations for 108 animals, with two rooms 10 X 9 X 9 ft. on east side used as a granary and as a Saddlers Shop, also four rooms on west side two each 9 X 12 X 9 ft.—1 room 8 X 9 X 9 ft. and 1 room 9 X 5 X 9 ft. used respectively as Granary, Harness room, Sleeping room and Sitting room.[29]

---

[26] December 31, 1875, ibid.

[27] Ibid.

[28] June 17, 1872, ibid.

[29] December 31, 1873, "Medical History," Fort Shaw Letters and Telegrams Sent and Received.

Assistant Surgeon John D. Hall recommended in his Monthly Sanitary Report for June 1875 that "There should be a new locked privy to each company for the women and children." Here he was doubtless referring to the families of the married enlisted men. Each officers' quarters was already provided with a privy. On December 31, 1875, he also noted, "Married-soldiers Quarters...Accommodations insufficient. Some families much crowded...Officers Quarters...Accommodations insufficient. Out of 13 houses there are 6 occupied by single families, the rest are occupied by two officers together."[30]

As previously stated, most of the post buildings were originally constructed of adobe with lumber roofs. Such structures will suffice many years in a dry climate such as that of Montana. However, the area experienced some highly unusual weather in May 1876, while most of the garrison was out in the field on the Yellowstone and Bighorn Expedition against the hostile Sioux and Northern Cheyenne, a campaign we will discuss later. Assistant Surgeon Paul R. Brown reported in the May 1876 Sanitary Report:

> Post Adjutant
>
> Sir:
>
> I have the honor herewith to forward monthly Report for the month ending May 31st, 1876.
>
> The buildings of the post generally are in an unsafe condition, especially those which are constructed of "Adobe". The two violent storms of the month just passed occurring so closely together have injured the "Adobe" buildings to such an extent that it is imperatively necessary that many new buildings should be constructed and others repaired. There is no a single water-closet connected with the Officers Quarters which can be entered without imminent danger of the walls falling upon the occupant, and several of the closets are simply piles of mud. Those which remain standing are dangerous and unfit for use, and it is absolutely necessary both for the sake of comfort and decency, that this matter should be attended to at once.
>
> Parts of the Quarters occupied by "H" Co. have fallen down and likewise parts of the building occupied by the Regimental Band are in a ruinous state. The almost phenomenal character of these storms will be evident from the enclosed table of statistics taken from the Post Hospital Meteorological Register, showing the amount

---

[30] June, December 1875 Fort Shaw Sanitary Reports.

of rainfall for the month of May during the last six years and likewise the rainfall of May 1876...

May 1871	.48
May 1872	.34
May 1873	3.38
May 1874	1.06
May 1875	.80
May 1876	7.19

...during the past two weeks nearly twice as much rain has fallen as in the whole of each of the two preceding years. I would most strongly recommend on the ground of safety to life and health, that new outbuildings of brick or wood be constructed, the sides and rear of all quarters weather boarded and piazzas placed in front of all quarters facing east or north.[31]

We may assume, of course, that nothing happens fast in a bureaucracy. Although Assistant Surgeon Brown noted in his July 1876 Sanitary Report that lumber had been purchased for boarding of houses and construction of new outhouses, these repairs were likely of a temporary nature. No doubt funding for such a large project had to be requested and authorized. Matters were further impeded by the fact that the Montana Military District commander, Colonel John Gibbon, was in the field with the troops on the Yellowstone and did not return to the post until early October 1876. The author will speculate that the necessary requests, i.e. paperwork, were sent forward during the winter months of 1876–1877. During the summer of 1877, the attention of the post and a great deal of the U.S. Army was taken up by the Nez Perce campaign. The years 1876 through 1877 were very busy Indian-fighting years. Finally, on April 30, 1878, Assistant Surgeon Brown reported that the weather-boarding of the buildings was in progress. We are also informed by Post Returns for April, May and June of 1878 that civilian employment increased by one supervisory carpenter and three carpenters.[32]

In April 30, 1883, Captain Henry S. Kilbourne, the post surgeon (Assistant Surgeon by title) reported that alterations were underway on the married soldiers quarters. On September 30, 1885, he also commented that new shingles were being put on the barracks roofs.[33]

---

[31] May 1876 Fort Shaw Sanitary Report.

[32] April, May, June 1868 Fort Shaw Post Returns.

[33] April 1883, September 1885, Fort Shaw Sanitary Reports.

During the entire period in which the army was stationed at Fort Shaw, some twenty-four years, the post utilized drinking water pumped from the Sun River. The post surgeons monitored it on a regular basis for cleanliness and the possible appearance of any detriment to health. Occasionally, they would comment on the water becoming turbid during periods of high water in the river, but in their view it always remained healthful. In fact, Captain Kilbourne commented in his report for November 1882 that the water supply was "...one of the purest potable waters I have seen at any post in the Army."[34] On July 1, 1872, L.K. Werner noted, "Water is kept in barrel; leather buckets in hospital to be used in case of fire, (which can be filled from irrigating ditches in front and rear of hospital) also at post several fire extinguishers, and powerful pump with requisite hose..."[35] Captain Kilbourne commented in his entry dated April 30, 1883, that there were some dead animals present in the Sun River both above and below the water pipe intake, and he recommended their removal and burial. He also noted that litter from the engine house (steam engine) had accumulated above the intake. On December 31, 1884, he commented that due to the cold weather the hospital water barrel for fire prevention use was frozen solid. He questioned what they would do in case of fire. On January 18, 1885, the water intake became blocked and had to be replaced. A hand pump was driven through the ice to serve as a temporary solution. By February 1, 1885, a new intake was in place. Apparently, during the following summer it was decided to lay a new line underground extending farther out into the river and insulated with hay and fresh earth. This was reported completed on September 30, 1885.[36]

A small crisis of the water supply occurred in 1886. Captain Kilbourne wrote in his Monthly Sanitary Report for January 1886 that "During the month the inside painting of the water wagon with red roofing paint gave the supply an unusual appearance and afforded some consternation to the consumers. The cause was traced to its source and abated without detriment."[37] One can well imagine that this paint contained a considerable amount of lead, totally unacceptable by today's drinking water standards!

As previously described, drainage of the post was provided by irrigation ditches that flowed past most of the buildings and carried waste water

[34] November 1882 Fort Shaw Sanitary Report.

[35] July 1, 1872, Fort Shaw Letters and Telegrams Sent and Received.

[36] September 30, 1885, ibid.

[37] January 1886 Fort Shaw Sanitary Report.

off and into the Sun River. In November 1884, work was underway lining these ditches with cobblestone. On February 28, 1886, it was reported that "During the month drain pipes were laid from the wash room of the north barracks to the river bank." Garbage disposal was dealt with by throwing the refuse into the Sun River about a quarter mile below the post. This certainly would not have met with today's EPA standards but was considered sufficient at the time. The practice was given some thought, however, by Captain Kilbourne in 1885. "The disposal of refuse of the post by throwing it into the river below might give way with advantage, in a sanitary way, to its destruction by fire: for the river water is, for those who use it below the post, more or less polluted by what it receives in its flow through the post." It is unknown if this recommendation was ever followed up on.[38]

One of the medical problems that frequently confronted the post surgeon was frostbite emanating from exposure to the oftentimes severe winter climate in Montana. This problem as well as the inadequate protection provided by military issue clothing received special attention in a report by Assistant Surgeon Clark K. Werner in November 1871:

> Nov. 24. 71. Companies "B" and "H" 7th Infantry consisting of 82 enlisted men and 4 commissioned officers were en route to Fort Shaw, on the Fort Benton road, returning from detached service. When the command left camp at "Tingley's" or 28 mile ranche the thermometer indicated 33°. On the open prairie about 10 miles from the leavings of Sun river and 13 miles from Fort Shaw [This must be an error—23 miles would be correct!], the Troops were overwhelmed by a sudden snow storm, the wind blowing from the N.W. at an estimated velocity of 5, the mercury falling at noon to -30°, and to -19° at night. The majority of the men were frostbitten in all grades of severity, before reaching shelter at the "leavings".

> Nov. 25. 71. Early on the 25th instant when their condition was known, and all the requisite supplies were sent from Fort Shaw and transportation having been procured, many were sent into the hospital; the Thermometer indicating during the day, at the stated hours of observation -30° -21°, -37°. (The minimum thermometer does not register below -37°.)

> Nov. 26. 71. On the 26th inst. the remaining frostbitten men were transferred from ranche at "Leaving" to hospital, thermometer indicating

---

[38] December 31, 1875, November 13, 1884, August 31, 1885, February 28, 1886 Fort Shaw Sanitary Reports.

-37°, -34°, -37°, at hours of observation. The thermometer observations are of course taken from the register at the post. Although a storm of such unexampled severity could not be foreseen at this season of the year, yet its lamentable results show how sparingly Troops can be used in an advanced season of the year, in this latitude, and how entirely inadequate for the protection of the men, is the clothing furnished by the government, including Buffalo shoes etc.[39]

One can only imagine how miserable these men must have felt. The author has, as have most Montanans, personally experienced the harshness of the environment in similar storms, but while enjoying the advantage of modern down-filled parka coats, thermal underwear and insulated boots!

In 1883 Captain Kilbourne, responding to the request of higher headquarters, drafted a report on the winter clothing. The following letter provides the reader with a great deal of insight into the winter clothing worn at the time by not only soldiers but by civilians as well:

Fort Shaw, M.T.
August 31, 1883

To the Medical Director
Department of Dakota
Fort Snelling, Minn

Sir:

I have the honor to acknowledge the receipt of Circular Letter from your office dated Fort Snelling Minn., Aug. 21, 1883, referring to the use of overcoats by the troops at this post and reply to state as follows: An opinion is requested on the following points—[Question #1] What would be the effect upon the health of the men exposed during drill, fatigue, and stable duty, woodcutting or in fact any duty requiring them to be in the open air with only the regulation overcoat?

In reply I would respectfully state that, in my opinion, when troops are on any duty requiring prolonged exposure in the open air in this climate in the severest winter weather with only the regulation overcoat some will be frozen to death, some will become so chilled as to cause fatal illness, some will frostbitten on face, hands, feet, scrotum or any part least protected, and a few will escape any severe consequences. In a word, the soldier protected only by the regulation

---

[39] November 1871 Fort Shaw Sanitary Report.

overcoat is in constant jeopardy of life and limb, when deprived of fire and shelter. The opinion of the men as to the protective value of the regulation overcoat is illustrated by their practice of wearing the buffalo coat over it when on detached service in coldest weather.

It is the general opinion of officers and others of experience in this latitude that on account of sudden and extreme variations of temperature it is hazardous to be exposed during the winter on the prarie, however mild the weather may be, without adequate protection for any contingency.

When on any duty in and about the post not requiring prolonged exposure and demanding bodily exercise the regulation overcoat is, in my opinion, a sufficient protection for any but the severest cold weather.

[Question #2] Please give your views as to the best servicable overcoat to insure protection to the men at your post when upon any kind of duty which requires them to be in the open air.

My opinion on this point is offered with the hesitation due to an experience and observation somewhat limited.

The buffalo skin coat is the one generally worn and preferred by civilians whose choice is not restricted. This is commonly lined with a heavy flannel throughout having a high collar of same or some finer skin made close well around the front of the neck. The pattern of the garment is double breasted and long enough to reach well below the knees. Closed in front by buttons and cords.

The coat now issued to the troops here is substantially of this sort. It appears to be generally satisfactory to both officers and men. The following defects are noted. It is heavy and cumbrous as compared with other furs, hindering movements of the body in any sort of exercise. The seams rip before the coat is much worn. Buttons fall off readily and are too few in number to close completely. In snow and rain they become very wet and heavy and dry slowly, but as the winter climate here is generally dry the latter objection is not a mighty one. Another coat here worn by civilians is made of heavy water proofed canvas, lined with a blanket, cut very long in the body and belted at the waist. This is said to be a comfortable coat even in severe weather but I have no personal experience with it. It is somewhat less heavy than the buffalo coat and restricts less the movements of the wearer.

I am informed that sample coats of similar pattern were issued last winter to the troops and that a favorable report of the trial was made by one company commander.

Another sample coat issued by the Quartermaster Department for trial, at the same time, was made from the water-proofed canvas, or duck and lined with sheepskin tanned with the wool on. This coat, I am informed by two company commanders, was much liked by the men who wore them, and found them to be lighter than the buffalo coats and sufficiently warm, while at the same time permitting greater freedom of movement of the body, the canvas however, was found to add greatly to the stiffness of the garment.

Another coat, the so-called Russian coat issued for trial at the same time, was made from sheepskin tanned with the wool on and worn with wool inside. This coat is said to be very pliable, warm and comfortable. The objections to it were that it absorbed moisture readily and unless kept quite dry, constantly gave out a disagreeable odor. If it were practicable to render this coat water repellant and free from oder, it would, in my opinion, prove to be the best substitute for the buffalo coat...

(Sgd.) H.S. Kilbourne
Capt. and Asst. Surgeon U.S. Army[40]

The post hospital especially and the post in general became a source of a streptococcus infection described at the time as "erysipelas." Although it was seldom fatal, the post surgeon was frequently combating outbreaks of this infection. Modern medical dictionaries describe erysipelas as an infection of the face caused by streptococcal bacteria, which are thought to enter the skin through a small wound or sore. Today it is readily treated by penicillin and successor drugs.

In June 1874 an outbreak of measles was reported among the children at the post. Care was also taken to see that the soldiers and civilians were adequately immunized against smallpox. Smallpox vaccination was available at the time. In the winter of 1869–1870 there was an outbreak of smallpox among the Indians in the area, and two stage drivers operating on the route between the Leavings of Sun River (near present-day Vaughn) and Fort Benton died of the disease.[41] In his November 1876 report

---

[40] August 31, 1883, Fort Shaw Letters and Telegrams Sent and Received.

[41] Vaughn, Then and Now: 88.

Assistant Surgeon Paul R. Brown noted, "During the past month 300 enlisted men have been vaccinated, of which the number 184 have taken. Twenty children of laundresses have also been vaccinated successfully."[42] On December 6, 1881, Post Surgeon Greenleaf directed a letter to Colonel Brooke, the post commander, advising him of an outbreak of smallpox in the territory around Fort Shaw. The surgeon recommended vaccination of the troops and a quarantine of citizens, Indians and half-breeds wishing to stay at the post. In January 1882 the contingent at the post (since 1878 members of the 3rd Infantry Regiment) was vaccinated. Apparently, the post at Fort Shaw remained entirely free of smallpox during its twenty-four-year duration. The November 1882 Sanitary Report noted that variola (smallpox) cases had appeared in Helena, Fort Benton and Missoula as well as one fatal case on the stage line between Fort Shaw and Helena.

On August 30, 1885, personnel at the post were forbidden to have intercourse with anyone in the St. Peter's Mission area, due to an outbreak of scarlet fever. This quarantine was lifted on September 13, 1885. The January 1890 report noted an outbreak of *la grippe* (flu) among twenty officers and enlisted men as well as fourteen civilians.[43]

As might be expected, the troops at Fort Shaw suffered from the results of sin with ladies of ill repute. Although it did not appear to be a matter of great import in the realm of post medical problems, medical personnel noted the presence of syphilis (two cases) and one case of gonorrhea among incoming recruits on September 30, 1882. The presence of venereal disease among recruits was mentioned again in October 1883.[44] One can only speculate on this matter, but it is reasonable to assume that the opportunity for illicit sexual activity was very limited at Fort Shaw when compared to other posts collocated with large cities and towns. This was aided by the fact that the only civilian settlement existing outside of the post at Fort Shaw was Sun River Crossing—too far away to be frequented on a daily basis. Frequent comments were often made of the readily available opportunity for drunkenness and sinful behavior available to the occupants of the post at Fort Benton, and to a more limited extent Sun River Crossing. Of course, many of the troops readily availed themselves of such opportunities.

---

[42] November 1876 Fort Shaw Sanitary Report.

[43] January 1890 Fort Shaw Sanitary Report; August 30, 1885, September 13, 1885, Fort Shaw Letters and Telegrams Sent and Received.

[44] September 30, 1882, October 10, 1883, Fort Shaw Letters and Telegrams Sent and Received.

The post Medical History contains frequent references to patients admitted to the Fort Shaw Hospital, both civilian and military. Some of these entries are described herein. There were a number of women at the post: either officers' wives, enlisted men's wives or civilian employees. There were numerous births at the post hospital. The frequent occurrence of death in childbirth underscores a stark reality of life for women in those days. Entries are frequently seen such as the following: "March 13, 1879 Born to the wife of Serg. R. Cunliff, Co. J. 7th Inf. a daughter—forceps delivery—post partum hemorrhage...March 26, 1879 Mrs. Cunliff died. 6:25 A.M. Asst. Surgeon Paul R. Brown"[45]

In almost every entry, with few exceptions, a birth that involved a postpartum hemorrhage was eventually followed by the death of the mother, leaving behind a motherless child to the care of a widower. Sometimes the mothers would linger for weeks before dying, unable to recover their strength from the loss of blood. The stark reality of those days meant that every childbirth was virtually a life and death matter and every bit as risky to the female of the species as the prospect of heavy combat was to the male. The attempted remedy for postpartum hemorrhage was hot water.

I am quoting some of the more interesting entries in the Medical History of the post regarding patients admitted to the post hospital:

JANUARY 1875 Pvt. John Winston, Co. G., 7th Inf. In a quarrel with another soldier in the afternoon of 12 Jan. he received a kick in the abdomen. He died within 24 hours of a ruptured bladder.

OCTOBER 4, 1879 Died at this Hospital John Kreger, freighter, 43 years of age, admitted to Hospital August 18th with compound comminuted fractures of both legs.

JANUARY 1880 Lucas Conant Citizen of Sun River Valley. Fracture of right thigh from horse kick. Discharged March 5, 1880.

JANUARY 1880 Charles Gilbert, Dearborn, M.T. Incised wound. Right foot from axe. Discharged February 8, 1880.

MARCH 1881 Pvt. John Mitchell, Co. G., 3rd Infty. Died in Post Hospital on 23 inst. at 9 P.M. from gunshot wound, received while endeavoring to escape while under arrest for desertion.

45 January 1875, October 1879, January 1880, March 1881, March 1885, March 1879 Fort Shaw Medical Reports.

> MARCH 1885 William Lee, a civilian under treatment in Hospital for severe injury, caused by the passage of a wagon over the abdomen, died of shock March 22, 1885, and was buried in Post Cemetery March 24, 1885[46]

The Medical History lists the most common activities of the troops, not surprisingly, as guard duty, fatigue duty, drills and target practice, although we will note later that target practice was sorely lacking when compared to that received by the modern-day soldier. Recreational activities were described on January 31, 1875, as walking, riding and hunting, with frequently utilized temperance lodge, theater and glee club.[47]

During 1888, the 3rd Infantry was relieved of duty at Fort Shaw by the 25th Infantry, an all African-American unit with white officers. The following entry in the post Medical History by Captain George F. Wilson, assistant surgeon, reveals that racist, prejudiced behavior was not limited to Southerners only.

> JUNE 11, 1888 Pvt Wm Robinson, Co. E, 25th Infantry was demanded, June 10th, by the Civil Authorities for the alleged murder of a citizen of Sun River, M.T., on the night of June 9th, and turned over to them. It is reported on reliable authority that on the morning of June 11th he was taken out of the jail by unknown persons (presumeably citizens of Sun River) and hung (lynched).[48]

Two additional entries involving African American soldiers at Fort Shaw, one humorous and one tragic, are of interest:

> MARCH 21, 1889 Private Jefferson Talton, Co. B., 25th Inftry, was admitted to Hospital at 4:30 A.M. for an acute oblique…hernia, left side,…Patient states he received his injury during the night of Mar. 20-21st at Sun River, M.T. while "skylarking with women".

> FEBRUARY 28, 1890 Private John Mack, Co. B., 25th Inftry, who was absent without leave was brought to the Hospital, Feb. 16th, (1 ocl) A.M. Pvt. Mack was thrown from his horse about ½ mile from the post where he was found by the guard. Both hands and feet were frozen solid. He was doing as well as might be expected, when Feb. 21 pneumonia set in which caused his death Feb. 23. 90 at 2:45 ocl. A.M.[49]

---

[46] Fort Shaw Medical Histories, Fort Shaw Letters and Telegrams Sent and Received.

[47] January 31, 1875, ibid.

[48] June 11, 1888, ibid.

[49] March 21, 1889, February 28, 1890, ibid.

CHAPTER SEVEN

Operations and Events in the Montana Military District, Summer 1867 to June 1869

T HE PRIMARY ACTIVITY FOR ALL CONCERNED DURING the summer and fall of 1867 was the construction of the new posts at Fort Shaw and Fort Ellis and the transfer of men, equipment and supplies up the Missouri from Camp Cooke and from stateside. On July 13, 1st Lieutenant William Spencer, who was responsible for the movement of some of these supplies, reported problems with his mules and the relative lack of experience among his men in handling them. He stated that they knew as much about handling mules "…as the Sioux knew about Hebrew!" He then requested the assignment to his unit of soldiers more experienced in handling his uncooperative U.S. Army mules.[1]

As work on the post construction proceeded, the army had its usual share of problems with discipline and desertions. The temptation for a poorly paid and overworked frontier soldier to desert and strike it rich in the gold fields was great. The post stockade was never unoccupied. The following letter written on July 13, 1867, to the post commander by Private Leroy Waller expresses the sad state of affairs for many of these prisoners:

> Sir,
>
> I, Private Leroy Waller, of Co. F, 13th Inft., after a long period of confinement, request that I may be released and returned to duty

---

[1] July 13, 1867, Records of Posts, Continental Army Command 1820–1920, Fort Shaw Letters and Telegrams Sent and Received, Record Group 393.7, National Archives.

in my Company. The failing state of my health induces me to make this request.

I was arrested for desertion on the 12th of May 1866 and I have been a prisoner ever since. The anxiety of my mind has been most intense during that whole of that time, and at the present moment I feel its effects upon my constitution. I do not ask my release as a right, but simply as an act of clemency for which I shall be ever grateful. I will return to my duty as a good soldier; being willing to meet all demands the government may make on me as a deserter. I am willing to make good the time I was absent and pay every expense accruing from my arrest.

I will do all and everything but I beg to be released. Under any conditions, I beg you will release me from the miserable state of mind I am now in.

> I am, Sir
> Very Respectfully
> Your Obt. Servant[2]

Desertion was so prevalent that at one point 1st Lieutenant Spencer wrote from Fort Benton that he had a deserter by the name of Patrick Kelly in his custody, but he could not accurately identify the deserter because the army sought two Patrick Kellys for desertion![3]

On July 14, 1867, a citizen physician, Mr. R.B. Hitz, arrived for duty at Fort Shaw.[4]

On July 23 a letter was received from George Wright, Indian Agent at Fort Benton requesting that troops arrest one "…Frederick Walker who is engaged as a cook for a lame Frenchman who keeps the Dearborn Ranche and who I accuse of selling the Indians of my agency whisky, and taking a squaw for the purpose of living off her relatives in the Indian camp."[5] The author was unable to determine from available records whether this request was granted.

In August, Major General Alfred H. Terry, then commanding the Department of the Dakota, and Major General Comstock, Inspector General

---

[2] Ibid.

[3] August 4, 1867, Fort Shaw Letters and Telegrams Sent and Received.

[4] July 1867 Fort Shaw Post Return, Records of the Adjutant General's Office, ca. 1775–ca. 1928, Record Group 94, National Archives.

[5] July 23, 1867, Fort Shaw Letters and Telegrams Sent and Received.

of the U.S. Army, arrived to inspect progress of construction at Fort Shaw. On August 15th, Companies D and F departed Fort Shaw for the Gallatin Valley to a site at present-day Bozeman to establish a new post. This post would be designated Fort Ellis in honor of Colonel A.V.H. Ellis, killed at the Battle of Gettysburg. A third company, Company G, followed them to Fort Ellis, departing Fort Shaw on August 25th. On August 31, 1867, the post commander of Fort Ellis, Captain R.S. LaMotte, filed the following report to his headquarters at Fort Shaw:

> Sir:
>
> I have the honor to report that in accordance with Special Orders No. 15 Hd Qrs Dept of Dakota Fort Shaw MT August 7th 1867 I proceeded with Co's D and F 13th Infy to Gallatin Valley arriving at this place on the 27th inst., and on examining the surrounding country, I have located and commenced building a Post, which I have called Fort Ellis, subject to the approval of the proper authority in honor of Colonel A.V.H Ellis 124th NY Volunteers, who fell at the Battle of Gettysburg.
>
> The Post is situated in Gallatin Valley at the extreme eastern end, at the opening of Bozeman's Pass and about three miles from the town of Bozeman, Bridger's Pass is about three miles west or northwest, and Flathead Pass about fifteen miles northwest. These are the only known passes through the mountains between here and the Missouri River through which Indian incursions might be made from the valley of the Yellowstone. To the southeast no passes are known within twenty five miles. The Gallatin Valley stretches away to the west and is thickly settled with farmers. The population is estimated about fifteen hundred, principally engaged in farming and raising stock...A private express will bring all letters from Virginia City, but as the charge is half a dollar/gold I shall not avail myself of the facility.
>
> Gallatin City exists only on the map, there being but one log hut there inhabited by the ferryman...
>
> There is an abundance of pine, spruce and fir trees of suitable size for huts, within three miles and a half of the location selected, but to get them on the ground ox teams will have to be hired, which can be done here at reasonable prices, say five yoke of oxen with heavy timber wagon and driver for ten dollars a day; if without driver two or three dollars less.

> Hay will have to be contracted for, as it is too late to cut green, even if there were any fit to cut. I think hay can be delivered here for twenty dollars per ton. Beef can be purchased at about ten cents on the block. Flour and grain at less than the freight from St. Louis to Benton.[6]

The headquarters staff for the District of Montana arrived at Fort Shaw on August 21st and set up their operations. These headquarters would command all posts in Montana Territory until 1876[7] and report to the Department of Dakota headquarters at Fort Snelling in St. Paul, MN.[8] The chain of command for each unit in the field was first to the post commander, then the district commander, the department commander, the Division of the Missouri commander at Chicago, and then to the War Department, Washington, D.C. As of the close of 1867, the District of Montana consisted of three posts: Fort Shaw, Fort Ellis and Fort Benton. The latter was usually never staffed with more than one company and this for the primary purpose of securing government supplies being brought upriver by steamboat.

During the summer and fall of 1867 Colonel I.V.D. Reeve, the first regimental commander at Fort Shaw, moved to disband and retrieve Army issued weapons from the Montana militia. The short-lived militia had been organized to protect anxious citizens from a real and sometimes perceived Indian threat, but with the arrival of federal troops the General of the Army, William Tecumseh Sherman, lost no time in disbanding them. Captain R.S. LaMotte's opinion of the militia on his arrival to establish Fort Ellis was not good. He wrote on August 30th:

> The Montana Militia are located about eighteen miles beyond this [post] on the Yellowstone and are as much dreaded by the people as the Indians, being a disorganized lawless set of desperados under no sort of discipline whatever. Out of about five hundred sent there, about fifty are all that remain, the rest either being on indefinite furloughs, prospecting or riding public horses back and forth between Bozeman and their camps for whisky. I understand there is an effort to turn the horses belonging to the Militia over to the U.S. at the pricces contracted to be paid. I would especially state that very

---

[6] August 31, 1867, Fort Ellis Letters and Telegrams Sent and Received, Records of Posts, Continental Army Command 1820–1920, Record Group 393.7, National Archives.

[7] In 1876 a separate District of the Yellowstone was created for Fort Keogh and Fort Custer.

[8] August 1867 Fort Shaw Post Return.

few of them are serviceable, the best having been stolen, the prices at which they were contracted for were from $200 to 240 while the prices paid by the contractors were $40 to $50. A considerable number of horses have been stolen lately in the vicinity and I see the Montana papers are filled with accounts of these "Indian depredations", I noticed, however, that in this vicinity the depredators are strongly suspected of being Montana Militia.[9]

On September 13, 1867, Territorial Governor Green Clay Smith sent a telegram to Department of Dakota headquarters in St. Paul protesting the disarming of the militia. The army was not to be deterred and on October 1, 1867, Colonel Reeve could report that the militia had been discharged.[10]

Hardships for the army servicemen were many, and affected all ranks and dependents. On September 10th, 1st Lieutenant Thomas J. Lloyd submitted an explanation for his failure to report for duty at Fort Shaw on the date specified. The lieutenant had been granted leave to travel to Camp Cooke and meet his wife to bring her to Fort Shaw. He accomplished the trip to Camp Cooke in two days. The couple then boarded the steamer *Zephyr* bound upriver for Fort Benton. Unfortunately, after twelve days travel, due to low water the *Zephyr* made it only as far as the mouth of the Marias River some eighteen miles below Fort Benton. The lieutenant then walked to Fort Benton, secured a wagon and team, then returned to retrieve his wife and baggage and eventually bring her to Fort Shaw, obviously arriving well past his granted term of leave.[11]

Sometime during September the troops at Fort Shaw received new breech-loading rifles, which greatly increased their fire power. (Note: See the comments on the new breech-loaders in chapter 5). On September 23rd, Colonel I.V.D. Reeves made an inquiry to the Department of Dakota headquarters requesting guidance on the disposal of his surplus muzzle-loading arms. He noted that the Indian Agent at the Flathead Agency had asked for arms.[12]

Until the arrival of a telegraph at Fort Shaw, there was considerable delay in communications. For example, the July Post Return forwarded to Washington, D.C., in early August did not arrive there until August 28th,

9 August 30, 1867, Fort Ellis Letters and Telegrams Sent and Received.

10 September 13, October 1, 1867, Department of Dakota Letters and Telegrams Sent and Received, Record Group 393.4, National Archives.

11 September 10, 1867, Fort Shaw Letters and Telegrams Sent and Received.

12 September 23, 1867, ibid.

at which time an acknowledgement of receipt was sent out, arriving at Fort Shaw on September 15th. Mail was carried by stagecoach during the summer months, from Fort Shaw to Fort Benton then downriver by steamer to Sioux City or Omaha and then onward by train. In the winter months the steamers could not operate on the Missouri, and the mail was carried by stage via Helena and Virginia City, onward down the Corinne Road to Fort Hall then eastward on the Oregon Trail to points in the East. After completion of the transcontinental railroad in the summer of 1869, the mail was carried by stage from the Corinne, UT, railhead northward. This stage, traveling twenty-four hours per day with stops to change horses and obtain meals, took five days to reach Helena and eighteen additional hours to reach Fort Shaw.[13]

Edward J. McClernand, who in 1870 as a young 2nd lieutenant traversed the new transcontinental railroad to Corinne, UT, and then traveled northward by stagecoach to Helena and Fort Shaw, wrote:

> Thirty miles northwest of Ogden at a place called Corrine…we left the railway intending to take a stagecoach on the following day, and late in the afternoon saw the Montana coach arrive. It turned the corner near our hotel with the horses on a full gallop, and the air made merry with the crack of the driver's whip. I learned afterwards that this speed was attained only while passing through a village. Doubtless the autocrat of the ribbons imagined he increased his importance thereby among the villagers.[14]

McClernand described Corinne as a rough town full of mule skinners, gamblers and toughs. The lieutenant gives us a good account of the meals and the relay stations:

> The four horses were changed every ten or fifteen miles, the distance between stations varying somewhat with the nature of the road and the location of water. The buildings were nearly all constructed of rough logs, and erected in the most primitive way. Where food was served, one end of the cabin was assigned as a kitchen and eating room, while the other was used as a stable, the dividing wall between the two being of the most flimsy material. Meals were served three times a day, and a half hour allowed for each. The breakfast hour varied from 5 to 9 A.M., and supper from 5 to 10 P.M., according to the location of the particular station, with

[13] Edward J. McClernand, *On Time for Disaster:* 21.

[14] Ibid.: 19.

dinner sandwiched in between without any apparent endeavor to divide the hours equally. The menu was simple, but not good. The frying pan seemed to be the favorite utensil with every cook, while the amount of grease supplied was enough to eat up all the profits derived from economies practised elsewhere. Perhaps my experience on one occasion will suffice to give a general idea of the food furnished. We arrived at the supper station with our lips, nostrils and throats sore and feverish from alkaline dust; everyone wishing for something cool and refreshing. The food put before us was, as usual, swimming in grease and most uninviting, but at the end of the meal our hopes were raised by the waitress asking me if I would have some fruit. "Fruit," said I, "Have you fruit?" "Oh, yes," replied the haughty damsel who condescended to serve us, "we have dried peaches."[15]

The entire distance between Corinne and Helena was occupied by only by an occasional house, aside from the relay station buildings.

> Travelling as we did, day and night, we caught on the morning of the fifth day our first glimpse of Helena...a welcome sight. On entering the village the driver applied the whip unmercifully, frightening the broken down horses into a gallop; we dashed through the streets in becoming style to the great delight of numerous small boys. It was a repetition of the grand entry into Corinne.

The lieutenant then boarded another stagecoach for an eighteen-hour ride to Fort Shaw.[16]

Speed of communication with headquarters in St. Paul and Washington, D.C., was greatly improved with the arrival of telegraph by December 1869.[17] The telegraph would serve Virginia City, Helena, Fort Ellis at Bozeman, Fort Shaw, Deer Lodge and Fort Benton. The line emanated from the transcontinental line in Utah and paralleled the Corinne Road into Montana. Over the years that Fort Shaw served as an active post, 1867–1891, the line was frequently downed and interrupted by weather. During the earlier years, in particular, the line from Fort Shaw to Fort Benton was frequently downed by buffalo exercising their right to rub against the poles! On April 17, 1871, the post commander reported, "Operators from Benton and Shaw have

---

15 Ibid.: 20–21.

16 Ibid.: 21–22.

17 December 1869 Fort Shaw Post Return.

been at work putting up line. Buffaloes rut the poles down and break wire so that it is impossible to keep it in order."[18]

On January 1, 1868, Captain N.S. Constable, post quartermaster, reported the following buildings completed at Fort Shaw:

2 Officers Quarters	50 x 65 feet	Pine and Adobe
1 Officers Quarters	50 x 65 feet	Pine and Adobe
5 Outhouses	8 x 12 feet	Willow and Adobe
1 Storehouse	90 x 90 feet	Willow
4 Company Quarters	102½ x 90 feet	Pine and Adobe
1 Cellar	18 x 30 feet	Underground
1 Corrall	220 x 150 feet	Pine Slabs
1 Stable	165 x 30 feet	Pine Slabs
2 Stables	10 x 30 feet	Pine Slabs
1 Granary	30 x 30 feet	Pine Slabs
1 Saddler Shop	15 x 30 feet	Pine Slabs
1 Corrall Office	15 x 30 feet	Pine Slabs
1 Blacksmith Shop	40 x 30 feet	Pine Slabs
1 Bakery	40 x 20 feet	Willow and Adobe
1 Hospital	40 x 30 feet	Pine and Adobe
1 Magazine	18 x 12	Underground
1 Sawmill	120 x 30	Pine Slabs

Pine and willow wood were cut at the sawmill and adobe was made at the post.[19]

As quoted earlier, timber was scarce in the vicinity of Fort Shaw. On January 29, 1868, the commander of the Montana Military District sent the following instructions to the post commander, Major William Clinton:

> The Colonel commanding directs you to make a detail of (2) officers and (25) men, mounted, to proceed up Sun River to the mountains to examine the timber and to report its kind and fitness for building, quantity, and the practicability of putting it in the river, and floating it to this post, and whether there are any important obstructions now in the river between the points.[20]

This task fell to 1st Lieutenant E.H. Townsend, commander of Company C. His report is quoted in full:

---

[18] April 17, 1871, Fort Shaw Letters and Telegrams Sent and Received.

[19] January 1868, ibid.

[20] January 29, 1868, ibid.

Sir,

In compliance with Special Orders No. 12 Headquarters, Fort Shaw, M.T. Jan. 30 1868 I have the honor to report.

On the 31st day of Jan. 1868 I started up Sun River in company with 1st Lieut. J. S. Stafford, Commanding Detachment of (25) mounted men 13th Infantry and proceeded to examine the river and the timber along its banks to the mountains. Feb. 1st on the afternoon of second day's travel we crossed what is termed as the South Fork of Sun River, but which is in real[i]ty a mere brook compared with the main stream, and which is impracticable at its mouth for floating timber of any size. Besides this small stream branches out into four spring brooks before reaching the mountains. There is a fine belt of Cotton-wood timber along this branch which is plainly seen from the road and the course of the same can be traced for many miles by the timber along the banks.

From Fort Shaw to this branch of Sun River the quantity and size of the timber along the river gradually diminishes, but the kind is about the same—being principally Cotton-wood and Willow with some Elm, which is still seen along the banks of Sun River clear to the mountains. This first branch of Sun River is about twenty three miles from Fort Shaw, and eight miles further is Willow Creek, the highest point on the river that a wagon can go, although by following up the south branch about eight miles then striking straight across the country for the Canyon, a team can go nearly to the first Falls of the Sun River taking one day long to travel it.

Leaving the wagon and part of the Command at Willow Creek and taking two pack mules we proceeded across the country to the foot of the mountains, and after travelling about twelve miles over a very rough country we went into camp near the first falls of Sun River about a mile below the wall—on the third day out Feb. 2nd 1868.

Upon examination there was little or no timber fit for building purposes below the falls or on this side of the wall although there is no perceptible difference in the size of the river there and at this post, yet much more rapid. At the falls the river has worn its way down through the solid rock, and shoots through a wall several hundred feet in thickness and height much like pouring through a tunnel. The present bed is worn much wider through the wall than for several feet above the water, the rocks nearly forming an arch above, and the falls commence about halfway through the wall and end at the foot of it. The main fall is about ten feet over very large rocks and is entirely impassable for anything up or down. The wall on the east side is solid rock several hundred feet high and perpendicular and is impassible for two miles on either side of the river and only then by climbing the steep mountainside. Above the wall is plenty of fine timber, pine and a kind of fir, and these groves extend down to within half a mile of the river above the falls. But the hills and ravines are so precipitous that the timber cannot be got out with any kind of stock. In fact it would be very difficult to get pack animals over the wall down to where a lumbering camp ought to be, and highly impracticable to attempt it at all with a team. Yet if it was possible to get this timber out of the canyon, through the wall and over the falls, the rapid stream, the numerous sloughs and beaver dams, and the low timbered bottom lands so difficult to get logs out of in high water, together with the great distance for floating timber to this post, renders the whole impracticable.

> I am Sir Very Respectfully Your Obdt. Servt.
> E.H. Townsend
> 1st Lieut. 13th Infantry
> Commanding Company C[21]

Although the summer of 1867 passed without the feared general Indian uprising, by February 1868 problems between the Indians, in particular the Piegans, and settlers in the territory were increasing in intensity. The post commander received the following letter written on February 12th from Tingley and Smith of Tingley's Ranch, a stage way station on the road between Fort Benton and Fort Shaw:

> To the Commander of Fort Shaw on Sun River.
>
> Dear Sir. We had a visit last night of 22 Indians. The same took a vote to see whether they should kill us or not and finally left but took everything that we had amounting to about $100 worth. This is the third time they have been here and I think something ought to be done. They threatened to steel the stage horses to. If there is not something done I will get some men and kill every damned Indian that comes here for I have troubled enough. P. S. I hope that you will attend to this for a man is in danger of his life and I would not be surprised to hear of the stage [illegible] stopped and they made their brag that they would have the horses before long.[22]

---

[21] February 12, 1868, ibid.

[22] Ibid.

About the same date information arrived at the post that Indians had also committed "outrages" near Kennedy's Ranch (a stage station near the northern entrance to Little Prickly Pear Canyon) in the direction of Helena. There were also reports of horses stolen from citizens in the Little Prickly Pear Valley. Responding to the request for assistance, the post commander immediately dispatched a mounted patrol to Tingley's Ranch under Lieutenant William Sanborn. On February 15th, Lieutenant Sanborn made the following report:

> Sir,
>
> ...I left this post on the morning of the 13th, inst., with a Corporal and ten men and proceeded to what is known as Tingley's ranch, arriving there on the evening of the same day. In obedience to instructions, I immediately proceeded to inquire into the outrages reported to have been committed there by a party of Indians a few nights previous and find that the damage consists of the loss of some five hundred pounds of Buffalo meat and other supplies and destruction of wooden benches; these are the extent of damages as far as I could ascertain from Mr. Smith, a partner of Tingley's, who was present at the time. The Indians were some twenty-two in number and some of them were a portion of the same party who have visited the house several times before this winter and boasted of [having] stolen horses from the Mission. They came to the house about dusk on the 11th, inst., and left early the next morning going in the direction of the Missouri river, but as I found it would be useless to pursue them, I returned to this post, arriving here at six o'clock last evening. The proprietor of the ranch is anxious that a party of soldiers may be stationed there...the Indians have informed him that it is their intention to return and take the stage stock.[23]

Also on February 15th, Lieutenant Stafford reported patrolling to the old St. Peter's Mission site, near present-day Ulm, then about ten miles up the Missouri to a place called "The Boom" without spotting the Indians. Another mounted unit under 2nd Lieutenant Guthrie was dispatched up the Sun River in an attempt to intercept any hostile Indians moving northward from the Little Prickly Pear to their encampments north of the Sun River in the Teton and Marias river regions. On the 16th, Lieutenant Guthrie reported a lack of success as well as some additional hardships encountered:

---

[23] February 15, 1868, ibid.

Sir,

In obedience to Special Orders…Feb 12th 1868 I proceeded in pursuit of a band of Indians, who had stolen horses from citizens living on the Little Prickley Pear River. On leaving this post our object was to intercept, if possible, the Indians at the crossing of Sun River near the mountains, or if too late to do this, to follow the trail and bring back the stolen property. After travelling two days without finding any signs of the horses having crossed Sun River, the citizens who accompanied this expedition, declared it was useless to go any further, and that they would return home. I returned to this post on the morning of the 15th.

On the morning of the 14th, inst., about 3 o'clock, the grass took fire near our camp, and although every exertion was made to save the public property in my charge, yet there was some…destroyed among which were 4 cavalry saddles and bridles, 6 nose bags, 7 horse blankets, and two picket ropes. Several of the men lost all their own blankets, arms and accoutrements.

I experienced great difficulty in travelling with the pack saddles in use at this post, and would respectfully recommend that where these pack saddles are used again that the packs consist of not more than 150 pounds to the animal, and that corn and oats be placed in two bags with not more than 75 pounds to a sack, as by this means they can be more securely packed on the saddle.[24]

Responding to increased Indian hostilities and the threat to the integrity of the transportation route from Helena to Fort Benton, the district commander issued orders on February 15th to maintain

…mounted patrols on the road as far as Tingley's Ranch in the direction of Fort Benton and as far as Kennedy's Station in the direction of Helena…the patrols to be sent out under the charge of commissioned officers; that they may be started from this post every alternate day in each direction: that all possible protection be afforded to the mail route and the stations thereon, within the limits above named; and also a other points in their vicinity, if known to be threatened by Indians.[25]

All present-day Montanans can only well imagine the comforts of

---

[24] February 15, 16, 1868, ibid.

[25] February 15, 1868, ibid.

riding and walking a horse all day long in all types of weather during the cold winter. Even for the hardy types of the days of old this was no pleasant task, other dangers aside. Great care had to be given to the animals as well as the men. For example, a young and relatively inexperienced 2nd Lieutenant Guthrie, charged with patrolling toward Kennedy's Ranch, received the following instructions:

> Your attention is called to the fact that this patrol must necessarily be very hard on the horses, you will therefore give them a large share of your attention. Except in cases of emergency, the Command will not move faster than a walk, the men should be dismounted at intervals and compelled to walk for say about two miles and then ride three or four.[26]

One may speculate that the horses in question may have already been in run-down condition prior to the lieutenant's departure, thus the necessity for this order.

Apparently the operators of the stage way station at Tingley's, who were understandably quick to demand the aid of the army, were not so hospitable to the troops engaged in the effort to protect them from the Indian threat. On February 26th a 2nd lieutenant (last name illegible) submitted the following report:

> Sir,
>
> I have the honor to report that I reached Tingley's Ranch on the evening of the 24th, inst., at about 5 o'clock P.M. with my command. The weather was very cold and having been informed as well as seen that there were several vacant stables in the stable owned by Wells, Fargo & Co., I respectfully asked that the horses of my command might be sheltered therein for the night. The answer I received to my request was—"No sir, Wells, Fargo & Co. did not keep stable room for government stock." The horses in consequence remained out in the cold.
>
> I would also report that it seems to be a great [illegible] on the part of the Ranche keepers to furnish fuel sufficient for the men to cook their rations and for their comfort during the short time they remain there.[27]

---

[26] February 1868, ibid.

[27] February 26, 1868, ibid.

This report prompted Major Clinton, post commander, to request of the Wells, Fargo & Co. supervisor in Helena that such accommodations be provided. On February 28th the supervisor, Mr. C.M. Pollinger, responded declining the request, stating that to furnish accommodations to non-company stock was against company rules.

The post commander had not only Indian horse thieves to deal with but white ones as well. On March 7, 1868, a detail was sent out to recover a stolen U.S. Army horse and a U.S. Army mule from a man named Garrison encamped about three miles above the Old Mission (Ulm) and place him and any other guilty parties under arrest.[28]

On a lighter note, 1st Lieutenant Townsend requested six days' leave to go to the head of the Sun River, to collect specimens for the Smithsonian Institution. Also, in early April, garden seeds were ordered for Fort Shaw's post garden from D.H. Cuthert, Saul Louis Drug Store, Helena, MT.[29]

The post commander continued to respond to reports of Indian hostilities and the general supposition that spring would bring increased Indian depredations. Mr. William McCormick, special Indian agent for the Flathead Agency, requested a supply of arms and ammunition by which his charges could defend themselves from forays by their traditional enemies, the Blackfeet.[30]

On April 2, 1868, 1st Lieutenant Townsend was once again ordered out on patrol with a detachment of three non-commissioned officers, seventeen privates and a guide. He was directed to take this patrol,

> …All mounted with rations and forage for ten days packed upon 6 pack mules toward the Big Blackfoot valley for the purpose of visiting McClellan, Lincoln and other gulches in that country, and of ascertaining the damage done to the miners and citizens and the number of depredations committed upon them by marauding bands of Indians in the vicinity of Cadotte's Pass.

The lieutenant's report follows:

> The first night I camped at Dearborn River learning from hunters and others that it was impossible to cross the range at Cadotte's Pass with pack animals loaded, I followed up the Little Prickley Pear and camped near Trinity and Silver City. Finding the Trinity Trail to

---

[28] March 7, 1868, ibid.

[29] April 1868, ibid.

[30] April 3, 1868, ibid.

McClellan Gulch passable I followed it up through Canyon [illegible] and crossed the divide with much difficulty, the snow being so deep and heavy on the eastern slope in timber and so difficult for the men to break through and pack down sufficiently for the animals to pass over. After crossing the [illegible] I followed down Poor Man's Gulch and reached McClellan Gulch the third night, making a distance of about one hundred and five (105) miles by this pass.

...I visited Lincoln and passed Stonewall and Keep Cool gulches and from the principal men of these gulches several of whom I saw had signed a petition to the Territorial Governor for military aid and protection. I could only learn that Indian troubles were only anticipated this coming season. The season before last [1866] there were about one hundred and fifty (150) horses stolen by Indians up the Blackfoot valley near Keep Cool Gulch, and it is a very convenient place for Indians to do mischief by dodging through Cadotte's Pass, into the head of this valley and out again with what stock they can run off, some trouble is anticipated from this quarter, and only this.

The supplies to this valley and all [illegible] gulches do not come by way of the "Trinity Trail" but through a well settled country and up California and Peagan and down Jefferson gulches to McClellan and the other mining camps all of which naturally protect themselves. The fourth night I camped on the Blackfoot River about twelve miles above Keep Cool Gulch and the fifth after following up this stream and crossing the [illegible] at Cadotte's Pass I camped on South Fork of Dearborn River. In the vicinity of this pass I saw numerous fresh signs of Indians and it is evidently a favorite haunt of theirs. The sixth day I followed down the South Fork of Dearborn to the main stream...and camped near Bird Tail Rock & the seventh day reached this post.

The distance to Cadotte's Pass is about fifty miles and to Keep Cool Gulch seventy-five (75) miles, from here to McClellan, eighty.[31]

On April 16th, Lieutenant William Spencer continued efforts to intercept the Indians. His report follows:

Sir,

I left the post about 5:50 P.M. on the 16th, inst., with a party consist-

---

[31] April 1868, ibid.

ing of two non-commissioned officers and eight privates, and the post guide —Vielle.

That evening, after crossing, we proceeded up Sun River a few miles where we encamped. In the morning we made an early start, heading Northwest, for the Teton intending to strike it well up, crossing any trails that would be made by Indians, heading over toward the Marias River, or bound north. We found no trace of any. About 9:20 A.M. we saw some object upon the hills to our right, in which direction the guide and two men were sent. This object proved to be an antelope, but upon their return they reported that they had seen six objects, which they supposed to be horsemen, and at a distance of four or five miles, heading in an easterly direction and making off with great rapidity—No trail was found, and if they were Indians, they must have crossed Sun River east of Fort Shaw.

Reaching the Teton at 2 P.M. the party camped and took dinner. After which the river was examined for several miles, without finding any indication of the party of which we were in search. The only indication of Indians was the remains of a dead buffalo, which might have been dead a week, and had evidently been killed by Indians *on foot*. Leaving camp at an early hour this morning, we found a trail which was followed about three quarters of an hour. The guide was satisfied that it led to the Blood Indian Camp, which, he said, was located about twelve miles from Tingley's Ranch. As the indications were not such as to lead us to believe it to have been made by the stock we were hunting, we changed our course and made for the post, which we reached at 2:20 P.M.

The Post Return for April 1868 states, "The mounted detachment of the post, 1st Lieutenant J.S. Stafford in command, left the post on the 19th inst. In pursuit of a band of Indians who had stolen horses and mules from [a] citizen at Dearborn on the route from Ft Benton to Helena…" The May 1868 Post Return reports the departure of Company C to Fort Benton, "… to receive and take care of gov. stores as they come up the river for the different posts within the District of Montana."[32]

On April 21st, the post commander at Fort Ellis received a report that hostile Indians had committed depredations on settlers and herders in the Yellowstone drainage, presumably near present-day Livingston and the Shields River. A twenty-two-man detachment was dispatched, and located

---

32 April, May 1868 Fort Shaw Post Returns.

the body of a herder named Wyatt, who had been shot through the heart. Although his body was still warm, the detachment was unable to continue pursuit, since they had just ridden forty miles to reach that location. On April 23rd, a man was found shot and killed within two miles of Fort Ellis. During the month of May, Sergeant Floyd Keating with five men pursued Indian horse thieves over to the Yellowstone, where a skirmish took place. The sergeant's horse was killed and another wounded. The guide counted eleven Indians. In June there was another brief skirmish with Indian horse thieves near Fort Ellis, with no casualties. In August a unit from Fort Ellis was again sent out in pursuit of Indians who had stolen stock near Flathead Pass, with results unknown.[33]

On August 9th the post commander at Fort Shaw, Colonel George S. Andrews, received more news of Indian troubles. It arrived in the form of a letter out of Diamond City, MT, written by Edward Lowlack, sheriff of Meagher County:

> My dear Sir,
>
> The Indians have been committing depredations in this vicinity stealing some 25 head of horses and killing one man by the name of Cameron and wounding another by the name of Bohannan. The object of this note is to draw your attention to the conduct of those Red Devils hoping that it may be in your power to retake the stolen stock as they have been tracked on the Benton Trail.... Enclosed you will find the horses descriptions...The animals in question were stolen on the 5th of this month. This is the third trip they made here this season. Should you be fortunate enough to get those animals you will please notify me by mail or otherwise the parties interested will go after them. Those Indians have driven all the [illegible] miners in to this place from Benton Gulch, Elk creek and Slug gulch.
>
> I am respectfully yours,
> Ed Lowlack
> Sheriff of Meagher County[34]

On August 15th another letter was directed to Colonel Andrews from Diamond City:

---

[33] April, May, June, August 1868, Fort Ellis Post Returns.

[34] August 9, 1868, Fort Shaw Letters and Telegrams Sent and Received.

Dear Sir:

Enclosed please find dispatch from Col. Head who is following the Indians to their camp. Please give it your attention and aid him if possible and chastize the red devils.

> Yours
> J.R. Weston
> Chairman of Com

The enclosure is quoted as follows:

> In Camp
> August 15, 1868

J.R. Weston, Esq.

Dear Sir:

Yours of the 13th, inst., enclosing dispatch from Judge Barron at Ft. Shaw I read on march late on yesterday evening. I am very happy to know that the soldiers at Ft. Shaw have so promptly responded to our call and hope that it will prove an incentive to them in future to more carefully guard and protect these settlements. Their cooperation, however, is likely to be of little service to us directly as the Indians have without doubt have crossed the MO River at least from 50 to 75 miles below the points they are guarding near Dearborn. Should they cross the river at Dearborn and come down on this side they will do us the very greatest service. The Indians have gone in the direction of Fort Benton & will cross not [illegible] than the mouth of the Belt River & may go below Benton altogether. We are directly on their trail and are pushing ahead with the full intention of following them to their camp be it where it may if it be anywhere short of the British possessions. We have [difficult to read but appears to be the number 33] men all told. All are well and every duty is performed with the greatest cheerfulness and alacrity. We have not made great progress from the fact that we have had to march mostly by night and consume the day in scouting and trailing. On yesterday, however, we struck the main trail and will push forward more rapidly. The last Indians are not more than 36 hours in advance of us.

> Very respectfully yours,
> Your obt. Servt.
> C.P. Head[35]

---

[35] August 15, 1868, ibid.

On August 22nd, Colonel Andrews received another letter from concerned settlers at Sun River Crossing:

> Sun River House MT
> August 22, 1868
>
> Col. Geo L. Andrews
> Fort Shaw MT
>
> Sir,
>
> We have just learned from good authority that there is a war party of Indians numbering 20 camped near the leaving of Sun River. They have been seen coming from the direction of the Teton this evening and are doubtless on their way again to the vicinity of Diamond City. They are all armed, have also lauriettas & no horses as yet. We can raise about ten saddles in this vicinity & intend starting after them in the morning. Should you be able to send a small detachment we may possibly be able to detain the Indians.
>
> We remain very respectfully, Your obt. Servts.
> John Largent   A.B. Hamilton
> J.M. Clarke   Wm Lillard
> Floyd Keaton   Josef Largent
> and ten others[36]

The Post Return for August reveals that on August 24th, just two days later, settlers brought into Fort Shaw twenty-one Indians that they had captured near the Old Mission (Ulm) some fifteen miles from the post. The settlers "…earnestly request[ed] that they be summarily dealt with. The Indians are now in custody at the post awaiting the return of three of their band who were sent to their camp to recover the stolen animals."[37] Nathaniel Pope, U.S. Indian Agent at Fort Benton, later identified these Indians as Piegans, whom he described as "…mostly boys…" The three released Indians proceeded to the Piegan camp, at the time about 150 miles to the north. Pope further reported that about the last week of September,

> … a party of Indians came in, bringing 32 horses, which were turned over to the commanding officer of Fort Shaw, who immediately released the prisoners. Mountain Chief [a Piegan chief] has sent word that he will send thirty more horses shortly. As yet, however, they

---

36 August 22, 1868, ibid.

37 August 1868 Fort Shaw Post Return.

have not appeared, and I think it is owing to the fact that the released prisoners were threatened with killing, and their interpreter came near being hanged, by whites on Sun river, for an alleged attempt to shoot a white man shortly after their release.[38]

Another letter originating at Fort Benton and received at Fort Shaw further explains the delivery of the stolen animals:

> Benton Sept. 30th 1868
> Col G.S. Andrews
> Com.ding Dist Montana
> Fort Shaw
>
> Sir:
>
> The Mountain Chief, Chief of the Piegans, is here with a large number of his people. They brought in about thirty head of horses belonging to whites. And now the bearer, Almost-a-Dog, goes to Shaw, with said horses, being all he could recover. The warriors having traded their stolen stock off to the Bloods as fast as they brought them into their camp. He has turned over three head to me which was stolen from my wagons at Ellis and he has posted me in regard to who has two more making out the number lost to me.
>
> I write you this upon the request of Almost-a-Dog, who I think has done everything in his power for the recovery of horses.
>
> I am respectfully your obt. Srvt.
> George Steell[39]

Learning of the recovery of some horses at Fort Shaw via the *Montana Post*, a Virginia City newspaper, Judge E.H. Barron at Diamond City sent an inquiry to Fort Shaw asking if Mr. Rosenbaum's "excellent span of mules" were among the animals recovered. On October 14th the post responded:

> Sir,
>
> The Brevet Colonel Comd'g directs me to acknowledge the receipt of your communication dated Diamond City, M.T. Oct. 11th, 1868, and in reply to state, that there are now at this post seventeen horses and no mules.

---

[38] Annual Report to the Commissioner of Indian Affairs for Year 1868: 215, Annual Reports of the Commissioner of Indian Affairs, Record Group 75, SuDocs Number I 20.1, 1824–1920, National Archives.

[39] August 30, 1868, Fort Shaw Letters and Telegrams Sent and Received.

> When the Indians were released they promised to bring in some thirty more, but owing to the action of the citizens at Sun River, I fear they will not do as they promised.
>
> A board of three officers has been appointed, for the purpose of investigating the evidence of those who claim the horses,—by describing marks, brands, etc. to the satisfaction of the board, the horses will be delivered up.[40]

The practice of stealing horses belonging to other outside entities, whether they were other Indian tribes or whites, was simply an honorable and accepted way of life to the Plains Indians. An abundance of horses in the vicinity of Diamond City, at the time a boomtown, offered a convenient target of opportunity. Of course, in this clash of cultures, the whites did not see it that way. The Piegans, having stolen the horses, swiftly moved them north into the area of the Teton and Marias rivers and beyond. They then traded them to the Bloods. The Bloods tended to occupy the country northward into Canada, where they had good ties with Hudson's Bay traders at, for example, the Edmonton House. As we shall see later, the army developed sufficient evidence to show that these traders readily accepted stolen U.S. horses from the Indians. Therefore, should the Piegans obtain more horses than they needed for their own use, they could readily trade them off for cash, guns and other desirable goods.

On October 9, 1868, Nathaniel Pope, U.S. Indian Agent at Fort Benton, directed a letter to his superiors describing the Indian problems of the past summer. He stated that on July 3, 1868,

> ... the principal chief of the Piegans, Mountain Chief, while visiting this place [Fort Benton] was insulted and abused in an outrageous manner by some whites, whose only reason for their conduct was the fact that this chief, in council, had asked the commissioner to have certain men sent out of the Indian country, and all good citizens agree that these men are not fit to be in an Indian country. As soon as the young men of the Piegans heard of the ill treatment of their chief, they were naturally very indignant, and made no secret of their determination to be avenged. The consequence was that about 80 horses were stolen from whites living in the neighborhood of Diamond City, in this Territory, and the Piegans boasted of having taken them.[41]

---

[40] October 14, 1868, ibid.

[41] Annual Report to Commissioner of Indian Affairs, 1868: 215–216.

Pope's report might lead one to believe that all the horse stealing by the Piegans in the summer of 1868 emanated from this ugly event at Fort Benton. We note, however, from previous documentation that horse theft was ongoing well prior to the events of July 3rd. We also have ample documentation of a rowdy, lawless element existing in Fort Benton at the time, which showed little respect for Indians.

Aside from their efforts to curb depredations by the Indians, the frontier army had its share of problems emanating from illegal activities on the part of the settlers and also within its own ranks. On August 8, 1868, Colonel Andrews received a request from the Indian agent at Fort Benton, who was having trouble enlisting the aid of civil authorities to arrest whiskey peddlers active in his area of responsibility. The army did act upon such requests upon occasion, but it was felt that they lacked clear authority to do so.

On August 11th Lieutenant Guthrie reported from Fort Benton that Private George Hagadon, Company C., 13th Infantry, had been causing problems at that post: "…he has been drunk several times…has been in several street brawls, struck a woman with his pistol and [boasted] that he cared for noone."[42] Obviously, not all enlisted men fit this picture. Many were interested in legitimate diversions; for example, on August 21st, enlisted men at Fort Shaw requested that they be provided materials with which they could construct a theater for the post.

On the uglier side of soldierly behavior, however, a killing occurred at Sun River Crossing. On September 4th, Colonel Andrews wrote to the sheriff of Edgerton County, Helena, MT: "Sir, Pursuant to the 33rd Article of War, it becomes my duty to inform you that, Private Mathew McManus, Co. J, 13th Infty., shot with a pistol and killed Corpl. Thomas Welsh of Co. K., 13th Infty. on the 3rd, inst., while both men were at Sun River Crossing… McManus (now in confinement at this post) will be delivered over to the Civil Authorities, in order to bring him to trial: together with the names of [illegible] witnesses."[43]

On October 20, 1868, the Department of Dakota ordered all its posts, including all in the District of Montana, to clearly mark or stake out roads on the prairie so they could be more easily followed in the winter snow. On October 22nd, 1st Lieutenant Townsend returned to Fort Shaw with a command of twenty-eight men after escorting a government wagon train from Fort Peck on the Missouri. It may be assumed from this that some of the

---

[42] August 11, 1868, Fort Benton Letters Sent and Received.

[43] August 21, September 4, 1868, Fort Shaw Letters Sent and Received.

necessary supplies could not be brought any farther up the Missouri than Fort Peck Indian Agency, due to low water in the late summer season. It was therefore necessary to bring them all the way to Fort Shaw from Fort Peck on freight wagons, a distance well in excess of 300 miles.

As with the previous winter and, indeed, most winters in the late 1860s and 1870s, Indian problems subsided. The Indians were fully occupied with surviving the harsh northern winters. There had been, beginning in the fall of 1868, problems from another quarter. On March 17, 1869, Colonel George S. Andrews sent a letter to Ales A. Mayhew, U.S. district attorney, Helena, MT, reporting the arrest of Floyd Keating and two Indian boys while they were en route to Helena with stolen government supplies. The stolen property had been secreted on the premises of John J. Healy at Sun River Crossing. At the time of arrest, Sam Woods was able to escape the scene and was believed to have fled to Helena. Keating made statements to the effect that he was acting at the direction of John Kennedy of Kennedy's Ranch, one of the stage way stations between the Dearborn River and Helena. Keating stated that Kennedy was awaiting him in Helena where they were to distribute the stolen property. John J. Healy and his brother, Joseph Healy, were later placed under arrest. Colonel Andrews further advised that the thieving had gone on since the past autumn. He requested prosecution and stated that the arrests had been carried out by Captain Constable, Lieutenant Sanborn, Privates Augustus Grube and Jeremiah Kline, and U.S. Deputy Marshal Charles D. Hard. He further stated that besides those persons affecting the arrests, two Sun River Crossing residents, Peter Conly and Tom Duffy, would also make good witnesses.[44]

During March 1869, Indian hostilities occurred in the Fort Ellis area of operations. On March 17th the post commander, Captain R.S. LaMotte, telegraphed headquarters at Fort Shaw that

> ... on the morning of the 12th Inst four citizens came in and reported that while herding cattle on Shields River (or twenty five Yard Creek) for Mr. P.W. McAdow they were attacked on the 11th by a large number of mounted Indians, variously estimated between fifty and seventy five. That four men of their party were out looking after the herd—and from firing having been heard in their direction, were supposed to have been killed. On seeing the Indians approach the four men who were in the cabin, seized their arms and ran into the bushes where the[y] concealed themselves until night...

---

[44] March 17, 1869, ibid.

Saturday morning I sent Captain Clift with fifty men to endeavor to recover the cattle, and ascertain the fate of the missing men. He went to the spot, found and buried the two who were killed and while searching for the missing [two] was attacked by double or trible his force. The Indians were splendidly mounted on large fliet horses that could outrun ours easily—and as they had the Captain surrounded in a country broken into knolls and ravines he fell back to the ridge near the old militia camp. The Indians followed him up, constantly charging, but though they kept up a steady fire none of our men were wounded or killed, though several had narrow escapes. Four Indians were killed and several of their horses. All that we lost was one horse that bucked his rider off and a mule's pack of rations.

Captain Clift remained at the Militia Camp and got in to this place Sunday afternoon. This morning I sent out Major Horr with fifty soldiers and fifty citizens from the valley who will leave their rations and teams under guard at the stockade, and pursue the Indians. Another party of fifty or sixty citizens are expected from West Gallatin and the lower part of the valley this afternoon or tomorrow.

It is not known to a certainty what tribe these Indians belong to some suppose them to be Sioux from various reasons—others think there Arapahoes while the majority think they are Nez Perces. I am inclined to the latter theory from the fact that eighty lodges of Nez Perces have been encamped since last fall with the Crows, and have been trying to persuade the latter to join them in war against the whites. I understand that a large number of Nez Perces consisting altogether of old men, squaws and children passed narrows warm spring ranch[45] within a few days. If such is the case it may well be supposed that the warriors are in some mischief.[46]

On March 18th Captain LaMotte again cabled regarding potential problems with the Nez Perce who frequently traveled into his area of operations for seasonal hunts and visits with the Crows. "The Crows have several times reported to me that the Nez Perces were urging them to join them and the Sioux in a war against the whites." One month later LaMotte requested that his post be reinforced by an additional fifty men from Fort Shaw. He also reported additional Indian incursions near Flathead Pass.[47]

---

[45] Might be Hunters Hot Springs.

[46] March 17, 1869, Fort Ellis Letters and Telegrams Sent and Received.

[47] March 18, April 18, 1869, ibid.

On March 31, 1869, Mr. Benjamin F. Marsh, the U.S. Deputy Surveyor stationed in Helena, made a request for a military escort for his surveyors who were planning to work in the Fort Shaw area.

Colonel Andrews replied:

> Sir,
>
> I have the honor to acknowledge receipt of your communication of March 31, 1869, and in reply to say. I do not consider it extra hazardous at this time in the vicinity of this post, but there is always danger in traveling in Indian country. The force under my command at this time is so small as to forbid detachments being made from it whenever it can be avoided. An application to the Commanding Officer, District of Montana, for a guard, would probably be favorably entertained next fall.[48]

Meanwhile, on April 5, 1869, at Fort Ellis, Captain Clift was ordered out once again in pursuit of Indians who had raided a ranch in the Gallatin Valley, stealing livestock. This pursuit resulted in another hot fight with the Indians. The captain filed the following report on April 10, 1869:

> I have the honor to report that, pursuant to your instructions of the 5th inst., I left the post that evening with a detachment consisting of one lieutenant, one surgeon, one sergeant, two corporals and 40 men,...and proceeded to the residence of Judge Sheels where I was joined by several citizens from the valley. I learned that on the night of the 4th inst. seven head of cattle and one horse had been driven off. We found their trail and followed it to the foot of the mountains about two miles north of the Flathead Pass....From this point I took the trail of the Indians and followed it over an almost impassable country until about noon on the 7th inst. Those in advance came in sight of the Indians near a mountain on the north fork of Sixteen-mile Creek and near the headwaters of the Muscleshell River. The party consisted of 13 Indians, two of whom made their escape with the horse they had taken....The eleven remaining took to a mountain about 1500 feet between them and the creek. The mountain was a narrow ridge and could only be ascended at two ends. On the north side the comb of rock was at least 100 feet in height perpendicularly; on the south side it was not so abrupt.
>
> I immediately divided the party, leaving a few below on the north

---

side, and they ascended both from the east and west ends. The Indians could be plainly seen on the peak of rocks, defying us in the most insulting manner. The position chosen by the Indians afforded them complete shelter and at the same time commanded the mountain on all sides. There were three holes on the summit around which they built up walls, leaving port-holes through which they kept up an incessant fire. We got to within 150 yards on each end and worked for two hours to dislodge them but with no effect. Finding that there was no resource left except by assault, I directed Lieutenant Thompson to lead the men on the east, while I would direct on the west end. As soon as Lieutenant Thompson could get around to his position the assault was made from both sides, and in a few minutes we had the satisfaction of putting an end to the affair....We killed nine Indians on the spot. They were all armed with rifles and revolvers, and had an abundant supply of ammunition.

The casualties on our side were one private killed and two badly wounded. Two citizens were wounded.

When all did so well it is difficult to particularize. Lieutenant Thompson conducted his part of the action in a manner highly satisfactory. Surgeon C. Ewen attended to the wounded in the best possible manner. Sergeant J.P. Sullivan, Company G; Corporal B. Sheridan, Company D; Private C. Thompson, Company F; Citizen T. King and two others, names unknown, were conspicuous for daring and bravery. Private Conry, who died so nobly at the same instant with his antagonist, should be remembered. I suggest therefore that the mountain upon which the engagement took place be named after him.[49]

The Indians involved in this engagement were not identified by tribe. On April 19, 1869, 1st Lieutenant H.C. Pratt was ordered to proceed from Fort Shaw with Lieutenant William Sanborn and a detachment to American Bar, located some fifteen miles from the Clarke's Ranch, to search for four deserters, results of search unknown.[50]

---

[49] James B. Goe, History of 13th Regiment of Infantry, Center for Military History website.

[50] April 19, 1869, Fort Shaw Letters Sent and Received.

CHAPTER EIGHT

Operations and Events June 1869 to June 1870; Colonel Trobriand Takes Command; Origins, Conduct and Repercussions of the Piegan Campaign

O N JUNE 4, 1869, COLONEL PHILIPPE REGIS DE TROBRIAND arrived at Fort Shaw and assumed command of the Montana Military District. Colonel Trobriand was an individual of very unique background, in particular when one views it with the U.S. frontier as a backdrop. He was born to wealth and fame in France. His family history contained a long line of French military personages. His father had fought in the armies of Napoleon, was wounded eleven times and participated in Napoleon's disastrous retreat from Moscow. He later forbade his son to make a career of the military. The younger Trobriand was to spend a significant portion of his life as a journalist, author, painter and sometimes world traveler, thanks to significant family wealth and great personal talent.

Trobriand moved to the United States in 1841 and was occupied principally as a journalist until the outbreak of the Civil War in 1861. He then joined the Lafayette Guard and served in the battles of Fredericksburg, Chancellorsville and Gettysburg. After the war he remained in the army and was posted as commanding officer at Fort Stevenson, Dakota Territory, arriving there on August 19, 1867. He had been vacationing in Paris when he received word of his new command and commented:

> I left Paris Tuesday, June 11, 1867, to go straight to the Upper Missouri. From the brilliant peaks of civilized life, I was to plunge straight into the dark pit of savage existence. Never was there a greater contrast, but contrasts are the spice of life; they banish

monotony and boredom, and give life a variety that cannot be found in a settled existence.[1]

Fort Stevenson was located on the Missouri perhaps thirty to forty miles upriver from present-day Bismarck, ND. The Sioux were still very troublesome and hostile there at the time. Trobriand served almost two years at Fort Stevenson, maintaining a diary, from which would spring a book written in French entitled *Vie militaire dans le Dakota*. It was translated into English and published as *Military Life in Dakota*. This book paints a vivid picture of life in frontier military posts at the time of the establishment of the Montana Military District. Unfortunately, the book terminates upon Colonel Trobriand's transfer from the Dakota Military District to Fort Shaw and command of the Montana Military District.

An aristocrat to the core, but a man of adventure, one can gain some insight into his personality by reading the following quote from his diary during his journey to Fort Stevenson. It provides a vivid description of his fellow travelers aboard the train crossing Iowa en route to Council Bluffs and Omaha, the rail terminus at that time.

> The travelers match their country. They are for the most part rough Westerners, men who are not at all refined, who are still crude physically and morally, but who are gifted with tremendous energy, and who utilize fully the gifts that God gave them. Inside the car as well as in the surrounding country, it is evident that the centers of civilization are far away, although here, as everywhere else, one meets the ingenious Yankee, the precocious fruit of Eastern culture.
>
> In the group of fortune seekers, there are some who have already found it. They are more easily identified by their air, their jewelry, and their language than by their manners. Almost without exception, these men are adventurers who have earned their money by the sweat of their brow and at great personal risk. They have come up from the dirt and have never had time to dust themselves off. Because they live among savages, or half savages, and are completely absorbed with business affairs, they do not worry very much about elevating themselves above the material comforts and crude pastimes they can buy with their money. They may be clever, intelligent, energetic, and even honest, but they are not gentlemen, although they often assume the title. In fact, they do not even know

---

[1] Philippe Regis de Trobriand, *Military Life in Dakota*: 3.

the real meaning of this word which has been so distorted since it left England and arrived on the banks of the Missouri.[2]

One deduces from the above passage that Trobriand, the true aristocrat, is not simply an arrogant individual looking down his nose at people he considers of lesser worth; there is a deep respect for these crude Westerners! One quote in his diary, however, will not please Irish Americans. While journeying about the outskirts of Omaha, awaiting the departure of his steamer upriver, he came across an Irish settlement. "We came upon some miserable Irish shanties by a muddy stream, where some geese and ducks were playing and the inevitable hogs were wallowing. Irishmen and hogs always go together."[3]

Colonel Philippe Regis de Trobriand—commander, Montana Military District.
PHOTO COURTESY OF THE NATIONAL ARCHIVES.

Attempting to learn as much as possible about his potential antagonists, the American Indians, he queried those he encountered while en route to Fort Stevenson.

> Most of them [the frontiersmen] believed that the only way to settle the Indian question was to exterminate all this vermin. ...Others who were more moderate or more just held that the white man was far from being blameless and that he was really responsible for the outbreaks during the war and now. These people were not numerous, and I believe that even if they did maintain that the poor Indians had been treated like dogs, deceived, cheated, pillaged and massacred, they would have been just as quick as anyone else to shot on sight any suspicious looking redskin who appeared on their road.[4]

Later, during his tour at Fort Stevenson, Trobriand offered his own opinions on the Indian problem, recognizing that at the root of many Indian out-

[2] Ibid.: 13.

[3] Ibid.: 20.

[4] Ibid.: 18.

breaks was theft of their intended annuities by unscrupulous Indian agents.

> This is nothing unusual, and it can even be said that it is the general custom on all frontiers. If one were to go to the heart of the matter, he would find that the hostilities of most of the tribes and the troubles that result from them are hardly more than the result of the notorious bad faith in which the agents steal from them the greatest part of the annuities sent by the government.[5]

This was an opinion felt by the majority of army officers stationed on the frontier, no less among them than George Custer, John Gibbon or Nelson Miles.

In commenting on the plight of the Ree (Aricara) Indians near Fort Berthold, Dakota Territory, Trobriand offered the following opinion:

> The migration of the Buffalo west of the Yellowstone leaves them almost without game and consequently without food, for deer and antelope are much more difficult to hunt and kill…The fleetness of these animals makes any pursuit impossible, while, on the contrary, the buffalo can be easily overtaken by a horse of average speed. This is why the Indian lives on buffalo meat and why, when there is no buffalo, the Indian must disappear.

> The pity that one would feel for the periodic famine that decimates a part of the Indians almost every winter is dulled considerably when one remembers that it is caused by their incorrigible laziness and their incurable dislike for all work. The most severe ordeals teach them nothing. At Berthold they agreed to grow corn because they themselves did not have to turn a hand. Their women, those two-footed beasts of burden, do all the work of cultivation, planting, hoeing, harvesting, husking, and packing of the corn, while their lords and masters, draped in their blankets, sun themselves, smoke, and watch them work.[6]

Turning to some more mundane events in the Montana Military District during the spring, summer and autumn of 1869, on May 28th a payment of $50 was sent to Messrs. Oakley and Mason in New York for a magazine subscription for the Fort Shaw post library. Also, sometime during this period a contract was signed with Messrs. Hubbell and Cullen for the delivery to Fort

---

[5] Ibid.: 156.

[6] Ibid.: 230.

Shaw of 200,000 feet of sawed lumber. There was mention of a steam engine arriving from Camp Cooke and being placed in operation.[7]

On June 29th Major General John Hancock arrived to inspect the post. He had just been assigned command of the Department of Dakota. Students of military history will recall that it was General Hancock's 2nd Corps that held the Union line at Gettysburg against the Confederate assault led by General George Pickett in July 1863. On September 12th the post commander reported that the post had on hand 135,660 lbs of corn, 9,955 lbs of oats and 11,285 lbs of barley.[8]

In July, elements of the 2nd Cavalry Regiment began arriving at Fort Ellis, augmenting the force available in the District of Montana. Lieutenant Colonel A.G. Bracket, 2nd Cavalry, then became post commander at Fort Ellis.[9]

As Colonel Trobriand assumed command of the Montana Military District, the problems with the Piegans continued and increased in intensity throughout the summer of 1869. In August, Indians were reported stealing horses in the Gallatin Valley. Recently promoted, Captain Lewis Thompson was dispatched in pursuit with two officers and thirty-seven men. After a seven-mile night march they located a band of Indians and searched their herd. No stolen animals were located. "Upon investigation it was found that these Indians were a band of friendly Nez Perces, and the command returned to the post."[10]

Excessive drinking and desertions were an ongoing problem in the district. On September 13th the post adjutant at Fort Shaw sent the following communication to Mr. Chas A. Bull, Esquire:

> Sir,
>
> In reply to your communication of September 11, 1869, the Bvt. Brig. General Commanding directs me to state that it is a notorious fact that you have been guilty of selling bad whisky to the soldiers of this garrison at any and all times, also that you have assisted them in getting to the crossing [Sun River], by allowing them to ride in your

---

[7] The author presumes that this was a second steam engine or a replacement for the one already on hand at Fort Shaw.

[8] May 28, June 29, September 12, 1869, Fort Shaw Letters and Telegrams Sent and Received, Records of Posts, Continental Army Command 1820–1920, Record Group 393.7, National Archives.

[9] July 1869 Fort Ellis Post Return, Records of the Adjutant General's Office, ca. 1775–ca. 1928, Record Group 94, National Archives.

[10] August 1869 Fort Ellis Post Return.

wagon, this too while they were under the influence of liquor from you & without proper authority.[11]

One can only speculate and perhaps sympathize with the desire of the soldiers to break away from the monotony of post life and get down to the saloon at Sun River. They were, of course, granted leave from time to time to do so, but Mr. Bull's ready assistance was obviously not appreciated by the post commander, whose mission it was to maintain order and discipline among his troops.

During October seventy-nine recruits arrived at Fort Shaw. They had marched from Custer's Station on the newly constructed Union Pacific Railroad via Fort Bridger, Wyoming Territory, to Fort Ellis and then on to Fort Shaw. Distance marched was 617 miles! One might presume that by the time of their arrival they had become thoroughly accustomed to long marches! Late in October, Company L, 2nd Cavalry, commanded by Captain Thompson, visited Fort Shaw while surveying a new road from Fort Ellis and Helena to Fort Benton. In November, Company G, 2nd Cavalry was ordered to Diamond City from Fort Ellis to provide additional security against Indian depredations in that area. A telegraph operator commenced employment at Fort Shaw during the month of December 1869, an obvious indication that the line had reached Fort Shaw.[12]

On January 23, 1870, the U.S. Army would strike a Piegan camp on the Marias River with bloody results. The attack sparked much bitterness and controversy, but also resulted in a more peaceful co-existence between the whites and the Blackfoot Nation, in particular the Piegans in subsequent years. Most modern authors and historians refer to the incident as the Baker Massacre. The origins and the results of this campaign are described in the following pages.

On August 3 and August 18, 1869, General Alfred Sully, Superintendent of Indian Affairs for Montana Territory, sent two very important letters to Elias S. Parker, the Commissioner of Indian Affairs, in Washington, D.C. Students of American history will recall that Mr. Parker, whose name was sometimes spelled Ely S. Parker, was himself a full-blooded American Indian (Seneca). He had risen to the rank of general during the Civil War and was present as a member of General Grant's staff at General Lee's

---

[11] September 13, 1869, Fort Shaw Letters and Telegrams Sent and Received.

[12] October, December 1869, Fort Shaw Post Returns, Records of the Adjutant General's Office, ca 1775–ca. 1928, Record Group 94, National Archives; November 1869 Fort Ellis Post Return.

surrender at Appomattox. Now a recently elected President Grant had appointed him Commissioner of Indian Affairs.

General Sully's initial letter is quoted as follows:

General Alfred Sully—Superintendent of Indian Affairs, Montana Territory.
PHOTO COURTESY OF MONTANA HISTORICAL SOCIETY RESEARCH CENTER PHOTOGRAPH ARCHIVES, HELENA, MONTANA.

> Helena, Montana Territory
> August 3, 1869
>
> Sir: I feel it is my duty to report to you that I fear before long we may have serious difficulties between whites and Indians in this Territory, and I would urge upon you the necessity of applying for an immediate increase of military force in Montana to prevent this. There is no section of the country that has more Indians in it than Montana, taking into consideration those who permanently reside here, and those who visit the Territory peaceably or with hostile intentions. I think, taking them all together, I can safely say that about from 50,000 to 60,000 men, women, and children, is the total of Indians frequently located here, and yet there is, if I am not mistaken, no section of Indian country that has fewer troops in it.[13] At present there are not over four hundred men in the Territory, inclusive of the four companies of the 2nd Cavalry which have recently arrived, and, as I understand, are to leave and rejoin the department of the Platte before winter...
>
> My reasons for apprehending trouble are that war parties of Indians from the Powder River country, the British Possessions, and from Idaho and Washington Territories, frequently visit this Territory and often commit depredations on the whites. The whites retaliate by killing any Indians they may chance to meet, sometimes in the most brutal and cowardly manner...There is a white element in this

---

[13] If any credence can be given to figures provided in the Report of the Indian Peace Commission, the figure of 50,000 to 60,000 appears far too high; Report to the President by the Indian Peace Commission. As a matter of fact, the Annual Report to the Office of Indian Affairs for 1872 listed the Montana Indian population as 30,412.

country which, from its rowdy and lawless character, cannot be excelled in any section, and the traffic in whiskey with Indians in this Territory is carried on to an alarming extent. This frequently causes altercations between whites and Indians, resulting often in bloodshed, and as they occur in sections of the Territory where the civil authorities acknowledge themselves powerless to act, nothing but military force can at present put a stop to it…

From reliable reports that increase daily, it is a wonder to me that open war with the Indians has not broken out already, but as yet only several skirmishes between Indians and soldiers and citizens have occurred…I intend to do all I can to arrest some of the citizens, who, about ten days ago, committed the cowardly murder of a harmless old man and a boy about fourteen years old, at Fort Benton. They were Piegans, (a part of the Blackfoot Nation.) These Indians were shot in broad day-light in the streets of the town. I think I can arrest the murderers, but doubt very much if I can convict them in any court.[14]

One may note from the tone of this letter that General Sully probably did not have a punitive campaign in mind at that time, but held out the hope that the presence of additional troops to control the hostile Indian element and the lawless white element might improve the state of affairs in the territory. However, the machinery of government had been set in motion in Washington, D.C. Shortly after receipt of the above letter, the Commissioner of Indian Affairs, Mr. Parker, wrote on August 16th to his superior, William T. Otto, Acting Secretary of Interior:

Sir:

I have the honor to transmit herewith copy of communications just received from General A. Sully, Superintendent of Indian Affairs for Montana, which I respectfully request be submitted for the consideration and action of the War Department. I may add that, upon information received from other sources, I regard the apprehensions entertained by General Sully as well founded. A considerable number of the Sioux are still roaming and hostile, coming in only occasionally to the settlements of located Indians on the Missouri, and almost always boasting of their continued hostility, besides committing acts of lawlessness, which, because we cannot punish, we must

---

[14] Alfred Sully, Superintendent of Indian Affairs for Montana Territory, Record Group 75, SuDocs Number I 20.1, 1824–1920, National Archives.

endure. These Indians roam far into Montana, and will lose no opportunity to commit acts of hostility upon the remote and exposed settlements.

There is also serious danger to be looked for from the local Indians of Montana.

The Crows have a treaty which embodies a stipulation for feeding them specific quantities of food for a certain length of time. Congress, however, neglected to make any appropriation to carry this stipulation into effect, and the Indians are consequently disappointed and dissatisfied. They regard it as a breach of faith and a just cause for a general war. The same may be said of the Piegans, Bloods, and the Blackfeet, with some of whom the citizens have already come in conflict even in the streets of Benton.

I regard it therefore of great importance that every precautionary measure should be taken to guard against an outbreak, and I heartily endorse General Sully's views and recommendations, and trust that favorable action may be taken by the War Department on his letter.

Very respectfully, your obedient servant,
E.S. Parker Commissioner[15]

Upon receipt of Mr. Parker's request, Mr. Otto promptly forwarded it to the Secretary of War:

Department of Interior Washington, D.C., August 17, 1869

Sir,

I have the honor to transmit herewith a copy of a letter dated the 16th instant, from the Commissioner of Indian Affairs, and accompanying copy of a communication to him from General Alfred Sully, Superintendent of Indian Affairs for the Territory of Montana, in relation to Indian affairs in said Territory, and respectfully request that the recommendations of the Commissioner may receive the favorable consideration of the Secretary of War.

Very respectfully, your obedient servant,
W.T. Otto Acting Secretary[16]

---

[15] Annual Report of the Commissioner of Indian Affairs 1869, ibid.

[16] W.T. Otto, ibid.

On August 17th the Secretary of Interior received a response from the Secretary of War advising that the request for an increase in military presence in Montana Territory had been forward to the General of the Army, William Tecumseh Sherman. It was then referred for action to General Philip Sheridan, Commander, Division of the Missouri. In the interim, on August 18th, General Sully sent his second telegram to Commissioner Parker:

Helena, Montana August 18, 1869

Sir:

I fear we will have to consider the Blackfeet in a state of war. In addition to the late attack by these Indians on a train[17] near Fort Benton a large number of horses have been stolen within fifty miles of here, and early this morning a ranch twenty-five miles from here was attacked and two men shot. The miners are very much exasperated.

General Sully Superintendent of Indian Affairs[18]

The two men shot twenty-five miles distant from Helena were a well-known citizen, Mr. Malcolm Clarke and his son, Horace. Mr. Clarke had first arrived in Montana in 1839 employed as a young clerk for Alexander Culbertson, who was in charge of all American Fur Company interests in the future territory. Not unlike his employer, who had married the daughter of a Blood chief, Clarke would marry the daughter of a Piegan chief. Her name was Kahkokima, "Cutting-off-Head Woman." He would eventually control all American Fur Company interests on the Marias and gain great personal wealth in the process. Around 1864 Clarke moved with his family to Little Prickly Pear Creek and established a fine ranch—the site known today as the Sieben Ranch, near where present-day northbound traffic on Interstate 15 enters the Little Prickly Pear canyon. Clarke, together with other notables in Montana history such as Granville Stuart, Horace Sanders and others, would found the Montana Historical Society.[19] He was also named as one of the first county commissioners for Lewis and Clark County, at the time known as Edgerton County.[20]

---

[17] Refers to a wagon train; there were no railroads.

[18] Sully, ibid.

[19] Robert J. Ege, *Tell Baker To Strike Them Hard!* 1–7.

[20] *Grass Range* (MT) *Review*, reprint of Helen Clarke's Contribution to Montana Historical Society on the occasion of her death, March 23, 1923.

As fate would have it, we are provided with a fine historical record of events surrounding the murder of Malcolm Clarke and the attempted murder of his son, Horace. Malcolm's daughter, Helen Clarke, a lovely well-educated, half-white, half-Piegan Indian woman, witnessed this tragic episode. She later provided the Montana Historical Society with a well-written version of the events that was also reprinted in a newspaper, the *Grass Range Review,* upon her death in 1923. There is no better record than this account written by a person of mixed white and Indian blood, very familiar with both the white and Indian lifestyles and mores, and apparently lacking in prejudices toward members of either race. Not only did this handsome woman move in the finest circles in Helena, but she also spent the last days of her life living on the Blackfeet Reservation. She also served as the first superintendent of public schools for Lewis and Clark County.

According to Helen, events leading to her father's murder began to unfold in the spring of 1867 when the Clarke family was visited on their ranch by some Pi-kan-i (Piegan) relatives. Principal in this group was Ne-tus-che-o, a cousin of Helen's Indian mother. He is also known as Pete Owl Child. Ne-tus-che-o was accompanied by his wife, his mother, his sister and a brother. After several days' visit, a group of unidentified whites stole horses from the corral of Malcolm Clarke, Mr. Clarke's horses and Pete Owl Child's horses included. Mr. Clarke's horses were recovered but Pete's horses were not. Helen wrote:

> Had these white men gone into the Pi-kan-i village, "bearded the lion in his den," and stolen this man's horses, it would have presented a very different phase of the matter and, according to the Indian's standpoint and code of honor, would have been right proper and just. They were, however, stolen while he was enjoying a white man's hospitality. Stolen in a white man's country; therefore it could never be forgiven. The was the primary cause of the tragedy enacted two years later.[21]

Acting in revenge while Malcolm Clarke was briefly absent from his home, Pete Owl Child and his party departed in the dark of night, stealing some of Malcolm Clarke's horses and his spy glass. He then proceeded down the Little Prickly Pear canyon en route north to a Piegan village. In the dark of night they passed close to a freighter's camp at one of the crossings of the Little Prickly Pear (no doubt the confines of the canyon necessitated their

---

[21] Ibid.

Helen P. Clarke.

passing close to the whites). Referring to the freighters hearing the passing of riders in the night, Helen stated, "No one they knew could be out at that unseemingly time, and acting upon this supposition they fired, and were answered by a woman's scream."[22] Fleeing the scene Pete's group lost possession of some of Clarke's horses, and the freighters, later recognizing his brand, returned them to the Clarke ranch.

Upon Malcolm's return he and Horace rode north to the Piegan village where they located Pete Owl Child astride Horace's horse (In Horace Clarke Reminiscences, MHS, Horace states that this was the village of Chief Heavy Runner[23]—Helen does not identify the village). Horace struck Pete and Malcolm insulted him, both nearly losing their lives in the encounter; they were saved by the intervention of the Piegan elders. Later, during the winter of 1867–1868 Malcolm would spend time in the Piegan village and he and Pete made amends, or at least Clarke thought so. However, in the summer of 1869, other events served Pete's pent-up desire for revenge. Helen wrote:

> …near the middle of July [1869], about fifteen miles from Benton, four or five wagons were attacked by Indians who proved afterwards to be Crows, and one or more white men killed. The news came into Benton. The citizens were highly excited, and while laboring under this high pressure, chance threw in their way the mountain chief's brother and a young Blood Indian of fourteen years, sent by Alexander Culbertson to the town with special instructions. Some of the residents shot these Indians down with as little mercy as they would take the life of a wolf. Both were harmless. This, remember, was done in the name of self protection.[24]

---

22 Ibid.

23 Horace Clarke Reminiscences, SC 540: 4, Montana Historical Society Archives.

24 Helen Clarke, *Grass Range Review*.

Mountain Chief, even previous to the murders of his brother and the young boy, had little love for whites. He had on one occasion stated to Malcolm Clarke:

> I despise the whites; they have encroached on our territory; they are killing our buffalo, which will soon pass away; they have treated my nation like dogs, and hereafter I shall no longer be responsible for depredations which may be committed by my young men; for we, the Pi-kan-ies, have been made to suffer for the bad deeds of the other tribes. We do not wish these pale faces to come to our villages. If we desire to trade, we will go into their forts, dispose of our robes and leave. There is nothing in common between us. With you, my friend, it is far different; you have identified yourself with us by marrying into the nation and have children. Therefore we suffer you among us.[25]

In spite of his dislike for whites and the murder of his brother, Mountain Chief allowed whites present in his camp to depart in safety upon the arrival of the news of the killings. Helen wrote:

> When news of this cold-blooded murder reached the Pi-kan-i village, preparations for war commenced. What mercy could be expected from infuriated savages? None, one would naturally reply. Yet mercy was shown to the whites in the camp. The Mountain Chief told them that he would not be responsible for what his young braves might do: therefore he wished them to leave, and would provide them with an escort until they were beyond their enemy's country.[26]

Also according to Helen, more of Clarke's horses were stolen within two weeks of the death of Mountain Chief's brother, and within one month some 800 horses had been stolen from whites and Pend d'Oreille Indians.

On the night of August 17, 1869, at about 9 P.M., the Clarke family was once again visited by Pete Owl Child and three other Piegan friends, among them Bear Chief, Black Weasel, Crowfoot and another son of Mountain Chief. They gave as a reason for their visit their intention to return to the Clarkes horses that Blood Indians had stolen from them three years previous. After some time in the house enjoying the hospitality of the Clarke family, young Horace Clarke and one of the Piegans left the house to ride to a point some two miles distant where the recovered horses allegedly were

[25] Ibid.
[26] Ibid.

located. As they rode some distance from the house, the Piegan shot Horace in the face. Falling from his horse, he was left for dead. Because Piegan blood flowed in his veins, he was not scalped. Almost at the same time back at the house, Malcolm Clarke stepped outside with Pete Owl Child and another Indian identified by Helen as Crowfoot. Crowfoot shot Malcolm through the heart and Pete Owl Child brained him with an axe. Some twenty to thirty Indians then appeared on the scene. They had been lurking in the neighborhood. As luck would have it, Helen, her Indian mother and her sister were not killed. They were saved by the intervention of Black Bear, a Piegan woman friend of the family. Pete Owl Child, Bear Chief and the others then departed. Helen, her sister and her mother managed to find the badly wounded Horace and eventually get help through distant neighbors and Dr. Glick from Helena. Horace recovered.[27]

Clarke's murder, although not the only incident in recent months involving Piegan renegades, sparked considerable attention in the territorial press and spread fear through the ranks of the white populace. Although frequently portrayed by historians in the modern era as the sole cause of what would be later termed the "Piegan Massacre," this was not the case. This was but one of many incidences that eventually led to the attack on the Marias River. In fact, subsequent to his murder, Clarke was seldom mentioned by name in the messages sent by General Sully and Colonel Trobriand to their respective superiors. The incident was, however, one of the few in which the perpetrators were accurately identified—in this case most of them were well known to the survivors, Helen and Horace Clarke. Helen would later testify before the grand jury in Helena, identifying many of the perpetrators.

Returning to General Sully's August 18th message, Commissioner Parker forwarded it on the 19th to his superior, Secretary of Interior J.D. Cox, with the recommendation that it be forwarded to the Secretary of War, "…for such action as he may deem necessary in the premises."[28]

On August 31st Lieutenant F.D. Pease, Acting Agent for the Blackfeet Indians, wrote General Sully from Fort Benton:

> Blackfoot Agency, Montana Territory
> August 31, 1869

---

[27] Ibid.

[28] Annual Report of the Commissioner of Indian Affairs 1869, Record Group 75, SuDocs Number I 20.1, 1824–1920, National Archives.

Sir:

I have the honor to report the following in regard to the feeling and condition of the Indians of this agency:

The depredation committed upon the whites, so far, has been done by the Piegans. The Bloods and the Blackfeet have had nothing to do with it whatever, and the Bloods, in particular, are very anxious to come to this agency and comply in all respects to the conditions of the treaty made with them last year, provided they can be feed and taken care of, according to the promises made them.

In fact, by what I can learn, there is, so far, only a small band of the Piegans that are, or that have been interested in the depredations lately committed, and their moving north with their families has been caused by fear of being accused of having something to do with these depredations, and the false reports of irresponsible, mischief-making whites...[29]

This letter identified the perpetrators of the depredations as a band of Piegans. Although the last quoted paragraph is a little unclear, Mr. Pease appears to be saying that those not involved were Piegans moving north to avoid retaliation by whites.

On September 2nd Mr. Alexander Culbertson sent a letter to Superintendent Sully. As we may note from earlier references, Mr. Culbertson was widely recognized as very knowledgeable of Indian affairs in Montana.

Blackfoot Agency September 2, 1869

Dear Sir:

Having met with Major Pease, your special agent for the Blackfeet Indians, and from whom I learned your arrival in the country, I thought it would not be amiss for me to drop you a few lines on the subject.

I have recently arrived from the interior, where I have been since last winter, with the Bloods and Blackfoot Indians. These people are perfectly friendly to the whites, and up to the time I left there, they evinced no disposition to be otherwise. They were no little surprised to hear of the frequent raids made upon the whites by the Piegans. These people have always professed to be the friend and protector

---

[29] F.D. Pease, in Annual Report of the Commissioner of Indian Affairs 1869.

of the whites, living as they have in almost constant communication with Benton. I have not seen those Indians to know for what reason they are now committing these depredations upon whites, but really my knowledge of their character for a great many years will not permit me to think that there exists a general hostile feeling among them. On the contrary, these depredations have been committed by a portion of the young rabble over whom the chiefs have no control, and nothing but the strong arm of government can control...

The Bloods and Blackfeet, who are distant and live remote from each other, have no sympathy with the Piegans, and of course will take no part with them in any way...[30]

Mr. Culbertson goes on to state that non-ratification of the recent negotiated treaty with the Blackfoot Nation, had, in the eyes of the Piegans, given them free rein to steal any horses they please. Once again, we see that the horse theft problem was laid squarely at the feet of a band of Piegans.

Colonel Trobriand, commander of the District of Montana, was not in complete accord with General Sully, the territorial Superintendent of Indian Affairs. On September 9th he forwarded an extensive report on the Indian problem to his superiors. As compared with General Sully's report, it was far more informative and insightful.

> Headquarters
> District of Montana
> Fort Shaw, M. T., September 9, 1869

Sir: I have the honor to report that I returned yesterday, after an absence of fourteen days, to visit and inspect Fort Ellis, traveling ten days and staying two days at Ellis and two at Helena, (one each way.) This journey was hastened by circumstances of which the major general commanding was kept informed by my previous communications either by mail or telegraph.

During my journey to and from Fort Ellis I saw many different people, had long talks with most of them, and neglected no opportunity of gathering full and reliable information about the real facts which gave rise to the excitement in regard to Indian hostilities; what part was to be attributed to exagerated reports, and what part to interested speculations. What conclusions I came to is the principal object of this report.

---

[30] Alexander Culbertson, in Annual Report of the Commissioner of Indian Affairs 1869.

The facts are those that I reported previously and no more, that is: The attack on two white men, who died of their wounds, at Benton; the execution of two bad Indians, and the murder of two other innocent ones at the same place; the attack on one of the government trains at Eagle Creek, between Cooke and Benton; the murder of Mr. Clarke, and the attempted murder of his son by a party of Piegans, led by Peter, and the Indian brother-in-law of Mr. Clarke, the sons of Mountain Chief, Bear Chief, and others not well known. This, as I mentioned previously, is the bloody denouement of a long-standing family quarrel. The party being in for two murders (as they believed they had killed the young Horace Clarke, who has since recovered) thought they might as well steal as many horses as they could in their way toward the Yellowstone, where they took refuge. Hence the depredations committed at different points in that direction, especially at or near Diamond City. The band must have divided into several parties, or some other Indians seized the opportunity of doing mischief, since, at the time, horses were also stolen at the Mission, fifteen miles from Shaw, and near Deer Lodge, about thirty miles from Helena. These are the only facts ascertained so far, for I cannot include in the Indian hostilities the highway robbery of the mail and express, twice repeated, for it was done by white brigands, and in the Territory of Utah.

The Blackfeet, the Pend d'Oreilles, the Bloods, and even part of the Piegans, remain still perfectly quiet, protesting that they have nothing to do with these attacks on the persons or properties of white men; that they want no war, but peace, and that they are ready to come and stay on whatever reservation may be assigned to them. These assurances come to me through the agencies, and are so far corroborated by the peaceful attitude of the tribes above named. The responsibility of the recent hostilities and depredations seems therefore to rest exclusively on a band of Piegans and some roaming vagabonds of different tribes, acting on their own hook, and independently of their own people, as is often the case in Indian country.

This is not altogether very formidable, but was enough to spread terror between Benton and Helena and scare the greater part of the Territory, as shown by the rush upon me from all sides for military protection. Could I then have disposed of only fifty mounted men by sending them promptly, part toward Benton and part toward Helena, fears would have been allayed, some depredations prevented, and some chastisement possibly inflicted. But the information that I was utterly powerless, without soldiers left for patrols, escorts, or guards, made the people more uneasy, the Indians more impudent, and several farmers sent their families to Helena for safety.

This caused some commotion and a good deal of talk at Helena. Of course there was a cry for more troops and a corresponding blame upon the government for leaving the frontier so unprotected. For it is a remarkable fact that whenever there is no apparent danger and no cause for apprehension, people will think that there is always too much of military, while if a handful of redskins appear upon the bluffs, shaking their buffalo robes, it turns out suddenly that there is never enough of it, according to the same people. In this case I strongly suspect that there was some interested scheme on the part of some parties to magnify the danger, exaggerate the reports, and through the general excitement to bring the governor, then just arrived, to issue a proclamation to raise a regiment of mounted volunteers. This, if successful, would have procured some fat jobs to somebody or other at the expense of the government. But when I broke the subject to Governor Ashley, I found at once that he had seen through the game, and that no proclamation would be issued, at least, without real necessity.

There was also another proposition discussed freely, not only in Helena, but along the road to Benton and the Gallatin Valley. This was simply an authorization asked by certain men to organize in companies and chase and fight the Indians wherever they might find them. They asked for no pay, no arms, no equipments, no horses, but only for whatever captures they could make from the enemy. This was, I think, still more dangerous to the white farmers than to the red Indians, and no doubt that such bands let loose through the Territory would soon make the matters worse than anything else, therefore it could not be entertained.

I do not believe much in the genuiness of the fear expressed by the people along the road from Helena to Fort Ellis, through the Missouri, the Crow Creek [area west of Toston and around Radersburg], and the Gallatin Valley. Everywhere I saw them attending to their usual business, traveling with their wives and children, driving isolated wagons with twelve or fourteen oxen, without arms, and without any apparent concern about Indians. Horses were grazing as usual at rather great distances from the ranches, and I found the wife of a farmer traveling alone, on foot, with her carpet bag, from Morse's Store to Forster's bridge. Still, all considered, I am under the impression that, if any serious danger was to be apprehended, it would come more properly in that direction, from the Yellowstone River, where hostile Sioux are roaming, more than anything else...

> Respectfully submitted.
> I am, general, your obedient servant,
> P.R. De Trobriand,
> Col. Thirteenth Inf.,
> Bvt. Brig. Gen. USA[31]

It becomes obvious upon comparing General Sully's report to the Commissioner of Indian Affairs, Department of Interior, dated August 18, 1869, with that of Colonel Trobriand to his superior in the U.S. Army's Department of Dakota, dated September 9, 1869, which would be forwarded to General Sheridan commanding the Division of the Missouri and eventually to the War Department, that these two men did not entirely agree in their description of the current Indian problem in Montana Territory. In fact, during the entire run up and aftermath of the raid, they disagreed in the approach taken as well as in judging its results. Some of this may have arisen from the natural tensions always present between the military and the representatives of the Office of Indian Affairs, many of them themselves military men. However, we cannot discount the fact that a dislike for one another existed in the relationship. Trobriand may have felt that Sully, a general, while not his commander, was overbearing and inclined to interfere in the military affairs of the territory, which were the responsibility of the colonel. This is, however, purely speculation on the part of the author.

Trobriand did not believe that a "state of war" existed between the Blackfoot Nation and the whites. His description of the state of affairs was far more complete. General Sully's reports did more to convey a sense of panic and a rush to judgment. It is interesting that the man responsible for Indian affairs in the territory failed to differentiate the various Blackfeet tribes and bands from one another, but rather, perhaps unintentionally, painted them all with a broad brush in describing those responsible for the depredations simply as "Blackfeet." This describes Bloods, Piegans and Blackfeet—perhaps even Gros Ventres.

Colonel Trobriand's description was much more balanced. He pointed

---

[31] Quoted in Ege, *Tell Baker To Strike Them Hard!* 75–78.

out those members of the Blackfoot Nation whom he believed responsible for the recent depredations. Obviously, the colonel was not champing at the bit looking for an excuse to kill Indians. Of course, neither was Sully. Trobriand's mission was to preserve peaceful relations between the whites and the American Indians insofar as this was possible, recognizing that rogues existed on both sides of the equation. In fairness to General Sully, he faced far greater pressure from the populace and politicians at his post in Helena. Trobriand, stationed at Fort Shaw, was more distant from public pressure calling for action. The reader must also consider in reading the colonel's report that the vast majority of white settlers in the territory at that time in our history would have cried few tears if the Indian population had disappeared—no matter in what fashion, be it massacre, starvation or expulsion. It was the mission of the frontier army not only to fight Indians but also to protect them when necessary. Prospects for success in both tasks were never good, and, of course, the Indians were usually the losers.

We note the colonel's skepticism regarding calls for granting authority for the formation of a territorial militia or even the authorization of certain bands of whites to roam the countryside looking for Indians and any booty they might confiscate from whatever action they pleased to take. The U.S. Army was loathe to see a repetition of the Chivington raid conducted by territorial militia at Sand Creek in Colorado Territory only five years earlier.

On September 27th another communication from Superintendent Sully to Commissioner Parker to his superiors in Washington, D.C., reported additional depredations:

> Superintendent of Indians of Montana
> Helena, Montana, September 27, 1869
>
> Dear Sir:
>
> I have to report two more depredations committed by the Indians and supposed to be Blackfeet. [Once again the broad brush addressing the perpetrators as Blackfeet and not Piegans!] This occurred four days ago at a place not over seven miles from this city. A citizen by the name of James Quait, well known to all the people here, lost some horses and mules. He started out to look for them, and not returning, search was made for him, and his body found pierced with arrows and horribly mutilated. Nine Indians were seen a few days

before driving off the stock from that direction. The Indians have now been at this work for over two months, and as no one, neither the military nor citizens, have made any attempts whatever to check them, they are daily becoming more bold in their operations.

I am told by those who have lost stock that they ride up boldly, in daytime, in presence of citizens, and take what animals they please. Of course, this all comes to me with their complaints, thinking it is my duty to punish the Indians and recover their stolen property.

There are already over four hundred horses and mules known to have been stolen lately. That number, at $150 each, will make an expensive claim against the government.

> With much respect, your obedient servant,
> Alfred Sully, U.S.A. Superintendent Indian Affairs[32]

This letter prompted another message from Commissioner Parker to the Secretary of Interior:

> Department of Interior Office of Indian Affairs
> Washington, D.C., October 7, 1869

> Sir:

> I have the honor to transmit herewith copies of communications received form General Sully, Superintendent of Indian affairs for Montana Territory, giving information of extensive depredations by Indians of that Territory, of the Blackfeet and Piegan tribes.

> This bureau is powerless to control and prevent these depredations, and I respectfully suggest the communications above referred to be transmitted to the Secretary of War, with the request that the military take prompt measures to check them.

> Very respectfully your obedient servant,
> E.S. Parker, Commissioner[33]

The U.S. Army began laying plans for an effective response. On October 21, 1869, General Phillip H. Sheridan sent General of the Army William Tecumseh Sherman a proposed battle plan:

---

[32] Sully, Sen. Exec. Doc. 49, 41st Congress 2nd Session.

[33] Parker, ibid.

Headquarters Military Division of the Missouri
Chicago, Illinois
October 21, 1869

General:

I have the honor to acknowledge the receipt of a letter from the Secretary of Interior, with accompanying reports of General Sully, Mr. Pease, and Mr. Culbertson, Indian Agents in Montana, on the subject of depredations by the Piegan tribe of Indians.

We have so few troops in Montana on account of expiration of enlistments, as to have been unable to do much against these Indian marauders; but the regiments are now filling up and I think it would be the best plan to let me find out exactly where these Indians are going to spend the winter, and about the time of a good heavy snow I will send out a party and try to strike them. About the 15th of January they will be very helpless, and if where they live is not too far from Shaw or Ellis, we might be able to give them a good hard blow, which will make peace a desirable object.

To simply keep the troops on the defensive will not stop the marauders; we must occasionally strike where it hurts, and if the General in-chief thinks well of this, I will try and steal a small force on this tribe from Fort Shaw or Ellis, during the winter.

It numbers about fifteen hundred men, women, and children, all told.

Very respectfully
P.H. Sheridan
Lieutenant General[34]

On November 4, 1869, General Sheridan received permission from his superior, General of the Army William Tecumseh Sherman, to proceed with his plan to strike the Piegans:

Headquarters of the Army Adjutant General's Office
Washington
November 4, 1869

Sir:

Referring to your communication of the 21st ultimo, relative to the depredations by the Piegan Indians, in Montana, I have the honor

---

[34] P. H. Sheridan, ibid.

to inform you that your proposed action, as stated therein, for the punishment of these marauders, has been approved by the General of the Army.

> Very respectfully, your obedient servant,
> E.D. Townsend
> Adjutant General[35]

Subsequent to the decision by the army to strike at the opportune moment, Commissioner Parker sent the following communication to General Sully:

> Department of the Interior
> Office of Indian Affairs,
> November 6, 1869

> Sir;

> I enclose herewith, for your information, copy of correspondence between Lieutenant General P. H. Sheridan and the adjutant general United States Army, relative to punishing the Piegan Indians in Montana for depredations committed by them, and have to request that you will report to this department any further information you may have of said Indians, and also see that peaceable Indians are not molested by the invading troops.

> Very respectfully, your obedient servant,
> E.S. Parker
> Commissioner[36]

Colonel Trobriand continued to disagree with General Sully's description of affairs. On November 22, 1869, he sent a telegram to his superiors with the following information relative to the murder of James Quait near Silver City:

> ...You will recall that a great commotion was caused in Helena about the last days of September by a murder committed near Silver City. It was taken at once for granted that this was the work of Indians, and highly colored descriptions of the barbarous mutilation of the body were reported in every part; whereupon a meeting took place, the committee wrote to me for protection, the grand jury took the

---

[35] Sen. Exec. Doc 49.

[36] Parker, House Exec. Doc. 185.

matter in hand, &c. Now it turns up that said murder was, according to all probabilities and circumstancial evidence, committed by white men, and that the Indians had nothing whatever to do with it. The murdered man was known to have in his possession a gold watch and the sum of four or five hundred dollars in greenbacks, all of which were stolen when the body was found. It is not true that the body was scalped. It is not true that it was cut or mutilated in any way. It is not true that the horses of the man were stolen; they were all found grazing quietly within some three or four hundred yards of where he fell, and no Indian was seen anywhere near the place all day.

These precise details were reported to me by Major Hanna, of the Pay Department, who has them direct from one of the residents of the place where the murder was committed. Any report of Indian disturbances since that date up to [this] present time [this would be from August 18th to November 22, 1869] is absolutely false, and without foundation whatever...[37]

Plans for a punitive strike were being made, but there was some concern by the military that a strike on a select band or group of Piegans might ignite a more general war with all tribes of the Blackfoot Nation. The Department of Dakota inquired as to the availability of arms for issuance to civilians should the need arise. On October 3, 1869, Colonel Trobriand responded that Fort Shaw had no surplus arms available. Forty-two needle guns had been issued to the wagon trains to and from Fort Peck and eight had also been issued to a surveying party. He added that all surplus breech-loaders were being held by the company commanders and that the mounted detachment possessed fifty carbines.[38]

The citizens' committee referred to by Colonel Trobriand in his November 22nd telegram had requested that the colonel direct his 200-man cavalry contingent to conduct a general sweep through Indian country, i.e. "...drive to their reservations and homes the squads or bands of Indians now scattered through the Territory, and that, having done this, you will station parties of troops for the time being at the principal passes through which they are want to make their incursions."[39] Trobriand knew that although he now had 200 cavalrymen at his disposal, a general sweep of Indian country in

---

[37] Quoted in Ege, *Tell Baker To Strike Them Hard!* 88.

[38] October 3, 1869, Fort Shaw Letters and Telegrams Sent and Received.

[39] Quoted in Ege, *Tell Baker To Strike Them Hard!* 79.

an attempt to force the Indians to stay on their reservations was bound to fail. The Indians had often enough demonstrated with sufficient warning an amazing ability to break up into smaller groups and disappear in varying directions before oncoming troops. Whites had earlier observed the ability of the Blackfeet to break up and move their entire village out in a matter of hours, i.e. the departure witnessed by Governor Stevens' envoy in 1853. Instead of a general sweep or general campaign against all Blackfeet, Trobriand sought to be more specific and precise in seeking out his target for punishment. He refused to be stampeded into conducting a fruitless and, also, unjust campaign. If the opportunity arose to launch a precise strike at the offending band or bands, only then did he feel there existed a chance of success. He wrote his superior on November 26th:

> ...I do not see, so far, an opportunity for striking a successful blow. The only Indians within reach are decidedly friendly, and nothing would be worse, I think, than to chastise them for offenses of which they are not guilty... In any case I deem it of importance not to make any demonstration without a reasonable chance of success; for an unsuccessful attempt would only have the bad effect to alarm those we have an interest to bring peacefully to their reservations, and to encourage those who are ill-disposed and inclined to war.[40]

On November 26th Trobriand telegraphed a response to the query made by the Department of Dakota regarding the location of the hostile Piegans. He stated that most of the Piegan tribe, with the exception of a smaller friendly band under Heavy Runner, was located north of the frontier in Canada. He added that most of the rogues were with either Bear Chief's or Mountain Chief's bands north of the frontier. Trobriand reported that a meeting had taken place between Lieutenant Pease and Heavy Runner at the agency in which Heavy Runner promised to have Pete Owl Child killed. Pete had murdered his own father-in-law, who happened to be the brother of Heavy Runner.

Colonel Trobriand further stated:

> Those who are known or suspected to be hostile are scattered along or beyond the frontier line. The arrival of several hundred recruits, in three detachments, is known to them and keeps them on the alert. At the first move they would disappear in the British Territory. But

---

40 Ege, *Tell Baker To Strike Them Hard!* 92.

let everything remain quiet during three or four months, and in the spring they will come back, supposing we will let bygones be bygones. Then I think will be the best chance to give them a lesson of good effect towards putting an end to the murders and depredations among the settlements. This of course with all reserve for any good occasion which may present itself in the meantime to catch any offending party venturing within reach at a proper distance inside of the line. Those offending parties are either with Mountain Chief or Bear Chief, and number but a few lodges in each band.[41]

On December 6, 1869, General Sully requested that the Department of Dakota place a sufficient number of troops under his command in order for him to visit the Blackfeet and demand the surrender of the rogue Piegans and any stolen property, i.e. for the most part horses and/or mules. The Department of Dakota complied with his request by ordering Trobriand to furnish the assistance, somewhat to the chagrin of the colonel. (Note Trobriand's report dated January 13, 1870).

In December the Piegans, unexpected by Trobriand, moved back onto the Marias for the winter. Depredations immediately resumed. On December 14th Colonel Trobriand sent the following message to the Department of Dakota:

Sir:

I have the honor to report that yesterday evening about 8 O'Clock, a party of eleven hunters were attacked by a party of Piegans at the head of the Sun River Valley about 45 miles from this post. The marauding party did not number more than twelve or fifteen and were driven back, not however without having seriously wounded one of the white men, a Mexican known as Johnny the Spaniard.

The news was brought this morning by one of the party and a mounted detachment, thirty-nine men under the command of 2nd Lieut. J.B. Guthrie, 13th Inft., was dispatched at once.[42]

On December 27th General Philip Sheridan, commanding the Division of the Missouri from his headquarters in Chicago, realizing that Colonel Trobriand and General Sully were frequently not on the same page, dispatched Inspector General James A. Hardie to Montana Territory. A section of General Sheridan's instructions to General Hardie is quoted below:

---

[41] Ibid.

[42] December 14, 1869, Fort Shaw Letters and Telegrams Sent and Received.

It will be seen by the accompanying papers that General De Trobriand and General Sully differ very much in their judgement in reference to the condition of Indian affairs in the district of Montana. From these papers it appears that General Sully so represented affairs in Montana as to cause the Secretary of Interior to apply to the General-in-chief for additional protection for the people, and on this application as a basis, the General authorized me to punish the Piegan Indians, and orders were sent accordingly to General De Trobriand. On the date of November 22, General De Trobriand makes a report on the condition of Indian affairs, from which it will be seen that the reports of Indian depredations are exaggerated; and also a second report of the date of November 26, from which it appears that the condition of Indian affairs is by no means alarming.

After a careful examination of the correspondence, I desire that you proceed without delay to Montana, and make a thorough examination of the subject, and if there is any danger of Indians being molested who are friendly, you are authorized to suspend all operations under the orders emanating from the General-in-Chief, until your report is received, or until you return to these headquarters.[43]

Traveling west on the new transcontinental railroad, then north by stage from Corrine, Utah Territory, General Hardie reached Helena on January 5th, commenced his investigation and then continued it from Fort Shaw, after arriving there on January 7, 1870.

In the meantime, as per his request on December 6th, General Sully, accompanied by Marshal Wheeler,[44] was supplied with a sufficient troop escort and conducted his visit to the Piegans on January 1 and 2, 1870. His report dated January 3rd follows:

I left [Fort Shaw] on the 1st instant with twenty-five men, and reached the Teton the same afternoon; [The agency was located near present-day Choteau, MT] there I met a very few Blackfeet; among them were Heavy Runner, Little Wolf, and Big Lake, Piegan chiefs, and Gray Eyes, a Blood chief. I was disappointed at not meeting more of the principal men of the nation; but when my messenger reached the camp he found the Indians very much intoxicated, and some of the head men so overcome with the effects of liquor that it was

---

43 Ege, *Tell Baker To Strike Them Hard!* 94.

44 As the territorial marshal, Wheeler was responsible for the enforcement of civil law, that is to say, had the murderers of Clarke and others been turned over to him by the Piegans, he would have taken them, assisted by the military, to Helena for prosecution.

impossible for them to meet me… I had a talk with what Indians that were there the night of my arrival and the next morning at the agency. I told them that the government, tired out with repeated aggressions of their people, was determined to make war against them as the only way to protect the lives and property of whites; that if we made war they need not think that the northerly boundary would stop our troops from pursuing them; that we intended to cross the line and pursue them into the British possessions…[45]

Sully managed to extract a promise from those few chiefs present to kill the rogues should the opportunity arise and bring in their bodies. We may note, of course, that Colonel Trobriand had reported on November 26th that this same promise had been made during a meeting between Heavy Runner and the Blackfeet agent, Lieutenant Pease. Of course, Sully was bluffing about crossing the boundary. Permission for such a move would have required diplomatic negotiations between Washington and the British government. The likelihood that the British would allow such an incursion was next to nil. Sully stressed the fact that rogue Indians could readily sell their stolen horses to British traders north of the line and seemed to be attempting to make the British the reason for the problem rather than the Indians carrying out the murders and thefts in the United States. He wrote:

From all I can learn, the difficulties with the Indians are more a matter between the United States and English government than between the United States and the Indians; and if the English government cannot protect their savages and half-breeds, they should at least allow our troops to cross the line into that unsettled portion of their territory, to deal with these robbers ourselves. Any war commenced against the Blackfeet will be a farce and a useless expenditure of money, without we can follow them up into their own country.

Sully concluded his report with a degree of pessimism:

I hope my mission to the Piegans and the Bloods may be a success, yet I am not over-sanguine; two or three weeks will determine. In the meantime I would recommend the commander of the district not to retard any preparation he may contemplate, so that he may be ready to strike, if necessary, should it prove that these chiefs cannot carry out their good intentions with their own people.[46]

[45] Quoted in Ege, *Tell Baker To Strike Them Hard!* 99 –102.
[46] Ibid.

Subsequent to his arrival at Fort Shaw, General Hardie continued his investigation. Colonel Trobriand had employed the services of a half-white, half-Mandan Indian named Joseph Kipp, who had known the Piegans from his earlier employment with the American Fur Company at Fort Benton. Kipp spoke their language fluently. In early January General Hardie and Colonel Trobriand dispatched the young Kipp, about twenty-two years old at that time, north to the Marias River country to collect the latest intelligence on the Piegans. General Hardie later wrote to his superior, General Sheridan. A portion of that report describing efforts to follow up on General Sully's conference as well as an expression of opinion regarding its results is quoted below:

> General Sully's conference with the Indians at the agency took place on the 1st instant. He had allowed then two weeks for compliance with their promises. I had not expected any efficacious result from this conference; it was a failure at the start. General Sully himself, indeed, was not sanguine of any success. General De Trobriand, as I have said, thought nothing would come of it. But, this much was done; the Indians were distinctly informed that "the government was tired out with repeated aggressions of their people," and had "determined to make war against them, as the only way to protect the lives and property of the whites," and warned of what would follow, if they did not furnish the guarantee of future good conduct demanded of them. They agreed to effect the restitution of all the stolen stock they could get, and try to have the murderers killed.

> To verify accounts derived from various sources pertaining to the subjects of the inquiry and to get fresh information as to what progress was being made by the Indians to carry into effect their promises as to their present dispositions and the places of encampment of the obnoxious bands, I caused a messenger [Joseph Kipp] to be sent to the Marias. This messenger, who knew the Indians well, whom I had heard generally well spoken of, and who had the confidence of General De Trobriand, left Fort Shaw January 8, and reached the agency on the Teton [near present-day Choteau], thirty-five miles from Fort Shaw, the same day, and the Northwest Fur Company trading post [Riplingers], seventy-five miles from Fort Shaw, the next day; went among the Piegans that and the following day, and returned January 12. The trading post is on the Marias River, seventy-five miles from Benton, and about the same distance from Fort Shaw. It is situated above the Dry Fork, and five miles below Medicine Creek. The messenger reported that the Bloods were near

the trading post, and that the Piegans were also trading there. He saw Mr. Riplinger, agent of the Northwest Fur Company, at the post, who is well acquainted with the Blackfeet tribes. Mr. Culbertson, whom General Sully advised me to see, had left for Belly River, north of the line; but his report is on file. From what the messenger saw and heard, it was clear that the Indians did not seem to be seriously trying to affect anything toward the fulfillment of their promises. They had talked about doing something. But there was stolen stock (some he saw and recognized) distributed through the different bands on the Marias and south of the line, both among the Bloods and the Piegans, there was no effort to get it and bring it in. Mr. Riplinger told him about the same thing. He found out that the Piegans had some stock in their possession belonging to white men – some out with a buffalo party, some also with their bands on the Marias. He saw horses among the Bloods that had been stolen, and he heard from the traders that there were some stage horses there. Among the Indians he saw were Little Wolf and Heavy Runner, whom General Sully had met at the agency. Little Wolf told him he had sent two lads to Bow River to try and get back some mules stolen from the train of a government contractor; and that they were among the Piegans and Blackfeet north of the line. The name of the Piegan who stole them is White Man's Dog. This Indian had killed another Piegan, and had to leave camp and go north. The contractor had got permission to send a man north, prepared to offer a reward for the recovery of the mules. The Indian boys [lads] went with him. This, properly, cannot be claimed as a mission undertaken in furtherance of the chief's promises to General Sully. Little Wolf said that General Sully demanded Pete, Star, and Crow Top, all concerned in murders. Pete is the only one there. He said he could not give them up alive, as they might kill him; yet if Pete were killed no one would care, as he is sort of a renegade, and does not always sleep in the same lodge, for fear of being attacked at night. He was with the Bloods when the messenger was there. The messenger learned from the Bloods that they thought they were not going to be molested by the troops, but they believed the Piegans would be punished, or those of the Piegans who had committed the crimes, because General Sully had told them so. The Bloods, therefore, seemed indifferent to the matter. They were camped above and near the trading post. That is the reason they gave for being separated from the Piegans, who were camped below the post. This differed from what the Indians told General Sully at the conference, where they claimed that the South Piegans were innocent as well as the Bloods, thus throwing all the blame on Indians not so generally ranging south of the line. The Piegans were encamped on the Marias all the way down from the trading post to the Goose Bill, thirty miles from Benton. The messenger gave the localities of the particular encampments of Mountain Chief's, Bear Chief's and other bands of Piegans, both those called friendly and unfriendly, and, what was important, informed me that if sent with any expedition against the Piegans,—and it was designed to send him – he thought he could distinguish the marauding bands it was contemplated to strike from those not intended to be punished upon seeing the Indians, and could inform the commanding officer. His statements were sufficiently confirmed by other testimony to entitle them to credit...[47]

On January 10th General Hardie, still at Fort Shaw, telegraphed General Sully in Helena:

I would be glad to know what definite period you fix as that beyond which you will wait no further for the compliance of Indians with their promises to bring in property, &c. If you have any information touching this point please let me know.[48]

Sully responded the same day:

Two weeks is the time I thought to give the Indians. Better send message to Riplinger, trader on the Marias, to see what the Indians are doing toward carrying out their promises.[49]

Of course, General Hardie had already dispatched young Joe Kipp. On the 11th General Sully sent additional intelligence received from a Mr. Eastman, manager of the Northwest Fur Company at Fort Benton. The crux of this intelligence was that the Indians believed the whites would not fight. "Mr. Riplinger tells me that the only thing you can't make them believe is that the whites will fight..."[50]

Following Kipp's return to Fort Shaw on January 12th, Hardie telegraphed Sully:

Your letter received [referring to Sully's telegram of the 11th]. Messenger to the Marias and the agency returned last night. No serious efforts among Piegans generally to comply with promises to you. Little

[47] Ege, *Tell Baker To Strike Them Hard!* 105–107.

[48] Ibid.: 108.

[49] Ibid.

[50] Ibid.: 109.

Wolf has sent two boys to Belly River for mules. Mountain Chief and other doing nothing. No great hope. Mountain Chief encamped serparately from the Bloods. Two weeks up tomorrow. What do you say the best policy now? You know the situation. Reply by telegraph.[51]

Hardie's statement, "You know the situation," doubtless refers to the fact that Major Baker (brevet colonel) had just passed through Helena en route to Fort Shaw from Fort Ellis with four companies of cavalry. Baker had departed Fort Ellis on January 6th and marched to Fort Shaw via Helena in extremely cold weather. He would arrive at Fort Shaw with his force on January 14th. Sully would have been well aware of this movement, but, in the interests of secrecy, the less said about it the better. Sully responded with two messages, both on the 13th. The first message read: "Under the circumstances as you telegraph, I would, if possible, capture Mountain Chief and some of his principal men, and hold them as hostages until the nation [once again the broad brush] fulfill their promises to me." In the second, more extensive message, Sully fell back on his newfound notion of cross-border incursions into Canada and then concluded with a sentence seemingly designed to cover his backside should bloodshed occur:

I am still of the same opinion in regard to a campaign against the Blackfeet. That the parties most deserving punishment will not receive their just rewards without we can cross the frontier into the camps of the Blackfeet there [Here Sully not only paints the whole Blackfeet nation with the broad brush, but appears in favor of action which could possibly incite a war with Great Britain]; until this can be done no permanent good will result from any movements of troops. However, as some of the most active members of the late marauding parties did belong to Mountain Chief's band—although it is said that these individual Indians are, at present, north of the line—it would be well to show them that we are in earnest; and the seizure of old Mountain Chief, and about half-dozen other principal men of his band, would, I think, cause the rest to go after stolen animals. It will be a difficult matter to make any movements without the Indians getting information through the half-breeds and whisky sellers at Sun River and Benton...but whatever is done, precaution should be taken to give Mr. Riplinger and his trading party of ten men, who are now on the Marias, military protection, for it won't do for them to remain there after any move is made; they would likely be massacred, and all their very valuable stock of goods destroyed....

---

[51] Ibid.: 110–111.

I also gave a wagonmaster of Mr. Kirkendahll's permission to go north with the Indians to see if he could not get some of the mules stolen lately. For these reasons I would recommend that, for the present, no blood should be shed, if it is possible to avoid it.[52]

General Hardie was obviously becoming frustrated with General Sully's persistent vacillations of opinion regarding exactly what action should be taken. He would later write:

> I was quite unprepared for this recommendation, in view of the opinions and recommendations of General Sully up to the 13th of January. He had left an official copy of his report of Janaury 3 with General De Trobriand, at about its date, wherein he recommends the commander of the district (General De Trobriand) not to retard any preparation he may contemplate, so that he may be ready to strike, if necessary, should it prove that the chiefs cannot carry out their good intentions with their own people. The papers show that through his reports to the Indian Bureau (backed by the representations of the citizens of Montana) of the bad acts and dispositions of these Indians, and of his inability to mend matters without military activity and assistance, he had, in fact, procured the issuing of an order from the War Department for military action. He had been so convinced that a campaign was called for that he thought considerable additions should be made to the troops in the Territory. He had contemplated, if authorized, to conduct the operations himself. Before final measures were taken, he had resorted to negotiations; that had failed. The chiefs could not carry out their "good intentions." The necessary inference was that the time had come for General De Trobriand to "strike" as contemplated.

> The experience and character of General Sully, as well as his official position, lent his recommendation due weight in my mind; but I could not feel that the measure now proposed would fully meet the case.

> It certainly was very desirable that blood should not be shed if it were possible to avoid it, for other considerations beside those brought forward by General Sully those of humanity and duty. But then there is the duty of providing security for the lives and property of the citizens of Montana, and that is imperious. To shrink from doing what the occasion called for as necessary, no matter how severe is to incur responsibility for future massacres of men, women,

---

[52] Ibid.

and children, for the destruction of homes and the plunder and ruin of settlements. The question then was, what did the occasion call for as necessary? To this General De Trobriand had answered. A sharp and severe blow upon some guilty bands as an example to the rest. A view of the situation seemed to me to justify his opinion.[53]

General Hardie could have added another reason to proceed promptly with the strike—the simple fact that over 200 cavalrymen were now on the move in extremely cold weather and had been for nearly two weeks, since January 6th. These troopers lacked sufficient barracks space at Fort Shaw for any prolonged stay that would have been necessary had General Sully's most recent recommendation been followed. In his report of inspection General Hardie emphasized the rationale for the strike:

> …it is to be remembered that the object is to stop aggressions for the future, not to punish for the past. To bring these reckless and deluded savages to their senses, a single blow on any guilty band would be probably as efficacious as more extended operations.[54]

The arrival of the Piegans back on the Marias, the resumption of hostile actions by members of their tribe, and the potential for a successful strike had now convinced Colonel Trobriand that action as envisioned by General Sheridan and authorized by General-in-Chief Sherman was now not only possible but necessary.

Fort Shaw, M.T. January 13, 1870

Sir:

I have the honor to acknowledge receipt of your communication of the 11th inst. In which referring to my reports of September 9th and November 26th, 1869, on the Indian affairs in this District, you asked me to inform you if, since the dates cited, events have occurred to modify the conclusion of these reports, what they are and what are my present views.

In answer I have to state that events have occurred since November 26th which materially alter the condition of things. The first of which is the return of the Indians (Piegans and Bloods) on the Marias River about the middle of December, when, as seen by my

---

[53] Ibid.: 111–112
[54] Ibid.: 113.

previous reports, they were not expected to come there before the end of January or the month of February. This created an opportunity to strike the Piegans at once, which did not exist before. How I intended to promptly avail myself of it…is explained in my report of December 21st, 1868, to Department Headquarters.

In the meantime, General Sully, superintendent of Indian Affairs in the Territory, proposed to make a demand on the Indians for the delivery of the murderers of Mr. [Malcolm] Clarke and some other white men, and the recovery of animals stolen during last summer. This demand was to be backed by a military force, and the plan being approved in Washington, I received the following orders by telegraph:

St. Paul, December 16th

Furnish Gen. Sully what military assistance he may request to support any demand he may make for culprits for stolen horses with Indians in his jurisdiction. Place troops at such points as he may indicate during the operation. Acknowledge receipt by telegraph (Confidential).

By command of Mj. Gen. Hancock. O.D. Greene

This telegram had of course the effect of paralyzing any independent action on my part, by putting the military forces of my command virtually at the disposal of the superintendent of Indian affairs in Montana. As this was, in my opinion, calculated to defeat the success of the contemplated expedition by giving alarm to the Indians and driving them back beyond the frontier line, without (as I believed) securing the compliance by them with the demands of Gen. Sully, I attempted by a telegram to Gen. Hancock to obtain a prevention of the interference of Gen. Sully, but without success, and Gen. Sully arrived at Fort Shaw on December 25th.

What took place in his council with four Indian chiefs at the agency on the Teton River is stated in his report to the commission of Indian Affairs, a copy of which was furnished to this headquarters. I do not think it necessary to add anything as to the present condition of affairs as your arrival at this post enabled you to ascertain it directly in all its details.

To come back to the object of your communication: the other events which took place to alter the condition of affairs during the month of December are:

1st. An attack on a party of hunters at the head of Sun River Valley 45 miles from Fort Shaw on the evening of Dec. 13th in which one man was killed and another wounded by a band of Piegans.

2nd. The loss of a herd of thirty mules belonging to Mr. Kirkendahl, government contractor, stolen during the night of December 16th near Dearborn, by the same band of Piegans,—and not of Blackfeet as erroneously reported by Gen. Sully.

3rd. The breaking open of a log house and stealing or destroying the provisions and other articles contained therein near Camp Cooke, the pursuit of the marauders by wood-choppers reinforced by a small detachment from Camp Cooke, and the fight which lasted several hours without result ascertained. This on the evening of the 22nd and during the 23rd of December.

These attacks on White men or on their properties without any sort of provocation whatever and occurring almost simultaneously and immediately upon the arrival of the Indians on the Maria [Marias] River show in what disposition they have returned and how prompt they are to resume their murderous and plundering incursions,— unfortunately unchecked during the past summer for want of means of repression. It is my belief that they are greatly encouraged by their past impunity and that to prevent the recurrence and in- crease of those depredatory raids upon the residents of the Territory, it has become necessary to inflict a punishment on the guilty par- ties.—Mostly Piegans. This not only to chastise the culprits, but also as a warning to prevent others unconcerned so far in the past aggres- sions, to become accomplices and participators in new ones which seem to be contemplated by young red warriors, judging by their open boasts, as I am informed from various sources.

This General, does not imply that my views are changed reflecting the general disposition of the Blackfeet Nation, including the three tribes, the Blackfeet proper, Bloods, and Piegans. It is still my opinion that no state of war actually exists in the Territory, and that the majority of the Indians, especially among the Bloods, are peacefully disposed. But among them all, and principally among the Piegans, there is a certain number of ill-disposed and positively hostile young men who must be punished as they cannot be controlled by the friendly chiefs and are even openly sustained and protected by other chiefs, the most conspic- uous of whom are Mountain Chief and his sons with their followers. These we must strike, and strike hard so as to make an example.

As far as the striking goes (provided the action of Gen. Sully does not scare them away) I can do it with the forces now at my command as explained in my dispatch to Gen. Hancock of December 21st, with this modification that I will operate from the trading post down towards Benton instead of from Benton's up towards the trading post. In that way I would cut the line of the Maria [Marias] River where the Indians are scattered, so as to leave out the Bloods, who are encamped up the river above, and peaceably disposed, limiting the punishment to the Piegans who are all below that point. And even then I would be careful that the two friendly bands of Heavy Runner and Big Lake be left unmolested, so as to single out Mountain Chief and his followers, who were two days ago still at a place known as the Big Bend.

This successfully accomplished, would not, according to all probabilities short of a certainty, bring any general war. The Blackfeet [Blackfeet Proper] are all far away on the British possessions and would not be touched. The Bloods would be left out, and, as they all expect it, the hostile Piegans would be punished alone, while friendly ones would be spared. The moral and material result would therefore be, I am confident of it, what we may desire, and peace and security would be secured in the Territory, at least for a time.

Still, every possible contingency must be taken into consideration, even the least probable according to our calculations. Therefore, I would respectfully submit that, in case of an extensive war and serious hostilities in the spring, I shall need reinforcements, principally cavalry, to carry it with vigor and effect. Until then, with my infantry stationed by detachments at different points, which I can indicate to you on the map, and with the cavalry on the move, I shall be able to sufficiently protect the settlements by a strong defensive.

In conclusion, convinced that it is better to strike at once than to preserve indefinitely a passive attitude, and judging the present opportunity the best we can reasonably hope for, I have the honor to inform you that I am ready for action, and after mature consideration, in no fear of the consequences.

I am General, [your obt. Svt.,] R. De Trobriand[55]

Major Eugene Baker arrived at Fort Shaw with his four troops (companies) of cavalry on January 14, 1870. He then spent several days meeting

---

[55] Marie Caroline Post, *The Life and Memoirs of Comte Regis de Trobriand*: 413–414.

with Colonel Trobriand and General Hardie as well as the guide, Joseph Kipp and another guide, Joe Cobell.[56] Cobell had also been hired on as a guide to accompany the force. In the interim General Hardie telegraphed to General Sheridan a summarization of his report and conclusions. On January 15th General Sheridan responded with final instructions. "If the lives and property of citizens of Montana can best be protected by striking the Indians, I want them struck. Tell Baker to strike them hard."[57]

On January 16th Colonel Trobriand issued clear and concise orders to Major Baker:

Fort Shaw, M.T., January 16th, 1870

Colonel,

In compliance with instructions from superior headquarters you will proceed with your command without any more delay than may be required by the present condition of the weather, to chastise that portion of the Indian tribe of Piegans which under Mountain Chief or his sons committed the greater part of the murders and depredations last summer and last month in this District. The band of Mountain Chief is now encamped on the Maria [Marias] River about 75 miles from this post at a place called the Big Bend, and can be easily singled out from other bands of Piegans, two of which should be left unmolested as they have uniformly remained friendly, viz: the bands of Heavy Runner and Big Lake. These two chiefs and Little Wolf are the three who met Gen. Sully at the agency a short time ago. All the Piegans now on the Territory of the U.S. are encamped along the Maria [Marias] River from the trading post near the Red Coulee down to near the mouth of the river. And this section of the country up to the frontier line of the British possessions will be the field of your operations.

Above the trading post and at a short distance is encamped about one-half of the Bloods. This tribe is peacefully inclined and although a number of stolen horses are reported to be in their camp, they should be let alone, and not included in your expedition for the present. The Blackfeet proper being far away in the British

---

[56] Joe Cobell was also a former employee of the American Fur Company. He later settled on a ranch near Rock Creek, which flows from the northwest into the Missouri about halfway between the present-day towns of Wolf Creek and Craig. His second wife, Mary, was a younger sister of Mountain Chief. Ege, *Tell Baker To Strike Them Hard!* 40.

[57] J.P. Dunn, Jr., *Massacres of the Mountains:* 453.

possessions, and not considered as hostile, will not come in your way. All necessary information in regard to the location of the several Indian encampments and the character of the roaming Indians who may fall into your hands during your operations will be furnished to you by the guide who is ordered to report to you.

When you strike the Maria [Marias] River, or such time when it may not any more convey a premature information, you will leave or send a small detachment of ten men under a non-commissioned officer to the trading post of the N.W. fur company for the protection of the establishment during your operations.

Besides your command of four companies of cavalry, Captain and Bvt. Lieutenant Col. Higbie is ordered to report to you with the mounted detachment at Fort Shaw, and the necessary transportation. Captain Torrey, 13th Inf., is also ordered to report to you with his company as a guard and escort for the train of supplies that you will have to leave behind, so as to leave the whole of your cavalry disposable for action. A guide will also be furnished to you to go with the train.

Beyond these general instructions it is deemed unnecessary to add anything. The details as to the best way to surprise the enemy and to carry on successfully the operations, is confidently left to your judgement and discretion according to circumstances, and to your experience in such expeditions.

> R. De Trobriand Col. 13th Inf., Bvt. Brig. Gen.
> Commanding Military District of Montana[58]

General Hardie departed Fort Shaw on January 17th en route back to Chicago via Helena and Corrine, Utah Territory. While in Helena he sent the following telegram to General Sheridan:

Reached here last night from Fort Shaw. Lieutenant General's telegram of the 15th instant received. I think chastisement necessary. In this Colonel Baker concurs. He knows the General's wishes. He will move today. Some horses and mules stolen from citizens in various Indian camps on the Marias; among them camps of Indians pretending to be innocent. Also murderers there. The stock the Indians promised Sully to deliver up, the latter to have killed. I thought, well, Colonel Baker's design should be extended to include the coercion of

---

[58] Post: 414–415.

Indians to keep this promise, if he could do so prudently. Hence, my suggestion at close of long dispatch. But this is only following up of stroke directed by the Lieutenant General, and Colonel Baker may be relied on to do all that the General would wish in the way of vigorous and sufficient action. If the Indians do not get wind of movement and the weather has been opportunely severe, so as to measurably prevent that danger, I anticipate best results. in any case good, and no harm, will be done. I leave for Corrine in the morning.[59]

On January 19th Colonel Trobriand sent the following telegram to the Department of Dakota:

Fort Shaw, Jan. 19th, 1870, 9 A.M.

Cavalry arrived here on the fourteenth instant. Detained by excessive cold. Thermometer fell to forty-three degrees below zero. Starting now with mounted detachment, and a Company of Infantry (seventy-five men) as escort to wagons. General Hardie left on seventeenth.

R. De Trobriand Bvt. Brig.
General Commanding[60]

Present-day Montana residents can well imagine what it would be like to ride a horse and/or walk from Bozeman to Fort Shaw, then on to the Marias River during a cold January! A picnic it was not. Major Baker's force, now accompanied by guides Joe Kipp and Joe Cobell as well as young Horace Clarke and Nathan Clarke, departed Fort Shaw early on January 19th with the temperature near 30 below, crossed the Sun River, and marched some twenty miles north-northwest, to a point near Priest's Butte (near present-day Choteau, MT). They halted there until the evening of January 20th, then marched in darkness northeasterly about twenty-two miles to a point where Muddy Creek empties into the Teton River. There they camped during daylight hours on the 21st and that evening commenced their march in darkness for about twenty miles to a point about "…seven miles northeast of present-day Conrad, Montana."[61] Once again they spent the daylight hours in the greatest possible concealment with fires kept to a minimum. At darkness they resumed the march down the Dry Fork of the Marias.

---

[59] Quoted in Ege, *Tell Baker To Strike Them Hard!* 121–122.

[60] Post: 415–416.

[61] Ege, *Tell Baker To Strike Them Hard!* 42.

During the entire march Kipp and Cobell scouted forward watching for signs of Indians.

Major Baker could not be certain that this mission would be a cake walk. For one thing, the Montana reader will be well aware of the climatic conditions that could not only work for the major but also against him. His entire command could have become engulfed in a blizzard—not uncommon to the northern plains of Montana. The possibility also existed that the Piegans had gotten word of his intentions and prepared an ambush for his troops. Just four years prior, in December 1866, Captain Fetterman's entire command of some eighty men had been massacred by Sioux and Northern Cheyenne warriors. The reader should not assume via marvelous 20-20 hindsight that Major Baker need not be concerned that he was not leading his troops to a similar fate.

Upon reaching the mouth of the Dry Fork, the force came upon a small Piegan encampment consisting of five lodges. They surrounded it without gunfire and ordered the inhabitants out. This was the camp of the Piegan Gray Wolf. Faced with annihilation if he failed to cooperate, this chieftain stated that the village of two hostile chiefs, Bear Chief and Bighorn, was located six or seven miles down the Marias. Upon learning this, Major Baker left the supply wagons under the guard of Captain Torrey's company of infantry and moved the remainder of his command, all mounted (four cavalry troops and one mounted infantry company), out at a rapid gait down the Marias. Gray Wolf and his small band were kept under observation by Captain Torrey's command to prevent anyone from departing to warn the hostiles. As previously ordered, Baker also dispatched a sergeant and ten enlisted men to ride to Riplinger's Trading Post to provide the traders with protection from any counter strike by hostiles.

Just before dawn Baker's force came upon the village, which consisted of thirty-seven lodges—some near a bluff on one side of the Marias and some on the other bank of the river. Baker's men took concealed positions on the bluffs and two smaller forces were detached, one to cross the river and move around behind the village on the opposite bank, thus blocking escape in that direction, and another to separate the horse herd from the Indians in the village. Major Baker had about 250 mounted personnel available. Surprise was complete. It was about 8 A.M. Firing commenced on the surprised Indians, but reports vary as to the manner in which the fight, which was destined to be one-sided, began. The *Helena Gazette* reported on February 1st that as one detachment galloped across the river to surround the village it was fired upon by an Indian, killing one soldier, Private Walter McKay. Other versions will be discussed later. Author Robert Ege offered a plausible description of the battle:

> The Piegans, seeking any means to escape the deadly hail of lead, scattered into the brush that fringed the flat on which their camp was situated. Panic stricken Indians ran in every direction. Many were dropped in their tracks. Across the river a warrior, obviously wounded, dragged himself to a horse, mounted and rode wildly down the river. Several Indian riflemen, cut off from further retreat, took refuge behind a small cutbank and attempted to return the soldier's fire. However, a detachment of Higbee's sharp-shooters worked around behind them and finished them off in short order.[62]

The Piegans were taken completely by surprise and, in spite of some effort to do so, were unable to organize an effective resistance. They were, of course, being fired upon by a large number of soldiers who had the good fortune to be able to mount the greater part of their attack from concealed positions. These soldiers were armed with breach-loading carbines and rifles, which could be fired at the rate of as many as ten rounds per minute. Although this author has no documentation regarding the amount of ammunition carried on this particular expedition, there is documentation available from numerous other expeditions of that era describing how each cavalry soldier was supplied with one hundred rounds of carbine ammunition and twenty-four rounds of pistol ammunition on his person and in his saddlebags. Custer's men also had additional carbine ammunition on the pack mules at the Little Bighorn, but Baker had no pack mules; he had wagons and they had been left under guard next to Gray Wolf's camp six or seven miles distant. Certain versions of the event report that the firing continued for about an hour. The volume of firing was likely initially heavy for a few minutes, then sporadic in nature. Firing at a heavy volume, the troopers would have expended nearly all their ammunition in about thirty minutes. This was certainly not the case, for once Major Baker had secured the village, he promptly moved out his force, now reduced in size by one company, or about fifty men, without resupplying them, in an effort to engage another village of unknown size. This indicates that he had ample ammunition available for this potential second attack.

The troopers then moved into the village destroying the tepees and supplies. One may be certain that no quarter was given to Indian males or

---

[62] Ibid.: 43–44.

anyone else who resisted regardless of their age and sex. The village consisting of thirty-seven lodges contained about 315 persons, mostly Piegans but also a few whiskey runners. All males were killed. It may be safely stated that they were given no quarter and expected none. Surrender by a Plains Indian male to his Indian enemies had always meant certain death, usually by torture. For most women and children this was also true, although if the conquerors had the need, some were kept as slaves. Although there were doubtless cases of cold-blooded slaughter of some unresisting women and children, most of them were taken captive and cared for as the circumstances permitted. At the conclusion of the battle 173 were killed and 140 women and children taken prisoner. One soldier was killed.

Major Baker left Lieutenant Doane and his company to continue the destruction of the village, and to secure and care for the prisoners. It was determined either during the course of the attack or after the attack that the friendly chief, Heavy Runner, and his band was also encamped with the bands of Bear Chief and Bighorn, both indicted hostiles. Heavy Runner was killed in the course of the attack as were Bear Chief and Bighorn and another indicted hostile, Red Horn. An additional indicted hostile, Black Eagle, was wounded but managed to escape on horseback. Mountain Chief and Pete Owl Child were not present in this village. Baker learned that Mountain Chief was encamped an additional four miles downriver. He promptly moved out with his remaining companies in an attempt to reach Mountain Chief's village. After traveling what seemed to Baker to be about sixteen miles, they came upon seven hastily abandoned lodges, believed to be Mountain Chief's village. Baker had the lodges and equipment destroyed and, for the first time on the entire journey from Fort Shaw, allowed his troopers to warm themselves by ample campfires and rest, spending the night at the site of Mountain Chief's abandoned village.[63]

The next day Baker marched his column back to Lieutenant Doane's position and learned that some of the women and children prisoners had smallpox. The troopers did not have sufficient supplies to escort them all the way back to Fort Shaw, and having them held at the post with smallpox among them was not desired. They were provided with some rations and released to join other neighboring tribes. No doubt some died in the cold weather while making their way to the shelter of neighboring bands. The horse herd was secured to be driven to Fort Shaw.

---

[63] Ibid.: 44–45.

Baker then moved his column back to the freight wagons still under guard by Captain Torrey's company of infantry and resupplied. He then marched to Riplinger's Trading Post, summoned the various Blood chieftains, and demanded that they surrender all stolen horses and mules or face a similar fate. The Bloods quickly delivered up more stolen animals. Baker then marched his tired troopers back to Fort Shaw, arriving there on January 28th and bringing with him a total of about 300 horses captured from the Piegan village. This number also included some stolen animals surrendered by the Bloods.

Meanwhile, back at Fort Shaw word of the attack began to reach Colonel Trobriand, who promptly reported to his headquarters:

Fort Shaw, M.T. January 26th, 1870

On Sunday morning, the twenty-third instant at daybreak Colonel Baker surprised the camp of Bear Chief, a hostile Piegan—thirty lodges—on the Marias. The attack was a complete success, no more than four or five escaped. Three Bloods and one whiskey trader happening to be in the camp are reported killed. Some wounded soldiers said to be with the train. The column was going on to strike the camp of Mountain Chief when last heard of.

This news is not official, but was brought from the trading post by Mr. Riplinger who had it from runaway and wounded Indians.[64]

On January 28th Major Baker returned to Fort Shaw with his command and Colonel Trobriand reported to the Department of Dakota:

Fort Shaw, M.T. January 28th, 1870

The expedition a complete success. Col. Baker just returned having killed one hundred and seventy-three (173) Piegans, destroyed forty-four (44) lodges with all their winter supplies, robes, etc. and captured over three hundred (300) horses.

The Bloods turned over to him all the horses from white people which were in their hands. The most of the murderers and marauders of last summer are killed.

Pete and Mountain Chief escaped with a few followers, losing everything but the horses they were on.[65]

[64] January 26, 1870, District of Montana Letters and Telegrams Sent, Department of Dakota, Record Group 393.5, National Archives.

[65] January 28, 1870, ibid.

Officers at Fort Ellis, July 1871: Left to right: 1st Lt. Frank C. Grugan, Captain Lewis Thompson, 2nd Lt. George H. Wright, 2nd Lt. Gustavus C. Doane, Captain Lewis Cass Forsyth, Assist. Surgeon A.B. Campbell, Dr. R.M. Whitefoot, 1st Lt. Sam T. Hamilton, Major Eugene Baker, Post Commander–Captain Edward Ball, 2nd Lt. Lovell H. Jerome, Captain George L. Tyler (front), 2nd Lt. Edward J. McClernand and 2nd Lt. Charles B. Schofield.

On January 30th Major Trobriand sent another telegram to the Department of Dakota advising that Major Baker had not yet made his report and commending the men and Major Baker. He predicted, "I am confident that peace and safety is secured for a long time to the Territory. I should mention that about one hundred squaws and children captured in action were turned loose unhurt."

On the same date he responded to a query from General Sully regarding Big Lake's camp, advising that Big Lake was safe as long as he remained friendly. He added "Unless you intend to feed them at the Agency, I would rather have them on the other side of the Marias, where I intend to keep all Indians as much as possible."[66]

On January 31st, after a brief rest at Fort Shaw, Major Baker's 2nd Cavalry departed for Fort Ellis. They arrived back there on February 5th.

On February 18, 1870, Colonel Trobriand forwarded Major Baker's report to the Department of Dakota:

> Hd. Qts. Dist. Of Montana
> Fort Shaw, M.T., Feb. 18th, 1870

> Sir:

> I have the honor to forward herein enclosed report of Bvt. Col. Baker, 2nd Cavalry, on the expedition against the hostile Piegans, under his command.

> To this report I have but little to add, as the Major General commanding the Department has already been informed by me of all the dispositions made to prepare and organize the expedition at these headquarters, and to secure its success, as far as possible with the means at my command.

> It is most gratifying that my previsions were fully realized, and complete success was attained not only in the severe punishment of the Piegans, but in the telling effect of that manifestation of our power on the whole of the Blackfeet nation, Bloods and Blackfeet proper, who henceforth will carefully avoid bringing upon themselves a similar retribution by murders of white men and depredations on the settlements. This has given the chiefs friendly disposed, the power of controlling their wild young warriors much better, and inspired those ill disposed with a salutary fear which will coerce

---

[66] January 30, 1870, ibid.

them into good behavior in the future. The peace and security of the Territory may therefore be considered as restored, at least for a pretty long time, and maybe forever, if judicious measures are taken to prevent occasions of no troubles as well from lawless white men as from wild Indians...

Colonel Trobriand then commended Major Baker for his performance of duty:

...The presence of smallpox among the Piegans and Bloods, which induced Col. Baker to turn loose the women and children captured in the hostile camp, was also the cause of his ordering everything to be destroyed. I may add that the expeditionary column had not surplus rations enough to feed that crowd on their way back to Fort Shaw, and that it would have been extremely inconvenient in several ways to keep them at this post, as there was no provision for them at the Indian agency on the Teton River.

The number of horses captured which was originally over three hundred (300) was reduced to two hundred and eighty-five (285) when the herd arrived at this post. The balance were either lost on the way, having gone astray in the bushes, or perhaps stolen during the night. Eighteen (18) were taken by Col. Baker as pack animals with his command. Thirty-four (34) horses and one (1) mule were claimed since that time and returned to known resident citizens who proved property. Two (2) died, which leaves two hundred and thirty horses in my keeping. They are nearly all Indian ponies in a poor condition and of but little value. I would respectfully request to be instructed what ultimate disposition is to be made of them.

I remain, [your obt. svt.] R. De Trobriand[67]

The enclosed report by Major Baker reads:

Fort Shaw, M.T. February 18, 1870

Sir:

I have the honor to submit the following report of a scout made by me against the hostile Piegan and Blood Indians.

Pursuant to Special Orders No. 62, Headquarters District of Montana, I left Fort Ellis on the 6th of January with two squadrons

---

[67] Post: 417–418.

of the 2nd Cavalry, consisting of H Company, Captain Edward Ball, L Company, Brevet Major Lewis Thompson, G Company, Captain S.H. Norton, and F Company, under the command of Lieutenant G. C. Doane; arrived at Fort Shaw on the 14th. On our arrival at Fort Shaw, Brevet Lieutenant Colonel G.H. Higbee was ordered to report to me with a detachment of fifty-five mounted infantry, and Captain R.A. Torrey, with his company of the Thirteenth Infantry.

I left Fort Shaw on the 19th, and marched to the Teton River, where we remained in camp until the evening of the 20th, when we left camp and made a night march to the mouth of Muddy Creek, a branch of the Teton. I remained in camp there until the evening of the 21st, then marched for the Maria's River, expecting to be able to reach the Big Bend on the next morning, having understood from the guide that was where the Indians were encamped.

We were obliged to camp in a ravine on the Dry Fork of the Maria's till the night of the 22nd, when we broke camp and marched to the Maria's River, arriving there on the morning of the 23rd. We succeeded about 8 o'clock in surprising the camp of Bear Chief and Bighorn. We killed one hundred and seventy-three Indians, captured over one hundred women and children, and over three hundred horses.

I ordered Lieutenant Doane to remain in this camp and destroy all the property, while I marched downriver after the camp of Mountain Chief, who, I understood, was camped four miles below.

After marching sixteen miles I found a camp of seven lodges that had been abandoned in great haste, leaving everything. The Indians had scattered in every direction so that it was impossible to pursue them. The lodges were burned the next morning, and the command started for the Northwest Fur Company's station, arriving there on the 25th.

I sent for the chiefs of the Bloods and had a consultation with them, making them give up all their stolen stock. They promised that they would be responsible for the good behavior of their tribe.

On the 25th, started for Fort Shaw, where we arrived on the 29th January.

The cavalry command left for Fort Ellis on the 31st, arriving there on the 6th February, having made a march of about six hundred miles in one month, and this in the coldest weather that has been known in Montana for years.

Too much credit cannot be given to the officers and men of the command for their conduct during the whole expedition.

The result of the expedition is one hundred seventy-three Indians killed, over one hundred prisoners, women and children; these were allowed to go free, as it was ascertained that some of them had the small-pox; forty-four lodges with all their supplies and stores destroyed, and three hundred horses captured.

Our casualties were one man killed, and one man with a broken leg from a fall of his horse.

> Very respectfully, your obedient servant,
> E.M. Baker Major 2nd Cavalry, Bvt. Col. U.S.A.[68]

As soon as the news came out, the great majority of white settlers and miners in Montana Territory were elated. Back in the eastern states, however, a scandal arose over the alleged slaughter of helpless Indian women and children. On February 23, 1870, the *New York Times* published a letter from Mr. Vincent Collyer, Secretary, Board of Indian Commissioners, Department of Interior, quoted as follows:

...At last the sickening details of Colonel Baker's attack on the village of the Piegans, in Montana, on the 23d of January last, have been received. Of the 173 killed, only fifteen were what might be called fighting men, that is, men between the ages of 12 and 37 years. Ten were from 37 to 60 years, and eight additional were over 60—in all, fifty-three. There were ninety women killed, fifty-five, or over one-half, of whom were over 40 years of age, and the remaining thirty-five were between 12 and 40 years. Lastly. There were fifty children under 12 years of age killed; many of them were in their parents' arms. The whole village had been suffering for over two months past with smallpox, some half-dozen dying daily...[69]

Inquiries were made in the House and Senate. U.S. Representative Vorhees stated:

When Indians were a power in this land we made war on them according to civilized warfare. We struck them in manly battle. Now,

---

[68] E.M. Baker, House Exec. Doc. 197, 41st Congress, 2nd Session: 41–42, National Archives.

[69] *New York Times*, February 23, 1870.

when they are poor, broken, and miserable remnants, corrupted and demoralized, it is proposed to change our mode of warfare, and smite not merely the warrior, but the woman and babe in her arms...[70]

The scandal spread throughout the East, and the military was heavily criticized. The House and Senate demanded copies of all pertinent reports on the affair from the Commissioner of Indian Affairs and from the Secretary of War. Citizens on the frontier, however, remained very supportive of the action. Their sentiment was shared by the press in Montana Territory. One Montana newspaper wrote of the raid:

> ...Besides this, the utter destruction of their villages, their winter stores, their furs, and everything that goes to constitute an Indian's property, all going to make it a terrible and fatal blow at the impudent and bloody marauders that have during the past summer ravaged our northern frontier.

> Col. Baker was in immediate command of the expedition, which was organized by General de Trobriand, commander of this Military District. He has been its head and projector, as Baker has been its right arm. To them hundreds of men, women and children in Montana, who can now sleep with a greater feeling of security than ever before, can render their thanks; and to the gallant officers and men of the command that faced the open prairie in the midst of winter to hunt these savages in their lair.

> ...Every effort was made to keep the destination of the troops secret. It was late at night when they marched to the point the guides intended to take them. On account of the frost in the air and a few inches of snow on the ground they had some difficulty in keeping the right course. Finally, the command arrived at the bluffs overlooking the Marias River, the tepees of the enemy were hardly observable, but the scouts had located the Indian villages, and, before daylight, they were completely surrounded by soldiers. At an early hour the firing commenced and before the bugle called a halt nearly two hundred Indians had joined their ancestors in their happy hunting grounds. Two soldiers were killed in this terrible battle.[71]

---

[70] Dunn: 452.

[71] Post: 419.

As late as 1900, Montana pioneer Robert Vaughn praised the action of the military:

> When the news reached the stations along the Helena and Benton road, there were a few who became alarmed for fear that retaliation would be made by the Indians. But they did not retaliate; the battle was the best thing that ever happened to Northern Montana at that time. For several years afterwards the Indians were very shy, although some roving war parties of different tribes would cross the country and kill people and steal horses and cattle.[72]

On February 6, 1870, approximately two weeks after the raid and just as Major Baker's command arrived back at Fort Ellis, Lieutenant Pease reported to General Sully on a visit to the Piegan camp of Big Lake. While there he had spoken with some of the survivors of the raid on the Piegan camp. He reported as a result of information gathered at this camp that of the 173 Indians killed, 33 were men and of this number only 15 were young fighting men between the ages of 12 and 37. Eighteen of the men were between the ages of 37 and 70 and of this number 8 were between the ages of 60 and 70. He further reported that 90 were women; of these, 35 were between the ages of 12 and 37 and 55 were between the ages of 37 and 70. There were 50 children less than 12 years old "… and many of them in their mothers' arms." This report was obviously the source of the information provided by Mr. Vincent Collyer.

On February 10th, eight days before Major Baker's report dated February 18th, General Sully, now in receipt of Lieutenant Pease's report, wired Commissioner Parker, his superior in Washington, D.C.:

> Superintendency Montana,
> Helena, M.T. February 10, 1870
>
> Sir:
>
> I have delayed any official report to you concerning the late attack of Colonel Baker's command on a camp of Blackfeet. [Again the broad brush] I did this as I had so many conflicting reports, from various sources, of this affair; some of them apparently were so greatly exaggerated that I withheld making any report till I could get something more definite; so I directed Lieutenant Pease, United States Army,

---

[72] Robert Vaughn, *Then and Now*: 49. Vaughn established one of the earliest ranches in the Sun River Valley near present-day Vaughn, MT, in 1869. In early 1889 he sold the ranch to Thomas Couch for $46,000 (reported by the *Madisonian*, Virginia City, in January 1889). Thereafter he made his residence in Great Falls.

Agent for the Blackfeet, to proceed to a camp of these Indians, who were on the Marias River about thirty miles from Benton, of which camp Big Lake was the chief. Herewith I have the honor to inclose you a copy of the result of his visit and interview with these Indians.

The report that Lieutenant Pease sends is entirely what the Indians say of the affair and of course it is natural to suppose it is prejudiced in their own favor. It is the Indians side of the question, and, as I am here as their only representative, I consider it my duty to give them a hearing.

Colonel Baker's attack was a complete surprise, and the punishment he gave them was one of the most severe lessons that Indians have received. It is to be hoped that this lesson will inspire them with some respect for the government, which heretofore the majority of the nation did not seem to have. In addition to this punishment, the smallpox, which they had at the time, has since spread fearfully among them. This may strike so much terror among them, and make them so dejected, that they will be comparatively quiet this winter, and there may be no difficulty in making arrangements with the nation next spring that will secure peace in this section of the country, at least for a year or two. I should have said, comparatively speaking, for I do not believe perfect peace can be preserved until measures are taken to stop the Indians north of the line from stealing horses and selling them in the British Possessions. However, in about two months, matters will more fully develop themselves, and we will be able to better form an opinion of what will be the future conduct of these Indians.

It is perhaps to be regretted, since it was necessary to chastise a portion of the Piegans, that Mountain Chief's band was not the band that suffered. The young men of this band have been lately notoriously the worst of the Blackfeet in committing depredations on the citizens. I know that General De Trobriand, commanding this district, so considered them, as well as myself; but they, the most guilty, escaped, and got across the line.

I refrain from making any comments on the reported unnecessary and uncalled for cruelty on the part of the soldiers. Both sides should be heard before one can justly make up his mind on the subject.

With much respect, your obedient servant,
Alf. Sully, U.S.A. Superintendent Indian Affairs[73]

---

[73] Sully, House Exec. Doc. 185, 41st Congress, 2nd Session: 41–42.

On February 18, 1870, the *New York Times* reprinted an article that had originated in the *Helena Daily Rocky Mountain Gazette* on February 1st:

The expedition against the hostile Indians set out from Fort Shaw on Wednesday. The weather was fearfully cold, the thermometer ranging from 10° to 20° below zero, and the icy winds swept across the exposed and bleak plains with a keenness and penetration that defy description. About dawn on Sunday morning they reached the tepee of an Indian called Gray Wolf, who was encamped alone, with his family, in which there were two cases of smallpox. Extorting from Gray Wolf the intelligence that Red Horn and Bear Chief's camp was about eight miles further on the Big Bend of the Marias, the command started at a gallop and came upon the camp like a whirlwind about 7 o'clock A.M. There was only one Indian stirring, and he, seeing the cavalry as they dashed across the creek, fired and killed a soldier. The next second the command were in the camp, around every tepee, in front of every lodge door, and opening a fusilade from their repeating rifles. The awakened Indians jumped to their feet with terrific yells; but no sooner would one put his head out of the lodge door than he was riddled. Some fired through the lodges, others endeavored to escape by running. One "buck" was found alive afterwards, in his tepee, who had killed two of his squaws with his knife and piled their dead bodies over himself to hide him. This is an act of stratagem, meanness and cowardice unexampled even in Indian history. It is unnecessary to say that the wretch did not live long after he was found in this condition. Soon it appeared that the warriors of the camp were thoroughly wiped out, and the troops took a view of the situation. The camp consisted of 37 lodges, with a wealth of buffalo robes, furs, meat, whiskey and everything that an Indian considers necessary to make him rich, that astonished the troops. They found they had killed 173 Indians, and had, besides, between 130 and 140 captives, women and children. These they had no use for; and, assigning them a lodge for their shelter, with such necessaries as they needed, the troops burned the robes, furs, peltries, meats, arms, lodges and everything else.

While a detachment remained at the work of destruction, the main command had resumed the march to attack the Mountain Chief's band, which they supposed was only three miles further, but a march of sixteen miles scarcely brought them to the camp. The Indians here had received the alarm and fled, barely taking their ponies with them. The lodges were struck, but nothing had been moved. The pots were still burning on the fires. There were forty-four lodges in this camp, with a similar wealth of Indian goods, proving that they were the richest Indians in America. Everything was destroyed. The guides and citizens were much disgusted at the destruction of bales of buffalo robes and rich furs; but the doctor announced that they all had smallpox contagion in them. Then the command made for the Blood camp near the agency. Here the smallpox was raging fearfully. The warriors had skedaddled, but Colonel Baker sent a half-breed after them, who induced them to come back. They came back to their camp, mighty good Indians, delivered up about a dozen American horses that they had, including Broadwater's brown horse, and were for peace all the time. They then brought meat and all sorts of presents to the soldiers—being the first Indian treaty on record where presents were not made by the whites. Colonel Baker made a speech and told them that as they had taken no part in the murder he would spare them, and warned them never to trespass on the whites. The command was then gathered up and went into camp where they got a square meal, the first they had had for thirty-six hours. From the camp they returned to Fort Shaw, bringing with them over three hundred captured horses. All these particulars are authentic, received from officers of the command.[74]

After reading the above article, which reveals a strong dislike and disregard for Indian life among many white settlers and miners at that time in Montana Territory, one needs no imagination to realize that had not a degree of military discipline prevailed during this strike, i.e. if it had been carried out by an undisciplined citizen militia, the likelihood is great that even more Indian blood would have been shed. One can well imagine that the Blood camp might have been attacked as well. Conversely, and in all fairness to our early settlers and miners, hatred and disregard for the life of one's enemy usually springs forth from a fear of that enemy as well as the strong prospect and, in some cases, certain knowledge that the enemy also has little regard for one's own life. Residents of the East, having "solved" their problems with the American Indian inhabitants of their geographical areas some one hundred years prior, largely by expulsion and/or extermination, now found no reason to fear them.

One may be certain that the initial assault on the village did not go forward as described in the *Gazette*. Most commanders would not expose their troops Hollywood style in such an assault if they had the option of firing on the village from an effective range and concealed positions. We may

---

[74] *New York Times*, February 18, 1870.

be certain that had the attack gone forward as described by the *Gazette*, Major Baker's losses would have been much higher. Such an assault likely took place only after pouring heavy fire into the village from positions on the bluff.

The scandal continued in the East, and in response to House and Senate demands, the military leadership requested more specific information on the age, sex, and number of Indians killed and captured. Generals Sherman and Sheridan steadfastly refused, however, to criticize the conduct of the operation or its results. As late as March 17, 1870, Colonel Trobriand sent the following response to a request from the Division of the Missouri:

> Your telegram of March 16th received. The band of Piegans struck by Baker was guilty. Lots of murderers and thieves among them. They boasted of it themselves, and announced that in early spring, they would be down upon the settlements murdering and plundering.
>
> Baker never knew the state, age, sex, or condition of the Indians killed. How could he? Quarter was given to all known in time as women and children. Peace and security returned to the Territory. All residents grateful, and will show it.[75]

On March 12th General of the Army William Tecumseh Sherman forwarded Major Baker's report to the Secretary of War:

> In submitting to the Secretary of War the within report of Colonel Baker and of Inspector General Hardie, I will remark that they are this moment received, and will bear careful perusal, on account of the unusual severity with which the matter has been treated, both by Congress and the press.
>
> General Sheridan took the precaution to send General Hardie, a most humane and considerate officer, well known here in Washington, to Montana, to judge on the spot between the conflicting statements of parties there, and he justified the expedition against Mountain Chief's band of the Piegan tribe.
>
> Colonel Baker followed the instructions of his immediate commander, Colonel de Trobriand, but he does not report in detail, as is proper and usual, the sex and kind of Indians actually left dead at the camp on the Maria's. I will instruct General Sheridan to call on Colonel Baker for a fuller report on this point, to meet the

---

[75] March 17, 1870, Fort Shaw Letters and Telegrams Sent and Received.

*General Philip H. Sheridan—
commander, Department of Dakota.*
PHOTO COURTESY OF THE LIBRARY OF CONGRESS.

public charge, that of the number killed the greater part were squaws and children.

W.T. Sherman General[76]

General Sheridan complied with his superior's request and ordered a more complete report from Major Baker. In response Major Baker telegraphed General Sheridan on March 23rd:

Fort Ellis, M.T. March 23rd, 1870

General,

In answer to your telegram dated March 14th, 1870. I report that after having made every effort to get the judgement of the Officers of my Command. I am satisfied the following numbers approximate as nearly to the exact truth as any estimate can possibly be made.

That the number killed was (173) one hundred and seventy-three: of these there were 120 able men. (53) Fifty-three were women and children. That of captives afterwards released there were of women and children (140) one hundred and forty.

I believe every effort was made by Officers and men to save the Noncombatants and that such women as were killed were killed accidentally.

The reports published in the eastern papers purporting to come from General Alfred Sully are wholly and maliciously false, and if he has authorized them he knew them to be false.

If he has given authority to these slanders. I can only suppose it is that attention may be drawn away from the manifest irregularities that mark the conduct of Indian Affairs under his direction in this Territory.

It seems incredible that the false accusations of two Officers. General Sully and Lieut. Pease neither of whom have made any effort to

[76] House Exec. Doc. 197: 41st Congress, 2nd Session: 41–42, National Archives.

inform themselves in the matter. Should outweigh the reports of those who were engaged in the fight. And who feel that they have nothing to [illegible] or conceal in their conduct.

All that the Officers of this Command ask at the hands of the authorities is a full and complete investigation of the campaign, and less than this cannot in justice be conceded to them.

> E.M. Baker
> Major 2nd Cavalry Bvt. Col.
> Commanding Post[77]

Noting from the language in his report as it refers to General Sully, Major Baker must have been boiling over with anger and disgust at General Sully's professed "neutrality" in this entire affair. After all, General Sully, who had set the whole affair in motion, was now pretending to sit on the sidelines while others bore the blame for his actions. Baker's language is unusually harsh for a communiqué from a lower-ranking officer to his superiors at headquarters. It must have fallen on sympathetic ears, however, for little love was lost between the Office of Indian Affairs and the U.S. Army. Correspondence from General Sheridan to General Sherman on February 28th and excerpts from Sherman's reply on March 5th, sum up their feelings on the matter:

> Headquarters Military Division of the Missouri
> Chicago, Illinois, February 28th, 1870

> General W. T. Sherman
> Commanding U.S. Army, Washington, D.C.

> General: I have your telegram of the 26th instant, and will make the necessary reports and furnish you with all the facts in the case as soon as Colonel Baker's report is received. Colonel Baker could not make out his report at Fort Shaw, as he was obliged to return immediately to Fort Ellis to get shelter for his horses and men. I see that Mr. Vincent Collyer is out again in a sensational letter. Why did he not mention that Colonel Baker had captured over one hundred women and children? This he suppressed in order to do in-justice to that officer by deceiving the kind-hearted public, and to further the end of the old Indian ring, doubtless in whose interest he is writing.

> So far as wild Indians are concerned, the problem which the good

[77] March 23, 1870, Records of Posts, Continental Army Command 1820–1920, Fort Ellis Letters and Telegrams Sent and Received, Record Group 393.7, National Archives.

people of the country must decide upon is, who shall be killed, the whites or the Indians, they can take their choice.

Since 1862, at least eight hundred men, women, and children have been murdered within the limits of my present command, in most fiendish manner, the men usually scalped and mutilated, their — cut off and placed in their mouths, women ravished sometimes fifty and sixty times in succession, then killed and scalped, sticks stuck up their persons before and after death. I have myself conversed with one woman who, while some months gone in pregnancy, was ravished over thirty times successively by different Indians, becoming insensible two or three times during this fearful ordeal; and each time on recovering conciousness mutely appealing for mercy, if not for herself, for her unborn child. Also another woman ravished with more fearful brutality, over forty times, and the last Indian sticking the point of his saber up the person of the woman. I could give the names of these women were it not for delicacy.

It would appear that Mr. Collyer wants this work to go on. I mention these two cases especially, because they came under my own personal examination, and can give them as ample of what has occurred to hundreds of others.

The old Indian ring has again set itself to work to get possession of Indian affairs, so that the treasury can be more successfully plundered, and are printing and circulating throughout the country specimens of doggerel poetry, such as I inclose to you with this communication…

> I am, General, very respectfully,
> your obedient servant,
> P.H. Sheridan
> Lieutenant General[78]

On March 5th General Sherman responded to Sheridan's letter by stating:

…don't be unhappy about Indian affairs. There are two classes of people, one demanding the utter extinction of the Indians, and the other full of love for their conversion to civilization and Christianity. Unfortunately, the army stands between and gets the cuffs from both sides.[79]

---

[78] Quoted in Ege, *Tell Baker To Strike Them Hard!* 136–137.

[79] Ibid.: 138.

In another communication to General Sherman on March 18th, General Sheridan discussed the deaths of the Piegan women and children:

> During the war [Civil War, 1861-1865], did anyone hesitate to attack a village or town occupied by the enemy because women and children were within its limits? Did we cease to throw shells into Vicksburg or Atlanta because women and children were there? If women and children were saved in these places, it was because they had cellars to go into; and should any of the women and children of the Piegans have lost their lives, I sincerely regret that they did not have similar places of refuge. Though I doubt they would have availed themselves of them, for they fight with more fury than the men. The soldiers do not want to kill Indians. After long years of Indian frontier service, I am satisfied that they are the only good, practical friends that Indians have. We cannot avoid being abused by one side or the other. If we allow the defenseless people on the frontier to be scalped and ravished, we are burnt in effigy and execrated as soulless monsters, insensible to the sufferings of humanity. If the Indian is punished to give security to these people, we are the same soulless monsters from the other side. This is a bad predicament to be in; but, as I have said, I have made my choice, and I am going to stand by the people the government has placed me here to protect.

General Sheridan then expounded on the other role of the U.S. frontier soldier—the protection of the Indian from overzealous whites:

> The reservation is the last ditch to the wild Indian, but to get him there he must be forced on by the troops. Those who think he can be induced to go there by other means are mistaken.[80] When on the reservation he will have to be kept there by the presence of troops, and thus become tangible for the good work of civilization, and he can only be protected in his rights while there by the troops keeping off the emmigrants who encroach on his land. All these points are practically exhibited each year. The Cheyennes, Arapahoes, Comanches, Kiowas, and Apaches have just been forced on by the troops. During the last year, as soon as I withdrew the troops from the Sac and Fox reservation, the emigrants took possession. A flood of immigration, almost ten thousand strong, moved in solid mass and occupied the Osage reservation, because there were no troops to keep them off. All the other reservations on which the Indians

---

[80] Here the general overlooks the demise of the buffalo, which, along with the efforts of the U.S. Army, also played a role in forcing the Indians onto the reservations.

may yet be placed will be lost in the same manner, unless guarded by the military.[81]

On April 1, 1870, Colonel Trobriand wrote to the Department of Dakota: "Father Imoda just arrived from among the Indians. All Piegan chiefs sue for peace. Pete, the murderer of Malcolm Clark died of the small-pox. All news satisfactory from that quarter."[82]

On April 10, 1870, the *New York Times* printed the following article under the title:

> The Piegan Massacre—
> A Memorial from Wyoming—
> Gen. Sheridan Indorsed

> Chicago, Ill., April 9.—Gen. Sheridan has received a communication in the form of a petition signed by several hundred residents of Wyoming Territory relative to Indian difficulties and outrages in that region. They heartily approve of the Indian policy pursued by the Lieutenant-General, and indorse the so-called "massacre of the Piegans by Col. Baker." They also state that, while the settlers in Wyoming are constantly suffering by unprovoked depredations from Indians, they ask that sufficient military force, under the command of Col. Baker or some officer like him, be stationed in the Wind River Valley, to protect the white people and punish the Indians for any further atrocities which they may commit.[83]

The investigation requested by Major Baker and his officers never took place, and the scandal in the East abated. Eleven years later, in its May 8, 1881, issue, Fort Benton's newspaper the *River Press* still wrote in positive terms about Baker's attack on the Piegans. While presenting an argument for the preservation of a military post at Fort Benton in the face of plans by the U.S. Army to move the troops to other posts, the *River Press* wrote:

> Does anyone suppose that the civil authority could render the assistance it has, had it not been for the strength that is known to exist behind it, and which these Indians of the North have known how to respect since the so-called Piegan Massacre taught them that there was terrible force in a few cavalry troopers well led.[84]

---

[81] Quoted in Ege, *Tell Baker To Strike Them Hard:* 141–142.

[82] April 1, 1870, Fort Shaw Letters and Telegrams Sent and Received.

[83] *New York Times*, April 10, 1870.

[84] *River Press*, May 8, 1881.

Major Baker's Attack on Piegans on Marias River 1/19–1/29/1870

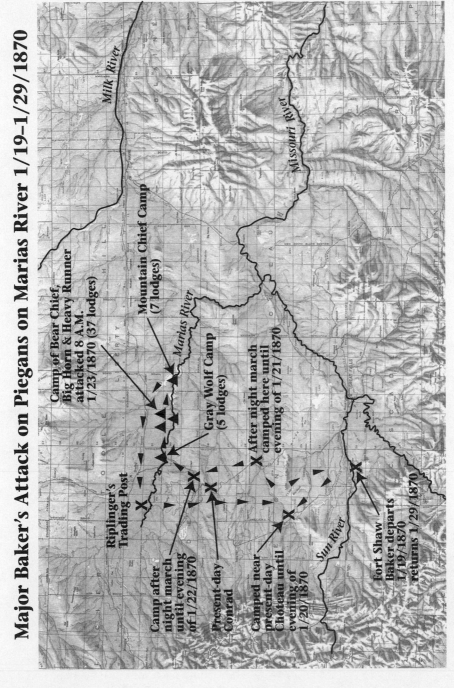

Milk River

Missouri River

Marias River

Sun River

Camp of Bear Chief, Big Horn & Heavy Runner attacked 8 A.M. 1/23/1870 (37 lodges)

Mountain Chief Camp (7 lodges)

Gray Wolf Camp (5 lodges)

After night march camped here until evening of 1/21/1870

Riplinger's Trading Post

Camp after night march until evening of 1/22/1870

Present-day Conrad

Camped near present-day Choteau until evening of 1/20/1870

Fort Shaw Baker departs 1/19/1870 returns 1/29/1870

Background map courtesy of USGS

CHAPTER NINE

The Piegan Campaign;
Latter-Day Reverberations;
Colonel Trobriand and 13th Infantry
Transfer to Utah Territory

O N FEBRUARY 8, 1913, SOME FORTY-THREE YEARS AFTER
Major Eugene Baker's attack on the Marias, one of his guides,
Joseph Kipp, now about sixty-five years old and by then married
to one of Chief Heavy Runner's daughters, forwarded the following affidavit
to the Indian Claims Commission:

> The Blackfeet Indian Agency
> Browning, Montana
> February 8, 1913

To Whom It May Concern:

I was employed at Fort Shaw, Montana as a guide and interpreter
in 1869-70. At that time there was not a very friendly feeling existing between the Whites and the Indians owing to the killing of
one Malcolm Clark[e]. The Whites took offense and the Indians
became aggressive, and the matter ran a long time without definite
action being taken against Pete Owl Child (Indian), the murderer
of Clark. The Civil Authorities and the United States Marshal were
powerless. Col. [W.F.] Wheeler [U.S. Marshal at the time] consulted me in regard to bringing Pete Owl Child to trial. I heard it said
that Pete Owl Child had stated that he would never be taken alive.
Thus matters drifted along. I made several trips to Pete's camp to
try and locate him but could not do so because nobody would give
me any information as to his whereabouts. I returned to the fort

each time and made my report that I could not locate the man, Pete Owl Child. I could see no other way than for the military to arrest Pete and so recommended. I was consulted several times as to what course to pursue to effect the arrest of Pete Owl Child. I told the Commanding Officer at Fort Shaw, Gen. De Tri Briand [sic], that the best way to arrest Pete Owl Child was to employ the military force. General Canby [this is referring to General Hardie]...was sent out from Washington, D.C....[actually Chicago]...to try to ascertain the best way to effect this arrest. My recollection is that after several days of consultation, the United States Marshal ordered the soldiers to go to the camp of Pete Owl Child and demand his surrender, and, if the Indians refused to give him up, and he refused to submit to arrest, to take him forcibly, and if the Indians opened fire to return their fire. These soldiers were under the command of Col. E. M. Baker of Fort Ellis.

An Indian chief, employed by the Government to try to effect the arrest of Pete Owl Child peaceably, Heavy Runner by name, had a camp something like six or eight miles distant from the camp of Pete Owl Child. When the soldiers reached the camp of Chief Heavy Runner, this chief went toward them as if to tell them who he was and to explain his mission there, but the soldiers opened fire and I myself counted two hundred and seventeen dead bodies after the firing.—Chief Heavy Runner was shot and killed during this firing. The able-bodied Indians at that time were out hunting and those who were killed were the Chief and such Indians as could not hunt, being the old men, women, and children. The Indians did not return the fire of the soldiers. Only one shot was fired by any of the Indians, this was after the general firing had ceased when one of the soldiers rode through the camp and shot everything and every person that was alive if he saw they had been injured. The soldier opened the flap of one of the tents and after shooting inside started to ride away when an Indian inside the tent drew his gun on this soldier and shot him in the back of the head or neck and knocked him from his horse. This was the only shot fired by any of the Indians.

After the firing was over, the soldiers gathered up the clothing, bedding, and subsistence and piled them up with a lot of wood and set fire to the pile and burned everything up. The soldiers then rounded up something like 5,000 head of horses belonging to the Indians, among which were some 400 or 500 head of horses belonging to Chief Heavy Runner, and drove these horses off.

Pete Owl Child got away from his camp and the soldiers returned to Fort Shaw without making his arrest. At the time Chief Heavy Runner was shot and killed I was distant from him, probably fifty or sixty yards. After the chief fell, some of the soldiers came his body and went through his pockets, taking papers of recommendation, etcetera. At the time the manner of burial among the Indians was to place the dead bodies in trees. The soldiers, however, on reading the papers taken from the body of Chief Heavy Runner, dug a grave and he was buried in the ground.

(signed) JOSEPH KIPP[1]

This and other versions of the event around the turn of the 20th century portray the village of Bear Chief and Bighorn as the village of Heavy Runner—a friendly village, in which only innocents were slain, i.e. helpless old men, women and children. That Heavy Runner was present in this village there is no doubt. That this was solely his village, containing innocent friendlies, is far less likely. That 5,000 horses were taken from the scene is a ridiculous exaggeration. That the able-bodied men were all out hunting is not likely for at least two reasons: one, it was extremely cold and the Indians would have been hunkered down riding out the harsh weather in their village; and two, the high number of Indians in the number of lodges. By the official count of 173 dead and 140 prisoners we arrive at a total of 313 inhabitants housed in 37 lodges. This is an average of nearly 8.5 Indians per lodge. If we return to Governor Stevens's report on the Piegans, we note his tally of 2,450 individuals housed in 350 lodges. This comes out at seven Indians per lodge. Also, among this number he calculated 875 warriors, or about 2.5 per lodge.[2] Thus for two reasons, one the extreme cold, the other the high number of persons occupying the 37 lodges, it is highly unlikely that very many warriors, if any, were out on a hunt.

Kipp makes no mention of the seizure and interrogation of Gray Wolf, who reported that Bear Chief and Bighorn[3] were encamped some six or eight miles distant. Kipp would have been the interpreter present at the

---

[1] Quoted in Robert J. Ege, *Tell Baker To Strike Them Hard!* 55–57.

[2] Isaac I. Stevens, in Report of the Commissioner of Indian Affairs 1853: 402. Annual Reports of the Commissioner of Indian Affairs, Record Group 75, SuDocs Number I 20.1, 1824–1920, National Archives.

[3] Bighorn was a signatory to the Treaty of 1865 and the Treaty of 1868, both unratified. Heavy Runner also was a signatory to both unratified treaties. Treaties Between the United States and the Nation of Blackfeet Indians, Oklahoma State University Library website.

time. If anything had been said about its being Heavy Runner's band, Kipp could have imparted this information to Major Baker then. It is far more likely that Chief Heavy Runner had moved his smaller band from their location near Riplinger's Trading Post (this was where Kipp had last reported it as of January 9th) some twenty miles or more downstream on the Marias to make common camp with Bear Chief and Bighorn, both indicted hostiles. Of the some 300 horses captured from this village, about 30 head were stolen from settlers, miners and freighters. Heavy Runner's reasons for being present with his band in this village will probably never be known, but that he was there to effect the arrest of Pete Owl Child is highly unlikely. He was not an agent of the government, as claimed by Kipp. Also, the time allowed the Indians by General Sully had expired.

It is of interest to note that not one government communication this author has been able to locate in the National Archives, for the period immediately following the attack, makes any mention of Chief Heavy Runner. General Sully describes his early January meeting with Heavy Runner and others, and Colonel Trobriand states in his orders to Major Baker that Heavy Runner's band is not to be attacked. But in all the U.S. Army communications following the attack, as well as all the Office of Indian Affairs letters this author has read, no mention is made of the death of Heavy Runner or a misguided attack on his band. Sully does state in his February 10th letter to Commissioner Parker that it was unfortunate that Mountain Chief's band was not the one that suffered. (This is not entirely true, since their tepees and supplies were destroyed following their successful flight.) Yet Sully makes no mention of Heavy Runner. Nor does Lieutenant Pease make any reference to Heavy Runner in his letter to Sully on February 6th, just after visiting survivors of the attack at the camp of Big Lake. Yet nearly all the modern literature describing the bloody event labels it an attack on the friendly village of Heavy Runner. Major Baker is now popularly described as a hard-drinking, craven killer of innocent Indians. That he was a hard-drinking soldier is very likely true; that he was a craven killer of innocent Indians is likely far from the truth.

On September 27, 1924, Horace Clarke was interviewed by David Hilger. Horace Clarke stated:

> As a matter of history, I will say that Col. Baker was after Mountain Chief and his band of Indians and we struck the wrong camp and finished the job...I don't mean to say that Col. Baker's charge was not justified as all these Indians needed a severe drubbing but it was

intended to get Mountain Chief as he had many desperate Indians with him and was a real warrior himself, but as it came about he got away.[4]

In this same interview, Horace Clarke, now an old man of some seventy-eight years, also exaggerated the number of horses captured as about 1,200. This was likely not intentional, since he probably did not have access to military reports or notes to recall events some fifty-four years past. He was also not seeking compensation for losses to family members, as was Joe Kipp.

Let us attempt to view the matter from the perspective of Major Baker. When the small camp of Gray Wolf was discovered, the major was told that the camp of Bear Chief and Bighorn, two indicted hostiles, was located about six or seven miles distant. From Baker's standpoint, surprise was of the essence. He moved rapidly to this camp and surrounded it, preparing to attack. Let us assume that upon his arrival at this camp he was informed of Heavy Runner's presence there. Was this sufficient reason to call off the attack on an otherwise hostile village? Had Baker done so, word would have quickly spread to the other bands—friendly and hostile; they would have scattered, and the expedition would have failed. Baker had one camp of hostiles before him; to bypass it and attempt a strike on Mountain Chief's camp (assuming he even knew where it was at that particular moment in the chain of events) would likely have resulted in no hostiles being struck at all. As Horace Clarke stated, the "drubbing" of Bear Chief's and Bighorn's camp was justified.

Major Baker was not on a civil law enforcement mission to "arrest" Pete Owl Child as stated later by Joe Kipp. His force was not accompanied by U.S. Marshal Wheeler or any of his deputies. He was out on a punitive military mission to strike Mountain Chief's or other hostile bands and inflict severe damage. If this village had consisted solely of Heavy Runner's band, then this author finds it of interest that Colonel Trobriand made no documentary comment on that fact. After all, a part of Major Baker's orders directed him to leave Heavy Runner's band unmolested. Yet Colonel Trobriand steadfastly defended Major Baker's actions. Along with representatives of the Office of Indian Affairs, Lieutenant Pease and Superintendent (General) Sully, he never made any mention of Heavy Runner being a casualty of the attack.

---

[4] Horace Clarke Reminiscences, SC 540, Montana Historical Society.

Modern-day historical writers have claimed that Baker was incapacitated by alcohol at the time of the attack. Baker did have a drinking problem, as was common among many in the military of his day. He was criticized, and, I might add, also defended for his reaction to a Sioux attack on his troops at the Yellowstone River on August 12, 1872.[5] There is, however, no concrete evidence that drinking impaired his judgment during this particular campaign. He had moved his command in stealth and in extreme cold for several days prior to the attack. At Gray Wolf's camp, he had the presence of mind to move quickly and decisively, acting on the latest intelligence he had received. Adhering to his orders he dispatched a sergeant and ten men to Riplinger's Trading Post. He also directed a rapid and efficient deployment of his troops around the hostile camp upon locating it. From the standpoint of an efficient military operation, the Indians were completely surprised and for the most part confined in a well-set trap as the attack commenced.

Modern writers often make much of the one-sided nature of the fight. In this case Baker's force was stronger, but there is possibly another reason for the one-sided results of the battle and the apparent helplessness of the Indians—alcohol consumption in the Piegan camp. General Sully's meeting with the Piegan chiefs had failed due to overindulgence of alcohol by many of the chiefs. He reported that they were too drunk to meet with him. If the Piegan leaders in the camp under attack were still in such an inebriated state, then they were possibly incapable of mounting an effective defense. Later in this book, we will discuss the attack on the Nez Perce village at the Big Hole Basin. Although taken completely by surprise in a dawn attack, the Nez Perce leaders rallied their people to an effective defense, causing heavy casualties in Colonel John Gibbon's command.

Some modern writers scoff at the fact that Baker lost only one man killed out of a force of some 250 men. Consider the far more recent Gulf War. With some 500,000 servicemen and -women deployed for the attack, we had fewer than 200 killed. This represents one death for every 2,500 troops deployed. At Baker's casualty rate, we would have lost over 2,000 killed in the Gulf War.

Joe Kipp offers us his latter-day version of events in which Heavy Runner advances from his tepee toward the troops with a document in his hand only to be shot down, this shot causing the troops to open fire on the camp.

---

[5] Baker was criticized by Lieutenant James Bradley, 7th Infantry, and defended by Lieutenant Edward McClernand, 2nd Cavalry. Edward J. McClernand, *On Time for Disaster.* 2–30.

Joe Cobell, also present, would many years later, in 1931, confide to a friend that he had fired the shot killing Heavy Runner in hopes that this would cause the soldiers to open fire on the village, thus giving his brother-in-law, Mountain Chief, a chance to escape.[6]

To return to events in the Montana Military District: on March 5, 1870, Colonel Trobriand reported to his superiors the theft of Indian horses by whites.

> Two white residents of the Crossing and an Indian from the Old Mission have stolen about twenty (20) horses from friendly Bloods on the Marias. On their return, I seized all horses to be returned to the owners, and caused the parties to be arrested by civil authorities. I leave tomorrow for Helena to appear as a witness against them. Justice must be done to all. Whites or Reds.[7]

Also in March, construction of a new post, Camp Baker, was commenced by Captain Clift and a company of soldiers from Fort Ellis. On March 10, 1870, Captain Clift advised that due to lack of sufficient transportation, which was needed for camp supplies, he had been unable to make "… a thorough examination of the valley of Smith's River." He reported that the Camp Baker site was located some ten miles north of the road to the Musselshell River and expressed his belief that a more suitable location could be found. He was also hopeful of establishing a shorter route back to Fort Ellis. "From here to Fort Ellis via Diamond City and Indian Creek Ferry, M.T. the distance is about 110 miles. I think the route through Blackfoot Pass will cut off 30 to 40 miles of travel."[8]

On May 2nd, mention was made of a public auction in which all the remaining unclaimed Indian ponies that had been seized from the Piegans by Major Baker were sold.[9]

The summer of 1870 saw a change of command in the Montana Military

---

[6] Robert J. Ege, *Tell Baker To Strike Them Hard!* 126. I feel that Mr. Cobell's claim is extremely far-fetched, especially coming some sixty-one years after the fact from an obviously very old man. Besides, if Joe Kipp was surprised by Heavy Runner's presence in the village, how could Joe Cobell know Mountain Chief was present? Furthermore, the village was already totally surrounded and the troops were preparing to open fire in any case. It is doubtful that had Mountain Chief been present, this alleged warning shot could have benefited him in any way.

[7] March 5, 1870, Fort Shaw Letters and Telegrams Sent and Received, Records of Posts, Continental Army Command 1820–1920, Record Group 393.7, National Archives.

[8] March 10, 1870, Camp Baker Letters Sent and Received, Records of Posts, Continental Army Command 1820–1920, Record Group 393.7, National Archives.

[9] May 2, 1870, Fort Shaw Letters and Telegrams Sent and Received.

District. The 13th Infantry Regiment along with its commander, Colonel Trobriand, was transferred in June to the Department of the Platte. On the morning of June 11th, "Hqts, NCO Staff, Band and Companies A, F, J, & K…" marched out of Fort Shaw, a post the regiment had occupied since the summer of 1867, en route to the Department of the Platte. They were replaced by the 7th Infantry Regiment commanded by Colonel John Gibbon. In keeping with the general sentiment of white Montana residents at the time, Colonel Trobriand was saluted upon his departure by a Helena newspaper:

> For His New Command. We yesterday met our friend Gen. De Trobriand, on his way to Utah with his command, which was encamped near the Widow Durgin's ranch on Ten Mile, last night. A number of his friends here pressed him to stay and partake of a little farewell festivity, but he preferred to stay in camp with his command, and declined their invitation with sincere thanks for their generous intentions. Gen. De Trobriand leaves the Territory with the kindest regards and best wishes of all good citizens. He has been an active and efficient commander of this district, has put forth zealous endeavors to preserve us from Indian depredations, and through his endeavors Baker's successful and efficacious expedition was organized and sent out against the murdering Piegans. His courtesy as a gentleman equaled his efficacy as a commander, and no citizen has ever had any business to transact with him, but was kindly received and attended to. He goes to his new command followed by the best wishes of the people of Montana.[10]

In examining available documentation, I noted a few other events occurring at Fort Shaw prior to Colonel Trobriand's departure. A letter dated December 26, 1869, identifies one Mr. Cutter as the post sutler. A letter dated February 2, 1870, notes that there had been no target practice at the post for the past two quarters and that an officer was now assigned to superintend target practice.[11] A letter from Colonel Trobriand to the adjutant general, Department of Dakota, discusses a dispute that arose between two officers at the post, 2nd Lieutenant Guthrie and Brevet Lieutenant Colonel Higbee, while at the table of Captain Constable. The dispute centered on Colonel Higbee's dog.

---

[10] Marie Caroline Post, *The Life and Memoirs of Comte Regis de Trobriand:* 422.

[11] Target practice in those days nowhere near approached the standards of our modern army.

Colonel Trobriand reported that Colonel Higbee stated, "If you kill my dog, I'll kill you!" whereupon 2nd Lieutenant Guthrie retorted, "Look out! When I kill your dog not to come near me, for I will have the first shot at you sure as I live!" 2nd Lieutenant Guthrie brought charges against Colonel Higbee, but Colonel Trobriand recommended dismissal since Brevet Colonel Higbee would soon be leaving the post and military service.[12]

---

[12] December 1869 through June 1870, Fort Shaw Letters and Telegrams Sent and Received.

CHAPTER TEN

Colonel John Gibbon Assumes Command of the Montana Military District; Operations and Events June 1870 to June 1872

THE ARRIVAL OF COLONEL JOHN GIBBON ALONG WITH components of his 7th Infantry Regiment in June 1870 commenced an extended period in the history of Fort Shaw under the command of a very experienced and competent officer. Gibbon would remain the Montana Military District commander, stationed at Fort Shaw, for almost eight years with the exception of a one-year stint in 1873–1874 when he served as superintendent of the army recruiting service in New York City.[1] During this period the troops at Fort Shaw, and at other posts in Montana Territory, were involved in two significant Indian campaigns: one against the Sioux and Northern Cheyenne in 1876 and later years, and the second against the non-treaty Nez Perce under Chief Joseph in 1877.

John Gibbon, born in 1827, was approximately forty-three years old on his arrival at Fort Shaw. His tour as commander of the Montana Military District was only part of an exceptional military career spanning forty-nine years from his appointment at West Point in 1842 until his retirement from the service in 1891. As a young officer he saw service in the Mexican campaign and, later, the campaign against the Seminole Indians in Florida. In 1860 he was assigned to a frontier post at Camp Floyd, Utah Territory. His diary of travel with his family over the Oregon Trail to the new assignment was later printed, along with a series of his other writings, in a book entitled *Adventures on the Western Frontier*. He also wrote other articles that enlighten

---

[1] John Gibbon, *Adventures on the Western Fronter:* xiv.

us about his experiences in Montana and during the campaigns against the Sioux and their Northern Cheyenne allies and, later, the Nez Perce.

At the onset of the Civil War, Gibbon had been assigned as General McDowell's chief of artillery, with the rank of brevet colonel. Gibbon was promoted to brigadier general in May 1862 and initially commanded the Iron Brigade, which he led in the battles of Second Manassas and Antietam. By the time of the Battle of Fredericksburg in December 1862, he had become a division commander. He was wounded at Fredericksburg, but recovered in time to lead his division, the 2nd Division, and also serve as acting corps commander of General John Hancock's 2nd Corps during a crucial phase of the Battle of Gettysburg. It was the 2nd Corps that bore the brunt of and threw back General Pickett's charge on July 3, 1863, deciding that pivotal Civil War battle.

Lieutenant Frank Haskell provided us with an excellent account of the battle. He served as Gibbon's aide-de-camp during the entire engagement and would later fall himself in 1864 at the Battle of Cold Harbor. He reported the losses to the 2nd Corps as nearly three-eighths of the entire force either killed or wounded, and summed up the accomplishment of Gibbon's 2nd Division:

> At Gettysburg its loss in killed and wounded was over one thousand seven hundred, near one half of all engaged; it captured seventeen battle-flags and two thousand three hundred prisoners. Its bullets hailed on Pickett's division, and killed or mortally wounded four Rebel generals, Barksdale on the 2d of July, with the three on the 3d, Armistead, Garnett and Kemper. In losses, in killed and wounded, and in captures from the enemy of prisoners and flags, it stood pre-eminent among all the divisions at Gettysburg....Under such Generals as Hancock and Gibbon, brilliant results may be expected. Will the country remember them?[2]

General Hancock was wounded in the thigh and Colonel Gibbon was shot through the left shoulder.[3]

Lieutenant Haskell described John Gibbon as weighing less than 150 pounds and noted that he was

> ... compactly made, neither spare nor corpulent, with ruddy complexion, chestnut brown hair, with a clean-shaven face, except his moustache, which is decidedly reddish in color, medium sized, well-shaped head, sharp, moderately-jutting brow, deep blue, calm eyes, sharp,

---

[2] Frank Aretas Haskell, "The Battle of Gettysburg," *The Harvard Classics*: 403.

[3] Ibid.: 406.

slightly aquiline nose, compressed mouth, full jaws and chin, with an air of calm firmness in his manner. He always looked well dressed.[4]

Haskell was near Gibbon during the two-hour bombardment by approximately 125 Confederate cannon of the 2nd Corps position on Cemetery Ridge. He reported that during the bombardment the general remarked to him:

> I am not a member of any church, but I have always had a strong religious feeling; and so in all these battles I have always believed that I was in the hands of God, and that I should be unharmed or not, according to His will. For this reason, I think it is, I am always ready to go where duty calls, no matter how great the danger.[5]

After his wounds healed, Gibbon once again returned to service and led his division through the Wilderness Campaign and the bloody battle at Cold Harbor, both fought in the summer of 1864. From there the Union Army moved on to the siege of Petersburg. By January 1865, Gibbon had been promoted to corps commander.[6]

The vast majority of Union officers who chose to continue their military careers at the close of the Civil War were required to accept considerable reduction in rank as the army was reduced in size from over 500,000 men to around 25,000. Therefore Brevet Major General Gibbon, as had been the case with General Trobriand, Custer, Miles, and numerous others, was reduced to the permanent rank of colonel for continued service in the army. Having commanded perhaps 20,000 to 30,000 men in the closing days of the Civil War, he now commanded only slightly more than 400 men in the District of Montana.

In examining Gibbon's long career with the army and his very extensive combat experience—wounded three times, twice during the Civil War and the third time at the much smaller but, for those involved, very intense Battle of the Big Hole in Montana Territory—one wonders why he is not better known. One thing is certain: he was a dedicated soldier with a breadth of combat and leadership experience few could match. Perhaps he did not exude the self-aggrandizement and self-promotion that some of his contemporaries such as George Armstrong Custer and Nelson Miles did. His contribution to the Union cause was certainly recognized by no less than Robert E. Lee's

4 Ibid.: 359.

5 Ibid.: 377.

6 Paul T. Schieps, "Darkness and Light": 1.

General John Gibbon with his granddaughter—commander, Montana Military District.

PHOTO COURTESY OF MONTANA HISTORICAL SOCIETY RESEARCH CENTER PHOTOGRAPH ARCHIVES, HELENA, MONTANA.

second in command, Confederate General James Longstreet, who frequently mentioned Gibbon in his memoirs *From Manassas to Appomattox: Memoirs of the Civil War in America* and praised him as an able enemy commander. John Gibbon served his country long and he served it well. He died on February 6, 1896, at his home in Baltimore. He is buried at Arlington National Cemetery.

Shortly after his arrival at Fort Shaw, Colonel Gibbon sent a letter to his superiors at the Department of Dakota in St. Paul, MN, outlining shortcomings at his new post. He noted that some quarters were still unfinished, with all four company quarters not yet shingled but covered with boards. He wrote that only two buildings were protected by outside plaster, and recommended it for the remainder. He further advised that the storehouses were inadequate and that more work was needed on the stable and corrals. The steam-powered sawmill was up and running but the current sawyer was incompetent. Gibbon advised that in about three weeks "water will be directed into garrison from Sun River…" and wells would not be needed (thus indicating completion of the post irrigation canal from the Sun River). He requested authority to hire nine citizen mechanics, six carpenters, two plasterers or masons and one sawyer. Another letter dated September 6, 1870, mentions the assignment of lots for the post garden to the various companies, water for irrigation now being available.[7]

On July 29, 1870, the Department of Dakota directed Gibbon to dispatch a cavalry detail to Cadotte Pass. From this point the army could monitor or check the movement of Indian tribes from west of the Rocky Mountains,

---

[7] June 30, September 6, 1870, Fort Shaw Letters and Telegrams Sent and Received, Records of Posts, Continental Army Command 1820–1920, Record Group 393.7, National Archives.

such as the Flathead and Nez Perce, as they moved east to the buffalo hunting grounds. Further, they could also check any movement of war parties from the east headed west, such as the Blackfeet, whose custom was to conduct raids on the Flathead Indians. Gibbon would later request permission to withdraw this force and put it to work on a new road leading from Fort Shaw to Camp Baker.[8]

Desertion and pilferage problems continued. On August 28, 1870, Colonel Gibbon ordered the post commander at Fort Benton to search all discharged soldiers headed downriver from that location, noting, "Spencer and Sharps carbines have been stolen from here." Also in August a request was made for one machinist and five men to operate the post sawmill.[9]

On October 5, 1870, a Board of Survey was requested to examine the quantity and condition of hay delivered to the post by Nimrod Ford of Sun River Crossing. Tragically, on October 12, 1870, the paymaster, Colonel Steinberger, was thrown from his horse while in Helena and died of his injuries. Three days later Colonel Gibbon wired a response to a message from Steinberger's brother, A.B. Steinberger, who lived in the East, that the steamers were no longer operating downriver from Fort Benton (due to low winter water levels). It was impractical to attempt to send the colonel's remains down the Corinne Road for shipment east on the transcontinental railroad. The colonel advised that Steinberger would be buried at Fort Shaw, then disinterred in the spring and shipped downriver on a steamer. Although hard to imagine in this day and age, such were the solutions demanded by the times and circumstances.[10]

Meanwhile, on October 18, 1870, the Superintendent of Indian Affairs for Montana Territory, General Alfred Sully, was replaced by J.A. Vaill.[11]

On October 24, 1870, the post requisitioned an allowance for 3,575 cords of firewood (fuel) for one year's use.[12] One can imagine that very little firewood remained in the general area of the post along the Sun River. In November the army intercepted and seized a shipment of buffalo robes at Sun River Crossing on suspicion that they originated with Indians and were infected with smallpox. Mr. J.A. Vaill, the new Superintendent of Indian Affairs, certified that they were all right for further shipment; however, the

---

8 July 29, August 24, 1870, Fort Shaw Letters and Telegrams Sent and Received.

9 August 28, 29, 1870, ibid.

10 October 5, 15, 1870, ibid.

11 House Exec. Doc. 1, 42nd Congress, 2nd Session, National Archives.

12 October 24, 1870, Fort Shaw Letters and Telegrams Sent and Received.

army surgeon recommended that the shippers be required to certify all means used to disinfect.[13] The eventual disposition of this shipment is unknown.

On November 16, 1870, a letter was received from Captain George S. Hallister at Camp Baker advising on the status of construction at that post. He also requested that he be allowed to permit members of his command to explore the surrounding area up to Judith Basin and "... also to watch the movements of the Indians. The lat[t]er are in great force near the 'basin'. I am informed that some strange tribes are there—although to all appearance these Indians are friendly, it would do no harm and perhaps some good to be prepared for any emergency."[14] The Judith Basin was a very popular buffalo hunting ground for numerous tribes.

In December 1870, U.S. Marshal Chas D. Hard requested that the army provide him with one noncommissioned officer and six enlisted men to assist in arresting whiskey smugglers, doubtless for illegal sale of whiskey to Indians. The issue of whiskey trade with the Indians was regulated by the Commissioner of Indian Affairs. When he needed someone arrested, he turned first to civil and not military authority. Civil authority was represented by the U.S. marshal and his deputies in Helena. The marshal frequently turned to the army for assistance, and military personnel were often detailed to assist the U.S. marshal or his deputies in effecting arrests. It was the preference of Colonel Gibbon that civil authority took the lead in these matters.[15] Although whiskey peddlers were seldom prosecuted, not all were able to escape justice. In his annual report for the year 1870, the Superintendent of Indian Affairs reported that two men were convicted in court at Deer Lodge for sale of whiskey to Indians. One received a sentence of eighteen months and the other six months. They were convicted on Indian testimony.[16]

In February 1871 an incident was reported, exact date of occurrence unknown, that certainly must have become a lasting topic of conversation among the troops at Fort Shaw. In discussing the ill effects of alcohol among the personnel, Post Surgeon Town reported that "One man ran five miles to the post in a maniacal condition one afternoon the past fall without any clothing whatever on his person, except a pair of stockings—the

---

[13] November 7, 1870, ibid.

[14] November 16, 1870, ibid.

[15] December 5, 1870, April 26, 1871, ibid.

[16] Alfred Sully in Annual Report of the Commissioner of Indians Affairs 1870, Annual Reports of the Commissioner of Indian Affairs, Record Group 75, SuDocs Number I 20.1, 1824–1920: 826.

temperature at the time being chilling and raw, he recovered his reason during the subsequent day."[17] Doubtless, this soldier became the subject of many jokes.

In March 1871, work was being carried out surveying and mapping roads between Fort Shaw and Camp Baker. As reported in an earlier chapter, problems arose with the telegraph line between Fort Shaw and Fort Benton. Captain W.B. Freeman, then acting post commander at Fort Shaw, telegraphed the assistant adjutant general of the Department of Dakota in St. Paul: "Operators from Benton and Shaw have been at work putting up line. Buffaloes rut the poles down and break wire so that it is impossible to keep it in order. Severe storms prevailing. Shall start out party to repair as soon as it is over."[18]

In May 1871, the Fort Shaw post ordered a small one-horse plow for use in the post garden. According to the communication, this type of plow was referred to in the south as a "bull tongue" and in the north as a "shood plow." Also in May, the post commander at Fort Shaw was contacted by Mr. Billing, Justice of the Peace at Brown's Creek, Montana Territory. Apparently, there had been words between one Mr. Jacob Smith and U.S. Army personnel at Smith's Ranch, a stage stop between Fort Shaw and Fort Benton, located about fifteen miles from Fort Benton near present-day Carter, MT. It would appear that this is the same stage station referred to in February 1868 as Tingley's Ranch, where one Mr. Smith was a partner of Tingley. In any case, relations between Mr. Smith and the U.S. Army were obviously not good. The reader will recall their refusal to allow the troops who were providing requested protection to bed their horses in extreme cold weather in vacant Wells Fargo stables![19]

On March 17, 1871, Mr. J.A. Vaill, the Superintendent of Indian Affairs for Montana, reported that he had removed one M.M. McCauley from his position as agent for the Blackfoot Nation for criminal conduct. In support of his action, he submitted the text of an affidavit sworn by Mr. Hugh Kirkendall on March 7, 1871, before Mr. W.S. Scribner, Clerk, Third Judicial District Court of the Territory of Montana, County of Lewis and Clark.

Mr. Kirkendall, thirty-five years old at the time, possessed a freighting business that had operated in Montana Territory for the past ten

[17] February 26, 1871, Fort Shaw Letters and Telegrams Sent and Received.

[18] March 7, April 17, 1871, ibid.

[19] May 6, May 30, 1871, ibid.

years. His business consisted of 300 head of mules and sixty wagons. He often hauled Indian goods to the various agencies. In his affidavit, Mr. Kirkendall stated that after initially meeting Mr. M. McCauley, U.S. Agent for the Blackfeet Indians, at Mr. J.A. Vaill's office in Helena about December 1, 1870, he was approached in a saloon by Mr. McCauley. McCauley asked him to go for a walk.

> We walked out alone, and McCauley informed me that he had made a requisition on the superintendent for a large lot of provisions for the Blackfeet agency; that he desired I should freight them. Said that he was afraid to talk with L. M. Black or Superintendent Vaill, because they were old fogies; that he wished to effect a private arrangement with me about the goods; that he would not want but a small portion of the amount purchased delivered at the agency; that he wished me to receipt for and take the whole amount from the superintendent, and leave part of them on the way, at a place he would thereafter designate…

Mr. Kirkendall further swore that it was his understanding that Indian agent McCauley intended to split the profits from a future sale of the diverted goods with him.[20] The author was unable to determine if Mr. McCauley was ever prosecuted for this scheme.

On May 11, 1871, Gibbon cabled W.F. Wheeler, U.S. marshal in Helena, that five deserters were possibly en route to Helena. In June 1871 a communication mentions the purchase of an advertisement in the *Helena Herald* offering a $30 reward for information leading to the capture of army deserters. The young, poorly paid soldiers were always tempted to desert and try their luck in the nearby gold fields. The following month the post provided engineers working for U.S. Surveyor General John Blaine at Dearborn Crossing with six breech-loading rifles and 600 rounds of ammunition.[21]

Once again word of Indian problems began coming in. On July 25, 1871, Colonel Gibbon sent a telegram from Fort Ellis to the Department of Dakota: "Yesterday a party of Indians made a raid into the valley eighteen miles below [Gallatin Valley] killing two men and stealing a number of horses. Parties left here last night and are now in hot pursuit. It is not known what Indians they were, nor how many."[22]

---

[20] House Exec. Doc. 81 (42-2): 2

[21] May 11, June 14, July 30, 1871, Fort Shaw Letters and Telegrams Sent and Received.

[22] July 25, 1871, Fort Ellis Letters and Telegrams Sent and Received, Records of Posts, Continental Army Command 1820–1920, Record Group 393.7, National Archives.

Mr. J.A. Vaill, Superintendent of Indian Affairs, reported that a party of Piegan marauders was intending to cross the Missouri near the mouth of the Sun River, allegedly en route to the Diamond City area, as in the past. Lieutenant Bomford rode out from Fort Shaw with thirty men and covered fords above and below this crossing point, but saw no evidence of Indians. The army disputed the possibility that the reported marauders could have been Piegans, for the tribe was believed to be north of the Canadian line at that time.[23]

In spite of the reported Piegan activity and the incident in the Gallatin Valley, later attributed to hostile Sioux under Sitting Bull, Colonel Gibbon remained confident that most of the countryside was secure. On August 22, 1871, he sent a telegram to the Department of the Dakota advising against the construction of a block house at Camp Baker. He suggested that a block house would be bad for trooper morale and

> "... calculated to bring the military into contempt in a country oc-
> cupied in every direction by women and children in ranches...I
> brought my family over direct road from Ellis." He noted that the
> country was free of Indians and scouting parties were chasing the
> marauders.[24]

In August 1871, a local Sun River Valley rancher, Mr. Robert Vaughn, visited Colonel Gibbon at Fort Shaw and informed him that Indians had stolen a team of his horses. The colonel dispatched the post guide, Hiram Bostwick, with six men to the camp of the Piegan Chief Gray Eagle, who was encamped upriver from the post on the Sun River. After discussion with Colonel Gibbon, Gray Eagle arranged the return of Mr. Vaughn's horses some eleven days after the theft.[25]

In September 1871, Colonel Gibbon continued some explorations in western Montana that he had commenced the previous autumn. These events are described in the book *Adventures on the Western Frontier* and make interesting reading for residents of Montana. One year earlier, in the autumn of 1870, the colonel had set out to locate and explore Lewis and Clark Pass. Riding up to Elk Creek or the South Fork of the Sun River and from there close by Haystack Butte, he wrote that there were a few settlers' cabins in the area. No one, however, seemed to know of Lewis and Clark

---

[23] July 28, 1871, Fort Shaw Letters and Telegrams Sent and Received.

[24] August 22, 1871, ibid.

[25] Robert Vaughn, *Then and Now:* 91–93.

Pass. The pass known to some residents of the area was Cadotte Pass, and Gibbon explored the approaches to both passes. For the modern reader familiar with the area, Lewis and Clark Pass crosses the Continental Divide into the Dearborn drainage from the head of Alice Creek. Cadotte Pass crosses the divide at the head of Cadotte Creek just west of present-day Rogers Pass (Montana Highway 200) and descends on the eastern slope to the Middle Fork of the Dearborn River. It is of interest that Colonel Gibbon, fond of hunting, sighted very little game on his ride from Fort Shaw to the present-day Augusta area in 1870—certainly not the massive buffalo herds reported by Captain Meriwether Lewis when his party rode through the area in 1806.

On September 23, 1871, Colonel Gibbon continued his hunting and exploration trip by traveling with a small party to Helena. He noted that on the night of September 30th to October 1st he was kept awake most of the night by a fire that threatened to engulf the entire town. Departing Helena they traveled west over the divide to Deer Lodge "…over a winding, well-graded road …" At Deer Lodge he stayed in Sam Scott's Hotel. He spent several days in this area exploring and hunting. He described Deer Lodge as a "…pretty little town…" and the valley as being "…dotted with farm houses, grain and grass fields…" He also noted that a survey team for the Northern Pacific Railroad was camped in the area seeking out a rail route.[26]

Upon leaving Deer Lodge, the party headed up the Little Blackfoot River to the mining town of Blackfoot City.[27] From there the group traveled over to the Blackfoot Valley and visited Lincoln Gulch, which Gibbon described as a "… somewhat dilapidated mining camp …" They were able to take a wagon up to the head of the Blackfoot, but wagons could not be taken over the pass. The party then crossed Cadotte Pass and traveled down the eastern slope. They spent one night at a ranch on the Dearborn River then returned to Fort Shaw.[28]

In October 1871 there was a meeting held at Fort Shaw between Colonel Gibbon, some Indian chiefs and Mr. J.A. Vaill, Superintendent of Indian Affairs. The author was unable to ascertain the purpose of the meeting, but we may assume that it was a routine matter.

---

[26] Gibbon: 42–43.

[27] As in the case of Diamond City, Blackfoot City has long since disappeared from Montana maps; it was populated by about 1,000 souls in 1870. It was located five to six miles north-northeast of present-day Avon and can be found on the current Helena National Forest map.

[28] Gibbon: 36–56.

CHAPTER ELEVEN

The Northern Pacific Railroad Survey in 1871; Operations and Events 1871–1872; Battle with the Sioux 1872

IN THE YEARS 1871–1873 AS WELL AS SUBSEQUENT YEARS, survey work was under way on the proposed Northern Pacific Railroad, which would lead from the rail terminus at Bismarck, then up the Yellowstone Valley and on west to Deer Lodge, Missoula and beyond. The Yellowstone Valley was occupied to the west by relatively friendly Crow Indians, but the greater portion to the east was hotly contested by the Sioux and their Northern Cheyenne allies. The U.S. Army was responsible for providing security for the railroad surveyors. This effort emanated primarily from Fort Abraham Lincoln (at Bismarck, ND) and Fort Rice, another Missouri River post some forty to fifty miles south of Abraham Lincoln, and Montana's Fort Ellis, with crews working their way from west to east and east to west toward each other. Plans were to meet at the mouth of the Powder River, just southwest of present-day Terry, MT. Troops from Fort Abraham Lincoln and Fort Rice provided protection for the westbound crew, and troops from the Montana Military District via Fort Ellis were tasked with the protection of the eastbound crew. This task would occupy Colonel John Gibbon's Montana forces for a portion of the summer and fall of 1871 and the greater part of the summer of 1872. It involved considerable hardship on troopers from Fort Ellis in the fall of 1871 and resulted, in August 1872, in a pitched battle between forces from Fort Shaw and Fort Ellis and the Sioux, about ten miles northeast of present-day Billings (near present-day Huntley, MT). In 1873 the troops of the Montana Military District would not be involved in the railroad survey efforts; this role was fulfilled by a much larger contingent of troops from Fort Abraham Lincoln and Fort Rice in the Dakota Military District.

In 1871 the eastbound survey was escorted from Fort Ellis to a point near present-day Billings by two companies of 2nd Cavalry under the command of Captain Edward Ball. In early November, their task fulfilled, Captain Ball's troops headed back to Fort Ellis. On the return march a tent caught fire, and the flames, fanned by high winds, destroyed a great deal of their equipment and supplies. Additionally, they were overtaken by extremely cold weather and deep snow. A troop under the command of Lieutenant Edward J. McClernand was sent out to meet them with supplies and assist in their return. This unit had great difficulty in crossing Bozeman Pass just east of Fort Ellis (now traversed by Interstate 90 between Bozeman and present-day Livingston). McClernand wrote:

> ...the deep snow greatly impeded our progress. Frequently it was necessary to dig out a horse or pack-mule that had sunken to his back, and in spite of our earnest efforts all day, night overtook us when only eight miles out; utterly worn out we went into camp in a little grove of pines just below the summit of the divide...That night the thermometer at Ellis, a thousand or more feet below us, fell to forty-eight degrees below zero, and the wind blew a gale. The cold was intense and sleep out of the question; even the animals huddled around the fire in seeking protection from the bitter blasts.[1]

The next day the rescue troop pressed on and later that afternoon met up with Ball's command near present-day Livingston. Both commands then marched back toward Fort Ellis but were overtaken by a blizzard that obscured all vision, with many of the troopers becoming disoriented and losing their way.

> Many troopers became numb, and a few threw themselves from their saddles and had to be lifted back and forced to follow...Some men wept and begged to be permitted to lie down and die; others wandered from the column and were forced to return by those who kept their heads.[2]

After five hours they went into camp. Trumpeter Page, who would

---

[1] Edward J. McClernand, *On Time for Disaster:* 24–25.

[2] Ibid.

later fall in 1877 at the Battle of the Big Hole, signaled with his trumpet, guiding many into the campsite. They reached Fort Ellis the next day. "...[F]ifty-three men out of the one hundred and fifty in the command had their extremities frozen, many of them severely."[3]

This same weather system also inflicted damage on two companies of the 7th Infantry from Fort Shaw. They had departed Fort Shaw on October 20th and proceeded to the Milk River country. Their mission was to drive whiskey smugglers identified as "Red River half-breeds" out of the area. They sold whiskey to various Indian camps with often disastrous results.

> The command struck the half-breed camp on the 2d of November, capturing and burning their supplies and ordering them out of the country. Here it remained until the 16th, when it broke camp en route to Fort Shaw. On the 24th, about noon, the command was overtaken while on the march, by a most terrific storm...[4]

Colonel Gibbon would later cable the Department of Dakota, "The Milk river expedition returned on the 25th. One half of the men were badly frozen the 24th in a terrible storm with the thermometer 35 degrees below zero. They are now all in and doing well. Expedition successful."[5]

In an aside, it will be of interest to the reader that Sitting Bull's camp also fell victim to these whiskey peddlers in the autumn of 1872 while camped on the Dry Fork of the Missouri. As a result, numerous Sioux killed or harmed one another after becoming intoxicated. This event was witnessed by Frank Grouard, who was a prisoner in Sitting Bull's camp at the time.[6]

On April 3, 1872, Company K under Captain James M. Sanno, consisting of two officers and thirty-two enlisted men, departed Fort Shaw en route to the vicinity of Badger Creek near present-day Browning, MT, to arrest illegal whiskey traffickers. They arrived in Badger Creek on the 4th. On the 5th they arrested the traffickers (number unknown) and the following day departed for Fort Shaw. They arrived back at Fort Shaw with the prisoners on April 8th, having marched 212 miles.[7]

---

[3] Ibid.: 25–26.

[4] A.B. Johnson, History of 7th Inf. Regt., U.S. Army Center for Military History website: 505.

[5] November 27, 1871, Fort Shaw Letters and Telegrams Sent and Received, Records of Posts, Continental Army Command 1820–1920, Record Group 393.7, National Archives.

[6] Joe DeBarthe, The Life and Adventures of Frank Grouard: 106–108.

[7] April 1872 Fort Shaw Post Return, Records of the Adjutant General's Office, ca. 1775–ca. 1928, Record Group 94, National Archives.

In May 1872, Colonel Gibbon acted to squelch a rumor of an Indian atrocity. He wrote to the editor of the *Helena Herald*, "Please publish the fact that the report in regard to the murder of Mr. Simmons and party is totally without foundation. They are on their way up on the *Nellie Peck* [a steamer], which will probably reach Benton tomorrow."[8]

On June 10, 1872, local Indian problems and illegal whiskey sales had to be addressed once again. Gibbon wrote to Mr. J.A. Vaill, Superintendent of Indian Affairs in Helena, that "Some fifteen lodges of Piegans are camped on the South Fork of Sun River. The whiskey traffic is active and should be stopped or the Indians sent away from there." By the 27th of June, Gibbon was at Fort Ellis. He ordered the post commander at Fort Shaw to provide protection for surveying parties under the surveyor general of Montana.[9]

The Northern Pacific Railroad survey was continued in the summer of 1872. Gibbon began preparations for this expedition in early July. Since the survey would be pressing farther east down the Yellowstone, to the mouth of the Powder River from the mouth of the Bighorn, there was greater potential of conflict with the hostile Sioux and Northern Cheyenne. More troops would be needed. Colonel Gibbon advised the Department of Dakota that the effective strength at Fort Shaw was 268 men including twelve officers, and that he had ordered that 8,000 pounds of hard bread be shipped from Fort Shaw to Fort Ellis in support of the expedition. He further ordered that fifty-three mules be sent from Fort Shaw to Fort Ellis. On July 5th, while at Fort Ellis, Gibbon cabled E.G. Maclay & Company in Helena: "Have mule transportation at Shaw on the 13th instant to bring sixty thousand (60,000) pounds to this post, and mule transportation here (Ellis) on the 22nd instant for two hundred thousand (200,000) pounds to go down the Yellowstone."[10]

Also on July 5th, Gibbon cabled the post commander at Fort Shaw:

> Hold four companies, filled up by detachments from other companies, to a total enlisted of 200 in readiness to leave for this post [Fort Ellis] to go down the Yellowstone, as soon as transportation can be sent you. Report the number of wagons available to bring your companies this far. The men are to be in light marching order without knapsacks, and

---

[8] May 16, 1982, Fort Shaw Letters and Telegrams Sent and Received.

[9] June 10, 27, 1872, ibid.

[10] July 4, 5, 1872, ibid.

with overcoats, rolled blankets and extra shoes and stockings. One
hundred rounds of ammunition will be taken per man.[11]

Gibbon further advised the Department of Dakota that 200 infantrymen were available at Fort Shaw and 200 cavalry troopers at Fort Ellis for
the expedition. This would leave sixty-eight men at Fort Shaw and remove
every effective man from Fort Ellis. He further advised that he would have
to bring in the company currently guarding Flathead Pass. He reported having no Gatling guns in the Montana Military District.[12]

On July 7th Gibbon sent a telegram to Samuel Hauser in Helena and
requested that the bridges over the Little Prickly Pear be repaired in preparation for the expedition. He offered the assistance of troops to complete
necessary repairs. Two days later he cabled the post commander at Fort
Shaw and requested that he send one lieutenant, two NCOs and fifteen
enlisted men to cover Flathead Pass against possible incursion by hostile
Indians into the Gallatin Valley while the force at Fort Ellis was drawn down
for the survey expedition.[13]

On July 16, 1872, it was reported that 11,000 pounds of freight had
to be left behind at "the Birdtail." It was too much weight. The freight
would eventually be recovered. It was also reported that the ox train
was presently "in the canyon" (likely referring to the Little Prickly Pear
canyon) and the freight would be transferred to the mule train upon
arrival in Helena.[14]

On July 27, 1872, Colonel Gibbon was able to report to the Department
of Dakota that the infantry had departed Fort Ellis for the Yellowstone
and that the cavalry would follow the next day. He reported his aggregate
strength as 382 men, plus 30 citizens with the freight train. He further advised that the unit from Fort Shaw was in place at Flathead Pass and that the
original Flathead Pass detail of 41 men would now man Fort Ellis while the
expedition was absent.[15]

The force escorting Ferdinand V. Hayden and his corps of surveyors
consisted of Companies C, E, G and I of the 7th Infantry from Fort Shaw

---

[11] July 5, 1872, ibid.

[12] July 7, 1872. District of Montana Letters and Telegrams Sent, Department of Dakota, Record
Group 393.5, National Archives.

[13] July 7, 9, 1872, ibid.

[14] July 16, 1872, ibid.

[15] July 27, 1872, ibid.

and Companies (Troops) F, G, H and L of the 2nd Cavalry from Fort Ellis. The force was commanded by Major Eugene M. Baker, who had led the attack on the Piegans in 1870.[16] The men marched down the Yellowstone to a point just above the mouth of Pryor's Creek.[17] They arrived there on August 12th. It was at this point that the eastbound survey had discontinued work the previous autumn. Two days later, at this position, they would come under attack by a large force of Sioux Indians.

Lieutenant James H. Bradley, who accompanied the force from Fort Shaw, provided us with a fine historical record of the battle in his diary later published as *The March of the Montana Column*. Also present was Lieutenant Edward J. McClernand, who gave an informative but more brief account of the fight in his book *On Time for Disaster*, which he wrote many years later in 1926. McClernand was an officer with the 2nd Cavalry from Fort Ellis.

Bradley describes the rationale for the fight:

> … a heavy force of Sioux warriors, variously estimated at from eight hundred to one thousand strong, were ascending the river upon a hostile incursion against the Crows; and about the twelfth of August discovered that they were in the presence of Baker's command. This unexpected recontre created a division in their councils, many being anxious to give over their former design and measure powers with the troops, while the more prudent minority were disposed to avoid so hazardous an enterprise and continue their advance on the less prepared and unsuspecting Crows. At length, however, tempted by the large spoils in horses which they hoped by dexterous management to secure at little cost to themselves, they declared in favor of an attack upon the troops, and fixed upon the morning of August 14th [1872] for carrying the plan into effect.[18]

Baker's force, about 400 men, soldiers and citizens, were encamped on an open field, about forty to sixty acres in size, alongside the Yellowstone. This field was surrounded by a slough timbered with willows and, at one end, a line of cottonwood trees. Farther back, the camp was somewhat enclosed by the bluffs extending along the river, but they were at long-range rifle distance. The camp contained about one hundred wagons, which "…were parked in the form of an ellipse with one end open, so as to form a corral into which

---

[16] James H. Bradley, *The March of the Montana Column*: 56.

[17] McClernand, *On Time for Disaster*: 28.

[18] Bradley: 56–57.

the wagon mules, left out to graze [in the field] during the night, could be driven if necessary."[19]

It was the objective and hope of the Sioux to capture a large number of animals with as little fighting and loss to themselves as necessary. They concealed a large force behind the screen of cottonwood trees on one end of the camp and moved another sizable force into the willows growing along the slough. The plan was to rush the camp, causing great confusion, and simultaneously swarm across the field, driving off or otherwise secur- ing as many government animals as possible, then quickly withdraw with their booty at little or no loss to life to themselves. Prior to their attack, a few

Lieutenant James H. Bradley.
PHOTO COURTESY OF MONTANA HISTORICAL SOCIETY RESEARCH CENTER PHOTOGRAPH ARCHIVES, HELENA, MONTANA.

of the hostiles actually crept into the midst of the camp, killing a dog and stealing saddles from under the noses of some sleeping prospectors, who were camped with the column.

Fortunately for the army and unfortunately for the Sioux, the command- er of the guard detail, Lieutenant William Logan, among others in the camp, had become suspicious that Indians were present in the area. Earlier that day a couple of stray Indian dogs had been spotted near the camp. Major Baker, however, was not overly concerned about an attack and that evening had, in Bradley's words, "...permitted himself to become unfitted for the proper performance of his duties by an over-indulgence in strong drink."[20] In spite of the commander's lack of concern, Lieutenant Logan posted his guard, consisting of twenty-six men drawn from both the cavalry and the infantry, between the field and the slough some 300 yards from the camp. A squad of herders also moved about among the animals as they grazed in the field. At approximately 3 A.M. the hostiles commenced their attack with a volley of gunfire. As they moved onto the field to capture the animals, the herders fired on them and quickly drove most of the herd into the camp

[19] McClernand, *On Time for Disaster:* 28.

[20] Bradley: 56–57.

Captain William Logan.

enclosure. Lieutenant Logan's guards then opened a hot fire on the hostiles moving about in the darkness, causing them to withdraw out onto the prairie. Initially confusion reigned among the men and officers in the main portion of the camp, and there was some delay in receipt of commands from Major Baker. In the interim the prospectors, about twenty in number, quickly formed up under Lieutenant Jacobs and provided valuable assistance to the guard force. After recovering from their repulse, the hostiles moved back into the cottonwoods and attacked the guard in heavy force. "But the citizens with Lieutenant Jacobs poured in a rapid fire upon their flank while the guard received them firmly in front, handling their breech-loaders with such effect that again the Indians speedily withdrew."[21]

By this time Major Baker had ordered the remainder of the command into action. Shortly before daylight, Lieutenant Reed discovered movement in the willows near the camp as the Sioux were again attempting to approach and rush the camp. He ordered a heavy volley of fire into the willows and the surprised Indians quickly retreated. As they withdrew across the prairie toward the bluffs, they were observed to carry "…with them their killed and wounded slung across their horses in their front, Lieutenant Quinton, who occupied a favorable position for observing their movements, counted eighteen thus borne from the field."[22]

The Indians then sniped at the soldiers from the bluffs, with an occasional warrior tempting fate by riding his pony rapidly along the front while fired upon by the troops. Lieutenant McClernand would later describe the horsemanship skills demonstrated by the hostiles in this particular action. "I do not recall that any were killed, but several were wounded. One pony

21 Ibid.: 58–60.

22 Ibid.: 61.

was killed; his rider picked up by two braves dashing along in rear, and by them carried away, one on either side of the dismounted warrior." Finally, at about 6:30 A.M. the hostiles withdrew down the valley.[23]

Lieutenant Bradley reported that the hostiles left three dead on the field. The actual number of dead and those who later died from wounds was no doubt much higher. Sergeant McLaren of Company C, 7th Infantry was killed during the action. A citizen named Francis would later die of wounds received in the battle. Three privates were wounded: O'Mally of Company C, Ward of Company L, 7th Infantry, and Cox of Company F, 2nd Cavalry.[24]

Lieutenant Bradley, an infantryman, was critical of Major Baker's conduct prior to and during the fight, but Lieutenant McClernand, a cavalryman, would years later describe the onset of the action from his perspective in the camp:

> At first the confusion was great owing to the difficulty of distinguishing friend from foe. Some people thought the pickets were deceived as to the presence of Indians, and that they were firing at imaginary red-skins, but a volley from the latter, together with their demoniacal yells and war-whoops did away with that belief.

McClernand defended Major Baker:

> This engagement caused much controversy, and the commanding officer was criticised by many, but in my opinion this criticism was largely unjust. The critics charged, with other censure, that bad judgment was shown in the selection of the camp-ground. With that view I distinctly disagreed.[25]

The survey was resumed the next day, but Colonel Hayden had become concerned that the troops available could not provide adequate protection for his surveyors. It was necessary, on occasion, to have the surveyors dispersed over distances as great as two to three miles.[26] On August 20th, some six miles above Pompeys Pillar, he chose to abandon the Yellowstone and instead ran a line northward to the Musselshell River and then westward along that stream and up its south fork toward the Missouri. On

---

23 McClernand, *On Time for Disaster:* 29–30.

24 Bradley: 63.

25 McClernand, *On Time for Disaster:* 29–30.

26 Ibid.

September 25th the expedition was terminated, with the Fort Shaw contingent marching via Camp Baker back to Fort Shaw and the Fort Ellis contingent proceeding directly to that post. According to Lieutenant Bradley, the army had been more than willing to continue down the Yellowstone but Hayden's "…fears got the better of him."[27] Bradley later noted, "Engineer Hayden, though wholly responsible for the failure to prosecute the survey to Powder River as had been originally designed, afterwards endeavored to shirk it upon the military."[28] The railroad survey would resume the following summer, but be escorted by a much larger contingent of troops from Forts Abraham Lincoln and Rice in Dakota Territory.

---

[27] Ibid.: 30–31.

[28] Bradley: 63.

Northern Pacific Railroad Survey of Summer 1872

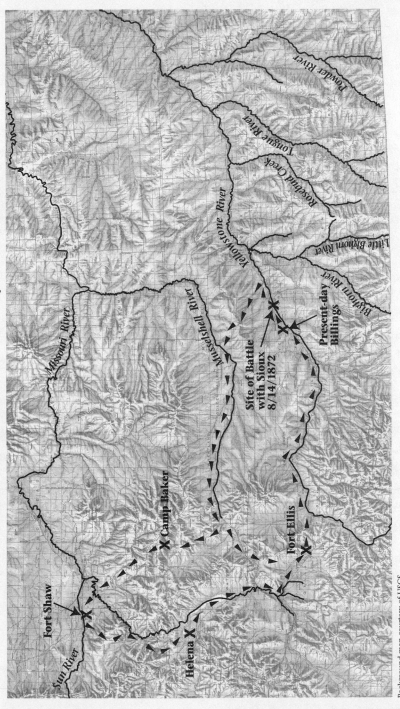

Background map courtesy of USGS

7th Infantry departs Fort Shaw 7/28, marches to Fort Ellis, then with 2nd Cavalry moves down Yellowstone. After battle on 8/14 survey is moved up Musselshell, then on 9/25 the units return to their posts.

CHAPTER TWELVE

Operations and Events
Autumn 1872 to Autumn 1873;
The Stanley Expedition and the
N.P.R.R. Survey Summer 1873; Custer
Battles Hostiles Under Sitting Bull

I N NOVEMBER 1872, THE FORT SHAW TROOPS TOOK UP MORE routine duties as Company D, 7th Infantry, under Captain Richard Comba, escorted a delegation of Sioux chiefs, along with Indian agent A. Simmonds, to Fort Browning, Montana Territory. Fort Browning, located on the Milk River, served as an agency for the Gros Ventres but was also populated by other Indian tribes. The chiefs were returning from Washington, D.C., to their reservation.

Also in November, the post commander at Fort Shaw telegraphed Fort Ellis advising, "There is a considerable body of Crow Indians in this section and their presence is causing complaint and alarm among the settlers."[1] This information was obviously intended for forwarding to the Indian agent at the Crow Agency. The results of the concern are not known, but certainly no serious incident occurred, as it did not appear in the annual report of operations covering this period.

On November 25th, the District of Montana headquarters received the following cable from department headquarters in St. Paul: "It is reported that Bull Eagle a [illegible] Sioux Chief last summer captured a wagon on the Musselshell containing two men, one woman and several children all of whom he murdered. Ascertain if such an occurrence transpired and report by telegraph." The author was unable to locate a response that would either verify or deny this information.[2]

---

[1] November 11, 1872, Fort Shaw Letters and Telegrams Sent and Received, Records of Posts, Continental Army Command 1820–1920, Record Group 393.7, National Archives.

[2] November 25, 1872, ibid.

Relieved from providing a large escort for the Northern Pacific Railroad survey, the military personnel stationed at Fort Shaw, Fort Ellis and Camp Baker experienced few Indian problems during most of 1873. Colonel John Gibbon was absent from Fort Shaw during the period November 1872 to August 1874, assigned to recruiting duties in New York City. The district was commanded in his absence by Lieutenant Colonel C.C. Gilbert.[3] On September 14, 1873, Captain D.W. Benham, acting post commander at Fort Shaw, submitted Fort Shaw's annual report of operations, which covered the first eight months of that year. With reference to Indian problems, he reported none of importance. "The Indians generally remain in a satisfactorily quiet condition."[4]

The troops were occupied with routine maintenance, scouting and escort duties. From April 30 to May 27, 1873, Company K, 7th Infantry, commanded by Captain James M. Sanno, escorted Indian supplies to the Assiniboine Agency at Fort Belknap and supervised their distribution. From July 31 to August 28, 1873, Company F, 7th Infantry, led by 1st Lieutenant Burnett, made repairs to the telegraph line between Helena and Fort Shaw. Simultaneously, Lieutenant J.T. Van Orsdale and his Company D conducted repairs on that portion of the line between Fort Benton and Fort Shaw. During August and September, Company C under Lieutenant Quinton escorted supplies to the Fort Peck Agency for delivery to the Teton Sioux and other Indians.

Captain Benham also reported the following improvements made at Fort Shaw and vicinity during the year 1873:

> The Engine house repaired, a new steam engine received and placed
> in running order for sawing wood and supplying the garrison with
> water. Fences constructed in rear of officers' quarters and around
> the cemetery...A ferry boat with capacity for one six mule team and
> waggon, has been constructed at the crossing of the Missouri river,
> on the road leading to Camp Baker, M.T.[5]

This ferry was likely located at or near the site of the present-day bridge over the Missouri River at Ulm, MT.

On May 23, 1873, the commander at Camp Baker reported that thirty lodges of Nez Perce under Chief Looking Glass had wintered with the

[3] November 1872 through August 1874, Fort Shaw Post Return, Records of the Adjutant General's Office, ca. 1775–ca. 1928, Record Group 94, National Archives.

[4] September 14, 1873, Fort Shaw Letters and Telegrams Sent and Received.

[5] Ibid.

Crows and then returned to Lapwai in western Idaho.[6] About thirty Nez Perce remained behind in the Crow camp. Later that year, Captain W.B. Freeman, post commander, would cable the adjutant general of the army in Washington, D.C., requesting the discharge of three men of H Company, 7th Infantry—Privates Richard Templeton, Thomas Vaughan and William Willis.

> These men are completely under the domination of their appetite for liquor as to be totally unfit for service, they cannot be trusted on detached service of any kind, where there is the possibility of obtaining liquor,—They are simply a nuisance to the Company and I think the service would be the gainer from their discharge."[7]

In September, the Camp Baker commander wrote his annual report stating that there were no Indian problems in his area of operation, i.e. for one hundred miles from his post in every direction. He added that the only Indians that might cause concern in the area were Blackfeet and Piegans and that they had not been present in the area for three years.[8] Earlier that summer, sixty cavalry troopers had been dispatched from Fort Ellis down the Corinne Road to Corinne, UT, to receive and drive back 134 head of cavalry horses. They departed Fort Ellis on June 12, 1873, and arrived in Corinne on July 9.[9]

The N.P.R.R. survey resumed in the summer of 1873. The escort was provided that year by the District of Dakota, with a much larger force than could be mustered from the small contingents manning the Montana Military District. The expedition was under the command of Colonel David S. Stanley and comprised of ten companies of the 7th Cavalry commanded by Lieutenant Colonel George Armstrong Custer, plus a number of infantry companies: the 8th and 9th, commanded by Lieutenant Colonel L.P. Bradley, three companies of the 17th Infantry and one company of the 6th commanded by Major R.E.A. Crofton, and five companies of the 22nd Infantry commanded by Captain C.J. Dickey. Also included in this force were twenty-seven Indian scouts and two three-inch Rodman

---

[6] May 23, 1873, Camp Baker Letters Sent and Received, Records of Posts, Continental Army Command 1820–1920, Record Group 393.7, National Archives.

[7] August 3, 1873, ibid.

[8] September 18, 1873, ibid.

[9] June 12, 1873, District of Montana Letters and Telegrams Sent and Received, Record Group 393.5, National Archives.

artillery pieces. "The transportation, including every wheeled vehicle, amounted to 275 wagons and ambulances. The civilian employees numbered 353 men. The number of mules and horses to be foraged was 2,321."[10] Seven hundred head of beef cattle were also driven along to provide beef as needed. The engineers conducting the survey were under the direction of Thomas L. Rosser, the chief engineer.[11]

Lieutenant Colonel Custer would, of course, fall with a large portion of his command at the Little Bighorn some three years later and be forever etched into the history of Montana Territory.

Lieutenant Colonel George A. Custer.
PHOTO COURTESY OF MONTANA HISTORICAL SOCIETY RESEARCH CENTER PHOTOGRAPH ARCHIVES, HELENA, MONTANA.

Custer, raised in northern Ohio, had barely made the required academic grade at West Point, graduating last in his class just prior to the commencement of the Civil War. Once in the field as a young lieutenant, however, his boldness and daring coupled with considerable military talent quickly caught the attention of the higher-echelon commanders—no less than General George B. McClellan, early in the war, and General Philip Sheridan in the latter portion of the war. Serving in the Union cavalry, he quickly rose to the rank of brevet brigadier general, in fact the youngest general in the Union army. At the conclusion of the war, Custer was reduced in rank to lieutenant colonel. Such reductions were the case with most professional officers who wished to continue service in the army. He would attain de facto command of the 7th Cavalry Regiment, which was stationed in Kansas, the unit's official commander, a colonel, always being absent on other assignments.

While stationed in Kansas he made a name for himself as a well-known Indian fighter. Although his regiment spent a great deal of time chasing

[10] David Sloan Stanley, *Personal Memoirs:* 244–245.

[11] Ibid.: 247.

war parties about Kansas, Oklahoma and Colorado territories, usually with little effect, as was the case with most army units on the frontier, Custer managed on one occasion, after tracking hostiles for over a hundred miles, to locate an Indian camp, capture some of their chiefs and force them to surrender white female captives—in effect, a bloodless coup. On another, more famous, occasion Custer and his 7th Cavalry tracked hostiles to a Cheyenne encampment on the Washita River in northern Oklahoma and struck it on November 27, 1868, inflicting heavy casualties, seizing 700 Indian ponies and taking prisoner a large number of women and children. Ironically, this was the village of Cheyenne Chief Black Kettle, whose village had been razed a few years earlier at Sand Creek by the Colorado militia under John Chivington.

Latter-day writers and some serious historians have criticized Custer for his raid at Washita. The fact remains, however, that the Cheyenne at Washita held a number of white captives in their camps, which were strung out along the Washita River. During the attack, one of Custer's soldiers witnessed an Indian woman running away, gripping a young white male captive. Upon seeing that she could not escape, she stabbed the young boy to death, then was shot down by Custer's troopers. Also in searching through tepees in the next encampment along the river, Custer's troopers found several white scalps and further evidence of white captives' being held in this series of encampments.

Custer had split his command prior to the surprise attack at Washita. One portion of that command, an eighteen-man contingent, was surrounded and wiped out by the Cheyenne. Custer would later be criticized for not making a greater effort to locate these missing soldiers before departing from the area. As Custer's troopers were consolidating their victory, i.e. destroying Indian supplies and eventually shooting the 700 captured Indian ponies, (for fear they would fall back into Indian hands), ever larger numbers of warriors began to appear on the slopes, coming in from neighboring camps downriver. Fearing that his command might be surrounded, he opted to withdraw with his captives over the frozen ground the many miles back to his base camp. He correctly assumed that if the troopers had not yet appeared, they were probably already dead anyway.

His successful raid at the Washita River was widely acclaimed. Among the soldiers and officers on the frontier, he had many admirers as well as critics inside and outside the U.S. Army. He was admired by many senior officers, no less among them than Sherman, Sheridan and Terry. He was also disliked by numerous other ranking officers, who likely viewed Custer as a young upstart who had gained the favor of the top echelon and thus rank well beyond his years. He also knew how to advertise himself to the public, writing numerous magazine articles of his and the 7th Cavalry's exploits and finally publishing a book entitled *My Life on the Plains*. It is of note that in his writings he did not solely heap praise upon himself but also frequently credited, by name, the brave deeds and accomplishments of many of his subordinates, including enlisted men.

His attractive young wife, Elizabeth (nicknamed Libby), would, after Custer's tragic death, also become an accomplished author. For years after his death in 1876, Custer was considered a national hero. Then, in the early 20th century and thereafter, many citizens of the United States began to have second thoughts regarding the white man's treatment of the Indians. It became popular to condemn Custer for many of his actions, primarily his decisions and actions at the Little Bighorn—once again with a marvelous amount of 20-20 hindsight. These criticisms seldom take into account the conditions Custer faced at the time, as well as his orders.

To return to the N.P.R.R. survey in the summer of 1873: It is obvious, from the size of the escort force, that the U.S. Army was taking the presence of hostile Sioux along the Yellowstone River very seriously. The force was formed from contingents at Fort Rice and Fort Abraham Lincoln in Dakota Territory. On July 13, 1873, after hard going in muddy, rainy weather, the expedition including the surveyors' escort reached the Yellowstone River in Montana Territory at a point between Glendive and Cedar creeks. Colonel Stanley established a stockade some eight miles upriver from Glendive Creek, which could be resupplied by steamboats coming up the Missouri and Yellowstone. On July 26th, Stanley left one company of the 17th Infantry and two companies of the 7th Cavalry behind to man the stockade while the main body proceeded on up the Yellowstone.[12]

On August 4th, while scouting up the Yellowstone opposite the mouth of the Tongue River some eight to ten miles in advance of the main party, a portion of Lieutenant Colonel Custer's force was attacked by the Sioux. No one could describe this event better than Custer himself. His report of the action is included in its entirety. It does much to enhance the reader's understanding of the manner in which the cavalry operated when engaged in battle, as well as Custer's combat leadership.

---

[12] Ibid.: 248.

Headquarters Battalion 7th Cavalry,
Pompey's Pillar, Yellowstone River, Montana,
Aug. 15, 1873

Acting Assistant Adjutant-General Yellowstone Expedition

Sir.—Acting under the instructions of the Brevet-major general commanding [Colonel Stanley], I proceeded at five o'clock, on the morning of the 4th instant, with one squadron of my command, numbering about ninety men, to explore a route over which the main column could move. Having reached a point on the Yellowstone River, near the mouth of the Tongue River, and several miles in advance, and while awaiting the arrival of the forces of the expedition, six mounted Sioux dashed boldly into the skirt of timber within which my command had halted and unsaddled, and attempted to stampede our horses. Fortunately our vedettes discovered the approach of the Indians in time to give the alarm. A few well-directed shots soon drove the Indians to a safe distance, where they kept up a series of yells, occasionally firing a few shots. As soon as the squadron could mount, I directed Captain Moylan to move out in pursuit, at the same time I moved with the troops in advance, commanded by 1st Lieutenant T.W. Custer. Following the Indians at a brisk gait, my suspicions became excited by the confident bearing exhibited by the six Sioux in our front, whose course seemed to lead us near a heavy growth of timber which stood along the river bank above us. When almost within rifle range of this timber, I directed the squadron to halt, while I with two orderlies, all being well mounted, continued after the Sioux in order to develop their intentions. Proceeding a few hundred yards in advance of the squadron, and keeping a watchful eye on the timber to my left, I halted. The six Indians in my front also halted, as if to tempt further pursuit. Finding all efforts in this direction unavailing, their plans and intentions were quickly made evident, as no sooner was it seen that we intended to advance no farther, than with their characteristic howls and yells over three hundred well-mounted warriors dashed in perfect line from the edge of the timber, and charged down upon Captain Moylan's squadron, at the same time endeavoring to intercept the small party with me. As soon as the speed of the thorough-bred on which I was mounted brought me within hailing distance of Lieutenant Custer's troop [Thomas W. Custer, George's brother], I directed that officer to quickly throw forward a dismounted line of troopers, and endeavor to empty a few Indian saddles. The order was obeyed with the greatest alacrity, and as the Sioux came dashing forward, expecting to ride down the squadron, a line of dismounted cavalrymen rose from the grass and delivered almost in the faces of the warriors a volley of carbine bullets which broke and scattered their ranks in all directions, and sent more than one Sioux reeling from his saddle. This check gave us time to make our dispositions to resist the succeeding attacks, which we knew our enemies would soon make upon us. The great superiority of our enemies in numbers, the long distance separating us from the main command, and the belief, afterwards verified, that the woods above us still concealed a portion of the savage forces, induced me to confine my movements, at first, strictly to the defensive. The entire squadron (except the horse-holders) was dismounted and ordered to fight on foot. The Indians outnumbering us almost five to one were enabled to envelop us completely between their lines, formed in a semi-circle, and the river which flowed at our backs. The little belt of timber in which we had been first attacked formed a very good cover for our led-horses, while the crest of a second table-land, conveniently located from the timber, gave us an excellent line of defence. The length of our line and the numbers of our enemy prevented us from having any force in reserve; every available officer and man was on the skirmish-line, which was in reality our line of battle, even the number of men holding the horses had to be reduced, so that each horse-holder held eight horses [the usual number was four]. Until the Indians were made to taste quite freely of our lead they displayed unusual boldness, frequently charging up to our line and firing with great deliberation and accuracy. Captain Moylan exercised command along the entire line; Lieutenant Custer commanded the center; my adjutant, Lieutenant James Calhoun, commanded the right; and Lieutenant Charles A. Varnum, the left. The first Indian was shot from his pony by "Bloody Knife," the Crows who acted as my guide and scout. Soon after Private Charles P. Miller, of "A" troop, 7th Cavalry, succeeded in sending a carbine bullet directly through the body of a chief who had been conspicuous throughout the engagement. At the same time it was known that our firing had disabled many of their ponies, while owing to our sheltered position the only damage thus far inflicted upon us was one man and two horses wounded, one of the latter shot in three places.

Finding their efforts to force back our line unavailing, the Indians now resorted to another expedient. By an evidently preconcerted plan they set fire in several places to the tall grass which covered the ground in our front, hoping by this means to force us back to the rear, and thus finish us at their pleasure. Fortunately for us there was no wind prevailing at the time, while the grass was scarcely dry enough to burn rapidly. Taking advantage of the dense curtain of smoke which rose from the burning grass, the Indians, by following the course of the flame, could often contrive to obtain a shot at us at comparatively close range; but my men, observing that there was no danger to be apprehended from the slowly advancing flames, could frequently catch an opportunity to send a shot through a break in the curtain of smoke, and in this way surprised the Indian by the adoption of his own device.

The fight began at 11:30 A.M., and was waged without cessation until near three o'clock, all efforts of the Indians to dislodge us proving unsuccessful. The Indians had become extremely weary, and had almost discontinued their offensive movements, when my ammunition ran low. I decided to mount the squadron and charge the Indians, with the intention of driving them from the field.

Captain Moylan promptly had his men in the saddle, and throwing forward twenty mounted skirmishers, under Lieutenant Varnum, the entire squadron moved forward at a trot. No sooner did the Indians discern our intentions than, despite their superiority in numbers, they cowardly prepared for flight, in which preparation they were greatly hastened when Captain Moylan's squadron charged them and drove them "pell-mell" for three miles.

Five ponies killed or badly wounded were left on the battleground or along the line of their flight. So rapidly were they forced to flee that they abandoned and threw away breech-loading arms, saddle equipments, clothing, robes, lariats, and other articles comprised in an Indian outfit.

Among the Indians who fought us on this occasion were some of the identical warriors who committed the massacre at Fort Phil. Kearney, and they no doubt intended a similar programme when they sent the six warriors to dash up and attempt to decoy us into a pursuit past the timber in which the savages hoped to ambush us. Had we pursued the six warriors half a mile further, instead of halting, the entire band of warriors would have been in our rear, and all the advantage of position and numbers would have been with them.

So far as the troops attacked were concerned, the Indians, to offset their own heavy losses, had been able to do us no damage except to wound one man and two horses; but unfortunately two noncombatants, Veterinary Surgeon John Honsinger, 7th Cavalry, and Mr. Baliran, of Memphis, Tenn., in endeavoring to come from the main column to join the squadron in advance, were discovered by the Indians during the attack, and being unarmed were overtaken and killed almost within view of the battle-ground. Fortunately, the Indians were so pressed as not to be able to scalp or otherwise mutilate the remains...

> Respectfully submitted.
> (Signed) G.A. Custer
> Lieutenant-colonel 7th Cavalry
> Brevet-major-general, U.S.A., commanding[13]

Four days later, on August 8th, components of the expedition discovered the trail of what was, in the words of Colonel Stanley, a "very large Indian village...fleeing before us."[14] At this point the expedition was farther upriver, opposite the mouth of the Rosebud. Stanley ordered Custer to move out with a 450-man force of 7th Cavalry and a detachment of Indian scouts, and locate and destroy the village. The trail was believed to be about two days old. Custer's force departed at 10 P.M. on the evening of the 8th with seven day's rations and one hundred rounds of ammunition per man. By daylight they had marched thirty miles. They then stopped for three hours to rest and graze the horses. At 8 A.M. they resumed the march, stopping again at noon and concealing the force in timber until nightfall. They resumed the march at 6:30 P.M. and soon discovered that the Indians had forded the Yellowstone at a point some three miles below the mouth of the Bighorn River. Custer wrote:

> In following their trail to this point it was evident that the movement of the Indians was one of precipitate flight, the result of the engagement on the 4th. All along the trail and in their camping-places were to be found large quantities of what constitutes an Indian's equipments, such as lodge-poles, robes, saddle equipments, arms, and cooking utensils. In a hastily abandoned camp-ground nearly two hundred axes, besides a great many camp-kettles and cups, were found.[15]

Custer attempted for one entire day to cross the Yellowstone with his force, but the water proved too deep and swift. There had recently been rainy weather, and the river was running high. He eventually abandoned the attempt by the evening of the 10th. Very early the next morning a large force of Indians came to the opposite bank and opened fire on the troopers at

---

13 Quoted in Elizabeth B. Custer, *Boots and Saddles:* 237–241.

14 Stanley: 250.

15 Quoted in Elizabeth B. Custer, *Boots and Saddles:* 241–242.

long range. As groups of Indians moved to points within rifle range, Custer employed his best marksmen to fire upon the Indians from across the river and disperse them. Indian warriors then began recrossing the river above and below Custer's force. Now that their families were safe on the other bank, they were returning to do battle. Custer later wrote, "It would have been possible, perhaps, for us to have prevented the Indians from effecting a crossing, at least when they did, but I was not only willing but anxious that as many of them should come over as were so disposed."[16]

Watched by Custer's scouts, warriors collected on the bluffs behind his main force, which was situated near the riverbank. In the meantime, Indian sharpshooters using long-range rifles continued to fire on the troops from across the river.

> It was at this time that my standing orderly, Private Tuttle, of "E" Troop, 7th Cavalry, one of the best marksmen in my command, took a sporting Springfield rifle and posted himself, with two other men, behind cover on the river bank, and began picking off Indians as they exposed themselves on the opposite bank…It was while so engaged that he observed an Indian in full view near the river. Calling the attention of his comrade to the fact, he asked him "to watch him drop that Indian," a feat which he succeeded in performing. Several other Indians rushed to the assistance of their fallen comrade, when Private Tuttle, by a skilful and rapid use of his breech-loading Springfield, succeeded in killing two other warriors. The Indians, enraged no doubt at this rough handling, directed their aim at Private Tuttle, who fell pierced through the head by a rifle-bullet. He was one of the most useful and daring soldiers who ever served under my command.

> About this time Captain French, who was engaged with the Indians who were attacking us from below, succeeded in shooting a warrior from his saddle, while several ponies were known to be wounded or disabled. The Indians now began to display a strong force in our front on the bluffs.[17]

Colonel Stanley summarized Custer's subsequent action:

> …Custer found himself assailed from the bluffs 600 yards in his rear; pushing up a skirmish line on foot in the latter direction, Colonel Custer formed each squadron in a separate column, and charged the

---

[16] Ibid: 243.

[17] Ibid.: 244.

Indians, driving them eight or ten miles from the field. The main column came within sight of Colonel Custer's position at 7 A.M. Indians in large groups had collected on the high bluffs across the Yellowstone. I directed Lieutenant Webster, Twenty-second Infantry, in command of the section of artillery, to shell these groups; he threw several shells, well aimed, producing a wonderful scampering out of sight.[18]

Sitting Bull—Sioux chief.
PHOTO COURTESY OF MONTANA HISTORICAL SOCIETY RESEARCH CENTER PHOTOGRAPH ARCHIVES, HELENA, MONTANA.

Regarding the observers across the river, Custer wrote, "The Indians had evidently come out prepared to do their best, and with no misgivings as to their success, as the mounds and high bluffs beyond the river were covered with groups of old men, squaws, and children, who collected there to witness our destruction."[19]

Stanley reported one officer severely wounded (Lieutenant Charles Braden, shot through the thigh bone) and one private killed (Tuttle) and two wounded, "... summing the two engagements, we lost four killed, four wounded and five horses killed."[20] Stanley deferred to Custer's report regarding the number of Indian casualties. Custer estimated the number of Indians engaged at between 800 and 1,000 as opposed to his force of 450 men. He believed that the Indians lost about forty warriors killed and wounded and lost a much higher number of ponies.

Summing up his report on the battles Custer wrote:

> The Indians were made up of different bands of Sioux, principally Uncpapas, the whole under the command of "Sitting Bull" who participated in the second day's fight, and who for once has been taught a lesson he will not soon forget. [Obviously Sitting Bull did not for-

---

[18] Stanley: 251. Stanley would later comment that many of the shells supplied for the Rodman gun failed to explode.

[19] Quoted in Elizabeth B. Custer, *Boots and Saddles*: 246.

[20] Stanley: 251.

get; he would avenge himself three years later at the Little Bighorn.] A large number of Indians who fought us were fresh from their reservations on the Missouri River. Many of the warriors engaged in the fight on both days were dressed in complete suits of clothes issued at the agencies to Indians. The arms with which they fought us (several of which were captured in the fight) were of the latest improved patterns of breech-loading repeating rifles, and their supply of metallic rifle-cartridges seemed unlimited, as they were anything but sparing in their use. So amply have they been supplied with breech-loading rifles and ammunition that neither bows nor arrows were employed against us. As an evidence that these Indians, at least many of them, were recently from the Missouri River agencies, we found provisions, such as coffee, in their abandoned camps, and cooking and other domestic utensils, such as only reservation Indians are supplied with. Besides, our scouts conversed with them across the river for nearly an hour before the fight became general, and satisfied themselves as to the identity of our foes. I only regret that it was impossible for my command to effect a crossing of the river before our presence was discovered, and while the hostile village was located near at hand, as I am confident that we could have largely reduced the necessity for appropriation for Indian supplies the coming winter…[21]

Commenting on the origin of the hostiles Colonel Stanley reported:

… from two new Winchester rifles found on the first field, it is certainly true that these Indians were recipients of the bounty of the United States government; and as they were mostly Uncpapa Sioux they had no long time since come from the center of iniquity in Indian affairs, Fort Peck.[22]

The expedition experienced no further Indian hostilities beyond one minor harassment, which occurred on August 16th in the vicinity of Pompey's Pillar. There, a small group of Indians fired on some soldiers bathing in the Yellowstone. There were no casualties. From Pompey's Pillar, Stanley's column moved some sixty miles "west of northwest" to the Musselshell River, joining the route taken by Major Eugene Baker while escorting Ferdinand Hayden's surveyors in 1872. At this point, Colonel Stanley's report becomes confusing regarding directions taken once reaching the Musselshell. After

---

[21] Elizabeth B. Custer, *Boots and Saddles*: 247.

[22] Stanley: 251.

reporting their arrival on the Musselshell on the 19th, he wrote, "Setting out the morning of the 20th, we continued down the Musselshell River 65 miles, mostly due west." He reports slow progress and then announces their arrival at the Big Bend of the Musselshell "...where this river turns a little west of north to its junction with the Missouri."[23] Following his description of the route over the Musselshell from Pompey's Pillar, the expedition should have struck the river somewhere near present-day Cushman, MT. Had they continued west up and not down the Musselshell for 65 miles, they would have come near the forks of the river where the survey escort had been discontinued the previous year. Yet Stanley reports that on August 27th, after slow going along the river, they departed the Musselshell heading east. If they had, in fact, traveled west up the Musselshell for those 65 miles, they could not have returned to the Big Bend, i.e., the easternmost point of the river, by the 27th. Therefore, it is likely that the expedition traveled eastward down the Musselshell after intersecting it on the 19th.

Upon reaching the Big Bend, the expedition started back toward the stockade on the Yellowstone, which was still over 150 miles east of their position. The animals were now suffering from lack of good grazing. Stanley commented that "The Muscle sell valley is fertile, and, uninhabited by game, would furnish good grazing; but our march had been preceded by thousands of buffaloes, and the grass was completely exhausted."[24] After marching easterly into unknown country for one day, Colonel Stanley became concerned that the animals would suffer too greatly if the force continued directly through unfamiliar terrain to his stockade on the Yellowstone. He therefore opted to proceed with the main body down the Porcupine drainage to the Yellowstone. There good grass would be available. Custer was allowed to march with six companies of the 7th Cavalry and the engineer contingent by direct route to the stockade. He accomplished the trip in five days without incident.

Stanley's main body arrived at the north bank of the Yellowstone, across from the stockade, on September 9th. A steamer, the *Josephine*, arrived on the same day and ferried them across to the stockade. Custer departed on the 11th, escorting the engineers to the Little Missouri River (Dakota Territory), where they had additional work to accomplish. Other components of the expedition were loaded on the steamboat for the journey downstream.

---

[23] Ibid.: 252.

[24] Ibid.: 253.

Colonel Stanley departed on the 14th with the remaining components and, after a nine-day march, arrived back at Fort Abraham Lincoln. This concluded the Yellowstone Expedition of 1873.[25] One note of interest regarding the amount of suffering on the part of the seriously wounded during such movements: Lieutenant Braden, shot through the upper third of his thigh, the bone shattered, was transported 400 miles "…upon a litter made by connecting the front and rear axles of an old spring-wagon by lodge poles sixteen feet long, and swinging a stretcher bed from and underneath the poles."[26]

---

[25] Ibid.: 252–254.

[26] Ibid.: 271.

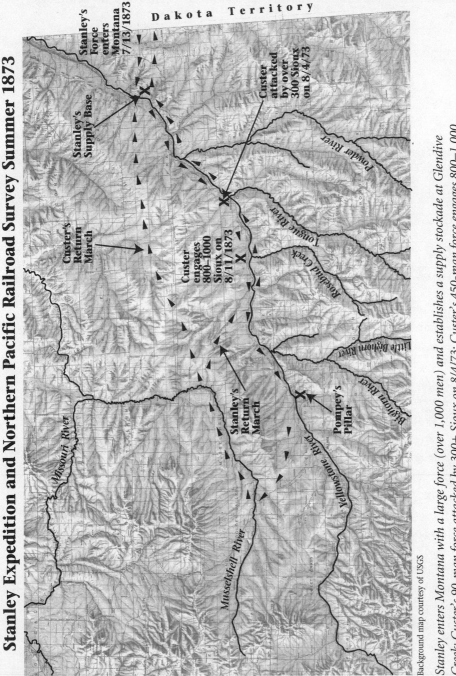

Stanley Expedition and Northern Pacific Railroad Survey Summer 1873

Background map courtesy of USGS

Stanley enters Montana with a large force (over 1,000 men) and establishes a supply stockade at Glendive Creek; Custer's 90-man force attacked by 300+ Sioux on 8/4/73; Custer's 450-man force engages 800–1,000 Sioux on 8/11/73; survey reaches Pompeys Pillar, crosses over to the Musselshell River, then returns to the supply stockade by separate routes and departs Montana for Dakota Territory posts on 9/9/1873.

CHAPTER THIRTEEN

Operations and Events 1874–1876

EVEN AS CONCERNS GREW ABOUT THE HOSTILE SIOUX in eastern Montana Territory, contingents of the Montana Military District had to handle many routine duties. In September, Crow Indian Agent Wright reported that the road between the Crow Agency (located on Mission Creek southeast of present-day Livingston) and Bozeman was infested with hostile Indians. Later that year, obviously aware of potential danger, Mr. C.A. Broadwater of the Diamond R Freight Company requested a military escort while he located a new road via the Musselshell River to the Missouri. He was advised that it would take too long to arrange for an escort. Nevertheless, he proceeded with construction of the new road, later referred to as the Carroll Road. It was located (i.e. surveyed, cleared and graded where necessary) and in operation by the spring of 1874.[1]

It was also reported that some of the soldiers assigned as guards to the stockade at Fort Shaw were reluctant to fire on escaping prisoners. We know, however, that at least one soldier at Fort Shaw was shot and killed attempting to escape. On October 8, 1873, Lieutenant Colonel C.C. Gilbert, the military district commander during Colonel Gibbon's absence, complained in a telegram to the Department of Dakota about leniency in punishing guards who failed to shoot escaping prisoners. Another cable to the Department of Dakota on November 18th commented on the results of target practice, something our frontier army soldiers received far too infrequently.

---

[1] September 27, November 20, 1873, Fort Shaw Letters and Telegrams Sent and Received, Records of Posts, Continental Army Command 1820–1920, Record Group 393.7, National Archives.

It was stated that one soldier was only allowed two shots at practice because "...his firing endangered the lives of the markers."[2]

The year 1874 commenced with routine duties in the district. A 2nd Cavalry major filed a report of some interest on his supervision of the distribution of annuities and supplies to the Indians at the Crow Agency. He reported that the Mountain Crows had 230 lodges and numbered 2,400 people. Their chiefs were Iron Bull, Show his Face, Blackfoot, Bull Goes Hunting, Long Horse, Bear in the Water, Tin Belly, Good Heart, Crazy Head, Pretty Bear, Bear Wolf, and Under the Ridge. They numbered 500 fighting men and were armed with 630 breach-loading guns. Of these, 300 were needle guns and the remainder Spencer and Henry rifles. This tribe possessed 7,000 to 8,000 horses. He added that the River Crows had 110 lodges with 1,100 people. The chiefs were Horse Guard, White Wizzle, Black Head, Big Bellies Woman, Hunts His Enemy, Bear Head, Little Soldier, and Wolf Bow. This tribe could muster 250 fighting men armed with 250 to 300 breachloaders. They possessed 1,200 to 1,500 horses. Major A.B. Sweitzer, Fort Ellis post commander, viewed the Crows as friendly. They were at war with the Sioux, but Sweitzer also suspected that some Crows might be trading ammunition with the Sioux on occasion.[3]

Also in January, a 500-head beef herd was reported stampeded by Indians about thirty miles east of Fort Benton. It was being driven by three herders from Fort Benton to the Fort Peck Agency for distribution to the agency Indians. Of the three herders, two were reported missing. A mounted party was dispatched from Fort Benton to collect the animals and investigate the incident.[4]

On January 22, 1874, Major Sweitzer reported that some citizens in the Bozeman area were organizing an expedition down the Yellowstone to establish a commercial stockade in the vicinity of the mouths of the Powder and the Tongue rivers.[5]

---

[2] October 8, November 18, 1873, District of Montana Letters and Telegrams Sent and Received, Department of Dakota, Record Group 393.5, National Archives.

[3] January 5, 10, 1874, Fort Ellis Letters and Telegrams Sent and Received, Records of Posts, Continental Army Command 1820–1920, Record Group 393.7, National Archives. The reader will note the advanced level of armament among the Crows and, perhaps, draw some conclusions regarding the likely level of armament of the Sioux and Northern Cheyenne at the Battle of the Little Bighorn in 1876. The Crows had been in continual conflict with the Sioux and Northern Cheyenne for many years prior to that battle.

[4] January 17, 1874, District of Montana Letters and Telegrams Sent and Received.

[5] January 22, 1874, Fort Ellis Letters and Telegrams Sent and Received. This was to become the ill-fated Fort Pease enterprise.

In February 1874, problems arose with the telegraph line between Virginia City and the Pleasant Valley station on the Corinne Road, and a repair party was dispatched from Fort Ellis.[6]

The newly constructed Carroll Road, completed by the spring of 1874, would shorten the distance for wagons from areas such as Diamond City, Bozeman and Virginia City, to a more reliable Missouri River port at Carroll's Landing, located on the Missouri River just north of present-day Winifred, MT. The Camp Baker annual report for 1874 describes the new Carroll Road as crossing the Big Belt Range fifteen miles south of Camp Baker, then following the north fork of Deep Creek to the summit of Copperopolis Divide and down the north fork of the Musselshell to the forks of that river, then through Judith Gap into Judith Basin and via Camp Lewis near present-day Lewistown, MT, to Carroll's Landing. As of August 4th, Camp Baker reported that the Indians had caused no problems on this new road. There had, however, been considerable concern regarding the safety of the new route when it was initiated. In April the post commander at Camp Baker had reported that "…during the past ten days, not less than seventy five teams; in squads of from two to twenty, have passed this post en route to Carrol." He expressed concern that many were very lightly armed and provided a tempting target for Indians in the area, particularly once warm weather arrived.[7] It is known, however, that district headquarters at Fort Shaw ordered that Fort Ellis provide a two-company cavalry escort for freight on this road in March 1874, in response to a request by citizens and businessmen utilizing the route.[8] Fort Shaw also dispatched two infantry companies to assist in escorting an E.G. Maclay & Company train down the Carroll Road from Brewers Springs (near Camp Baker) to the Missouri landing.[9]

To turn to more mundane events at Fort Shaw: Lieutenant Colonel Gilbert's servant was fired on March 3rd, "…Morris Ward colored servant to Lieutenant Colonel C.C. Gilbert 7th Infantry, is this day discharged for incorrigible neglectfulness of household duties, and for persistently staying out at night."[10]

---

6   February 1, 1874, ibid. Pleasant Valley was located in Idaho a few miles south of present-day Monida, MT, on Interstate 15.

7   April 19, August 4, 1874, Camp Baker Letters Sent and Received, Record Group 393.7, Records of Posts, Continental Army Command 1820–1920, National Archives.

8   March 21, 1874, Fort Ellis Letters and Telegrams Sent and Received.

9   March 1874 Fort Shaw Post Return, November 20, 1873, Records of Posts, Continental Army Command 1820–1920, Record Group 94, National Archives.

10 March 3, 1874, District of Montana Letters and Telegrams Sent and Received.

On March 29, 1874, a woodcutter was killed by Indians on the site of present-day Great Falls, MT. Lieutenant Colonel Gilbert sent the following cable on April 8th:

Headquarters Fort Shaw M.T.
April 8th 1874

The Assistant Adjutant General
Department of Dakota
Saint Paul, Minn

Sir:

On the 30th Ultimo. Deputy U.S. Marshal Hard and a citizen from Sun River Crossing came to the post about 2:30 AM and stated that a man by the name of John Rock had been killed by Indians just below the mouth of the Sun River on the Missouri River. It seems that these two men were employed by Mr. John Sargent of Sun River Crossing to cut and cord wood, and were out hunting geese on the 29th when the one on this, the north side, was fired upon by a party of twelve or fifteen Indians, concealed in a cabin near the river. It does not appear that any of the Indians were mounted. Mr. Hard and the citizen accompanying him asked to have a party sent out to recover the body.

Lieut. Jacobs, Commanding the Mounted Detachment, was ordered out to recover the body and then to take the necessary steps to identify the purpetrators of the act of violence complained of. The body was brought to the Crossing of Sun River near this post and during the day seen by several of the officers, who described it as bearing many wounds but not scalped.

The fact that the body was not scalped and mutilated may be accounted for by the Indians having been surprised in their act of violence, by the brother of the murdered man firing his gun at them. It is likely that they did not return to the body after running away...I have delayed this communication for the purpose of sending with it the statement of the brother of the murdered man James Rock and that of Mr. C.D. Hard, Deputy U.S. Marshal who went out with the citizens to recover the body...It is understood that a party of citizens traced the track of 12 Indians from the vicinity of the dead body, down the Missouri River opposite the Falls and thence north as far as the lakes on the Benton Road, where it was lost on account of the vast herds of buffalo

roaming over this country. Please observe the promptness with which
Lieut. Jacobs moved at so early an hour in the morning.

C.C. Gilbert
Lieutenant Colonel 7th Infantry
Commanding Post[11]

Also in late March, another tragic incident occurred at Fort Ellis when a soldier was killed, this time at the hands of a comrade-in-arms. On the 31st, Private Daniel J. Daily, Company F, 2nd Cavalry, was teasing Private James Murphy, also of Company F, while preparing for inspection. Murphy loaded his gun and fired at Daily, striking him in the shoulder. The bullet passed through Daily's shoulder and struck and killed Sergeant William Baker, Company F. Murphy was later prosecuted. Results of prosecution unknown.[12]

On April 18th, Fort Shaw dispatched Captain Constant Williams with Company F, 7th Infantry, to march to Storey's Trading Store on Trout Creek in Judith Basin and go into camp in that area to provide security for the new Carroll Road. They would remain in the area referred to as Camp Lewis until November, when they marched back to Fort Shaw.[13]

Concerns about the hostile Sioux on the Yellowstone continued to mount. In April, Major Sweitzer, post commander at Fort Ellis, wrote to Crow Indian Agent Wright regarding a request for military protection by Dr. Andrew Jackson Hunter and his family, known to reside deep in Indian country at Hunter's Hot Springs. This isolated location was some thirty miles east of Fort Ellis near present-day Springdale. The major advised that he could not provide protection for the doctor and his family at such an exposed location and suggested that he and his family move into the settlement.[14]

On May 1, Major Sweitzer cabled information on the progress of the commercial enterprise down the Yellowstone.

> Couriers from the Yellowstone party of Citizens report them retreating up the Yellowstone with frequent skirmishes with the Indians. They turned back near Tongue River after a fight, and have reached a point about 195 miles from here. One man killed and two wounded, and, considerable stock killed. A number of Indians reported killed, and stock captured.

---

[11] April 8, 1874, Fort Shaw Letters and Telegrams Sent and Received.

[12] April 13, 1874, Fort Ellis Letters and Telegrams Sent and Received.

[13] April, November 1874, Fort Shaw Post Returns.

[14] April 24, 1874, Fort Ellis Letters and Telegrams Sent and Received.

The following day he telegraphed Territorial Governor Potts that the party had requested no aid but had reported that if more hard fighting took place they would run short of ammunition.[15] Apparently members of this expedition returned to Bozeman by autumn and began preparations for another expedition the following summer.

On May 6, Fort Shaw dispatched Company I, 7th Infantry, commanded by 2nd Lieutenant Albert V. Amet to Carroll's Landing to provide additional security for the new Carroll Road. This company remained on station there until November, when it marched back to Fort Shaw. It is also of note that Amet died of consumption on December 16th while at Fort Shaw.[16]

Also in May 1874, Fort Ellis dispatched a small detachment of troops to the Crow Agency to provide protection. Meanwhile, Corporal Plant and three privates from Fort Ellis continued to work on the telegraph line between Virginia City and Pleasant Valley.[17] Work on this stretch of line would also be carried on in the summer of 1875.

On June 2nd, Companies G and K, 7th Infantry, commanded by Captain G.L. Browning, arrived at Camp Lewis to provide further escort duty on the Carroll Road. Further Indian hostilities occurred in July:

> On the 7th of July a war party of from fifty to eighty hostile Sioux made their appearance within a mile of Camp Lewis, firing upon a fatigue party procuring wood for the camp, and also upon a small number of recruits who were fishing in the creek near the wood party. A detachment of mounted men from the two companies, under Lieutenant Wright, 7th Infantry, proceeded at once to the scene of the attack, followed by the companies under Captain Browning. The Indians being mounted on fleet ponies and the companies on foot, they were unable to intercept them. The mounted men however followed on the trail and overtook them in a ravine about fifteen miles from camp, immediately opening fire upon them, which was returned by the Indians. After a sharp skirmish of a few minutes, the Indians fled. The detachment recaptured eight head of stock which had been run off from a ranch near camp. The horses of the detachment being too much jaded to follow the Indians any further, the command returned to camp. Three unassigned recruits were killed in this affair, one of whom

---

[15] May 1, 2, 1874, ibid.

[16] May, November, December 1874, Fort Shaw Post Returns.

[17] May 1874, Fort Ellis Post Returns.

was scalped. Private Davis, Company G, was severely wounded in the right hand, while bravely defending himself with his fishing pole, that being his only means of defense.[18]

On July 6, 1874, Captain Daniel W. Benham departed Fort Shaw with four officers and seventy enlisted men in two companies to escort a supply train from Fort Benton to the mouth of Box Elder Creek on the Milk River. These supplies were destined for use by the British Boundary Survey Commission. On July 24th, Colonel John Gibbon resumed command of the Montana Military District on his return from detached service in New York City. Lieutenant Colonel Gilbert was then made post commander at Camp Baker.[19] As of August, Camp Baker reported no Indian problems during the first eight months of the year, but the small detachment sent to the Crow Agency from Fort Ellis had a skirmish with hostiles on July 8th. There were no casualties.[20] Also during August, in response to a message of concern from Territorial Governor Benjamin Potts in Virginia City, Colonel Gibbon cabled him, "Everything is being done to protect Gallatin Valley."[21]

On November 23, 1874, Lieutenant Colonel Gilbert noted that wild game was disappearing in Camp Baker's area of responsibility, a much utilized hunting area for numerous Indian tribes, and that the Indians in his area would soon be tempted to eat cattle. He requested that the various agents representing those tribes, some as far away as Idaho, Washington and Oregon, whose hunting parties frequented the Judith Basin area, be forewarned.[22]

In the spring of 1875, Colonel Gibbon addressed a letter to the Department of Dakota describing the methodology employed by whiskey traffickers in northern Montana Territory:

Sir:

I have the honor to report, for the information of the Department Commander, that I am frequently called upon by the U.S. Indian Agents for the Blackfeet for military assistance in arresting parties engaged in illicit traffic with the Indians.

---

[18] A.B. Johnson, "History of 7th Inf. Regt.," U.S. Army Center for Military History website: 506.

[19] July 1874, Fort Shaw Post Returns.

[20] August 4, 1874, Camp Baker Letters Sent and Received; August 10, 1874, Fort Ellis Letters and Telegrams Sent and Received.

[21] August 3, 1874, District of Montana Letters and Telegrams Sent and Received.

[22] November 23, 1874, Camp Baker Letters Sent and Received.

I have today had a full conference with Captain Dusold, a Deputy U.S. Marshal, under whose directions these operations are usually conducted. He informs me that the Indian Department, grants to certain parties, licenses, to trade with the Indians, and that by the regulations of the Department the licensed traders are not permitted to trade in whisky, ammunition, etc. The practical operation of this traffic however is as follows. The licensed trader establishes himself or his agent on or near the line of the Reservation on the north bank of the Marias River. Directly in the vicinity of this licensed trader and on the south bank of the river/that is off the Reservation/ the illicit trafficer establishes himself and exposes his vile poison for sale or exchange for robes. The licensed trader receives, entertains and harbors the illicit trader and his wares and receives from the latter the robes, etc., which he gathers in from the Indians in trade for whisky and ammunition.

On a recent occasion Captain Dusold found a quantity of ammunition concealed at Baker's Trading Post.

In this way the object of the law is defeated and the regular trader licensed by the Indian Department not only encourages the violation of the law, but reaps advantages from it. In addition to this it is more than suspected that the very men in whose interests these licensed Traderships are established are the people from whom the illicit trafficer obtains his contraband goods.

The whole country along the Teton River and north to the Marias is reported to be occupied by Indian camps and Whisky Traders. The Indians are permitted to come on to this country and the whiskey trading cannot be stopped because [it is] not in the Indian country.

This state of affairs will, of course, ultimately produce trouble. I am not only willing but anxious to do everything in my power to aid in putting an end to this infamous traffic, but I think the Indian Department should do its part too, and strike at the root of the evil, by revoking the licenses of those traders known by its own officers to be connected with and reaping and reaping advantages from this illicit traffic.

> I am Sir
> Very Respectfully
> Your Obd. Servt.
> John Gibbon[23]

---

[23] March 6, 1875, District of Montana Letters and Telegrams Sent and Received.

On April 14, 1875, Major Sweitzer reported from Fort Ellis that another commercial expedition down the Yellowstone was being prepared by a civilian, Major F.D. Pease. On June 15th, Major Pease passed through Fort Ellis on his way to the Yellowstone with plans to establish a post at the mouth of the Bighorn River. Later in June, Fort Ellis received word from Dr. Hunter at Hunter's Hot Springs that he had been visited by two Crow Indians. They had informed him that there had been three days of fighting between some Crows and the Sioux farther down the Yellowstone and that the Crows were now all banding together to fight the Sioux. Dr. Hunter added that the boat *Bozeman*, belonging to the Pease expedition, had wrecked near his location and was being repaired.

On June 30, 1875, Captain D.W. Benham, now post commander at Fort Ellis, provided additional information on Major Pease's enterprise. He stated that Pease had expected to act in concert with the Crows against the Sioux after a rendezvous with them at some point below the Bighorn River. But Pease had bad luck, losing two out of his three boats on the way down and arriving at the rendezvous too late. The Crows had clashed with the Sioux prior to Pease's arrival and were forced to retreat. Regarding potential military aid from Fort Ellis to the Pease expedition, Captain Benham wrote:

> Making due allowance for exageration in the reported number of Sioux warriors on the Yellowstone, it would take every available man at this post to penetrate the country as far as Major Pease now is with safety and would leave this whole section open to the hostiles. I am of the opinion that Pease will stockade his party in case he is annoyed by Sioux and await the arrival of the boat that is expected to bring up supplies for the Custer expedition.[24]

It is of interest to note that Major Pease is the same individual who was an agent to the Blackfeet Indians at the time of Major Baker's raid on the Piegans in 1870. The reader will recall that he was highly critical of the army's conduct of this raid.

In the spring of 1875, the Office of Indian Affairs decided to move the Crow Agency to a location on the Stillwater River near present-day Absarokee, MT, some sixty to ninety miles eastward from its original location on Mission Creek. It was a move obviously favored by the Crow Indian Agent, Dexter Clapp, but opposed by the army. On June 18, 1875,

---

[24] April 14, June 15, 23, 30, 1875, Fort Ellis Letters and Telegrams Sent and Received.

Captain Benham wrote the district headquarters expressing his opposition to the move and his mounting concern about activities of the hostile Sioux:

Head Qrs. Fort Ellis M. T.
June 18, 1875

To the Acting Assistant Adjutant General
District of Montana
Fort Shaw, M.T

Sir:

I have the honor to forward herewith a copy of a letter from J.V. Bogert Esq. of Bozeman M. T. touching the condition of Indian Affairs.

Mr. Bogert is a citizen of Bozeman and a reliable man, I deem his report worthy of serious consideration [the author was unable to locate a copy of this report], and think the fact should not be overlooked, that the Crow Indians are in a very disturbed condition notwithstanding their Agent's (Mr. Clapp's) report to the contrary. I know from personal knowledge that they were bitterly opposed to the removal of their agency, and in a council at which I was present, they advanced many good reasons why it should not be moved.

It seems that any action of the Indian Department, liable to destroy the good feelings which have existed between the Crow Indians and the Whites would be very disastrous to this section of the country and should be suspended at once.

I believe that were it not for the Crow Indians this country would be constantly ravaged by the Sioux and it would take double the number of soldiers now in the District to protect the people of Montana from their depradations.

I have ordered out a scouting party consisting of a Sergeant and nine (9) men with directions to scour the country in the direction of the Yellowstone then around Sheep Mountain and north towards the Crazy Woman's range thence across to the Camp Baker road and back to this post.

I have also directed Lieutenant Jerome who is stationed between Flathead and Blackfoot passes, with fifteen (15) men, to be on the alert and at all times watchful for Indians.

I will do all that is possible to do with the men at my disposal for the protection of the settlers in the valley.

> I am, Sir, Very Respectfully
> Your Obedient Servant
> D.W. Benham
> Captain 7th Infantry
> Commanding Post[25]

Captain Benham continued to receive numerous reports of Sioux coming up the Yellowstone, and he requested that the post be reinforced by the cavalry company then on detached service at Fort Benton. On July 8th, thirty-five horses and mules were stolen from the stage station and a train (a freight-wagon train) at Box Elder on the Carroll Road. A posse of citizens pursued the hostiles, presumed to be the same band, for some fifty miles in the direction of Pompey's Pillar.

> A few days later another party made a raid upon Carrole formed a skirmish line between the town and…horses which were leisurely gathered up and driven off. On the 26th [of July] stage stock was stolen from the station at Judith Gap. On the 12th of July a party of herders were attacked near the Fort Ellis and Baker road about sixty miles from this post [Camp Baker], on Flathead Creek by sixty Indians who at the same time drove off ninety head of cattle.[26]

On July 8th, a small band of Indians killed one man and drove off several head of stock at Quinn's ranch in the Fort Ellis area. Lieutenant Edward J. McClernand was sent out in pursuit of the hostiles. Results unknown. In his annual report covering the first eight months of 1875, the post commander at Camp Baker stated, "It is certain that all depredations were committed by the Sioux whose villages are supposed to be located between Tongue and Powder Rivers…"[27]

The rash of hostile activity by the Sioux raised the concern, particularly in the Judith Basin area, that members of the numerous friendly tribes hunting in the area, i.e. Nez Perce, Flatheads, Pend d'Oreilles and other tribes, could be mistaken by angry settlers for hostile Indians and attacked. Therefore, the military attempted to provide escorts for parties of friendly

---

[25] June 18, 1875, ibid.

[26] August 1875 Post Return, Camp Baker.

[27] July 6, 7, 8, 9. 1875, Fort Ellis Letters and Telegrams Sent and Received.

Indians when passing through or near settlements. For example, from March 28th to May 17th, Lieutenant W.H. Nelson and five enlisted men escorted Flathead Indians back to their agency from Camp Baker. Later, in January 1876, Lieutenant Colonel Gilbert, post commander at Camp Baker, reported that numerous small bands of friendly Indians were passing his post and likely to do so for the next four months. He added that each band required the escort of one officer and four enlisted men, and requested that more men be provided to him for this purpose. Naturally these Indian tribes bristled at restrictions placed on their travel to and from their traditional hunting grounds, but generally remained peaceful.[28]

On July 13, 1875, the garrison strength at Fort Ellis was reduced by the tragic drowning of four soldiers when their ferry across the Yellowstone gave away. They were en route back to Fort Ellis from duty at the Crow Agency on Mission Creek (soon to be referred to as the Old Agency).[29]

On July 16, 1875, Fort Shaw experienced an invasion of grasshoppers. Colonel Gibbon wrote:

> The grasshoppers made their appearance in large numbers here on the 16th of July and every man that could be raised was occupied in driving them off the post gardens with the assistance of bon fires, drums, brushes and the firing of cannon. With constant labor the vegetables were saved from destruction and the pest finally on the 25th disappeared, not having done us any great harm although they have injured more or less all the farms in this vicinity.[30]

In the meantime, at district headquarters at Fort Shaw, Colonel Gibbon sought to take advantage of the presence of friendly Indians. On July 19th he queried the Department of Dakota, "Can I have authority to employ one or two hundred of the friendly Indians now in the Judith Basin?"[31] This authority was eventually granted the following year, with a number of Crow Indian scouts employed by the Montana Military District.

Meanwhile, Crow agent Dexter Clapp was pressing the military for more protection from Sioux depredations committed on the Crow Indians. In a letter dated June 18th, he requested a military escort for the agency school

---

[28] August 1875 Post Return, Camp Baker; January 4, February 21, 1876, Camp Baker Letters Sent and Received.

[29] July 14, 1875, Fort Ellis Letters and Telegrams Sent and Received.

[30] August 26, 1875, Fort Shaw Letters and Telegrams Sent and Received.

[31] July 19, 1875, District of Montana Letters and Telegrams Sent and Received.

and Indian families from the Old Agency to the New Agency. Colonel Gibbon could not provide it. On July 18th, in response to a query from his superior in St. Paul, Colonel Gibbon wrote:

> Agency not attacked when last heard from. My troops are too much scattered now. Ft. Ellis has all it can do to furnish scouting parties in pursuit of raiding bands and a guard at the Old Agency, where Agent Clapp is calling for more. Lt. Jerome with a party is now down in the direction of the new agency and will probably bring some news when he returns. I may have to withdraw the 2 companies on the Teton to place them on the Carroll route. If Custer is out and could manage to capture the home camp of Sitting Bull's band and ship their families down the river it would do more to bring these rascals to terms than anything but a sound thrashing.[32]

On July 23, 1875, Gibbon proposed to go on the offensive with his available forces against the hostiles. He cabled the Department of Dakota:

> Your telegrams of 19 and 21 received. I have already ordered the companies on the Teton withdrawn. When they arrive here, I propose with the cavalry company and about 100 infantry, to move rapidly across to Lewis [Camp Lewis] direct, if the Missouri is fordable, then sweep up the Carroll road [southward] as far as the fork of the Muscleshell and from there down the Shields River to the front of Ellis, hoping to strike one of the hostile bands and thus relieve both Ellis and the Carroll route. Should the Missouri not be fordable at mouth of Sun River, or reports from Ellis render quicker aid necessary I should go by the ferry direct to Boxer and so on to Ellis. I would be in better shape and have a more efficient force, if I could employ some of the friendly Indians in Judith Basin as auxiliaries and scouts. I telegraphed Gen. Terry on the 19th asking for authority to employ these Indians. Let me know his answer as soon as possible and also if he approves my plan as above.[33]

The author was unable to determine if this plan was executed as described. The August and September post returns for Fort Shaw indicate, however, that Captain Charles Rawn departed Fort Shaw on August 1st with one hundred men en route to the forks of the Musselshell to guard the Carroll Road. His contingent returned to Fort Shaw on September 29th,

---

[32] July 18, 1875, ibid.

[33] July 23, 1875, ibid.

having marched 184 miles. The marching distance reported would indicate that his contingent went on station near the forks of the Musselshell. Colonel Gibbon would, however, eventually receive authority to employ some friendly Indians as scouts—and none too soon.[34]

---

[34] August, September 1875 Post Returns, Fort Shaw.

CHAPTER FOURTEEN

Origins of the 1876 Campaign Against the Hostile Sioux and Northern Cheyenne

C OMMENCING IN 1876, THE U.S. ARMY ENTERED A PERIOD of continuous warfare against hostile Sioux and Northern Cheyenne bands when and where they could be found. This open warfare would continue until the last of the hostiles under Sitting Bull surrendered at Fort Buford on July 19, 1881. Most of the fighting would occur within the bounds of Montana Territory. Elements of the District of Montana, a newly formed District of the Yellowstone (also in Montana), and units from other areas in the Department of Dakota (headquartered in St. Paul, Minnesota) and the Department of the Platte (headquartered in Omaha, Nebraska) would be involved in this struggle.

In his annual report for the year 1871, J.A. Vaill, Superintendent of Indian Affairs for Montana Territory, noted that 1,000 lodges of "Teton Sioux," under the leadership of Sitting Bull, were occupying the territory near the juncture of the Yellowstone and Powder rivers (near present-day Terry). According to Vaill, these Indians maintained no relations with whites or friendly Indians. He added that they were believed to have conducted a raid into the Gallatin Valley on July 24, 1871, in which two whites were killed and some forty horses stolen. Further, they had killed two men named McKnight and Lee and wounded another named Williams near the mouth of the Musselshell River (the present Fort Peck Lake area). Vaill reported that Sitting Bull was not loyal to Red Cloud, the recognized Sioux leader, and predicted that he would have to be brought to heel. "Red Cloud claimed to represent them in his negotiations with the department [1868], but since

Red Cloud's treaty [negotiated after the Sioux had wiped out the Fetterman command] they repudiate his authority and leadership and acknowledge no chief but Sitting Bull."[1]

Sitting Bull refused to submit himself and his band to white rule on the reservation, preferring instead to roam free in the last great buffalo hunting grounds of eastern Montana, western North and South Dakota, northern Wyoming, and portions of northern Nebraska. Acclaimed for his bravery and prowess as a young man, he was much respected by members of the Sioux nation. Although the permanent members of his band were relatively small in number as compared to the greater Sioux nation, their ranks swelled during the summer months, when large numbers of disaffected young warriors arrived from the various Sioux agencies. Most of these agencies, such as Pine Ridge, Standing Rock, Red Cloud, Spotted Tail, Lower Brule, Crow Creek, Cheyenne River and Devil's Lake, were located in central and western Dakota Territory.

These young Indian men, some living the red man's bachelor existence but many others accompanied by their wives and children, could winter at the agencies and then resume the life of the hunt with Sitting Bull during the summer months. They could also conduct raids on whites and friendly Indians and collect scalps and booty as the opportunity presented itself, and this they frequently accomplished.

Gradually the patience of the Office of Indian Affairs grew thin in regards to Sitting Bull and other hostile chiefs, the most prominent among them being Crazy Horse, who also shared Sitting Bull's defiance of the white man's rule. These Indians were referred to as "hostiles." Interestingly enough, the Commissioner of Indian Affairs, Edward P. Smith, in his annual report of November 1, 1874, held a somewhat low opinion of the military strength of the hostile bands still active in the United States. He wrote, "the hostiles themselves are so scattered and divided in cliques and bands that, except under extraordinary provocation, or in circumstances not at all to be apprehended, it is not probable that as many as 500 Indian warriors will ever again be mustered at one point for a fight."[2] Obviously, the commissioner had not read or discounted Custer's report of his clash with 800 to 1,000 Sioux on the Yellowstone just a little over one year prior, on August 11, 1873.

---

[1] Annual Report to the Commissioner of Indian Affairs for 1871, Annual Reports of the Commissioner of Indian Affairs. Record Group 75, SuDocs Number I 20.1, 1824–1920, National Archives.

[2] Annual Report to the Commissioner of Indians Affairs for 1874, ibid.

Sitting Bull was about forty-two to forty-three years old at this time. Although he led the Uncpapa Sioux—this sometimes disputed by a rival faction under Chiefs Gall and No Neck—he had earned a reputation for fearlessness and prowess in battle among all members of the Sioux nation. Once, during a standoff with a group of Crow warriors on the Porcupine in Montana Territory, Sitting Bull challenged the Crow leader to one-on-one combat. Sitting Bull began to get the upper hand and the Crow warrior, in desperation, seized a nearby rifle and fired just as Sitting Bull sank his knife into the Crow's chest. The bullet struck the sole of Sitting Bull's left foot. Thereafter, Sitting Bull always walked with a limp.[3]

On another occasion around 1870, Sitting Bull and some of his warriors had surrounded a group of thirty-one well-fortified Crow warriors. Sitting Bull called upon his men, about equal in number to the Crows, to follow him in a charge and wipe out the Crow Indians. He led the way far ahead of the other Sioux warriors, breached the Crows redoubt, and killed several Crows in hand-to-hand combat before the other Sioux warriors could join the fight. All the Crows were wiped out. Two Sioux warriors fell in the fight. Frank Grouard, who had lived with the Sioux for six years and was well acquainted with Sitting Bull, stated:

> Some men who have written of Sitting Bull, claiming that he was a medicine man and not a warrior, are unacquainted with the circumstances surrounding his life among the Indians themselves. No man in the Sioux nation was braver in battle than Sitting Bull, and he asked none of his warriors to take any chances that he was not willing at all times to share.[4]

Grouard provided us with a description of Sitting Bull as he appeared in 1870:

> His head was crowned with a profusion of long, black hair, which he wore brushed from a low forehead. His face was massive and swarthy. His eyes were large and expressive, while the mouth was large and the lips thin, indicating cruelty. His shoulders were broad and heavy, and his body tapered symmetrically...The only bodily defect Grouard noted was a well-defined limp... a wound in the left foot.

---

[3] Joe DeBarthe, *Life and Adventures of Frank Grouard*: 79–81.

[4] Ibid.: 103–105.

Grouard also stated that Sitting Bull had been badly wounded in a fight with General Harney's contingent at Lookout Buttes, but survived.[5]

Sioux depredations in Montana Territory resulted in public and military pressure on the Office of Indian Affairs to take action against the hostiles. E.C. Watkins, U.S. Indian Inspector, conducted an inspection tour of the Montana and Dakota territories and, on November 9, 1875, provided the following report to Commissioner Smith:

> Sir: I have the honor to address you in relation to the attitude and condition of certain wild and hostile bands of Sioux Indians in Dakota and Montana, that came under my observation during my recent tour through their country, and what I think should be the policy of the government toward them.
>
> I refer to "Sitting Bull's" band and other bands of the Sioux nation, under chiefs or "head-men" of less note, but no less untamable and hostile. These Indians occupy the center, so to speak, and roam over Western Dakota and Eastern Montana, including the rich valleys of the Yellowstone and Powder rivers, and make war on the Arickarees, Mandans, Gros Ventres, Assiniboines, Blackfeet, Piegans, Crows, and other friendly tribes on the circumference.
>
> ... they openly set at defiance all law and authority, and boast that the United States authorities are not strong enough to conquer them. The United States troops are held in contempt, and surrounded by their native mountains, relying on their knowledge of the country and powers of endurance, they laugh at the futile efforts that have thus far been made to subjugate them, and scorn the idea of white civilization.
>
> ...They are rich in horses and robes, and are thoroughly armed. Nearly every warrior carries a breech-loading gun, a pistol, a bow and quiver of arrows. From their central position they strike to the east, north and west, steal horses and plunder from all the surrounding tribes, as well as frontier settlers, and luckless white hunters or emigrants who are not in sufficient force to resist them; and fortunate, indeed, is the man who thus meets them if, after losing all his worldly possessions, he escapes with his scalp.
>
> And yet these Indians number, all told, but a few hundred warriors, and these are never all together or under the control of one chief. In

---

[5] Ibid.: 79–81.

Frank Grouard—U.S. Army scout.
PHOTO COURTESY OF WWW.WIKIPEDIA.ORG.

my judgment, one thousand men, under the command of an experienced officer, sent into their country in winter, when the Indians are nearly always in camp, and at which season of the year they are most helpless, would be amply sufficient for their capture or punishment.

...In interviews with Indians along the Missouri River and through Montana, during my recent tour of inspection, they invariably spoke of this subject, and complained bitterly that the Government was not protecting them as it had promised, and frequently closed the case by saying they might just as well go out and kill white men as to try to be good Indians, for they got no protection or extra reward for being good. When I told them that these Sioux would be punished, they said, "We have heard that before; we'll wait and see." While I am not disposed to be needlessly alarmed, and do not agree with the writers of articles in numerous territorial papers of a sensational character on this subject, yet I think there is danger of some of the young warriors from friendly tribes falling off and joining with these hostile bands, until with these accessions they would be somewhat formidable, and might make a simultaneous attack on white settlers in some localities, if they are thus allowed to gather head.

The true policy, in my judgment, is to send troops against them in the winter, the sooner the better, and whip them into subjection...[6]

On November 27, 1875, Commissioner Smith forwarded Inspector Watkins's recommendations to his superior, Zachariah Chandler, Secretary of Interior, recommending that:

...this communication be referred to the War Department for consideration and such action as may be deemed best by Lieutenant-General Sheridan, who is personally conversant with the situation

---

[6] Fay, George E., *Military Engagements Between United States Troops and Plains Indians*: 15–16.

on the Upper Missouri, and with the relations of Sitting Bull's band to the other Sioux tribes.[7]

On December 3, 1875, Secretary of Interior Chandler informed Secretary of War William W. Belknap that he had directed the Commissioner of Indian Affairs to notify the Indians that they must go onto the reservation by January 31, 1876, or be declared hostiles and "...a military force will be sent to compel them to obey the orders of the Indian Office."[8]

On December 11, 1875, the War Department forwarded copies of the above to the General of the Army, William T. Sherman, on whose authority all pertinent correspondence was referred down the chain of command to General Philip H. Sheridan, "...commanding Division of the Missouri, for report as to the feasibility of military operations against Sitting Bull and his tribe this winter."[9] General Sheridan then contacted his subordinates, Generals Alfred H. Terry in St. Paul and George Crook in Omaha, the former commanding the Department of Dakota and the latter commanding the Department of the Platte, both having responsibility for portions of the geographical area utilized by the hostile Sioux bands. He requested they report regarding the feasibility of military operations against the Indians.

On December 22, 1875, General Crook briefly responded that:

> ...military operations may be commenced against them whenever, in the opinion of the Department, such action becomes necessary. I recommend that the Department communicate their decision at the earliest date practicable, in order that preparations may be commenced before spring weather comes.[10]

On December 28, 1875, General Terry responded in detail as quoted:

> Sir: Referring to your indorsement of the 20th instant, upon a copy of correspondence between the War and Interior Departments, relative to operations against Sitting Bull and his band, in case they should refuse to obey the order of the Commissioner of Indian Affairs, directing them to move to the reservation which is set apart for them in common with other bands of the Sioux Nation, I have the honor to report that information from various sources tends to show that these Indians are now encamped for the winter on

---

7 Ibid.: 14–15.

8 Ibid.: 17.

9 Ibid.: 18.

10 Ibid.: 24.

the Little Missouri; it is believed that they are near the mouth [just north of present-day Twin Buttes, ND]. If this information is correct it will be possible in ordinary winter weather to reach their camp by a rapid march from Fort Abraham Lincoln [an approximately straight-line distance of 150–160 miles]. For such an operation there are available five well-mounted companies of cavalry at Lincoln and two at Fort Rice; a force which I think would be sufficient. Such an operation must, of course, be conducted with secrecy and rapidity, for it would not be possible for cavalry to follow the Indians for any considerable distance should they receive notice of the approach of troops and seek safety in dispersion and flight. It would be impracticable to carry supplies of food and forage for more than a very few days.

In view of the conversation which I had with the Lieutenant-General upon this subject when I was in Chicago week before last, I have not felt at liberty to communicate even to any of my staff that such operations have been contemplated, nor have I felt at liberty to take any steps to ascertain the precise position of Sitting Bull's camp.

I think that this information can be obtained by sending out scouts from Fort Stevenson [straight-line distance of 35–50 miles] without exciting suspicion. Sitting Bull doubtless knows that the garrison of that post consists entirely of infantry, and that he has nothing to fear from it. He will pay little attention to a movement from that quarter, even if it were discovered. If the Lieutenant-General shall approve of this suggestion, I will send confidential instructions to Lieutenant-Colonel Huston, the post commander, to obtain this information as if for his own purposes.[11]

Unfortunately for the U.S. Army, General Terry's assumption that Sitting Bull's camp could be quickly dealt with by a strike in the winter months from Fort Abraham Lincoln was incorrect. The first hints that Sitting Bull was no longer encamped on the Little Missouri in western North Dakota were enclosed in a report from the Indian agent for the Crow Agency in Montana, Dexter E. Clapp, written on January 10, 1876. Clapp reported that a large number of Sioux were in the Bighorn River area and had killed two whites near Fort Pease, the temporary stockade for the civilian enterprise that had gone down the Yellowstone River. This post was located on the north bank of the Yellowstone not far from the mouth of the Bighorn River.

---

11 Ibid.: 23–24.

Since Clapp's agency was located on the Stillwater River over 110 miles east of the nearest telegraph at Fort Ellis, his report did not reach the telegraph lines until January 20th.[12]

A few days earlier, on January 16th, another report had arrived with information originating with C.W. Darling, Indian agent, Fort Berthold Agency, and forwarded by Lieutenant Colonel Dan Houston from Fort Stevenson that Sitting Bull's camp was now located at Calf's Ear Butte[13] on the Yellowstone River about ninety to one hundred miles southwest of Fort Buford (between Glendive and Terry, MT). Thus, even before the January 31st deadline could expire or before it could be ascertained that Sitting Bull would not accede to the deadline, General Sheridan now knew that the possibility of an easy solution to this military problem was not at hand.

It is necessary to pause at this point and review the geographical and logistical situation as it existed at that time in our history. First and foremost, the hostile bands not residing on the reservations had to stay close to the buffalo for subsistence. The last great herds still roamed in an area bounded more or less on the east by the Little Missouri Valley, which ran south to north somewhat parallel to and slightly east of the Montana–North Dakota border; on the south it extended perhaps fifty miles into northern Wyoming; and on the west it was more or less bounded by the 110° meridian running north from present-day Big Timber, MT, and passing just west of present-day Havre, MT, and on up into Canada. The area south of the Yellowstone River, running from the Bighorn River west, in particular the area around the Stillwater River and farther west, was still occupied and strongly contested by the Crow Indians. The north was bounded by the Canadian border, but only for the U.S. Army. The hostiles could move across the boundary at will, provided buffalo were available, and, if buffalo were available, grass for the Indian ponies would likely also be available. All in all, this geographical area is approximately 400 miles east to west and 500 miles north to south. The hostiles could hold forth almost anywhere in this vast unsettled region, quickly moving their villages and camps by use of their ponies and travois. The Indians, living with the bare essentials, were not encumbered by the need to provide shoes for soldiers and grain for the soldiers' horses. Although far less so than today, the U.S. Army still had considerable logistical needs that the American Indian in his wild state was capable of forgoing.

---

[12] Ibid.: 61.

[13] The author was unable to locate Calf's Ear Butte on a map.

General George Crook—commander, Department of the Platte.

PHOTO COURTESY OF THE NATIONAL ARCHIVES.

Improved roads and railroads were virtually nonexistent in this entire area. The closest railheads in the east were at Bismarck, ND, near Fort Abraham Lincoln, and in the south at Sidney, NE, and Cheyenne, WY. The closest telegraphs were at Fort Abraham Lincoln in the east, in the south at Fort Fetterman (seven miles north of present-day Douglas, WY), and in the west at Fort Ellis. It should be noted that this latter line ran north into Montana Territory from Fort Hall in Idaho and the Corinne, UT railhead. There was a summertime water transportation route up the Missouri and Yellowstone to the mouth of the Bighorn River and, in periods of relatively high water (1876 was a very wet spring), a short distance up the Bighorn to the mouth of the Little Bighorn.

General Crook's Department of the Platte, based at the Union Pacific Railroad in Omaha, would move north from the Union Pacific Railroad at Fort Russell (Cheyenne, WY) and from Fort Sidney (Sidney, NE) via Fort Fetterman. Straight-line distance from Fort Fetterman to the Little Bighorn battlefield (the actual location of any battle could not be foreseen—the Little Bighorn location is only given as a point of reference) is approximately 230 miles, most of it unimproved wagon road, with about 30 to 50 miles of it no road at all, in very rugged, ravine-filled country. Additionally, most of the troops would have to travel over unimproved wagon roads for at least 185 miles from Fort Russell and over 200 miles from Fort Sidney just to reach Fort Fetterman.

General Terry's Department of Dakota was faced with a distance of 300 to 350 miles from Fort Abraham Lincoln to the Little Bighorn battlefield, with virtually no roads at all and, in some parts, very rugged country. The march from Fort Ellis to the Little Bighorn battlefield was over 190 miles, most of it over very rugged terrain, with large, swollen streams to overcome. In addition to this, the forces at hand in Montana were small in number, and their logistical base, i.e. supplies available in Montana Territory, was much smaller than that available to the contingents at Fort Abraham Lincoln and Forts Russell and Sidney.

On January 20, 1876, Colonel John Gibbon, at the Fort Shaw headquarters, District of Montana, forwarded a message to General Sheridan from Captain D.W. Benham, post commander, Fort Ellis, advising he had, pursuant to instructions from the Secretary of War, turned over a quantity of arms and ammunition to Mr. Clapp at the Crow Agency for use in their defense against incursions by the hostile Sioux.[14] Increasing incursions by the Sioux into that territory still held by the Crow Indians had caused great anxiety among the Crows, and was strong potential for disaffection with the whites to whom they looked for protection and assistance.

Two days later, Colonel Gibbon cabled the post commander at Fort Ellis, inquiring about the situation at Fort Pease. "Report the condition of the ranges east of Ellis. Is it passable for wagons?"[15] Gibbon had received a preliminary notification from General Terry before the January 31st deadline, regarding possible future movements against Sitting Bull. On January 12, 1876, Gibbon had sent a message to Dr. A.J. Hunter in Bozeman advising him that troops might be sent down the Yellowstone in the spring pending receipt of orders from the department commander, General Terry.

In the meantime, the deadline imposed on the hostiles by the Office of Indian Affairs drew nearer. On January 21, 1876, the newly appointed Commissioner of Indian Affairs, Mr. J.Q. Smith, sent a letter to Mr. Z. Chandler, Secretary of Interior, regarding steps taken to notify the hostiles of the deadline.

> ...on the 6th ultimo, my predecessor, acting under your instructions, directed the agents at the Red Cloud, Spotted Tail, Lower Brule, Crow Creek, Cheyenne River, Standing Rock, Devil's Lake and Fort Peck agencies to communicate, if practicable, to Sitting Bull and the other hostile Indians, the requirements of the Government that they return to the bounds of their reservation on or before the 31st instant.[16]

Agent Howard of Spotted Tail Agency expressed his belief that the message had reached Sitting Bull. Agents were also asked to report any news

---

[14] Fay: 61.

[15] January 22, 1876, District of Montana Letters and Telegrams Sent and Received.

[16] Fay: 21.

*General Alfred Terry—commander,
Department of Dakota.*

PHOTO COURTESY OF THE LIBRARY OF CONGRESS.

of Sitting Bull's movements and intentions. The commissioner further advised that he would forward any such news immediately to the Secretary of Interior for forwarding to the Secretary of War.[17]

As of February 4, 1876, however, word had not yet been received by the U.S. Army's Division of the Missouri from the Office of Indian Affairs as to whether the deadline had been met by the hostiles. On that date, General Sheridan cabled the following through the chain of command for the Secretary of Interior:

Respectfully returned. General's Terry and Crook notified these headquarters on December 28th and 22nd respectively, that they could move against these Indians…It is now for the Indian Bureau to make its decision on the subject. The matter of notifying the Indians to come in is perhaps well to put on paper, but it will be regarded as a good joke by the Indians. If it is intended that the military should operate against these Indians, I may safely say that every possibility of success will vanish unless directions are immediately given. I fully comprehend the difficulties of the country inhabited by these hostile bands, and unless they are caught before early spring, they cannot be caught at all. General's Terry and Crook should be notified, one way or the other, without delay.[18]

It appears, however, that General Sheridan's message to his superiors arrived in Washington about the same time as he received official authorization of the Secretary of War to move against the hostiles. On February 3rd, the secretary communicated with General Sheridan via the General of the Army, Sherman, ordering him "…to take immediate measures to compel these Indians to return to and remain upon their reservation…"[19]

---

[17] Ibid.

[18] Ibid.: 23.

[19] Ibid.: 29.

Preparations could now begin in earnest to initiate movements by Crook and Terry. Word went out in the Department of Dakota and the Department of the Platte to initiate action against the hostiles.

The larger portion of Terry's troops would have to march over inhospitable terrain for hundreds of miles from Fort Abraham Lincoln near present-day Bismarck, ND, to the area of the Bighorn River's junction with the Yellowstone, if that was where the Indians were to be located. It must be emphasized that no one knew at the time where the hostiles might be encamped; however, the Yellowstone drainage presented the greatest likelihood. Supplies could be brought all the way up to the Bighorn by steamboat, but not before the spring thaw. In other words, steamboats were not available for a winter campaign. General Sheridan, commanding the Division of the Missouri from Chicago, had in earlier years pushed for the establishment of posts and supply depots in the area of the Tongue and Bighorn river junctions with the Yellowstone, but these had not been funded. Further, that territory had up to this point been ceded, by the Treaty of 1868, to the Sioux and their allies. Portions of Terry's troops were located in the Montana Military District; although relatively small in number, they were ready to move out in the winter.

Naturally the military commanders also had to concern themselves with the protection of settlements and agencies in their areas of responsibility. For Terry these areas were around Bismarck and down along the Missouri in the Dakotas and those previously described in Montana Territory. Crook had to concern himself with the settlements along the new transcontinental railroad in Wyoming and Nebraska. There were also a considerable number of miners in the Black Hills, but these were all illegal settlements whose settlers had been informed by the army to vacate the area—warnings most people ignored. Eventually, political pressure resulted in the army's providing protection to the routes into the Black Hills, even though such movement and settlement were treaty violations. Both generals also had to remain cognizant of the fact that initiation of hostilities with the popular Indian leaders Sitting Bull and Crazy Horse might lead to a general uprising among the powerful Sioux tribe, which numbered in the thousands, the greater portion of them still residing in a peaceful state at the various Indian agencies in Dakota and Nebraska territories.

In his excellent book *On the Border with Crook*, John G. Bourke, at the time a young lieutenant on General Crook's staff, summarized problems faced and noted a possible key to victory.

The Sioux and Cheyenne whom we were soon to face were "horse" Indians, who marched and fought on horseback; they kept together in large bodies, and attacked by charging and attempting to stampede the herds of the troops. They were well armed with the newest patterns of magazine arms [repeating rifles], and were reported to be possessed of an abundance of metallic cartridges. Their formidable numbers, estimated by many authorities at as many as fifty thousand for the entire nation, had given them an overweening confidence in themselves and a contempt for the small bodies of troops that could be thrown out against them, and it was generally believed by those pretending to know that we should have all the fighting we wanted. These were the points on which the pessimists most strongly insisted. The cloud certainly looked black enough to satisfy any one, but there was a silver lining to it which was not perceptible at first inspection. If a single one of these large villages could be surprised and destroyed in the depth of winter, the resulting loss of property would be so great that the enemy would suffer for years; their exposure to the bitter cold of the blizzards would break down any spirit, no matter how brave; their ponies would be so weak that they could not escape from an energetic pursuit, and the advantages would seem to be on the side of the troops.[20]

---

[20] John G. Bourke, *On the Border with Crook:* 248.

CHAPTER FIFTEEN

Fort Pease Expedition and Pre-Campaign Logistics in Montana; General Crook's Winter Campaign

O N FEBRUARY 19, 1876, MAJOR JAMES BRISBIN, POST commander, Fort Ellis, cabled news of the Pease expedition.

> Letters appealing for help received here yesterday from Fort Pease, state all the men have abandoned the fort except 14, who are surrounded by Indians! Couriers in last night confirm the above report, and say one man [illegible] killed since letters were written and fighting going on. One man is wounded at the fort and unable to travel and another wounded man was brought as far as Baker's Battle ground and left in log cabin with two men. Citizens of Bozeman ask me to go to the relief of the men at Fort Pease. Fifty citizens will go with me and I can take two hundred soldiers from Ellis. Please instruct me what action I shall take?[1]

General Alfred Terry ordered Colonel John Gibbon to dispatch a rescue column for the beleaguered occupants of Fort Pease. On February 24th, Gibbon reported from Fort Shaw to Terry in St. Paul:

> The Cavalry left Fort Ellis on 22nd with 30 days rations. If the Dept Cmdr approves I will as soon as transportation can be obtained of the contractor, concentrate all available force in the District at Ellis,

---

[1] February 19, 1876, Fort Ellis Letters and Telegrams Sent and Received, Records of Posts, Continental Army Command 1820–1920, Record Group 393.7, National Archives.

join the Cavalry down the Yellowstone, and strike the Indians who have been making all this trouble. They will unless punished give us great trouble this summer. I would be able to take 450 or 500 men, and would be able to go with two months rations. The weather is fine with no snow on the ranges and although we are liable to have storms, they probably would not last long. If the plan is approved, I should have authority to employ about 50 Crows as scouts and guides, and an interpreter.[2]

The Fort Pease rescue force consisted of 14 officers, 192 enlisted men and 15 Bozeman citizens making up four companies of the 2nd Cavalry and a detachment of one company of 7th Infantry. Major James Brisbin commanded the column. The infantry "…was placed in charge of one 12-pounder Napoleon gun and one Gatling gun." A chronology of the march was cabled by Major Brisbin after his return on March 21.

FEBRUARY 22.—The command marched over the divide between the post [Fort Ellis] and Yellowstone River; distance, 14 miles.

FEBRUARY 23.—Marched to a point on the Yellowstone River opposite the Old Crow Agency [Springdale area]; distance, 22 miles.

FEBRUARY 24.—Marched downriver 15 miles, crossed to right bank, and camped 2 miles below crossing; distance, 17 miles.

FEBRUARY 25.—Marched to the "Bowlder," 7 miles; thence to Big Deer Creek, 2 miles; thence to Little Deer Creek, 2 miles; thence to Point of Rocks, on Yellowstone, 4 miles; total distance, 20 miles.

FEBRUARY 26.—Marched to Bridger's Creek, 3 miles; thence downriver 11 miles; total, 14 miles.

FEBRUARY 27.—Crossed to left bank of river and marched 9 miles; recrossed to right bank and camped 2 miles below crossing, near mouth of "Stillwater;" total, 11 miles. [Columbus area near site of Crow Agency located at that time on Rosebud Creek, a branch of the Stillwater.] At this point the command was joined by Lieutenant [Charles B.] Schofield, 2nd Cavalry, with twenty-five citizens and thirty Crow Indians, from the Crow Agency, I having sent Lieutenant Schofield in advance of the command to that point to secure as many citizens and Indians as he could to accompany the expedition.

2 February 24, 1876, District of Montana Letters and Telegrams Sent and Received, Records of Posts, Continental Army Command 1820–1920, Record Group 393.7, National Archives.

FEBRUARY 28.—Marched downriver 5 miles; crossed to left bank, thence down 9 miles; total, 14 miles. At this point the command was joined by twenty-four Crow Indians, making in all fifty-four.

FEBRUARY 29.—Marched down left bank 20 miles.

MARCH 2.—Marched down right bank to "Pompey's Pillar," 20 miles [about 30 miles down the Yellowstone from present-day Billings, MT].

MARCH 3.—Crossed river and marched on "Stanley's" road of 1873, 20 miles and camped about 6 miles from the river.

MARCH 4.—Marched to river, 6 miles; crossed to right bank; thence down 2 miles; crossed to left bank; thence down left bank 8 miles to Fort Pease; total, 16 miles.

MARCH 5.—Remained in camp at Fort Pease [near present-day Bighorn, MT]. The original garrison consisted of forty-six men, of whom six were killed and eight wounded. Twenty-one men had left the fort and gone through to the settlements by night. I found at the fort eighteen white men and one negro.

MARCH 6.—The fort was evacuated, and all the men started back with my command. I brought away all the valuable property belonging to the men at Pease and took it to the mouth of the Stillwater, where there is no danger of hostile Indians at present, and unloaded it. I saw no Indians, and but small parties are about. My scouts report the Indians have removed their villages from the Big and Little Horn Rivers and are camped on the Rosebud. The command marched back 8 miles and crossed to the right bank.

MARCH 7.—Marched up right bank 12 miles; crossed and marched up left bank 2 miles; crossed to right bank, and camped 4 miles above crossing; total, 18 miles. A scouting party was sent out during the night to go across the country to where the mouth of the Little Horn could be seen, the Crows having reported that a camp of Sioux was probably located near that point. The party returned the afternoon of the 7th, having been in full view of the Valley of the Bighorn, both above and below the mouth of the Little Horn, but saw no sign of hostile Indians.[3]

Major Brisbin's command arrived back at Fort Ellis on March 17th, reporting a total distance marched outbound of 208 miles and homebound 190 miles

[3] George E. Fay, *Military Engagements Between United States Troops and Plains Indian:* 64–66.

for a total marching distance of 398 miles. "The crossings of the Yellowstone were all made upon the ice, except the first [a ferry may have been utilized at this crossing]. One mule gave out, and had to be abandoned on the road."[4]

In the meantime, back at district headquarters in Fort Shaw, Colonel Gibbon was busy pulling together the necessary men and supplies for a major movement down the Yellowstone. On February 27, 1876, he requested permission from his department commander to order 11,000 pounds of hard bread at 8½ cents per pound. This was granted and the bread was ordered from Mr. T.H. Kleinschmidt at the 1st National Bank in Helena. On March 1st, Gibbon requested permission to secure contract wagons for freighting supplies under the same arrangements as during the 1872 expedition, or $5 per day per 2,500 pounds. He added that the contractor could not move before March 1st, since his animals were still out to pasture and had not yet been shod. Gibbon planned to freight supplies forward to the New Crow Agency on the Stillwater. On March 4th he telegraphed the post commander at Fort Ellis:

> The Contractor has been called upon to transport one hundred thousand pounds from Ellis to the New [Crow] Agency. If you can get a part of this transportation, send to the New Agency thirteen thousand complete rations and forty thousand pounds of grain under the escort of the Co. from Camp Baker as soon as it reaches Ellis. Send all your hard bread and complete the ration with flour. Answer.[5]

On March 6th, Gibbon cabled the commander at Fort Ellis asking him to order Major Brisbin to leave any extra supplies he may have on hand at the New Crow Agency (Brisbin would be passing the agency on his return from Fort Pease). Additionally, the post commander was to inform Mr. Dexter Clapp, the Indian agent, that Gibbon would need twenty-five good Crow scouts and would also like to meet with Mitch Boyer and Pierre Chien upon his arrival while en route down the Yellowstone. On the 7th, Colonel Gibbon queried Fort Ellis about the amount of grain, flour and bacon they had on hand, to determine if he should ship some in from Fort Shaw.[6]

On the 14th, Gibbon notified the post commander at Fort Ellis that the contractor's train had departed Fort Shaw on that date and should reach Fort Ellis by the 20th. Gibbon ordered the commander at Ellis to load on as

---

[4] February 27, 29, March 3, 4, 1876, District of Montana Letters and Telegrams Sent and Received.

[5] March 4, 1876, ibid.

[6] March 6, 7, 1876, ibid.

many extra rations and grain as the wagons would bear and move the train out immediately for the New Crow Agency. On the same date, he reported that Captain Comba was in Helena to take delivery of the hard bread and get it on the train upon its arrival in Helena. Of course, red tape existed even in the days of old. It was necessary for Colonel Gibbon to get Department of Dakota authorization for the purchase of some much needed grain sacks at Fort Ellis![7]

On March 17, 1876, Gibbon telegraphed Terry from Fort Shaw that the troops had "… marched [from Fort Shaw] this morning, twelve officers and one hundred and ninety four men, weather clear, but cold. I will be here till Tuesday, after that the telegrams can reach me at Helena, or be forwarded to Ellis. If possible, I should get your answer to my dispatch of the 4th regarding hire of transportation before leaving Helena."[8] Two other events of significance occurred on March 17, 1876: 1) Major Brisbin's expedition arrived back at Fort Ellis from Fort Pease, and 2) six cavalry companies of General Crook's command under Colonel Reynolds struck Crazy Horse's village on the Powder River in far southeastern Montana Territory near present-day Broadus, MT. The Bighorn–Yellowstone Campaign had begun in earnest.

General Crook was considered the U.S. Army's most experienced commander in Indian warfare. He had spent many years in the Southwest campaigning against hostile Apaches in Arizona as well as the Paiutes and Snakes in northern Nevada and Idaho. His philosophy of Indian fighting dictated that the U.S. soldier get by with as few supplies and other encumbrances as possible while pursuing hostile Indians. He was also prepared to suffer miserable weather and food and supply shortages equally with his men, and demanded the same of his officers. Consequently, his plan was to move his wagon and pack train as far north as feasible along the old Montana Road up into the areas around the abandoned Forts Reno and Phil Kearny. This area had been heavily contested by the Sioux and Northern Cheyenne some ten years earlier and eventually ceded to them by treaty in 1868. At this point Crook planned to establish a base camp from which to move out in light, swift mounted columns and mule pack trains with limited rations and supplies, seeking out and striking the hostiles.

While gathering his troops and supplies at Fort Fetterman, General Crook received a visit from an Arapahoe chief, "Black Coal," who informed him that the hostiles were located on the lower Powder River in Montana

---

[7] March 14, 16, 1876, ibid.

[8] March 17, 1876, ibid.

Territory some 150 miles from Fort Fetterman and 90 miles below old Fort Reno. The general also received a telegram informing him that 300 lodges of northern Sioux had just come in to the Red Cloud Agency, apparently in response to the January 31st deadline, but that supplies for the Indians were running short there. Upon learning this, Lieutenant Bourke wrote:

> This news was both good and bad, bitter and sweet; we should have a smaller number of Sioux to drive back to the reservation; but, on the other hand, if supplies were not soon provided, all the Indians would surely take to the Black Hills and Bighorn country, where an abundance of game of all kinds was still to be found.[9]

On March 1, 1876, after marshalling his forces and supplies at Fort Fetterman, following overland marches from the rail terminals at Fort Russell (present-day Cheyenne, WY) and Fort Sidney (present-day Sidney, NE), General Crook commenced his march north. His force consisted of ten full companies (troops) of cavalry and two companies of infantry. The column also included "eighty six-mule-team wagons loaded with forage and three or four ambulances carrying as much as they safely could of the same." Also included were 400 pack mules divided into five divisions of 80 mules each.[10]

The wintertime countryside provided poor sustenance for the animals, making forage an absolute necessity in order to maintain their strength in the bitter cold weather. This lack of winter forage was also a major problem for the hostiles.

> Winter campaigning was an entirely different matter; even the savages hibernated during the cold months, and sought the shelter of friendly cliffs and buttes, at whose feet they could pitch their tepees of buffalo or elk skin, and watch their ponies grazing upon the pasturage. The ponies of the Indians, the mares and foals especially, fare poorly during this season; they have no protection from the keen northern blasts, but must huddle together in ravines and "draws," or "coulees" as the French half-breeds call them, until the worst is over. They become very thin and weak, and can hardly haul the "travois" on which the family supplies must be packed. Then is assuredly the time to strike, provided always that the soldiers be not caught and frozen to death by some furious storm while on the march, or after being wounded.[11]

---

[9] John G. Bourke, *On the Border with Crook:* 250.

[10] Ibid.: 254.

[11] Ibid.: 251.

The expedition was accompanied by several half-breed scouts, among them Frank Grouard (sometimes spelled Gruard), half-Hawaiian and half-French, born in Hawaii. He had been captured by the Sioux but had the good fortune to escape death and spent many years living among them, becoming personally acquainted with Crazy Horse and Sitting Bull. He was held in high regard by General Crook and other members of the expedition. Crook's efficient scouting contingent was also staffed by Louis Richard, Baptiste Pourrier, Baptiste Garnier, Louis Changrau, Speed Stagner, Ben Clark and others. These scouts had been recruited at the Red Cloud and Spotted Tail agencies.[12]

Crook's column proceeded up the Montana Road from Fort Fetterman and immediately encountered hostile Indian activity. On the evening of March 1st, one of the herders was wounded as Indians attempted to stampede some of the stock, and on March 5th, the expedition was struck by a small group of Sioux while encamped, suffering one man wounded. On March 6th, Crook established his base camp near old Fort Reno and the wagon train was sent back to Fort Fetterman under infantry escort. He issued his instructions to the men:

> He said that we should now leave our wagons behind and strike out with the pack trains; all superfluous baggage must be left in camp; every officer and every soldier should be allowed the clothes on his back and no more; for bedding each soldier could carry along one buffalo robe or two blankets; to economize transportation, company officers should mess with their men, staff officers or those "unattached" with the pack-trains; officers to have the same amount of bedding as the men; each man could take one piece of shelter tent, and each officer one piece of canvas, or every two officers one tent fly. We were to start out on a trip to last fifteen days unless the enemy should be sooner found, and were to take along half-rations of bacon, hard tack, coffee and sugar.[13]

Commencing their march from the Fort Reno site on the evening of March 7, 1876, the column crossed over the divide at the head of the Clear Fork of the Powder River, marching thirty-five miles in a northwesterly direction. Camp was made on the Clear Fork, where the ice was found to be eighteen inches thick! It was bitter cold, and at 8 A.M. on the 8th, a

---

12 Ibid.: 255.

13 Ibid.: 259.

snowstorm commenced. During the day the column moved another five miles down the fork to a more suitable camp site. Snowy blustery weather continued all through the night of the 8th–9th of March. The column pushed on north, and scouts were sent forward in search of the hostile village. On the 10th of March they reached the Tongue River Valley, which provided a good supply of grass for the animals. The weather was bitter, -20 and -30 degrees Fahrenheit, but not one man suffered frostbite. "The exception of the command from frost-bite was not more remarkable than the total absence of all ailments of a pneumonitic type; thus far there had not been a single instance of pneumonia, influenza, or even a simple cold."[14]

On March 10th, the bitter cold weather continued as the column marched north. Scouts came in and reported finding a recently abandoned village. All evidence indicated it had been well-stocked with food, as the scouts brought back an amount of venison the Indians had abandoned. This was readily consumed by the troops. On March 11th, the column continued down the Tongue River toward the Yellowstone, with the scouts being sent west toward the Rosebud in search of the Indian camp. The weather remained bitter cold. Several abandoned villages were located along the Tongue closer to the Yellowstone. "Cottonwood by the hundreds of cords lay scattered about the villages, felled by the Sioux as food for their ponies, which derive a small amount of nourishment from the inner bark."[15] The troops enjoyed a two-day pause in the bitter cold as the temperature rose to +20 degrees!

On March 16th, the column was moving eastward from the Tongue toward the Powder River when area forward elements spotted two Sioux warriors observing them from a distance. General Crook ordered the column to set up camp, hoping that the Indians would assume he was en route to the Yellowstone and therefore not a threat to their village. It was believed that these Indians would return to their camp, thus revealing its exact location. This assumption would prove correct; these Indians were part of a forty-man hunting party. At dusk General Crook ordered Colonel J.J. Reynolds to take six troops of cavalry with scouts, march rapidly following the Indians' trail and, if the village could be located, strike it. Colonel Reynolds's force commenced a rapid night march eastward along the trail of the hunting party over very difficult terrain filled with ravines and gullies on slippery snow and ice, in a bittercold snowstorm. By 1 A.M. they sighted the bluffs

---

14 Ibid.: 263.

15 Ibid.: 266.

on the east side of the Powder River. Before daylight on March 17, 1876, a substantial village of an estimated one hundred lodges was located at the base of a cliff on the west bank of the Powder.

Colonel Reynolds divided his six troops into three battalions of two troops (companies) each. These battalions were commanded by Captain Anson Mills, Major H.E. Noyes and Colonel Alex Moore. A plan of battle was drawn up. The force was located above the village behind the cliff. The Indians were unaware of their presence. The battalions under Noyes and Moore would work their way down through a draw in the bluffs to the valley bottom. This draw was located to the right side of the force. Once on the bottom and in position, Captain James Egan's company, belonging to Noyes's battalion, was to ride into the village using revolvers and firing from horseback, thereby stampeding the Indians while Noyes with his remaining company drove off the horse herd, estimated at 700 ponies. "Mills was to move in the rear of Noyes, and, after the village had been charged, move in and take possession of it, occupy the plum thicket surrounding it, and destroy all the "tepis" and plunder of all kinds."[16]

Since the lodges were scattered in among boulders at the base of the cliff, it was correctly presumed that the hostiles would flee upslope into the boulders for protection once driven out of their tepees. Colonel Moore's battalion was ordered to move to the left of the force and take positions in the bluffs above the village from where they could fire down on the retreating hostiles, thus providing valuable support for the attacking battalions. On the face of it, the plan seemed to be a good one, but as all experienced soldiers will say, once the battle commences the best-laid plans go awry. Egan's company attacked as planned but made the mistake of discarding some of their warmer clothing just prior to the charge for the sake of mobility. Lieutenant Bourke participated in the daylight assault with Egan's company.

> Just as we approached the edge of the village we came upon a ravine some ten feet in depth and of a varying width, the average being not less than fifty. We got down this deliberately, and at the bottom and behind a stump saw a young boy about fifteen years old driving his ponies. He was not ten feet off. The youngster wrapped his blanket about him and stood like a statue of bronze, waiting for the fatal bullet; his features were as immobile as if cut in stone. The American Indian knows how to die with as much stoicism as the East Indian. I leveled my pistol. "Don't shoot," said Eagan, "We must

---

[16] Ibid.: 272.

make no noise." We were up on the bench upon which the village stood, and the-war whoop of the youngster was ringing wildly in the winter air, awakening the echos of the bald-faced bluffs…The ponies closest to the village trotted off slowly to the right and left as we drew near; the dogs barked and howled and scurried out of sight; a squaw raised the door to her lodge, and seeing the enemy yelled with all her strength, but as yet there had been not one shot fired. We had emerged from the clump of cottonwoods and the thick undergrowth of plum bushes immediately alongside the nearest "tepis" when the report of the first Winchester and the zip of the first bullet notified us that the fun had begun.[17]

The Indians fled from their tepees to the safety of the rocks, firing back at the attacking troopers and their horses as they went. Noyes's other company succeeded in driving off all the horses as planned, and Mills's battalion moved in, seized and began destroying the village. All the while the Indians poured fire on them from positions among the boulders. The plan, however, began to go awry when Colonel Moore's battalion failed to get into a good position from which to fire down on the Indians. When some of his battalion did fire, the rounds went high and actually fell among the attacking troopers.[18] In spite of this failure, the attack was proving successful. Lodges were being systematically destroyed, although Captain Egan's men were now suffering frostbite due to insufficient clothing.

> [The lodges] exploded as soon as the flames and heat had a chance to act upon the great quantities of powder in kegs and canisters with which they were all supplied. When these loose kegs exploded the lodge-poles, as thick as a man's wrist and not less than eighteen feet long, would go sailing like sky-rockets up into the air and descend to smash all obstacles in their way. It was a great wonder to me that some of our party did not receive serious injuries from this cause.[19]

Suddenly, in the middle of the fight, Colonel Reynolds ordered his forces to break off contact and, along with the captured ponies, move rapidly up the Powder to a rendezvous point with General Crook's remaining forces. This inexplicable move caused considerable dismay and bitterness in the ranks. Lieutenant Bourke exclaimed:

---

[17] Ibid.: 273–274.

[18] This is a common problem when firing downhill and calls for considerable adjustment in aim, to which many are not accustomed.

[19] Bourke: 276.

General Reynolds concluded suddenly to withdraw from the village, and the movement was carried out so precipitately that we practically abandoned the victory to the savages. There were over seven hundred ponies, over one hundred and fifty saddles, tons upon tons of meat, hundreds of blankets and robes, and a very appreciable addition to our own stock of ammunition in our hands, and the enemy driven into the hills, while we had Crook and his four companies to depend upon as a reserve, and yet we fell back at such a rate that our dead were left in the hands of the Indians, and, as was whispered among the men, one of our poor soldiers fell alive into the enemy's hands and was cut limb from limb. I do not state this fact of my own knowledge, and I can only say that I believe it to be true.[20]

Lieutenant Bourke reported that a wounded Indian woman in one of the tepees stated that the village was led by Crazy Horse, an Ogallalla Sioux chief. He added that among the lodges some forty were made of canvas and that they belonged to Cheyenne hostiles who had just arrived from the Red Cloud Agency. It is of interest to note that the Cheyenne warrior Wooden Leg, who was present at the time, stated to Thomas B. Marquis in the late 1920s, while about seventy years old, that this was a Cheyenne village of about forty lodges. Wooden Leg did, however, state that some Ogallallas were present in the village, although he stated that they comprised only three or four lodges. He also mentioned a wounded Indian woman was left alone in her lodge unharmed by the troopers.[21] While it is unlikely that Lieutenant Bourke would describe a village containing forty lodges as containing one hundred lodges, especially when he specifically stated that there were forty lodges of Cheyenne present, we may assume that there were more Ogallallas present than Wooden Leg recalled. Further, the wounded woman may have been an Ogallalla, who would naturally identify her village as belonging to Crazy Horse's Ogallallas.

Reynolds marched his force rapidly to the juncture of Lodge Pole Creek and the Powder River and went into camp, awaiting the arrival of Crook. The troops had suffered four killed and six wounded as well as some sixty-six cases of frostbite to feet, hands and fingers. Upon going into camp at Lodge Pole Creek, they were much fatigued and no guard was placed on the captured ponies. The Indians arrived that night and were able to recapture nearly all of them. Crook and his four companies arrived at the

---

[20] Ibid.: 278–279.

[21] Thomas B. Marquis, *Wooden Leg:* 168–170.

rendezvous on March 18th. On the way they had encountered a party of Indians with some recaptured ponies and managed to recover about one hundred of them. General Crook, disgusted with the turn of events, now had an exhausted force in hostile country some ninety miles from his base camp and a herd of captured ponies. During their march back to the base camp, they were frequently harassed by the Indians attempting to recover their ponies. General Crook ordered the ponies killed to keep them out of hostile Indian hands.[22]

Crook then retired his force to the base camp at Fort Reno, where he wrote the following telegram to General Sheridan for transmission from Fort Fetterman:

> Had terrible severe weather during absence from wagon-train; it snowed every day but one, and the mercurial thermometer on several occasions failed to register. Will be at Fetterman on the 26th instant, and if you desire me to move these Indians, please have instructions for me by this date, or else I shall return the cavalry to railroad at once for recuperation.[23]

General Crook was not happy at the loss of the captured Indian ponies and sought to court-martial Colonel Reynolds. He was of the opinion that if Reynolds was unable to hold them he should have ordered them all shot as Custer had done at the Battle of the Washita in northern Oklahoma on November 27, 1868. "After a long trial...Colonel J.J. Reynolds was found guilty and sentenced to be suspended from rank and command for the period of one year." Colonel Moore and Major Noyes were found guilty of lesser charges.[24]

In view of the less than satisfactory results of the first major battle of the Bighorn–Yellowstone Campaign, General Crook now made preparations for a spring and summer campaign. Crazy Horse, no doubt, wanted to avenge the attack on his village. Instead of forcing the Indians to return to the reservation or face starvation, this battle had left Crazy Horse and his band feeling victorious. The white invaders had been beaten off. As soon as the spring thaw and green grass allowed, Crazy Horse and Sitting Bull were soon joined by hundreds of young warriors arriving from among disaffected agency Indians. The white man was invading their hunting ground,

---

[22] Ibid.: 260–282.

[23] Fay: 67.

[24] Crook, George. *General George Crook: His Autobiography*: 192.

which had been granted to them nearly ten years prior by the Treaty of 1868. Further, an ever increasing influx of white prospectors was arriving in their sacred Black Hills. On his march from Fort Fetterman back to Fort Russell in late March, Lieutenant Bourke reported large parties of whites en route to the Black Hills.[25]

---

[25] Bourke: 281–282.

CHAPTER SIXTEEN

Colonel Gibbon's Montana Column Marches Down the Yellowstone— Spring 1876

WHILE GENERAL GEORGE CROOK WAS WITHDRAWING in preparation for a spring campaign, the Fort Shaw troops were marching to Fort Ellis. The soldiers, five companies of infantry and a mounted detachment, were "…accompanied by ten wagons containing camp equipage, extra ammunition, the personal effects of officers and men, and ten day's rations—which are expected to last until the command reaches Fort Ellis."[1] The troops experienced cold, wet, muddy weather during their entire 185-mile march. Simultaneously, another company of infantry was making its way from Camp Baker toward Fort Ellis.

As the Fort Shaw contingent departed, there were several inches of snow on the ground. After marching eleven miles, some of it in cold, drifting snow, the troops made camp at Eagle Rock. During the night two men deserted, taking with them two government horses. 1st Lieutenant James H. Bradley, in charge of the mounted infantry detachment, was sent forward with eight men to capture them, and after an exhausting ride in bitter cold weather, with short rests at Krueger's Ranch, thirty miles from Eagle Rock, John's Ranch and at Widow Durgin's (four miles outside of frontier Helena on Ten Mile Creek), the lieutenant and his small command overtook the deserters some four miles beyond Helena. Only twenty-seven hours had passed since Lieutenant Bradley's departure from Eagle Rock. Bradley then delivered the deserters to the Helena jail and he and his men rested, awaiting the arrival of the infantry.[2]

---

[1] James H. Bradley, *March of the Montana Column*: 7.

[2] Ibid.: 8–9.

Departing Eagle Rock, the infantry marched seventeen miles to the Dearborn River on March 18th, thirteen miles through deep snowdrifts to Krueger's Ranch on the 19th, eighteen miles to a cove on Little Prickly Pear Creek on the 20th, five miles on the 21st to John's Ranch, and seventeen miles to Widow Durgin's near Helena on the 22nd. On the 23rd, the troops marched eighteen miles to the Spokane House, and on the 24th another seventeen miles to Indian Creek Ferry on the Missouri River. The next day they covered twenty-one miles to Galen's residence, followed by a fourteen-mile march to Gallatin City on the 26th. On the 27th, they marched eighteen miles to Cockerill's Bridge on the West Gallatin. On the 28th, a sixteen-mile march took them through the town of Bozeman and into Fort Ellis four miles beyond.[3] Anyone familiar with March weather in Montana can well imagine what a joyous experience this trek must have been! After that, a small, dry corner in a drafty wood-stove–heated barracks would seem like heaven on earth.

Meanwhile, Colonel Gibbon continued to wrestle with the logistics of the operation. On March 18, 1876, he telegraphed the post commander at Fort Ellis, "Contractor's train should be at Ellis tomorrow. Push it out at once with all the supplies you can get on it using Benham's company as an escort, if the company from Baker has not arrived. It is important we should get supplies to the Agency [New Crow Agency] before 1st of April." On the following day he cabled General Terry, "Have arranged to throw forward about two months' supplies. Will this be sufficient? Arrangements for further supplies, if needed, should be made before I leave Ellis, for after the streams rise it will be difficult to get them forward." Five days later, on the 23rd, he cabled Terry from Helena, "Roads very bad. I cannot get transportation here on the terms you authorize. Am I to accept the best terms I can get? Infantry left here today, and one Company with a contract train containing one hundred thousand pounds of supplies left Ellis today"[4]

The contract train was issued arms for its protection and was escorted by Captain Telifford's company to the New Crow Agency and then as far back as the Yellowstone River on the return leg. By the 24th, Gibbon was advising Terry that his troops would not get to the Yellowstone crossing before April 1st. On March 27th, prior to getting word of Colonel Reynolds's battle with Crazy Horse, Gibbon predicted that the purpose of the expedition could

---

[3] Ibid.: 9–23.

[4] March 18, 23, 1876, District of Montana Letters and Telegrams Sent and Received, Records of Posts, Continental Army Command 1820–1920, Record Group 393.7, National Archives.

be fulfilled in two months—somewhat optimistic in hindsight! On March 29th, he cabled Terry from Fort Ellis that he had hired twenty-two wagons, each capable of transporting 4,500 pounds. He further advised that the infantry would march out of Fort Ellis on March 30th en route to the Yellowstone.[5]

It was originally intended that the Montana Column would store supplies at the New Crow Agency on the Stillwater River south of the Yellowstone and then follow the old Bozeman Trail down to the vicinity of Fort C.F. Smith, which had been abandoned in 1867. It would then operate in that general area attempting to strike the hostiles.[6] However, by March 30th, Gibbon received the news of Reynolds's fight with Crazy Horse and Crook's decision to prepare for a spring campaign. He cabled Terry:

> In view of the information from General Crook am I not operating on a wrong line by go[ing] south of the Yellowstone instead of north of it? Brisbin reports a large fresh lodge [trail] leading north from the mouth of the Rosebud. He thinks Sitting Bull is on Big Dry Fork toward which this trail leads. Must I limit my offensive operations to Indian Reservation lines, or may I strike Sitting Bull wherever I can find him?[7]

General Terry concurred that Gibbon should now remain on the north side of the Yellowstone once he reached the presumed area of operations. This meant that Gibbon would now have to transfer his supplies, already en route to the Crow Agency south of the Yellowstone, to a location on the north bank. Once the floodwaters of the spring thaw had commenced, it would be impossible or, at best, extremely difficult to move them to the north bank as needed.

As for Gibbon's suggestion that he strike Sitting Bull wherever he could find him, in view of all that actually transpired during the next six months, Gibbon certainly cannot be faulted for lack of an aggressive war-fighting spirit. His total command as it marched out of Fort Ellis amounted to only 409 men and 27 officers. Compare this to Custer's force of over 700 men and Crook's summer campaign force of 1,100 men eventually engaged at the Battle of the Rosebud!

---

[5] March 23 through 30, 1876, ibid.

[6] James H. Bradley, *The March of the Montana Column*: 31–32.

[7] Big Dry Fork is located well to the north of the Yellowstone, north-northeast of present Jordan, and flows north into the Missouri. March 30, 1876, District of Montana Letters and Telegrams Sent and Received.

By April 3rd, all elements of Gibbon's command had departed Fort Ellis.[8] The Montana Column now entered that portion of Montana Territory east of Fort Ellis that was totally devoid of settlers with the exception of two or three scattered establishments. Their route of travel took them along the wagon road through the pass between Bozeman and present-day Livingston now traversed by Interstate 90, then up over the divide between the Gallatin and Yellowstone rivers (Bozeman Pass), then down Billman's Creek, arriving at Benson's Landing shortly after crossing Fleshman's Creek in present-day Livingston. At that time, Benson's Landing "...served as the head of Mackinaw-boat navigation..." on the Yellowstone.[9]

On April 1, 1876, Lieutenant James H. Bradley, traveling with the infantry, noted in his diary, "Passed two occupied places today, Quinn's ranch, in the gap, and the rather extensive establishment at the Yellowstone Ferry."[10] By this time they had overtaken the wagon train, which the lieutenant referred to as Power's contract train. On April 2nd they passed the Shields River. This stream flowed "...through an extensive and fertile section of the country, which for some years past has furnished pasture for large herds of cattle."[11] The next day they arrived at Hunter's Hot Springs where Dr. Hunter, residing with his family, was attempting to operate a summer resort for the afflicted, i.e. brave souls who were willing to risk attack by the Sioux while seeking the healing powers of the water! This would be Hunter's Hot Springs on Hunter's Creek about three miles northwest of present-day Springdale, MT.

On April 3rd, the infantry reached the ford across the Yellowstone, one and one quarter miles beyond Duck Creek. This location was approximately four miles east of present-day Springdale, MT. They made the crossing in twenty minutes without mishap. They then marched down the right bank in nasty, snowy weather, before making camp on the Big Boulder River.[12] Colonel Gibbon, having departed Fort Ellis at a later date with the cavalry, took four days to cover the first thirty miles due to the severity of a snowstorm in the mountains.[13] On the 4th Lieutenant Bradley reported,

---

8   April 3, 1876, ibid.

9   Edward J. McClernand, *On Time for Disaster:* 116–117.

10 Bradley: 29.

11 McClernand, *On Time for Disaster:* 117.

12 Ibid.: 118.

13 Bradley: 27–31.

> [General Gibbon] has changed his plan of operations in conse-
> quence of the news received from General Crook. As it is feared that
> the Indians defeated by [Crook] will endeavor to escape toward the
> north, we are now to keep down on the Yellowstone with a view to
> intercepting them, instead of turning off toward Fort C.F. Smith as
> originally planned.[14]

On April 5th the infantry arrived at Bridger Creek. Here they encountered a large group of hardy prospectors on their way to the gold fields in
the Black Hills. On the 6th they arrived at a location some two miles above
the mouth of the Stillwater where they were joined on April 8th by Colonel
Gibbon and Major Brisbin's 2nd Cavalry companies. Near the mouth of
the Stillwater, they encountered the last occupied establishment to be seen
while going down the Yellowstone. It was a whiskey trading post known as
Countryman's Ranch near present-day Columbus, MT.[15] Its clientele were
no doubt thirsty Crow Indians from the nearby new agency.

At this location Colonel Gibbon was visited by Mitch Boyer, sometimes
spelled Bouyer, one of the half-breed scouts whose services he had requested in
his cable to Fort Ellis on March 6th. Gibbon describes his meeting with Boyer:

> This man I had never seen, but he had served with troops before, and
> bore the reputation of being, next to the celebrated Jim Bridger, the
> best guide in the country. Whilst seated in my tent…a man with the
> face of an Indian and the dress of a white man approached the door,
> and almost without saying anything seated himself on the ground,
> and it was some moments before I understood that my visitor was
> the expected guide. He was a diffident, low-spoken man, who ut-
> tered his words in a hesitating way, as if uncertain what he was going
> to say. He brought the news that the Crows were waiting to see me,
> and mounting my horse I was with a small party soon on the road
> to the agency, which we reached after a disagreeable ride of eighteen
> miles through a severe storm of wet snow.[16]

Lieutenant McClernand would later write that he believed Boyer's
father was French-Canadian and his mother, Sioux. Boyer was married to a
Crow woman.[17]

---

[14] Ibid.: 31–32.

[15] Ibid.: 32–38.

[16] John Gibbon, *Adventures on the Western Frontier:* 113–114.

[17] Edward J. McClernand, "With the Indian and Buffalo in Montana," *Journal of the United States Cavalry Association* 1927: 16.

In the midst of some 3,000 Crow Indians camped at the New Crow Agency at Rosebud Creek (a branch of the Stillwater near present-day Absarokee, MT), Colonel Gibbon met with the Crow leaders, in particular, the two principal chiefs, Blackfoot and Iron Bull. After much negotiation he was able to secure twenty-five Crow scouts to accompany the expedition. "They thus became United States soldiers for three months, and were to receive soldier's pay, rations and clothing."[18] Each scout also received forty cents per day for horses provided.[19] The Crow scouts were placed under the command of Lieutenant James H. Bradley, who also commanded Gibbon's mounted infantry detachment. He wrote:

> The [scouts] were mostly young men of less than thirty years of age, but two are veterans of middle age and two more, old men over sixty, who are expected to do little service beyond giving the young fellows the benefit of their encouragement and advice.[20]

Gibbon emphasized the difficulty in communicating through the available interpreters:

> These Indian interpreters are a peculiar institution. As a class they are an interesting study, and will bear generally a good deal of watching. A white man, usually a renegade from civil society, takes up his abode with a tribe of Indians, adopts their mode of life, takes unto himself a squaw, picks up gradually enough of their signs and words to make himself understood, and when the Indians come in contact with the whites becomes, in the absence of any other means of communication, an interpreter. Frequently these "interpreters" were barely fluent in their native English or French tongues, let alone the Indian tongues. For this reason it is a matter of importance in communicating with Indians to make use of the plainest language and the shortest sentences.[21]

On April 10, 1876, Gibbon wrote Terry from the Crow Agency:

> Will establish my depot twenty five miles from here north of Yellowstone, and then move down the river with all the rations and grain I can carry. Additional supplies, if sent to us, can now follow

---

18 Gibbon: 115.

19 September 27, 1876, District of Montana Letters and Telegrams Sent and Received.

20 Bradley: 48–49.

21 Gibbon: 114.

the river as we do. After the river rises they must keep north of the Yellowstone. Have engaged Crow scouts here, but can get no news of matters beyond the Bighorn. Two hundred prospectors left yesterday for Fort Phil Kearney via Fort C.F. Smith.[22]

The reader must bear in mind that this message would not reach the telegraph terminal at Fort Ellis for several days. Also, even though Gibbon's forces were now in the Yellowstone Valley, they were still some one hundred miles from the Bighorn River and even farther from the Rosebud, Tongue and Powder River drainages. They did not anticipate locating large numbers of Sioux, i.e. villages, before reaching the Bighorn. Regarding the prospectors— even though the Montana (Bozeman) Road was officially closed, hardy souls continued to use this route. They were, however, careful to travel well armed and in sufficient numbers. The prospectors mentioned were probably en route to the Black Hills.

On April 11th, the wagons were loaded with the supplies, which had been stocked at the Crow Agency and, battling deep snow, moved the eighteen miles back to the Yellowstone, forded it with the loss of two mules to drowning, and arrived at the new base camp site on the north bank. The camp was dubbed "Camp Supply." Leaving one infantry company and one Gatling gun under Captain William Logan to secure Camp Supply, Gibbon headed on downriver with the remainder of his force on April 12th.[23] The going was muddy and difficult. On April 15, 1876, after covering some forty-three miles they reached "Baker's Battlefield," near present-day Billings, MT. Once there, they were forced by the geography along the river to cross to the south bank and work their way across a flooding Pryor Creek. Marching on to Pompey's Pillar and beyond, they were again forced to ford the Yellowstone twice due to high bluffs on both banks.

> Our guide, Mitch Bouyer, is of inestimable value now, for he rides forward to search for a crossing, and is an indefatigable worker, riding his hardy little pony into the ice-cold water, sometimes to a swimming depth, testing the crossings where anybody thinks there is a chance to get our wagons over.[24]

Of course, these were not warm tropical waters but rather freezing

---

[22] April 10, 1876, District of Montana Letters and Telegrams Sent and Received.

[23] Bradley: 50–51.

[24] Gibbon: 118.

floodwaters from the snowmelt in the mountains. Gibbon describes one crossing in detail:

> At last the shallowest point is found, and although deeper than is comfortable, we must take to the water, for we cannot afford to wait another day. A company of cavalry, with its old soldier captain at its head, mounted on his old and long-time favorite, "Dick", enters the ford, stringing out in a long curved line as brave old "Dick" breasts the rushing and rapidly deepening stream. Higher and higher rises the water, and just as we begin to think some of the smaller horses will have to swim, "Dick's" shoulder commences to emerge and the worst is past. Now the wagons, covered with infantrymen, start in, and as they approach the deepest part some of the smaller mules barely have their backs above the water, but still they struggle on, seeming to understand as well as their drivers that when crossing a river is no time "to swap horses." Suddenly down goes the forepart of one of the wagons, and for a moment it is a matter of doubt whether a wheel is broken or is in a hole. The mules struggle and plunge, fall down and get up again, the drivers, outsiders [sic], and men shout at their loudest yells to encourage the frantic animals, and at last the long line of wagons reaches the opposite shore, water pouring from every crack of the wagon-bodies, which makes us hope that the bottom layer of each load is bacon, rather than "hardtack" and bedding. The dripping teams are given a short rest, mounted officers and men pour the water from their boots, and we all feel relieved that we are on the right bank of the river at last.[25]

Gibbon maintained a steady and cautious vigilance to prevent surprise by hostiles. Whenever the main force was on the move, Bradley's scouts were posted well to the front, sometimes as much as eight to twelve miles distant, scouting the countryside for signs of the enemy. During the river crossings they were posted forward on the opposite bank, covering the force against possible surprise attack. On April 17th two scouts were sent across into the Bighorn area. They returned on the 18th, reporting no signs of Indians. Also on the 18th, scouts were sent back along the trail to check for any Sioux who might be shadowing the force. Only a few days before, these scouts had discovered a party of five bold white men out on a hunting expedition![26]

---

[25] Ibid.: 119–120.

[26] Bradley: 52, 63–65.

The base camps were also situated and fortified to avoid successful surprise attack by the hostiles. 1st Lieutenant John F. McBlain, who accompanied the expedition, would later describe one of the encampments:

> This camp was arranged nicely for defensive purposes, and as we were in the heart of Sioux country the fine soldierly instincts of the commander appreciated the necessity for constant vigilance and preparation for any attack that might be made. The wagon train was in an almost circular corral, around which were camped the six companies of infantry; at the open or entrance side of the corral was camped the four troops of cavalry, two on each side, the flanks furthest from the corral being thrown back so as to form a funnel-shaped driveway to the corral, through which would be driven all the animals in case of a threatened attack on the herds. The defensive strength of a camp like this can be readily seen.[27]

On April 21st, Gibbon wrote a message to Terry from Fort Pease, "Reached here yesterday. Fort standing with flag flying. No sign of Indians being here since Brisbin's visit, and we have seen none. Send any intelligence or instructions you may have for me quickly. The further we proceed the more uncertain and slow our communication with Ellis becomes." Gibbon also asked Terry if he could now depend on steamers for supplies or if he should continue to rely on wagon trains from Fort Ellis.[28]

Before the day was out, however, a courier, identified by Lieutenant Bradley as Will Logan, the son of Captain William Logan, arrived from Camp Supply with a message from Terry via Fort Ellis. The message was dated April 15, 1876. It was six days old. Gibbon wrote that the message

> … informed me that General Crook would not be prepared to take the field before the middle of May, that the third column had not yet started [Terry's force from Fort Abraham Lincoln], and directed that I proceed no farther that the mouth of the Bighorn unless sure of striking a successful blow."[29]

Receiving this news, Lieutenant Bradley noted in his diary on April 21st, "General Crook's victory was not so decisive as we have regarded it, while the fighting seems to have demonstrated that there are heavier forces of

---

[27] John F. McBain, "With Gibbon on the Sioux Campaign of 1876," Part I, *Journal of the United States Cavalry Association*, Vol. 9 (June 1896): 140–141.

[28] April 21, 1876, District of Montana Letters and Telegrams Sent and Received.

[29] Gibbon: 120.

warriors to encounter than had been counted upon. General Terry fears the Indians may combine and get the better of us..."[30]

The 7th Cavalry at Fort Abraham Lincoln had not moved out simultaneous with the Montana Column and Crook's movements in the south. We may assume that Terry was delayed by logistical problems, severe North Dakota weather and, possibly, a desire to have better intelligence on the location of the hostiles before dispatching his major elements. One thing is certain. Steamboats could not get up the Yellowstone until spring, thus rendering resupply of a large body of troops extremely difficult.

Another dispatch from Terry requested an additional fifty Crow scouts to be sent to the aid of General Crook's forces. On April 21st, Gibbon responded to Terry's messages:

> Have just received your two dispatches of the 15th. Have established my camp alongside of Fort Pease where I can leave a single company and strike out with the rest if any opportunity offers. Meantime I will have this vicinity thoroughly scouted, bring up more supplies, and be ready to start the moment you notify me to do so. I will write the Crow Agency regarding the Scouts, but fear fifty cannot be got to go, and advise Gen'l Crook to send the Officer to Missoula and get Flatheads through their Chief Adolph. They know this country as well as the Crows and, I hear, are better scouts.[31]

Colonel Gibbon now knew that it would be at least three weeks before his force would be expected to move in coordination with Crook's and Terry's elements. He utilized this time to scout the area and to move his stores down from Camp Supply, now one hundred miles to his west. He sent his wagon train, escorted by one infantry company, Company H, 7th Infantry, under Captain W.B. Freeman, to retrieve the supplies and bring them down to the Fort Pease camp.

On April 24th, Colonel Gibbon dispatched Captain Edward Ball with two troops (companies) of cavalry, Ball's own Company H and Lieutenant Roe's Company F, 2nd Cavalry, total strength eighty men, to cross the Yellowstone and ride south to old Fort C.F. Smith, then scout the Bighorn and Little Bighorn areas for signs of the hostiles. Lieutenant McClernand, who accompanied this scout, wrote, "It was not desired that Captain Ball should engage the Indians, but only to discover, if possible, their

---

[30] Bradley: 68.

[31] April 21, 1876, District of Montana Letters and Telegrams Sent and Received.

whereabouts, at the same time keeping his command as well concealed as possible."[32] Gibbon also dispatched scouts out to the Rosebud drainage. On April 30th, the scouts returned from the Rosebud, reporting no signs of the hostiles.

On May 1st, Captain Ball's two companies returned from their reconnaissance. They had ridden to Fort Smith, then over to the Little Bighorn, actually bivouacking at a spot very near the later battlefield site. This scout was accompanied by Lieutenant McClernand and George Herendeen.[33] On their arrival, Gibbon sent the following message to Terry:

> Captain Ball just in with two companies from C. F. Smith. Went out on Phil Kearney road as far as Rottingrass, thence over to Little Bighorn, and Tullock's Fork's and down that. He saw no signs of Indians. My scouts report none on Rosebud. As soon as my supplies reach here, say in four days, I propose, if no news comes from you, to move down the river.[34]

In the meantime, there were signs of small parties of Sioux around Gibbon's camp. During the early hours of May 3rd, one group of hostiles managed to steal thirty ponies belonging to Gibbon's Crow scouts, as well as a mule and a horse belonging to the Fort Shaw post guide, Hiram S. Bostwick. These horses had been kept overnight outside the picket area.[35] When referencing signs of Indians, Gibbon obviously meant signs of large camps or villages.

On the night of May 7th, Lieutenant Bradley, with seventeen mounted infantry, Hiram Bostwick and Thomas LeForge, the latter a white who resided with the Crows, and four Crow scouts conducted a reconnaissance down the north bank of the river, traveling some eighty-five miles round-trip to Porcupine Creek and back. They returned on the 9th, having sighted the fresh trail of the Sioux party that had stolen the animals.[36]

In the meantime, Captains Freeman and Logan had arrived the previous day with the wagon train from Camp Supply and two companies of infantry—the one company originally left to secure the camp and the other company that had escorted the wagons back to Camp Supply. On May 10th,

---

[32] McClernand, "With the Indian and Buffalo in Montana": 11.

[33] Edward J. McClernand, *On Time for Disaster:* 43.

[34] May 1, 1876, District of Montana Letters and Telegrams Sent and Received.

[35] Bradley: 87.

[36] Ibid.: 90.

Gibbon began moving his forces down to a point opposite the mouth of the Rosebud. If Indians attempted to cross the Yellowstone to the north, it was reasoned that they would utilize the more popular fords in that area. On the previous day, he had notified Terry:

> Leave here tomorrow with my entire command. Small war parties have been in vicinity, and this place is too far up the river to produce any effect. A scouting party under Lieut. Bradley just came in from the Porcupine, forty miles below, saw no Indians, but found the fresh trail of a war party of thirty leading down the river. This party ran off some Crow ponies from the vicinity of this camp on the night of the 2nd. We shall be short of rations before our train can reach us, but buffalo are plenty and we will not suffer.[37]

By May 15, 1876, Gibbon's force was now encamped on the Yellowstone's north bank just above the mouth of the Rosebud, which flowed into the Yellowstone from the south. Operating on a hunch that there might be a hostile village on the Tongue River, Gibbon directed Lieutenant Bradley, with a twenty-seven-man mounted force made up of infantry volunteers and Crow scouts, to ford the Yellowstone and conduct a scout in that direction. On the afternoon of May 16th, they spotted a very large Sioux village some twelve to fifteen miles above the mouth of the Tongue River. Bradley's Crow scouts believed the village contained no fewer than 200 to 300 lodges. Lieutenant Bradley would later note, "It afterward turned out that this camp contained about four hundred lodges, or from eight hundred to a thousand warriors..."[38] This village was about thirty-five miles distant from Gibbon's main force. Upon receiving Bradley's report on May 17th, Gibbon decided to send a force out to strike it, which was news well received among most of the men. Lieutenant Bradley wrote:

> It was two months to a day since we had left Fort Shaw for the purpose of cleaning out the Sioux nation, and during all that time we had done nothing but march, march, and rest in camp; but now the enemy had been found and we were going over to whip them. The accumulated satisfaction of the sixty blessed days that had preceded, if combined in a single lump, could have equaled that with which this order was received. Not that there were no soreheads who were personified gloom and despondency and whispered of dire

---

[37] May 9, 1876, District of Montana Letters and Telegrams Sent and Received.

[38] Bradley: 101.

overthrow and dreadful disaster; but the great majority were hopeful, jubilant, and full of fire of battle. Everybody fell to with a will, and there was more real good feeling and enthusiasm in the camp than I had witnessed in a body of men for a long time. But there came a sober, serious time to most of us, and that was when we sat down to pen to the far-off loved ones letters that might be the last they would ever receive from us. We did not then credit the Sioux with the prowess we have since learned to, but still we did not despise our foe, and felt that the fight would probably be well enough contested to make some vacancies among us.[39]

Unfortunately, or fortunately with perfect 20-20 hindsight, Gibbon found it impossible to move his force across the Yellowstone, which had continued to rise since they had made their last crossing on April 21st. After hours of failed attempts and the drowning of four horses, plans to cross and strike the Sioux were abandoned. Even before the attempt was abandoned, a large party of Sioux, presumably from the Tongue River village, was spotted watching Gibbon's force. Gibbon had planned to conduct a night march and strike the Indians at dawn, giving his 392-man force the advantage of surprise. Losing hope of surprising the Indians as well as determining the extreme difficulty in getting across the river, Gibbon decided to abandon the effort.[40]

---

[39] Ibid.: 102–103.
[40] Ibid.: 105–106.

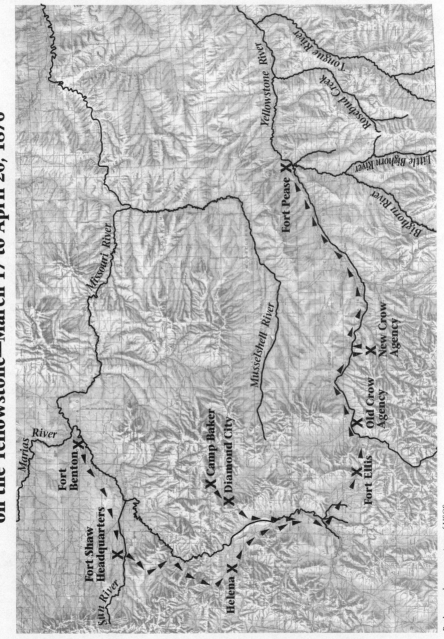

Gibbon's Montana Column Marches to Fort Pease on the Yellowstone—March 17 to April 20, 1876

Marias River

Fort Benton X

Fort Shaw Headquarters X

Sun River

Missouri River

Camp Baker X
Diamond City X

Helena X

Musselshell River

Yellowstone River

Tongue River

Rosebud Creek

Little Bighorn River

Bighorn River

Fort Pease X

New Crow Agency X

Old Crow Agency X

Fort Ellis X

Background map courtesy of USGS

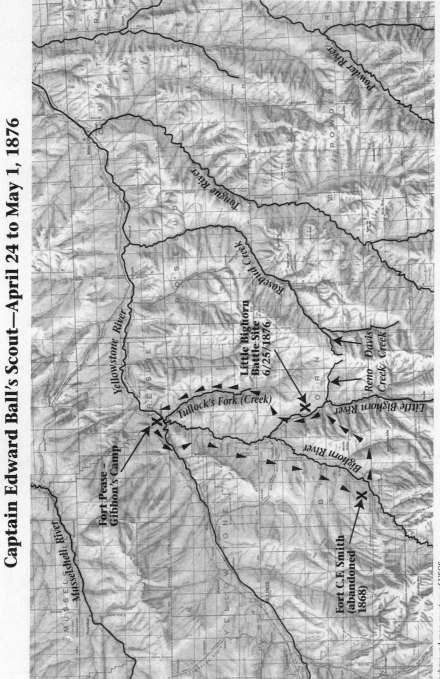

Captain Edward Ball's Scout—April 24 to May 1, 1876

Background map courtesy of USGS

General Terry's Force Departs Fort Abraham Lincoln and Joins Gibbon; Crook Commences Summer Campaign

G ENERAL ALFRED TERRY'S COLUMN MARCHED OUT OF Fort Abraham Lincoln on May 17th, simultaneous with John Gibbon's attempt to do battle. He planned to coordinate operations with Gibbon's force, which was situated over rugged country some 350 miles to the west, and George Crook's force, which was still forming up at Fort Fetterman far off over equally rugged country to the southwest. Terry's column

> ...consisted of the 7th United States Cavalry, commanded by General George A. Custer, 28 officers and about 700 men; two companies of the 17th United States Infantry, and one company of the 6th United States Infantry, 8 officers and 135 men; one platoon of Gatling guns, 2 officers and 32 men (of the 20th United States Infantry); and 40 "Ree" [Arikara] Indian scouts.[1]

This amounted to a total strength of about 870 men, 38 officers and 40 Indian scouts. The column also contained about 150 wagons, including two-horse wagons carrying from 1,500 to 2,000 pounds and six-mule wagons, which could carry 3,000 to 5,000 pounds. The smaller wagons were contracted and the larger were U.S. government wagons.[2]

Custer's command of the 7th Cavalry on this expedition had been very

---

[1] E.S. Godfrey, *Custer's Last Battle*: 5.

[2] Ibid.: 7.

much in question right up to its date of departure from Fort Abraham Lincoln. He had incurred the wrath of President Ulysses Grant by becoming involved in the congressional investigation of Secretary of War William W. Belknap. As a consequence, Grant had ordered Custer to remain at his post while his regiment took to the field against the hostiles. However, Custer's presence as commander was much valued by his superiors. General Terry and his superior, General Sheridan, as well as General of the Army Sherman interceded on Custer's behalf and finally convinced the president to allow Custer to accompany the expedition. Thus, Custer was able in the nick of time to march out of Fort Abraham Lincoln in command of the 7th Cavalry.[3]

On May 18, 1876, Colonel Gibbon sent two companies of the 2nd Cavalry under Captains Thompson and Wheelan down the north bank to scout the mouth of the Tongue River. On the same day, Gibbon sent Lieutenant James Bradley with a detachment on a three-day scout upriver in an effort to locate couriers, who were due from Fort Ellis. The couriers were located and arrived at the base camp with Bradley's detachment on the 19th. They brought news of Terry's planned departure from Fort Abraham Lincoln, and that Gibbon could now expect the 7th Cavalry under Custer to reach them in about one month. Gibbon was also informed that Terry had secured two steamboats, the *Josephine* and the *Far West,* to assist in moving troops and supplies into the area.[4]

On the 19th, Crow scouts reported sighting some 200 to 300 hundred Sioux warriors moving across the Wolf Mountains in the direction of the Rosebud River. This was confirmed by a later scout, according to Lieutenant Bradley, on the 27th. On May 21st, Thompson's command of cavalry returned from their scout. They had spotted about forty to fifty Sioux warriors attempting to cross the Yellowstone to the north side. The Indians gave up their effort due to the high water and departed southward without spotting the cavalry, which had taken up positions on the north bank to give them a surprise reception.

Once again, the Sioux made an appearance near Colonel Gibbon's camp. Two soldiers, Privates Raymeyer and Stoker, Company H, 2nd Cavalry and one teamster, Mr. Quinn, out hunting near the base camp on the 23rd, were ambushed and killed by a small party of Sioux.

---

[3] J.P. Dunn, Jr., *Massacres of the Mountains:* 513–515.

[4] James H. Bradley, *The March of the Montana Column,* 108–109.

On reaching the foothills [near the base camp, the hunting] party found itself in the midst of a succession of knolls rising higher and higher and forming a number of narrow valleys. The men appear to have entered one of these blindly without taking any precaution in the way of a lookout. They were doubtless watched from the high ground, and parties of Indians posted out of sight behind the hills on each side permitted the three hunters to advance until surrounded on all sides, and then making their appearance, delivered their fire from several directions upon the doomed men. The bodies were found stripped, shot in several places and horribly mutilated, with heads beaten in, and one of the men had two knives, taken from the bodies of his dead comrades and driven into the sides of his head. The knife of the third man was afterwards recognized and picked up on Custer's battle-field.[5]

On May 24th, a lone Sioux scout appeared within one-half mile of the base camp but fled upon approach. On the 27th, Lieutenant Bradley was again ordered to cross the river and conduct a nighttime scout southward, in an attempt to locate the Sioux. He was accompanied by thirteen men of his mounted infantry detachment, plus LeForge and five Crow scouts. After penetrating some fourteen miles to the south, observing numerous Indian signs, and reaching a point in the Little Wolf Mountains that he had reconnoitered on the 16th, Bradley discovered a very large Indian village located along the Rosebud.

[We] found ourselves again in the vicinity of an immense Indian camp. In numerous places up and down the valley the smoke was rising in columns and blending in a cloud over the camp, the break in the bluffs revealed the tops of several lodges—in a few instances, the entire lodge. The plain above the camp was dotted with hundreds of moving black specks that could only be horses, and while we gazed, there came distinctly to our ears from the broken ground at the base of the hills the sounds of several rifle shots, showing that the Sioux hunters were at work. [The camp previously sighted had been] about thirty-fives miles from our command, but now they were only eighteen; and the fact that they had moved down within easy striking distance seemed to prove that they held us in no awe.[6]

---

5 John Gibbon, *Adventures on the Western Frontier:* 125.

6 Bradley: 122–124. Gibbon had, of course, already attempted one crossing in his effort to attack the village when it was spotted on the Tongue River. At this juncture, he knew that reinforcements and steamboats were on their way. It is therefore understandable that he did not attempt another crossing. It is of further interest that Gibbon makes no mention of this second sighting of the village, this time on the Rosebud. Bradley alludes to a degree of doubt among some of his colleagues back at the base camp, who were skeptical of his original sighting of the Tongue River camp.

In the meantime, Gibbon had received new word from Terry that he expected to reach the Yellowstone at Glendive Creek, near present-day Glendive, MT, on about May 27th or 28th. Gibbon asked for two volunteers to float down the river to meet Terry with dispatches. "Two men who afterwards became quite noted for a deed of great daring, offered their services for the trip. Their names were Evans and Stewart, both soldiers, belonging to Captain Clifford's company of the Seventh Infantry."[7] These men were accompanied on their journey by a white scout, Williamson.[8]

On May 28th, Gibbon received word that General Terry had departed Fort Abraham Lincoln on the 15th (in fact, the force moved out from Fort Abraham Lincoln on the 17th). The message informed Gibbon that Terry now had intelligence that the hostiles were concentrated on the Little Missouri River and between there and the Powder River. Thus, Terry expected fighting in that area and ordered Gibbon to march his forces about 150 miles downriver to Stanley's Stockade near present-day Glendive, MT, and cross, if possible, to link up with Terry on Colonel Stanley's "trail" (route) of 1873. A steamer would likely be awaiting Gibbon's command at the crossing, and ferry his forces across.

This order placed Gibbon in somewhat of a dilemma, for he was still awaiting the arrival of his supply train from Fort Ellis, under escort by Lieutenant William English. To hasten its arrival, he dispatched an infantry company and Lieutenant Roe's cavalry company, under the command of Captain Sanno, along with all available wagons on hand in the base camp to meet up with them and hasten their return back to camp.[9] Terry, of course, had not yet received the latest information regarding the movement of the Indian village on the Tongue and its current position on the Rosebud. The first sighting of this village was on May 16th, and Gibbon learned of it on the 17th. Allowing at least six days for the message to arrive at Fort Ellis and be transmitted to Fort Abraham Lincoln, it could not have arrived there before the 23rd. However, General Terry had departed Fort Abraham Lincoln on the 17th, so now the message had to overtake him.

Simultaneous with Gibbon's preparations to march downriver to meet Terry's column, General Crook's column once again marched north out of Fort Fetterman on the morning of May 29, 1876. This time his force

---

7 Ibid.: 125.

8 Ibid.: 126.

9 Gibbon: 126; Bradley: 127.

consisted of fifteen companies (troops) of cavalry under Colonel William B. Royall and five companies of the 9th and 4th Infantry under Colonel Alexander Chambers. The train contained 103 six-mule wagons and several hundred pack mules. Crook's force would later be joined by 175 Crow and 86 Shoshone scouts.[10] Now all three columns were in the field. It was, of course, no longer the planned winter campaign.

On May 27th, General Terry's column reached the Little Missouri River badlands. On the 30th he ordered Lieutenant Colonel Custer to take four companies and scout up this river for twenty miles. Custer returned later that same day, having found no sign of Indians. The column then continued its march west toward the Powder River, still finding no Indians. They eventually struck the Powder about twenty-five miles above its confluence with the Yellowstone.[11] While en route they encountered a snowstorm and as a result remained in camp on June 1st and 2nd.[12]

On the 1st, Gibbon's force had to endure the same heavy snowstorm that had stopped Terry, but the wagon train and escort made it to the base camp by June 4th. On the 5th Gibbon moved his forces out, heading downriver, but was only able to make forty miles in three days—one hill alone took four hours to overcome. Mitch Boyer told Gibbon that the trail ahead would be even worse. By June 8th, white scouts from General Terry's command attempted to make contact, but were frightened off by Gibbon's Crow scouts, mistaking them for hostiles. Later that day contact was made and Gibbon received a message that Terry was on a steamboat at the mouth of the Powder awaiting him. Gibbon then moved out on June 9th with a company of cavalry to meet Terry, and on his way down encountered the steamboat, the *Far West*, slowly making its way upriver toward his command.[13]

Terry had established a temporary base camp after reaching the Powder River at a point about twenty-five miles above its mouth on the Yellowstone. He and an escort had then moved down to the Yellowstone, where a steamboat awaited him, then hooked up with Gibbon. Upon his meeting with General Terry, Gibbon noted:

---

[10] John G. Bourke, *On the Border with Crook:* 289–291.

[11] We may assume that the column entered Montana along the course of present-day U.S. Highway 12, which crosses the Powder River approximately twenty-five miles above the Yellowstone River.

[12] Godfrey, *Custer's Last Battle:* 9.

[13] Gibbon: 126–127.

The existence of any large camps of hostile Indians in this region is now more than ever a matter of doubt; for General Terry has discovered no trace of any on his march from Fort Lincoln to the Powder River, which he had reached at a point twenty-five miles above its mouth. He…had heard nothing from General Crook, and intended on his return to Powder River to send a cavalry command on a scout up that river and across it west to the Tongue and the Rosebud.[14]

Apparently Colonel Gibbon did not consider the village located by Bradley and his scouts on the Tongue and later on the Rosebud to be the "large" village the campaigners were hoping to strike.

Terry still expected Crook to be pushing up from the south. He therefore instructed Gibbon to move his troops back to their old position opposite the mouth of the Rosebud and continue to scout the north bank for signs of hostiles attempting to cross. Terry would join Gibbon later at his Rosebud camp. General Terry needed guides familiar with the country south of the Yellowstone, and Gibbon provided him with some of his Crow scouts along with his best scout, Mitch Boyer.[15] By June 14th, the whole Montana Column would be back operating out of its old base camp opposite the mouth of the Rosebud and scouting the north bank of the Yellowstone, per Terry's instructions.

On June 10th, Terry returned to his column on the Powder and ordered Major Marcus Reno with six troops of Custer's 7th Cavalry to conduct the above-described scout of the Powder, Tongue and Rosebud. Reno departed at 3 P.M. with pack mules and twelve days' rations. Terry then moved the remainder of his column down to the mouth of the Powder to set up a new supply camp.

General Edward S. Godfrey, at the time a young 2nd Cavalry lieutenant serving in Terry's column, would later write:

Up to this time we had not seen an Indian, nor any recent signs of them, except one small trail of perhaps a half dozen tepees, evidently of a party of agency Indians on their way to join the hostile camps. The buffalo had all gone west; other game was scarce and wild. The indications were that the Indians were west of the Powder, and information from General Gibbon placed them south

---

14 Ibid.: 127.

15 Ibid.: 128.

of the Yellowstone. Some of the officers of the right wing [that portion of the command on the scout with Reno] before they left expressed their belief that we would not find any Indians, and were sanguine that we would all get home by the middle of August.[16]

Reno was to follow the Powder up to its forks near present-day Broadus, MT, and then cross over to Mizpah Creek (present-day Olive, MT), then follow Mizpah Creek back down to its confluence with the Powder (present-day Mizpah, MT). From here he was to head west to Pumpkin Creek, following this stream down to the Tongue River at a point some twelve miles above the Yellowstone, then head up the Tongue and eventually rejoin the regiment at the mouth of the Tongue, unless an important discovery warranted otherwise.[17]

Major Marcus A. Reno.
PHOTO COURTESY OF MONTANA HISTORICAL SOCIETY RESEARCH CENTER PHOTOGRAPH ARCHIVES, HELENA, MONTANA.

In the meantime, after establishing a supply camp at the mouth of the Powder secured by his infantry, Terry moved by steamboat to the mouth of the Tongue while Custer marched along the south bank of the Yellowstone to that location with the remaining left wing of the 7th Cavalry. Once they arrived at the mouth of the Tongue, they waited until June 19th to hear from Reno. Godfrey noted that there were numerous Indian graves near the site of the camp, which were plundered by some of the troopers:

> Several persons rode about exhibiting trinkets with as much gusto as if they were trophies of their valor, and showed no more concern for their desecration than if they had won them at a raffle.

[16] Godfrey: 10.
[17] Ibid.

> Ten days later I saw the bodies of these same persons dead, naked, mutilated.[18]

On June 18th, Reno's scouting command arrived opposite Gibbon's camp at the mouth of the Rosebud, and on the 19th he reported back to Terry's column farther down the Yellowstone at the Tongue River camp. While scouting the Tongue, he had come across a large trail, which he followed over to the Rosebud and then to a point about forty miles above the mouth of the Rosebud, likely somewhere just north of present-day Lame Deer, MT. Lieutenant Bradley later wrote that Mitch Boyer, traveling with Reno, counted 360 lodge fire sites and some 40 other fire sites, indicating a village of about 400 lodges—some 800 to 1,000 warriors. The lodges had been arranged in circles scattered along the valley but close enough to provide support to one another if attacked. Bradley wrote, "A well-defined trail led from the site of the village across the plain toward the Little Bighorn, and it is now thought that the Indians will be found on that stream."[19]

On June 17, 1876, just one day after Reno had reached his farthest point up the Rosebud (approximately June 16th), General Crook's command was struck at the headwaters of the Rosebud by a large force of Sioux and Northern Cheyenne under Crazy Horse and lesser-ranking Sioux and Northern Cheyenne chiefs, resulting in the Battle of the Rosebud. Although Reno was likely only about a two-day ride from Crook at this time, news of this battle did not reach division headquarters in Chicago until June 23rd.[20] On that same date it was forwarded to Terry's headquarters in St. Paul and also to Fort Abraham Lincoln and Fort Ellis. Of course, it would be at least five or six days before it could reach either Terry or Gibbon from those points, in other words, after the Battle of the Little Bighorn (June 25, 1876) had already taken place.

---

[18] Ibid.

[19] Bradley: 142.

[20] Finnerty, *War Path and Bivouac*: 448–449.

CHAPTER EIGHTEEN

Crook Marches North; Crazy Horse Attacks Him on the Rosebud

AFTER ITS DEPARTURE FROM FORT FETTERMAN, GENERAL George Crook's column followed the same route taken earlier—up the Bozeman Road. They encountered and suffered through the same snowstorm that had struck Gibbon's and Terry's forces on June 1. On that date, scouts Frank Grouard, Louis Richard and Big Bat were sent out to attempt to locate an expected force of Crow scouts. On June 2, 1876, Crook's column reached Clear Creek on the Tongue River drainage, where they encountered sixty-five Montana miners on their way from the Black Hills gold fields back to the Yellowstone. The miners joined Crook's column.

On June 9th, the column came under attack by a small Sioux war party while camped on the upper Tongue River. This skirmish resulted in two soldiers being wounded. Lieutenant Bourke wrote of this skirmish:

> This attack was only a bluff on the part of "Crazy Horse" to keep his word to Crook that he would begin to fight the latter just as soon as he reached the waters of the Tongue River; we had scoffed at the message at first believing it to be an invention of agency half-breeds, but there were many who now believed its authenticity.[1]

This was to be the site of the base camp, but since grass was scarce, Crook moved his troops to a better location on Goose Creek near present-day Sheridan, WY. Here he awaited the arrival of his Crow scouts. On June 14th, after an absence of two weeks, Frank Grouard and the others returned with 176 Crow scouts under the leadership of three chiefs, Old Crow, Medicine

---

[1] John G. Bourke, *On the Border with Crook*: 296.

Crow and Good Heart. Lieutenant Bourke described the reaction of the soldiers to their newly arrived allies:

> A curious crowd of lookers-on—officers, soldiers, teamsters, and packers—congregated around little squads of Crows, watching with eager attention their every movement. The Indians seemed proud of the distinguished position they occupied in popular estimation, and were soon on terms of easy familiarity with the soldiers, some of whom could talk a sentence or two of Crow, and others were expert to a slight extent in the sign language.[2]

Shortly after the arrival of the Crows, eighty-six Shoshone scouts arrived. Finerty wrote that "The chiefs of the Snakes [Shoshones] present were Wesha and Nawkee, with the two sons of old Washakie."[3] They had ridden sixty miles that day and were accompanied by Tom Cosgrove, Nelson Yurnell, Ulah Clairs, and Luisant, a French Canadian half-breed.[4] The Crows considered the Shoshones allies against a common enemy, the Sioux, and welcomed them with enthusiasm. Bourke described their armaments as "…of the latest model —calibre .45."[5] These were likely repeating rifles, probably Winchesters.

Shortly after the arrival of the Indian scouts, General Crook gathered his officers and issued his marching instructions:

> We were to cut loose from our wagons, each officer and soldier carrying four days rations of hard bread, coffee, and bacon in saddle pockets, and one hundred rounds of ammunition in belts or pouches; one blanket to each person. The wagons were to be parked and left behind in a defensible position on the Tongue or Goose and under the protection of men unable for any reason to join in the forward movement; all infantrymen who could ride and who so desired were to be mounted on mules from the pack-trains with saddles from the wagons or from the cavalry companies which could spare them.[6]

The general, having drawn a lesson from his last foray into Crazy Horse country, added that:

> If successful in attacking a village, the supplies of dried meat and other food were to be saved, and we should then, in place of

---

[2] Ibid.: 302.

[3] John Finerty, *War Path and Bivouac*: 103.

[4] Bourke: 306.

[5] Ibid: 305.

[6] Ibid.: 302–303.

returning immediately to our train, push on to make a combination with either Terry or Gibbon, as the case might be.[7]

June 15th was spent preparing for departure. The unfortunate infantry soldiers who had to be mounted on mules did not have a very pleasant time of it. *Chicago Times* correspondent John Finerty, who accompanied the expedition, described the brief interval when pack mules were expected to become accustomed to saddles and riders, and riders had to learn, on short notice, to master the unwilling mules. Many of the unhappy infantrymen were promptly bucked off their rebellious beasts of burden.[8] Eventually, by the conclusion of a harrowing day, 175 infantry troops, or approximately four companies, had become mule-mounted infantry.[9] Bourke wrote:

> At 5 AM on June 16th the column departed, 1,100 men strong, and proceeded in a northwesterly direction crossing tributaries of the Tongue. Late that afternoon the Indian scouts, who had been riding out to the front of the column reported evidence of a large Indian village nearby. As the column moved over a table land toward the Rosebud Creek drainage, Lieutenant Bourke reported that buffalo were encountered and some thirty were killed,
>
> …and the choice pieces—hump, tenderloin, tongue, heart, and rib steaks—packed upon our horses. The flesh was roasted in the ashes, a pinch of salt sprinkled over it, and a very savory and juicy addition made to our scanty supplies. The Indians ate the buffalo liver raw, sometimes sprinkling a pinch of gall upon it; the warm raw liver alone is not bad for a hungry man, tasting very much like a raw oyster. The entrails are also much in favor with the aborigines; they are cleaned, wound round a ramrod, or something akin to it if a ramrod is not available, and held in hot ashes until cooked through; they make a palatable dish…[10]

While Bourke relished in the feast of buffalo, Mr. Finerty reported that the Indian scouts, "Contrary to their general custom,…killed the animals with sheer wantonness, and when reproached by the officers said, "better kill the buffalo than have him feed the Sioux!"[11]

---

[7] Quoted in Bourke.

[8] Finerty: 112.

[9] Bourke: 305.

[10] Ibid.: 309–310.

[11] Finerty: 118.

The night of the 16th to 17th of June, the column made camp at the headwaters of Rosebud Creek. At dawn on the 17th, it moved out heading down the Rosebud. At approximately 8 A.M. a halt was ordered in a portion of the valley described by Lieutenant Bourke to be somewhat shaped like an amphitheater, bordered on the sides, front and rear by hills cresting within rifle range, probably at 500 to 1,000 yards. The horses were unsaddled and allowed to graze, attended by their riders. Mr. Finerty sat down to rest with several officers. Suddenly, rifle fire was heard to the front, evoking the comment that the Indian scouts had once again located buffalo, but the shooting increased and shortly thereafter a group of Indian scouts came galloping rapidly over the hill crest toward the front and down to the troops, crying "Sioux, Sioux!"

Washakie—Shoshone chief.
PHOTO COURTESY OF THE LIBRARY
OF CONGRESS.

> "Saddle up, there—Saddle up, there, quick!" shouted Colonel Mills, and immediately all the cavalry within sight, without waiting for formal orders, were mounted and ready for action. General Crook, who appreciated the situation, had already ordered the companies of the 4th and 9th Infantry, posted at the foot of the northern slopes, to deploy as skirmishers, leaving their mules with the holders.[12]

No sooner had the cavalry mounted when hundreds of Sioux began to appear on the slopes to the front, rushing down on the troops and firing at them at full gallop.

Mr. Finerty was an eyewitness to the preceding and following sequence of events. Shortly after Colonel Anson Mills had saddled up his troopers, regimental adjutant Lemly rode rapidly up to his position, his horse heavily lathered from his dash from General Crook's position, "The commanding officer's compliments, Colonel Mills!" he yelled. "Your battalion will charge those bluffs on the center!" Finerty then describes the charge, which he accompanied:

---

12 Ibid.: 123.

Mills immediately swung his fine battalion, consisting of Troops A, E, I and M, by the right into line, and, rising in his stirrups, shouted "Charge!" Forward we went at our best pace, to reach the crest occupied by the enemy, who, meanwhile, were not idle, for men and horses rolled over pretty rapidly as we began the ascent. Many horses, owing to the rugged nature of the ground, fell upon their riders without receiving a wound. We went like a storm, and the Indians waited for us until we were within fifty paces. We were going too rapidly to use our carbines, but several of the men fired their revolvers, with what effect I could neither then nor afterward determine, for all passed "like a flash of lightning or a dream."[13]

The troopers carried the crest, driving the Sioux back. General Crook then ordered Lieutenant Colonel Guy V. Henry's 2nd Battalion, 3rd Cavalry, Company B, D, F and L, to charge the Sioux lines, likewise driving the Sioux back. Company C and G of the 3rd Cavalry under Captain Frederick Van Vliet and Lieutenant Crawford were ordered to occupy the heights to the left rear, from which a good view of the battlefield existed.

The Crow and Shoshone scouts, under Major George M. Randall, chief of scouts, assisted by Lieutenant Bourke, were ordered to charge into a second line of defense of the Sioux. Bourke accompanied the attack with the Shoshones under their chief, whom he identified as "Luishaw" (probably Chief Washakie):

I went in with this charge, and was enabled to see how such things were conducted by the American savages, fighting according to their own notions. There was a headlong rush for about two hundred yards, which drove the enemy back in confusion; then was a sudden halt, and very many of the Shoshones jumped down from their ponies and began firing from the ground; the others who remained mounted threw themselves alongside their horses' necks, so that there could be few good marks presented to the aim of the enemy. Then, in response to some signal or cry which, of course, I did not understand, we were off again, this time for good, and right into the midst of the hostiles, who had been halted by a steep hill directly in their front. Why we did not kill more of them than we did was because they were so dressed like our own Crows that even our Shoshones were afraid of mistakes, and in the confusion many of the Sioux and Cheyennes made their way down the face of the bluffs unharmed.[14]

---

[13] Ibid.: 124–125.

[14] Bourke: 312–313

Finerty described the rescue of a sergeant by a Crow scout from the clutches of the Sioux. Sergeant Van Moll had been accidentally left on foot within the grasp of the Sioux as the Indian scout force withdrew from the fight described above.

> Major Randall and Lieutenant Bourke…who in the crisis, recognized his stature and his danger, turned their horses to rush to his rescue. They called on the Indians to follow them. One small, misshapen Crow warrior, mounted on a fleet pony, outstripped all others. He dashed boldly in among the Sioux, against whom Van Moll was dauntlessly defending himself, seized the big Sergeant by the shoulder and motioned him to jump up behind. The Sioux were too astonished to realize what had been done until they saw the long-legged Sergeant, mounted behind the little Crow, known as "Humpy," dash toward our lines like the wind. Then they opened fire, but we opened also, and compelled them to seek higher ground. The whole line of our battalion cheered "Humpy" and Van Moll as they passed us on the home-stretch. There were no insects on them either.[15]

As the day progressed Crook's troopers pushed the hostiles from ridge to ridge and crest to crest some five miles back toward their village, which was believed to be located about eight miles down the Rosebud at the end of Dead Canyon. Crook then decided to split his force and launch a rapid thrust through the canyon toward the village. He assigned Colonel Mills's Company A, E and M and an additional five troops under Major Henry E. Noyes, in all around 350 to 400 men, to press this attack. After they had pushed some distance into the canyon, they began to notice an ever-increasing number of hostiles on the surrounding slopes, directing harassing fire at them. Shortly after Crook had launched this thrust, Colonel Royall's 3rd Cavalry troopers, a part of Crook's main body, came under heavy attack and in need of reinforcements. Crook then dispatched couriers to overtake the troopers in the canyon and order them back. He would later note in his autobiography:

> To this end I sent Captain Mills with his squadron up a cañon in the proposed direction. I noticed some Indians who were just above where he passed, and who could have inflicted much damage to his troops without any danger to themselves. Instead of doing this, they sneaked off the hill, keeping in advance of the troops, which showed

---

[15] Finerty: 128.

me plainly that we were doing just what they wanted us to do. So I recalled the squadron.[16]

Upon receipt of these orders, the troopers turned left and climbed out of the canyon, returning to their previous battleground and relieving the hard-pressed 3rd Cavalry troopers. The hostiles were beaten off.[17]

General Crook then decided to retire his forces some five miles back up the canyon, to where the day's fighting had begun. He had used up about 25,000 rounds of ammunition and had some seriously wounded troops to care for.[18] The next day he marched his force back to their base camp at Goose Creek. Arriving at Goose Creek, General Crook dispatched the following telegram to Fort Fetterman for transmission to his division commander, General Sheridan, in Chicago:

> Camp on the South of Tongue River, Wyoming, June 19th via Fort Fetterman, June 23rd.—Lieut.-Gen. Sheridan, Chicago, Ill: Returned to camp today having marched as indicated in my last telegram. When about forty miles from here on Rosebud Creek, Montana, on the morning of the 17th inst., the scouts reported Indians in the vicinity, and within a few moments we were attacked in force, the fight lasting several hours. We were near the mouth of a deep cañon, through which the creek ran. The sides were very steep, covered with pine and apparently impregnable. The village was supposed to be at the other end, about eight miles off. They displayed a strong force at all points, occupying so many and such covered places that it is impossible to correctly estimate their numbers. The attack, however, showed that they anticipated that they were strong enough to thoroughly defeat the command.

> During the engagement, I tried to throw a strong force through the cañon, but I was obliged to use it elsewhere before it had gotten to the supposed location of the village. The command finally drove the Indians back in great confusion, following them several miles, the scouts killing a good many during the retreat. Our casualties were nine men killed and fifteen wounded of the 3rd Cavalry; two wounded of the 2nd Cavalry, three men wounded of the 4th

---

[16] George Crook, *General George Crook: His Autobiography:* 195.

[17] On October 31, 2008, the author visited the Rosebud Battlefield. With the exception of a fence or two and isolated ranch buildings, the area still exists much as it did at the time of the battle. Unfortunately, the markers and the road around Royall's Ridge were in very poor condition. A visit to this site is highly recommended.

[18] Quoted in Finerty: 135.

Infantry, and Captain Henry, of the 3rd Cavalry, severely wounded in the face. It is impossible to correctly estimate the loss of the
Indians, many being killed in the rocks, and others being gotten off
before we gained possession of that part of the field, thirteen dead
bodies being left.

We remained in the field that night, and, having nothing but what
each man carried himself, we were obliged to retire to the train to
properly care for our wounded, who were transported here on mule-
litters. They are now comfortable and all doing well.

I expect to find those Indians in rough places all the time and so have
ordered five companies of infantry, and shall not probably make any
extended movement until they arrive. The officers and men behaved
with marked gallantry during the engagement.

Crook,
Brigadier General[19]

John Finerty noted that the general reported only those wounds that
rendered the men incapable of action. Lieutenant Bourke reported the losses
at fifty-seven killed and wounded, although some of these wounds were slight.
Crook does not give an estimate of the Indian force, but Lieutenant Bourke
wrote that the general at the time believed them to number about 2,500.[20]

Of particular interest is Lieutenant Bourke's report of an interview with
Crazy Horse at the Red Cloud Agency after his surrender. Crazy Horse
claimed he had 6,500 warriors present during the Battle of the Rosebud.
He had planned to draw Crook's troops into the canyon, cut them off and
overwhelm them. The force he had displayed immediately to the front of
Crook had numbered about 1,500.[21] We may assume with perfect 20-20
hindsight that Crook's force sent into the canyon withdrew before Crazy
Horse could close the trap and wipe out a force of 350 to 400 men, even
more than fell with Custer! What he failed to accomplish at the Rosebud,
he, Chief Gall and other Indian allies would make good at the Little Bighorn
just eight days later.

---

[19] Finerty: 448–449.

[20] Bourke: 315.

[21] Ibid.: 311.

Terry's Force Enters Montana and Reno's Scout June 10–June 19, 1876

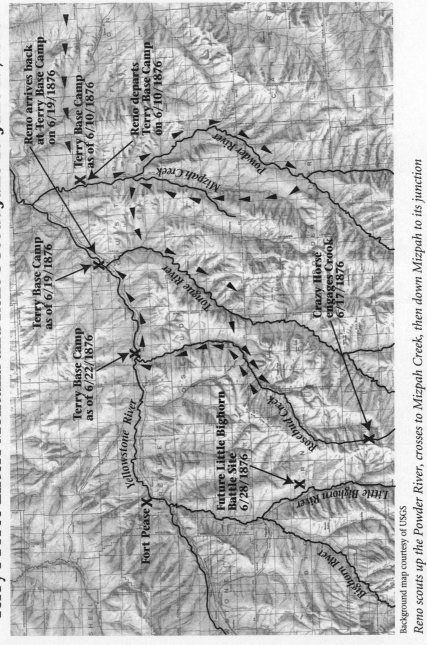

Reno arrives back at Terry Base Camp on 6/19/1876

Terry Base Camp as of 6/10/1876

Reno departs Terry Base Camp on 6/10/1876

Terry Base Camp as of 6/19/1876

Terry Base Camp as of 6/22/1876

Crazy Horse engages Crook 6/17/1876

Future Little Bighorn Battle Site 6/28/1876

Fort Pease

Powder River

Mizpah Creek

Tongue River

Yellowstone River

Rosebud Creek

Little Bighorn River

Bighorn River

Background map courtesy of USGS

Reno scouts up the Powder River, crosses to Mizpah Creek, then down Mizpah to its junction with the Powder, then up the Tongue, where he locates an Indian trail. He follows it to and up Rosebud Creek to the site of present-day Lame Deer, MT. Reno then turns back down the Rosebud to the Yellowstone and over to Terry's base camp at the mouth of the Tongue River.

CHAPTER NINETEEN

Terry Moves Against the Hostiles at Little Bighorn

TOTALLY IGNORANT OF GENERAL GEORGE CROOK AND the Wyoming Column's setback at the headwaters of the Rosebud, General Alfred Terry made preparations to locate and strike the hostile Indian camp, the traces of which had been discovered during Major Marcus Reno's scout. On June 21st, Colonel John Gibbon ordered three companies to move back up the north bank of the Yellowstone, repairing the road and bridges along the way in preparation for moving the entire Montana Column back to Fort Pease, just across from the mouth of the Bighorn River. Later on the same day, Terry arrived at Gibbon's camp on the steamer *Far West* and met with Gibbon. After the meeting, Gibbon ordered the remainder of his force to proceed to Fort Pease, while he accompanied General Terry back downriver aboard the steamer for a general conference with Lieutenant Colonel George Custer. In the meantime, Custer was marching with his cavalry regiment up the Yellowstone to the mouth of the Rosebud from the mouth of the Tongue.[1] Custer's 7th Cavalry Regiment arrived at the mouth of the Rosebud about noon on the 21st.

On the afternoon of June 21, 1876, as Gibbon's forces were marching back to Fort Pease, General Terry conferred with his subordinates Gibbon and Custer aboard the *Far West* at the mouth of the Rosebud. Gibbon later described the results of the meeting:

---

[1] John Gibbon, *Adventures on the Western Frontier*: 129.

The large trail found by Colonel Reno leading up the Rosebud and the fires seen in that direction by my scouts led to the belief that the Indians, if overtaken at all, would be found somewhere on the Little Bighorn, a favorite resort, where the grazing was good and the game close by. It was therefore arranged that General Custer would start the next day with the whole of his regiment, take up the trail on the Rosebud, and follow it; that my command should march to the mouth of the Bighorn [Fort Pease], something over sixty miles distant, be there ferried [by steamboat] across the Yellowstone, and march from there to the valley of the Little Bighorn, and up that stream to cooperate with Custer's command.[2]

It was believed that if the Indians attempted to withdraw from the Little Bighorn, should they be located there, they would likely attempt to move south and thus encounter General Crook's forces, coming up from that direction.[3]

After the conference, Custer assembled the officers of the 7th Cavalry Regiment and gave them instructions, as later described by then-lieutenant (later general) E.S. Godfrey:

We were to transport on our pack-mules fifteen days' rations of hard bread, coffee and sugar; twelve days' rations of bacon, and fifty rounds of carbine ammunition per man. Each man was to be supplied with 100 rounds of carbine and 24 rounds of pistol ammunition,[4] to be carried on his person and in his saddle-bags. Each man was to carry on his horse twelve pounds of oats. The pack-mules sent out with Reno's command were badly used up, and promised seriously to embarrass the expedition. General Custer recommended that some extra forage be carried on the pack-mules...some troop commanders...told the General that some of the mules would surely break down, especially if the extra forage was packed. He replied in an excited manner, quite unusual with him: "Well, gentlemen, you may carry what supplies you please; you will be held responsible for your companies. The extra forage was only a suggestion, but this fact bear in mind, we might follow the trail for fifteen days unless we catch them before that time expires, no matter how far it may take us from our base of supplies; we may not see the supply steamer

---

2 Ibid.: 130

3 Ibid. The reader should realize that the vastness of the country would make it very easy for the Indians to avoid Crook's force during any such withdrawal to the south. The notion that they would be trapped between Custer's, Gibbon's and Crook's forces with no avenue of escape is not a realistic one. Unless surprised, the highly mobile Indians could easily avoid any fight in the summer months, or pick one on the grounds of their choosing. They were not forced to fight on the Rosebud; they chose to fight there.

again;" and, turning as he was about to enter his tent, he added, "You had better carry along an extra supply of salt; we may have to live on horse meat before we get through."[4]

On the morning of June 22nd, Custer received his written orders from General Terry:

>Camp at the Mouth of the Rosebud River
>Montana Territory
>June 22nd, 1876

Lieutenant-Colonel Custer, 7th Cavalry

Colonel: The Brigadier-General Commanding directs that, as soon as your regiment can be made ready for march, you will proceed up the Rosebud in pursuit of the Indians whose trail was discovered by Major Reno a few days since. It is, of course, impossible to give you any definite instructions in regard to this movement, and were it not impossible to do so the Department Commander places too much confidence in your zeal, energy, and ability to wish to impose upon you precise orders which might hamper your action when nearly in contact with the enemy. He will, however, indicate to you his own views of what your action should be, and he desires that you should conform to them unless you see sufficient reason for departing from them. He thinks that you should proceed up the Rosebud until you ascertain definitely the direction in which the trail above spoken of leads. Should it be found (as it appears almost certain that it will be found) to turn towards the Little Horn, he thinks that you should still proceed southward, perhaps as far as the headwaters of the Tongue, and then turn towards the Little Horn, feeling constantly, however, to your left, so as to preclude the possibility of the escape of the Indians to the south or southeast by passing around your left flank. The column of Colonel Gibbon is now in motion for the mouth of the Bighorn. As soon as it reaches that point, it will cross the Yellowstone and move up at least as far as the forks of the Big and Little Horns. Of course, its future movements must be

---

[4] E.S. Godfrey, *Custer's Last Battle:* 14. Custer's troopers were equipped with single-shot Springfield Model 1873 carbines and Colt caliber .45 revolvers. "[The carbine]...weighed 7 pounds and had an overall length of 41 inches. It used a .45-caliber copper-cased cartridge, a 405 grain bullet and a charge of 55 grains of black powder. The best effective range for this carbine was less than 300 yards, but significant hits still could be scored out to 600 yards. A bullet was driven out of the muzzle at a velocity of about 1,200 feet per second, with 1,650 foot-pounds of energy. The trapdoor Springfield could hurl a slug more than 1,000 yards and, with proper training, could be fired with accuracy 12 to 15 times per minute." (Dave Higgenbotham, "General George Custer: An Overview of the Weapons Used, www.lonestarrifle.com/Custer, accessed February 24, 2006.)

controlled by circumstances as they arise, but it is hoped that the Indians, if upon the Little Horn, may be so nearly inclosed by the two columns that their escape will be impossible.

The Department Commander desires that on your way up the Rosebud you should thoroughly examine the upper part of Tulloch's Creek, and that you should endeavor to send a scout through to Colonel Gibbon's column, with information of the result of your examination. The lower part of this creek will be examined by a detachment from Colonel Gibbon's command. The supply steamer will be pushed up the Bighorn as far as the forks if the river is found to be navigable for that distance, and the Department Commander, who will accompany the column of Colonel Gibbon, desires you to report to him there not later than the expiration of the time for which your troops are rationed, unless in the meantime you receive further orders.

Very respectfully, your obedient servant,
E.W. Smith, Captain 18th Infantry,
Acting Assistant Adjutant-General.[5]

Since Custer's Ree (Arikara) scouts were unfamiliar with the country, Gibbon's Montana Column provided him with its six best Crow scouts and Mitch Boyer, referred to by Lieutenant Bradley as "…one of the very best the country affords…Surely [Custer] is being afforded every facility to make a successful pursuit."[6] One of these scouts was Curly, the only known survivor of that battalion of Custer's regiment, otherwise slaughtered to the last man. At noon on the 22nd, Custer's 7th Cavalry Regiment moved out in a column of fours and passed in review before General Terry, Colonel Gibbon and Major John S. Brisbin. The column marched twelve miles up the Rosebud and made camp at 4 P.M. Custer's packers were not as experienced as General Crook's, and had considerable trouble keeping their packs from falling off during that first afternoon's march. This problem was for the most part remedied by the second day.

In the meantime, the Montana Column continued its march up the north bank of the Yellowstone and arrived at Fort Pease about 5:30 P.M. on June 23rd. The column was also accompanied by a battery of three Gatling guns commanded by Lieutenant Low, 20th Infantry. Custer had decided not

---

[5] Ibid.

[6] James H. Bradley, *The March of the Montana Column*: 143–144.

Captain Frederick William Benteen.
PHOTO COURTESY OF MONTANA HISTORICAL
SOCIETY RESEARCH CENTER PHOTOGRAPH
ARCHIVES, HELENA, MONTANA.

to take these guns with him for reasons of mobility.[7] These three guns were mounted on carriages, each pulled by four condemned cavalry horses. The entire battery was manned by two officers and thirty-two men.[8]

At the end of their first day's march, Custer summoned his officers for a conference, best described by Lieutenant Godfrey, who commanded Company K:

When all had assembled the General said that until further orders trumpet-calls would not be sounded except in an emergency; the marches would begin at 5 A.M. sharp; the troop commanders were all experienced officers, and knew well enough what to do, and when to do what was necessary for their troops; there were two things that would be regulated from his headquarters, i.e. when to move out and when to go into camp. All other details, such as reveille, stables, watering, halting, grazing, etc., on the march would be left to the judgment and discretion of the troop commanders; they were to keep within supporting distance of each other, not to get ahead of the scouts, or very far to the rear of the column…He thought, judging from the number of lodge fires reported by Reno, that we might meet at least a thousand warriors; there might be enough young men from the agencies, visiting their hostile friends, to make a total of fifteen hundred. He had consulted reports of the Commissioner of Indian Affairs as to the probable number of "Hostiles" (those who had persistently refused to live or enroll themselves at the Indian agencies), and he was confident, if any reliance was to be placed upon those reports, that there would not be an opposing force of more than fifteen hundred. General Terry had offered him the additional force of the battalion of the 2nd Cavalry, but he had declined it because he felt sure that the 7th Cavalry could whip any force that would be able to combine against him; that if the

---

[7] Ibid.: 144, 146

[8] E.S. Godfrey: 5.

regiment could not, no other regiment in the service could; if they could whip the regiment, they would be able to defeat a much larger force, or, in other words, the reinforcement of this battalion could not save us from defeat. With the regiment acting alone there would be harmony, but another organization would be sure to cause jealousy. He had declined the offer of the Gatling guns for the reason that they might hamper our movements or march at a critical moment, because of the difficult nature of the country through which we would march. The marches would be from twenty-five to thirty miles a day. Troop officers were cautioned to husband their rations and the strength of their mules and horses, as we might be out for a great deal longer time than that for which we were rationed, as he intended to follow the trail until we could get the Indians, even if it took us to the Indian agencies on the Missouri River or in Nebraska. All officers were requested to make to him, then or at any time, any suggestions they thought fit.[9]

Godfrey reported that Custer's tone was unusually conciliatory and subdued during this meeting. One officer in attendance, Lieutenant Wallace, voiced his premonition that Custer would be killed in the coming fight because he had never heard him talk that way before. Wallace would also fall fourteen years later at the Battle of Wounded Knee.[10]

At 5 A.M. sharp on June 23rd, Custer's regiment mounted and moved out. After marching about eight miles, they encountered the first of a series of three recent Indian encampments. They went into camp at 5 P.M. after marching up the Rosebud for thirty-three miles. About this time Gibbon's force was arriving at Fort Pease. On the following day, June 24, 1876, Godfrey reported:

> ...we passed a great many camping places, all appearing to be of nearly the same strength. One would naturally suppose these were the successive camping-places of the same village, when in fact they were the continuous camps of the several bands. The fact that they all appeared to be of nearly of the same age, that is, having been made at the same time, did not impress us then.[11]

At one larger camp they found the scalp of a white man, believed to be from one of the three men killed from Gibbon's command while out

---

[9] Ibid.: 365.

[10] Ibid.

[11] Ibid.: 366.

Gall—Sioux chief.
PHOTO COURTESY OF MONTANA HISTORICAL
SOCIETY RESEARCH CENTER PHOTOGRAPH
ARCHIVES, HELENA, MONTANA.

hunting. "The march during the day was tedious. We made many long halts so as not to get ahead of the scouts, who seemed to be doing their work thoroughly, giving special attention to the right, toward Tullock's Fork (Creek), the valley of which was in general view from the divide."[12] At sundown they camped under a bluff after marching twenty-eight miles. Captain Benteen would later state that this campsite was located at the intersection of Muddy Creek and the Rosebud River. They were now seventy-three miles up the Rosebud from their point of origin.[13]

After dark, Custer met with his officers and informed them that the trail led across the divide to the Little Bighorn. He stated that they would march to a point as close to the divide as possible that evening, concealing the command as much as possible before daylight on the 25th. Then they would reconnoiter the surrounding area during the day, locate the village, and launch an attack on June 26th. The command then took up the march in darkness, moving about ten miles and stopping at 2 A.M. on the 25th.

Also on the 24th, at 11 A.M., twelve of Gibbon's remaining Crow scouts were ferried across the Yellowstone and ordered to scout up Tullock's Fork until they hit the trail, then locate the Sioux village. They would make a disappointing reappearance at the camp of the command later that same evening, having sighted nothing but a buffalo killed by Sioux. That same day, Gibbon left Captain Kirkland's Company B behind to guard the base camp and ferried the remainder of the Montana Column and Lieutenant

---

12 Ibid.

13 W.A. Graham, *The Custer Myth:* 178.

Low's battery of Gatling guns across to a point just below the mouth of the Bighorn. They then marched, accompanied by four pack mules to each infantry company and six to each cavalry troop, a few miles up the Bighorn, then to the left about one mile up Tullock's Fork, and made camp at 5:30 P.M., having marched just over four miles. The wagons were left behind at the Fort Pease base camp. General Terry and his staff accompanied the column. Prior to their departure, Colonel Gibbon had become ill and remained for the time being on the steamer.[14]

Lieutenant Bradley made the following entry in his diary:

> We are now fairly en route to the Indian village, which is supposed to be on the Little Bighorn. It is undoubtedly a large one, and should Custer's command and ours unite, we, too, will have a large force numbering all told about one thousand men, armed with the splendid breech-loading Springfield rifles and carbines, caliber forty-five, and strengthened by the presence of Low's battery of three Gatling guns. Should we come to blows, it will be one of the biggest Indian battles ever fought on this continent, and the most decisive in its results, for such force as we have if united will be invincible, and the utter destruction of the Indian village, and overthrow of Sioux power will be the certain result. There is not much glory in Indian wars, but it will be worth while to have been present at such an affair as this.[15]

Meanwhile, the troops of Custer's command had spent an uncomfortable night. "After daylight [June 25, 1876] some coffee was made, but it was impossible to drink it; the water was so alkaline that the horses refused to drink it."[16] Shortly before 8 A.M. Custer rode around bareback and informed the various troops that the scouts had located the Indian camps on the Little Bighorn about twelve to fifteen miles away. He ordered the troops to take up the march at 8 A.M. At one point Lieutenant Godfrey overheard an interpreter passing a remark of the Ree scout Bloody Knife to Custer. "He says we'll find enough Sioux to keep us fighting two or three days." Custer smiled and remarked, "I guess we'll get through with them in one day."[17]

The march was commenced at 8 A.M. and continued without pause until about 10:30 A.M., at which time the command concealed itself in a

---

[14] Bradley: 147–148; distances and times from Edward J. McClernand, *On Time for Disaster*: 144.

[15] Bradley: 148.

[16] Godfrey: 19.

[17] Ibid.

Bloody Knife—Custer's scout.
PHOTO COURTESY OF THE NATIONAL ARCHIVES.

ravine, having marched about ten miles. At this point information was received effecting a change in the plan of approach and attack:

Captain Yates's troop had lost one of its packs of hard bread during the night march from our last halting-place on the 24th. He sent a detail back on the trail to recover it. Captain [Myles] Keogh came to where a group of officers were, and said this detail had returned and reported that when near the pack they discovered an Indian opening one of the boxes of hard bread with his tomahawk, and that as soon as the Indian saw the soldiers he galloped away to the hills out of range and then moved along leisurely. This information was taken to the General at once by his brother, [brevet] Colonel Tom Custer. The General came back and had "officers call" sounded. He recounted Captain Keogh's report, and also said that the scouts had seen several Indians moving along the ridge overlooking the valley through which we had marched, as if observing our movements; he thought the Indians must have seen the dust made by the command. At all events our presence had been discovered and further concealment was unnecessary; that we would march at once to attack the village; that he had not intended to make the attack until the next morning, the 26th, but our discovery made it imperative to act at once, as delay would allow the village to scatter and escape.[18]

---

[18] Godfrey: 19.

Custer's command was divided into three battalions, one commanded by himself consisting of Company I under Captain Myles Keogh and Lieutenant James Porter, Company F under Captain George Yates and Lieutenant Reilly, Company C under Captain Tom Custer and Lieutenant Harrington, Company E under Lieutenants Smith and Sturgis, and Company L under Lieutenants James Calhoun and Crittenden, with Lieutenant Cook as adjutant and Dr. G.E. Lord as medical officer. Major Marcus Reno commanded another battalion consisting of Company M under Captain French, Company A under Captain Miles Moylan and Lieutenant Charles DeRudio, Company G under Lieutenants McIntosh and Wallace, and the Indian scouts and the interpreter Girard (not to be confused with General Crook's scout Frank Grouard) under Lieutenants Charles Varnum and Hare, with Lieutenant Hodgson as acting adjutant and medical officers Doctors DeWolf and Porter. The third battalion was commanded by Captain Frederick W. Benteen and consisted of Company H under Captain Benteen and Lieutenant F. Gibson, Company D under Captain Thomas Weir and Lieutenant Winfield Edgerly, and Company K under Lieutenant E.S. Godfrey. The pack train was escorted by Company B under Captain Thomas McDougall. Lieutenant Edward Mathey was in charge of the pack train itself.[19]

At approximately 11:45 A.M. the battalions marched up to the divide between Davis Creek and Reno Creek, arriving there about noon.[20] The precise location on the Little Bighorn of the village or encampments was not known for certain at the time. From the divide, Captain Benteen was ordered to march with his battalion toward a line of bluffs to the south of Custer's and Reno's line of march and continue until he reached full view of the Little Bighorn valley. Presumably, Custer ordered this maneuver in an effort to cut off any hostiles attempting to escape up the Little Bighorn to the south. Years later, in 1892, Captain Benteen would estimate the distance from this point of departure to the later location of Custer's body as about fifteen miles.[21]

Custer and Reno then proceeded with their battalions down what is now known as Reno Creek, which flowed in a west-northwest direction down to the Little Bighorn, emptying into it at a point later learned to be upriver from the Indian encampments. Trumpeter Giovanni Martini (also called

---

[19] Godfrey: 21.

[20] Times taken from map in Graham: 288.

[21] Graham: 194.

John Martin) had been detailed from Captain Benteen's battalion to accompany Custer at his side as an orderly. He later reported, "Reno was on the left bank and we on the right. All the time, as we rode, scouts were riding in and out, and the General would listen to them and sometimes gallop away a short distance to look around."[22]

As Custer's and Reno's troops moved down Reno Creek, they came upon an abandoned tepee containing a dead Indian. Custer's scouts, moving farther in advance, had set it on fire. Trumpeter John Martini later stated:

> Just a little off from that [the tepee] there was a little hill, from which Girard, one of the scouts, saw some Indians between us and the river. He called to the General and pointed them out. He said they were running away. The General ordered the Indian scouts to follow them but they refused to go. Then the General motioned to Colonel Reno and when he rode up [better said while he was riding up since Reno and Custer did not actually speak at that time] the General told the Adjutant to order him to go down and cross the river and attack the Indian village, and that he would support him with the whole regiment. He said he would go down to the other end and drive them, and that he would have Benteen hurry up and attack them in the center.[23]

---

[22] Quoted in Graham: 289.

[23] Ibid.

CHAPTER TWENTY

Battle of the Little Bighorn: Reno's Battalion Attacks Hostiles from Upriver, June 25, 1876

S COUT GEORGE HERENDEEN, ACCOMPANYING MARCUS Reno's battalion at the Little Bighorn, later reported, "From this point we could see the Little Horn valley, and observed heavy clouds of dust rising about five miles distant. Many thought the Indians were moving away, and I think General Custer believed so, for he sent word to Colonel Reno…to push on the scouts rapidly and to head for the dust."[1] Lieutenant E.S. Godfrey would later report that Custer ordered Reno "to move forward at as rapid a gait as he thought prudent, and charge the village afterward and the whole outfit would support him."[2]

Reno moved his battalion rapidly some three miles down Reno Creek to a ford across the Little Bighorn, where he crossed and then deployed for battle on the plain or valley bottom, which was about three-fourths of a mile wide. He sent word back to George Custer "…that he had everything in front of him and that the enemy was strong."[3] He then charged in a downriver direction toward the dust raised by the retreating hostiles, who fired back at his command as they retreated. After charging forward for about a mile downriver the hostiles' resistance became stronger. Reno then dismounted his men to fight on foot in a skirmish line while the horse holders moved the horses into some timber that extended out into the valley bottom from the right of the line near the Little Bighorn River. Lieutenant George D. Wallace later wrote a friend:

---

[1] W.A. Graham, *The Custer Myth*: 258.

[2] E.S. Godfrey, *Custer's Last Battle*: 22.

[3] Ibid.: 23.

… we were now in a rather hot place. The Indians were all around and bullets whizzing uncomfortably close. We got behind some trees, dismounted, and threw out skirmishers. We now discovered that just beyond the woods was a village of over a thousand lodges, and that with less than a 100 men we were fighting the whole Sioux nation.[4]

Sergeant John M. Ryan of M Company described events just before and after dismounting:

When we got to the timber we rode down an embankment and dismounted. This was where the channel of the river changed and was probably several feet lower than the level of the prairie. We dismounted in haste, number four of each set of four holding the horses. We came onto higher ground forming a skirmish line…facing down stream in the direction of the Indian camp. This was our first view of the Indian camp from the skirmish line. Some of the men laid down while others knelt down. At this particular place there was a prairie-dog town and we used the mounds for temporary breastworks. We got the skirmish line formed and here the Indians made their first charge. There were probably 500 of them coming from the direction of their village. They were well mounted and well armed. They tried to cut through our skirmish line. We fired volleys into them repulsing their charge and emptying a number of their saddles. Lieutenant Hodgson walked up and down the line encouraging the men to keep cool and fire low. Finally when they could not cut through us, they strung out in single file, lying on the opposite side of their ponies from us, and then they commenced to circle. They overlapped our skirmish line on the left and were closing in on the rear to complete the circle. We had orders to fall back to our horses. This was where the first man was killed, Sergt. Miles F. O'Hara of my Troop M.[5]

The Indians moved to Reno's left and rear, appearing to attempt to cut him off from the ford. Most of the Ree scouts fled the field, some not stopping until they reached the Yellowstone, while the Crow scouts remained with the command. Lieutenant Varnum, having lost control of his scouts, reported to Captain Moylan, Company A, for duty.[6] As stated above, Reno had ordered his troops to fall back into the timber where the horses were being held. He could not see any additional support from Custer arriving

---

[4] George D. Wallace to Dr. Charles Knoblauch, July 4, 1876, in Douglas Paul Westfall, *Letters from the Field:* 22. Reno's force consisted of about 150 men, but Lieutenant Wallace's point is well taken.

[5] Quoted in Graham, *The Custer Myth:* 242.

[6] Graham, *The Custer Myth:* 342.

and became concerned that his command would be overwhelmed. Some of Reno's troopers later reported sighting Custer and a small group on horseback atop the ridge on the opposite side of the river, cheering and waving Reno's men on. According to Lieutenant Edward J. McClernand, Lieutenant Wallace later reported to members of John Gibbon's command upon meeting them after the battle that "we" had sighted Custer on the ridge waving to them as they moved to the attack with Reno.[7] However, Wallace makes no mention of sighting Custer in his letter to Dr. Charles Knoblauch, dated Yellowstone Depot, MT, July 4, 1876.[8] Custer had then disappeared from view behind the ridge. Trumpeter Martini later reported being present with Custer at this point, but stated that Custer had not seen any of Reno's command at that time. He did, however, report that Custer turned in his saddle and looked back down the opposite slope toward his men, waving his hat and shouting something like "Hurrah, boys we've got them...!"[9] Doubtless, some members of Reno's battalion, observing this from a distance, thought Custer had seen them and was cheering them on. We may also speculate that Custer turned away from them just as they rode into his field of view and therefore did not see Reno's troopers as Martini reported. Of course, it is also possible that Martini did not see Reno's troopers while Custer did.

Reno, feeling much in need of support he did not see coming, decided to withdraw his command to a more defensible position on the bluffs across the river. According to Lieutenant Varnum, they had been in action about a half hour at this point.[10] Reno ordered his men to mount, but, as scout Herendeen later reported, at that moment a group of hostiles who had managed to close in on the command, delivered a fusillade that killed the Ree scout, Blood Knife, and a trooper as they sat on their horses near Reno.[11] Reno hastily ordered the men to dismount, then, abruptly, to mount again. He then led the troops out onto the open prairie and headed toward the ford, leaving a large number of soldiers, believed to be thirteen in all, some wounded, behind in the woods. Many of them had not heard the com-

---

7 McClernand, *On Time for Disaster:* 61.

8 In Westfall, *Letters from the Field*, and Wallace's testimony at the Reno Inquiry, he made no mention of sighting Custer on the ridge; however, at least two other lieutenants in Reno's battalion did: Charles DeRudio and Charles Varnum. This is likely what Wallace meant in his statement quoted by McClernand, the "we" meaning that members of the battalion had seen Custer on the ridge.

9 Graham, *The Custer Myth:* 289–290.

10 Ibid.: 342.

11 Ibid.: 263.

mand to withdraw. His retreat rapidly turned into a headlong rout, with Indians riding up on their flanks and shooting, some reported to be rapidly firing their Winchester repeaters into the column as they rode alongside,[12] and/or clubbing soldiers off their mounts, the mounted white soldier being no match for a mounted Indian. Lieutenant Godfrey would later report one exception, "…Private Dalvern, troop 'F,' had a hand-to-hand conflict with an Indian; his horse was killed; he then shot the Indian, caught the Indian's pony, and rode to the command."[13] Wooden Leg, a Cheyenne warrior, reported:

> Suddenly, the hidden soldiers came tearing out on horseback, from the woods. I was around on that side where they came out. I whirled my horse and lashed it into a dash to escape from them. All others of my companions did the same. But soon we discovered they were not following us. They were running away from us. They were going as fast as their tired horses could carry them across an open valley space toward the river. We stopped, looked a moment, and then we whipped our ponies into swift pursuit.[14]

Pressure by the hotly pursuing hostiles on the right flank of the retreat forced Reno's command to the riverbank at a point short of the original ford, with the soldiers all bunching up on the bank and no semblance of organized resistance. Most of them managed to cross at this point and rapidly make their way up a ravine on a very steep trail to the top of the bluff. Lieutenant Wallace wrote, "The Indians stopped at the bank and shot men & horses as they rode up the other bank."[15] Wooden Leg reported clubbing two soldiers off their horses into the river with his rifle butt.[16] Upon reaching the top, some 700 yards from the river and about 200 feet up, Godfrey wrote:

> Reno's casualties were…three officers, including Dr. J.M. DeWolf, and twenty-nine enlisted men and scouts killed; seven enlisted men wounded; and one officer, one interpreter, and fourteen soldiers and scouts missing. Nearly all the casualties occurred during the retreat and after leaving the timber.[17]

---

[12] W.A. Graham, *The Reno Court of Inquiry:* 52, 216.

[13] Godfrey: 25.

[14] Thomas B. Marquis, *Wooden Leg:* 220–221.

[15] In Westfall: 22.

[16] Marquis: 223.

[17] Godfrey: 25.

One of Reno's company commanders, Captain Thomas French, would later write:

> I thought we were to charge headlong through them all—that was the only chance. To turn one's back on Indians without being better mounted than they is throwing away life. When he started to that hill he had told me, not one minute before, that he was going to fight—this was in reply to a question of mine.[18]

Herendeen, who accompanied Reno's command, was quoted less than a month later on July 7, 1876, by a reporter of the *New York Herald*:

> ...a good many [men] were killed when the command left the timber. Just as I got out [of the timber] my horse stumbled and fell and I was dismounted, the horse running away after Reno's command. I saw several soldiers who were dismounted, their horses having been killed or having run away. There were also some soldiers mounted who had remained behind. I should think in all there were as many as thirteen soldiers...Three of the soldiers were wounded, two of them so badly they could not use their arms.[19]

Herendeen and the others concealed themselves in the woods as the hostiles left in pursuit of the remainder of Reno's command. Shortly after the retreat from the woods, Herendeen and the others still in the woods began to hear heavy firing from about two miles downriver. Herendeen said, "...I learned afterwards, it was Custer's command. Nearly all the Indians in the upper end of the valley drew off down the river, and the fight with Custer lasted about an hour when the heavy firing ceased."[20] Herendeen and eleven others then managed to move out of the timber and rejoin Reno's command on the bluff some hours later after a brief scrap with five mounted Sioux. The withdrawal downriver of most of the hostiles who had been pressing Reno's force gave Reno and the survivors of his command time to secure a position on the bluffs. Some of Reno's men could also hear heavy firing from downriver (about three miles from their location) but could see nothing. They knew, however, that Custer's command was in action.

---

[18] Quoted in Graham, *The Custer Myth:* 341.

[19] Ibid.: 258.

[20] Ibid.: 259.

CHAPTER TWENTY-ONE

Battle of the Little Bighorn: Custer's Battalion Maneuvers to Attack Hostile Village and Is Annihilated

AFTER ORDERING RENO ACROSS THE LITTLE BIGHORN River in pursuit of the hostiles, Custer marched his command to the right, away from the Reno Creek drainage and along the back side of the ridge and bluffs that abutted the east bank of the Little Bighorn. Trumpeter Giovanni Martini reported that, after Custer had given Reno his orders, his command followed Reno's a few hundred yards, then bore off to the right at a gallop, stopping once to water the horses. He then marched one or two miles and halted his troops behind the ridge. Custer then climbed with his orderly, Trumpeter Martini, and others to the top of a hill overlooking the valley. Martini later reported:

> … he could see the village in the valley on the other side of the river. It was a big village, but we couldn't see it all from there, though we didn't know it then; but several hundred tepees were in plain sight. There were no bucks to be seen; all we could see was some squaws and children playing and a few dogs and ponies. The General seemed both surprised and glad, and said the Indians must be in their tents, asleep. We did not see anything of Reno's column when we were up on the hill. I am sure the General did not see them at all, because he looked all around with his glasses, and all he said was that we had "got them this time." He turned in the saddle and took off his hat and waved it so the men of the command, who were halted at the base of the hill, could see him, and he shouted to them, "Hurrah, boys, we've got them! We'll finish them up and then go home to our station.[1]

---

[1] Quoted in W.A. Graham, *The Custer Myth*: 290.

Martini stated that Custer rode down to his troops and talked a minute to the adjutant, explaining what he had observed. The command then rode rapidly, trotting and galloping, about one more mile downriver to a large ravine leading down to the Little Bighorn and the village. Custer pointed down the ravine, then called Martini over to him, saying:

> "Orderly, I want you to take a message to Colonel [Frederick] Benteen. Ride as fast as you can and tell him to hurry. Tell him its a big village and I want him to be quick and to bring the ammunition packs." He didn't stop at all when he was telling me this, and I just said, "Yes, sir," and checked my horse, when the Adjutant said, "Wait, orderly, I'll give you a message," and he stopped and wrote it in a big hurry, in a little book, and then tore out the leaf and gave it to me. And then he told me, "Now, orderly, ride as fast as you can to Colonel Benteen. Take the same trail we came down. If you have time and there is no danger, come back; otherwise stay with your company."[2]

Martini then departed the command. His last glimpse of them was as they galloped down the ravine. Just before Martini arrived back at the hill from where Custer had viewed the valley, he heard firing commence from the direction of Custer's command. As he reached the area of the hill, Martini sighted Reno's command.

> When I got up on the hill, I looked down and there I saw Reno's battalion in action. It had not been more than ten or fifteen minutes since the General and I were on the hill, and then we had seen no Indians.[3]

Reno's troops were on foot deployed in a skirmish line. By the time Martini lost sight of them, he could see Reno's men were falling back (presumably to the trees). Martini came under fire by some Indians, and his horse was wounded in the hip, but he kept going, eventually locating Captain Benteen coming down the trail riding ahead of his command.

> I saluted and handed the message to Colonel Benteen, and then I told him what the General said—that it was a big village and to hurry. He said, "Where's the General now?" and I answered that the Indians we saw were running, and I supposed that by this time he

---

[2] Ibid.

[3] Ibid.: 290.

had charged through the village. I was going to tell him about Major Reno being in action, too, but he didn't give me the chance…and told me to join my company.[4]

Martini did not have a good command of English at the time. He had arrived from Italy and joined the U.S. Army in 1873.[5]

Captain Benteen, without question a brave and competent leader, but a man who had little positive to say about any of those with whom he served, would later refer to Martini as a "…thick headed, dull witted Italian, just about as much cut out for a cavalryman as he was for a King: he informed me that the Indians were "skidaddling"; hence less the necessity for retracing our steps to get the Packs."[6]

Trumpeter Martini's account seems to indicate that Custer's command and Reno's command became engaged with the Indians almost simultaneously, or, to say the least, that Custer had commenced to encounter some degree of opposition within ten or fifteen minutes of the beginning of fighting by Reno's command. Those men in Reno's command who observed Custer on the hill must have come into Custer's field of view just as he turned and waved his hat to his troops. Custer knew by this time that he faced a lot of Indians but felt that he had the element of surprise. As he headed down the ravine to the attack, he was still unaware of the actual extent of the hostile village and the number of enemy combatants it contained.

A participant in the Montana Column, Lieutenant John McBain, later wrote:

> [Custer] cannot be blamed for mistaking their strength, for there is no place in the surrounding country from which the extent of the camp could be observed. With Gibbon's command was an odometer cart, and the instrument registered the camp as four and three-quarters miles long; now let anyone familiar with the Indian ways of camping picture to himself the fighting strength of that camp. I never did and do not now believe that there was a soul less than 6,000 fighting men.[7]

---

[4] Ibid.: 290–291.

[5] Ibid.: 288.

[6] Ibid.: 180. If this was Captain Benteen's honest opinion of Trooper Martini, then it is, indeed, a poor reflection on Benteen to have selected Martini to serve in such an important position as Custer's orderly, i.e., his link of communication with his commander.

[7] John F. McBain, "With Gibbon on the Sioux Campaign of 1876," Part l, *Journal of the United States Cavalry Association*, Vol. 9, June 1896: 148.

In 1892, Captain Benteen later estimated the strength of able-bodied Indians at 8,000 or 9,000.[8] Lieutenant Winfield Edgerly, with Benteen's battalion, stated, "From what I saw, I think there were as many as 7,000 warriors. I judged from seeing Terry's command—about 500 men—the size of which I knew, ride down where I saw the Indians the day before. Terry's command looked like a handful compared to the Indians."[9]

Crazy Horse, in an interview by a *Chicago Times* correspondent at Fort Robinson (located in the northwestern corner of Nebraska Territory) after his surrender less than one year later, reported that the hostile camps consisted of seven different bands of Indians. They were all commanded by their own chiefs:

> First, the Uncpapas, under Sitting Bull; second, the Ogalallas, under Crazy Horse; third, the Minneconjous, under Fast Bull; fourth, the Sansarcs, under Red Bear; fifth, the Cheyennes, under Ice Bear, their two principal chiefs being absent; sixth, the Santees and Yanktonias, under Red Point, of the Santees; seventh, the Blackfeet [Blackfeet Sioux, not to be confused with members of the Blackfeet Nation in Montana], under Scabby Head. The village consisted of eighteen hundred lodges, and at least four hundred wickayups, a lodge made of small poles and willows for temporary shelter. Each of the wickayups contained four young bucks, and the estimate made by Crazy Horse is that each lodge had from three to four warriors. Estimating at three made a fighting force of seven thousand Indians.[10]

We will recall that Crazy Horse told Lieutenant Bourke that he had 6,500 warriors at his disposal during the Battle of the Rosebud just eight days prior to Custer's attack, and now this force had combined with Sitting Bull's.

The wife of Tatanka-he-gle-ska (Spotted-Horn-Bull) and a cousin of Sitting Bull, whose later accounts of the battle were deemed likely the most thorough, truthful, and accurate, drew a map indicating six separate camps commencing from Reno's point of attack upriver and extending downriver. According to her, those camps closest to Reno's onslaught were the Blackfeet Sioux and the Uncpapas. Below them were the Ogallallas, Sans Arcs and Brules, with the Cheyennes and the Minneconjous immediately below. This somewhat matches the later account of Chief Gall of the Uncpapas, who stated that two of his wives and three children were killed in the trees by

8 Graham, *The Custer Myth:* 194.

9 Ibid.: 221.

10 Quoted in Graham, *The Custer Myth:* 62–63.

Reno's troops as they made their assault on the upper end of the village. He also stated that he was with Sitting Bull near the point where Reno attacked. Scout George Herendeen later stated, "Our men did not kill any squaws, but the Ree Indian scouts did. The bodies of six squaws were found in the little ravine." Gall's family members may have been among them.[11]

Mrs. Spotted-Horn-Bull reported that seven Cheyennes had departed the camp earlier, en route to the southeast, when they spotted Custer's troops approaching the village. Two of them returned and, with blankets, signaled a warning to the encampments from the ridge that a large number of troops were approaching. Great confusion ensued, with the women and children attempting to flee the camp toward the north, and many warriors moving out to secure their horses grazing to the north and west, or already taking positions to block Custer's approach. It may have been at this time that Custer observed the seemingly quiet camp. Also, even though Custer could see several hundred tepees from his vantage point, he may have only been looking at a fraction of the village, reported by Crazy Horse to contain 1,800 lodges. About this time Reno's troops struck the encampment on the up-river side. "The camp…was in the wildest commotion and women and children shrieked with terror. More than half the men were absent after the pony herd."[12] It may be deduced that at this point those warriors still available in the upriver camps were sufficiently organized under Gall and other chieftains to overcome Reno's assault and panic him to a greater extent than they were panicked themselves, thus causing him to retreat.

Chief Gall, the warrior chief and real field commander of Sitting Bull's Uncpapas, at least during the Battle of the Little Bighorn, reported that he was moving to cut off Reno before he could get to the bluffs when one of his lieutenants, Iron Cedar, rode up to him and reported that another body of troops was approaching the encampment farther downriver.[13] Upon confirming this report, Gall with most of the warriors broke off the attack on Reno's retreating troopers and headed downriver. The Indians no longer perceived Reno's badly chewed-up force as a serious threat to the encampment. This, no doubt, kept Reno's men from being wiped out as they attempted to cross the river and organize an effective defense on the bluffs.

Exactly what transpired when Custer pressed his attack cannot be reported by any of the military participants, for they were wiped out to the

---

[11] Ibid.: 83, 90, 260.

[12] Ibid.: 84.

[13] E.S. Godfrey, *Custer's Last Battle:* 33.

last man. The sole survivor of this command was the Crow scout, Curly, who did not witness the entire struggle. He hid himself in a ravine and later blended with the hostiles to make his escape. He later gave contradicting accounts, and sensational but inconsistent stories of his exploits were published, making it unclear exactly what action he witnessed. Shortly after the battle, he stated to Lieutenant James Bradley that he had done nothing; that he was not in the fight. Various versions of Curly's experience appeared in publications in the years following the battle.[14] Since Curly did not speak English, at least not at the time of the battle, it is more likely that these inconsistencies were more attributable to overzealous reporting and, perhaps, faulty interpreting, than to Curly's own statements. One thing is certain: He was there at the beginning of the battle and he survived it. (Major Reno later filed a report on carbine failure that refers to an observance by Curly.)

It is believed that after sending Trumpeter Martini to Captain Benteen with the dispatch, Custer started to approach the river and the encampments by coming down Medicine Tail Coulee, but his force was checked by hordes of warriors coming up to meet him. Custer's troops deployed in skirmish lines over an area about three-quarters of a mile long, parallel to, but still about a half mile from the river, along the ridge—with the horse holders (every fourth man) behind the ridge—and began advancing toward the village. Large numbers of warriors under Crazy Horse began forming just behind a second lower ridge between Custer's troops and the river. In the meantime, Gall led his warriors up and around the south side of the troopers and stampeded most of the horses and overwhelmed the horse holders. As Gall's forces were accomplishing this maneuver and gradually pushing the troopers north or to their right, Crazy Horse's Sioux and their Northern Cheyenne allies encircled Custer's troops around their right flank on the north side.[15] We might also speculate that Custer, seeing the strong force before him, had reduced the ratio of horse holders from four-to-one down to eight-to-one, as he had done in his battle with the Sioux in 1873. This would have placed more men in the line but would also have rendered it easier for Gall's warriors to stampede the horses, thus depriving Custer's men of the portion of the allotted one hundred rounds of carbine ammunition per man that still remained in their

---

14 Graham, *The Custer Myth:* 9. Major Reno later filed a report on carbine failure, which refers to an observation by Curly.

15 These maneuvers were later interpreted by Lieutenant Godfrey in *Century* magazine, and agreed to by Benteen (see Graham, *The Custer Myth:* 193).

saddlebags. Major Reno would later testify that his men had "…100 rounds each, 50 in their belts and 50 in the saddle bags."[16] We will recall that an additional fifty rounds per man were still with the pack train. Therefore, it is entirely possible that Custer's ammunition supply had been quickly reduced to fifty rounds of carbine ammunition and twenty-four rounds of pistol ammunition per man.

Wooden Leg reported that the Indians were able to conceal themselves for the most part in the ravines, sagebrush and tall grass. They were able to creep up on the soldiers and shoot arrows in high arches that rained down on the soldiers, striking and panicking their horses. Those Indians using rifles had to rise up and expose themselves to shoot. Using bows and arrows, the Indians could remain concealed from the fire of the troopers.[17]

Many of the soldiers held their ground and were shot down, while others became disorganized in their final moments, possibly already out of ammunition. Some, doubtless, saved their last bullet for themselves to avoid torture. The Indians reported many suicides, although this phenomenon, unusual as it was for the Indians, was likely exaggerated in numbers. The battle lasted no more than an hour, maybe less, with many of the troopers running out of ammunition to be dispatched with war clubs and hatchets. Chief Gall claimed to have killed a number himself with his hatchet.[18]

As in most great battles, some participants died by friendly fire. Horned Horse with the Ogallalla warriors under Crazy Horse later related, "…the smoke and dust was so great that foe could not be distinguished from friend. The horses were wild with fright and uncontrollable. The Indians were knocking each other from their steeds, and it is an absolute fact that the young bucks in their excitement and fury killed each other, several dead Indians being found killed by arrows."[19]

Some of the soldiers are known to have had problems with jammed weapons. In the final analysis, however, brave troopers were simply overwhelmed by overpowering numbers of brave warriors, and Custer's entire battalion, five troops, I, F, E, C and L were wiped out to the last man. With their deaths they instantly became subjects of glowing praise or victims of unwarranted criticism; all this, of course, based on marvelous 20-20 hindsight and/or exaggerated imaginations for the ages since passed.

---

[16] W.A. Graham, *The Reno Court of Inquiry:* 214.

[17] Thomas B. Marquis, *Wooden Leg:* 230.

[18] Ibid.: 91–92.

[19] Ibid.: 63.

CHAPTER TWENTY-TWO

Battle of the Little Bighorn: Captain Benteen's Movements, June 25

CAPTAIN FREDERICK BENTEEN'S BATTALION HAD ENCOUN-tered very difficult terrain as it marched toward the Little Bighorn River to the south or left of Reno Creek. Crossing the first of two lines of bluffs, they were forced northward by the terrain and eventually came to a point about a mile from the track made down Reno Creek by Lieutenant Colonel George Custer's and Major Marcus Reno's battalions. During his march Benteen received two additional orders from Custer through the chief trumpeter and then through the regiment's sergeant major. Obviously, Custer had noted during his march down Reno Creek, as this stream is known today, that Benteen would encounter a second line of bluffs before reaching the Little Bighorn. Benteen wrote:

> ...the first [order] to the effect, that, should I not find anything at the first line of bluffs, then, to go on to the second line of bluffs, to pitch in, and notify him at once, being included: the order through Sergeant Major received 15 or 20 minutes later, was, if nothing could be seen from the second line of bluffs, then, go on until I came to a valley, to "pitch in," and to notify him at once...[1]

The going became very difficult, and Captain Benteen sent Lieutenant Samuel Gibson forward to see if anything could be seen from the second line of bluffs. Gibson reported back in the negative, so Benteen opted to follow the trail of Custer and Reno, "...we got out of the hills to the trail;

---

[1] Quoted in W.A. Graham, *The Custer Myth*: 179–180.

my command getting to it just ahead of the train of Packs, the horses not having been watered since evening before, and this being along about one o'clock P.M. of a hot June day, they were needing it badly." They stopped to water their horses, and Captain Thomas Weir, tired of waiting on the others, moved out in the advance with his Company D, apparently moving ahead out of sight and contact with Captain Benteen.[2] Benteen's column then continued on down the trail, coming upon an abandoned tepee after a few miles. A couple miles beyond the tepee a sergeant arrived with orders for the pack train. Benteen advised him that it was coming on behind, and the sergeant proceeded up the trail to meet it. "Another couple miles brought an order to me thro' the orderly trumpeter of the day [Martini], from the adjutant of the regiment, to the effect: "Benteen, Big Village, Be Quick; Bring Packs. P.S. Bring Packs, W.W. Cooke, Adjt."[3]

Upon receipt of this order, Benteen moved his command out at a trot, eventually arriving at the ford. From that point he observed the immediate aftermath of Reno's rout. "...[W]e saw going on what evidently was not 'skedaddling' on the part of the indians, as there were 12 or 14 dismounted men on the bottom, and they were being ridden down and shot by 800 or 900 indian warriors..."[4]

Benteen then encountered a group of Crow scouts who informed him of the great numbers of Sioux and the location to which Major Reno's command had retreated on the bluffs. Remaining on the east, or right, side of the river, Benteen then marched downriver and located Reno in the bluffs.

> Reno, knowing of course we were soldiers, came riding to meet me as I moved towards him. My first query of Reno was—where is Custer? Showing him the last order received from the Adjutant of the Regt., Reno replied he did not know, that Custer had ordered him across the river to charge the indians, informing him that he would support him with the whole "Outfit," but he had neither seen nor heard from him since:—Well, our battalion got just in the nick of time to save Reno's. After a few words with Col. Reno I inquired as

---

[2] On Benteen's arrival at Reno's position, he was unaware of Captain Weir's location. The author finds it strange, indeed, that Captain Benteen would allow one entire company to depart his command without explicit permission. Either Weir was disobedient or Benteen was failing to exercise command. We will recall that Custer had ordered his subordinate commanders to remain within supporting distance of one another.

[3] Quoted in Graham, *The Custer Myth*, ibid.

[4] Ibid.: 180.

to the whereabouts of "D" Troop of my Battn.—and was informed that Capt. Wier had, without orders, gone down the river. This being the case, I sallied after Wier, and about 3/4ths of a mile lower down, from the top of the highest point in the vicinity, saw Wier's troop returning; hordes of indians hurrying them somewhat.[5]

Heavy firing could still be heard from downriver at the time of the arrival of Benteen's battalion with some but not all of his men. After an additional hour, the pack train arrived in its entirety. The ammunition-bearing mules had been cut out earlier and hurried to Reno's command. Lieutenant E.S. Godfrey believed the pack train arrived at 4:20 P.M. It is unclear, however, if this signified the arrival of the first mules of the train or the last, it being a fairly long train. By seven o'clock the hostiles, having wiped out the battalion with Custer, were moving in ever-greater numbers around Reno's command, which now included Benteen's troopers.

The position came under heavy fire until darkness fell. Of course everybody was wondering about Custer—why he did not communicate by courier or signal. But the general opinion seemed to prevail that he had been defeated and driven down the river, where he would probably join General Terry, and with whom he would return for our relief.[6]

The Indians did not fire on the beleaguered troops during the night. The men could see numerous bonfires in the Indian encampment below and hear them celebrating throughout the night of June 25th to 26th. Attempts were made to send scouts out to make contact with Custer, but these were forced to turn back by the immense number of Sioux about the area. The troopers spent the night digging in with what little trenching equipment they had on hand. "The ground was hard and dry. There were only three or four spades and shovels in the whole command; axes, hatchets, knives, table-forks, tin cups and halves of canteens were brought into use."[7] Captain Benteen later wrote that many of the men were so tired after having missed a great deal of sleep that it was difficult to keep the sentries awake.[8]

---

[5] Ibid.: 181.

[6] E.S. Godfrey, *Custer's Last Battle:* 28.

[7] Ibid.: 30.

[8] Quoted in Graham, *The Custer Myth:* 182.

CHAPTER TWENTY-THREE

Battle of the Little Bighorn: Terry Approaches the Battlefield, June 25

URNING TO GENERAL ALFRED TERRY'S COLUMN ON THE morning of June 25th: Lieutenant James Bradley started the day at 4 A.M. by sending six Crow scouts up Tullock's Fork then following them at 4:30 with the remainder of his scouts and mounted detachment. The column marched at 5:30 A.M., continuing about two miles up Tullock's Fork, then turning right to cut across the country back to the Bighorn valley. After going nine miles up Tullock's Fork, Lieutenant Bradley was notified that the command had turned right. Bradley overtook them and found them

> …involved in a labyrinth of bald hills and deep precipitous ravines completely destitute of water. The men had emptied their canteens of the wretched alkali water they started with and were parched with thirst as well as greatly fatigued…a worse route could not have been chosen, but destitute of a guide as we are, it is not to be wondered that we entangled ourselves in such a mess of physical obstacles.[1]

Lieutenant Edward McClernand described how it was necessary at one point to lower the Gatling gun carriages down a slope hand-over-hand with lariats tied together. The infantry reached the Bighorn and made camp at 6:50 P.M. after marching twenty-three miles. Bradley's Crow scouts reported sighting smoke toward the Little Bighorn. General Terry pushed on another twelve miles with the cavalry and Gatling battery, but found the going very

---

[1] James H. Bradley, *The March of the Montana Column*: 149.

difficult, maneuvering in the dark among the bluffs and broken country on the east side of the Bighorn. "The battery [Gatling gun battery], especially, had great difficulty in keeping up. Several times it was lost only to be brought back by repeated trumpet calls."[2] Rain fell that evening, making the going even more difficult. One of Bradley's old Crow scouts, Little Face, provided invaluable assistance in leading these troops down through the bluffs to a camping place on the Bighorn.[3] Lieutenant John McBain reported that shortly after Little Face took over the task of guiding the troops, "…we were to abandon the three Gatling guns that we had with us in a ravine, from which it seemed impossible to extricate the command."[4] At the conclusion of marching on the 25th, Terry's cavalry was still about twenty-two miles from the Custer battlefield. His infantry was thirty-four miles distant. Custer's battalion lay dead on the battlefield and the troops with Reno and Benteen were fighting for their survival.

---

[2] Edward J. McClernand, *On Time for Disaster:* 49–50.

[3] Bradley: 151.

[4] John F. McBain, "With Gibbon on the Sioux Campaign of 1876," Part l, *Journal of the United States Cavalry Association*, Vol. 9, June 1896: 143.

CHAPTER TWENTY-FOUR

Battle of the Little Bighorn: Reno's and Benteen's Battalions Fight for Survival on the Bluffs, June 26

O N JUNE 26TH, THE HOSTILES RESUMED FIRING ON THE beleaguered troopers with Major Marcus Reno and Captain Frederick Benteen as soon as morning light appeared. At first, it was only light incoming fire, but it increased as more Indians took up positions surrounding the troopers. They occupied the heights to the north and east from which they directed long-range rifle fire at the soldiers, particularly Benteen's men, who held the hill on the southern side of the perimeter. Their backs were thus exposed to fire from the hills to the north of the perimeter. Also, many of the animals within the perimeter were hit by long-range fire from the east side of the perimeter. Upon his arrival at this site after the battle, Colonel John Gibbon reported counting forty-eight dead animals.[1]

Captain Benteen noted, "I dropped on the hill-side, determined to gather what [sleep] I could, in; but some wakeful red skin had pretty nearly my exact range, plumping me in the heel of the extended foot; another bullet scattering the dry dust under my arm pit…"[2] Lieutenant E.S. Godfrey stated, "Of course, it was [the Indians'] policy to draw our fire as much as possible to exhaust our ammunition. As they exposed their persons very little we forbade our men, except well-known good shots, to fire without orders."[3] Benteen's position became precarious and he went to Reno and

---

[1] John Gibbon, *Adventures on the Western Frontier:* 139.

[2] Quoted in W.A. Graham, *The Custer Myth:* 182.

[3] E.S. Godfrey, *Custer's Last Battle:* 30.

asked that his position be reinforced. After considerable urging by Benteen, the latter finally ordered Captain Thomas French to take M Company over to the south side. On returning to his lines, being temporarily commanded by Lieutenant Gibson, Benteen found

> ... an Indian had shot one of Gibson's men, then rushed up and touched the body with his "coup stick", and started back to cover, but he was killed. He was in such close proximity to the lines and so exposed to the fire that the other Indians could not carry his body away. This, I believe, was the only dead Indian left in our position.[4]

Benteen, fearing the Indians were preparing to rush his line en masse, readied his men with their reinforcements for a charge, which he led, forcing the Indians almost back to the river dragging their dead and wounded along with them. This stabilized the situation for a while, and then the Indians resumed their siege with even greater intensity. Again Benteen became concerned that the Indians were preparing to rush the lines, and he went back to Reno recommending that a charge be made before the Indians could overrun the command. Godfrey would later report:

> Waiting a short time, and no action being taken on his suggestion, [Captain Benteen] said rather impatiently: "You've got to do something here pretty quick; this won't do, you must drive them back." Reno then directed us to get ready for a charge, and told Benteen to give the word. Benteen called out, "All ready now, men. Now's your time. Give them hell. Hip, hip, here we go!" and away we went with a hurrah, every man, but one who lay in his pit crying like a child. The Indians fired more rapidly than before from their whole line. Our men left their pits with their carbines loaded [This would mean that they had chambered rounds in their single-shot rifles.], and they began firing, without orders, soon after we started. A large body of Indians had assembled at the foot of one of the hills, intending probably to make a charge, as Benteen had divined, but they broke as soon as our line started. When we had advanced 75 to 100 yards, Reno called out "Get back, men, get back," and back the whole line came.

The charge resulted in no casualties but, ironically, the man who had failed to charge was struck by a hostile round a short while later and killed.[5]

---

4 Ibid.

5 Ibid.: 31.

By 11 A.M. on the 26th, the intensity of the enemy fire diminished somewhat. The troops were short of water, and volunteers braved enemy fire to retrieve it from the river below. Several were wounded in these attempts, but sufficient water was procured. By 1 P.M. most of the Indians left, although they still harassed the water detail at the river. They returned at 2 P.M. and opened fire, sending the troops to cover, and by 3 P.M. they stopped firing and withdrew, leaving a few mounted Indians below on the river bottom to maintain a watch on the troops. The Indians then set fire to the grass in the valley and withdrew their camp under the cover of the smoke. "At 7 P.M. we saw emerge from behind this screen an immense moving mass crossing the plateau, going toward the Bighorn Mountains. A fervent 'Thank God' that they had at last given up the contest was soon followed by grave doubts as to their motive for moving."[6] The hostiles had observed Terry's force approaching from the north up the Bighorn. Their leaders determined it prudent to withdraw from the area toward the Bighorn Mountains.

---

[6] Ibid.: 379.

CHAPTER TWENTY-FIVE

Battle of the Little Bighorn: Terry's Movements on June 26, 1876; Hostiles Withdraw from Battlefield Area

O N JUNE 26, LIEUTENANT JAMES BRADLEY WAS ORDERED to send his Crow scouts up the Little Bighorn. He sent six of them forward at 3:30 A.M., following with the rest of his detachment at 4 A.M., with no opportunity to eat breakfast even after having marched about fifty-five miles the previous day. After moving about three miles upriver, they encountered the tracks of four Indian ponies. They also observed heavy smoke rising to their front some fifteen to twenty miles distant. Bradley followed the tracks for two miles to a point where the riders had crossed the Bighorn River, discarding some equipment in apparent haste. He discovered that the equipment belonged to the six Crow scouts Colonel John Gibbon had loaned to Custer's column. Three men were then spotted on the opposite bank of the Bighorn, and signal communications were established between them and the Crow scouts with Bradley. Eventually, Little Face and some of the other Crow scouts went down to the river and spoke with the three men on the other side, who turned out to be three Crow scouts from Custer's command. Bradley remained with his detachment on the bluffs. Little Face and the other Crows returned to the detachment wailing and sobbing with word of the battle and the massacre of Custer's column. "They were the first listeners to the horrid story of the Custer massacre, and, outside of the relatives and personal friends of the fallen, there were none in this whole horrified nation of forty millions of people to whom the tidings brought greater grief."[1]

---

[1] James H. Bradley, *The March of the Montana Column*: 153–154.

Members of the Crow nation had suffered greatly at the hands of the Sioux. Now all hopes that the U.S. Army could defeat their bitter enemy had been dashed. Six Crow scouts had accompanied Custer, and two of them— White Swan and Half Yellow Face—were dead, and Curly was still missing. (He would later ride up to the *Far West* at its anchorage near the mouth of the Little Bighorn.) Bradley rode two miles back to the command and reported the news to General Alfred Terry and staff:

> … accompanied by General Gibbon, who had that morning joined [them], and for a moment there were blank faces and silent tongues and no doubt heavy hearts in that group…But presently the voice of doubt and scorning was raised, the story was sneered at, such a catastrophe it was asserted was wholly improbable, nay, impossible; if a battle had been fought, which was condescendingly admitted might have happened, then Custer was victorious, and these three Crows were dastards who had fled without awaiting the result and told this story to excuse their cowardice. General Terry took no part in these criticisms, but sat on his horse silent and thoughtful, biting his lower lip and looking at me as though he by no means shared the wholesale skepticism of the flippant members of his staff.[2]

One officer, Captain James Whelan, was frowned upon by the others for insisting that the Crows were telling the true story. "In fact Custer command-ed the admiration, and excited the enthusiasm of most of the young men in the army. His well known reputation for courage and dash was contagious and caught the fancy of even those among us who had never met him."[3]

General Terry nevertheless had little choice but to press forward regardless of the validity of the report. If true, he had to rescue what remained of Custer's 600 men, if any, even though he would likely be facing with his 400 men the same force that had allegedly dispatched Custer's 600! By noon the infantry, as well as the Gatling guns left behind the night before,[4] had caught up with the cavalry. Terry's command entered the valley of the Little Bighorn and, eventu-ally, crossed over to the left bank of that stream (the right side when moving upriver). At 3 P.M. they stopped and rested for about two hours and moved out again at 5 P.M. In the meantime, Lieutenant Bradley had sent the Fort Shaw post guide Hiram Bostwick and another citizen guide, Muggins Taylor, on

---

[2] Ibid.: 155.

[3] McClernand, *On Time for Disaster:* 52.

[4] John F. McBain, "With Gibbon on the Sioux Campaign of 1876," Part I, *Journal of the United States Cavalry Association,* Vol. 9 (June 1896): 143.

separate routes toward the position of the Sioux village, as later determined, in an attempt to make contact with Custer. After moving out, Bradley saw several ponies toward his left front near the river and a while later sighted three or four mounted men about two miles ahead of him. He had

> ... deployed [his] detachment as skirmishers; and soon afterward Bostwick came into view down the valley galloping at full speed. As he came up, he paused long enough to say that he had proceeded cautiously up the valley for several miles until all at once he came plump on a considerable body of Indians.[5]

Bostwick had then beat a hasty retreat.

From this point forward, the entire column marched in fighting order, aware that there were hostiles to their front. Three troops of cavalry and the Gatling battery advanced on the left bank of the river, with four companies of infantry on the right and the pack mules escorted by one company of infantry in the center. One troop of cavalry under Lieutenant Roe was positioned about one-half mile ahead of the main column in the bluffs on the right, with Lieutenant Bradley's mounted detachment also out about one-half mile to the front on the left. Toward dusk, as Bradley's mounted detachment approached a timbered spot at a narrow point on the floor of the valley, large numbers of Indians were observed riding down out of the hills and into the trees as if preparing to meet the troops there in force. Small groups of Indians also exchanged a few shots with Lieutenant Roe's troop as it pressed forward. Bradley wrote:

> As I had this timber to go through with my detachment, it was not pleasant to think of the storm of bullets that would undoubtedly be hurled in our faces as we rode up to its dark border or of the painted hundreds that would rise suddenly on all sides of us...and cut off the whole of us in a moment. I have been in several engagements and participated in several charges upon intrenched positions, but in my whole career as a soldier never did anything call for so much nerve as the riding slowly up with eleven men, half a mile from the rest of the column, on this body of ambushed warriors [warriors lying in ambush]. My men sat in their saddles with pale faces but closed lips with stern determination, expecting in a few minutes more to be shot down, but resolved not to flinch though the cost were death.[6]

---

[5] Bradley: 157.

[6] Ibid.: 158–159.

Scarcely fourteen months later, Lieutenant Bradley would be shot and killed while advancing on the Nez Perce camp at the Battle of the Big Hole.

From his position up on the bluffs on the left bank[7] of the Little Bighorn, Lieutenant Roe could observe a dark moving mass crossing the plateau between the Little Bighorn and the Bighorn. This was the hostile encampment moving toward the Bighorn Mountains. The lieutenant's troops then spotted groups of mounted men in the distance, difficult to make out in the gathering darkness, but appearing to be mounted cavalrymen in blue uniforms. A small detachment was sent forward to meet them, but was greeted with a volley of gunfire.[8] Scout Muggins Taylor returned to the command, stating that he had been fired upon by some of Custer's scouts after attempting to make contact with them. Obviously, he had been fired upon by the Sioux wearing captured clothing. As the command moved forward, some officers spotted through their field glasses objects on the hills farther upriver on the opposite side, which appeared to be buffaloes lying down.[9]

About 9 P.M. the evening of the 26th, General Terry, fearing that members of his command and Custer's command might fire on each other in the dark, made camp in the valley of the Little Bighorn, at the site of the present-day town of Crow Agency. The infantry had marched over twenty-nine miles, and the cavalry and the Gatling detachment about seventeen miles. They were still about four to five miles from the location of Custer's body. As a halt was called, Bradley's mounted detachment was still about one-fourth mile from the timber he had been advancing on. Some riderless horses were spotted about an eighth of a mile from the timber. The Fort Shaw post guide Bostwick and Will Logan boldly rode forward and drove them back to the command. They were not fired upon. Lieutenant McClernand recalled, "The command formed a hollow square, with the Gatling guns placed to the best advantage to repel a possible attack....Whatever the result of Custer's fight had been, everyone anticipated another on the morrow."[10] Lieutenant Bradley would later go over the ground they had been advancing on and assert:

> ... I am convinced there were not less than a thousand of these ambushed savages, with plenty more to co-operate with them...they would have given our whole command a desperate fight had we ad-

---

[7] The right-hand side of Terry's column as it moved up the river.

[8] Bradley: 158–159.

[9] McClernand, *On Time for Disaster:* 57–58.

[10] Ibid.

vanced that evening another mile. Their village was retreating, and they were there to cover it, and it was only for lack of an hour or two more of daylight that we did not come upon them in force and prove once more the terrific gallantry with which they can fight under such an incitement as the salvation of their all.[11]

11 Bradley: 161–162.

CHAPTER TWENTY-SIX

Terry's Column Finds Bodies of Custer and His Men; Terry Makes Contact with Reno, June 27

ARLY ON JUNE 27, GENERAL ALFRED TERRY'S COMMAND resumed their advance, passing through the wooded area that had by that time been reconnoitered by Lieutenant James Bradley's scouts. They soon entered the lower area of the village, which they described as immense, but now deserted. The Indians had obviously left in a degree of haste leaving a few tepees standing, several dead Indians, at least fifty ponies and some equipment and supplies scattered about, including large quantities of dried meat. A blood-stained buckskin shirt with bullet holes in it was located and identified as having belonged to Lieutenant Sturgis of Custer's command. An army horse was also found grazing in the village area; Lieutenant Edward McClernand believed that this was probably Comanche, Captain Myles Keogh's mount. "All were horrified by a message received at this time from Lieutenant Bradley, our chief of scouts, saying he had counted 196 dead cavalrymen on the hills across the river. The objects seen the day before looking like buffaloes lying down were probably dead comrades and their horses."[1]

Bradley would later report:

> I was scouting the hills some two or three miles to the left of the column upon the opposite bank of the river from that traversed by the column itself, when the body of a horse attracted our attention to the field of Custer's fight, and hastening in that direction the

[1] McClernand, *On Time for Disaster*: 59.

appalling sight was revealed to us of his entire command in the embrace of death. This was the first discovery of the field, and the first hasty count made of the slain, resulting in the finding of 197 bodies reported by General Terry.[2]

Shortly after receiving the bad news from Bradley, two riders were sighted galloping down the valley toward the column.

As the hurrying riders drew nearer we discovered they were riding bare-back, then that they were white men, and finally two lieutenants, [George D.] Wallace and Hare, sent by [Major Marcus] Reno to tell of the desperate fight by his own detachment, and to point out their present position on the bluffs up, and across the river. "Where is Custer," they were asked. Wallace replied, "The last we saw of him he was going along that high bluff (pointing in a general direction to the bluffs down stream from the position where he had located Reno), toward the lower end of the village. He took off his hat and waved to us. We do not know where he is now." General Terry responded sorrowfully that Custer had been found, now certain that Custer's body lay on the field found by Bradley's detachment. Reno's messengers sat their horses aghast at the information given them, and seemed slow to grasp the fact that their detachment had not played a major role in the drama that had been enacted.[3]

Dawn on the morning of June 27th had been a quiet one for Reno's command on the bluffs. During the previous evening four more men had entered Reno's lines from the valley bottom, where they had been left by Reno's retreat. They were Lieutenant Charles DeRudio, Private O'Neal, the interpreter, Mr. Girard, and a scout named Jackson. No Indians were in sight, but Reno held his troops in readiness, fearing a ruse on the part of the hostiles. Dust was sighted down the valley and the command prepared for action, fearing that the Indians were returning. After some time it became apparent that a body of troops was approaching from downriver. Reno sent out two lieutenants to make contact. A while later, a civilian scout arrived from Terry's command with a note for Custer, followed by the arrival of Lieutenant Bradley. Lieutenant E.S. Godfrey wrote:

Greeting most cordially my old friend [Lieutenant Bradley], I immediately asked, "Where is Custer?" He replied, "I don't know, but I

---

[2] Bradley, *The March of the Montana Column:* 172.

[3] McClernand: 61.

suppose he was killed, as we counted 197 bodies. I don't suppose any escaped." We were simply dumfounded. This was the first intimation we had of his fate. It was hard to realize; it did seem impossible.[4]

The rest of the day the united commands cared for the wounded, destroyed surplus supplies and also destroyed supplies left behind by the Indians. On June 28th, they buried the dead. Lieutenant McClernand related, "As we had but a few spades, the burial of the dead was more a pretense than a reality. A number were simply covered with sage brush. Yet we did our best."[5]

The Montana Column's favorite scout, Mitch Boyer, was also found among the dead. Colonel Gibbon praised him, "He was a half-breed Sioux, and they had often tried to kill him. He was the protegé and pupil of the celebrated guide Jim Bridger; was the best guide in this section of the country, and the only half-breed I ever met who could give distances to be passed over with any accuracy in miles."[6]

Lieutenant Godfrey stated the entire command had lost 265 killed and fifty-two wounded during the battle. Care for the wounded now became the primary task of the unified command. Lieutenant Godfrey related one humorous note:

> Among the wounded was saddler "Mike" Madden of my troop, whom I promoted to be sergeant, on the field, for gallantry. Madden was very fond of his grog. His long abstinence had given him a famous thirst. It was necessary to amputate his leg, which was done without administering any anesthetic; but after the amputation the surgeon gave him a good stiff drink of brandy. Madden eagerly gulped it down, and his eyes fairly danced as he smacked his lips and said, "M-eh, doctor, cut off my other leg."[7]

---

[4] Godfrey, *Custer's Last Battle:* 36.

[5] McClernand: 94.

[6] Gibbon, *Adventures on the Western Frontier:* 150.

[7] Godfrey: 36–38.

Terry, Gibbon and Custer Approach to Little Bighorn Battlefield

C1-Custer departs 12 p.m., 6/22 and marches 12 miles; C2-departs 5 a.m., 6/23 and marches 33 miles; C3-departs 5 a.m., 6/24 and marches 28 miles; C4-departs at sundown and marches 10 miles, halts at 2 a.m., 6/25 (C5); (See map of Battlefield Maneuvers on 6/25).

TG1-6/24, Terry/Gibbon ferry across Yellowstone and march 4 miles; TG2-depart 5 a.m., 6/25, cavalry reaches TG3 still 22 miles from battlefield, infantry is 34 miles distant; departs 5 a.m., 6/26 and by nightfall reach TG4; morning of 6/27 they make contact with Reno on the bluffs.

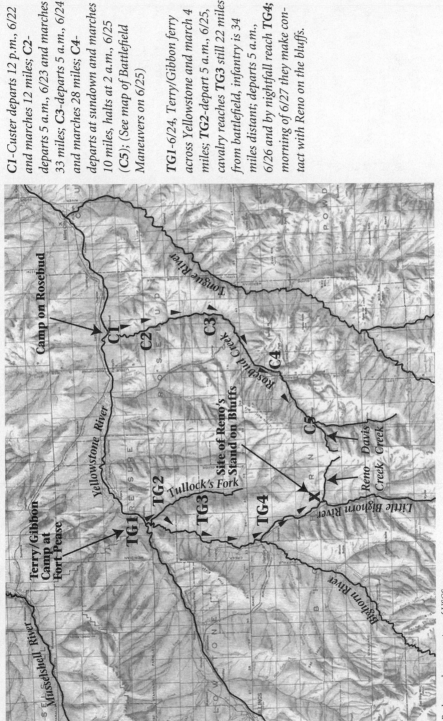

Background map courtesy of USGS

Little Bighorn Battlefield Maneuvers 6/25/1876

12 Noon 6/25 Custer divides his force. Reno to proceed and cross Little Bighorn River and attack village; Benteen to probe toward bluffs on the left. Custer's battalion proceeds down Reno Creek alongside Reno then veers right behind the hills out of view of the village. Reno crosses and charges village, halts (R1), then retreats to the bluffs across the river (R2). Approximately the same time as Reno's retreat, Custer engages Indians and is annihilated (C). Benteen (B) joins Reno on bluffs to fight a defensive battle until Indians draw off evening of 6/26. Reno/Benteen joined by Terry/Gibbon morning of 6/27/1876.

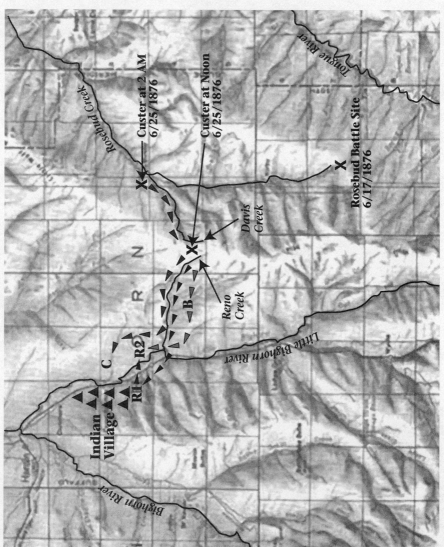

Custer at 2 AM
6/25/1876

Custer at Noon
6/25/1876

Rosebud Battle Site
6/17/1876

Rosebud Creek

Tongue River

Davis Creek

Reno Creek

Little Bighorn River

Bighorn River

Indian Village

C R2 R1 B

Background map courtesy of USGS

Terry Evacuates Wounded Back to the Yellowstone; Awaits Reinforcements; Indian Force Dissipates; Terry Makes Contact with Crook

COLONEL JOHN GIBBON WOULD LATER REPORT THAT there was some concern in the command that any display of haste to retreat from the area would likely invite attack by the hostile force; nevertheless, the needs of over fifty wounded men had to take priority. Colonel Gibbon also made a somewhat revealing statement on the mental state of the wounded troopers. "Poor fellows, an impression had, in some way, gained a footing amongst them during the long weary hours of the fight on the 26th that, to save the balance of the command, they were to be abandoned." Many of the men had lost confidence in Major Marcus Reno as a battlefield commander and obviously were aware that wounded had been abandoned at the onset of his retreat to the bluffs.[1] Later, in testimony at the Reno Inquiry in 1879, Lieutenant Winfield S. Edgerly stated that another wounded man of Company D had been abandoned as Reno's command, which then included Benteen's battalion, withdrew from its attempt to move down the ridge toward what was believed to be Custer's position.[2]

The Fort Shaw post guide, Hiram Bostwick, and Private Goodwin of the 7th Infantry were dispatched on June 29th to make contact with the steamer *Far West* and ensure that it remained on station at the mouth of the Little Bighorn, assuming it had reached that position, until the wounded could be transported to it and placed on board. Arriving at the junction of the two rivers, Bostwick and Goodwin did not sight the steamer. Unknown

---

[1] John Gibbon, *Adventures on the Western Frontier*: 145–146.

[2] W.A. Graham, *The Reno Court of Inquiry*: 162.

to them, it had progressed another ten miles up the Bighorn before the captain decided that he had passed the mouth of the Little Bighorn and returned. Thinking that the steamer was farther *down*stream, Bostwick and Goodwin rode all the way to the supply camp on the Yellowstone. They then learned that the boat was still up the Bighorn and returned upriver, finally locating it now at the mouth of the Little Bighorn. After delivering their message to Captain Grant Marsh to stand by, they returned to the battlefield, having ridden 140 miles in forty-eight hours. Colonel Gibbon wrote, "Their names deserve to be preserved in the records of the campaign."[3]

At 6:30 P.M. on June 28th, the command departed for the *Far West*. Initially, the troops transported the wounded by hand litters. This, however, proved too difficult, and they were able to advance only four and one-half miles before stopping. They spent June 29th preparing litters sufficient to meet the task. Mule litters were built by attaching Indian tent poles to the sides of two mules, one standing directly in front of the other with sufficient space in between to lay a man on a litter. This design proved efficient. They then moved out again at 5 P.M. on June 29th, and by 1:30 A.M. on the 30th they reached the *Far West*, placing the wounded aboard. Eight of the wounded eventually died of their wounds. Of Custer's battalion, 13 officers, 191 enlisted men and 4 citizens were killed, for a total of 208. Of Reno's portion of the command (including Benteen's troopers), 3 officers, 48 enlisted men, and 5 citizens and Indian scouts were killed and 67 wounded, including those who died later of wounds. For the 7th Cavalry Regiment as a whole, out of a total strength of 655 men, including 25 Crow scouts and 6 Ree (Arikara) scouts, 260 were killed and 51 wounded.[4] This represented a battle casualty rate of over 47 percent for the regiment (Indian scouts and citizens included).

As the *Far West* made her way down the Bighorn to the Yellowstone, Terry marched and ferried his troops back to the Fort Pease area, where he set up a temporary base to await reinforcements. On July 3, 1876, the *Far West* departed with the wounded and dispatches of the disaster for Bismarck, Dakota Territory. It arrived there at 11:30 P.M. on July 5th, with heartbreaking news for thirty-nine widows and numerous fatherless children at Fort Abraham Lincoln.[5]

General Terry also forwarded a dispatch reporting the battle to Fort Ellis, carried by scout Muggins Taylor. From there it could also be telegraphed to

3 Gibbon: 152.

4 James H. Bradley, *The March of the Montana Column:* 164.

5 W.A. Graham, *The Custer Myth:* 148.

St. Paul and Chicago. Taylor arrived in Bozeman on July 3rd. Captain D.W. Benham, in command at Ellis, immediately went to the telegraph office and delivered the dispatch. He discovered later, however, to his dismay, that it did not go out on the 3rd for technical reasons, but rather was forwarded by mail. The news did, however, reach the *Bozeman Times* and the *Helena Herald*, the *Times* reporting late on the evening of July 3rd and the *Herald* reporting the story on July 4, 1876—the first national centennial. Upon the arrival of the *Far West* in Bismarck, news was rapidly transmitted throughout the entire nation and received with shock and dismay, particularly in the frontier areas.[6]

In the years immediately following the defeat of Custer's troops, many Indian participants in the battle were interviewed by various persons: military officers, scholars, correspondents, etc. In his excellent book, which he described as a "Source Book of Custeriana," Colonel W.A. Graham, U.S. Army retired, quoted numerous interviews of American Indian participants in the battle, including those of the two principals, Sitting Bull and Crazy Horse. While acknowledging contradictions in the various Indian versions of the battle, as well as many of the white man's versions, the interviews published by Colonel Graham give us an accurate picture of the actions of many warriors during the battle. We must also remember that the battle extended over an area some four and one-half miles long. Just as Reno's men in the bluffs had no certain knowledge of what had happened to Custer, it is equally understandable that a warrior, who may have been involved in considerable combat in one sector, would have no first-hand knowledge of what occurred in another.

Obviously the entire U.S. Army, from the high command down to the lowest ranks, was taken by complete surprise at the overwhelming numbers of warriors available to Sitting Bull and Crazy Horse at the Little Bighorn and, to a lesser extent, at the Battle of the Rosebud. To return to the January 31, 1876, deadline imposed on the hostiles, principally Sitting Bull of the Uncpapas and Crazy Horse of the Ogallallas as well as Northern Cheyenne hostiles, one must assume that word of this became widely known by most Plains Indians, in particular within the realm of the Sioux and Northern Cheyenne Indian universe. Indeed, with General Crook's attack on Crazy Horse's village on the Powder River on March 17, 1876, every Sioux and Northern Cheyenne knew that the U.S. Army was invading the last great hunting ground—the place where those agency (reservation) Indians could ride out to in the summer months and still live their old lifestyle of the hunt while conducting occasional raids on the

---

[6] Ibid.: 349–351.

Crow and other Indian bands as well as whites, as the opportunity arose. In the autumn, they could return to the reservation and live on government beef, albeit scarce at times, obtain tent canvas for their tepees (since buffalo hides were becoming ever scarcer), and, in the spring, with green grass for their horses, return once again to the summer camps.

Now that their sacred territory was being invaded, many young warriors answered the appeals of Sitting Bull and Crazy Horse to rise against the whites. Had the original plans of General Philip Sheridan come to fruition and a winter campaign been successfully carried out against the hostile holdouts—i.e. those who never came to the agencies—the number of hostiles encountered might not have been much more than intelligence collected by the army, and reiterated by Custer, had indicated. We will recall that Custer believed he would encounter at the most 1,500 warriors.

Warriors residing at the agencies could not easily move to the aid of the hostiles on half-starved horses, as was usually the state of their animals in the winter. However, even before the commencement of the army's summer campaign, with the grass now green and the horses in good condition, reports began to filter in indicating a large exodus of young warriors, and in some cases their families, departing the agencies—along the Missouri River, near the Black Hills in Dakota Territory and in northern Nebraska Territory—and heading west to join the hostile camps. As early as April 27th, Major Reno, then acting commander at Fort Abraham Lincoln, reported the following provided to him by a scout: "…all young men are leaving reservation with best ponies. They report going to fight Crow Indians, he says they are going to join Sitting Bull."[7]

Apparently these agency Indians had little trouble procuring a plentiful supply of arms and ammunition from traders at or near their respective agencies. They carried on trade with those Indians who remained permanently hostile under Sitting Bull, Crazy Horse and other hostile chiefs. The extent of this trade was outlined by Captain John S. Poland, 6th Infantry, who was stationed at the Standing Rock Agency in Dakota Territory. On December 30, 1875, he had sent a telegram to his superiors with an estimate of the extent of the ammunition trade carried on by Indians residing at Standing Rock Agency:

> I here submit an item which will, perhaps, show how extensive this trade might be. Six thousand beeves [beef cattle] are supposed to be

---

[7] George E. Fay, *Military Engagements Between United States Troops and Plains Indians*: 67.

sent to this agency annually, yielding 6,000 hides. The trader pays for each hide, say, 50 rounds of ammunition. Deduct, say, one-half for hides sold to Mrs. Galpin [According to Captain Poland, she did not sell ammo]; then 3,000 x 50 = 150,000 (one hundred and fifty thousand) rounds would correctly represent the total sales. I am of the opinion, however, that 100,000 (one hundred thousand) rounds of ammunition is nearer the total of his [referring to trader J.R. Casselberry] annual sales. If we suppose that 25 percent of this amount is taken out to Sitting Bull for trade, and a proportional amount from other agencies, can we wonder how the hostiles procure arms and ammunition?[8]

The exodus of warriors from the agencies placed more firepower at the disposal of Sitting Bull, Crazy Horse and the other leaders than they likely had ever possessed at any previous given time. Crazy Horse was able to check Crook at the Battle of the Rosebud on June 17, 1876, with a much larger force than he had had available when General Reynolds attacked his village on the Powder River on March 17th. Mrs. Spotted-Horn-Bull reported that, about eleven days before the Battle of the Little Bighorn, the Sioux had held a Sun Dance. Although she did not give the location, it was doubtless the one ridden through by Custer's men as they advanced up the Rosebud. "... Sitting Bull, the medicine man and counselor more than a warrior, was one of those tied to the pole of suffering, and the pierced muscles of his breast still show the scars of that dire observance."[9] While others succumbed to the self-imposed suffering, Sitting Bull held out, fainting on the third day. In the course of these events he had a dream that "...his people were soon to meet Custer[10] and his followers and annihilate them." Mrs. Spotted-Horn-Bull continued that about that time a great battle with thousands of Crows took place. It lasted all day and the Crows were defeated. (Here she is likely referring to the Battle of the Rosebud with Crook's forces, as there was no large battle with the Crows at that time nor did the Crows have thousands of warriors at their disposal). She stated that the distance from the fight with the Crows was about thirty miles from the site of the Battle of the Little Bighorn. This corresponds with the distance to the Battle of the Rosebud (as the crow flies, about thirty-two miles) in which, we will recall, 176 Crow

---

8 Ibid.: 45.

9 Graham, *The Custer Myth*: 82–83.

10 The Indians had no way of knowing they would meet "Custer." That they would meet troops, yes. But not even Custer, himself, knew he would be on the expedition until very shortly before its departure from Fort Abraham Lincoln. Once again, that marvelous 20-20 hindsight is at work.

scouts were involved. She added that the morning after the battle (with the Crows), the Sioux encampment was moved to the Little Bighorn site.[11]

If we return to the Battle of the Rosebud, General George Crook thought that the Indian village was about eight miles down the Rosebud from his location. The approximate location of the Sun Dance lodge seen by Custer's troops was some thirty to thirty-five miles down the Rosebud from Crook's battlefield. Thus, Crazy Horse was doubtless able to draw on considerable reinforcements from the more distant camp. In any case, by the time of the Battle of the Little Bighorn eight days later, Crazy Horse's Ogallallas were encamped with Sitting Bull on the Little Bighorn. A company of the 2nd Cavalry, while scouting the trail of the withdrawing hostiles on June 28th, discovered a very large lodge-pole trail coming down the valley of the Little Bighorn from the south and leading to the encampment near the battle-field. Colonel Gibbon surmised that this was the trail of Crazy Horse's camp coming from the site of the Rosebud battlefield to join Sitting Bull.[12]

Upon sighting the approach of Terry's column on June 26th, the leaders of the hostiles, principally Sitting Bull and Crazy Horse, opted to withdraw to the Bighorn Mountains.[13] The Indians, although much more at home in the wilds than the soldiers, also had their logistical problems, particularly when attempting to sustain such a large encampment merely from the fruits of the hunt. Smaller bands that were still large enough to defend themselves were more mobile and more easily sustained. The large gathering began to dissipate. The aforementioned company of the 2nd Cavalry sent out to scout the Indian trail on the 28th of June followed it about ten to twelve miles from the battlefield, then found that it forked into two trails, one heading southwest and one southeast.[14]

Northern Cheyenne Chief Two Moon departed eastward from the Bighorn Mountain encampment with his thirty lodges,[15] while a large body eventually moved over to the Rosebud in late July and followed it down-stream, then crossed over to the Tongue River valley, where the trail split up with one going downstream, one upstream and the main trail leading east-ward toward the Powder River. Horny Horse would tell Lieutenant James Bourke one year later that the bands broke up at Bluestone Creek. Thus, by

---

[11] Graham, *The Custer Myth:* 81–87.

[12] Gibbon: 145–146.

[13] Two Moon (Cheyenne), quoted in Graham, *The Custer Myth:* 101–103.

[14] Ibid.

[15] Graham, *The Custer Myth:* 101–103.

around August 1st, the great American Indian fighting force had dissolved into numerous bands, with most of the participants in the great battle returning to the agencies while the original hostiles under Sitting Bull and Crazy Horse and other lesser leaders remained in the field living by the hunt as they had always done.[16]

Some forty to fifty years later, the Cheyenne warrior Wooden Leg would report the larger bands' movements as follows: First night of movement away from the Little Bighorn Battlefield was spent in the area of present-day Lodge Grass, MT; second night the camp moved farther south to near present-day Wyola, MT; the next day they moved over the divide into the Rosebud drainage; the next day they moved down the Rosebud, camping two more nights en route then one night near present-day Busby, MT; the next day they moved farther down the Rosebud to its junction with Muddy Creek. They continued down the Rosebud, then turned eastward to the Tongue valley and eventually the Powder River valley where, according to Wooden Leg, it was decided that the various bands would go their own ways. Wooden Leg estimated that this division of the bands occurred about sixteen days after departing the battlefield camp.[17]

Terry's command, including Gibbon's Montana Column and remnants of the 7th Cavalry now commanded by Major Reno, remained in the Fort Pease area until July 26th awaiting reinforcements. As with the hostiles, good grass for the animals was always a necessity, and the army shifted the camp from time to time to nearby areas not yet grazed off. For obvious security reasons, it was not desirable to drive the herds great distances from the main camp for grass; thus, the camp had to move to good grass.[18]

The Crow Indians were camped at Pompey's Pillar, some twenty-five miles up the Yellowstone. They learned of the Battle of the Rosebud via Crow scouts who had participated in it with General Crook and informed Terry's command of the battle on July 7, 1876.[19] Ten days had passed since the Custer disaster. General Terry, anxious to open communication with General Crook, attempted to induce the Crows to carry a message through, but to no avail. After an unsuccessful attempt to send an enterprising civilian scout, volunteers from Colonel Gibbon's command were selected. They were Privates Evans, Stewart and Bell, all of Company E, 7th Infantry. They volunteered to

---

[16] John G. Bourke, *On the Border with Crook:* 347, 353, 417.

[17] Thomas B. Marquis, *Wooden Leg:* 272–280.

[18] Edward J. McClernand, *On Time for Disaster:* 149–150.

[19] Gibbon: 154.

ride south through approximately one hundred miles of Sioux-infested country, essentially from present-day Bighorn, MT, to Sheridan, WY, and deliver dispatches to General Crook. Colonel Gibbon described these brave men:

> Evans and Stewart were both tall, gaunt, lank specimens of humanity, and looked as if a hard day's ride would use them up completely. Bell was short, and more stoutly made…Evans was apparently the leader of the party, and to him I gave full instructions as to how he was to travel. I also placed in his hand a section of a map of the country he was to pass over, marking upon it the supposed location of General Crook's camp. He looked at this in a stolid sort of way, and I began to think he did not even know the object in giving it to him. But he quietly stowed it away in his pocket, and after he came back to us, told me with a little smile he believed he could go anywhere in an unknown country if he had a map to travel by.[20]

The men were escorted a short distance up Tullock's Fork on July 9th and then, in darkness, departed on their own. They were not heard of for sixteen days.[21]

Upon receipt of the news of the disaster, the government and the army high command moved quickly to provide reinforcements and to lay plans for the construction of two permanent posts in the Yellowstone region— Fort Keogh near present-day Miles City, MT, and Fort Custer near present-day Hardin, MT. This task would fall to Colonel (Brevet General) Nelson A. Miles and his 5th Infantry Regiment, then stationed at Fort Leavenworth, KS. They were ordered upriver by steamboat, arriving at Terry's command on the Yellowstone around August 1, 1876.[22] Six companies of the 22nd Infantry also arrived at that time, following a skirmish with a party of hostiles at the mouth of the Powder River.[23]

General Crook, to the south in Wyoming, awaited reinforcements and word from General Terry. During the first days of July, he sent a party of twenty men and his best guide, Frank Grouard, under the command of Lieutenant Sibley, 2nd Cavalry, to reconnoiter around the base of the Bighorn Mountains to the headwaters of the Bighorn River. Upon reaching the headwaters of the Little Bighorn, they were attacked by about one

---

[20] Ibid.: 155.

[21] Ibid.

[22] McClernand, *On Time for Disaster:* 96.

[23] Gibbon: 159.

hundred Cheyenne warriors under Chief White Antelope and barely escaped with their lives. White Antelope was killed during the fight.[24]

Lieutenant Bourke later described the arrival of Colonel Gibbon's Montana messengers with news of Custer's defeat:

> On the 12th of July, 1876, three men, dirty, ragged, dressed in tatters of army uniforms, rode into camp and gave their names as Evans, Stewart, and Bell, of Captain Clifford's company of the Seventh Infantry, bearers of dispatches from General Terry to General Crook; in the dress of each was sewed a copy of the one message which revealed the terrible catastrophe happening to the companies under Custer. These three modest heroes had ridden across country in the face of unknown dangers, and had performed the duty confided to them in a manner that challenged the admiration of every man in our camp. I have looked in vain through the leaves of the Army Register to see their names inscribed on the roll of commissioned officers; and I feel sure that ours is the only army in the world in which such conspicuous courage, skill, and efficiency would have gone absolutely un-recognized.[25]

We may note that over two weeks had passed from the time of Custer's defeat until General Crook received word of it. On July 19th, four Crow messengers also arrived at General Crook's encampment. They had been sent by Terry, who, fearing that Evans, Stewart and Bell might not survive the trip, sent duplicate messages for Crook.[26] On July 25th, Evans and Stewart arrived back at Gibbon's camp. Colonel Gibbon later described the return of these brave messengers. Having sighted mounted persons arriving at the south bank of the Yellowstone, by all indications friendly, a boat was sent across to retrieve them.

> ... as the boat neared the opposite shore the conduct of the crew was narrowly watched through our glasses, for although some of the strangers were seen to be Indians at least two were recognized as white men...when they landed on our shore and presented me with dispatches from General Crook I greeted them almost like men risen from the dead. Bell's horse had broken down on the trip, and Evans and Stewart only returned, accompanied by the Crow scouts...[27]

---

[24] Bourke: 331–333.

[25] Ibid.: 335–336. Bourke was apparently unaware that these men were later awarded the Medal of Honor for their service.

[26] Ibid.: 339

[27] Gibbon: 157–158.

CHAPTER TWENTY-EIGHT

Crook Is Reinforced and Marches to Join Terry; After Fruitless Pursuit, Gibbon and Terry Depart the Field; Miles Builds Fort Keogh; Crook Follows Lesser Trail Southeast

G ENERAL GEORGE CROOK, IN CAMP IN WYOMING, continued to await the arrival of his own reinforcements, General Wesley Merritt and ten troops of the 5th Cavalry, who were en route from the Red Cloud Agency in northwestern Nebraska Territory. Shoshone Chief Washakie, leading the Shoshone scouts, advised General Crook,

> The Sioux and Cheyennes have three to your one, even now that you have been reinforced; why not let them alone for a few days? They cannot subsist the great numbers of warriors and men in their camp, and will have to scatter for pasturage and meat; they'll begin to fight among themselves about the plunder taken on the battlefield, and many will want to slip into the agencies and rejoin their families.[1]

Around August 1, 1876, scouting parties from Crook's command proceeded to the headwaters of the Little Bighorn and the Bighorn. One party found evidence of a very large Sioux camp "…of hundreds of lodges and thousands of ponies…" as well as further evidence of food shortages indicating that the hostiles were now eating their dogs and ponies. The camp had departed toward the northeast in the direction of the Powder River about the 25th or 26th of July. In the meantime, to prevent further exodus of warriors to the field, the War Department was given control of the Sioux agencies.[2]

---

[1] Quoted in John G. Bourke, *On the Border with Crook*: 341–342.

[2] Bourke: 342, 347.

On August 3rd, Crook's force was reinforced by General Merritt's cavalry companies. Merritt also brought along a famous white scout, William F. Cody, better known as "Buffalo Bill." General Crook commenced his march to join up with Terry by traveling down Prairie Dog Creek to the Tongue River and then down the Tongue. The column then crossed the Rosebud Mountains and followed the Rosebud River drainage downstream. Here they struck the main trail of the hostiles, believed to be about ten to twelve days old. The scouts estimated the number of pony tracks to be in the thousands.[3]

On August 11, 1876, Crook's column and Terry's column finally met. Earlier, Captain John Gibbon had moved his command downriver to meet Terry at Camp Supply on the Rosebud, arriving there on June 30th.[4] Terry's unified column had then departed up the Rosebud on August 8th. It now consisted of Gibbon's Montana Column (7th Infantry and 2nd Cavalry) as well as Colonel Nelson Mile's 5th Infantry and the remnants of the 7th Cavalry now under the command of Major Marcus Reno.

Upon his meeting with Crook's large force, General Terry ordered Colonel Miles to return to the north bank of the Yellowstone with his command and, utilizing a steamboat now available for the purpose, patrol the river on the lookout for any attempts by the Sioux to cross to the north bank. Of course, Miles also had additional responsibilities, namely the establishment of a new post at the mouth of the Tongue River. Terry, who had been accompanied by wagons, decided to send them back with Miles and proceed with Crook by pack train. Crook's and Terry's large unified command then continued to follow the hostile trail, which led from the Rosebud across to the Tongue River.

Lieutenant Bourke later wrote of his impressions of Terry's command:

> In two things the column from the Yellowstone was sadly deficient: in cavalry and in rapid transportation. The Seventh Cavalry was in need of reorganization, half of its original numbers having been killed or wounded in the affair of the Bighorn; the pack-train, made up, as it necessarily was, of animals taken out of the traces of the heavy wagons, was the saddest burlesque in that direction which it has ever been my lot to witness—for this no blame was ascribable to Terry, who was doing the best he could with the means allowed him from Washington. The 2nd Cavalry was in good shape, and so was

---

[3] Ibid.: 348–350.

[4] John Gibbon, *Adventures on the Western Frontier*: 158.

Gibbon's column of infantry, which seemed ready to go wherever ordered and go at once.[5]

Special pride was taken in Crook's pack train. "[It] was a marvel of system; it maintained a discipline much severer than had been attained by any company in either column; under the indefatigable supervision of Tom Moore, Dave Mears, and others, who had had an experience of more than a quarter of a century…"[6]

Once the unified commands arrived at the Tongue River, the hostile trail split three ways: one upriver, one downriver, and the main trail continuing east toward the Powder River. At the Tongue, the bodies of two prospectors were discovered. They had been captured by the Sioux and roasted alive.[7] According to the Crow scouts, the trail at this point was at least nine days old. The column followed it down to "Pumpkin Vine Creek," presumably Pumpkin Creek at the junction of present-day Montana Route 332 and Highway 59. They then turned up Pumpkin Vine and crossed over to the Powder River. Leaving the trail, they followed the Powder down to the Yellowstone, where a steamboat awaited them with supplies.[8]

They arrived at the mouth of the Powder on August 17th. General Crook's cavalry horses were nearly worn out.[9] Here the column spent about one week taking on supplies and recuperating the animals. On August 20th, Gibbon discharged his Crow scouts, who needed to go back to their homes, hunt buffalo and prepare for the winter. On August 24th, the unified commands headed back up the Powder to pick up the trail of the hostiles, which had turned east about fifteen miles above the Yellowstone. On the 25th, however, Buffalo Bill arrived with news that newly arriving reinforcements for Colonel Miles coming upriver on a steamer had been fired on by Indians at a point farther down the Yellowstone. News was also received that Indians were crossing the Yellowstone above Fort Buford, somewhere between present-day Glendive, MT, and the Montana–North Dakota border. Acting on this new intelligence, a decision was made to divide the commands, with Terry's column going to the north side of the Yellowstone to attempt to intercept hostiles moving toward the Missouri

---

5 Bourke: 352–353.

6 Ibid.: 353.

7 Ibid.

8 McClernand, *On Time for Disaster:* 153.

9 Ibid.: 154–155.

River and Canada, while Crook's column continued its pursuit eastward following the trail that, it was believed, would eventually lead to the Black Hills and the various agencies.[10]

The easterly trail led on O'Fallon's Creek and then to Beaver Creek near the present-day state border. By the time it reached this point, the trail showed definite signs of breaking up as the various bands split off, in many cases to go to their various agencies. Meanwhile, Terry's command reached the Yellowstone near the mouth of O'Fallon's Creek and on August 27th was ferried across by two steamers. They then marched toward the north, reaching Bad Route Creek on the evening of the 28th, some twenty-seven miles from the Yellowstone, then over seventeen miles to Rush Creek (no longer designated as such on the map), and arriving at Deer Creek on August 30th after marching another seventeen miles. On August 31st, they arrived back at the Yellowstone at the mouth of Deer Creek.[11] All in all, they had marched in a semicircle extending down the Yellowstone in an attempt to intercept a frequently utilized lodge-pole trail leading toward Big Dry Creek, known as a favorite camping area for Sitting Bull. A cavalry force was sent on a scout to the north of the main body and intercepted the lodge-pole trail, but it showed no signs of recent use. As the infantry approached the Yellowstone, another large cavalry scout was sent eastward, but also found no trail.[12]

Referring to the situation in the field as of early September 1876, Colonel Gibbon would later write:

> Our stern chase had thus proved a long and fruitless one, and we had no longer even a shifting objective point to move against; for the Indians had doubtless divided their forces in the wilderness to the south of the Yellowstone, and could at any time concentrate again or remain scattered, according to circumstances.[13]

The Yellowstone was rapidly dropping and would soon be no longer navigable for the steamers busily bringing in supplies for the new post at Fort Keogh. This new post was to be manned with about 1,500 troops, making up a new and separate District of the Yellowstone. It was decided to send the troops of the Montana Column back to their respective posts.

---

[10] Gibbon: 164–165.

[11] McClernand, *On Time for Disaster:* 157.

[12] Gibbon: 167–168.

[13] Gibbon: 168.

Gibbon's column departed Glendive Creek homeward bound on September 6, 1876, marching up the north bank of the Yellowstone until they reached Sweetgrass Creek opposite present-day Greycliff, MT. Here the Camp Baker and Fort Shaw companies turned north toward those posts, while the Fort Ellis contingent of infantry and cavalry continued up the Yellowstone to Fort Ellis, which was reached on September 29th. The others arrived at Camp Baker on October 2nd and Fort Shaw on October 6th. Distance from Glendive Creek to Fort Ellis was 449 miles, to Fort Shaw 586 miles. Surely, our frontier soldiers received sufficient walking exercise! From the dates of their respective departures from Fort Shaw (March 17, 1876), Camp Baker and Fort Ellis (April 1st), the infantry marched over 1,687 miles and the cavalry over 1,393 miles during the campaign.[14]

Colonel Gibbon made an insightful statement relative to the relationship between man and his beasts of burden in frontier campaigns; namely, that the men fared better on the long march back to their Montana posts than did the horses and mules. The men were conditioned to the extended marches throughout their long, hard period in the field with sufficient—albeit sparse—rations, whereas their animals were worked hard, but also had to struggle to obtain sufficient nourishment from the constantly varying grazing areas made available to them, usually over a limited amount of time. Thus, the overall quality of their feed was poor, causing them to become physically worn down.[15]

On September 27th, Gibbon sent the following telegram from Fort Ellis to Major J.E. Blaine in Helena. "Forty six Crow scouts will be at Ellis in a few days for muster out and payment. Make arrangements at once for their payment, so they need not be detained longer than necessary. They have pay due from April and are entitled to soldier's pay, forty cents per day for horses and some clothing…"[16]

In the meantime, General Crook's force pressed eastward on the fading trail, eventually reaching the headwaters of the Heart River in present-day North Dakota about September 5, 1876. His men and animals were worn out, and they were forced to butcher many of their horses to provide the men with food. At this point, only four or five day's march from Fort

---

[14] McClernand, *On Time for Disaster:* 160–164.

[15] Gibbon: 169.

[16] September 27, 1876, Letters and Telegrams Sent and Received, District of Montana, Department of Dakota, Record Group 393.5, National Archives.

Abraham Lincoln, they turned south toward the Black Hills. On September 9th, at Slim Buttes, approximately 120 miles southeast of present-day Miles City, MT, and near present-day Reva, SD, an advance guard of the column commanded by Captain Anson Mills surprised a Sioux band under Chief American Horse. Mills's men engaged the Sioux in a firefight and captured some 200 ponies and numerous supplies.[17]

This band of about thirty-five lodges belonged to the Spotted Tail Agency, but they had participated in the Battle of the Little Bighorn. Lieutenant Bourke described the items captured:

> Great quantities of furs—almost exclusively untanned buffalo robes and other skins...and several tons of meat, dried after the Indian manner...A cavalry guidon, nearly new and torn from the staff; an army officer's overcoat; a non-commissioned officer's blouse; cavalry saddles of the McClellan model...a glove marked with the name of Captain Keogh; a letter addressed to a private soldier in the Seventh Cavalry; horses branded U.S. and 7 C....These Indians had certificates of good conduct dated at Spotted Tail Agency and issued by Agent Howard.[18]

Chicago Times correspondent John Finerty placed the number of buffalo robes captured at 2,500. This band was part and parcel of a larger force, which later attempted a counterattack led by Crazy Horse that was beaten off by Crook's 2,000-man force. General Crook's casualties amounted to three killed (two military men and one civilian scout) and over seventeen wounded. Mr. Finerty estimated Crazy Horse's force at 600 to 800 in number.[19]

Indian losses were unknown, but several warriors including the mortally wounded Chief American Horse, over a dozen Indian women and a number of children were captured when they became trapped in a ravine they had withdrawn into during the battle. The hostiles attempted to make a stand in the ravine. Their gunfire killed one of the civilian scouts. Mr. Finerty described the results of a heavy concentration of fire that Crook's men placed on this target:

> The soldiers opened upon it [the ravine] an incessant fire...the shower of close-range bullets from the latter terrified the unhappy squaws, and they began singing the awful Indian death chant. The

---

[17] McClernand *On Time for Disaster:* 99.

[18] Bourke: 370–371.

[19] John Finerty, *War Path and Bivouac:* 252, 264, 450–451.

pappooses wailed so loudly, and so piteously, that even the hot firing could not quell their voices, and General Crook ordered the men to suspend operations immediately. Then Frank Gruard and Baptiste Pourier, both versed in the Sioux tongue, by order of General Crook, approached the abrupt western bank of the Indian rifle pit and offered the women and children quarter. This was accepted by the besieged, and Crook in person went to the mouth of the cavern and handed out one tall fine looking woman, who had an infant strapped to her back. She trembled all over and refused to liberate the General's hand. Eleven other squaws, and six pappooses, were then taken out...[20]

The women and children were later released.

Aside from Lieutenant Sibley's hot fight with White Antelope's band of Northern Cheyenne on July 17th, the engagement at Slim Buttes with American Horse's small band and the brief action with the reinforcements coming up the Yellowstone were the only post–Battle of the Little Bighorn encounters with the Sioux and their Cheyenne allies during the summer campaign of 1876. I emphasize summer, for in the autumn further action would take place. Crook's forces marched on to Deadwood, Dakota Territory, arriving in a famished, exhausted condition. Here they were resupplied, eventually returning to their bases in great need of rest and recuperation. The great Sioux and Northern Cheyenne fighting force had now dissipated with most of the Indians going back to their agencies for the winter. Crazy Horse and Sitting Bull, with other hostiles, remained in the field, ever hostile and ever determined to continue their old way of life. The fighting ability of these forces, while still formidable, was much diminished from the midsummer days on the Little Bighorn. Game, while still available in some quantities, was gradually becoming scarce.

---

[20] Ibid.: 254.

CHAPTER TWENTY-NINE

Colonel Miles Opens a Winter Campaign Against Sitting Bull, October 17, 1876

U NDER NORMAL CIRCUMSTANCES, IN THE AUTUMN OF 1876, the hostiles would now concentrate on building up a good winter supply of meat and furs, locate suitable winter camp sites, and sit out the winter without fear of attack by the army. But their great victory at the Little Bighorn also spawned the seeds of their demise. Throughout the remainder of the summer, the army had moved up reinforcements and supplies for two new posts: first Fort Keogh near present-day Miles City, MT, and Fort Custer, near present-day Hardin, MT.[1] Thus U.S. military power had been projected into the midst of the last great hunting ground claimed by the Sioux and the Northern Cheyenne. The supply lines for campaigns in the area were now much shorter. And, in Colonel Nelson Miles, the army had now permanently established another able and aggressive commander right in the midst of hostile territory. While the men of Colonel John Gibbon's Montana Column were back at their posts recuperating and carrying out their duties in their assigned areas of responsibility, Colonel Miles prepared his newly created District of the Yellowstone for a winter campaign, which would, with few exceptions, break the back of hostile resistance in the Yellowstone and Bighorn areas.

---

[1] Post Returns for the Cantonment on the Tongue River (Fort Keogh) revealed an aggregate force of 690 in February 1877 and 702 in November 1877, and for Fort Custer an aggregate of 490 in December 1877 and 412 in July 1878; Fort Keogh Post Returns, Records of the Adjutant General's Office, ca. 1775–ca. 1928, Record Group 94, National Archives; Post Returns for Fort Custer, ibid. The aggregate strength of these two posts in Colonel Miles's newly created District of the Yellowstone was about 1,100 men, as compared to Colonel Gibbon's District of Montana with never more than 450 men in the entire district.

In the course of these preparations, he sent a telegram on September 16, 1876, to the assistant adjutant general, Department of Dakota, in which he commented on the effectiveness of the artillery available to his command. (The reader should note that Gatling guns were classified as artillery.) Referring to a Rodman rifle gun with a sight for a 12-pound Napoleon gun and the eight .50 caliber Gatling guns available to his command, Miles stated that these weapons were

> ...extremely unsuitable, if not worthless...The Department Commander is aware that it is not practicable, or possible, to move [these guns] over this country where Indians would be likely to leave a trail, hence such ordinance may be considered at most worthless... The chief objections to our field guns is their great weight and to the Gatling Guns their weight and small calibre. I have used both in Indian fights, and it is impossible to determine the range of the latter at twelve or fifteen hundred yards.[2]

Miles went on to request a light steel or wire gun, breech loading, which could throw a small shell about two miles. He added, "...the gun which would be useful in this country should be drawn by two horses, and so light that it could follow a Company of Cavalry in any day's march."[3]

Upon his arrival in the Yellowstone country, Miles had the good fortune to recruit at least three very able scouts who were familiar with that region. One was Yellowstone Kelly, an educated white man who had hunted and trapped the area since 1868, another was John Brughier and the third was George Boyd, a gentleman with badly deformed club-footed feet. These men and others provided Miles with invaluable intelligence on the movements of the hostile leaders and their followers.[4]

Due to low water in the autumn, steamboats could no longer operate up to Fort Keogh. It became necessary to move freight in by wagon from Fort Buford at the junction of the Yellowstone and Missouri rivers. One of these trains was attacked by hostile Indians in early October. Colonel Miles had also received intelligence that Sitting Bull and his band, now separated from Crazy Horse and his followers, planned to move north of the Yellowstone and winter on the Big Dry. News of the attack on the train led Miles to

---

[2] September 16, 1876, Fort Keogh District Letters and Telegrams Sent and Received, Records of Posts, Continental Army Command 1820–1920, Record Group 393.7, National Archives.

[3] Ibid.

[4] Miles, *Personal Recollections:* 217, 229, 239–240.

believe that Sitting Bull might be, in fact, moving toward the Big Dry. The colonel decided to take to the field.

On October 17, 1876, Miles marched in a northeasterly direction from Fort Keogh with 394 infantrymen and one piece of artillery. By the 21st he had located the hostiles. After two fruitless meetings with Sitting Bull, conducted under a flag of truce, Miles attacked his village on the 22nd in what would later become known as the Battle of Cedar Creek. This stream parallels present-day Montana Route 253, flowing in a southeasterly direction and emptying into the Yellowstone near present-day Terry, MT. Sitting Bull's camp consisted of Uncpapas, Minneconjous and Sans Arcs under the ever-hostile chiefs Low Neck, Gall,

General Nelson A. Miles—commander, District of the Yellowstone.
PHOTO COURTESY OF MONTANA HISTORICAL SOCIETY RESEARCH CENTER PHOTOGRAPH ARCHIVES, HELENA, MONTANA.

Pretty Bear and others. Their fighting force amounted to about 500 to 600 warriors. Miles described the engagement between his foot soldiers and the hostiles:

> At one time the command was entirely surrounded by Indians, and the troops were formed in a large hollow square in open order and deployed at five paces, with all the reserves brought into action, yet not a single man left his place or failed to do his duty. The engagement demonstrated that the Indians could not stand artillery, and that there was no position they could take from which the infantry could not dislodge them.[5]

---

[5] October 1, 1877, Fort Keogh Letters and Telegrams Sent and Received. In this battle, one sergeant and one private were wounded, and five Indians killed.

Over the next two days, Miles's force pressed the Indians some forty-two miles northeastward and eastward over to the Bad Route Creek drainage.[6] The Indians then sent out a flag of truce, and 2,000 of them—men, women and children—agreed to surrender to their agencies. As a guarantee, they gave up five chiefs as hostages. "But Sitting Bull, Gall, Pretty Bear and several other chiefs, with nearly four hundred people, broke away from the main camp and retreated north toward the Missouri."[7] While losses to the Indians were small in number of warriors killed and wounded, they lost a large amount of supplies and equipment, which they had been counting on for winter survival. Sitting Bull himself unwittingly expressed his frustration when, during one of his meetings with Miles, he wanted "...to know what the troops were remaining in that country for, and why they did not go back to their posts or into winter quarters."[8]

Colonel Miles then withdrew his forces some eighty miles back to Fort Keogh for rest, recuperation and replenishment of supplies. In November he once again struck out to locate Sitting Bull and his remaining bands. With a force of 434 men, he marched north to the Big Dry area and picked up Sitting Bull's trail. However, it was soon lost in a heavy snowstorm. The infantrymen experienced severe cold and discomfort during this November march, which had at first been north from Fort Keogh toward the Missouri and then west about one hundred miles to the Musselshell River. In order to better scout the vast countryside between the Yellowstone and the Missouri, Miles decided to split his force into three columns: one under himself, one under Captain Simon Snyder, and one under Lieutenant Frank D. Baldwin. Lieutenant Baldwin's column marched from the Missouri south of present-day Popular, MT, southward up the valley of the Red Water River. Baldwin later described the inclement weather in a letter to a friend:

> There was not a night that I did not visit my pickets and men in their tents at least once every two hours, fearing they might freeze to death...From the day I left the Missouri River about the only subsistence my animals had consisted of cottonwood limbs, which were gathered and placed before them after arriving in camp.[9]

---

[6] Miles: 228.

[7] Annual Report for the Commissioner of Indians Affairs, November 1, 1877: 411, Annual Reports of the Commissioner of Indian Affairs. Record Group 75, SuDocs Number I 20.1, 1824–1920, National Archives.

[8] Miles: 225.

[9] Ibid., 230.

Baldwin's force located and struck Sitting Bull's camp on November 18, 1876, at the head of the Red Water, capturing some of his horses and a considerable amount of supplies. This added further hardship for the wintering hostiles. While not the death knell to Sitting Bull and his followers, Baldwin's attack made the Sioux's continued hostility ever more difficult. Sitting Bull is believed to have then moved his camp back to the south of the Yellowstone. He did not remain there for long.[10]

---

[10] Miles: 228–231, 244.

CHAPTER THIRTY

Colonel Mackenzie Strikes the Northern Cheyenne Chief Dull Knife in Northern Wyoming; Colonel Miles Opens Winter Campaign Against Crazy Horse

L ATE IN 1876, IN ADDITION TO THE ESTABLISHMENT OF two posts in the Yellowstone drainage, there was also a considerable buildup of force in the Department of the Platte, specifically in northern Wyoming. Troops were stationed at old Fort Reno to provide a supply base for operations in the northern part of the territory. By November about fifty companies were stationed at or near the Red Cloud Agency and nearby Camp Robinson in the northwestern corner of Nebraska Territory. They patrolled throughout the Black Hills area in the Dakota and northern Wyoming territories. On November 25, 1876, a sharp blow was dealt to a large number of hostile Northern Cheyenne under Dull Knife. Colonel Ranald S. Mackenzie struck Dull Knife's village, consisting of 205 lodges, on Willow Creek,[1] with a force of 818 men, destroying it and forcing the Cheyenne to retreat into the countryside in extreme cold. Mackenzie lost seven men killed and twenty-five wounded, but the losses to the Cheyenne were much higher, with some thirty bodies left on the field and large quantities of valuable winter supplies as well as over 750 ponies lost. The village contained numerous articles taken from Custer's men at the Little Bighorn.

Dull Knife's people suffered greatly from the severe cold after being driven from their village, "…eleven of their little babies having frozen to

---

[1] According to a Wyoming Historical Marker on I-25 near Kaycee, WY, this event took place about thirty miles west of Kaycee. The author located a Willow Creek about thirty miles west of Kaycee just west of Wyoming Highway 434.

death in their mothers' arms the first night and three others the second night after the fight."[2] The Cheyenne chief withdrew down the Powder River with his survivors to the village of Crazy Horse and sought assistance for his destitute flock. Crazy Horse, otherwise known among his people for his care and generosity, refused to assist Dull Knife. Now very bitter and a sworn enemy of his former ally, Dull Knife surrendered to the U.S. Army, pledging to assist them in their campaign against Crazy Horse.[3] This, of course, greatly increased the odds against Crazy Horse, but he continued to hold out.[4] Now it was Colonel Miles's turn at the chief.

After the engagement with Sitting Bull at the head of the Red Water, Miles's force returned to Fort Keogh. The colonel quickly replenished and reorganized it and, after only six days' rest and recuperation at the post, he departed with his command in the latter days of December. The command, now consisting of 436 men and two artillery pieces, marched south up to the headwaters of the Tongue River, frequently marching and hauling his wagons over the frozen river. Miles had information that Crazy Horse's Ogallallas and the remaining Northern Cheyenne allies, Dull Knife's band excepted, were camped on the Tongue

Dull Knife—Northern Cheyenne chief.
PHOTO COURTESY OF THE NATIONAL ARCHIVES.

---

[2] John G. Bourke, *On the Border with Crook:* 392–393.

[3] Wooden Leg reported the retreat of the Northern Cheyenne down the Powder to find the Ogallallas. He stated, however, that the Ogallallas met their needs generously. He makes no mention of Crazy Horse's refusing aid or, indeed, even of Dull Knife's surrender. Since Wooden Leg continued to remain with other Cheyennes as allies of the Ogallallas, he may have overlooked or taken lesser note of Dull Knife's surrender than the U.S. Army did. He also stated that Dull Knife was present in the winter camp of the hostile Cheyenne and Ogallallas on the upper Little Bighorn after the Battle of Hanging Woman's Fork, January 8, 1877. Thomas B. Marquis, ed., *Wooden Leg:* 286–288, 293–294.

[4] Bourke: 394.

River just above the mouth of Otter Creek. During the absence of most of Miles's command in pursuit of Sitting Bull, Crazy Horse's hostiles had been harassing the compound at Fort Keogh, stealing government horses and government beef.

As the column advanced up the Tongue, it was harassed by small parties of Crazy Horse's followers. Two of Miles's soldiers were surprised and killed by the Indians. Miles described a subsequent event:

> On January 7…the advance guard captured a small party of Indians, including one young warrior, four women and three children. This event afterward proved of considerable importance, as they were relatives of some of the most prominent men in the hostile camp. That evening an attempt was made by a band of about three hundred warriors to recapture them, which resulted in a sharp skirmish and the repulse of the Indians.[5]

The force continued its march up the frozen Tongue River, with the draft animals drawing the wagons over the ice on the river bed whenever possible. The two artillery pieces were concealed in the wagons. As the column approached Otter Creek, Crazy Horse and the others withdrew their camp farther up the Tongue to Hanging Woman's Fork. It was there that Miles's force engaged them on January 8, 1877:

> …the main body of warriors…[was] led by Crazy Horse, Little Big Man, White Bull, Big Crow, Two Moons, Hump and other prominent chiefs of the Cheyennes and Ogalallas. The country was very rough—mountainous in fact; and as the Indians moved down the valley to encounter the troops they evidently had every confidence of making it another massacre. They outnumbered us at least two to one, and must have had at least a thousand warriors on the field.[6]

Although the hostiles were able at one time to surround the column, the effect of the artillery on them was demoralizing. Miles later described the capture of a key ridge held by Chief Big Crow, which determined the outcome of the battle:

> The Indians who held it were led by Big Crow a "medicine man" who…had made the Indians believe that his medicine was so strong that the white men could not harm him. He rushed out in front

---

[5] Nelson A. Miles, *Personal Recollections:* 236–237.

[6] Ibid.

Wolf Mountains Campaign, December 29, 1876—Left to right: Lieutenant O.F. Long; Major H.R. Tilton, Surgeon; Lieutenant J.W. Pope; Colonel Nelson A. Miles, commanding officer, 5th Infantry; Lieutenant Frank O. Baldwin; Lieutenant Chas E. Hargous; Lieutenant H.K. Bailey.

PHOTO COURTESY OF MONTANA HISTORICAL SOCIETY RESEARCH CENTER PHOTOGRAPH ARCHIVES, HELENA, MONTANA.

of the warriors, attired in the most gorgeous Indian battle costume of the brightest colors, and with a headdress made of the waving plumes of the eagle falling down his back, jumped up and down, ran in a circle and whopped and yelled. Our men turned their guns upon him, but for several minutes he was unharmed, notwithstanding their efforts to reach him with their rifles.

Then a charge was made by troops under Majors [James S.] Casey and [Edmund] Butler, and Captains McDonald and [Frank D.] Baldwin. It was done with splendid courage, vim and determination, although the men were so encumbered with their heavy winter clothing, and the snow was so deep, that it was impossible to move faster than a slow walk. Captain Baldwin was conspicuous in this charge for his boldness and excellent judgement. In the very midst of his daring acts of bravado, Big Crow fell, pierced by a rifle shot, and his loss, together with the success of the charge...seemed to cause a panic among the Indians, and they immediately fled in utter rout up the valley down which they had come a few hours before with such confidence.[7]

Losses in this battle were not heavy to either side, but the morale of Crazy Horse's hostile bands was broken. According to Miles:

...[It] demonstrated the fact that we could move in any part of the country in the midst of winter, and hunt the enemy down in their camps wherever they might take refuge. In this way, constantly pursuing them, we had made them realize that there was no peace or safety for them while they remained in a hostile attitude.[8]

Referring to the battle, Miles would later comment in a telegram to his superiors:

This engagement was unlike any other Indian fight I ever witnessed, it was fought on ground where it would have been impossible to have maneuvered cavalry, they fought entirely dismounted not a single rifle being fired on horseback, their ponies only being used to carry them from one line of ravines or ledges and bluffs to others. They used loud shrill whistles to convey their orders.[9]

---

[7] Ibid.: 238. Wooden Leg also was present at this battle and reported on Big Crow's actions. He stated that Big Crow was a Cheyenne warrior.

[8] Ibid.: 238–239.

[9] January 23, 1877, Letters and Telegrams Sent and Received, District of Yellowstone, Department of Dakota, Record Group 393.5, National Archives.

The column retired to Fort Keogh with the prisoners they had captured on January 7th. These captives had been treated well, and it was time to attempt diplomacy. Scout John Brughier agreed to escort two of the prisoners back to Crazy Horse's camp with terms of surrender. The Indians had withdrawn to the Little Bighorn River at the base of the Bighorn Mountains. Miles wrote:

> This was a very daring expedition for Brughier to undertake, and he did not attempt it without serious doubts as to his being able to get into their camp. He believed that if he was once there, he would find some of his friends who would protect him; but what he feared was being killed as he approached the camp. However, he succeeded in reaching there safely, and found the Indians encamped in deep snow and suffering greatly from the cold, while their horses were dying from exposure...The captives themselves acted as messengers of peace, and were very active in assuring their hostile brethren that the Indians, who were still in our hands, had been equally well treated, and urged their people to accept the terms of the government and put themselves under its control.[10]

This trip resulted in a delegation of nineteen hostiles accompanying Brughier back to Fort Keogh, arriving there on February 19, 1877. Miles commenced negotiations with them, and, eventually, some 2,300 hostiles—men, women and children—surrendered at Fort Keogh, including Chiefs Two Moon, White Bull, Hump and Horse Road and other chiefs. Crazy Horse was encouraged to surrender by his uncle, Chief Spotted Tail, who along with Chief Red Cloud had remained at peace with the whites. On May 6, 1877, Crazy Horse led over 1,100 of his people and 2,500 ponies into Fort Robinson, located in the northwest corner of Nebraska Territory, and surrendered in person to General George Crook, the department commander.[11]

On Crazy Horse's first evening at Fort Robinson, Lieutenant John Bourke accompanied scout Frank Grouard to the famous chief's lodge for an evening meal. Bourke recalled:

> When we approached the chief's "tepi," a couple of squaws were grinding coffee between two stones and preparing something to eat. "Crazy Horse" remained seated on the ground, but when Frank

---

[10] Miles: 239–240.

[11] Bourke: 412–413.

called his name in Dakota, "Tashunca-uitco," at the same time adding a few words I did not understand, he looked up, arose, and gave me a hearty grasp of his hand. I saw before me a man who looked quite young, not over thirty years old, five feet eight inches high, lithe and sinewy, with a scar in the face…All Indians gave him a high reputation for courage and generosity. In advancing upon an enemy, none of his warriors were allowed to pass him. He had made hundreds of friends by his charity towards the poor, as it was a point of honor never to keep anything for himself, excepting weapons of war. I never heard an Indian mention his name save in terms of respect.[12]

In light of this description one might ask why Crazy Horse had refused help to Dull Knife's band. There were doubtless other factors, unknown to us, influencing his decision. Perhaps there had been previous bad blood between the two. Also, it is known that at the time, other Northern Cheyenne allies were among Crazy Horse's followers. They may have influenced his decision, or it is entirely possible that he had only sufficient supplies for his own people's survival and none to spare.

In the meantime, Sitting Bull, still holding out, had fled with his band north into Canada.

On the 11th of January, 1877, information was received from Inspector [James M.] Walsh, commanding the detachment of mounted police at Cypress Hills, Canada, that one hundred and nine lodges of American Sioux had crossed the Canadian boundary near Wood Mountain, and were camped on the British side, and that they declared themselves to be desirous of peace and to have no intention of returning to the United States to carry on war. Later the number was reported to have been increased to over two hundred lodges, and they had been joined by Sitting Bull.[13]

Colonel Miles sent another telegram to his superiors on April 7, 1877, commenting on the unsuitability of his artillery and expanding his request for light steel or wire guns:

Referring to the enclosed copy of communications forwarded by me on its date [September 16, 1876], I have the honor to state that

---

[12] Ibid.: 414–415.

[13] Report of the Commissioner of Indians Affairs 1877, Annual Reports of the Commissioner of Indian Affairs, Record Group 75, SuDocs Number I 20.1, 1824–1920, National Archives.

> the statements therein—known then to be true—have received cor-
> roboration during the six months that have since passed, during the
> greater part of which time this command has been in the field. I have
> now to request that instead of two (2), six (6) of the light Steel or
> Wire Guns—with necessary ammunition—be procured and sent to
> this command for use.[14]

Miles made no specific mention of Gatling guns in this telegram.

By the summer of 1877, the governor-general of Canada made a formal request that the United States attempt to induce Sitting Bull's Indians to return to U.S. territory. Their presence in Canada was causing apprehension among the local white and Indian populations.[15] In response to the request of the Privy Council of Canada, General Alfred Terry and A.J. Lawrence were appointed by President Grant to attempt negotiating the return of Sitting Bull and his followers to U.S. soil. A meeting with Sitting Bull and his chiefs took place in the British Possessions (Canada) on October 17, 1877, but the great chief and his followers remained defiant that they would forever remain on Canadian soil.

> After the close of the council [meeting], the Canadian authorities
> conferred with the Indians, warning them that after the extinction
> of the buffalo [rapidly approaching extinction] no help whatever
> beyond protection could be expected from the British Government,
> and that a crossing of the line [U.S.-Canada border] by any of their
> young men with hostile intent would be considered an act of hostil-
> ity by both governments.[16]

There now remained only one band of hostile Sioux still at large on U.S. territory in the Yellowstone drainage. The Minneconjou Sioux chief, Lame Deer, had refused to surrender his band of some fifty to sixty lodges. Miles, now reinforced by four troops of the 2nd Cavalry sent in from Fort Ellis by Colonel John Gibbon, marched back up the Tongue River on May 2, 1877, in pursuit of Lame Deer. He was also aided by three captured Sioux chiefs, who now served as scouts providing him with invaluable assistance in locating Lame Deer's camp. On May 7th, the camp was located on Big Muddy Creek, a tributary of the Rosebud at or in the near vicinity of present-day Lame Deer, MT.

---

[14] April 7, 1877, Letters and Telegrams Sent and Received, District of Yellowstone.

[15] Report of the Commissioner of Indians Affairs 1877: 412–413.

[16] Ibid.

Major James M. Walsh— Northwest Mounted Police.

During this operation Miles received a first-hand demonstration of the ability of his Indian scouts to see objects at far greater distances than the whites:

> When first seen the camp [fifteen air miles distant] was not recognized by the white men, but the Indians declared they could see the smoke over the village. To me it looked like mist or a white cloud against the side of the mountain until I examined it more carefully with a glass. The Indians also announced that they could see ponies grazing on the hills. This was discovered to be correct by their [white] companions, but not without using their field glasses.[17]

Miles described the attack:

> The mounted infantry and scouts under Lieutenants Casey and [Lovell H.] Jerome were ordered to charge directly up the valley and stampede the Indian horses, while the battalion of cavalry [2nd Cavalry] followed at a gallop and attacked the camp. The attack was gallantly made. The command under Lieutenants Casey and Jerome stampeded the entire herd of ponies, horses and mules, four hundred fifty in number, and drove them five miles up the valley, where they rounded them up and by a long circuit brought them around to the rear of the command which was engaging the Indians. When attacked the Indians fled from their camp, taking only what they carried in their hands, up among the high bluffs and rugged hills in that vicinity. Our loss was four soldiers killed, one officer and six soldiers wounded. There were fourteen Indian warriors killed and many wounded.[18]

Lame Deer was killed after nearly succeeding in killing Colonel Miles, his bullet narrowly missing Miles and killing a soldier at the colonel's side. Among the animals captured were horses bearing the brand of the

---

[17] Miles: 249.

[18] Ibid.: 250.

7th Cavalry—booty from the Battle of the Little Bighorn. Some 200 of the Indian ponies were later utilized to mount the foot soldiers of the 5th Infantry, thus increasing the mobility of this force, in particular for summer campaigns. These animals would be of particular value during the campaign against the Nez Perce, which, although not yet foreseen, would occur before that summer's end.[19]

In the opinion of General William T. Sherman, General of the Army, Colonel Miles's campaigns during the winter of 1876–1877 and the spring of 1877 had effectively put an end to the Indian problem in the Yellowstone country. On July 17, 1877, Sherman wrote the Secretary of War, "Boats come and go now, where a year ago none could venture except with strong guards. Wood yards are being established to facilitate navigation, and the great mass of the hostiles have been forced to go to the agencies for food and protection, or have fled across the border into British territory."[20] Mopping-up operations still continued throughout that summer in the Yellowstone country against small groups of hostile Sioux and Cheyenne. These were conducted by 2nd Cavalry commands under Captain Edward Ball, Major Lazelle, Major James Brisbin and Captain Snyder. By the middle of September 1877, the country was generally considered cleared of hostiles.[21]

General Philip Sheridan summed up the efforts of Colonel Miles's Yellowstone District and that of the Department of the Platte in his annual report to General Sherman on October 25, 1877:

> General: During the months of December and January the hostile Indians were constantly harassed by the troops under Col. N.A. Miles, Fifth Infantry; whose headquarters were at the mouth of the Tongue River, and who had two sharp engagements with them, one at Redwater, and the other near Hanging Woman's Fork, inflicting heavy losses in men, supplies and animals. This constant pounding and sleepless activity upon the part of our troops (Colonel Miles in particular) in midwinter, began to tell, and early in February, 1877, information was communicated which led me to believe that the Indians in general were tired of the war, and that large bodies heretofore in the field were beginning to break up.
>
> On the 25th of that month 229 lodges of Minneconjous and Sans Arcs came in and surrendered to the troops at Cheyenne agency,

---

[19] Ibid.: 252.

[20] Quoted in John Finerty, War Path and Bivouac: 451.

[21] Miles: 253.

Dakota. They were completely disarmed, their horses taken from them, and they were put under guard, and this system was carried out with all who afterward came in to surrender within the Departments of Dakota and the Platte. From the 1st of March to the 21st of the same month over 2,200 Indians, in detachments of from 30 to 900, came in and surrendered at camps Sheridan and Robinson, in the Department of the Platte, and, on the 22nd of April, 303 came in and surrendered to Colonel Miles, at the cantonment on the Tongue River, in the Department of Dakota, and more were reported on the way in to give themselves up.

Finally, on the 6th of May, Crazy Horse, with 889 of his people and 2,000 ponies, came in to Camp Robinson and surrendered to General Crook in person.

In the meantime, Colonel Miles having had information of the whereabouts of Lame Deer's band of hostile Sioux, surprised his camp killing fourteen, including Lame Deer and Iron Star, the two principal chiefs, capturing 450 ponies and destroying fifty-one lodges and their contents. I may mention here that this band commenced to surrender, in small squads, from two to twenty, immediately thereafter, until at length, on the 10th of September, the last of the band, numbering 224, constantly followed, and pressed by the troops from the command of Colonel Miles, surrendered at Camp Sheridan. The Sioux War was now over. Sitting Bull went north of the Missouri into British America with his own small band and other hostiles, the number of whom cannot exactly be told, and is now near the Woody Mountains...[22]

In spite of the proclamations by Generals Sherman and Sheridan, smaller-scale hostilities would occur with Sitting Bull's hostiles over the next two years. Throughout the winter of 1876–1877 and later, Colonel Gibbon maintained an active liaison from his Fort Shaw headquarters with Major Walsh of the Northwest Mounted Police and received information on the movements of Sitting Bull.

Once bitten, the army was taking no chances with the fabled Sioux leader. An example of the seriousness with which they now viewed Sitting Bull can be found in Office of Indian Affairs correspondence. On April 12,

---

[22] Quoted in Finerty: 452. John G. Bourke, in *On the Border with Crook*, states the 1,100 Indians surrendered with 2,500 ponies. It is entirely possible that more surrendered after the initial figures were submitted to General Sherman. The Woody Mountains likely are the Cypress Hills located near present-day Eastend, Saskatchewan.

1880, the commanding officer of Fort Missoula (established in 1877) reported information received from a seventeen-year-old Nez Perce Indian. The youth had recently been among the Blackfeet and the River Crows in the Judith Basin, and he alleged that they were planning to unite with Sitting Bull and make war on whites. The commanding officer at Fort Missoula forwarded this information to General Terry at Department of Dakota headquarters in St. Paul. General Terry placed little faith in this information, but, nevertheless, forwarded it to General Sheridan at Division of Missouri headquarters in Chicago. General Sheridan concurred with Terry. Such was the seriousness with which the U.S. Army now took any intelligence regarding Sitting Bull.[23]

Colonel Gibbon obviously did not fear that the Blackfeet were about to join Sitting Bull. On November 27, 1876, he had sent the following request to General Terry: "Piegan Chiefs here to request they be allowed to trade for ammunition. They can be trusted and should have it for hunting purposes. Have I your authority to allow them to trade for a limited supply? Please answer at once as I start for the Agency in a few days."[24]

[23] April 12, 1880, Letters Received by the Office of Indian Affairs, 1824–1880, National Archives.

[24] January 27, 1876, District of Montana Letters and Telegrams Sent and Received, Department of Dakota, Record Group 393.5, National Archives.

CHAPTER THIRTY-ONE

The Nez Perce Campaign of 1877; Origins of the Conflict; The Battle Opens

URING THE SUMMER AND AUTUMN OF 1877, THE SOLDIERS in Montana Territory, now consisting of the Montana Military District and the District of the Yellowstone, would become engaged in a hard-fought campaign with a new enemy, non-treaty Nez Perce Indians from Idaho, Washington and Oregon. Generally speaking, the Nez Perce tribes, including the non-treaty Nez Perce, were viewed as "peaceful Indians" by the military and most white settlers. As we noted in prior chapters, there was some suspicion at Fort Ellis that elements of the Nez Perce had attempted to enlist the Crows as allies in war against the white man. The possibility exists, however, that some Nez Perce felt that eventually war with the whites would be inevitable and thus viewed the Crows, with whom they had good relations, as their most natural allies. We will recall Captain Clift's engagement in March 1869 with a large number of hostiles suspected of being Nez Perce. Also, Indian agent John Owen's 1859 comments about the "Buffalo Indians" (Nez Perce) who wintered in the upper Bitterroot Valley were not positive. Prior to 1870, however, there had been very few violent acts perpetrated between members of the Nez Perce tribes and whites. On the contrary, members of the Nez Perce nation, a confederation of numerous tribes, were generally viewed as among the most hospitable and "civilized" Indians in North America.

The Nez Perce had begun to have contacts with French traders and trappers in the late 18th century.[1] The first recorded contact with the white

---

[1] Chief Joseph, in Linwood Laughy, comp., *In Pursuit of the Nez Perces*: 280.

man occurred in September 1805 in western Idaho. The Lewis and Clark Expedition, half-starved, came upon a Nez Perce village after their nearly fatal crossing of the Bitterroot Mountains. After some debate within the tribe, these Nez Perce opted for a policy of friendship with these white men. They provided the nearly destitute members of the expedition with food and shelter. They later cared for horses and equipment belonging to the expedition while it wintered far to the west near the mouth of the Columbia River at Fort Clatsop. They further provided the whites with sound advice and guidance on their return journey over the Bitterroots in the spring of 1806.

The Nez Perce received high praise from members of the expedition. As the party separated from their five Nez Perce guides, who had accompanied them across the Bitterroots to the vicinity of present-day Missoula, MT, Captain Lewis would note, "These affectionate people our guides betrayed every emmotion of unfeigned regret at separating from us; they said that they were confidint that the Pahkees, (the appellation they give to the Minnetares) would cut us off."[2] The Nez Perce were fearful that the whites would encounter the warlike Minnetares, otherwise known as Hidatsas, as they proceeded up the Blackfoot River en route to Great Falls on the so-called Road to the Buffalo. Sergeant Patrick Gass, a member of the expedition, later reported, "It is but justice to say, that the whole nation to which they belong [Nez Perces], are the most friendly, honest and ingenuous people that we have seen in the course of our voyage and travels."[3]

In 1886, only nine years after the Nez Perce War, J.P. Dunn, Jr. wrote:

> ...the conduct of the Nez Perces had been of uniform friendship and kindness towards the Americans. Their call for missionaries, their support of the settlers against the overbearing Hudson's Bay Company, their offer of protection to the Lapwai when [Dr. Marcus] Whitman had fallen victim to the Cayuses, their protection and escort of Governor Stevens's party in 1855, their stand for peace when other tribes were for war in 1855 and 1856, their rescue of Steptoe's party in 1858, their assistance to our troops against hostile Indians, have all been recorded.[4]

One might ask how the Lower Nez Perce managed to maintain their homeland as late as 1877 against intruding white settlement, particularly

---

[2] Reuben Gold Thwaites, Vol. V., Pt II: 188.

[3] Ibid.: 340.

[4] J.P. Dunn. Jr., *Massacres of the Mountains,* 539.

Joseph—Nez Perce chief.
PHOTO COURTESY OF MONTANA HISTORICAL
SOCIETY RESEARCH CENTER PHOTOGRAPH
ARCHIVES, HELENA, MONTANA.

during the gold rush days of the 1860's when large numbers of whites moved into Idaho and then Montana. Due to the Nez Perce's reputation for peaceful behavior, the whites likely did not perceive them as threatening by their mere presence. Also, the land they occupied and loved was not felt by many whites to be of great value in terms of agricultural potential. Therefore, the natural tendency of the whites to push for settlement of Indian lands of agricultural value was in this case delayed by at least a decade. J.P. Dunn wrote:

[Chief] Joseph and his people seemed to love that country of theirs…On one side of it the Snake surges and foams over its rocky bed. On the other the Blue Mountains rise majestically, and along their eastern base the Grande Ronde River sweeps through its great arc to the Snake. Between them is a rugged country impossible of cultivation. Through it, towards the east, runs the Imnaha (Immaha), down a narrow, rugged vale; through it towards the northwest flows the Wallowa (Wall-low-how, Way-lee-way—the Winding Waters), with a valley larger and better than that of the other stream. The valley of the Wallowa was the very best of the land claimed by the Lower Nez Perces, and it was not much to be desired.[5]

By 1873, only about eighty-seven white settlers resided on the land of the Lower Nez Perce. A decade earlier, in 1863, the Upper Nez Perce, constituting the greater majority of the Nez Perce nation, had agreed by treaty to move to the Lapwai Reservation near present-day Lapwai, ID. The Lower Nez Perce refused to enter into this agreement, which had been accepted by the majority of the tribal chiefs of the Nez Perce nation. The Nez Perce

---

[5] Ibid.: 542.

nation had consisted since then of a majority "treaty" and a minority of "non-treaty" Nez Perce. The majority then sold all the Nez Perce land to the whites; this included the land owned by the Lower Nez Perce, although they had not been a party to the treaty. Joseph, chief of the Lower Nez Perce (Wallam-wat-kin), clung steadfastly to his land, claiming and believing that it had never been sold. In 1871, Joseph died and his son, Joseph, known by the Nez Perce as "…In-mut-too-yah-lat-lat—the-Thunder-Travelling-Over-the-Mountains…," a very prophetic name for future events in Montana Territory, took over the tribal leadership.[6]

There were other tribal groups of Nez Perce who belonged to the "non-treaty" Indians; the most significant of these were led by Chiefs Looking Glass, White Bird, Too-hul-hul-sote and Red Owl. With the exception of Looking Glass's band, the other non-treaties lived outside of the Lapwai Reservation. White Bird's band occupied the territory along the Salmon River and its tributaries in central western Idaho. Too-hul-hul-sote's band was located in the country between the Salmon and Snake rivers, also in central western Idaho.[7]

Throughout the early 1870's, pressure increased on the non-treaty Nez Perce.

> In 1871 an Indian was killed by a white man. The Indians took no revenge, but insisted that the whites should leave their country. Troops were sent into the country for the protection of both parties. In March 1875 a white man named Larry Ott killed a Nez Perce in a quarrel, and the grand jury returned no bill against him. In August, 1875, one Benedict shot at some drunken Indians who came to his house at night demanding admittance, and killed one and wounded another. This man was accused of selling liquor to the Indians. In June, 1876, a settler named Finley killed a brother of Joseph. None of these offenses were punished, and for none did the Indians take revenge, still urging only that the whites leave their lands.[8]

The outbreak of war in 1872 between the whites and the Modoc Indians (located in northern California and southern Oregon) also increased tensions. General Oliver O. Howard, U.S. Army commander, Department of the Columbia, wrote:

---

[6] Ibid.: 545–547.

[7] Howard: 14.

[8] Dunn: 546.

General Oliver O. Howard.
PHOTO COURTESY OF THE LIBRARY OF CONGRESS.

A year after the death of Old Joseph, the war with the Modoc Indians occurred, including the treacherous massacre of General Canby by this tribe. As is always the case in Indian wars, all Indians, far and near, were agitated by this outbreak. The non-treaties, now led by the ambitious young chief, Joseph, became suspiciously restless.[9]

An effort was made by the U.S. Department of Interior to buy back the land from the white squatters and set it aside as a reservation. However, Oregon's Governor L.F. Grover was opposed to this measure.[10] The price was estimated at $67,860, but Congress disapproved the request in 1875.[11] The subsequent military campaign would cost much more. Hindsight is, of course, always 20-20. At the time no military authority believed that such a formidable task awaited them. The Nez Perce had always been peaceful, bending over backwards to avoid conflict with the whites! The clamor for the forceful removal of the Lower Nez Perce increased.

General Howard offered the following opinion on this conflict:

> While admitting the injustice of the United States and of Oregon towards this band, when contrasted with the rights and privileges extended to citizens, still I do not think the real cause of the Indian war with the non-treaties came from the reduction of the reserve, nor from the immediate contact with immigrants and the quarrels that sprung therefrom. These, without doubt, aggravated the difficulty. The main cause lies back of ideas of rightful ownership, back of savage habits and instincts; it lies in the natural and persistent resistance of independent nations to the authority of other nations.[12]

---

9 Howard: 17–18.

10 Ibid.: 19.

11 Dunn: 547.

12 Howard: 22.

The Lower Nez Perce naturally did not want to give up old habits and become restricted in their freedom to roam. In the autumn of every year, it had been the habit of the Nez Perce to send parties to the buffalo country in Montana Territory for the fall hunt. Their route led through the Lolo country to the Bitterroot Valley, then by various routes to the buffalo country. A primary route called by the Nez Perce "The Road to the Buffalo" led from Missoula up the Blackfoot River to its headwaters, over either present-day Lewis and Clark Pass or Cadotte Pass and on past Fort Shaw to the Great Falls of the Missouri. Colonel John Gibbon wrote of one such trip when the Nez Perce visited his headquarters at Fort Shaw in the late fall of 1876:

> The various bands inhabiting the western part of Montana and eastern Idaho have been accustomed, for many years, to make this trip for procuring supplies of buffalo meat…This visit was, therefore, no novelty to the garrison of Fort Shaw, and derived its interest from future events, for the chief of the band was the since celebrated "Looking Glass." The chiefs called upon the commanding officer, as usual, were kindly received, and supplied with some necessary provisions, which, singular to say, they never asked for, but always took. They were invited to give us an exhibition of a sham battle. To this they consented, and, at the hour appointed, the whole garrison turned out, when the distant shouts and loud yells of the warriors were heard as they approached the post from their camp down the river [Sun River]. Firing their pieces in the air and uttering their peculiar yells, they approached the post in a motley crowd, their horses prancing, their drums beating and their gay, painted feathers fluttering in the breeze. After marching in this fashion entirely around the garrison, to show off their gay trappings and hideously painted faces, they assembled for the fight on the prairie outside the post. Dividing into two parties, they went through the manoeuvres of a supposed conflict…The whole thing was looked upon by the spectators as a ridiculous farce, and the remark was frequently heard, "If they do not fight better than that when they go into a real battle, they will not do much harm to the enemy.[13]

At that point in time, no one suspected, neither Indian nor soldier, that most of these Indians and the soldiers looking on would be locked in a deadly struggle with heavy losses to both sides less than one year later, at the Battle of the Big Hole in southwestern Montana Territory.

---

[13] John Gibbon, *Adventures on the Western Frontier*: 174–175.

Meanwhile, in Idaho, tensions continued to mount. On May 7, 1877, General Howard met in council at Fort Lapwai with Joseph and other non-treaty chiefs in a final attempt to persuade them to move onto the reservation. The Indians chose Too-hul-hul-sote as their speaker. He was so threatening and insolent in his bearing and speech that General Howard had him placed under arrest. After several days he was released. The general issued an ultimatum. The Lower Nez Perce must move onto the reservation within thirteen days or be compelled to do so.

On June 13th, hostilities broke out when two members of White Bird's band, identified by General Howard as Mox-mox and Wa-li-tits, and a third Indian from Joseph's band killed Richard Divine. On the 14th they killed Henry Elfers, Robert Bland and Henry Beckroge and wounded Samuel Benedict, who escaped to his home. It is of note that subsequent to the campaign, White Bird and other Nez Perce escapees in Canada informed reporter Duncan McDonald that the killers were Walitze, Tap-sis-ill-pilp and U-em-till-lilp-cown (the former two were later killed at the Battle of the Big Hole). After Benedict's escape, these Indians were joined by seventeen more from Joseph's band and proceeded toward Benedict's home. On the way, they encountered J.J. Manuel and his little girl, wounded both of them and also killed James Baker. At Benedict's home they killed him and August Bacon. They also took Mrs. Benedict, her baby and six-year-old daughter captive. On the following day they killed Mrs. Manuel, William Osborne and Harry Mason.[14]

Also on the evening of June 14th, Lew Day arrived at the Cottonwood House at today's Cottonwood, ID, and warned the occupants to flee to safety at Mount Idaho, approximately eighteen miles away. General Howard wrote:

> They set out in a wagon, with two on horseback, about ten o'clock that night and had traveled about ten miles when Indians came up at the rear and began firing at them. Soon [B.B.] Norton and [Joseph] Moore, the horse riders were badly wounded and compelled to abandon their horses and get into the wagon. Their team horses, however, were soon shot down, and the wagon came to a halt. Miss Bowers and little Hill Norton got out of the wagon and made their escaped unharmed. Mr. [John] Chamberlain, his wife and two children attempted to escape in the darkness, but had gone only a short distance when they were discovered by the Indians. Chamberlain

---

[14] Howard: 79–80; McDonald: 235, 261.

and his little boy were killed. The boy was murdered, according to the mother's statement, by having his head placed beneath the knees of a powerful Indian, and so crushed to death. The other child was torn from its mother and dreadfully wounded, piece of its tongue being cut and a knife run quite through its neck. Mrs. Chamberlain was repeatedly outraged by the Indians and received severe injuries. The remainder of the party sought shelter behind the dead horses. Here Norton was struck by a ball [bullet] and killed. Moore was shot through the hips, [Lew] Day through the shoulder and leg, and Mrs. Norton through both legs…Day died the following afternoon. Moore lingered for about six weeks and died. Mrs. Norton, Mrs. Chamberlain, and her child in time recovered.[15]

Looking Glass—Nez Perce chief.
PHOTO COURTESY OF THE NATIONAL ARCHIVES.

The die was cast. The war had begun. Upon receiving word of these hostilities while at Fort Lapwai, General Howard requested reinforcements and simultaneously dispatched most of his available force, two cavalry companies under Captain David Perry, to proceed with all haste to Mount Idaho to rescue frightened citizens and punish the Indians. Mount Idaho was sixty-two miles distant from Fort Lapwai. Upon reaching the small settlement of Grangeville, the troops encountered numerous beleaguered citizens, some ten of whom joined the force to proceed against the Indians. With the addition of these citizen volunteers, Captain Perry now had a force of 103 men. It was learned that Joseph had moved his Indians into White Bird Canyon, some sixteen miles distant, to await the U.S. Army. The troops marched all night, arriving at the canyon at daylight. As they descended into the canyon,

---

15 Ibid.: 80.

...a white woman, Mrs. Benedict, made her appearance from the slight brush-wood cover by the roadside, holding a baby in her arms and harboring a little girl about six years old by her side. Some of the Indians had released her from her horrid confinement, and she was hiding against recapture by the more brutal. She was burdened with her little ones and still more heavily with grief at her husband's death. Shivering with exposure, she was hastening as best she could to a settlement, the nearest being at least twelve miles distant.[16]

Thus, the first battle of the Nez Perce War began on June 17, 1877. It became known as the Battle of White Bird Canyon. To the surprise of the U.S. Army as well as the citizens of the surrounding area, the Nez Perce soundly defeated Captain Perry's troops, killing approximately thirty-five of them and pursuing them for twelve miles back toward Mount Idaho as the officers struggled to reorganize their routed men. There are differing accounts as to the size of the opposing forces. White Bird and other survivors reported later to Duncan McDonald from their exile in Canada that the Nez Perce had 75 warriors in this battle. In 1878, the editor of the *New Northwest*, a Deer Lodge, Montana Territory, newspaper reported an estimate of 125. Chief Joseph would later claim the Nez Perce had only 60 warriors in the battle. Although differing numbers are provided for the troop strength, the author believes it prudent to rely on the statistics provided by General Howard above. In any case, the U.S. Army was soundly defeated, undoubtedly as much to the surprise of the non-treaty Nez Perce as to anyone else![17]

Looking Glass and his band were not involved in this battle. He had been approached by Joseph and White Bird during the commencement of hostilities a day earlier and, according to the later report by the Nez Perce exiles,[18] had angrily rejected their plea to join them.

My hands are clean of the white man's blood, and I want you to know they shall so remain. You have acted like fools in murdering white men. I will have no part in these things and will have nothing

[16] Ibid.: 87.

[17] Duncan McDonald in Linwood Laughy, comp., *In Pursuit of the Nez Perces*: 236–237; Chief Joseph, ibid.: 291.

[18] "Exiles" refer to those Nez Perce who were not captured but escaped to Canada. We get their side of the story via the reporting of Duncan McDonald to the *New Northwest*, a Deer Lodge newspaper. McDonald, son of Montana pioneer Angus McDonald and a Nez Perce mother, Catherine McDonald, was well acquainted with members of the tribe and spoke their language. After Chief Joseph's surrender, McDonald journeyed to Canada and interviewed the Nez Perce exiles. He then reported the results of his interviews in the newspaper series.

to do with such men. If you are determined to fight, go and fight yourselves and do not attempt to embroil me or my people.[19]

General Howard was now confronted with a major campaign. He had to act as quickly as possible to subdue the hostile Indians, while providing as much protection as possible to the frightened white citizens and peaceful treaty Nez Perce of the area. By June 22nd, he still had only slightly more than 200 troops at Fort Lapwai at his disposal.[20] One week after the battle, troops returned to White Bird Canyon, now deserted by the Indians, to recover and bury the dead. The troopers found that Joseph and White Bird had moved their bands to safety across the Salmon River.

General Howard was informed by friendly treaty Nez Perce that forty warriors from Looking Glass's band had joined the hostiles. Since Looking Glass's band was located behind the troops on the Clearwater River, General Howard deemed it prudent to send forces to arrest Looking Glass and secure his band. On July 1, 1877, they arrived at Looking Glass's camp.

> An opportunity was given Looking Glass to surrender, which he at first promised to accept but afterwards defiantly refused. The result was that several Indians were killed, the camp, with a large amount of supplies, was destroyed, and seven hundred and twenty-five ponies were captured and driven to Mount Idaho.[21]

Looking Glass and his band escaped and joined Joseph and White Bird.

In the meantime, word of potential future problems for the army's District of Montana had reached Fort Shaw on June 23, 1877. It arrived in the form of a brief telegram from division headquarters in Chicago. "General McDowell requests [illegible] General to notify you of Indian disturbances in Northern Idaho and that one of the bands has fled northward by Spokane which he thinks may combine near Flathead Agency." This telegram was promptly forwarded to Fort Ellis and to Captain Charles Rawn at the new post under construction in the Missoula area.[22]

As the Indians and the U.S. Army maneuvered about in present-day Idaho, Lieutenant Sevier M. Rains with ten men and a scout, William Foster, were dispatched on July 2nd from Cottonwood toward Craig's Ferry to

---

[19] McDonald: 236.

[20] Howard: 99.

[21] Ibid.: 114.

[22] June 23, 1877, District of Montana Letters and Telegrams Sent and Received, Department of Dakota, Record Group 393.5, National Archives.

ascertain the location of Indians reported in the vicinity. The lieutenant and his entire party were wiped out. On July 5th, also in the area of Cottonwood, a company of volunteers, seventeen men, were surrounded on the Mount Idaho Road. Captain Randall and another man were killed and two wounded before they were rescued from certain massacre by a relief column.[23]

On July 3, 1887, Colonel Gibbon sent a telegram from Fort Shaw to Captain Rawn at his new Missoula post, Fort Missoula. The reader should note that telegrams to Missoula were transmitted to Deer Lodge and then forwarded by mail courier. "Send me by telegraph the first authentic intelligence from Indian troubles west of you." On the same date he telegraphed the following to General Terry at the Department of Dakota in St. Paul, responding to a query from Terry:

> Dispatch of today received. Capt. Rawn with two companies of infantry is now at Missoula. He has gone out with a small party mounted on citizen's horses to get information and quiet the apprehension of the settlers. I shall have early information from him of any important event. Should the hostile Nez-Perces invade the Bitterroot valley or threaten it I will do all in my power, but my force as you know, is very small and scattered for 250 miles. As early intelligence is of importance, I suggest I be sent any information received at Division headquarters during your absence, by telegraph. Our line does not reach beyond Deer Lodge.

General Terry was at the time preparing to visit the newly created post on the Bighorn, which was to be designated Fort Custer.[24]

On July 11, 1877, the Nez Perce and the U.S. Army fought a two-day battle on the Clearwater. General Howard engaged with about 400 troops, one howitzer, two Gatling guns and some teamsters. Joseph's forces numbered about 300 warriors, assisted by Indian women. The battle was a stand-off until the second day, when reinforcements in the form of a cavalry company arrived and turned Joseph's flank. By July 15th, the Indians had withdrawn to the entrance of the Lolo Trail.[25] General Howard wrote:

> We had, on our side, put into the engagement for these two days four hundred fighting men. The Indians, under Chief Joseph, [had]

---

[23] Howard: 116–117.

[24] July 3, 1877, District of Montana Letters and Telegrams Sent and Received.

[25] Dunn: 557–558.

over three hundred warriors, and a great number of women, who assisted in providing spare horses and ammunition—as did our packers and horse holders. They had twenty-three killed, about forty wounded, many of whom subsequently died, and some forty that fell into our hands as prisoners. Our loss was thirteen killed and twenty-two wounded.[26]

The Nez Perce exiles later claimed that no more than five Nez Perce warriors were killed by Howard's forces during the Idaho portion of the campaign. Chief Joseph in a later interview maintained that Nez Perce losses were four killed and several wounded. He also claimed that General Howard lost twenty-nine killed and sixty wounded. By all appearances, both sides were capable of exaggerating the losses of their opponent![27]

General Howard dispatched a scouting unit up the trail. This unit had a small engagement with Joseph's rear guard at Oro Fino Creek on July 17th. He could now be certain that Joseph was moving his forces over the trail toward Montana Territory. In the interim, word was reaching Colonel Gibbon at Fort Shaw, and he was rapidly setting his limited forces in motion. On July 20, 1877, Gibbon telegraphed the commander at Fort Ellis, "Send one of your companies together with all the cavalrymen you can mount to Missoula at once. Acknowledge receipt." On the 21st, in response to a question posed by Captain D.W. Benham, post commander at Fort Ellis, he wrote:

> Yours of yesterday received. Every man you can possibly spare must go with [Capt.] Browning as soon as possible. Start the command with your post teams in light marching order, and let their tents and balance of baggage follow in contract wagons. Since my telegram of yesterday, I have information that Howard is forcing the Indians towards the Bitterroot. I depend on you to hurry the movement and send every man you can possibly spare.[28]

On July 24th, Colonel Gibbon telegraphed division headquarters in Chicago and reported his movements toward the Bitterroot and added, "If Howard can reach the Hellgate with his troops he certainly should do so, as there is nothing there to cope with the mass of hostiles."[29]

---

[26] Howard: 128.

[27] McDonald: 245; Chief Joseph: 291.

[28] July 21, 1877, District of Montana Letters and Telegrams Sent and Received.

[29] July 24, 1877, ibid.

No stranger to the Nez Perce, Gibbon reported on July 24, 1877, to the Department of Dakota his plan to move to block the Indians at the Bitterroot, and countered rumors picked up by his superiors in St. Paul. "Later newspaper telegrams deny that Joseph's band is coming this way but I deem it best to carry out my original intention. The statement that Sitting Bull has come south of the line is not confirmed by news from the north." This cable was also repeated to Terry, who was visiting the new post on the Bighorn (Fort Custer); however, the circumstances of geography and the state of communications in Montana necessitated this telegram's being carried by horseback from Fort Ellis to the Bighorn, many days distant.[30]

The army was naturally fearful that the different Indian tribes might unite in their struggle against the whites. On July 26th, Gibbon moved to head off another potential problem by requesting that provisions be sent to the Gros Ventres, who were destitute and had no ammunition to hunt. Further, they did not have access to the Fort Peck Agency because of the hostile Sioux in that area. He ordered Major Igles at Fort Benton to request of the chief that he bring the Gros Ventres' main camp to the mouth of the Marias where they could be provided provisions.[31] Gibbon's request for Indian provisions went by necessity to his headquarters in St. Paul and then to the Commissioner of Indian Affairs. It is unknown if this request was ever responded to.

While General Howard made plans and preparations to follow the Indians up the Lolo Trail, Looking Glass doubled back on a horse-steal-ing expedition before re-entering the trail. General Howard summed up his plan of action:

> Hostile Indians, with few exceptions, (their rear guard back stealing ponies, causing the late alarm), had gone off by the Lolo Trail. My dispositions were to form two columns and a reserve, to accompany the right column myself, the left column to be in charge of [General] Wheaton, and the reserve to stay on Camas Prairie under [Colonel John] Green. The right column to take up the direct pursuit along the Lolo Trail; the left column to go eastward by Mullan Road, look after old "Columbia River renegades" and malcontent Indians, keep the peace, if possible, and then, like the right column, set out for Missoula, Montana. The reserve must watch out on all trails, keep intercommunication, be ready for hostile Indians should they

---

[30] Ibid.

[31] July 26, 1877, ibid.

double back, and give heart to all neighboring farmers, miners, prospectors, and friendly Indians by the show of protection at hand.[32]

On July 30th, General Howard's column entered the Lolo Trail in pursuit of Joseph's Indians.

The campaign had now entered a new phase and involved the participation of army units within the Montana Military District as well as those of General Howard. Also, the leadership of the combined Nez Perce non-treaty tribes had passed from Joseph to Looking Glass.

> …Looking Glass had sole control of the camp, although Joseph ranked as high, or perhaps higher, as chief. Joseph's reason for not leading the camp was that there was more or less discontent and growling among the warriors, and Joseph thought he had best have nothing to do with the camp except to follow the movements ordered by Looking Glass.[33]

---

[32] Howard: 134.

[33] Ibid.: 135; Duncan McDonald, in Linwood Laughy, *In Pursuit of the Nez Perces:* 244.

CHAPTER THIRTY-TWO

The Nez Perce on the Lolo Trail, July 15–25, 1877

THE NEZ PERCE EXILES IN CANADA LATER REPORTED THAT it took them nine days to traverse the Lolo Trail in July 1877. At the end of the first day, they camped at Weippe (WEE-*ipe*) Prairie, moving on the next day. The day after that, approximately July 18th, Looking Glass took a small force back to harass General O.O. Howard. Not finding him, since Howard had not yet entered the trail with anything but scouts, the Indians proceeded back to Camas Prairie and stole some sixty-five horses, then returned to the main body on the trail. They then made plans to ambush and destroy Howard's force on the trail, but Howard had still not yet entered the trail. When the Nez Perce reached the hot springs on the Lolo Trail (present-day Lolo Hot Springs in Montana), they met three Indians—one of them a Nez Perce who lived in the Bitterroot Valley. He warned them that the army had set up a blocking force at the end of the trail about four miles from the mouth of Lolo Creek. This was the force under Captain Charles Rawn stationed at Fort Missoula and ordered into position by Colonel Gibbon from his headquarters at Fort Shaw.

Looking Glass erroneously believed that if his forces proceeded on to the buffalo country in a peaceful manner they would have no further problems. He did not understand the federal concept. He failed to realize that the U.S. Army would pursue him anywhere on U.S. territory. Besides, he had traversed this area in the past without serious problems. This notion may have been somewhat reinforced by the fact that Howard's force had not yet made a serious attempt to pursue him.

> Looking Glass said he did not want any troubles on [the Montana] side of the Lo Lo range [present-day Bitterroot Range], that he did not want to fight either soldiers or citizens east of the Lo Lo because they were not the ones who had fought them in Idaho. The idea among the Indians, uneducated as they were, was that the people of Montana had no identity with the people of Idaho, and that they were entirely separate and distinct, having nothing to do with each other. If they had to fight, they believed it was Idaho people they should fight and not Montanans.[1]

This belief, however erroneous, would serve the Nez Perce and most citizens of the Bitterroot Valley well for the duration of the Nez Perce transit through the valley.

As they approached the exit of the trail they encountered a small group of four or five volunteers under Captain N.C. Kinney, located to the front of Captain Rawn's command. They stated their intentions to pass in peace, but Captain Rawn told them they would have to surrender their arms. The Indians were afraid they would be hanged if they fell into white custody. They knew this had happened in the past in a previous campaign in the Northwest. Members of the Sioux tribe in Minnesota had also been hanged after surrender or capture. The Nez Perce chose to bypass Rawn's fortifications by deviating around them through the hill country to the north of the trail. During this maneuver they captured several white citizen volunteers, among them Henry MacFarland and Jack Walsh. Looking Glass later released them saying, "Go home and mind your own business; we will harm no man."[2] General Howard later seemed critical of Captain Rawn when he wrote:

> Joseph and Looking Glass, with their hordes, had come up to the hastily-constructed fort in the Lolo Valley and had promised good behavior in consideration for a safe conduct through to the "Buffalo Illahee [Country]." Captain Rawn was there at the time, in command of a few regulars and many volunteers. It was judged best by him and those with him to let Joseph's band go by close on the right flank, and the whites promised not to fire. Who can think of the apprehension of a scattered population and blame these citizen volunteers for letting "General Howard's Indians" go on, provided they promised to do no damage?[3]

---

[1] Duncan McDonald, in Linwood Laughy, comp., *In Pursuit of the Nez Perces*: 245–247.

[2] Ibid.: 251.

[3] O.O. Howard, in Laughy, comp.: 141.

The author has been unable to locate any evidence of disciplinary or court-martial action against Rawn for cowardice in the face of the enemy, nor any criticism of him by his superior, Colonel John Gibbon. Rawn's decision to yield without resistance was likely based on the fact that once the intention of the Indians became known, supported by past peaceful experiences with them, most citizen volunteers abandoned his position. Further, Captain Rawn knew that he was heavily outnumbered and that his force would be wiped out, if he attempted to stop the Indians by anything beyond brazen bluff. He also knew that any help from either General Howard or Colonel Gibbon would not arrive for many days, perhaps a week. The Indians easily bypassed Rawn's small force on July 25th.

Rawn's closest relief or reinforcement was likely Captain Browning's company proceeding directly from Fort Ellis via the Helena-Missoula road. It had departed Fort Ellis, over 200 miles distant, on the 22nd at the earliest. Further, it was to be three more days before Colonel Gibbon's force left Fort Shaw, 150 miles distant, and five more days before General Howard's main force started up the Lolo Trail in Idaho, also 150 miles distant. In light of these facts and, of course, utilizing perfect 20-20 hindsight, we may conclude that a battle at this location would have resulted in a one-day delay for the Nez Perce, with death and destruction for Rawn's force and any assisting citizens. Further, there would likely have been numerous revenge killings and much destruction throughout the Bitterroot Valley by the Indians before relief forces could arrive. Nevertheless, Captain Rawn was initially criticized by the local citizenry for his failure to block the Nez Perce. The *New Northwest*, a Deer Lodge weekly, wrote on August 10, 1877:

> Capt. Rawn was at first very severely censured for his course. As yet there is no explanation of it, but the heat of public feeling has cooled and there is a disposition to await his report and give fair judgement… Capt. Rawn's record of fifteen years is that of a good fighting officer and it entitles him to a suspension of adverse expression until all the facts are known.[4]

On July 25, 1877, the Indians came out of the trail into the Bitterroot Valley and made camp the first night at McLain's Ranch eight miles south of the mouth of Lolo Creek. While the Indians were in camp at this location, about sixty citizen volunteers under W.J. Stephens stumbled into the Indian camp and were surrounded. Looking Glass released them and told them to

---

4 (Deer Lodge, M.T.) *New Northwest*, August 10, 1877.

go home, that he wished to pass through the valley in peace. During their encampment at McClain's Ranch, the Nez Perce leaders went into council to discuss their future direction of travel. One of the Indians, Grizzly-Bear-Youth, suggested to Looking Glass that the Nez Perce turn back northward and pass to Canada by way of Flathead Lake.

Looking Glass then told Joseph and the others what Grizzly-Bear-Youth had said. White Bird and Red Owl agreed; they wanted to go by the reserve (referring to the Indian reservation north of Missoula). Joseph did not say a word. Looking Glass wanted to go by the Big Hole and down the Yellowstone and join the Crows because the Crows had promised them that whenever the Nez Perce fought the whites they would join them. There was a disagreement, but after quarreling among themselves they concluded it was best to let Looking Glass have his way. This council was held about a mile or a mile and a half above McClain's Ranch on the Bitterroot River.[5]

---

[5] McDonald: 251–253.

Nez Perce Enter Montana Territory from Idaho Pursued by Howard. Gibbon Moves to Counter Nez Perce

Nez Perce bypass Captain Rawn on 7/25/1877 and enter Bitterroot Valley. Gibbon marches from Fort Shaw on 7/28 and units also proceed to Missoula from Fort Ellis and Camp Baker. Gibbon battles Nez Perce at Big Hole 8/9–8/10. Nez Perce draw off pursued by Howard. Gibbon and his wounded evacuate to Deer Lodge.

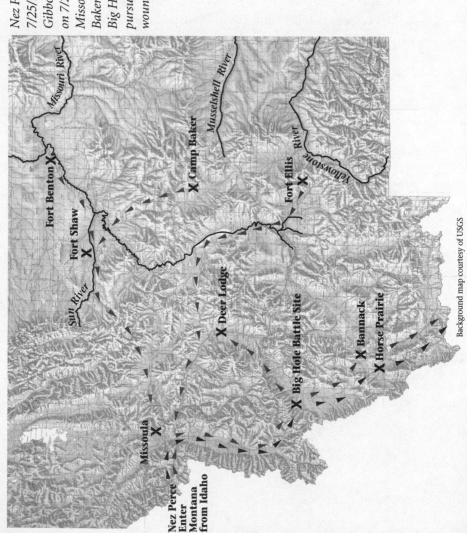

Background map courtesy of USGS

CHAPTER THIRTY-THREE

Gibbon Moves to Counter Nez Perce; March to the Bitterroot Valley

T HE MONTANA MILITARY DISTRICT HAD ESTABLISHED A new post, Fort Missoula, on June 9, 1877. Company A and Company I, 7th Infantry, under the command of Captain Charles Rawn, departed Fort Shaw to man this new post. The force consisted of six officers and sixty-eight enlisted men—three officers and thirty-one enlisted men from Company A and three officers and thirty-seven enlisted men from Company I commanded by Captain William Logan. Coincidental to this move, the Montana Military District began to receive word of hostilities in western Idaho.

In late July, while Colonel John Gibbon was on a fishing trip approximately twenty miles east of Fort Shaw and on the opposite side of the Missouri River, a messenger arrived for him with a telegram from headquarters in Chicago. The hostile Nez Perce were approaching Montana Territory's Bitterroot Valley via Lolo Pass. Since a large number of his troops were already committed to General Nelson Miles's Yellowstone Campaign, his Montana Military District had few troops remaining to confront the Nez Perce. Besides ordering Captain G.L. Browning's one company to proceed rapidly from Fort Ellis to Missoula, he also ordered Company D under Captain Richard Comba and twenty-seven enlisted men, then stationed at Camp Baker, and Company F with Lieutenant Hardin and twenty-two enlisted men, then stationed at Fort Benton, to proceed to Fort Shaw. These forces were joined by the officers and men of Company K, then stationed at Fort Shaw.[1]

---

[1] July 24, 1877, District of Montana Letters and Telegrams Sent and Received, Department of Dakota, Record Group 393.5, National Archives.

The approach of the Nez Perce hostiles had caused considerable apprehension among civilians in Montana Territory. In response, the territorial governor, Benjamin F. Potts, was busy attempting to raise a large number of militia volunteers to counter the Nez Perce. On July 27th, Gibbon sent the following telegram to Captain J.M. Mills, territorial secretary at Deer Lodge:

> Start tomorrow via Cadotte's Pass. Send word to Gov. Potts to give all the help he can to aid Capt. Rawn to hold the pass till I get there. If the Indians succeed in getting through they should be followed as closely as possible. I will come rapidly. I shall be without news after leaving here, if you get any send me a special courier through Lincoln. If the Indians get passed Missoula and start up the Blackfoot trail, any force you can bring from Deer Lodge across to Lincoln may be of material assistance to us.[2]

On July 28, 1877, Colonel Gibbon departed Fort Shaw for Missoula by the most direct route, via Cadotte Pass, a total distance of 150 miles, with a force consisting of eight officers and seventy-six enlisted men. This included most of the above-named officers as well as Lieutenant James Bradley and his mounted detachment. Since this route consisted of mostly rugged mountain trails (through an area now easily traversed on Montana Highway 200), all supplies were transported on a pack train of unruly, unpatriotic army mules whose previous assignments had been limited to pulling army wagons—not hauling packs. A few miles outside of Fort Shaw, a number of the mules bucked off their packs and galloped back to the fort before being rounded up and re-packed. Obviously, these mules felt that they had little quarrel with the Nez Perce!

Late on July 29th, they reached the Dearborn River about twenty-five miles from Fort Shaw. At the Dearborn, the force rested for three hours and dined on fresh trout, then proceeded on toward the pass, spending the night in the foothills of the eastern slope. An advance guard was placed on the pass. (Cadotte Pass is located just a short distance northwest of present-day Rogers Pass.) Gibbon had to assume that, should the Nez Perce overwhelm Captain Rawn's force at Missoula, which had moved up to block the exit of Lolo Pass, they might well proceed directly east over their "Road to the Buffalo" trail and meet his small force head on. In this case, he could not afford to be surprised, since his force was greatly outnumbered. He would need advance warning of the approach of the Nez Perce to set up a suitable

---

[2] July 27, 1877, ibid.

defense. While Colonel Gibbon's small force consisted primarily of infantry or foot soldiers, Lieutenant Bradley's mounted detachment functioned as his reconnaissance force. This group was undoubtedly kept well out in advance of the infantry to provided ample warning of any approach by the Nez Perce.

On reaching the summit of the pass the next day, Gibbon wrote, "There had been a slight rain the night before and the day was cold and cloudy, so that we felt but little disposition to stay and enjoy the view which opened out to the eastward. We quickly descended the slope on the other side and halted to rest and lunch at a clear little stream..."[3] This was, no doubt, Cadotte Creek. On this same day, General O.O. Howard's force entered the Lolo Trail in Idaho in pursuit of the Nez Perce, well over 200 miles to the west and some five days after the Nez Perce had bypassed Rawn's force near Fort Missoula.

Proceeding down the Blackfoot Valley, Gibbon's force noted numerous blue grouse along their path. They also found the trout fishing good during their occasional rest stops. By the close of the day on July 30th, they had marched twenty-seven miles and made camp at a point likely to have been near present-day Lincoln, MT. This was beyond the junction of their trail with that of the Lewis and Clark Pass trail, where, as Gibbon was aware, the Nez Perce may have turned off, crossed Lewis and Clark Pass and thus avoided his force. But Gibbon had, to his relief, seen no sign of a recent passing by Indians at this junction. This is the approximate location where Alice Creek now flows under Montana Highway 200, about fifteen miles east-northeast of present-day Lincoln, MT.

The next day, July 31st, they marched past the mining town of Lincoln Gulch,[4] located about four miles west of present-day Lincoln. Here the force entered the Blackfoot Canyon. During the course of this day, a courier arrived from Helena with news that Captain Rawn's fortifications had been bypassed, and that the Nez Perce were still in the Bitterroot Valley moving slowly southward. It is of note that Gibbon did not appear to have any questions regarding Rawn's failure to stop the Indians. He wrote:

> ...the Nez Perces, finding Captain Rawn's little force entrenched in the canyon at Lolo Fork, had displayed a force in his front, and then with their main body marched around his position over the hills,

---

[3] John Gibbon, *Adventures on the Western Frontier*: 177.

[4] According to the 1870 U.S. Census, Lincoln Gulch had then boasted a population of 188 souls; of these, 165 were white males, 21 white females and 2 Chinese males.

out of range of his rifles, and entered the valley of the Bitter Root in
his rear…[A] later dispatch received from Captain Rawn informed
me that the citizens who had accompanied him as volunteers to the
Lo Lo Pass had returned home, after making an agreement with the
Indians that their lives and property should be safe.[5]

Colonel Gibbon could now assume with a higher degree of certainty that
his force would not bump head on into the Nez Perce while en route down
the Blackfoot River to Missoula. On the evening of July 31st, after marching
twenty-seven miles from the Lincoln area, they camped on a lake, probably Brown's Lake or Kleinschmidt Lake near present-day Ovando, MT.
On August 1st, they marched only twenty-four miles, passing the North
Fork of the Blackfoot. Gibbon noted that the country was getting rougher
again. Once more he received word via courier from Captain Rawn that
the Nez Perce were moving slowly up the Bitterroot Valley southward from
Missoula toward present-day Hamilton, MT. The same messenger also carried a message from General Howard in Idaho, dated July 25th, advising
that he would depart Kamiah, ID, with his troops in pursuit up the Lolo
Trail on July 30th.

On August 2nd, Gibbon rode on ahead of the infantry with a small
party—although the troops were infantry, the officers were mounted—and
made all haste to reach Fort Missoula. This was a ride of some fifty miles,
much of it over very rough country. Arriving in the Missoula area just before nightfall, he observed farm houses and grain fields in the process of
harvest. He noted that these were the first houses he had seen since passing
Lincoln Gulch.[6]

Once at Fort Missoula, Gibbon arranged for wagons to be dispatched
to pick up the tired infantry. These troops finally reached Fort Missoula at

---

[5] Gibbon: 179. In spite of Howard's lament regarding events at the Lolo fortification, Captain
Rawn's version obviously makes more sense. First, it is entirely logical that the Nez Perce would
have displayed force to Rawn's front while bypassing his fortifications. It is also very likely that the
main body passed by out of rifle range and not, as Howard stated, "It was judged best by [Captain
Rawn] and those with him to let Joseph's band go by, close on the right flank, and the whites
promised not to fire"; O.O. Howard in Linwood Laughy, comp., *In Pursuit of the Nez Perces:* 141.
Since the Indians' main body consisted mainly of women and children, it was not likely that the
Nez Perce were prepared to pass within rifle range of Rawn's troops.

[6] Gibbon: 179; Bradley Manuscripts, Montana Historical Society. It is of interest that Lieutenant
Bradley, in a letter to his wife, which was written as the column passed the general area of Ovando,
noted that he had suggested the Nez Perce would go south, but that Colonel Gibbon and Lieutenant
Woodruff had disagreed with him, believing that they would, upon arrival in the Bitterroot, take
a more northerly course. He boasted to his wife that he was correct in his judgment. The fact is
that no one could have known for certain what the Nez Perce would do. In this case, Lieutenant
Bradley happened to be correct.

4 P.M. on August 3rd, after a 150-mile, seven-day march from Fort Shaw. He then sent a dispatch to Fort Ellis for relay to General of the Army, William T. Sherman, who was, together with the division commander, General Philip Sheridan, and the department commander, General Alfred Terry, conducting an inspection tour of the two new posts in eastern Montana. He informed Sherman that over 200 Nez Perce warriors and 1,200 horses were moving slowly up the Bitterroot Valley, approximately sixty miles south of him, en route toward the Big Hole basin. Gibbon advised he was pursuing with 125 men. He then ordered the post commander at Fort Ellis, that should information be received confirming that the hostile Indians had entered the Big Hole, to send Captain Randall Norwood's company of 2nd Cavalry in that direction.[7] He also sought out Chief Charlo of the Flathead tribe.[8]

On August 3rd, Colonel Gibbon met with Chief Charlo of the local Flathead tribe, which was camped near present-day Stevensville, MT. He knew that the Nez Perce would have spies throughout the valley monitoring troop movements. Since the whites could not differentiate the Nez Perce spies from friendly Flatheads, he asked Chief Charlo to order his people to arrest these spies and turn them over to the army. Chief Charlo declined to do so, stating that the Nez Perce had always been his friends and he did not have any part in the quarrel between the Nez Perce and the whites.

Colonel Gibbon then sent a citizen, Mr. Joe Pardee, over the Lolo Trail with a dispatch for General Howard, advising him of the strength of his force and that he was pursuing the Indians southward up the Bitterroot Valley and would need at least one hundred more troops as soon as possible. Also on August 3rd, far to the east at Fort Keogh, Colonel Nelson Miles began planning for a possible intercept of the Nez Perce. Anticipating that they would likely pass northward through Judith Gap toward Canada, if not stopped in the meantime, he dispatched Lieutenant G.C. Doane with Company E, 7th Cavalry, and Crow scouts to proceed to that general area.

---

[7] August 2, 1877, District of Montana Letters and Telegrams Sent and Received.

[8] Chief Charlo, often spelled Charlot, reigned over the Flathead tribe at its home in the Bitterroot Valley. As the towns of Stevensville and Corvallis grew, government pressure increased on Charlo to move his peaceful tribe onto the reservation at Jocko near St. Ignatius. In 1871, the president ordered them to move. Charlo remained at peace but refused to move. He had two sub-chiefs: Arlee and Adolph. Arlee, the war chief, agreed to move onto the reservation with a portion of the tribe about 1872. Charlo remained with followers in the Bitterroot. They continued their annual buffalo hunts. He held out in the Bitterroot with a dwindling band of followers until 1891, when he moved onto the reservation at Jocko. Chief Arlee had died on August 8, 1889. By that time, buffalo hunts were no longer possible, and Charlo's small band was faced with starvation and suffering from the ill effects of whiskey. Granville Stuart, *Forty Years on the Frontier*, Vol. II: 89–95.

On August 4th, Gibbon commenced his pursuit up the valley with 15 officers and 146 men. His force, now augmented by Captain Rawn's contingent, was concealed to the greatest extent possible in wagons. The supply train was operated by Hugh Kirkendall and a number of citizens.[9] That day they reached Stevensville, and Colonel Gibbon sought out Father Joseph Ravalli, a longtime resident of the area who was well acquainted with the Nez Perce. Here he learned that the Nez Perce force amounted to about 260 warriors. The next day, August 5th, the troops continued up the valley, marching thirty miles and passing the town of Corvallis. On their way, they had learned that great fear and apprehension existed among many of the citizens, while others, learning of Looking Glass's promise to pass through the valley peaceably, took every advantage and carried on a bustling trade in goods with the Indians. Much to the displeasure of the pursuing troops, some citizens had readily purchased some of the horses the Nez Perce had stolen from citizens in Idaho! Colonel Gibbon would later praise a certain Mr. Young, a Corvallis merchant, for defiantly refusing to trade with the Indians, even after they threatened to burn his establishment down.

At Corvallis the column was joined by six citizens, among them an invaluable guide by the name of Joe Blodget, a pioneer in the area who was well acquainted with a difficult but passable trail for wagons to Bannack...[10] Also among these citizens were a local rancher, Mr. Myron Lockwood, and his brother, Alvin Lockwood.[11]

Moving up the valley on August 6th, they reached Lockwood's ranch. His house and possessions had been thoroughly ransacked by the passing Nez Perce. This was, according to Colonel Gibbon, the last house observed as they moved up the valley toward the mouth of the pass leading across the mountains to the Big Hole basin. Also on this date, they passed what was known as the Southern Nez Perce Trail leading back to Idaho. At this point it was clear that the Nez Perce were not doubling back into Idaho although they may have received reinforcements via this trail. Gibbon noted that the Indians were moving slow, only about twelve miles per day, and he began to think he might have a chance of overtaking them.

---

[9] (Deer Lodge, M.T.) *New Northwest*, August 24 1877.

[10] Granville Stuart reported that Joe Blodget passed trough American Fork (Gold Creek) on October 9, 1861, with freight wagons loaded with supplies for Hellgate (Missoula area). Blodget was traveling with his partner Dempsey. Their trip had originated in Salt Lake City; Stuart, *Forty Years on the Frontier*, Vol. I: 188.

[11] According to the *New Northwest* (in August 1877), Alvin Lockwood had a wife and five children. He was killed in the Battle of the Big Hole. Myron was severely wounded through both thighs.

On August 7, 1877, as the force commenced its climb over the mountains, they were overtaken by two officers, one from Camp Baker and one from Fort Benton, and another party of local citizens. Although Gibbon does not name these officers, one was likely Captain Constant Williams, commander of Company F, who had arrived at Fort Benton on July 30th, several days after the departure of his company for Fort Shaw to join Colonel Gibbon.[12] The other was probably 2nd Lieutenant J.T. Van Orsdale, assigned to Company D, Camp Baker. The Post Return for Camp Baker for July 1877 reveals that this officer was under arrest during the period July 19th to the 31st. He was therefore unable to depart with his company for Fort Shaw, but was released and departed to join his company in the field on August 1st. The Post Return does not reveal the lieutenant's infraction, but it is of interest to note that he was promoted to 1st lieutenant in November 1877.[13]

On the evening of the 7th, Lieutenant James H. Bradley, in charge of the mounted patrol now numbering thirty-five soldiers and twenty-five citizens, among them Hiram S. Bostwick, the Fort Shaw post guide, moved on ahead of the column in an attempt to locate the Nez Perce and, if possible, stampede their horses. On August 8th, the main body struggled to get their wagons and their one howitzer over the steep mountains. Late in the day, Bostwick returned with a message from Lieutenant Bradley. The message is quoted in its entirety. It was the lieutenant's final communiqué. He was killed in action early the next morning. Bostwick was also killed in the fighting.

Aug. 8th, 1877

Battalion Adjutant,

Sir: I have the honor to report that I have personally seen the indications of an Indian camp situated in Big Hole, about three miles from my position. Lieutenant Jacobs accompanied me, and I have requested him to write a line in reference thereto. We saw horses grazing and mounted Indians, heard a gunshot, and the sound of axes. They evidently design staying all night, and from the anxious manner they have scouted the valley to the east, I judge that they have discovered a force in their front. They have seen my camp, but I do not expect them to attack me. Were the infantry to come up to-night we could attack them at daylight with great advantage, taking

---

[12] July 1877, Fort Benton Post Returns, Records of Posts, Continental Army Command 1820–1920, Record Group 393.7, National Archives.

[13] July and November 1877 Camp Baker Post Returns, Records of the Adjutant General's Office, ca 1775–ca. 1928, Record Group 94, National Archives.

them in rear, as we have scouted the country well and found a safe and concealed route over the hills.

Very respectfully,
James H. Bradley
[Marked Received August 8th, 5.10 P.M.][14]

Although Colonel Gibbon could not know it, General Howard's main body had on this same day reached the position where the Indians had by-passed Captain Rawn's fortifications and entered the Bitterroot Valley. Two days earlier, upon Howard's arrival at Lolo Hot Springs on August 6th, Joe Pardee had arrived in Howard's camp with Gibbon's dispatch. Howard then dispatched Sergeant Oliver Sutherland and an Indian scout with a message for Gibbon, informing him that he was coming at utmost speed with 200 cavalrymen.[15] However, Howard was still over one hundred miles behind Gibbon's force.

Gibbon knew well of the danger his force faced. He could be walking into an ambush. It was hard for him to believe, indeed hard for anyone to believe, that his force would be able to approach and surprise these Indians. If, however, he could gain the element of surprise, this could offset the fact that his force was outnumbered by nearly one hundred fighting men. His mission was to destroy the hostile Nez Perce as an effective fighting force and, thus, gain their surrender. If he exercised caution and opted to await the arrival of Howard's forces, the Nez Perce would surely discover his force and move on. Or worse yet, they could attack his force at their moment of choosing, putting him at a dangerous disadvantage and, possibly, wiping out his command.

The soldiers knew that they were facing a powerful and dangerous enemy. Word of the defeats in Idaho had surely impressed them. One need only recall that most of these same officers and men had been the first to arrive at the scene of the Custer disaster at the Little Bighorn less than fourteen months prior. They knew the odds were that they would not achieve a bloodless victory, that a number of them would die when they clashed with the Nez Perce. They could also lose the fight and be wiped out to the last man. Such is the role of the soldier—to follow orders and do his duty. Colonel Gibbon opted to attempt an approach under cover of darkness and attack the village at first light.

---

14 Gibbon: 190.

15 O.O. Howard, in Linwood Laughy, comp., *In Pursuit of the Nez Perces:* 143.

CHAPTER THIRTY-FOUR

The Battle of the Big Hole

A T 11 P.M. ON AUGUST 8, 1877, COLONEL JOHN GIBBON'S troops moved, under cover of darkness, eventually arriving just before dawn at the edge of the Indian camp. It was necessary to leave the supply train and howitzer about a mile behind with a small squad of troops. They could not be moved forward without the use of axes to clear the trail, thereby alerting the Nez Perce.[1] Gibbon's force succeeded in moving undetected by the Indians into an assault line between the Nez Perce horse herd and the village.[2] Shortly before dawn in semi-darkness, they launched their attack, advancing quietly forward down a small bluff, across the creek (Ruby Creek) and up to the edge of the village. As Lieutenant James Bradley, in charge of the left wing of the assault, entered the willows on the edge of the village, he was shot and killed by a Nez Perce warrior who was in turn shot dead by Private Philo Hurlbut.[3] The fight was on. Firing into the tepees, the soldiers rushed forward into the camp, scattering the surprised Indians in all directions. Gibbon later described the assault:

---

[1] The howitzer, had Gibbon been able to bring it up and deploy it, would have been a great asset in the fight. However, reality dictated otherwise. It was too big and too heavy to be brought forward without losing the advantage of surprise. Easily transportable mortars of the modern era did not exist in Gibbon's day.

[2] According to Gibbon and the (Deer Lodge, M.T.) *New Northwest*, the colonel originally wanted to drive the horse herd off, but was convinced by Hiram Bostwick that it was likely guarded and the village would thus be alerted to the troops. It turned out the herd was not guarded. Such are the fortunes of war. Bostwick's advice was sound and logical. Also, if Gibbon had sufficient strength, he could have scattered the horse herd simultaneous with his attack on the village.

[3] *New Northwest*, August 24, 1877.

The startled and completely surprised Indians rushed from the tents only to find themselves cut down by a withering fire from the brush, towards which some of them ran instinctively for shelter, whilst most of them scattered away from the fire out on the open prairie and up and down the creek. The last remaining company was sent in on the right at a run, and reached the upper end of the village, just where the creek, making a bend towards us, afforded by its steeply-cut bank admirable shelter to the Indians, who, huddling together, opened a fire upon our men as they entered the village about its middle at the apex of the "V." These were now taken in the rear, many of them slaughtered, and with loud shouts of triumph the whole command swept through the village. Many of the Indians still remained in the tepees, and some still alive and unwounded fired upon the men when tearing open the tents. One young officer narrowly escaped death at the hands of a squaw, who fired a pistol at him as he opened the door, and the next moment fell dead with a bullet through her brain. Some of the women and boys fought like men, while others sought safety behind the creek-banks, crouching down with the water up to their waists. In crossing the steam near the upper end of the village I saw three of these poor wretches, one with a baby in her arms, seated in the water behind a clump of bushes, and as I passed along one made a salutation with her hand, as if to claim my protection. I tried to explain to her that she was safe, and beckoned her to come out, but none of them moved, and they remained there till we left the village.[4]

According to a later account by Lieutenant Woodruff, the assault by Bradley's group against the lower end of the camp faltered upon his death, allowing many Nez Perce to escape downstream away from Gibbon's main force.[5]

The soldiers, once in possession of the village, began to set fire to the tepees and destroy supplies. As they moved about the village, they began to receive sporadic incoming rifle fire from Nez Perce scattered about in the brush, woods and hillsides on the outskirts of the village. The rifle fire gradually increased, and Colonel Gibbon began to realize that it was also very accurate. With almost every shot one of his men was hit. Courageous fighters as they were, the Nez Perce leaders, initially taken completely by surprise, had quickly regrouped their scattered warriors and begun to mount an offense. Gibbon decided that they had to move out of the village into a

---

4 Gibbon, *Adventures on the Western Frontier*: 193–194.

5 C.A. Woodruff Speeches, SC 1326, Montana Historical Society Archives: 12.

position providing them with cover or his command would be wiped out piecemeal. He ordered his troops to withdraw back up the bluff above and across the creek into a wooded area, which offered them some concealment. The bluff, already occupied by a number of Indians, was eventually secured by an assault across the creek. Once Gibbon's men had secured this position, the Indians gradually pressed in and sniped at the troops in their scant cover, which consisted of small trees no more than four inches in diameter and some stumps and fallen logs. Shortly after the troops reached this new position, they heard two shots from the howitzer and then silence. The Indians had located and overrun the howitzer contingent, killing Corporal Robert E. Sales and wounding Sergeants Patrick C. Daly and John W. Frederick. The howitzer team driver, Private John Bennett, and two other privates escaped unharmed. The Nez Perce rendered the howitzer useless and also seized over 2,000 rounds of rifle ammunition.[6]

Colonel Gibbon's force was now on the defensive and under siege by the Nez Perce. He would later write:

> Few of us will soon forget the wail of mingled grief, rage, and horror which came from the camp four or five hundred yards from us when the Indians returned to it and recognized their slaughtered warriors, women, and children. Above this wail of horror we could hear the passionate appeal of the leaders urging their followers to fight, and the war whoops in answer which boded us no good.[7]

The Nez Perce exiles would later state that upon regaining possession of the village, they captured one of the citizen volunteers, whom they interrogated. From him they learned that General Howard was on his way and would be arriving soon.[8] The fate of this captive is unknown by this author, but considering the emotional state of the Indians on returning to their destroyed village, it is highly unlikely that he survived.

The Nez Perce besieged the troops all day long, with deadly accurate fire from positions all around them, killing and wounding many soldiers and citizen volunteers. The troops now returned fire only sparingly, utilizing their best marksmen, for the ammunition supply was running low. One Nez Perce sharpshooter was particularly effective, killing and wounding a number of soldiers from his position behind a tree. He was finally killed.

---

6 Gibbon: 194–196, 199, 213–216; *New Northwest*, August 1877; Colonel Gibbon's Report.

7 Gibbon: 213–214.

8 Duncan McDonald in Linwood Laughy, comp., *In Pursuit of the Nez Perces*: 263–264.

After the battle, twenty expended cartridges were found in his position. At one point the Nez Perce attempted to drive the troops from their position by starting a fire in the grass and trees. Fortunately for Gibbon's men, the vegetation was not dry enough and the attempt failed. In their repeated charges across the creek, most of the rations carried by the men in their haversacks were ruined. The command killed a wounded horse and ate it, and obtained water from the creek some twenty yards below their position.

During the night, Colonel Gibbon dispatched a Mr. Edwards and another citizen to sneak out toward Deer Lodge, some seventy miles straight-line distance, with messages for General Alfred Terry and Governor Benjamin Potts requesting transport, medical supplies and doctors. Another group of citizens was less helpful. Fearful that the command would be rushed and wiped out the next day, they chose to slip out through Indian lines under cover of darkness.[9] General Howard later reported meeting seven citizens on foot late on the evening of August 10th, who had fled from the battlefield. The *New Northwest* later reported their number as five. No names were given. Howard later wrote:

> They enumerated those who had been killed in the battle, but even after they had been comforted by a night's rest and a warm breakfast, they gave us but gloomy views of the final situation at the time they themselves, for dear life, were making their escape to the brush. Now, no offer of favor or money, not even the attraction of a brother wounded and needy, could induce one of those brave men to go back and guide us to the battlefield.[10]

On the next day, while still maintaining a presence around Gibbon's troops, the Nez Perce, after burying their dead, began to strike what remained of their camp and, with what they could salvage of their possessions and horse herds, move off toward the southeast in the direction of Bannack. They hoped to put some distance between themselves and General Howard's oncoming forces. Shortly after daylight a citizen arrived in Gibbon's perimeter, followed shortly by Sergeant Sutherland, both with messages from General Howard advising that he was on the way.[11] Some hours earlier, Sergeant Oliver Sutherland had dispatched a message to General Howard, which the general received late that day:

---

[9] Gibbon: 214–217; *New Northwest*, August 17, 24, 1877.

[10] O.O. Howard in Laughy, comp.: 152.

[11] Gibbon: 198.

On the Big Hole Trail, about 20 miles
from Ross' Hole, 12 M., Aug. 9, '77

General: I arrived here en route to General Gibbon's command ten
minutes ago. I find the train of General Gibbon in camp, with a
guard of about eighteen men, citizens and soldiers. General Gibbon
left here last night, with a force of (say) one hundred and eighty
men, and had been fighting all day, but his exact whereabouts not
known to party here.

In conformity with orders from General Gibbon, a party of three
non-commissioned officers and seven privates started from here at
daybreak (with a 12-pounder mountain howitzer and ammunition)
and were attacked about three and a half miles out; one corporal
killed, two sergeants wounded, and two men missing. Howitzer
lost with fifteen rounds of ammunition; also two thousand rounds
calibre .45; pack mule killed. As near as I can learn, the sergeant in
charge scattered and destroyed the ammunition for the howitzer;
fired three rounds at the Indians. It appears from the attack that
Indians are between General Gibbon and this camp. I find the men
here somewhat uneasy, but determined to stand off the Indians at
all hazards. I take two men from here and start in five minutes to
endeavor to reach General Gibbon…

Would respectfully state, in explanation of seeming delay on my
part, that I was thrown from an unbroken horse…and my back severely hurt, my progress from that point [point of injury illegible]
attended with severe suffering. I am, General,

Very respectfully yours,
O. Sutherland
Sergeant Company "B," 1st Cavalry[12]

We may surmise from the time and place that this message was
composed and dispatched, at twelve midnight, that Sergeant Sutherland
knew that chances were good he would not reach Gibbon's command
alive. Being a loyal soldier, he wished to inform his general officer of what
he had learned before departing on this perilous journey. Colonel Gibbon
later learned the fate of the howitzer contingent from the sergeant. He
also learned that the pack train was safe. Although there were still a number of Indians in the area, he sent Captain Browning and Lieutenants

12 Howard: 154–155.

Wright and J.T. Van Orsdale with twenty-five men back to retrieve the supply train. The main body, which now contained about forty wounded, remained in position throughout August 10th, on the alert. Later that day, the supply train arrived with much needed food and supplies. At 11 P.M. the Nez Perce rear guard fired a parting volley into the perimeter as they withdrew from the area. The next morning, August 11th, the men were sent forward into the site of the village to retrieve and bury their dead. Gibbon sent the following dispatch to Captain D.W. Benham, commander at Fort Ellis:

> If you have not already done so send Norwood's company at once towards Bannock to act against the Nez Perce who have gone in that direction. Gen'l Howard will be here today and will doubtless pursue. Our fight with them here day before yesterday was a severe one. Our loss was two officers ([William] Logan and Bradley) and seventeen men killed. Four officers (Capt. [Constant] Williams, Lieuts Coolidge, Woodruff, [William] English and myself) and thirty six men wounded. The surprise was complete and many of the Indians were killed in their tepees or running from them. I know they suffered severely and think their loss greater than my own. They have all disappeared and I think Howard can catch them again. Furnish Gen'l [William T.] Sherman with a copy of this.[13]

Later that day, General Howard arrived with an advance party of soldiers and Bannock Indian scouts. Gibbon sent another dispatch to Fort Ellis for forwarding to General Terry, reporting his battle of August 9th and that seven officers and fifty-three men had been killed and wounded. He added that forty dead Indians had been found on half of the battlefield and that General Howard had just arrived.[14] All fallen soldiers and citizen volunteers, twenty-nine in all, were buried where they fell. Gibbon's men later counted eighty-nine dead Indian men, women and children on the field, most of them having been buried by the Indians. It is of note that Colonel Gibbon's first count of Indian dead ranged between eighty and ninety and he later corrected it to read eighty-nine. He wrote:

> The number of Indian dead would have remained a matter of conjecture to us, but for the fact that the Indian scouts who came with

---

[13] August 11, 1877, District of Montana Letters and Telegrams Sent and Received, Department of Dakota, Record Group 393.5, National Archives.

[14] Ibid.

the advance of the Oregon column, which reached our position that day, went upon the field, and with the triple purpose of recognition, scalping, and plunder, dug up the bodies. In this way the Indian loss became known with tolerable accuracy.[15]

The Battle of the Big Hole was, in the annals of U.S. military history, a very small battle, yet it was a very bloody battle for both sides—a struggle for survival. Colonel Gibbon went into this battle with approximately 180 men, soldiers and citizen volunteers. When the battle was over, there were forty wounded, among them Colonel Gibbon, who suffered a flesh wound in the thigh, and twenty-nine dead. Among the dead on the field were Captain William Logan, Lieutenant James H. Bradley, and Fort Shaw post guide Hiram Bostwick.[16] At least two of the wounded, Lieutenant William L. English and Sergeant William W. Watson, later died of their wounds, revising the casualty count to thirty-one dead and thirty-eight wounded for a total casualty count of sixty-nine, or over 38 percent of the colonel's fighting force. Contrast this casualty figure to a much more famous battle in U.S. history—the Battle of Gettysburg, in which Colonel Gibbon played a pivotal role as commanding general of the 2nd Division, 2nd Corps. This division bore the brunt of Pickett's famous charge on July 3, 1863. The Office of the Chief of Military History, U.S. Army, lists Union dead as 3,155 with 14,529 wounded for a total casualty count of 17,684 out of a force of approximately 90,000. This is a 19.6 percent casualty rate. On the Confederate side, 3,903 were killed and 18,735 wounded out of a force of approximately 75,000, for a 30 percent casualty rate. We therefore may conclude that those men engaged at the Battle of the Big Hole had a much higher chance of being killed or wounded than those soldiers on the losing side in the Battle of Gettysburg![17] The Big Hole casualties were later listed by name in the *New Northwest*. This list is provided in the Appendix.

---

[15] Gibbon: 199–201.

[16] Bostwick is known to have been an employee of the American Fur Company as of the year 1857. Late that year he accompanied Edward A. Lewis, Bill Atkinson and a Frenchman named Rinober on an overland journey hauling American Fur Company supplies from Fort Union to Fort Benton. Lewis referred to him as Bosdwike but he is the same man; Robert Vaughn: *Then and Now:* 118. The U.S. Census for 1870 reveals him employed as an interpreter at Fort Shaw and residing there with his Indian wife and children. According to the census, he was born in New York. Robert Vaughn mentions his employment at the fort as an interpreter in August 1871; Vaughn: 92. Another Bostwick bearing the first name of Ephraim was killed by Crow Indians while accompanying the Stuart prospecting party to the Yellowstone in the year 1863; Vaughn: 34–38. He may have been Hiram Bostwick's brother, but that is only speculation on the author's part.

[17] Office of the Chief of Military History, U.S. Army, American Military History, Army Historical Series, Chapter 11, The Civil War 1863: 253.

The Nez Perce exiles later reported that seventy-eight Indians were killed at the Battle of the Big Hole. Thirty of the dead were warriors, the rest women and children.[18] There is no doubt that some women and children were slaughtered without opportunity to surrender, in the heat of battle, while others were combatants. Colonel Gibbon wrote:

> The killing of women and children was, under the circumstances, unavoidable. The action commenced before it was fully light, and after daylight, when attempts were made to break open the tepees, squaws and boys from within fired on the men, and were, of course, fired on in turn; but the poor terrified and inoffensive women and children crouching in the brush were in no way disturbed, and a noted instance occurred under my personal observation when her sex saved the life of a woman. Whilst we were in possession of the camp a figure started to run from one of the tepees to the next. Instantly several rifles were brought to the aim, but amidst the cries, "It is a woman, don't shoot," the rifles were raised and she escaped unhurt.[19]

The Nez Perce exiles told of one young Indian woman who shot and killed an officer who had just shot down her warrior brother. She was in turn shot and killed by soldiers. It is believed that this officer was Captain William Logan. The exiles also commended Captain Browning for saving two Indian women in front of him who were about to be shot by soldiers.[20] The New Northwest later reported, "Enlisted men in the command say that the officers issued orders against killing non-combatant squaws or children and the order was respected, but that in numerous instances both were found fighting with pistol, gun and knife."[21]

There was plenty of blame to go around on both sides regarding the killing of wounded and innocent. After his capture, Chief Joseph was reported to have claimed that "Soldiers do not kill any Indians unless they are wounded and left upon the Battlefield."[22] This is, of course, an obvious exaggeration, but there are doubtless instances where this happened. If one takes some care to note how many U.S. Army "wounded" survived the

---

[18] Duncan McDonald, in Laughy, comp.: 262.

[19] Gibbon: 217.

[20] McDonald: 261–262, 264

[21] August 24, 1877, New Northwest.

[22] Chief Joseph in Laughy, comp.: 291.

Battle of White Bird Canyon and, also, the surrounding and annihilation of Lieutenant Sevier Rains's party of twelve men in Idaho, it defies logic that a number of these men were not first wounded and then later killed by the Indians. Granted the Nez Perce were better marksmen, but not every shot killed its intended target. Obviously, there were men left helpless by their wounds who were later killed outright. Most battles do not end with everyone on the opposing side dead, unless a number of them receive the coup de grace.

The Nez Perce camp is estimated to have contained approximately 700 Indians at the outset of the battle. Two hundred sixty of them were warriors. There is no record of the number of wounded Indians nor am I aware of any complete listing of the names of those killed. The exiles stated that this engagement had caused the loss of more warriors than any of the previous contests with the U.S. Army. As previously stated, two of the Indians involved in the murders of whites in Idaho, Walitze and Tap-sis-ill-i-pilp, were killed in this battle.[23]

Students of the Indian Wars have to ask themselves how it could be possible for Colonel Gibbon's force to so completely surprise these Indians, universally recognized as masters of the American woods and wilds. After all, this was not the first salvo in an unexpected war, or so it would seem to the casual observer. The fact is, however, that Chief Looking Glass, who was in command, did not believe that there would be further problems with the whites now that his people had left Idaho Territory. He had successfully brought his people through the Bitterroot Valley without bloodshed. He had not attacked the whites, and they had not attacked him. He had brought his people to this high mountain prairie in a very remote area with the closest houses or settlements many miles away. Although there were those Indians who later claimed to have disagreed with him, in particular Chief White Bird, Looking Glass sensed no danger of attack.

Somehow the Nez Perce spies left in the Bitterroot had failed to detect Gibbon's column, believing that Captain Charles Rawn's original force represented the total of all U.S. military in the Bitterroot Valley. Since Looking Glass had dealt with the U.S. Army before, he did not feel it to be much of a threat.[24] Colonel Gibbon noted after the battle that the Indians had been planning to spend some time at the Big Hole camp. "Many of

---

[23] McDonald: 261, 264.

[24] Ibid.: 258–259.

their tepee poles, in place of being dry poles, collected for temporary use, as in all their previous camps, were green, carefully peeled, and bored at the end for permanent use."[25]

By August 12th, all of General Howard's troops had arrived at the battle-field. On August 13th, he took up the pursuit of the Nez Perce with his forces now augmented by fifty of Colonel Gibbon's troops. Two days earlier in the eastern part of the territory, Colonel Miles had ordered Colonel Samuel D. Sturgis with six companies of the 7th Cavalry to move from Fort Keogh to Judith Gap. Miles presumed that, should the Nez Perce escape Howard's pursuit, they might pass through Judith Gap on their way to Canada. Lieutenant Gustavus Doane's company, with its Crow allies, later joined Sturgis's force.[26]

Colonel Gibbon's remaining troops, many of them wounded, departed for Deer Lodge. This force was to receive valuable assistance from a group of citizens, commanded by militia captain Stuart, whom they encountered when they were about twelve miles from the battlefield. These citizens were coming to aid in response to Colonel Gibbon's call for help. The combined columns then continued on to a point near Doolittle's Ranch on the Big Hole River and then made camp. Here surgeons from Deer Lodge, Helena and Butte attended to the wounded. The *New Northwest* identified the surgeons as Doctors Reese and Steele of Helena, Mitchell of Deer Lodge and Wheelock and Whitford of Butte.[27] When Gibbon's battered force arrived in Deer Lodge on August 15th, "The whole town turned out and gave us a reception, and, best of all, the ladies of the place came forward and took complete charge of all the wounded, feeding and fostering them until the unwounded ones sighed at the absence of wounds, which would have entitled them to such attentions."[28]

Lieutenant Bradley and Captain Logan were eulogized in the *New Northwest*. Bradley was well known in the territorial newspapers because of articles he had previously submitted, among them his description of the discovery of the bodies of Custer and his men. A few years earlier, while

---

[25] Gibbon: 201.

[26] In just one year, the balance of power between white man and red man in eastern Montana Territory had drastically changed in favor of the U.S. Army. Two posts had already been constructed and manned, Fort Keogh and Fort Custer, and Colonel Miles now had over 1,000 troops (Post Returns for Fort Keogh, February 1877; and Fort Custer December 1877, National Archives) under his command, where only one year earlier no posts had existed.

[27] August 17, 24, 1877, *New Northwest.*

[28] Gibbon: 202.

passing through Helena, he had fallen dangerously ill. This occurred as he and his young wife were arriving in Montana Territory from a previous posting in the south. His wife nursed him back to health. On August 24, 1877, the *New Northwest* reported that Mrs. Bradley and their small child had departed on a steamer from Fort Benton en route back to her home in Atlanta. The *New Northwest* also reported that Captain William Logan, just three years from retirement eligibility, had recently lost a grown daughter, Mrs. J.T. Van Orsdale, and a small grandchild.[29]

Lieutenant English died of his wounds in Deer Lodge on August 20th. Sergeant Watson passed away some days later. On September 14th, the *New Northwest* reported that Lieutenant English's wife had departed Fort Benton for her home in Illinois.[30]

[29] August 17, 24, 1877, *New Northwest.*

[30] August 24, 31, September 9, 1877, ibid.

CHAPTER THIRTY-FIVE

The Nez Perce on the Move Pursued by Howard, August 12–20, 1877; Battle of Camas Meadows, August 19–20, 1877

T HE NEZ PERCE HAD DEPARTED THE BATTLEFIELD IN A southerly direction toward the Bannack area. Suspecting that they would head east for buffalo country, General O.O. Howard held his column somewhat to the left of their track. Captain Randall Norwood arrived to join him with his company of 2nd Cavalry troops from Fort Ellis. The Indians passed through the gap between the Bannack valley and the Horse Prairie valley, bypassing to the west of Bannack, much to the relief of the frightened citizens of the area. Many had sought safety in Bannack, by that time a much smaller settlement than in its heyday.[1] Quite the opposite from many citizens of the Bitterroot Valley, most residents of the Bannack vicinity were very frightened. The Nez Perce were, under-standably, now in a vengeful mood. The residents of Bannack were happy to see the soldiers arrive.

Near Bannack, General Howard was met by some citizens from Idaho Territory who were fearful that Joseph's band would double back to Idaho over Lemhi Pass and threaten Salmon City. Some sixty Idaho volunteers had formed up under militia colonel George L. Shoup and prepared to meet the Indians in the Lemhi Pass area. However, the Indians took an easter-ly route toward the Corinne Road, which ran north from the railroad at Corinne, UT, through Fort Hall, ID, then past present-day Monida and on to Virginia City, MT.

---

[1] According to the 1870 U.S. Census, Bannack's population had declined to 359, of which 325 were white males, 29 white females, 1 an African American male, 3 Chinese males and 1 Chinese female.

General Howard had believed correctly that the Indians would cross the Corinne Road and head east for Tacher's Pass, located just east of Henry's Lake, and thus enter the Yellowstone Basin. They had a choice of two routes to get there: either by following a trail (present-day Montana Route 509 past Red Rock Lakes to Henry's Lake) that led alongside the north slope of the Centennial Mountains, or by following the stage route that led eastward from Dry Creek Station (approximately thirty miles south of Junction Station near present-day Spencer, ID) along the south side of the Centennial Mountains toward Tacher's Pass. Howard opted to take his main body along the easier but longer southern route, while dispatching Lieutenant August Bacon with forty men along the more direct trail route to Tacher's Pass (present-day Targhee Pass). Bacon was ordered to hold off the Nez Perce if they attempted to cross the pass.[2]

In the meantime, Howard's force had been further augmented by the arrival of fifty-five Montana volunteers under militia captain James F. Callaway. Callaway and his men were arriving from Virginia City.[3] On August 18th the Nez Perce crossed the Corinne Road just south of Dry Creek Station and went into camp on the Camas Meadows, about forty miles west southwest of Henry's Lake. Howard was relatively confident now that the Nez Perce were heading directly for Tacher's Pass, where they would encounter Lieutenant Bacon's small force as Howard pressed them from behind. The next day, August 19th, found Howard's force camped on Camas Meadows. The Indians had moved another fifteen miles toward Henry's Lake and made camp.[4]

Later interviewed in Canada, the Nez Perce exiles reported that after leaving the Big Hole camp their warriors attacked a group consisting of two Chinese males and about six whites with freight wagons and a large number of mules. Some of the Indians obtained whiskey from the captured freight and a drunken brawl ensued, in which one of their best warriors was killed by another of their number. The Indians shot up the group, believed to be the Jim Hayden train, but the exiles had no specific knowledge of the number killed. They did report killing two white men at a remote cabin. General Howard reported that the Nez Perce stole some 250 horses from settlers near Bannack. They did not enter Bannack, but rather briefly

---

[2] This was no small task. Colonel John Gibbon's force of 180 men had nearly been wiped out by the Nez Perce. At best, the lieutenant could stall the Nez Perce advance until Howard could come up from their rear. If Howard was really convinced that the Nez Perce would use Tacher's (Targhee) Pass, he should have pushed a larger force forward with Bacon.

[3] August 25, 1877, (Virginia City) *Madisonian.*

[4] O.O. Howard in Linwood Laughy, *In Pursuit of the Nez Perces:* 165–172.

occupied the area known as Horse Prairie commencing about eight miles south of Bannack.[5]

Perhaps our best insight into the situation around Bannack is provided by the Reverend W.W. Van Orsdel, who was in Bannack on the first Sunday following the Battle of the Big Hole. He wrote:

> On the next Sabbath we were at Bannock [sic], where we held service that evening. Some of the men and nearly all of the women from the surrounding country were there for safety and others came in that night. One young man was wounded in the arm, others had escaped almost miraculously. That night fifteen of us volunteered to go out to Horse Prairie. Melvin Trask was selected as Captain, and before sunrise we were on the move. We had information that some men were killed and others severely wounded at the ranches of Montague, Winters and Mr. Hamilton's. Mrs. Winters was in town. She said she was going with us; we said no, and persuaded her to remain, but when we were about twelve miles out she overtook us. She was a woman of fine form, her long, black hair hanging down her back, mounted on a very fine horse, and revolver buckled on, and she knew how and was not afraid to use it. When we arrived at the ranch, about sixteen miles from Bannock, it was plain to see that there had been trouble there. One of their fine cows was shot in front of the house, feather and straw ticks cut open and their contents emptied in the front yard. I was selected to go with Mrs. Winters into the house. Just as we went into the kitchen there lay a man who had been shot four times. On first sight he had the appearance of her husband. Some thought at this juncture she would faint, but she said she could stand it as well as any of us; that she loved her husband and her home, and the sooner she knew the facts in the case the more reconciled she would be. From there we passed into another room where we found the dead form of Mr. Montague, the partner of Mr. Winters. Everything in the house was upset and broken. The question then came as to where her husband was, and that was the particular object of the search just then. A short distance from the house we found the body of Mr. Smith pierced with five bullets. He left a widow and eight children. In another direction from the house was the body of Mr. Farnsworth, who was killed just before our arrival...During the time we were at the ranch, just across the creek (which was heavily skirted with willows and brush), there was a war party of Indians, from thirty to forty in number, yet they hesitated to

---

[5] Ibid.: 165; Duncan McDonald in ibid.: 264–267.

cross and meet us, for our party had now increased to eighteen men, well armed. Mr. Winters had a very narrow escape from the Indians, having reached Bannock just before our party came in, much to the relief of Mrs. Winters. At the next ranch—Mr. Hamilton's—he, with some others, also made narrow escapes. Mr. Cooper was killed close to his house.[6]

During their movement away from the Big Hole Battlefield, the Nez Perce watched for an opportunity to strike Howard's force. This came on the night of August 19th to August 20th, while Howard was encamped on Camas Meadows, east of Dry Creek Station in the vicinity of present-day Idmen and Kilgore, ID. The Nez Perce decided to strike Howard's encampment and capture his horses. Looking Glass, in tactical command, ordered that the Indians should concentrate on the animals and avoid a fight. He obviously saw much to gain by capturing Howard's animals and thus slowing him down or rendering his force incapable of further pursuit. Furthermore, additional animals only increased both the mobility and wealth of his tribe. As seen in the Bitterroot Valley, horses could be traded with non-combatants, white or Indian, for other much-needed supplies. There was little to be gained by becoming locked into a destructive battle with the troops, possibly costing him additional warriors, if Howard's force, could be immobilized by capturing their means of transportation.

The Indians hit the army camp under cover of darkness and drove off a large number of animals, horses and mules. They did become engaged briefly with Captain Norwood's 2nd Cavalry. Fifty to seventy-five animals were briefly recovered by the troopers but later stampeded toward the Indian camp. Bugler Bernard Brooks was killed and six troopers were wounded. The exiles later claimed that they carried out this attack with 225 warriors, captured approximately one hundred head of horses and one hundred head of mules, and suffered no losses. Chiefs Joseph and Looking Glass opted not to press the fight against Howard's now partially immobilized forces and withdrew toward Tacher's Pass.[7]

Following the attack at Camas Meadows, General Howard continued his pursuit of the Indians. On August 23, 1877, his forces camped at a tributary of the Snake River. This must have been Henry's Fork at a point near present-day Mack's Inn, ID. The following day they exited the forest onto

---

[6] Quoted in Robert Vaughn, *Then and Now:* 201–203.

[7] Howard: 173–177; McDonald: 267–269.

a beautiful plain with Henry's Lake in the distance on their left. The gap to Tacher's Pass (Targhee) lay before them, and smoke from an Indian camp could be seen near the pass. At this moment Howard thought he had the Indians between two forces: his main body and the small forty-man contingent under Lieutenant Bacon that he had earlier ordered to block the pass. Here Howard was to suffer another disappointment. He soon learned that Lieutenant Bacon had not received his earlier dispatches and had withdrawn from the pass, believing that the Indians and Howard had taken a different route. The pass now lay open before the Nez Perce.[8]

On the advice of his quartermaster and surgeon, a frustrated General Howard opted to rest and resupply his men. Leaving them camped near Henry's Lake, he accompanied wagons to the closest Montana settlement, Virginia City, some seventy miles distant, to procure fresh horses and supplies. Howard was relatively certain that the Indians would cross Yellowstone National Park, take the Clark's Fork of the Yellowstone down to the Yellowstone River, and cross to the north bank near present-day Laurel, MT. He therefore ordered two companies to proceed directly to Fort Ellis to procure supplies and take them to the New Crow Agency near the Yellowstone River, some thirty miles upriver of present-day Columbus, MT. He could resupply his force at this meeting place.

After a rough wagon ride, he reported arriving in Virginia City,

> …a mining village planted here in the midst of a wilderness of hills and mountains…Imagine the delight of the traders at this visitation, for shoes, clothes, and blankets we must have. We nearly bought them out. Our jaded cavalry horses were remembered, and a goodly supply of fresh animals were ordered from the most accommodating of ranchers, and I fear also from the shrewdest of jockeys.[9]

Howard stated that his group returned to Henry's Lake by crossing a divide and proceeding up the Gallatin River to another divide and then down to Henry's Lake. He refers to the Gallatin as a tributary of the Yellowstone. Here his geography fails him miserably. It is obvious that he followed the Madison River up to the divide near Henry's Lake. It would have been impossible for him to follow the Gallatin from Virginia City. Furthermore,

---

[8] Howard: 181–182. The topography of Targhee Pass is such that the Nez Perce could have easily engaged Bacon to his front with a small force and passed their main body around his flank with scarcely any delay in their progress. Therefore, Bacon's decision to withdraw prematurely likely did not deprive Howard of a victory at that point on the long march.

[9] Ibid.: 183.

he seemed not to be aware of the fact that the Madison and the Gallatin are two of the three main tributaries of the Missouri! Apparently, the general was relying on others to lead the way back. He arrived back at the Henry's Lake camp with supplies on August 27th after a round-trip of 120 miles. This entire trip was accomplished in only three days. Here he was greeted by dispatches from his superiors admonishing him to press the pursuit.[10]

---

[10] Ibid.

CHAPTER THIRTY-SIX

Gibbon Attempts to Coordinate Movements of Sturgis and Howard; Battle of Canyon Creek, September 13–14, 1877

I N THE MEANTIME, COLONEL JOHN GIBBON HAD TAKEN HIS wounded troops to Deer Lodge for medical care. By August 23rd he had arrived in Helena, where he remained until the 31st, attempting to coordinate the intercept of the Nez Perce by forces under Colonel Samuel Sturgis. On the 23rd he telegraphed Captain D.W. Benham at Fort Ellis:

> Dispatch received. Send word to Genl. Sturgis to push up the Yellowstone as rapidly as possible to Baronettes Bridge. He can take his wagons as far as Gardners River. If he does not meet the Indians before he reaches the bridge he should go on up the Yellowstone till he does meet them. He has a splendid chance now to capture the families and stock whilst the warriors are in front of Howard. Send at once some scouts up the Yellowstone to get information and communicate it to Sturgis.[1]

At this time, General of the Army William T. Sherman was also in Helena and added his endorsement to the dispatch.

The next day, acting on more recent intelligence, Gibbon sent a dispatch to Fort Ellis expressing his fear that Sturgis would reach the bridge too late, unless the Nez Perce halted in Yellowstone National Park. Should intelligence indicate that the Indians were continuing on, scouts should be sent to Sturgis advising him to proceed toward the Crow Agency for an intercept.

---

[1] August 23, 1877, District of Montana Letters and Telegrams Sent and Received, Record Group 393.5, National Archives.

On August 27th, Gibbon sent a cable to Virginia City advising Howard to communicate with Sturgis through Fort Ellis.[2]

In a related matter, Gibbon received word from Captain Charles Rawn, the post commander in Missoula, that a group of Spokane Indians were en route east, presumably a hunting party. On the 27th, Gibbon telegraphed Rawn, "Keep the Spokanes from coming east of Missoula if possible. Tell them in the present unsettled condition of affairs they will be mistaken for hostiles. Reports regarding 'Blackfeet' and 'Gros Ventres' are false." This latter line obviously referred to rumors the other Indian tribes might be opting for war in support of the Nez Perce.

Also on August 27th, Gibbon responded to Lieutenant Gustavus Doane, who commanded a company of 2nd Cavalry and one hundred Crow scouts out of Fort Ellis. We will recall that Colonel Miles had ordered Doane's force into the Judith Gap area to watch for the Nez Perce. "Your letter of 21st sent me from Baker [referring to Camp Baker, later Fort Logan] shows me you know exactly what is required to be done. Proceed to do it, using your force to obtain early information of hostile movements." Gibbon then addressed a concern of many army officers that the Crow Indians might provide aid to the Nez Perce, with whom they had friendly relations. "I do not fear the loyalty of the Crow nation, but individuals may prove traitors. Hence in using them as scouts let them know the penalty for treason and do not hesitate to shoot on the spot any Crows who betrays your movements to the Nez Perce." Gibbon then ordered Doane to get some scouts up the Clark's Fork as soon as possible.[3]

In another cable on the same date, Gibbon informed his division commander, General Phil Sheridan, of his belief that the Nez Perce would head out of the park toward the Wind River in Wyoming and stated, "I will push Sturgis at once up Clark's Fork." On August 30th, Gibbon sent a cable to Sheridan reporting that General Sherman had just departed Helena and disputing a report that Sitting Bull had moved south of the Canadian line. "Major Walsh (Canadian Police) is closely watching the camp and will give us early intelligence of any movement." Gibbon departed for Fort Shaw on August 31st.[4]

To return to Howard's forces: They crossed Tacher's Pass on the trail of the Indians. Once in Yellowstone National Park, they encountered survivors

[2] August 24, 27, 1877, ibid.

[3] August 27, 1877, ibid.

[4] August 27, 30, 1877, ibid.

of a group of tourists whom the Nez Perce had overrun—some tourists were killed and some captured and later released. One member of this party was identified as George F. Cowan, an attorney, and another as Albert Oldham. Chief Joseph later stated that they also captured two additional white men while crossing Yellowstone National Park. One escaped on a stolen horse and the other was released by the Indians. One of these men may have been a former soldier identified by Howard as Irwin. Howard also reported that the Nez Perce attacked four miners in the park, killing three of them, and attacked wagons and robbed stores at Mammoth Falls. Howard discovered too late that Lieutenant Colonel C.C. Gilbert had attempted to link up with him, with two cavalry companies from Fort Ellis. He had come as far as Mammoth Falls but missed Howard's force.[5]

By September 6, 1877, Howard's elements reached Baronet's Bridge, likely the present-day Fishing Bridge. Here Howard reported seeing his first house since leaving Henry's Lake! The bridge had been set on fire by the Indians and severely damaged. On September 9th, General Howard received some good news: A report arrived that Colonel Sturgis had marched his six-company force up the Clark's Fork and was now positioned near Heart Mountain, or "Hart" as Howard spelled it. This would be the Heart Mountain east of Yellowstone National Park and approximately twenty miles north of present-day Cody, WY. From this position Sturgis could block the Nez Perce if they attempted to move down the Clark's Fork of the Yellowstone to its juncture with the Yellowstone River.[6] However, Howard was to be eluded once again. As he emerged from the park on September 10th, he discovered to his disappointment that Sturgis had moved his force farther south toward the Stinking Water drainage (North Fork of the Shoshone), leaving the path open to the Nez Perce. Although later criticized for not remaining at Heart Mountain, Sturgis may have been relying on the information from Gibbon and Sheridan that the Nez Perce would likely head for the Wind River country. Captain Frederick Benteen happened to be serving as one of Sturgis's 7th Cavalry subordinate commanders. On November 17, 1891, some fourteen years later, he would write to Theo W. Goldin:

> I soon learned of the reports that were brought in by the detach-
> ments that had gone out under Lieutenants [Luther R.] Hare and

---

[5] O.O. Howard in Linwood Laughy, *In Pursuit of the Nez Perces:* 183–193; Chief Joseph in Laughy, comp.: 293.

[6] Howard: 260.

> Fuller…I "pumped" Hare, Fuller and the guides (?) and was the
> more convinced; so I went to the General on the march (it being
> then nearly dark) and told him that he was deliberately going away
> from the Indians. He said, "No, there is only one pass through which
> they can get; we will go up the Stinking Water and cut them off."…
> We went up the Stinking Water and crossed the mountain next day
> but found no pass; Sturgis and Major Merrill [Wesley Merritt] both
> telling me during the early forenoon that we were going to have a
> hell of a fight pretty soon. "No," said I, "you'll find an abandoned
> camp, and the Indians gone through the gap left by us.[7]

In another letter to Goldin on September 14, 1895, Benteen was even
more critical of Sturgis:

> Sam D. Sturgis should have been tried by G.C.M. [General Court
> Martial] for Clark's Ford Canyon idiocy. I labored the best part of
> the night we moved from there to get him to go where we knew
> Fuller had seen the Indian camp, but I couldn't phase him. Merrill
> was "working" him then, and from Aug. 10, '61, I knew neither of
> them would fight. They had never lost a Reb or an Indian![8]

This author doubts that Sturgis was a coward. It must also be stated that
Sturgis did not have any specific information regarding General Howard's
location nor was the reverse true. The intelligence received by Howard,
which revealed Sturgis's presence at Heart Mountain, had been the result
of Sturgis sending messengers to warn miners in the park that there was
danger from the Indians. Attempts by messengers from Howard to reach
Sturgis had failed. It is also true that there were several routes the Nez Perce
could have taken in passing through the park.

Sturgis, realizing his error, doubled back and overtook Howard's force
two days later, after it had emerged from the park and entered the upper
Clark's Fork drainage, still on the trail of the Nez Perce. Howard ordered
Sturgis ahead with additional troops from his own force. Sturgis followed
the Nez Perce down the Clark's Fork and crossed the Yellowstone near pres-
ent-day Laurel, MT. On September 13th, Sturgis caught up with the Nez
Perce at Canyon Creek, a few miles north of the Yellowstone River.[9] The
Nez Perce held fast to all approaches of the canyon and then fell back after

---

[7] W.A. Graham, *The Custer Myth:* 191.

[8] Ibid.: 198.

[9] Howard: 197.

dark. Sturgis lost three enlisted men killed, one officer (Captain Thomas H. French) and ten enlisted men wounded. The army claimed sixteen Indians killed and a large number of horses captured. Skirmishes continued the next day as the Indians withdrew north toward the Musselshell River. The army claimed five more Nez Perce killed on the second day of the battle, but had to cease the pursuit because their horses were exhausted. Ninety-three horses had to be abandoned and killed on the march.[10]

---

[10] E.A. Garlington, "History of the Seventh Regiment of Cavalry, Inspector General, U.S.A.": 17.

CHAPTER THIRTY-SEVEN

Colonel Miles Commences Pursuit; Skirmish at Cow Island, September 18, 1877

L
ATE ON SEPTEMBER 17, 1877, COLONEL NELSON MILES received a dispatch from Colonel Samuel D. Sturgis and General O.O. Howard at his headquarters in Fort Keogh. They informed him that their forces had now fallen hopelessly behind the Nez Perce. Miles was requested to mount a force and attempt to head off the Indians at the Missouri River, easily 200 miles distant from Miles's Fort Keogh, before they could cross and flee to Canada. Miles would write, "My command was then 150 miles east of where the Indians had crossed the Yellowstone, and this report was five days old."[1] Miles dispatched couriers to Forts Buford and Peck on the Missouri, ordering supplies to be shipped upriver by steamer to Cow Island for possible future use by the army, in particular General Howard's forces. Miles quickly readied his forces, and by the next morning they were ready to depart from the north bank of the Yellowstone.

> My command consisted of a small detachment of white guides and scouts and thirty Cheyenne Indian allies under the command of Lieutenant M.P. Maus, First United States Infantry; a battalion of Fifth Infantry mounted on captured Sioux ponies; Snyder's, Bennett's, Carter's and Romeyn's companies, Captain Simon Snyder commanding; a battalion of Second United States Cavalry, Tyler's, Jerome's and McClernand's companies, Captain George L. Tyler commanding; a battalion of the Seventh Cavalry, Hale's, Godfrey's and Moylan's companies, Captain Owen Hale commanding; one

---

[1] Nelson A. Miles, *Personal Recollections:* 261–262.

breechloading hotchkiss gun, Sergeant McHugh, Fifth Infantry commanding; the train escort, commanded by Captain D.H. Brotherton, Fifth Infantry, consisting of Company K and a detachment of Company D, Fifth Infantry, with one twelve-pounder Napoleon gun.[2]

One easily discerns that Miles had at his immediate disposal a considerable number of troops resulting from campaigns against the Sioux, particularly in the aftermath of the Custer defeat only fifteen months previous. Compare this to the difficulties faced by Howard, and then Gibbon, in pulling together forces. However, Miles, a very able commander, also employed his forces quickly and aggressively. After sending his scouts out to his front and left, scanning the countryside for signs of the Nez Perce, Miles marched northwest, arriving at the Missouri on September 22nd. Lieutenant Edward J. McClernand would later describe the route of travel: "Our route passed up Sunday Creek, over the divide to the Big Dry, across another divide to Squaw Creek, then to the Missouri."[3] They struck the Missouri at the mouth of the Musselshell River. There they were able to stop a steamer headed downstream, reportedly the last of the season. Miles used it to set Captain Tyler's battalion of 2nd Cavalry across to the north side; he planned to march the remainder of his force upriver along the south bank. Miles wrote:

> This was done for a double purpose. One was that they [Tyler's force] might move along the left bank and prevent the Nez Perces from crossing at any of the ferries above, and the other that they might continue the march to the northwest, where I had been ordered to send a battalion of cavalry to escort General Terry on his peace commission to meet Sitting Bull with the Canadian officers on Canadian soil.[4]

Just as Miles had completed this partial crossing and was preparing to move his forces out, news arrived from three men coming downriver in a boat. They reported that the Nez Perce had crossed the Missouri at Cow Island, some sixty miles upstream. The steamer had already departed, but Miles managed to signal it by cannon fire to return. Miles then ferried all his troops across to the north bank of the Missouri. The wagons were left at this point and pack trains formed for greater mobility and speed.

---

[2] Ibid.: 262–263.

[3] Edward J. McClernand, *On Time for Disaster:* 103–104.

[4] Miles: 264.

Leaving the scene of the Canyon Creek Battle, the Nez Perce had moved northward passing through Judith Gap. As they approached Cow Island, approximately twenty-five miles northeast of present-day Winifred, MT, they encountered a small detail of Company B, 7th Infantry, and some citizen volunteers. The following quote is from the September 1877 Post Return for Fort Shaw:

> Eight men of this company [Company B] have been stationed at Cow Island since Aug 18 guarding Government Stores, on the 28th of Sept this party which had in the meantime been increased to twelve enlisted men (all belonging to Co B) joined by 4 citizens (2 were discharged soldiers of Co B) were attacked by the hostile Nez Perce Indians, who charged seven times on their rifle pits and were repulsed. Two citizens seriously wounded. (Walter & Weimar). The Indians burned 30 tons of Government freight & 20 tons belonging to citizens and then left in the direction of the pass between Bear Paw and Little Rocky Mountains. Private Byron Martin Co B while in route from Dauphin Rapids to Cow Island was killed by Indians and buried one mile above Cow Island.[5]

Meanwhile Company F, 7th Infantry, had arrived back at Fort Benton on September 18th, returning from the Battle of the Big Hole. On September 21st, Major Guido Ilges marched toward Cow Island with Company F and twenty citizen volunteers. He encountered the Nez Perce and had one citizen killed and one horse disabled.[6] After this brief engagement, Major Guido Ilges continued to shadow the Nez Perce after their crossing at Cow Island, providing intelligence on their movements to Colonel Miles. On the 29th, Miles's force struck the Nez Perce trail on the north side of the Missouri.

> That night I received despatches from General Howard, stating that he had turned his cavalry back to Idaho, and was going to move his infantry down the Missouri River, leaving the battalion of Colonel Sturgis, six troops of the Seventh Cavalry on the Missouri River. This made it clear that whatever encounters we might now have with the Nez Perces we were entirely beyond support.[7]

---

[5] September 1877 Fort Shaw Post Return, Records of the Adjutant General's Office, ca 1775–ca. 1928, Record Group 94, National Archives.

[6] September 1877 Fort Benton Post Return.

[7] Miles: 266–267.

CHAPTER THIRTY-EIGHT

Miles Overtakes the Nez Perce; The Battle of Snake Creek, September 30 to October 5, 1877; Joseph Surrenders; White Bird Escapes to Canada

O N SEPTEMBER 30, GENERAL NELSON MILES'S TROOPS resumed pursuit of the Nez Perce, north of the Missouri River, at daylight. Later that morning, the Nez Perce camp was spotted. Miles described the reaction of his Cheyenne allies:

> Suddenly one of these advance scouts, a young warrior, was seen galloping at full speed back over the prairie. He said something in Sioux or Cheyenne to the Indians as he passed them, and it was evident that he had brought information of the discovery of the Nez Perce camp. Then an almost instantaneous transformation scene was enacted by these savages; hats, coats, leggins, shirts, blankets, saddles and bridles were quickly thrown into one great heap in a ravine or "cash" [cache] as the Indians call it. A lariat was placed over the neck of each war pony, with a double knot around his under jaw…They appeared perfectly wild with delight, and as unlike what they had seemed twenty minutes before as two scenes of a drama.[1]

The Nez Perce had camped along Snake Creek about forty miles from the Canadian border. The exiles would later report that Chief Looking Glass no longer felt any threat from the army. Their camp lay along the creek bottom in a north-south direction on the east bank of the creek. Their horse herd was grazing to the west of the creek. The Indians had either outfought or outdistanced every known threat, including the forces of Howard, Colonel John

---

[1] Nelson A. Miles, *Personal Recollections:* 267–268.

Gibbon and Colonel Samuel Sturgis. The military contingent encountered at Cow Island had been very small. The Indians were unaware that General Miles was coming on fast with a force in excess of ten companies, stronger than any they had before encountered. Looking Glass was very familiar with Montana Territory, as a result of numerous buffalo hunting expeditions undertaken by the Nez Perce in preceding years. He may not have been aware, however, of the existence of Fort Keogh, established the previous summer, and Fort Custer, under construction at the time. In the short period of one year, an area formerly seldom reached by the U.S. Army was now home to a strong contingent of troops. It is possible that Looking Glass had no knowledge of these new posts, or at the very least of the strong forces they contained.

Colonel Miles, approaching from the south, ordered the three companies of the 2nd Cavalry under Captain George L. Tyler to sweep to the left and capture or drive off the horse herd. Tyler was eagerly assisted in this effort by the Indian allies, who would not miss a chance to capture horses! Captain Owen Hale was ordered to charge straight into the village with his three companies of the 7th Cavalry. Captain Simon Snyder's four companies of mounted 5th Infantry troops followed hard on Captain Hale's heels and swept a little to his left. Miles would later write:

> The tramp of at least six hundred horses over the prairie fairly shook the ground, and, although a complete surprise to the Indians in the main, it must have given them a few minutes' notice, for as the troops charged against the village the Indians open a hot fire on upon them. This momentarily checked the advance of the Seventh Cavalry, which fell back, but only for a short distance and quickly rallied again and charged forward at a gallop, driving that portion of the camp of the Indians before it. At the same time the battalion of the Fifth Infantry under Captain Snyder charged forward up to the very edge of the valley in which the Indian camp was located, threw themselves upon the ground, holding the lariats of their ponies in their left hands, and opened a deadly fire with their long range rifles upon the enemy with telling effect. The tactics were somewhat in Indian fashion, and most effective, as they presented a small target when lying or kneeling upon the ground, and their ponies were so accustomed to the din and noise of the Indian camp, the buffalo chase and the Indian habits generally, that they stood quietly behind their riders, many of them putting their heads down to nibble the green grass upon which they were standing... As the battalion of 2nd Cavalry swept down the valley they became somewhat

separated; Captain Tyler captured some three hundred of the ponies; Lieutenant [Lovell H.] Jerome, another large bunch; and Lieutenant McClernand, who had swept on still further, finally secured upward of three hundred more some three or four miles down the valley.[2]

Nez Perce marksmanship was to prove very telling once again. The 7th Cavalry lost eighteen enlisted men and two officers killed, including Captain Owen Hale, and thirty-one enlisted men wounded—all in the first day of a battle that would later become a five-day siege. "Captain Carter [5th Infantry] in one charge had thirty-five percent of his men placed hors de combat [put out of action, disabled] …"[3] Miles's force, in sharp fighting with considerable losses, succeeded in surrounding the camp and capturing most of the horse herd. By the second day, snow covered the ground and a siege had set in. Miles was concerned that Sitting Bull, believed to have a force of 2,000 warriors just north of the boundary in Canada, might come to the assistance of the Nez Perce. Miles sent couriers to Howard notifying him of his position and to Sturgis, still on the Missouri one hundred miles south, ordering him to come up as soon as possible. Negotiations began with Chief Joseph for surrender terms. General Howard arrived on the evening of October 4th, escorted by twelve men. The next day Chief Joseph surrendered with over 400 Indians. "From where the sun now stands, I fight no more against the white man."[4]

Mr. Robert Ege, in his book *After the Little Bighorn: Battle of Snake Creek, Montana Territory, September 30 to October 5, 1877,* includes a report on that part of the battle involving the 7th Cavalry. Captain Myles Moylan, commanding Company A of the 7th Cavalry during the action, was ordered almost a year after the battle to report on the attack, up to the point when he was wounded and taken from the field. The battalion commander, Captain Owen Hale, had been killed in action on the first day of the battle. The report, submitted on August 16, 1878, at Camp J.G. Sturgis, Dakota Territory, is quoted from the time of the sighting of the Nez Perce camp:

> …The command was immediately given for the column to take the trot, and subsequently the gallop was taken up. About this time an order was brought to me from Captain Hale, commanding battalion, that the Seventh Cavalry would, by order of Colonel Miles, charge the village mounted with pistols. After passing over

---

[2] Ibid.: 271–273.

[3] Ibid.: 272.

[4] Ibid.: 275. For a detailed description of the battle and the battlefield terrain, the author recommends Robert J. Ege's *After the Little Bighorn.*

a divide which separated us from the Indian village, the battalion was formed in line about 1½ miles from the village. Company K on the right [commanded by Captain Hale], Company D in the center [commanded by Captain Edward S. Godfrey], Company A on the left [commanded by Captain Moylan]. The line being formed, the battalion moved forward at the trot, then the gallop and the charge. During the movement to the front in line, Company K, under Captain Hale, diverged to the right and struck at the Indians almost at right angles to the direction which Companies A and D charged. Company K struck the Indians first and was repulsed with some loss. The Company retired to a distance of about 250 or 300 yards, dismounted and deployed as skirmishers. After repulsing Company K, the Indians turned their attention to the other two Companies (A and D), which charged in front. These two Companies charged up to within twenty yards of a line of Indians that was concealed behind a high bank which overlooked their village (the village being situated in a deep ravine through which Snake Creek ran), and owing to the fact that this bank was at the point charged by the companies almost perpendicular, they could not dislodge the Indians, neither could they charge through them, owing to the nature of the ground. Taking in the situation at once and seeing the hoplessness [sic] of being able to do anything at this point mounted, I gave the order for the Companies to fall back [Moylan was the senior Captain of Companies A and D]; the movement was executed by "fours left about." In the execution of this movement some confusion occurred for the very good reason that the men were under a heavy fire from the Indians and that a large majority of them had never been under fire before, being mostly all recruits. [After the heavy loss at Little Bighorn just a little over fifteen months prior, a considerable number of replacements had been necessary.] The loss of the Companies in the action thus far was not so great as might have been expected for the reason that a heavy depression in the ground between them and the Indians protected them somewhat, the Indians over-shooting them. The movement was executed, however, and the Companies reformed on the right of the line occupied by the Fifth Infantry, some 200 or 300 yards to the rear. The loss thus far in Companies A and D was three men killed and four wounded. During the movement to the rear, Captain Godfrey, who was riding in rear of this Company and watching the Indians, had his horse killed under him. The fall of the horse was so sudden that Godfrey was thrown heavily to the ground, falling upon his shoulder and was partially stunned for a moment. Captain Godfrey would most certainly have lost his life at this time, as the Indians were advancing in his direction, but for the gallant conduct of Trumpeter Thomas Herwood, Company D, Seventh Cavalry, who, seeing Captain Godfrey's danger, separated himself from his Company and rode between where Captain Godfrey was lying and the Indians, thereby drawing the attention of the Indians to himself till Captain Godfrey was sufficiently recovered from the effects of his fall to get upon his feet and join his Company. In his gallant attempt to save his officer, Trumpeter Herwood was wounded through the body, and, I believe, since discharged from the service on Surgeon's Certificate of Disability.

An order was at the time received from Colonel Miles to dismount the Companies and that they be deployed to the right and make connection with Company K, that Company at this time being severly [sic] handled by the Indians. The Indians, not being particularly engaged at any other point, concentrated most of their force upon it and succeeded in driving back its skirmish line, also in driving the horse holders who were dismounted, from their lead horses. Having thus far been successful in driving the men away from their horses, the Indians attempted to lead into their village several of the horses of Company K, and were only prevented from accomplishing their purpose by the rapid advance of Companies A and D on foot at the double time. It was during this movement that Companies A and D suffered their heaviest loss. The Indians poured heavy cross fire into them as they advanced, killing and wounding a great many of the men. It was in this advance that Captain Godfrey was wounded, he having mounted another horse, was gallantly cheering on his men to the assistance of their comrades of Company K. Being mounted, he was a conspicuous mark for the Indians to shoot at.

It is but proper that I should here mention the gallantry and coolness of Captain Godfrey throughout the action up to the time of his being wounded and taken from the field. His conduct was brave, cool and soldierly throughout and added very materially to the success of the movement of the Companies to the assistance of Captain Hale's Company. The connection with Company K was made with considerable loss. Having established my line I reported to Captain Hale for further instructions and was in the act of receiving orders from him when I was shot through the upper part of the right thigh and had to be taken from the field. Farther than this I have no personal knowledge of the part taken by the Companies of the Seventh Cavalry in action...[5]

[5] Quoted in Ege, *After the Little Bighorn*: 5–7.

The number of Nez Perce taken prisoner totaled, per the War Department as of December 4, 1877, 431 individuals—79 men, 178 women and 174 children.[6] There were doubtless a few more taken prisoner, for Colonel Miles reported that some wounded Nez Perce died en route back to Fort Keogh.

> Several of our wounded died on the way before reaching the Missouri and had to be buried beside the trail. We did the same for the Indian wounded who expired along the way…Far from his loved ones, far from home, the wounded soldier, enduring while he lives intense pain, finally offers up his precious life as a sacrifice to duty and to his country. Equally melancholy were the scenes around the burial place of some Indian warrior who had been considered a pillar of his tribe and his race, the entire Indian camp enumerating his virtues, praising his prowess, chanting his requiem and bewailing his loss.[7]

Miles reported twenty-six Nez Perce killed and forty-six wounded.[8] Among those killed were Chief Looking Glass, Chief Too-hul-hul-sote and Joseph's brother, Ollicut. Although this was the final major engagement between the U.S. Army and the non-treaty Nez Perce, a considerable number of warriors under Chief White Bird managed to escape during the battle and make it into Canada. According to the Nez Perce exiles, White Bird escaped with 103 warriors, 60 women, 8 children and some 200 head of horses. They also reported that after

> … White Bird made his escape from the U.S. troops at Bear Paw and before he reached Sitting Bull's camp [north of the Canadian border], he lost seven warriors at the hands of the Assiniboines and Gros Ventres. One of those killed was Umti-lilp-cown [also U-em-till-lilp-cown], the third and last of the Nez Perces who had committed the murders in Idaho which brought on the war.[9]

Miles later wrote that Sitting Bull's Sioux, upon receiving word of the battle at Snake Creek, moved their camp forty miles farther back into Canada, rather than attempt to aid the Nez Perce.[10]

---

6 J.P. Dunn, Jr. *Massacres of the Mountains:* 568.

7 Miles: 277.

8 Ibid.: 275.

9 Duncan McDonald, in Linwood Laughy, *In Pursuit of the Nez Perces:* 271–272.

10 Miles: 273–274.

Returning southward to the Missouri River, the army shipped most of its surviving wounded downriver on the steamer that had, per Miles's earlier request, brought supplies upriver. Miles provided a vivid description of their movement across the prairie toward Fort Keogh:

> Crossing the Missouri the march was continued for several days over the trail we had made in coming up, until we reached the Yellowstone. As the force moved across the rolling prairie it appeared like a great caravan. There were three battalions of well-equipped, hardy, resolute soldiers, with artillery, besides upward of four hundred prisoners; and on the opposite flank, some distance away, were driven over six hundred of the captured stock, while in the rear were the travois and ambulances, bearing the wounded, followed by the pack trains and wagon trains, and all covered by advance guards, flankers, and rear guards.[11]

On arrival at Fort Keogh, Miles rewarded his Indian allies by giving them 150 of the best of the Nez Perce horses.[12] It is presumed that the government kept the remaining horses for future use or sale. Chief Joseph and his people were taken downriver to Fort Leavenworth, KS. In June 1879, they were moved onto the Ponce Agency on the Salt Fork of the Arkansas River. There they suffered greatly from the unfamiliar climate and surroundings. By 1881, this group numbered only 328 out of the original 431 captured. By late 1884, most of them were allowed to return to the Lapwai Reservation in Idaho; Chief Joseph, however, and a smaller number were sent to the Colville Agency in Washington Territory. By this time their numbers had dwindled down to 268 souls.[13]

The exiles with White Bird reached Sitting Bull's camp in Canada and remained there. By the following summer they had become disaffected with their Sioux hosts, and most attempted to return home to Idaho in small groups. This resulted in some additional theft and bloodshed, whether out of hatred for the whites or out of necessity for survival—or both. Those incidents occurring in Montana Territory are described in the next chapter.

---

[11] Ibid.: 277.

[12] Ibid.

[13] Dunn: 569–575.

Colonel Miles Intercepts Nez Perce

The Nez Perce come down Clark's Fork of the Yellowstone pursued by Sturgis; Sturgis engages them on 9/13 at Canyon Creek but the Nez Perce manage to outdistance him. Miles begins pursuit from Fort Keogh on 9/18. The Nez Perce skirmish with outpost at Cow Island on 9/18. Miles engages at Snake Creek on 9/30. Joseph surrenders 10/5. White Bird and approximately 170 Nez Perce escape to Canada.

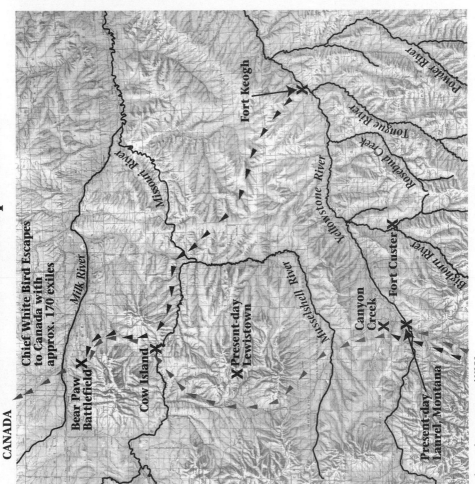

Background map courtesy of USGS

CHAPTER THIRTY-NINE

Events of 1878:
The Nez Perce Exiles; Hostilities with the Bannocks; Colonel Gibbon and 7th Infantry Transfer out of Montana

I N FEBRUARY 1878, COLONEL JOHN GIBBON AT FORT SHAW notified the army's Department of Dakota of an urgent need to cut through bureaucratic red tape and prevent starvation among the Assiniboines.

> Captain Williams reports from Belknap on the 6th that something should be done for the Assiniboines who are on the verge of starvation and urged by the Sioux to go to war. I should order the Commanding Officer of Fort Benton to issue one month's rations of flour and beef. (between twenty and thirty thousand rations) but am restrained by the lack of authority required in Par. 1. G.O. 78 A.G.O. 73 republished in G.O. 100 last year. What should I do? It is a matter of some importance and requires quick action.[1]

The outcome of this request is not known.

The year 1878 resulted in some lesser combat operations with hostiles. In May 1878, operating out of Camp Baker, since renamed Fort Logan in honor of fallen Captain William Logan, Captain Clift engaged a band of hostile Indians at the head of White's Gulch, killing at least one Indian. The identity of the tribe was not given.[2]

---

[1] February 9, 1878, District of Montana Letters and Telegrams Sent and Received, Department of Dakota, Record Group 393.5, National Archives.

[2] May 20, 1878, Fort Logan Letters Sent and Received, Records of Posts, Continental Army Command 1820–1920, Record Group 393.7, National Archives.

By the summer of 1878, telegraph lines had been constructed from Bismarck to Fort Keogh, and from Fort Keogh on to Fort Ellis. A line had also been constructed southeast from Fort Keogh to Deadwood, Dakota Territory. Relatively rapid communication between these posts and the remainder of the nation was now ensured. It is of interest that the soldiers utilized captured Indian ponies hauling travois, loaded with telegraph poles, to construct the lines. Obviously, these were not the large, heavy telephone or electric line poles with which we are familiar today, but more like the smaller, lighter standard lodge pole we nowadays see in fence construction.

During the summer of 1878, the 7th Infantry Regiment and its commander, Colonel John Gibbon, were transferred out of the District of Montana. The 7th was replaced by the 3rd Infantry Regiment commanded by Colonel John R. Brooke. An ever-watchful eye was kept on Sitting Bull. A site for a new post, Fort Assinniboine on the Milk River, was selected and construction commenced. This new post was located about six miles southwest of present-day Havre, MT, on present-day U.S. Highway 87.

Also during the summer of 1878, a small band of hostile Bannocks fled into Montana from Idaho Territory, where they had been on the warpath. Receiving intelligence that this band was headed into the Yellowstone country, Colonel Nelson Miles assembled a seventy-five-man force and moved to intercept them. Since it was believed they would cross into the Yellowstone basin at Boulder Pass or Clark's Fork Pass, Miles split his small force, sending Lieutenant Bailey with forty men to cover Boulder Pass. Colonel Miles then moved with his thirty-five men to Clark's Fork Pass, recruiting some Crow scouts along the way. The Bannocks were located in Clark's Fork Pass and surprised in their camp. During the engagement, eleven warriors were killed and a large number wounded, and 250 ponies were captured, along with the entire Indian camp. The army lost several killed, including Captain Andrew S. Bennett of the 5th Infantry. At least one Crow scout was killed. Also killed was an interpreter, whom Miles referred to as Rock. He had provided an invaluable service in scouting the camp prior to the attack.[3]

On July 20, 1878, the post commander at Fort Ellis forwarded a letter to Captain Edward Ball, then in charge of a contingent of troops temporarily assigned to Horse Prairie in the area of present-day Grant, MT. He had received reports that a band of Nez Perce, size unknown, was returning from Canada. They were in possession of seventy-five horses. They had

---

[3] Nelson A. Miles, *Personal Recollections:* 294–300.

reportedly killed John Worsham and Gus Cuttle on the Dearborn River, John Lynch and John Meyers on Deep Creek, and William Joyce and Amos Elliot on Rock Creek[4] as well as Dutch John on Elk Creek. The Indians were believed to be heading for the Horse Prairie area, and the captain was ordered to intercept them.[5] According to Leeson's *The History of Montana*, Lynch and Myers were killed on July 8th in their cabin at Beartown (vicinity of present-day Drummond) and Amos Elliot, William Elliot and Jack Hayes were killed on July 12th at Rock Creek near Philipsburg.[6]

Captain Ball was not able to locate and engage these hostile Nez Perce. Lieutenant George D. Wallace, however, commanding a small mounted detachment of thirteen men, one guide and two citizens, struck their trail while scouting the passes out of Fort Missoula. He managed to overtake the Nez Perce band and engage them on July 25, 1878, on the North Fork of the Clearwater (across the territorial boundary in present-day Idaho), killing six and wounding three. Lieutenant Wallace's force suffered no casualties. Deer Lodge's *New Northwest* reported, on August 2, 1878, that the band consisted of seventeen men and two women. Among the Indians killed was their chief identified as Ta-ba-bor.[7]

In October 1878, the post commander at Fort Logan reported a dispute between local ranchers and members of the Flathead tribe out on a buffalo hunt. These Indians were led by Chief Charlo. The commander advised that forty horses had been seized at Sherman's ranch some five miles east of "Hot Sulphur Springs." The horses were claimed by both the whites and the Indians. Captain Richard Comba later reported that the horses were believed to belong to the Flatheads.[8] The author was unable to determine the results of the dispute. Since no hostilities were reported, it apparently was resolved without armed conflict.

There is further evidence that liaison between the Montana Military District and the Canadian Mounted Police continued during the command of Colonel John R. Brooke. The following message was sent from Fort Shaw to St. Paul on December 10, 1878. It is not known if this movement was

---

[4] A third man, one Mr. Jones, managed to escape, according to the (Deer Lodge, M.T.) *New Northwest*, July 19, 1878.

[5] July 20, 1878, Fort Ellis Letters and Telegrams Sent and Received, Records of Posts, Continental Army Command 1820–1920, Record Group 393.7, National Archives.

[6] Michael A. Leeson, *The History of Montana*: 180.

[7] August 2, 1878, *New Northwest*.

[8] October 23, 29, 1878, Fort Logan Letters Sent and Received, Records of Posts, Continental Army Command 1820–1920, Record Group 393.7, National Archives.

verified or any further action resulted. However, a watchful eye was maintained on the movements of the Sioux, in particular Sitting Bull.

> A letter from Colonel [Atcheson G.] Irvine, Commanding Fort Walsh, dated Dec. 1st, says a rumor has reached him within a few days, that two Sioux arrived at the camp of the American Sioux now in British Territory and stated they had left a large camp, about five hundred lodges on Powder River, who intend crossing the Missouri when it freezes. They expect to reach British Territory in about thirty days. Colonel Irvine does not vouch for this, but considers it advisable to communicate letter by mail.[9]

---

[9] December 10, 1878, Fort Shaw Letters and Telegrams Sent and Received, Records of Posts, Continental Army Command 1820–1920, Record Group 393.7, National Archives.

CHAPTER FORTY

Events of 1879:
Sitting Bull Ventures South from Canada into Montana; Engagement at French Creek

THE WINTER OF 1878–1879 PASSED PEACEFULLY IN THE Yellowstone country, with Sitting Bull and his hostiles remaining north of the Canadian line and encamped on Mushroom Creek in the Woody Mountains area. Here they were closely watched by Major James M. Walsh and his small contingent of Northwest Mounted Police. From time to time, small raiding and hunting parties from the Sioux camp would venture across the line, but were usually driven back or captured. For example, in April 1879 Lieutenant Loder, operating out of Fort Logan with eighteen enlisted men, encountered a band of hostile Sioux on Careless Creek in the Musselshell River country. The entire band was killed, with no casualties to the soldiers. Also in late June or early July of 1879, settlers clashed with a band of Indians (tribe unidentified) on Sixteen Mile Creek, killing all but one, who escaped.[1] One notes that most Indian bands were now faring badly in clashes with the whites, as compared to clashes five to ten years earlier. This might indicate that these warriors and, perhaps, their animals were now often in a worn-out and destitute condition. Game was getting scarce, and cattle ranching was much more extensive.

Settlement of the Yellowstone Valley was occurring at a rapid pace, but settlers along the Missouri and Milk rivers were constantly in danger of raid forays south by Sitting Bull's followers. At the time of his flight to Canada, Sitting Bull had only some 400 followers, but by the summer of 1879 this

---

[1] April 17, July 3, 1879, Fort Logan Letters Sent and Received, Records of Posts, Continental Army Command 1820–1920, Record Group 393.7, National Archives.

number, augmented by disaffected U.S. agency Indians, had risen to about 2,000.[2] During the summer of 1879, intelligence was received that Sitting Bull had moved south of the line onto Frenchman's Creek, a tributary of the Milk River. In July, Colonel Nelson Miles marched his command north to the Missouri at Fort Peck. On July 15th, the command marched from Fort Peck up the right bank of the Milk River and made camp on Box Elder Creek. Miles made use of a heliostat station that he had set up on Tiger Butte, south of present-day Glasgow, MT. It was described by John Finerty as "... the same kind of apparatus used by the English in Afghanistan and Zululand. It is an idea borrowed from the Indians of both hemispheres, and is simply a method of telegraphing information by reflections of the sun in small mirrors."[3]

As Miles moved up the Milk River, his advance guard under Lieutenant W.P. Clark, 2nd Cavalry, surprised a band of Sioux warriors on Beaver Creek. He pursued them several miles to where they were joined by the main band under Sitting Bull. Upon sighting the hostiles, Clark had sent a courier back to notify Miles of the engagement, but he now became hard pressed by the reinforced hostiles. Upon arrival of the urgent dispatch from Clark, Miles moved his command rapidly forward. Lieutenant Edward McClernand describe the movement:

> For some miles broken hills caused a little delay, increased sligtly [sic] by two pieces of artillery with us. However, the men realizing their importance quickly pulled them out of ravines no matter how deep they were. One of these pieces was a Hotchkiss. A second courier arrived, his pony panting and covered with foam, bearing a message from Clark saying that he was nearly surrounded and asking for speedy help. We had now reached smooth ground. Three troops were deployed as skirmishers. In the rear of this line were three more in column of fours, and still further back were four companies of mounted infantry, also in fours. In this order we galloped [or trotted] about 12 miles.[4]

Upon the arrival of the main force, the Sioux retreated rapidly across the Milk River, leaving behind large quantities of buffalo meat and other supplies. Lieutenant Clark lost two killed and several wounded.[5] The Hotchkiss

---

[2] Nelson A. Miles, *Personal Recollections:* 306.

[3] John Finerty, *War Path and Bivouac:* 333.

[4] Edward J. McClernand, *On Time for Disaster:* 109.

[5] Ibid.: 110.

gun was deployed and had a considerable demoralizing effect on the Sioux. Joseph Finerty wrote:

> The new Hotchkiss revolver is a most remarkable piece of ordnance. It has five barrels of small diameter, and is fed by a kind of "hopper" at the left side of the breech. It can fling shell or shot with remarkable accuracy, to a great distance…and…proved very efficient agent of panic, if not of destruction. Our Indians [Indian scouts] regarded the weapon with awe, and did not care to be close when it was fired with rapidity. With all the extra trappings, this excellent canon does not weigh more than 3,500 pounds, and, like the single-barreled Hotchkiss, can be hauled along and handled without any particular embarrassment. Its range is 2,500 yards…Had Custer had this arm at the Little Bighorn, the issue of that disastrous day might have been reversed…I much doubt whether a better arm, for light field service in a difficult country, than the Hotchkiss gun could be devised.[6]

The Sioux continued their retreat on into the British Territories (Canada). Miles would maintain his force along the border for several weeks. While there, he rounded up a large number of Red River half-breeds whom he believed were supplying Sitting Bull with weapons. The reader will recall the earlier complaints of the Assiniboine Indians directed to General Isaac Stevens regarding the activities of the "Red River hunters." We will also recall Captain G.L. Browning's Milk River expedition in the autumn of 1871. Colonel Miles provided an excellent description of the Red River hunters:

> They were a very singular people in their mode of living. They had large bodies of strong, hardy, but small horses. They lived in tents and their principal mode of transportation was by what was known as the "Red River cart." A man with a knife and an axe could construct a cart and a harness, as there was no particle of iron used in either. Rawhide was occasionally used for binding them together and sometimes in the place of tires. The harness was entirely of rawhide. With this means of transportation they could carry from a thousand to fifteen hundred pounds over the prairies and when not heavily loaded the horses could, with these carts, swim any river, the carts having so much dry wood about them that they were very buoyant.[7]

---

[6] Finerty: 330–331, 338.

[7] Miles: 309–310.

Colonel Miles ordered Major Eugene Baker and his command of four companies of the 2nd Cavalry to round up the Red River half-breeds.[8] This was accomplished in late July 1879, with the troops rounding up about 1,000 of these people along with their horses and other supplies, including about 800 carts. Miles had them sent out of the area, hoping to deprive Sitting Bull of significant trading partners, i.e. a source of weapons and ammunition.[9]

While at the border, Colonel Miles also met with Major Walsh of the Northwest Mounted Police, whose detachment monitored the activities of Sitting Bull's hostiles then encamped in the Northwest Territory (in present-day Saskatchewan, on Mushroom Creek near the Woody Mountains). The Canadians were unwilling hosts to Sitting Bull's hostiles; nevertheless, peaceful relations existed between the Indians and Canadian authorities. Sitting Bull reserved his hatred for Americans. He also valued his good relations with the Canadian police force. Duncan McDonald reported in the *New Northwest* on August 9, 1878, that Sitting Bull had strongly advised the exiled Nez Perce Chief White Bird, whose band then resided among the exiled Sioux, not to allow his men to cross the line into the United States but to do as the Canadian police wished.[10]

Correspondent John Finerty, who had accompanied Miles's forces north to the border, was invited by Major Walsh to visit Sitting Bull's camp, and he accepted the invitation. He later described the camp as containing, as of late July 1879, nearly 1,100 lodges amounting to about 2,500 fighting men. "Arms and ammunition were plentiful, but food of any kind was scarce."[11] Meat was already in short supply, with the buffalo quickly disappearing from the plains. It was only a matter of time before starvation would force the surrender of those hostiles still attempting to live their old and free lifestyle.

---

[8] Finerty: 350. This was the same Major Baker, once again with four companies of the 2nd Cavalry, who had commanded the attack on the Piegans on January 23, 1870.

[9] Miles: 310.

[10] (Deer Lodge, M.T.) *New Northwest*, August 9, 1878.

[11] Finerty: 371.

CHAPTER FORTY-ONE

Events of 1880–1881:
Hostile Bands Face Starvation;
Miles Transferred out of Montana;
Sitting Bull Surrenders, July 19, 1881

D URING THE FOLLOWING WINTER OF 1879–1880, SMALL groups of Sioux hunters and raiders would venture south into Montana, but were usually driven back or captured by the constantly patrolling troopers. In February 1880, one such raiding party was discovered south of the Yellowstone River and pinned down by Sergeant Glover and troopers under his command. Upon the arrival of reinforcements under Captain Simon Snyder, a number of Sioux were captured. In late March and early April, a party of Sioux raided the Fort Custer military reservation, capturing some fifty horses. They were pursued over one hundred miles by Captain Huggins and troopers under his command. The captain eventually engaged them at the head of O'Fallon Creek on April 1, 1880. One trooper was killed, one Indian wounded and five Indians captured.[1] Miles then sent a message to Sitting Bull that the captured Sioux would be held until the hostile Sioux came in and surrendered.

A delegation of eight warriors later arrived at Fort Keogh to discuss terms of surrender. While there, they were allowed to use a new telephone system recently installed at Fort Keogh (for communication between the buildings only), thus being impressed with the white man's prowess. They returned north, urging the surrender of the hostiles. Eventually, some 2,000 Sioux came into Fort Keogh led by Chiefs "...Broad Trail, Spotted Eagle, Kicking Bear, Rain-in-the-Face and others."[2] This surrender, likely brought

---

[1] Nelson A. Miles, *Personal Recollections:* 310–316.

[2] Ibid.: 317–318.

about more by hunger than white technology, greatly eroded Sitting Bull's prestige and power.

In November 1880, Colonel Miles received a promotion to brigadier general commanding the Department of the Columbia. He departed Fort Keogh on November 20, 1880. Among the few remaining hostiles, hunger eventually became greater than the desire to roam free. On April 11, 1881, Chief Low Dog from Sitting Bull's camp in Canada surrendered with 185 men, women and children at Fort Buford, Dakota Territory.[3] He was followed by Sitting Bull with the remainder of his camp: 187 men, women and children on July 19, 1881. Arriving from his camp at Woody Mountain in the British Possessions, Sitting Bull also surrendered all arms and ponies to the U.S. Army.[4] The buffalo were now too few, even in Canada, to sustain free-roaming bands of Indians, both American and Canadian. By now, with few exceptions, the era of white-Indian hostilities on the soil of Montana Territory had come to an end, although a few lesser clashes would occur during the 1880's.

---

[3] April 1881, Fort Buford Post Returns, Records of the Adjutant General's Office, ca. 1775–ca. 1928, Record Group 94, National Archives.

[4] July 1881 Fort Buford Post Return.

Epilogue

T HE CESSATION OF HOSTILE INDIAN ACTIVITIES IN THE
eastern portion of Montana Territory had, commencing with the
arrival there of a substantial military presence in late 1876 and 1877,
led to a rapid influx of cattle ranchers all in search of choice range land. In
the spring of 1880, Granville Stuart traveled throughout the eastern portion of the territory searching for good range land for a cattle company he
and other partners had formed. After casting a wistful eye at the Bighorn
River country, Stuart noted that it "…would be ideal cattle range but it is on
the Crow reservation consequently out of the question."[1] Stuart eventually
settled on range land east and north of present-day Lewistown on Ford's
Creek. Stuart complained bitterly of the government policy of setting

> … apart for each [Indian] tribe enough of the choicest land to make
> a state…upon which the white man in search of homes may not put
> his foot, or even allow his domestic animals to feed upon the grasses
> which there grow up and decay without benefit to anyone, but the
> Indian who makes no use of this vast domain is allowed to leave at
> his own sweet will, and stay away for so long as he pleases and this he
> does for the well-known purpose of stealing the white men's horses,
> eating his cattle and robbing his cabin."[2]

One can easily deduce from this quote that many other ranchers no

---

[1] Granville Stuart, *Forty Years on the Frontier*, Vol. II: 122.

[2] Stuart, ibid.: 151.

doubt shared Stuart's point of view. Meanwhile the Indians, now all forced to make their homes on the reservations, still attempted to follow their old ways by going out on the hunt. By the fall of 1883, however, the buffalo had disappeared, to be replaced by range cattle. Indian parties away from the reservations, out on the hunt, were often forced to kill range cattle or starve. Stuart wrote, "Between the months of November 1880, and April 1881, three thousand head of cattle were wantonly butchered by Indians in Choteau and Meagher counties..."[3] This brought the Indians into conflict with ranchers trying to protect their property. One can well imagine that had the military not been present in force, ranchers may have pushed the Indians off their reservations, resulting in their starvation and, possibly, complete extermination.

Frontier Montana history now entered a period in which the presence of the U.S. Army provided direct and indirect protection to the Indian tribes in the territory by safeguarding and escorting reservation supplies and maintaining a watchful eye for potential white-Indian problems.[4] These were the years between the general cessation of hostilities and the gradual growth of public awareness among white Montana residents of the plight of the Indians in the state. This was a time of harsh transition for the Montana Indian tribes—away from the life of the hunt to a life of near total dependence on the white man for sustenance. Evidence of increased white sensitivity to the plight of the local Indians is revealed in articles by Fort Benton's newspaper, the *River Press*. During 1882, the *River Press* frequently published articles on a crisis faced by the Piegans. They no longer had any game on their reservation, and the allotments granted them by the Office of Indian Affairs were insufficient. The newspaper pointed out that in contrast to the Indians on the Fort Belknap Reservation, who still had some game in their area, the Piegans had none. In short, the Piegans were starving and were forced by circumstances to move off the reservation and butcher ranch cattle; thus, the threat of an Indian war loomed.[5]

On October 4, 1882, the *River Press* reported that the Commissioner of Indian Affairs had ordered a 25 percent increase in the allotment of beef and flour provided to the Piegans.[6] Whether this increase was brought about by the press reports or army post reports to headquarters, or both, the articles

---

[3] Ibid.: 154.

[4] The army was also, on occasion, utilized to project government force in territorial labor unrest.

[5] (Fort Benton, M.T.) *River Press*, September 6, 20, 1882.

[6] October 4, 1882, ibid.

reveal a degree of growing white concern for the plight of the Indians. Also during 1882, there were frequent forays by Cree Indians ranging southward into Montana Territory from their traditional homeland in the British Possessions. They would butcher cattle and frequently steal horses, returning with them to Canada.[7] Good cross-border relations continued, however, with the Northwest Mounted Police. On May 31, 1882, the *River Press* reported that Teton area ranchers, who had had horses stolen, followed the perpetrators back into Canada and reported the thefts to Colonel Irving, then the commanding officer at Fort Walsh. The colonel apprehended the thieves, members of the Cree tribe, arrested them and returned the horses to the ranchers.[8]

In the spring of 1883, Troop L, 2nd Cavalry, engaged a band of Crees near Wild Horse Lake, killing several of them.[9]

Ironically, at the close of the 1880's the threat of Indian hostilities arose among the two tribes most noted for their friendly relations with the whites—the Crows and the Flathead tribes. In 1887, trouble first flared up on the Crow Reservation. It culminated in a brief skirmish between the army and the Crow followers of Sword Bearer. He had succeeded in gathering a number of discontented reservation Crows and convincing them to clash with the U.S. Army. A firefight took place on November 5, 1887. One soldier was killed and two wounded. Seven Crow warriors are believed to have died as a result of the incident, among them Sword Bearer (Cheez-tah-paezh).[10]

Then in 1889, the threat of open armed conflict arose between the whites and the Flathead Indians. The majority of the Flatheads had moved with their war chief, Arlee, out of the Bitterroot Valley and onto their designated reservation at Jocko subsequent to a decision by the U.S. Department of Interior in 1872. Over the years, tensions had increased as a result of heavy white settlement in the area. In 1889 a Flathead Indian who was wanted for the killing of two prospectors the previous year was spotted on the

---

[7] This is, of course, a strong indication that the Crees themselves were now desperate to find sustenance wherever they could, thus the forays south into Montana.

[8] *River Press*, May 31, 1882.

[9] Edward J. McClernand, *A History of the Second Regiment of Cavalry*, II (1866–1891), http://www.army.mil/cmh-p./books: 190. There is a Wild Horse Lake located about twenty to twenty-five air miles northeast of present-day Grass Range, MT. There is also one north of Havre on the Canadian border. The author is uncertain as to the accurate location of the fight.

[10] Colin G. Calloway, "Sword Bearer and the Crow Outbreak 1887," *Montana: The Magazine of Western History*, Autumn 1986, Vol. 36, No. 4: 40–47.

reservation. Sheriff Daniel Heyfron, the civil authority in the area, proceeded to the reservation with a ten-man posse and placed the Flathead Indian under arrest. Subsequent to this arrest, the sheriff and his posse were surrounded by angry Flatheads, and the sheriff was reported to have shot and killed one Flathead in the confrontation before beating a hasty retreat with his posse and prisoner. Tensions simmered and the army was placed on alert at Fort Missoula, but calm returned before military intervention became necessary. The matter was successfully dealt with by civil authority and the Flathead Indian agent, Peter Ronan.[11]

Once again a degree of growing white sympathy for the plight of the Indians in Montana was revealed in this excerpt from an article in the *Helena Daily Independent* dated June 25, 1889:

> The outbreak of the Flatheads, albeit they are considered to be exceptionally friendly to the palefaces, is not altogether surprising. Since the advent of the Northern Pacific the country about them has been densely populated, and among the whites are many nefarious scoundrels who have been supplying the Indians with whiskey. This illegal traffic was the cause of the murder that resulted in the present trouble. The Indians are not wholly blameable in the matter. A short shrift and a long rope for the villains who caused them to commit the crimes of which they are accused would be a meting out of justice for the past, and effectively prevent future occurrences of like character.[12]

By 1881 Fort Benton and Fort Logan were abandoned as military posts. Also by 1881 a new post, Fort Maginnis, was established in the Judith Basin, and troops were stationed there until 1890, when it was also closed. This post was located near the town of Maiden on Ford's Creek along the eastern slope of the Judith Mountains, approximately twenty to twenty-five air miles northeast of present-day Lewistown, MT. Fort Assinniboine, which had been established in 1879 a short distance southwest of present-day Havre, MT, was abandoned in 1912. Fort Missoula, which had been established in 1877, eventually was abandoned by the active military in the early 20th century and serves today as a facility for reserve units. Fort Custer was abandoned by the military in 1898. Fort Keogh was abandoned two years later in 1900.[13]

---

[11] O.J. Taylor, *Montana–1889: The Centennial News Melange, Reprints from the* Madisonian: 101.

[12] Quoted in Taylor, *Montana–1889.*

[13] Michael J. Koury, *Military Posts of Montana.*

The 3rd Infantry Regiment would serve in Montana until 1888, when it was replaced by the 25th Infantry Regiment, an African-American unit with white officers. The 25th would remain on station until the abandonment of Fort Shaw in 1890. A portion of the 2nd Cavalry would remain at Fort Ellis until the summer of 1884, when it was transferred to the Division of the Pacific and stationed at Fort Walla Walla, Washington Territory. By 1887 the Great Northern Railroad had reached Great Falls, MT. This new railroad and the earlier Northern Pacific Railroad now provided the army with a quick entrance into Montana Territory should any trouble arise that would require a larger military force. All lesser problems could now be handled by the Indian Police and civil authority. In 1889, Montana became a state; the era of frontier Montana Territory had passed.

Of the three original Montana Military District posts, Fort Shaw would be utilized as an Indian school and later become property of the Fort Shaw Public School District. A portion of the old fort still stands today. Fort Ellis has completely disappeared. Its location would be unknown to most modern-day residents of the area but for a lonely stone and bronze marker erected by the Daughters of the American Revolution in 1926.[14] A portion of Fort Logan still stands.

---

[14] This marker is located on the frontage road (Old Highway 10) about 1.8 miles east of Interstate 90, Exit 309.

Appendix

Partial List of Killed and Wounded, Battle of the Big Hole

Killed

Captain William Logan, Company A
1st Lieutenant James H. Bradley, Company B
1st Lieutenant W.L. English, Company I, survived battle
    but died of wounds
1st Sergeant Robert L. Edgworth, Company G
1st Sergeant Fred Stortz, Company K
Sergeant W.H. Martin, Company G
Sergeant Michael Hogan, Company I
Sergeant William Watson, Company F, survived battle but died of wounds
Sergeant Ed Page, Company L, 2nd Cavalry
Corporal Robert E. Sale, Company G
Corporal Dominick O'Connor, Company G
Corporal Dan Hogan, Company I
Corporal Dan McCafferty, Company I
Corporal W.H. Payne, Company D
Corporal Isaac Eisenhart, Company D
Musician Michael Gallagher, Company D
Musician Thomas Steinbaker, Company K
Artificer John Kleiss, Company K
Private Matthew Batterly, Company E

Private William S. Pomeroy, Company F
Private James Maguire, Company F
Private Gottlien Mantz, Company G
Private John O'Brien, Company G
Private McKenzie L. Drake, Company H
Private Herman Britz, Company I
Citizen and Fort Shaw Post Guide Hiram Bostwick*
Citizen L.C. Elliot
Citizen Campbell Mitchell
Citizen Alvin Lockwood
Citizen John Armstrong
Citizen David Morrow

Wounded

Colonel John Gibbon, flesh wound left leg
Captain O. Williams, Company F, wounded above abdomen
1st Lieutenant C.J. Coolidge, Company A, shot through both thighs
    and wounded in left hand
2nd Lieutenant C.A. Woodruff, wounded in thigh, leg and head
Sergeant P.C. Dally, wounded in right temple
Sergeant James Bell, wounded in right shoulder
Sergeant William Wright, slight wound in forehead
Sergeant John W.H. Frederick, wounded in left shoulder
Private William Burk, shot through top of right lung, presumed mortal
Private John Erickson, wounded in right shoulder
Private L.D. Brown, wounded in left shoulder
Private R. M. Cunliff, flesh wound in left arm and left thigh
Private William Thompson, wounded in left shoulder
Private Philo O. Hurlbut, wounded in right shoulder
Private George Maurer, ball entered face at angle of jaw,
    carrying away cheek, roof of mouth and front teeth
Private George Berghart, wounded in right shoulder
Private Christian Lutman, shot through both thighs
Private Howard Clark, wounded in left foot and ankle
Private Edward Hunter, right arm badly shattered
Private John Murphy, wounded in right hip
Private Pat Fallin, shot through both hips
Private J.C. Lehmer, wounded in foot and ankle

Private David Healon, wounded in right wrist

Private Jas Keyes, wounded in left foot

Private M. Devine, left arm shattered

Private George Leber, wounded in head

Private Charles B. Gould, badly wounded in chest

Private Charles Davis, badly wounded in ankle and leg

Private Charles Alberts, shot through lungs

Citizen Myron Lockwood, shot through both thighs

Citizen O. Liefer, wounded in right foot and ankle

Citizen Fred Helt, wounded in foot and arm

From (Deer Lodge, Montana Territory) *New Northwest,* August 17 and 24, 1877. *Hiram Bostwick was not listed by the *New Northwest.*

Bibliography

Books

Ambrose, Stephen. *Undaunted Courage: Meriwether Lewis, Thomas Jefferson, and the Opening of the American West.* New York: Touchstone, 1996.

Beard, Charles A. and Mary R. *History of the United States: A Study in American Civilization.* New York: The Macmillan Company, 1933.

Bourke, John G. *On the Border with Crook.* New York: Charles Scribner's Sons, 1891.

Bradley, James H. *The March of the Montana Column: A Prelude to the Custer Disaster.* Norman: University of Oklahoma Press, 1961.

Brininstool, E.A. *Fighting Indian Warriors: True Tales of the Wild Frontier.* New York: Bonanza Books by arrangement with Stackpole Books, 1953.

Carrington, Margaret Irvin. *Absaraka: Home of the Crows.* 1868. Reprint, Lincoln: University of Nebraska Press, 1983.

Chief Joseph, in Linwood Laughy, comp. *In Pursuit of the Nez Perces.* Kooskia, ID: Mountain Meadow Press, 1993.

Chittenden, Hiram. *The American Fur Trade of the Far West.* 2 vols. 1902. Reprint, Lincoln: University of Nebraska Press, 1986.

Crook, George. *General George Crook: His Autobiography.* Martin F. Schmidt, editor. 1946. Reprint, Norman: University of Oklahoma Press, 1960.

Cummings, Luise K. *A Pictorial History of the Sun River Valley.* Shelby, MT: Promoter Publishing, 1989.

Custer, Elizabeth B. *Boots and Saddles: Life in Dakota with General Custer.* 1885. Reprint, Norman: University of Oklahoma Press, 1976.

_____. *Following the Guidon.* 1890. Reprint, Norman: University of Oklahoma Press, 1994.

Custer, George A. *My Life on the Plains.* 1874. Reprint, ed. by Milo Milton Quaife. Chicago: Lakeside Press, 1952.

DeBarthe, Joe. *Life and Adventures of Frank Grouard.* 1894. Reprint, New York: Time-Life Classics of the Old West, 1982.

De Smet, Pierre Jean. *Oregon Missions and Travels over the Rocky Mountains in 1845– 46.* Fairfield, WA: Ye Galleon Press, 1978.

DeVoto, Bernard, ed. *The Journals of Lewis and Clark.* New York: The Houghton Mifflin Company, 1981.

Dunn, J.P. Jr. *Massacres of the Mountains: A History of the Indian Wars in the Far West 1815–1875.* New York: Archer House, Inc., 1886.

Edgerton, Mary Wright. *A Governor's Wife on the Mining Frontier.* Edited by James L. Thane. Salt Lake City: Tanner Trust Fund, University of Utah Library, 1976.

Ege, Robert J. *After the Little Bighorn: The Battle of Snake Creek, Montana Territory, September 30 to October 5, 1877.* 2nd ed. Greely, CO: Werner Publications, 1982.

———. *Tell Baker To Strike Them Hard! Incident on the Marias, 23 Jan. 1870.* Bellevue, NE: The Olde Army Press, 1970.

Fay, George E., compiler and editor. *Military Engagements Between United States Troops and Plains Indians, Part IV, 1872–1890.* Museum of Anthropology-Ethnology Series, No. 29. Greeley: University of Northern Colorado, 1973.

Finerty, John. *War Path and Bivouac; or, The Conquest of the Sioux.* Chicago: M.A. Donohue & Co., 1890.

Garlington, E.A. "History of the Seventh Regiment of Cavalry, Inspector General, U.S.A." Bvt. General Theo F. Rodenbough and Major William L. Haskin, eds. *The Army of the United States: Historical Sketches of Staff and Line with Portraits of Generals-in-Chief.* New York: Maynard, Merrill & Co., 1896: 251–267. Accessed at U.S. Army Center for Military History. http://www.history.army.mil/books/R&H/ R&H-7Cav.htm.

Gibbon, John. *Adventures on the Western Frontier.* Indianapolis: Indiana University Press, 1994.

Godfrey, E.S. *Custer's Last Battle: Reprinted from Century Magazine, January 1892.* Olympic Valley, CA: Outbooks, 1976.

Graham, W.A. *The Custer Myth: A Source Book of Custeriana.* Harrisburg, PA: The Telegraph Press, 1953.

———. *The Reno Court of Inquiry: Abstract of the Official Proceedings.* Harrisburg, PA: The Telegraph Press, 1954.

Hamilton, James McClellan. *History of Montana: From Wilderness to Statehood.* 2nd ed. Portland, OR: Binford & Mort, 1970.

Haskell, Frank Aretas, "The Battle of Gettysburg" in American Historical Documents, 1000–1904. *The Harvard Classics.* Ed. by Charles W. Eliot, L.L.D. New York: P.F. Collier & Son, 1910.

Howard, O.O., in Linwood Laughy, comp. *In Pursuit of the Nez Perces.* Kooskia, ID: Mountain Meadow Press, 1993.

Irving, Washington. *The Adventures of Captain Bonneville.* 1837. Reprint, edited by Edgerly W. Todd. Norman: University of Oklahoma Press, 1961.

Klapper, Charles J., editor. *Indian Affairs: Laws and Treaties,* Vol. II (Treaties). Washington, DC: U.S. Government Printing Office, 1904.

Koury, Michael J. *Military Posts of Montana*. Bellevue, NE: Old Army Press, 1970.

Kuhlman, Charles. *Legend into History; and, Did Custer Disobey Orders at the Battle of the Little Bighorn?* First combined edition. Mechanicsburg, PA: Stackpole Books, 1994.

Laughy, Linwood, comp. *In Pursuit of the Nez Perces*. Kooskia, ID: Mountain Meadow Press, 1993.

Leeson, Michael A. *The History of Montana*. Chicago: Warner, Beers & Company, 1885.

Longstreet, James. *From Manassas to Appomattox: Memoirs of the Civil War in America*. Norwalk, CT: Easton Press, 1988.

Marquis, Thomas B., interpreter and editor, *Wooden Leg: A Warrior Who Fought Custer*. Lincoln: University of Nebraska Press, 1931.

McClernand, Edward J. *A History of the Second Regiment of Cavalry*. Vol. II (1866–1891): 179–192. Accessed at U.S. Army Center for Military History. http://www.army.mil/cmh-p./books/R&H/R&H-2CV.htm.

_____. *On Time for Disaster: The Rescue of Custer's Command*. 1969. Reprint, Lincoln: University of Nebraska Press, 1989.

McDonald, Duncan, in Linwood Laughy, comp. *In Pursuit of the Nez Perces*. Kooskia, ID: Mountain Meadow Press, 1993.

Meikle, Lyndel. *Very Close to Trouble: The Johnny Grant Memoir*. Pullman: Washington State University Press, 1996.

Miles, Nelson A. *Personal Recollections of General Nelson A. Miles*. 1896. Reprint, New York: Da Capo Press, 1969.

Mullan, John. *Report on the Construction of a Military Road from Fort Walla Walla to Fort Benton*. Fairfield, WA: Ye Galleon Press, 1994.

Office of the Chief of Military History, U.S. Army. *American Military History*. Army Historical Series, Chapter 11, The Civil War 1863, p. 253. Accessed at http://www.history.army.mil/books/AMH/AMH-11.htm.

Owen, John. *The Journals and Letters of Major John Owen*. 2 vols. Transcribed and edited by Seymour Dunbar and Paul C. Phillips. New York: Edward Eberstadt, 1927.

Post, Marie Caroline. *The Life and Memoirs of Comte Regis de Trobriand*. New York: E.P. Dutton & Company, 1910.

Raynolds, W. F. *Report on the Exploration of the Yellowstone River*. Washington, D.C.: U.S. Government Printing Office, 1868.

Schieps, Paul T. "Darkness and Light: The Interwar Years, 1865–1898." *American Military History*. Army Historical Series. Washington, DC: Office of Chief of Military History, U.S. Army. Accessed at http://www.army.mil/books/AMH/AMH-13.htm.

Sherman, William T. *Memoirs of General William T. Sherman*. 1875. Reprint, New York: Da Capo Press, 1984.

_____, and Gen. Philip H. Sheridan. *Reports of Inspection Made in the Summer of 1877*. Fairfield, WA: Ye Galleon Press, 1984.

Stanley, David Sloan. *Personal Memoirs of Major General David S. Stanley, U.S.A.* 1917. Reprint, Gaithersburg, MD: Olde Soldier Books, 1987.

Stuart, Granville. *Forty Years on the Frontier, as Seen in the Journals and Remembrances of Granville Stuart, Gold Miner, Trader, Merchant, Rancher and Politician.* 1925. Reprint, edited by Paul C. Phillips. 2 vols. in one, Northwest Historical Series II. Glendale, CA: The Arthur H. Clark Company, 1967.

Taylor, O.J. *Montana 1889: The Centennial News Melange.* Virginia City, MT: O.J. Taylor, 1989.

Thwaites, Reuben Gold. *Original Journals of the Lewis and Clark Expedition 1804–1806.* New York: Dodd, Mead & Company, 1905.

Trobriand, Philippe Regis de. *Military Life in Dakota.* 1900. Reprint, translated and edited by Lucille M. Kane. Lincoln: University of Nebraska Press, 1951.

Vaughn, Robert. *Then and Now: Thirty-Six Years in the Rockies, 1864–1900.* Foreword by Dave Walter. Helena, MT: Farcountry Press, 2001.

Westfall, Douglas Paul. *Letters from the Field: Wallace at the Little Bighorn.* Orange, CA: Paragon Agency Publishers, 1997.

Periodicals

Calloway, Colin G. "Sword Bearer and the Crow Outbreak 1887." *Montana: The Magazine of Western History,* Vol. 36, No. 4 (Autumn 1986), pp. 40–47.

Grass Range [Montana] *Review,* March 23, 1923. Reprint upon her death of Helen Clarke's *Contribution* to the Montana Historical Society.

Intharathat, Phisit. "Prisoner in Laos, Part 1." *Smokejumper: The National Smokejumper Association Quarterly Magazine,* October 2006: 10.

McBain, John F. "With Gibbon on the Sioux Campaign of 1876," Part I. *Journal of the United States Cavalry Association,* Vol. 9 (June 1896): 139–148.

McClernand, Edward J. "With the Indian and Buffalo in Montana." *Journal of the United States Cavalry Association* 1927.

Madisonian. Virginia City, Montana Territory.

Montana Post. Virginia City, Montana Territory.

New Northwest. Deer Lodge, Montana Territory.

New York Times.

River Press. Fort Benton, Montana Territory.

Documents

Montana Historical Society, Helena

Bradley, James H. Papers. SC 1616.

Clarke, Helen. Papers. SC 1153.

Clarke, Horace. Reminiscences. SC 540.

Woodruff, C.A. Speeches. SC 1326.

National Archives, Washington, D.C.

Annual Reports of the Commissioner of Indian Affairs. SuDocs Number I 20.1, 1824–1920. Record Group 75.

    1853. Annual Report of the Commissioner of Indian Affairs.

    1858. Annual Report of the Commissioner of Indian Affairs.

    1859. Annual Report of the Commissioner of Indian Affairs.

    1868. Annual Report of the Commissioner of Indian Affairs.

    1869. Annual Report of the Commissioner of Indian Affairs.

    1870. Annual Report of the Commissioner of Indian Affairs.

    1871. Annual Report of the Commissioner of Indian Affairs.

    1872. Annual Report of the Commissioner of Indian Affairs.

    1874. Annual Report of the Commissioner of Indian Affairs.

    1877. Annual Report of the Commissioner of Indian Affairs.

    1920. Annual Report of the Commissioner of Indian Affairs.

Letters Received by Office of Indian Affairs, 1824–1880. RG 75.

Record Group 94. Records of the Adjutant General's Office, ca. 1775–ca. 1928.

    Post Returns. Camp Baker, Montana Territory.

    Post Returns. Cantonment on Tongue River, Montana Territory.

    Post Returns. Fort Benton, Montana Territory.

    Post Returns. Fort Buford, Dakota Territory.

    Post Returns. Fort C.F. Smith, Montana Territory.

    Post Returns. Fort Custer, Montana Territory.

    Post Returns. Fort Ellis, Montana Territory.

    Post Returns. Fort Keogh, Montana Territory.

    Post Returns. Fort Logan, Montana Territory.

    Post Returns. Fort Missoula, Montana Territory.

    Post Returns. Fort Phil Kearny, Wyoming Territory.

    Post Returns. Fort Shaw, Montana Territory.

Record Group 393.4. Letters and Telegrams Sent and Received. Department of Dakota.

Record Group 393.5. Letters and Telegrams Sent and Received. District of Montana. Department of Dakota.

Record Group 393.5. Letters and Telegrams Sent and Received. District of Yellowstone. Department of Dakota.

Record Group 393.7. Records of Posts, Continental Army Command 1820–1920.

    Camp Baker Letters Sent and Received.

    Fort Benton Letters and Telegrams Sent and Received.

    Fort Custer Letters and Telegrams Sent and Received.

    Fort Ellis Letters and Telegrams Sent and Received.

    Fort Keogh Letters and Telegrams Sent and Received.

    Fort Logan Letters Sent and Received.

Fort Missoula Letters and Telegrams Sent and Received.

Fort Shaw Letters and Telegrams Sent and Received.

Fort Shaw Sanitary Reports, in Fort Shaw Letters and Telegrams Sent and Received.

Taylor, N.G., et al. Report to the President by the Indian Peace Commission, January 7, 1868. Transcribed by Carolyn Sims, Furman University Department of History, from the Annual Report of the Commissioner of Indian Affairs for the Year 1868.

U.S. Census of 1870, Territory of Montana.

U.S. House of Representatives, Exec. Doc. #185, 41st Congress, 2nd Session.

_____, _____ #197, 41st Congress, 2nd Session.

_____, _____ #1, 42nd Congress, 2nd Session, 1505.

_____, _____ #81, 42nd Congress, 2nd Session, 1510.

_____, _____ #1, 43rd Congress, 2nd Session, 1639.

_____, _____ #1, 45th Congress, 2nd Session.

U.S. Senate, Exec. Doc. #49, 41st Congress, 2nd Session.

Websites

"Captain Robert Gray becomes the first non-Indian navigator to enter the Columbia River, which he later names, on May 11, 1792." Essay 5051. HistoryLink.org. http://historylink.org/index.cfm?DisplayPage=output.cfm&file_id=5051.

Goe, James B. "History of the 13th Infantry Regiment." U.S. Army Center for Military History. http://www.history.army.mil/books/R&H/R&H-13IN.htm: 582.

Higgenbotham, Dave. "General George Custer; An Overview of the Weapons Used." Lone Star Rifle Company, Inc. www.lonestarrifle.com/Custer. Accessed February 24, 2006.

Johnson, A.B. History of the 7th Infantry Regiment. U.S. Army Center for Military History. http://www.history.army.mil/books/R&H-7IN.htm.

"Thrifty Innovation: Springfield's Search for Firepower, 1865–1872." Utah Gun Collectors Association. http://ugca.org/firepower/firepowermain.htm. Accessed February 24, 2006.

Treaties Between the United States and the Nation of Blackfeet Indians, November 16, 1865–September 1, 1868. Oklahoma State University Library.

Whitehorne, Joseph W.A. "The Battle of Second Manassas." Appendix on Personalities. U.S. Army Center for Military History, 1990. http://www.history.army.mil/books//staff-rides/2manassas/2mns-PER.htm.

Index

Italic page numbers indicate illustrations.